Teach Yourself
Oracle Power
Objects
in 21 Days

Teach Yourself
Oracle Power Objects
in 21 Days

Tom Grant

SAMS
PUBLISHING

201 West 103rd Street
Indianapolis, Indiana 46290

To Kathleen, for all the good times in the past, and all the better times to come.

To Sarah, the hope of the future, who makes life worth living.

Copyright © 1996 by Sams Publishing

FIRST EDITION

International Standard Book Number: 0-672-30868-1

Library of Congress Catalog Card Number: 95-72333

99 98 97 96   4   3   2   1

Interpretation of the printing code: the rightmost double-digit number is the year of the book's printing; the rightmost single-digit, the number of the book's printing. For example, a printing code of 96-1 shows that the first printing of the book occurred in 1996.

Composed in AGaramond and MCPdigital by Macmillan Computer Publishing

Printed in the United States of America

Trademarks

Publisher and President	Richard K. Swadley
Acquisitions Manager	Greg Wiegand
Development Manager	Dean Miller
Managing Editor	Cindy Morrow
Marketing Manager	Gregg Bushyeager

Acquisitions Editor
Rosemarie Graham

Development Editor
Keith Davenport

Production Editor
Tonya R. Simpson

Copy Editors
Mary Ann Faughnan
Jill Bond
Angie Trzepacz
Ryan Rader
Bart Reed

Technical Reviewer
Matthew D. Bennett

Editorial Coordinator
Bill Whitmer

Technical Edit Coordinator
Lynette Quinn

Formatter
Frank Sinclair

Editorial Assistants
Sharon Cox
Andi Richter
Rhonda Tinch-Mize

Cover Designer
Tim Amrhein

Book Designer
Gary Adair

Production Team Supervisor
Brad Chinn

Production
Carol Bowers
Jeanne Clark
Jason Hand
Mike Henry
Kevin Laseau
Casey Price
Nancy Price
Brian-Kent Proffitt
Bobbi Satterfield
Tim Taylor

Overview

Contents

Acknowledgments

Like all things in life, this book is one stop along a journey of serendipity. Although I owe many people a great deal, I'd like to especially thank several people.

Normally, acknowledgments in a book like this start with a paean to some long-suffering spouse, who waited patiently while the author went into a sensory deprivation tank for several months to finish writing the book. When at last you emerge, there is your significant other, happy that your long absence is finally over.

I won't break with tradition here, so to my very patient wife and daughter, thank you many times over for making it possible for me to write this book. I owe my daughter many long-postponed bike rides, and my wife many evenings together. You're the most important people in my life, and this book is rightfully dedicated to you. I did this book for you, and it's finished because of you.

I'd also like to thank Joan Nyland, the best boss any person could have, and a terrific friend. Joan gave me a start as a doc writer, and to her I am immensely grateful.

From the Oracle Power Objects team, special thanks to the following people:

- ☐ Mike Roberts and Steve McAdams, friends and developers extraordinaire, for working hard to build a great development tool.
- ☐ The development team, for their encouragement and help in putting together the documentation.
- ☐ Michael Weingartner and Adam Greenblatt, for their counsel and friendship when I needed it, and for nagging me to climb aboard the cruel Stairmaster on days when I might have otherwise slacked off.
- ☐ Jennifer Krauel, friend, confidante, and product manager, the lynchpin in getting the version 1.0 product finished, and a great believer in the humane.
- ☐ Chris Roberts, the other lead writer for the version 1.0 docs, one of the most dedicated and skilled people I've met.
- ☐ Marc Benioff, for his faith and support in the doc team.

Thanks also to Robbie Vann Adibe and Matt Bennett, both of whom made it possible for me to write this book, and to the ever-helpful staff at Sams.

Finally, to my good friends in Southern California—Maurice and Diane; Dennis, Sean, Chris, Brian, and John—thanks for your friendship and support through all my careers.

About the Author

Tom Grant

Tom Grant is the documentation manager for the Oracle Power Objects team, and was one of the lead writers on the version 1.0 doc set. He is now living in his favorite part of the United States, the Bay Area, where he enjoys being knee-deep in computers at Oracle Corporation.

When not at work, Tom's first pleasure is his family (his wife Kathleen, and his daughter Sarah). After that, he has earned the nickname "Mr. Games" for his abiding passion for games of all sorts. He also has a Ph.D. in political science, of which the lasting legacy is a fascination for politics, history, and current events.

Introduction

Welcome to Oracle Power Objects! This book will give you the guided tour of every part of this new development tool. By the end of these three weeks, you will have learned not only how to use the key features of this tool, but also how to use it to overcome some of the most common and important development challenges. The simple bookstore application you build will demonstrate all of the important capabilities of Oracle Power Objects, as well as some additional features that any self-respecting application should have.

The Oracle Power Objects Opportunity

This book is based on a bold premise: that people with little or no development experience can start building applications using Oracle Power Objects. In addition, experienced developers should look seriously at the shortcuts Oracle Power Objects provides to many of the most difficult development tasks, especially when the developers are building any application that uses a database.

For the Beginner

In many respects, Oracle Power Objects provides a startling opportunity for beginning developers:

☐ You can get a fully functional copy of Oracle Power Objects absolutely free. Really. You can download a trial version of Oracle Power Objects from the Oracle Web site, http://www.oracle.com. This trial copy (which you should register within 90 days) includes all the features of the product, such as Oracle7 and SQL Server database access, OLE support, and all the documentation in Adobe Acrobat format.

☐ Oracle Power Objects is designed to simplify development for everyone, including the uninitiated. There are several features of this toolset (for example, drag-and-drop development features) that provide powerful shortcuts for the types of development tasks that previously required a great deal of coding and an even greater amount of arcane knowledge. For example, the task of connecting an application to a database has been one of the most difficult development chores, fraught with frequent false turns and unexpected developments. In Oracle Power Objects, you connect a form to a database by dragging the icon for a table onto a form. That's it. Really.

☐ Every copy of Oracle Power Objects comes with a free copy of a relational database. The Blaze database technology that comes with Oracle Power Objects gives everyone the chance to play with a relational database—one of the most significant advances in software technology. An increasing number of organizations, both large and small, are placing their information in relational databases, most of which cost a considerable amount of money to install and maintain. With Blaze, you can learn the basics of how to develop an application that uses a relational database as a "back end" without having to invest thousands of dollars to install a more sophisticated relational database.

Therefore, Oracle Power Objects gives you the opportunity as a beginning developer to work with some state-of-the-art technology, without a huge up-front investment of time, money, or additional training. As Larry Ellison, CEO of Oracle Corporation, said during the Oracle Power Objects rollout, this product is designed for "mere mortals" to use.

I once had a disagreement with someone over how big an audience there was for tools such as Oracle Power Objects. Her argument was, "Why would you want to know how to build a car if you just want to drive one?" In other words, because cars and applications are fairly complex beasts, why not leave it to the experts?

Although not everyone will want to develop applications, there should not be artificial barriers erected against getting started as a developer. The thrust of the software revolution of the last decade has been to make everything you do on a personal computer as easy as possible. You cannot simplify everything about client/server application development, nor should you. However, new developers need to come from somewhere, and organizations often can't wait for someone else to develop an application for them. For beginning developers, therefore, an easy-to-use tool such as Oracle Power Objects puts them in command of powerful technologies without making it look like thaumaturgy.

For the Veteran

Whereas new developers want to ascend to higher levels of skill, experienced developers want to find easier ways to create applications. Organizations are depending increasingly on database applications, yet these are some of the most difficult applications to develop. You want to be especially careful about the quality, performance, and ease-of-use of these applications, because companies are often betting their business on them. If the general ledger system crashes every time it runs, the company's finances will be thrown into disarray.

The whole point of Oracle Power Objects is to simplify the task of developing database applications. By reducing the time it takes to create the basic features of the application, you enjoy more time to test it for bugs, enhance its performance, improve its usability, and add more features than the basics you knew had to be included. In other words, you can focus your attention on making the application work well, instead of simply working.

Focus on the Practical

Teach Yourself Oracle Power Objects in 21 Days is designed to give you a comprehensive look at all the major features of Oracle Power Objects. The lessons in this book teach you how to use

this tool, but they also show you how to use it to address real-world development challenges. Instead of telling you how to create a form that reads data queried from a database, many lessons show you how to add security to the form, increase the speed with which it accesses data, and handle any errors that might occur while the form is running.

In other words, the lessons in this book emphasize the practical whenever possible. Some lessons cover subjects that you will not see in a reference like the *Oracle Power Objects User's Guide*, such as usability, security, and performance.

Although learning the basics of how to use a development tool might be important, this basic knowledge is not sufficient to create real applications. For the beginning developer, seeing how to tackle a common development challenge such as improving the speed with which the application generates a report is just as important as learning how to create a new report. For experienced developers, a new tool is attractive only if you know that you can handle a particular task such as enforcing business rules better than you are now with an already familiar tool.

The goal of most exercises, therefore, is to add features to a sample application used to manage information for a bookstore. If this book has done its job, you should be able to add some of these features to your own applications. The procedures you will implement to check whether an employee should be viewing and editing sensitive information are generic enough to be used in nearly any application.

Windows Versus Macintosh Issues

This book is written for the Windows user. However, most of the lessons will work just the same on the Macintosh. The sections of the 21-day tutorial that you cannot do on the Macintosh include the following:

- ☐ OLE controls
- ☐ OCX controls
- ☐ Calling DLL procedures
- ☐ Calling Windows API procedures

Files Used in this Tutorial

During the lessons in this book, you will build everything in the Bookstore application from scratch. You don't need anything more than a copy of Oracle Power Objects and this book to finish the lesson plan.

At the end of every day, you will see a Workshop section suggesting some additional work you might do to reinforce what you learned during that day. In addition, the lessons reference some types of files you can use to increase the capabilities of your application, such as the custom controls (OCX files) discussed on Day 20, "Improving System Performance." If you want copies of some of these files, as well as application files containing solutions to some of the exercises, check the Sams Web site at http://www.mcp.com/.

Special Features of This Book

This book contains some special elements to help you understand Oracle Power Objects features as they are introduced. Specific features you'll see throughout the book are:

☐ **Notes:** These provide essential background information so that you not only learn to do things with Oracle Power Objects, but have a good understanding of what you're doing and why.

☐ **DO/DON'T boxes:** These give you specific guidance on what to do and what to avoid doing when you work with Oracle Power Objects.

☐ **Tips:** Tips are hints on how to use the features of Oracle Power Objects better.

☐ ➥ Sometimes, you need to type in a very long, single line of code. When you see this character, a code continuation character, it means the line is continued from the preceding line, and you should type in both lines as one.

Conventions Used in This Book

This book uses different typefaces to help you differentiate between code and regular English, and also to help you identify important concepts.

☐ Actual code is typeset in a special monospace font. You'll see this font used in code examples. In the explanations of code features, commands, statements, methods, and any text you see on the screen also is typeset in this font.

☐ Placeholders in code appear in an *italic monospace* font. Replace the placeholders with the actual filename, parameter, or whatever element it represents.

☐ *Italics* highlight technical terms when they first appear in the text and are sometimes used to emphasize important points.

Your First Form

Overview

Today you learn about the following topics:

- [ ] The Oracle Power Objects user interface
- [ ] Creating a new form
- [ ] Object-oriented development
- [ ] Properties and methods
- [ ] Writing code
- [ ] The Oracle Basic language
- [ ] Testing a form
- [ ] The importance of data types

Today, you will create a new application and add a form to it. The not-so-hidden motive behind this exercise is to teach you several important principles about Oracle Power Objects, and to get you comfortable with the Oracle Power Objects user interface. The form will include two objects: a pushbutton and a text field. By showing you how to display a message in the field by pressing the pushbutton, today's lesson teaches you the basics of object-oriented development with Oracle Power Objects.

Windows, Windows Everywhere

The focus of today's lesson is on the windows in the Oracle Power Objects interface, also called the *Desktop*. Oracle Power Objects can display a large number of *designer windows*, used to design forms, reports, database tables, and other objects. Other windows, such as the Property sheet and the Object palette, will also appear to help you design these objects. Additionally, the toolbar appearing near the top of the Desktop window displays a different set of shortcut buttons, depending on which window is selected.

For the first-time user, navigating among the windows, menus, and pushbuttons that appear can be confusing at first. This chapter will help dispel that confusion, so that the Power Objects interface provides a clear window into the application rather than a kaleidoscope of objects, like the Oracle Power Objects desktop shown in Figure 1.1.

The most important window in the Power Objects interface is the *Property sheet*. In the Property sheet, you define the characteristics of objects, such as the size and color of a form. Additionally, the Property sheet is where you write the code that performs actions at runtime (that is, while the application is running). By the end of the first day, you will understand how to use this all-important tool.

Figure 1.1.
A lot of objects!

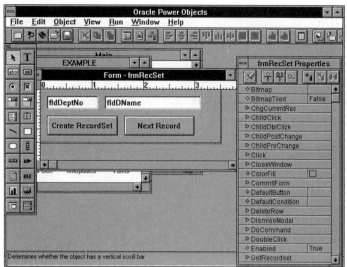

Some Preliminary Notes

In this first lesson, you do not need access to the database. The form you design will be *unbound*, meaning that it will not be connected to the database. On Day 4, "Connecting a Form to a Record Source," you will learn how to create a form that can read data from the database.

> **Note:** *A note to experienced developers.* Much of the material in this chapter is written for the beginning developer. However, included in the exercises for the first day is some important information about Oracle Power Objects. You might be able to skim this chapter to get the gist of object-oriented development with Oracle Power Objects. Be sure to do the exercises, so that you can get a good feel for how to use Oracle Power Objects.

Creating a Working Directory

Your first task is to create a working directory for your new application. Generally, you want to keep each application in a separate directory unless you are developing rather simple applications. You might prefer to maintain a common directory for all applications because some types of files (sessions and libraries, explained on Day 2, "Creating a Table") can be used in several applications. For the purpose of this lesson, however, you will maintain all the objects you create in the same directory: BOOKS.

To create the working directory, use the DOS command MD to create the new directory C:\BOOKS, or in Windows File Manager, select File | New Directory to create the C:\BOOKS directory. On the Macintosh, create a new folder, BOOKS, to contain these files.

This new directory will contain three important files:

☐ The *application file*, which contains the description of the application and all objects contained in it.

☐ The *session file*, which defines how the application accesses the database.

☐ The *library file*, which contains several objects used in multiple applications, but stored in the library.

You now are ready to start working in Oracle Power Objects.

Launching Oracle Power Objects

Assuming that you already have Oracle Power Objects installed, you now can launch it from the Program Manager group in Windows by double-clicking its icon. (For installation instructions, see the Oracle Power Objects *Getting Started* manual.) When you open Oracle Power Objects for the first time, you will see a screen similar to the one shown in Figure 1.2. (The sample applications that you can install with Oracle Power Objects have been removed from this window.)

Figure 1.2.
OPO opened for the first time.

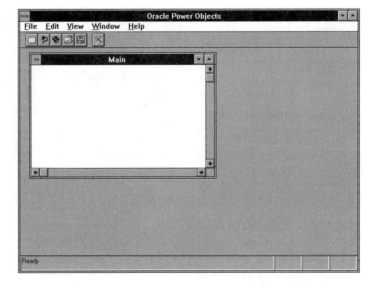

Table 1.1 summarizes the main components of the Oracle Power Objects desktop.

Table 1.1. Components of the Oracle Power Objects desktop.

Component	Description
Menu	The menu bar for Oracle Power Objects. The menu headings and menu commands beneath them change, depending on the active window.
Toolbar	The toolbar presents a series of buttons that provide shortcuts for frequently used menu commands. For example, the New Application pushbutton (which you will use in a moment) instructs Oracle Power Objects to create a new application.
Client area	This region is beneath the menu bar and the toolbar and is where the various windows used to design objects appear.
Main window	This window contains icons for applications, libraries, and sessions.

The objects in the Main window have corresponding files in the operating system. These files contain the description of the application, session, or library, including all the objects contained within it. For example, a library appearing in the Main window is described in a library file (with the extension .POL) stored somewhere on your hard disk. Therefore, applications, libraries, and sessions are called *file objects* because each one has a corresponding file in the operating system. Other objects stored within applications and libraries (such as a form) do not have their own operating system files. On the Macintosh, Oracle Power Objects does not add these filename extensions.

Additional Objects in the Main Window

If you installed the sample applications provided with Oracle Power Objects (not the one you'll be creating in this book), you also will see several icons in the Main window. These represent the applications, libraries, and sessions used in the sample applications.

You might want to remove some or all of these icons from the official Oracle Power Objects sample applications. If you install the sample applications provided with Oracle Power Objects, icons for these applications, as well as sessions and libraries, appear in the Main window. Fewer icons in the Main window will make it easier to find the objects you'll be creating in this book, and performance increases when you remove objects from this window.

> **Note:** Removing an application, session, or library does not delete its file from the operating system. When you remove an object from the Main window, Oracle Power Object no longer loads it at startup. Later, if you want to work with that file object again, you can add it to the Main window.

To remove a file object from the Main window, follow these steps:

1. Select the icon for the application, library, or session.
2. Click the Cut button.

The icon for the object no longer appears in the Main window.

Currently, you should not have any application open in Power Objects. When you create a new application, an icon for it will appear in the Main window. You then can open another window for the application that contains other icons for all the forms, reports, and other objects within the application.

If you have installed the sample applications included with Oracle Power Objects, icons for their applications, sessions, and libraries appear in the Main window. Before continuing, delete all of these icons by selecting each one in turn and pressing the Cut button.

Creating a New Application

Throughout the lessons in this book, you will be adding to an application created to help manage the information of a fictional bookstore, Logos Books. Now that you have Oracle Power Objects running, you can create the new file object for this application. Just follow these steps:

1. From the toolbar, click the New Application button, or select New Application from the File menu.

   The Create as dialog box appears requesting the name of the new application, as well as the directory in which it will appear. (See Figure 1.3.)

Figure 1.3.
The Create as dialog box.

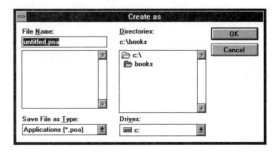

2. In the File Name text box, type BOOKS for the name of the application.

At this point, you also might enter the full filename of the application, which is BOOKS.POA. All applications have the extension .POA (short for Power Objects Application). If you do not add the extension, however, Power Objects appends it to the filename automatically.

3. Select the C:\BOOKS directory.

This is the directory in which the new application file object, BOOKS.POA, will appear.

4. Select OK.

The new file, BOOKS.POA, now appears in C:\BOOKS, and Power Objects opens the Application window for your bookstore application. This window currently is empty because you have not added any objects to the application. Later, as you build the application, several types of objects will appear in this window, as shown in Figure 1.4.

Figure 1.4.
Several types of objects
in the window.

Forms

In most applications, *forms* constitute the core of the interface. Forms can be bound to a table or view in a database, meaning that the user can view and edit data through the form. Additionally, forms can contain copies of other objects that appear in the Application window, such as user-defined classes and OLE objects.

Reports

Reports display data so that it can be printed in a meaningful, readable fashion. Reports can contain most of the same objects as forms (such as text fields and charts). As you shall see, reports share many similarities with forms, but also have some important differences. For example, reports are divided into several functionally distinct sections (often called bands), but forms are not.

Classes

A *user-defined class* is a reusable object that you can copy onto forms, reports, and other classes. Like a form, a class can be bound to a table or view; however, unlike a form, you can never open the class by itself at runtime. Instead, you must copy the class onto a form or report to view it.

Classes simplify the development process by defining in one place an object used repeatedly throughout an application (such as the customer information section of a form). By defining these frequently used objects as a class, you can make modifications to the class that then are immediately reflected in all copies (or *instances*) of the class.

OLE Data Objects

An *OLE data object* is a special type of object defined outside an Oracle Power Objects application, but used within that application. There are a wide range of possible OLE data objects, from QuickTime videos to Microsoft Word documents to Microsoft Excel spreadsheets. OLE data objects exist only in the Microsoft Windows environment. The Macintosh version of Oracle Power Objects does not support OLE objects.

Bitmaps

A *bitmap* is a graphic imported into the application from the operating system. Once imported, you can display the bitmap within objects in the application interface. Each type of object is described in greater detail later in this book, as you add it to the Bookstore application.

So far, your application has none of these objects displayed in the Application window. It's time to add the first form to the application.

Creating a New Form

The first form you'll create won't actually appear in the application. Instead, the form will illustrate some of the fundamentals of Oracle Power Objects.

To create the new form, follow these steps:

1. Open the Application window for BOOKS.

   If it is already open, simply select the Application window to make it the active window in Power Objects.

2. On the toolbar, click the New Form button.

   A new form now appears. Because this is the first object you have added to your application, the form is named Form1 (see Figure 1.5). Oracle Power Objects always assigns a default name to any new object you create.

Figure 1.5.
The new window for Form1.

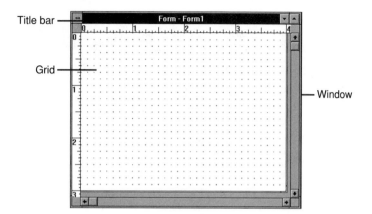

Although there is nothing on the form yet, the form already has several important features, as described in the following list:

Component	Description
Window	A moveable, resizeable window surrounds the form. This window is not the size of the window surrounding the form at runtime. Instead, when the user first opens the form, the window will appear around the edges of the form.
Title bar	The title bar appearing at the top of the window displays the type of object (in this case, Form) and its name. The name is used only within the application; it is not the label appearing on the title bar when the user sees the form at runtime.
Grid	The grid appearing on the form helps position the objects you will later add to the form. By default, Oracle Power Objects enforces the "snap to grid" rule.

However, as important as these visual features of the form are, the most important characteristics of the form are not yet visible. These are the properties and methods that define the appearance and behavior of the form. In a moment, you will begin working with these characteristics of the form. However, first click the Save button on the toolbar before continuing.

The Form Designer Toolbar

As you might have already noticed, the toolbar at the top of the Oracle Power Objects window changed when you created the new form. Several new buttons now appear on the toolbar, all of which provide more shortcuts for designing the form and the application (see Figure 1.6).

Figure 1.6.
The Form Designer window and toolbar.

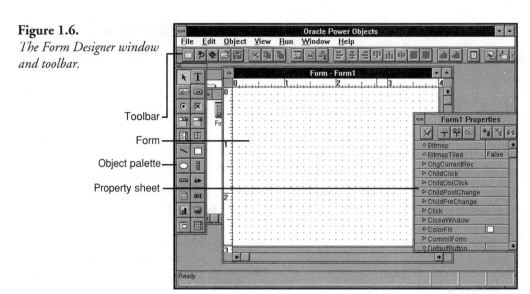

The window in which the form appears is called the *Form Designer window*, and the new toolbar is called (not surprisingly) the *Form Designer toolbar*. In Oracle Power Objects, this relationship occurs several times, in which a particular designer window has a special toolbar that appears when the window is selected. For example, when you start working with sessions (which provide the means to access the database), a different toolbar appears when you select the Session Designer window.

To see this type of relationship in action, select the Application window for BOOKS, and then reselect the Form Designer window for your new form. The toolbar changes, depending on which is the active window.

You also might have noticed that a floating toolbar displaying several buttons appears only when the new form is the active window. This toolbar is the *Object palette*, which you will use later today to add objects to the form. For the time being, however, move the Object palette to the left so that it does not obstruct the form.

Although the purpose of many of the buttons on the Form Designer toolbar might not be immediately apparent, you will learn what each button does as you work on the Bookstore application. If you are curious, you can look at the Quick Reference on the inside back cover of this book.

Opening the Property Sheet

At this point, click the Edit Properties button on the Form Designer toolbar. (If you don't see this button, make the new form the active window.) Another window, the Property sheet, now appears (see Figure 1.7).

Figure 1.7.
The form's Property sheet.

Title bar
Buttons

Property/method list

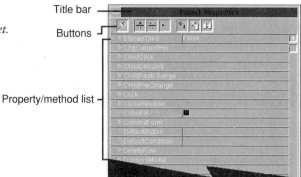

Unlike other windows you have seen, this one is divided into many sections.

Component	Description
Property/Method List	A scrolling list of the characteristics of the form that Oracle Power Objects recognizes.
Buttons	Several new buttons, all of which are related to the list of properties and methods on the Property sheet.
Title Bar	Like the title bar in the Form Designer window, this title bar displays the type of object you are viewing (in this case, a Form) and its name.

While you develop the application, you will spend a great deal of time, if not most of your time, working in the Property sheet. However, before you begin editing the properties and methods of the form, read a few quick words about what properties and methods really are, in an object-oriented world.

Changing Properties of the Form

Oracle Power Objects is an object-oriented development tool, meaning that it has been designed in a specific way. Power Objects represents everything in the application, from the application itself down to every pushbutton and text field, as an object possessing properties and methods.

What Is An Object?

An *object* is anything Oracle Power Objects recognizes as a distinct component of an application, library, or session. In addition, applications, libraries, and sessions are themselves objects.

Think for a moment of an application as a set of building blocks, or perhaps Lego blocks. You select each block not only for how it looks, but also for what it can do. You might add some objects simply for appearance: when you build a Lego car, for example, you might select a piece because it has an attractive color. You might select other blocks because of what they can do: to use the Lego car example, you might need a particular piece because it has a wheel attached to it.

Object-oriented development is much like building a Lego car. You start with a clear idea of what you want the final product to be. You then select components that you need to build the application, and then you fit together the pieces as needed to construct it.

The best test of whether you have succeeded in either case is whether it works: does the car roll on the floor, or does the application provide a meaningful way for bookstore owners to organize their data? Every piece of the application—each form, check box, or graph—is necessary to create the final product you have envisioned.

One of the chief advantages of object-oriented development is that it matches how you already think about application development. Before you begin developing, you have some idea of which pieces you need to build the application. During development, you add new pieces and frequently connect them to others. One connection might be that a pushbutton opens a form, or a form reads data from the database. Therefore, Oracle Power Objects organizes the pieces of the application in this object-oriented fashion, so that you can reach into your toolbox and get to work.

Unlike the Lego car, however, you will be doing a significant amount of customization on the individual pieces of the application. To perform this customization, you must modify the properties and methods of the object.

Objects and Properties

Consider real cars rather than Lego cars. Not all cars are built alike. For example, you would not use the same tires on a race car that you put on your family car. Similarly, it would be fruitless to put the race car's engine into the family car (at the very least, you would waste a lot of gasoline). However, both cars need wheels and engines. The race car's tires need a much thicker layer of rubber and steel, whereas the family car needs to get greater fuel efficiency. You could say, therefore, that the properties of the engines and wheels differ, but they're still wheels and engines.

When you modify an engine, you are changing the value of one of these properties. You can tinker with the engine to increase its fuel efficiency, for example, or reduce its emission level. In the same fashion, you change the value assigned to a property when you want an object to change its appearance or behavior. For example, you can indicate the database to which a form is connected through one property (RecSrcSession), or determine whether the user can edit the contents of a text field through another property (Enabled).

For this reason, you can understand a property as "a characteristic of an object that accepts a value." The height of a form (the SizeY property) can accept a value, as can the property that indicates where in the database the form gets its data (the RecordSource property).

You can change the value assigned to a property at design time (when you are still building the application) and at runtime (when the user is running the application). At design time, you set the properties of the object through the Property sheet. At runtime, you modify the properties of an object by executing code.

The Property sheet displays many properties for your new form. At the top of the Property sheet, you can see several properties (see Figure 1.8).

Figure 1.8.
The Property sheet for the form.

Some of the properties shown in Figure 1.8 include the following:

Property	Description
Bitmap	Identifies the bitmap to be displayed on the form, if any.
BitmapTiled	Indicates whether copies of the bitmap should be copied repeatedly across the form, in a "tiled" format.
ColorFill	Determines the form's background color.

Right now, you can change these properties through the Property sheet. First, change the background color of the form by following these steps:

1. Click the ColorFill property of the form.

   A palette of colors now appears in a drop-down window, as shown in Figure 1.9.

2. Click one of the colors in the palette.

   The background color of the form changes to match that color.

3. Click a different color in the palette.

   Again, the background color changes.

Figure 1.9.

ColorFill's color palette revealed!

In this case, the property changes only through the Property sheet. At other times, however, the Property sheet shows how the value of a property has changed through some other mechanism. To illustrate this point, follow these steps:

1. Scroll down the Property sheet until you find the SizeY property, shown in Figure 1.10.

   This property indicates the height of the form in pixels, inches, or centimeters (the unit of measurement is always displayed next to the value). Take note of the value currently assigned to the SizeY property.

Figure 1.10.

The Property sheet showing SizeY.

2. On the lower edge of the form, click and hold down the left mouse button.

   You have now grabbed the bottom edge of the form with the cursor.

3. Without releasing the mouse button, move the mouse upward.

   The height of the form decreases as you move the mouse. (See Figure 1.11.)

Figure 1.11.
Resizing the form.

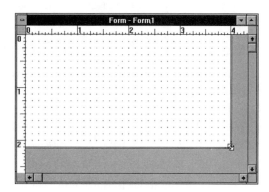

4. When the form is significantly shorter, release the mouse button.

5. Look again at the SizeY property of the form.

   The value assigned to this property has changed, reflecting the fact that the form is not as tall as it once was. (See Figure 1.12.)

Figure 1.12.
The new value for SizeY.

6. Click in the right side of the SizeY section of the Property sheet, where the value assigned to this property is displayed.

   The text in this section of the Property sheet should now be highlighted.

7. Type in the original value for the SizeY property and press Enter. (Refer to Figure 1.10.)

The form now returns to its original height.

This exercise illustrated how you can change a property's value at design time. Later, you will write code that evaluates and changes the values assigned to a property.

Changing the Name of the Form

While you still have the form's Property sheet open, you can modify other properties of the form. First, give the form a more descriptive name than Form1. With the form selected, scroll down the Property sheet until you reach the Name property and then perform the following steps. As mentioned earlier, this is the name the application uses to refer to the form, not the name displayed on the title bar while the form is running.

1. Click in the window to the right of the label Name in the Property sheet.

   The focus should move to the window, indicating that you can type a new value for the name (see Figure 1.13).

Figure 1.13.

Clicking in the Name *area of the Property sheet.*

2. In the window, type frmFirstForm and press Enter.

The new name of the form appears in both the Name section of the Property sheet, the title bar of the Property sheet, and the Application window. We gave the form the name frmFirstForm to follow some of the naming conventions suggested in Appendix A of the *Oracle Power Objects User's Guide.*

Additionally, you can change the label appearing on the title bar of the form at runtime by following these steps:

1. Move to the `Label` section of the Property sheet.
2. Click in the window next to the word `Label`.
3. Type `My First Form` in the window and press Enter.

Later, when you test the form, this text will appear in the form's title bar.

Other Changes to the Form

You'll notice that you have changed the value assigned to a property in two ways: by selecting a value from a drop-down list and by typing a value into the Property sheet. Now, you will use the third way to change the value assigned to a property at design time, by clicking on a value to toggle it.

Many properties have only two values, such as `True` and `False`. In these cases, you can switch between these properties by clicking the current value of the property displayed in the Property sheet. When you click, the value toggles to the other value—from `False` to `True`, or `True` to `False`.

To illustrate this, you will add and remove a scrollbar to and from your form.

1. Scroll through the Property sheet until you find the `HasScrollBar` property.
2. When you find it, click the right side of this section of the Property sheet, where the word `False` is currently displayed.

    The value assigned to `HasScrollBar` changes to `True` (see Figure 1.14). If you were to run the form at this point, it would display a vertical scrollbar on its window.

Figure 1.14.
The setting for
`HasScrollBar` *changed, so a*
scrollbar now appears on the
form.

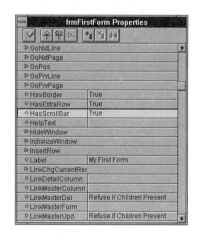

3. Click the same section of the Property sheet again.

   The property's value switches back to False.

You now have learned the three ways in which you can use the Property sheet to change the value assigned to a property:

☐ Type in a value. You renamed the form by typing in a value. Later, you will perform more significant development tasks using this technique, such as entering an equation that a text field uses to calculate the value assigned to it.

☐ Select a value from a drop-down list. In the case of ColorFill, the drop-down list displayed a color palette. For other properties, several lines of text might appear, each corresponding to a different value. For example, the WindowStyle property has several values (such as Standard Document, Fixed Dialog, and so on) you can select from the list.

☐ Click the current value to toggle it to another setting. Normally, the values are True and False.

So far, you have learned the techniques used to change the value of a property at design time. However, this begs an important question: How do you evaluate or change a property's value at runtime, when the user is running the application?

Objects and Methods

The only way you can read the value assigned to a property or change that value is by executing code. Because you can add code only to a method, code in Oracle Power Objects is often referred to as *method code*.

As described earlier, methods are as much a part of an object as properties. However, unlike properties, you call a method to tell the application that the method should start doing something.

Return to the world of automobiles for a moment. When you turn the key in the ignition, you are instructing the car to take an action. Turn the key, and the engine starts.

Similarly, you call a method to instruct it to perform some action that has been defined for it. Turning the key starts the engine, and calling the OpenWindow() method displays a form. In both cases, some action has already been defined: the engine starts, or the window appears. Figure 1.15 shows the Code Editor window for a form's OpenWindow() method.

As a mechanic or a developer, however, you can modify what happens. Perhaps you modify the car so that when the driver turns the key, the engine floods with gasoline rather than the normal flow of gasoline through the motor at startup. Similarly, as a developer, you can add code to the OpenWindow() method that not only opens the form, but displays the current date and time in a text field on the form.

1

Figure 1.15.
The form and its
`OpenWindow()` *method.*

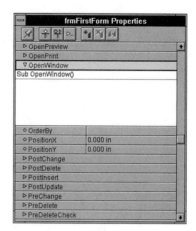

In the "Writing Code" section later today, you will begin working with methods. Here, it is only important to understand that methods are as much a characteristic of an object as are properties. Therefore, both properties and methods appear in the same Property sheet to signify that they are equally important features of the same object.

The form you created earlier has several methods intrinsic to it, such as the following:

`CloseWindow()`	Removes the window.
`DeleteRow()`	Deletes the data currently displayed in the form.
`PostDelete()`	Performs some actions after the data is deleted.

The application calls some of these methods automatically, when it detects that something has happened (in developer parlance, an *event*). For example, the application always calls the `PostDelete()` method after it deletes some related data (such as a record). Other methods never execute unless you call them from within code you write as a developer. To open a form, you must call that form's `OpenWindow()` method from within another method in another object.

If properties and methods still seem a little confusing, then perhaps a practical lesson will clarify these concepts. First, you must add some objects to the form. After you do that, you will add some code that calls a method and changes the value assigned to a property.

Adding Objects to the Form

As you might remember, a special floating toolbar, the Object palette, becomes visible when you select the form. The Object palette displays several buttons that, when pressed, enable you to add objects to the form. Each button corresponds to a different kind of object, as shown in Figure 1.16.

Figure 1.16.
The Object palette.

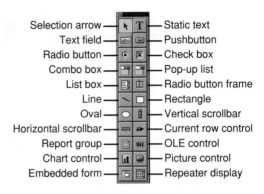

Selection arrow — Static text
Text field — Pushbutton
Radio button — Check box
Combo box — Pop-up list
List box — Radio button frame
Line — Rectangle
Oval — Vertical scrollbar
Horizontal scrollbar — Current row control
Report group — OLE control
Chart control — Picture control
Embedded form — Repeater display

When you click one of these buttons, the cursor changes to a *drawing tool* used to create a particular kind of object. For example, when you click the Text Field button on the Object palette, the cursor changes into the drawing tool for creating a text field (see Figure 1.17).

Figure 1.17.
The Text field drawing tool.

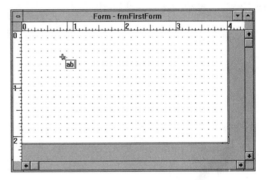

You then create the object by clicking and dragging across the face of the form. After you finish, the cursor reverts to the Selection tool (the standard arrow cursor, used for selecting, moving, and resizing objects).

In this exercise, you will add two objects to the form: a text field and a message box. Later, you will write code that displays a message in the text field when the user clicks the pushbutton.

Adding a Text Field

To add the text field, follow these steps:

1. Make the form the active window.

2. From the Object palette, click the Text Field drawing tool.

   The cursor now changes to indicate that you have selected the drawing tool.

3. Click the upper portion of the form.

The new text field appears on the form, as shown in Figure 1.18. The text displayed in it, Field1, is the name of the new object (that is, the value assigned to its Name property used when the application refers to the text field). The application gives the text field a default width and height, which you will change later.

Figure 1.18.
The new text field.

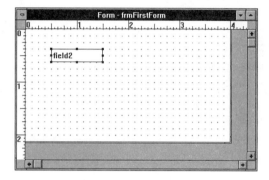

Adding a Pushbutton

To add the pushbutton, follow these steps:

1. From the Object palette, click the Pushbutton drawing tool.
2. On the lower portion of the form, click and hold down the left mouse button.
3. Drag the cursor across the lower section of the form.

   This technique is known as "click-and-drag" (see Figure 1.19). Here, rather than letting Power Objects assign a default width and height to the form, you are setting these dimensions yourself.

Figure 1.19.
Clicking and dragging.

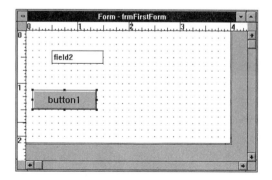

4. Move the cursor until the pushbutton has the width and height you want.
5. Release the mouse button.

In this case, the text appearing in the pushbutton is not its name, but the label appearing on the pushbutton at runtime. Obviously, in any application, you want to display a better title than Button1, so now you will change the label. In this case, however, instead of editing the value through the Property sheet, you can directly change the value assigned to the Label property through the pushbutton itself.

Changing the Label on the Pushbutton

To change the label on the pushbutton, follow these steps:

1. Click on the pushbutton repeatedly until you highlight the text appearing in the button (see Figure 1.20).

Figure 1.20.
Highlighted text.

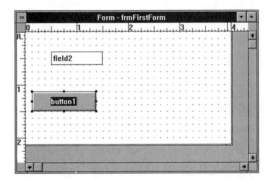

2. Type Hello in the pushbutton.

    Your text replaces Button1 as the value assigned to the Label property.

3. While you are here, change the name of the pushbutton to btnMessage.

4. Click the Save button.

Changing the Name of the Text Field

Now, using the same technique, you will change the text in the text field. However, in this case, you are editing the text field's Name property.

Why? Generally speaking, to avoid confusing the user, you do not want to change the label appearing for a pushbutton. You might, however, want the user to type any value into the field, or you might want the text field to display values that the application has read from the database.

Therefore, instead of a Label property, the text field has a Value property. Because the value is likely to change while the application is running, there's little point in assigning a value to it now.

However, it makes perfect sense to assign a new name to the text field. To change the name, follow these steps:

1. Click on the text field until you highlight the text appearing in it.

2. Type `fldMessage` in the text field.

The `Name` property of the text field has now changed. To confirm this fact, look at the Property sheet.

Viewing the Property Sheet for Different Objects

First of all, you might notice that the text in the title bar of the Property sheet has changed. When you have the text field selected, the Property sheet displays the properties and methods of the text field, not those of the form.

Click the pushbutton. The Property sheet changes again, displaying the properties and methods of this object, as shown in Figure 1.21. Not only do the values for some properties (such as `Name`) change when you click the pushbutton, but an entirely different set of properties and methods appear when you switch between the text field and the pushbutton. Some properties and methods appear only on the text field, whereas others appear only on the pushbutton.

Figure 1.21.
The new Property sheet.

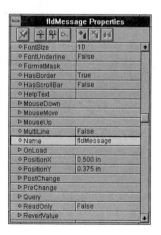

The mutating Property sheet might seem confusing at first, but when you think about these controls in terms of object-oriented development, it makes a great deal of sense. Some objects should have properties that other objects do not have. For example, a pushbutton has a very simple purpose: you click it, and something happens. Therefore, the text field does not need a `Value` property.

When the user types a value into a field, or the application assigns a value to that control (either by reading a value from the database or assigning a new value through code), however, you need some property of the text field to represent the value currently appearing in it. Therefore, the text field has a Value property, whereas the pushbutton does not.

To use the car analogy again, an engine has a property, RPMs, that indicates how hard the motor is working. The rearview mirror does not have the same property because no one ever needs to rotate it repeatedly. Similarly, a property appears on objects where it is appropriate, and not on the others.

Making Final Changes to the Text Field

Before continuing, you need to make a few modifications to the text field by following these steps:

1. Click the text field.

2. Holding down the mouse button, move the text field near the upper-left corner of the form. The text field should now be positioned as shown in Figure 1.22.

Figure 1.22.
The new position of the form.

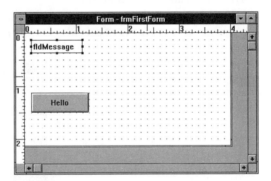

3. On the lower-right corner of the text field, on the rectangle appearing in that corner while the text field is selected, click and hold down the left mouse button.

   These rectangles, called *handles*, enable you to change the dimensions of the object by clicking and dragging (see Figure 1.23).

4. Drag the cursor across the form until it is twice as large, and then release the mouse button.

   You now have set the width and height of the text field, assigning new values to its SizeX and SizeY properties, respectively. If you are interested, look at the new values assigned to these properties in the Property sheet.

5. Scroll through the Property sheet until you find the Datatype property.

Figure 1.23.
Handles.

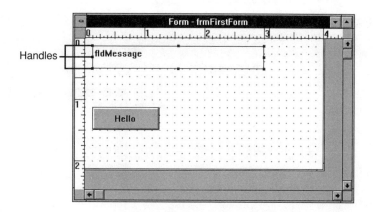

6. Click this property to display the drop-down window of all available data types.

7. From this list, select String.

    You need to select this data type so that the text field can properly display a message. For more information on data types, see the section "The Importance of Being the Right Data Type," later in this chapter.

8. In the window in the FontSize section of the Property sheet, shown in Figure 1.24, enter 18.

    This value is the new point size for text displayed in the field.

Figure 1.24.
Entering a font size.

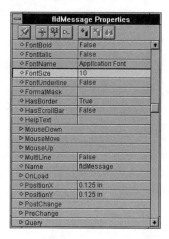

9. In the FontName section of the Property sheet, select Arial from the drop-down list of available fonts (see Figure 1.25).

    Arial is a more readable font than the default, System Font.

Figure 1.25.
The list of available fonts.

Note: The fonts available on your machine will differ from the ones shown in Figure 1.25. Many applications, such as Microsoft Word, come with additional fonts, and you can purchase new fonts from many companies.

10. Click Save to save your work.

So far, you have made several changes to the properties of the form, the text field, and the pushbutton. Now, you are ready to add some code to a method to change what happens when you press the pushbutton.

Writing Code

Right now, if you were to run the form and click the pushbutton, nothing would happen. Clicking the button would call a method of the pushbutton, Click(), but that method does not do anything unless you add code to it.

When other methods are triggered, however, they perform *default processing* that performs tasks without you, the developer, adding any code to them. In other words, Oracle Power Objects already has a set of actions predefined for these methods; you need only call these methods to perform these tasks. When the DeleteRow() method executes, for example, the application deletes a set of data (also called a *row* or a *record*), and the user sees the data disappear.

Most methods have some default processing associated with them. In fact, the Click() method has some default processing associated with it, but nothing relevant to your form. Therefore, when the user clicks the pushbutton, nothing happens.

Adding Method Code to the Pushbutton

There is no point in having a pushbutton unless it does something. First, you will write the code needed to display a message when the user clicks the pushbutton. Traditionally, the first thing programmers do when they work with a new development tool or programming language is write code that displays the message, Hello, world!.

First, you must see where you write this code by following these steps:

1. Select the pushbutton, and look at its Property sheet.

   If the Property sheet is no longer open, click the pushbutton and click the Edit Properties button.

2. Find the Click() method near the top of the Property sheet, and then click on its name.

   A drop-down window appears, as shown in Figure 1.26.

Figure 1.26.
The Code window for
Click().

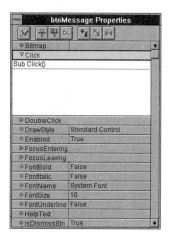

3. Click in this new window.

The focus moves within this window. This is is where you will type your code.

The reason why the code window is contained in the Property sheet is obvious, if you remember some of the basics of object-oriented development. Any code within this method executes only when this method is called. The code is completely self-contained within the method—when all the code inside the method finishes executing, the method is no longer called.

Additionally, the code you enter will execute only when the Click() method is called on this pushbutton. When the Click() method on other objects is called, the code added to the Click() method on the pushbutton does not execute. The instances of Click() on other objects are part of those objects, not of the pushbutton. Therefore, when you add method code to the pushbutton's Click() method, you are modifying what that method does only for that one

object, the pushbutton. Therefore, the method code you add to this method "belongs" to the pushbutton just as much as the new setting for its Label property. This is an important part of object-oriented design: an object's definition is completely self-contained, including changes you make to its properties and methods.

Enough abstraction. Now you are ready to enter and test the code by performing the following steps:

1. In the code window for the Click() method, enter the following code:

```
Sub Click()
MSGBOX "Hello, world!"
```

Now you can test the form to see if it behaves as expected.

> **Note:** Throughout this book, every time you are instructed to type in code, check the code window. Do not retype the first line of code if that line already appears in the window. For example, in the preceding code, the line Sub Click() should already appear in the code window. You simply need to type MSGBOX "Hello, world!".

2. With the form selected, click the Test Form button.

   The form now appears as it will at runtime. The Oracle Power Objects interface changes, replacing the toolbar you used to design the new application and form. The new toolbar displays several controls used to edit and view data. Additionally, when you click the Stop button (the one with the stop sign), the form stops running, and Oracle Power Objects returns to design-time mode, displaying all the windows and toolbars with which you are now familiar.

3. Click the Hello pushbutton.

   The message box now appears, as shown in Figure 1.27. Behind the scenes, Oracle Power Objects recognized that it was time to call the Click() method on the pushbutton. In this sense, Power Objects responded to an *event*, a concept discussed later in the next section.

Figure 1.27.
The message.

4. Click the OK button to dismiss the message box.

You might also notice a small palette near the form. This new palette controls the Run-Time Debugger, which you will use later today to help test and control the execution of method code.

Events Triggering Methods

In this exercise, the application called the `Click()` method of the pushbutton in response to an event. In Oracle Power Objects, an *event* is any occurrence that the application recognizes. Clicking the pushbutton is an event, as is deleting a record or opening a form. Generally, when an event occurs, Oracle Power Objects calls one or more methods in response. For example, when you click the mouse on an object, Power Objects calls up to four events: `Click()`, `MouseDown()`, `MouseUp()`, and (depending on whether you moved the mouse) `MouseMove()`. These methods are triggered in a specific sequence, each capturing a different part of the event (such as clicking the mouse).

By calling more than one method in response to the mouse click, Oracle Power Objects enables you to respond at exactly the right time. For example, if you want the application to do something while the mouse button is still pressed, you can add the necessary method code to `MouseDown()` or `MouseMove()`. If instead you want the application to respond after the mouse click has finished, you add the code to `Click()`.

Commonly, methods in this type of sequence already have default processing associated with them, which can include calling other methods. As you shall see later in this book, you can use these features of methods to intercept the processing normally performed by Oracle Power Objects. In other words, you can interrupt the chain of methods calling each other. For example, you can use the `DeleteRow()` method to check whether deleting the data breaks any business rules (that is, don't delete any outstanding orders) before allowing the application to perform the deletion.

To illustrate how methods can call other methods, you will now add some method code to the form that calls the `Click()` method on the pushbutton. This exercise illustrates that you can explicitly call other methods from within method code. Remember that some methods call other methods as part of their default processing; in this example, you will be doing the calling yourself.

Calling Methods from Other Methods

To illustrate this point, you will add some code to a method that Oracle Power Objects calls automatically when the user opens the form. This code will call the `Click()` method on the pushbutton whenever the form opens.

1. Select the form.

   You need to click on the form itself, not any object on the form, to select the form. Before you become accustomed to this technique, you might need to click around the face of the form a few times before you actually select the form. Once the form is selected, its name appears in the title bar of the Property sheet.

2. Open the code window for the OnLoad() method of the form.

The application calls the OnLoad() method whenever it first loads an object into memory and displays it. Figure 1.28 shows code added to the form's OnLoad() method that calls the pushbutton's Click() method whenever the form opens.

Figure 1.28.

The OnLoad() code window.

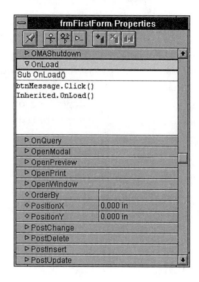

3. Enter the following code in the OnLoad() method, below the Sub OnLoad() line:

```
btnMessage.Click()
Inherited.OnLoad()
```

The first line of this method code calls the OnLoad() method. The second line calls the default processing for OnLoad(). For more information on default processing, see the section "Default Processing" later in this chapter.

4. Test the form by clicking the Run Form pushbutton.

The message box you saw before appears, because the application called the Click() method on the pushbutton when the form opened.

The Oracle Basic Programming Language

By now, you have had a small taste of the Oracle Basic programming language. Oracle Basic uses a syntax familiar to anyone who has programmed in Basic. In fact, the standard Basic commands and functions behave in exactly the same fashion as they do in Microsoft Visual Basic and Microsoft Access. The designers of Oracle Power Objects wanted the programming language to use this industry-standard Basic syntax, to flatten the learning curve for new users of Oracle Power Objects who had prior experience with these other development tools.

In addition to the standard Basic commands and functions, Oracle Basic also includes many *extensions*, or additions to Basic. Oracle Basic's extensions are the object-oriented terminology needed to identify objects by name, evaluate and set the values for properties, and call methods. Therefore, although Basic is not itself an object-oriented language, Oracle Basic includes extensions that are object-oriented. In addition to entering the name of an object, you can use several shorthands in Oracle Basic for quickly identifying objects.

Default Processing

Return for a moment to the `Inherited.OnLoad()` statement in the code you just wrote and tested. As you might remember from the earlier discussion of methods, most methods in Oracle Power Objects have default processing associated with them. In other words, if you do not add any code to it, the method performs some tasks automatically when called.

Remember this important rule: Whenever you add method code of any sort to a method, the code prevents the default processing from being performed.

The purpose of the `Inherited.method_name()` statement is that it enables the default processing for a method to occur. If `OnLoad()` has any default processing, it executes at the point in the code where the `Inherited.OnLoad()` statement appears.

To illustrate this point, perform the following steps:

1. Select the form and find the `OpenWindow()` method in its Property sheet.
2. Enter the following method code below the `Sub OpemWindow()` line in the code window for `OpenWindow()`:

   ```
   ' Nothing happening!
   ```

   Any text following an apostrophe is a comment, which means that the text doesn't do anything when the code executes. Comments serve an important purpose; they explain how method code works.
3. Click the Run Form pushbutton.

The form does not appear! The comment you added to `OpenWindow()` suppressed the method's default processing, which included opening the window.

To enable the form to open, enter the following last line in the code for `OpenWindow()`:

```
Sub OpenWindow()
' Nothing happening!
Inherited.OpenWindow()
```

Now, when you click the Run Form button, the form appears. The `Inherited.OpenWindow()` statement told the application to go ahead and execute the method's default processing, even though you added method code to it.

Displaying a Message in the Text Field

Finally, you will display the `Hello, world!` message in the text field on the form rather than in a message box. This exercise shows how to change the value assigned to an object at runtime.

1. Delete all the code added to the form's `OnLoad()` method.

2. Select the pushbutton and open its `Click()` method.

3. Replace the code you wrote earlier with the following code below the `Sub Click()` line:

   ```
   fldMessage.Value = "Hello, world!"
   ```

4. Run the form and click the pushbutton.

The message now appears in the text field (see Figure 1.29).

Figure 1.29.

The message in the text field.

Congratulations! You have learned several ways to succeed at the same task, displaying a message to the user. More important, you have become familiar with writing object-oriented code.

Object References in Method Code

By now, you have probably noticed that, in method code, references to objects take one of two forms: `object_name.property` for properties or `object_name.method()` for methods.

For example, to change the `Value` property of the text field (and by extension, the text it displays), you wrote the following statement:

```
fldMessage.Value = "Hello, world!"
```

This object-oriented syntax will appear in practically all your method code and is one of the important extensions in Oracle Basic to the Basic language. You also will use these object-oriented extensions when you test your application with the Run-Time Debugger.

Testing the Form

So far, you have tested a form by running it and seeing what happens. Although that's how you test forms about half the time, you use the Run-Time Debugger the other times you want to test

a form. While you are running the form, you can summon the Run-Time Debugger to perform the following tasks:

☐ Interrogate the value assigned to the property of an object.

☐ Interrogate the value assigned to a variable. When you create a variable in method code and assign a value to it, you can determine the current value of the variable through the Debugger.

☐ Track the value assigned to a property or variable. Using the Debugger (Expressions) window, you can keep track of the value as it changes.

☐ Observe the sequence in which the application calls methods. This sequence, also known as the *calling chain*, is visible through the Debugger.

In other words, the Debugger is a very useful tool. In this exercise, you will use the Debugger to view some of the values assigned to properties of the form and the text field.

Summoning the Debugger

To summon the Debugger, follow these steps:

1. Click the Run Form button to run the form.

   The form appears, along with the Debugger palette, as shown in Figure 1.30. The buttons appearing on this palette stop and restart the form, and they can summon the two windows that constitute the Run-Time Debugger.

2. Click the pushbutton on the form to display the message in the text field.

Figure 1.30.
The Debugger palette.

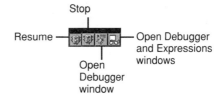

3. From the Debugger palette, click the Open Debugger window button.

The Debugger (Main) window now appears (see Figure 1.31). The form pauses execution while you use the Debugger (Main) window to interrogate the values assigned to properties, as well as control the execution of method code.

Figure 1.31.
The Debugger window.

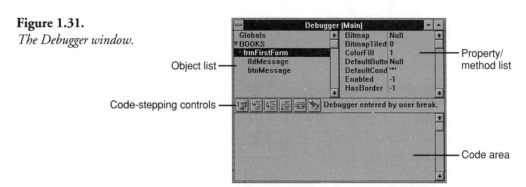

The Debugger window has the following components:

Component	Description
Object list	The list of objects within the application and the form, including the application and form themselves.
Property/Method list	The list of all properties and methods that belong to the currently selected object (chosen from the Object list). Methods do not appear in this list unless they have method code added to them.
Code area	The method code from the currently selected method. If no method is selected, then nothing appears in this area.
Code stepping controls	These buttons help test method code.

You are now ready to view the values assigned to properties of the form.

Interrogating Properties Through the Debugger

From the Object list, select the name of the form, `frmFirstForm`. The Property/Method list changes to show all the properties of the form and one of the methods. The `OpenWindow()` method appears in this list because it still has method code added to it. If you want to view this code, click the name of the method in the Property/Method list. The code then appears in the Code area of the Debugger (Main) window.

To get some experience using the Debugger, follow these steps:

1. In the Property/Method list, scroll down to the `Name` property.

   The name of the form appears here.

2. In the Object list, click the triangle next to the name of the form.

   An indented list of all the objects now appears. In this case, because you have added only the text field and pushbutton to the form, only two items appear in this new sublist.

3. Click the name of the text field, fldMessage, in the Object list.

   The Property/Method list now changes to show the properties and methods of the text field, not the form.

4. Scroll down the Property/Method list to see the Value property.

   The value now assigned to this property is the message displayed in the text field.

5. Once again, click the name of the form in the Object list, and then find the ColorFill property in the Property/Method list.

You might be surprised to find that, instead of displaying the name of a color (for example, blue, red, yellow), the Debugger displays a number. The reason for this is simple: Oracle Power Objects stores a numeric value for the ColorFill property rather than a string of characters. When the application displays the form, it interprets the value assigned to this property.

The Importance of Being the Right Data Type

Stop running the form for a moment (by first clicking the Continue button on the Debugger window, and then clicking the Stop button on the toolbar). In the form's Property sheet, click the ColorFill property and press F1.

The online help topic for the ColorFill property appears, including a table of the values that can be assigned to this property (see Figure 1.32). As you can see from the table, Oracle Power Objects interprets a specific value (12, for example) as a particular color (in the case of 12, Blue-Green). If you change the value of ColorFill to a different number, Oracle Power Objects then reinterprets the value as the new color and repaints the background of the form accordingly.

Data types are very important in Oracle Power Objects because your code will not run properly unless you assign the correct type of data to a property or a variable. The following are types of data types in Oracle Power Objects:

Data type	Description
Integer	A whole number between –32,768 and 32,767.
Long	A whole number between –2147483648 and 2147483647.
Float	A floating-point real number between –1.401298E45 and 1.401298E45.

continues

Data type	Description
String	A string of characters, which can be both alpha (letters and symbols) and numeric (numbers).
Date	A decimal value in which the number before the decimal defines the date and the number after the decimal defines the time.
Object	Identifies an object (that is, a form or a pushbutton).
Variant	A "catch-all" data type that can accept any type of data. As appealing as this sounds, however, you should use this data type only when absolutely necessary.

Figure 1.32.

The online help topic for ColorFill.

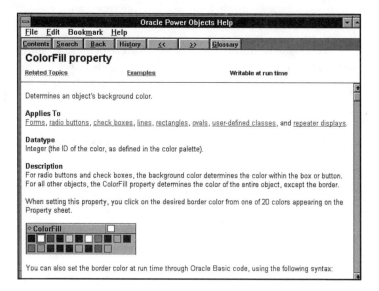

If you try to assign the wrong data type to a property or a variable (that is, a string of characters to a property that has the Integer data type), Oracle Power Objects will stop execution and display an error message. Additionally, when a method returns a value or takes a variable as an argument, you must be equally careful to use the right data type, or else you will suffer the same results.

To demonstrate the importance of using the right data for the right data type, perform the following steps:

1. Add a new pushbutton to the form.

2. In the Click() method of the pushbutton, add the following method code after the Sub Click() line:

```
frmFirstForm.ColorFill = "Blue"
```

3. Run the form and click the new pushbutton.

   The application immediately stops running, and you see an error message (see Figure 1.33).

Figure 1.33.
The application stopped running; the error message you see.

4. With the form no longer running, select the new pushbutton.
5. Press the Delete key.

The pushbutton now disappears. This step removes any further temptation you might feel to crash your program!

Summary

In this first day of instruction, you have learned a great deal about both object-oriented development and Oracle Power Objects.

☐ In an object-oriented environment, objects are self-contained components of the application.

☐ Objects have properties and methods. Properties are characteristics of an object that take a value. Methods are characteristics of the object that, when called, perform some processing.

☐ Events often trigger methods. Additionally, you can call a method from within method code.

☐ In addition to calling other methods, method code can evaluate and change the value assigned to a property.

☐ Many methods have default processing that automatically executes when you call the method.

☐ Method code suppresses a method's default processing unless you add the statement `Inherited.method_name()`.

☐ As part of their default processing, methods call other methods, or otherwise are called in some sequence.

☐ To test a form, you can run it. While it is running, you can perform additional tests through the Run-Time Debugger.

☐ You must be careful to use the right data type when you work with properties, methods, and variables.

You now understand the basics for working with Oracle Power Objects. However, the one topic that you conspicuously have not learned is databases, which are the topic of the next two chapters. Before moving on, however, a quick quiz will help cement your understanding of the Oracle Power Objects interface, object-oriented development, and programming in Basic.

What Comes Next?

Tomorrow, you take the first steps toward creating a database application by creating a new database and adding objects to it.

Q&A

Q There are a lot of windows open in the Desktop. How can I cut down on the clutter and confusion?

A Don't forget that you can always minimize or close windows that you're not using. Additionally, if you are not editing the properties or methods of an object, you can close the Property sheet.

Q There are a lot of properties and methods for some objects. How can I keep track of them all?

A The online help for Oracle Power Objects is context-sensitive, so you can quickly get the information relevant to whatever you're currently using. When you have an object selected and you press F1, the online help topic describing that object appears. Similarly, if you have a property or method selected in the Property sheet and you press F1, you get information on that topic.

Q How important is it for me to understand object-oriented development?

A Extremely! Although some elements of this approach might seem abstract, the whole point of object-oriented development is to make the development process as simple and practical as possible. In an object-oriented tool like Oracle Power Objects, you use the same techniques to work with any object, from forms to recordsets, from OLE objects to sessions.

Q What type of applications can I write with Oracle Power Objects?

A Any type of application that uses a database to store information. Like similar products (such as Microsoft Visual Basic and Sybase PowerBuilder), Oracle Power Objects is designed to be a multipurpose development tool. However, Oracle Power Objects

demonstrates its greatest power and potential when you connect the application to a database. Because of the advantages of modern database technology, an increasing range of applications rely on databases.

Workshop

The Workshop consists of quiz questions to help you solidify your understanding of the material covered. Try and understand the quiz questions before you go on to the next lesson.

Quiz

1. In object-oriented terminology, what is a property? A method?
2. Why do data types matter?
3. What happens when you add method code to a method?
4. What is the only way to change the value assigned to a property at runtime?
5. Is the application an object?
6. What usually happens when the application recognizes an event?

Quiz Answers

1. A property is a characteristic of an object that can accept a value. A method is also a characteristic of an object, but in contrast to a property, it takes some action when called.
2. Data types matter because your application crashes when you assign the wrong type of data to a property or variable.
3. The method code suppresses the method's default processing unless you add the `Inherited.method_name()` statement to the code.
4. As the developer, you can change the value of a property at runtime only through method code.
5. Yes, the application is an object, as are the other two types of file objects in Oracle Power Objects: libraries and sessions. You can view the Property sheet for all three kinds of objects.
6. Normally, the application calls one or more methods in response to an event.

Creating a Table

Overview

Before your application can talk to a database, it must have a database to which to talk. This book uses a local Blaze database that you will build from scratch. (Oracle Power Objects comes with a local database engine, Blaze, that you can use for a single-user application or to prototype database objects to be added later to Oracle7 or SQL Server.) This database will include all the database objects and data used in the Bookstore application.

At the beginning of this lesson, you will create the new database. Before you can add tables and data, however, you must first create a session, which provides the means for connecting the application to the database. After you create a session that can open this connection, you can begin adding database objects and data to the database. Today, you learn the following:

- [ ] An introduction to relational databases
- [ ] Creating a Blaze database
- [ ] Schemas in databases
- [ ] Connect strings and databases
- [ ] Sessions, databases, and applications
- [ ] Creating a session
- [ ] Viewing the objects in a session
- [ ] Tables and data
- [ ] Adding a table
- [ ] Entering data into the table

Oracle Power Objects and Relational Databases

Through Oracle Power Objects, you can create applications that use relational databases for storing, organizing, and protecting information. The current version of Oracle Power Objects can communicate with two types of remote servers, Oracle7 and SQL Server, as well as a local database, the Blaze database engine. Blaze databases are called "local" because they are stored as files on the same system as the application, Microsoft Windows or Macintosh personal computer. In the case of Oracle7 and SQL Server, the application must communicate across a network with a separate server machine.

If you're not familiar with this terminology, here's a quick summary of some of the important concepts.

What Is a Database Engine?

A *database engine* is any format for storing and maintaining information in a database. The engine not only includes the structure and organization of objects used to store information, but also the intelligence behind the database that makes sure that information gets stored, updated, or deleted properly.

Blaze is a database engine, as are Oracle7, Microsoft Access, Sybase SQL Server, and other database formats. Recently developed database engines like these often use a relational format for storing and maintaining information.

What Is a Relational Database?

A *relational database* stores information in a way that makes it easy to relate different pieces together. For example, information about books and publishers have an obvious connection: publishers manufacture books. Additionally, a list of books and a list of book topics have obvious relevance to each other, as do customer book orders and book titles. Ideally, you would like to have some way to quickly relate these separate but related pieces of information so that you can answer some important questions. Which types of books does a particular customer normally buy? In which type of books do particular publishers specialize?

A relational database stores information in a way that simplifies the task of answering these questions. Each category of information (such as book titles, publishers, and customers) is stored in a different table from the other. Each table is divided into several columns, each of which represents a different piece of information. In the case of book titles, a table might have columns for the title, the author's last name, the author's first name, and the price. Figure 2.1 shows rows and columns in a table.

Figure 2.1.
Rows and columns in a table.

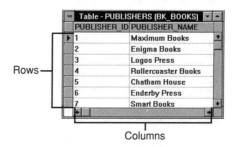

Each table stores data in records, or rows. Therefore, every book will have a record in the TITLES table, including information covering its title, author's last and first names, and price. Each of these components of the book's records is stored in a separate column in the table.

Tables: Separate but Related

The database you will build in this lesson will have a TITLES table that stores information on each book in this fashion. Information describing a publisher (name, address, company rep, and so on) will be stored in a different table, PUBLISHERS. Records for each customer will appear in the CUSTOMERS table, where there will be columns for the customer's name, address, and phone number.

At this point, you might ask yourself how you connect the information in one table, such as PUBLISHERS, to a related table such as TITLES. To give you a short preview, a relational database can look for matching information among records in two separate tables. When you ask the database for records (an act known as a *query* in relational database parlance), you specify the columns that will have matching values. In the case of TITLES and PUBLISHERS, for example, both tables will have a column containing an ID number for each publisher, PUBLISHER_ID. Figure 2.2 illustrates this relationship.

Figure 2.2.
Joining the two tables.

Column Name	Datatype
TITLE_ID	NUMBER
TITLE_NAME	VARCHAR2
AUTHLNAME	VARCHAR2
AUTHFNAME	VARCHAR2
PUBLISHER_ID	NUMBER
PRICE	FLOAT
WS_PRICE	FLOAT
PROMOTION_PRICE	FLOAT
PRINTING	INTEGER
TYPE_ID	NUMBER

Column Name	Datatype
PUBLISHER_ID	NUMBER
PUBLISHER_NAME	VARCHAR2

The two tables share a common column

The SQL Language

Whether you are interested in data stored in a single table or several tables, the instrument used to access these records is the same. Relational databases use the *Structured Query Language* (SQL) to query records. This language uses an English-like syntax to simplify the task of writing queries. When you ask for records from a single table (a relatively simple type of query), the SQL code might look something like the following:

```
SELECT PUBLISHER_NAME FROM PUBLISHERS WHERE PUBLISHER_ID > 100
➥ORDER BY PUBLISHER_NAME
```

The keyword SELECT tells the database that you want to query records. Immediately following that, you specify the columns that have information you want to view. You can specify each column by name, or you can select all of the columns using an asterisk (*) rather than the names

of the columns. For example, to get data from all the columns in PUBLISHERS, you would write the following:

```
SELECT * FROM PUBLISHERS
```

Following the list of columns to be queried, you enter the FROM statement, followed by the name of the table. Finally, you can enter conditions, and instruct the database how to sort the records returned from the query.

A *condition* tells the database to return only those records that meet some criteria. The condition always begins with the keyword WHERE and can include any number of criteria. For example, to find the record for a publisher named Big Books, you would enter the following:

```
SELECT * FROM PUBLISHERS WHERE PUBLISHER_NAME = 'Big Books'
```

Because the name of the publisher is a string, you need to surround (or *delimit*) it with quotes. In SQL, you use single quotes around strings; in Basic code, you use double quotes.

To sort records, you specify the column used for the sort. The keywords ORDER BY tell the database that you are identifying the column to sort records. For example, to sort by the names of publishing companies (in ascending alphabetical order), you would enter the following:

```
SELECT * FROM PUBLISHERS ORDER BY PUBLISHER_NAME
```

This section is intended to give you only a flavor of the SQL language. Oracle Power Objects is designed to save you the hassle of writing SQL code to query records for an application. Therefore, instead of writing a SQL query to display a list of books on a form, you will use some much simpler techniques.

There are several places in Oracle Power Objects, however, where you need some grounding in SQL. Fortunately, the online help provided with Oracle Power Objects includes a SQL language reference.

Breaking Down Your Data

Before continuing, take out a piece of scrap paper and write down all of the types of information a bookstore would need. You have already identified a few categories of information: books, publishers, and customers. What other functionally distinct categories of information can you think of?

Following are some other categories of data you might want to store in the bookstore's database:

- ☐ Employees
- ☐ Types of books

- ☐ Customer purchase histories
- ☐ Book orders
- ☐ Books in stock
- ☐ Books on order
- ☐ Marketing and promotions

In a relational database, you would store each of these categories of information in a separate table. All of these tables will have some potential relationship with one another; however, you need to keep their data separate. As long as there is some point of comparison between two tables (the ID number of a publisher, the name of the customer who placed an order), it is possible to relate information in the two tables.

This process of breaking down information into separate tables while you still make it possible to relate data stored in separate tables, is called *normalization*. This crucial technique of database design deserves a book to effectively describe it—in fact, there are quite a few textbooks on the subject. In trying to think of all the types of tables you might need in the Bookstore database, you were performing a simple kind of normalization.

As complex as normalization can be, following are a few simple rules to keep in mind:

- ☐ If the same information is duplicated in two tables (such as a customer's address), you should define it in a single table. This removes the headache of ensuring that the same information is stored identically in the separate tables. If you need a customer's address for an order, you can look up the address in the CUSTOMERS table.
- ☐ When you create a point of comparison (such as the name of a publisher), you must use the same data type. For example, if you identify publishers by a numeric ID, you should always use the same data type (such as Number).
- ☐ You should use some features of relational databases to ensure that information is stored in an intelligent way. For example, you might need a unique ID number for every publisher. A special database object, a *sequence*, can generate a new ID number every time you create a new publisher record in the PUBLISHERS table.
- ☐ Make the names of tables and columns descriptive but succinct. Remember, other people might need to look through the database, so you need to use self-explanatory names rather than cryptic ones.

Other Features of Relational Databases

Aside from storing data in tables, relational databases generally also have the following important features:

Constraints	When you define tables for storing information, you can often define constraints that limit what you can enter as part of a record. For example, you might want to prevent a user from entering a book price of zero, or less than zero. By adding a rule to the definition of a column, you can ensure that any record of a book includes a price greater than nothing!
Security	Relational databases use a variety of means for limiting the range of data the user can view and edit.
Server-based processing	You can often write code within the database itself to perform some task. For example, you can write a piece of SQL code stored within the database that checks to see whether a customer has any outstanding orders before a user deletes that customer's record. This small piece of code can help you to avoid having a very unhappy customer on your hands.
Views	One of the objects common to relational databases is a view, which provides a fast way to relate information in different tables and limit the amount of information in a single table a user can see.
Sequences	If you need to generate a unique numeric ID for each new record, a sequence is a special type of database object that automatically performs this task for you.
Indexes	An index is yet another database object that speeds up the database's capability to read and write records.

Note: Not every relational database has all these features. For example, SQL Server has indexes, but not sequences.

In this book, you will become very familiar with nearly all these elements of a relational database. For example, in tomorrow's lesson, you will create a view that will help you display information about book titles. However, today you will focus on the basics: creating a new Blaze database, adding a table to it, and entering records into this table.

Creating a Blaze Database

When you create a Blaze database, you make a new file on your system—usually in the same directory as your application. Normally, Blaze databases have the filename extension .BLZ, as will the database for this book, BOOKS.BLZ.

To create a new Blaze database, follow these steps:

1. Select New Blaze DB from the File menu.

   The Create Blaze Database File dialog box for creating Blaze databases appears (see Figure 2.3).

Figure 2.3.

The Create Blaze Database File dialog box for creating a new Blaze database.

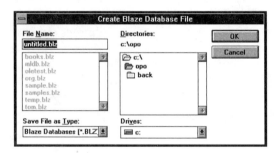

2. Select the C:\BOOKS directory as the location for your new database.

3. Enter the name of the new database, BOOKS.BLZ.

4. Click OK.

You have now created a Blaze database. It currently has no tables for storing data in it; without any tables, the database does not contain any data yet, either. The database does have two things, however: it has the means to understand SQL, and it has a schema.

Schemas and Databases

Most relational databases have *schemas* (often called *users*), which define who you are, and what you can see and edit in the database. Before giving yourself access, you need to provide the name of your schema (such as ClarkKent or SuperUser) and a password (such as Krypton).

The first schema created for a Blaze database is DBA (short for *database administrator*), and its password is DBA. Often, when you need to type in both the schema name and the password, you enter both on the same line, separated by a slash (for example, DBA/DBA). However, you do not need to specify a schema name and password for a Blaze database. You connect to the DBA/DBA schema by default.

At this point, you have a database but no way to access it. The next step is to create a session, a special type of object that gives you the capability to connect to the database.

Sessions, Databases, and Applications

As mentioned earlier, a session provides the means through which the application can communicate with the database. In a client/server setting, the application and the database must remain separate pieces: the database (or the server) stores and protects the data, while the application (or the client) gives users the means to request and edit this data from the database. Both can perform other tasks as well, but this relationship is the core of what it means to be client/server.

Ideally, you would like your applications to be able to talk to multiple databases and your databases to talk to multiple applications. For example, the same financial information might be used by your accounting staff, but some of it is also important for your executives to review. Therefore, you want to be able to write applications for both groups in the company that look at the same data in different ways. The accounting staff does not need to see information about an employee's history, so there should be some way to keep the EMP_HISTORY table invisible to the accounting department.

In addition to defining the range of information viewed by each user, you also need a simple way to connect to the database. If you install a new Oracle7 database, you want to be able to switch all the applications to the new server with a minimum of hassle.

To meet these goals, Oracle Power Objects connects to databases through a special kind of object, a session. The session does two things:

- [ ] Defines the location of the server, as well as a schema and password used to access data in it.
- [ ] Opens or closes a connection to the database. When the connection is open, you can read and write data; when it is closed, you can't.

Because the session can use any schema in the database, you can limit the information accessed through an application to whatever tables and views are visible to that schema. In addition, by making the information needed to connect to the schema a property of the session, Oracle Power Objects makes it easy to switch between databases as needed. Furthermore, because the session can determine when a connection is opened or closed, you can exert fine control over when the user can access the database.

Armed with this knowledge of relational databases and sessions, you are ready to create a connection to your new Blaze database.

Creating a New Session

To create the new session, follow these steps:

1. Select New Session from the File menu, or click the New Session button.

   The Create Session dialog box appears, in which you define the characteristics of the database session (see Figure 2.4). There are three different database types that you can specify in this dialog box: Blaze (the local database provided with Oracle Power Objects), Oracle7, and SQL Server.

Figure 2.4.

Creating a new session in the Create Session dialog box.

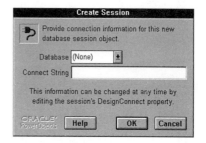

2. From the drop-down list of database types, select Blaze.

   The next step will be to enter a connect string for the session so that you can open a connection to the Blaze database. Connect strings use the following syntax:

   `schema/password@location`

   A connect string includes the components described in Table 2.1.

Table 2.1. The components of a connect string.

Component	Description
Schema	The database schema through which database objects will be accessed.
Password	The password for that schema.
Location	The address of the database on the network.

Because you are working with a Blaze database, you specify the directory and filename of the Blaze database file—in this case, C:\BOOKS\BOOKS.BLZ. Remember, you can omit the schema name and password so that you access by default the DBA/DBA schema.

When you work with connect strings, you must remember that if any part of the connect string is incorrect (that is, there is a typo in the password), you will be unable to connect to the database.

3. For the connect string, enter the following in the Create Session dialog box (see Figure 2.5):

```
C:\BOOKS\BOOKS.BLZ
```

Figure 2.5.

Entering the connect string.

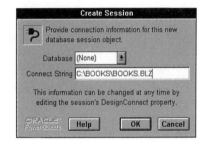

4. Click OK.

The common dialog box for creating files then appears, prompting you to name the new file containing the description of the session, as well as the directory in which you want to place it.

5. Enter the name of the session, BOOKS.POS.

By default, session filenames have the extension .POS (short for *Power Objects Session*).

6. Select the C:\BOOKS directory to be the location where the new session file will appear.

7. Click OK.

As shown in Figure 2.6, the new session, BOOKS, now appears in the Main window, and the Session Designer window for BOOKS is open. The name of the session (as shown in the Main window and in the Name section of the property sheet) is always the same as the filename, without the .POS extension. If you tried to rename the session through its Property sheet, the name would automatically revert to BOOKS.

Figure 2.6.

The new session in the Main window.

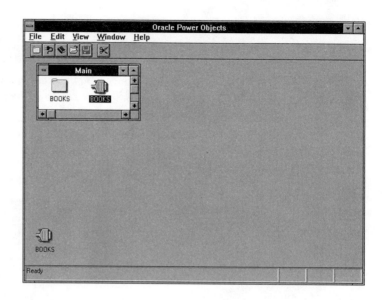

Connect Strings as Properties of the Session

If it is not open already, open the Property sheet for the session. Presently, only two of the properties have values assigned to them: Name and DesignConnect. It's easy to understand the Name property, but what does DesignConnect do?

Sessions have three different connect string properties, each corresponding to a different time when you can connect to a database, as shown in Table 2.2.

Table 2.2. The connect properties of sessions.

Property	Description
DesignConnect	Used when you work with database objects through the Session Designer window. Later in this lesson, you will add a new table to this window and add data to the table. If you don't enter any value for the other two connect string properties, the application uses the connect string assigned to the DesignConnect property.
DesignRunConnect	Used when you run a form or report connected to a table in the database. If you want a form to access a different schema in the database when you test a form, you must specify the connect

Property	Description
	string for that schema through the `DesignRunConnect` property. If you do not enter a connect string for the other two properties, the application uses the connect string entered for `DesignRunConnect`.
RunConnect	Used when the completed and compiled application attempts to connect to a schema in a database. Again, if you do not enter a connect string for the other two properties, the application uses the connect string assigned to `RunConnect`.

Why three different connect strings? Primarily, you might want to develop and test your application on one database (such as a Blaze database), and then connect the finished application to another database. You do not necessarily want to touch the data in the "real" database, so you use the other database for prototyping and testing your application. Later, you can connect the application to the other database, and make any modification to the tables, views, and other objects in it.

Therefore, you have connect strings for the following three uses:

☐ Connecting to the database directly through Oracle Power Objects

☐ Connecting to a database when you test a Power Objects application

☐ Connecting to a database when you run the finished, compiled application

Suppose that you wanted to deploy your Bookstore application on an Oracle7 server, used by a large company. You can specify the connect string for the Blaze database in the `DesignConnect` and `DesignRunConnect` properties, and the connect string for the Oracle7 server in the `RunConnect` property. While you are building your application, it connects to the Blaze database. When you are ready to deploy the finished application, it communicates with the Oracle7 server.

Now you're ready to start adding database objects to your Blaze database. By now, a few elements of our earlier discussion about relational databases should start making more sense. As you build the table, more aspects of relational databases should become even more clear.

Building Your First Table

First, you must get a connection to the database. Double-click the Connector icon in the Database Session window (see Figure 2.7). You now have a connection, although you don't see anything yet in the database.

Figure 2.7.

The connection opened to BOOKS.BLZ.

You'll start simple. The first table you will build contains information on publishers and contains only two columns.

1. Click the New Table button on the Session Designer toolbar.

   A spreadsheet-like window, the Table Editor window, opens (see Figure 2.8). Then the Property sheet for the new session also appears. Each row in this spreadsheet defines a new column in the table, as you shall soon see.

Figure 2.8.

The Table Editor window.

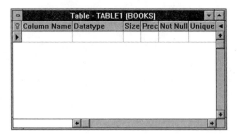

2. In the Property sheet, type PUBLISHERS as the name of the new table.

   By default, the name is TABLE1. However, you want to give your table a more descriptive name. Remember that as you develop databases and applications, you might need to come back to an object and remember what it does. After a few weeks, you might not remember what TABLE1 is supposed to do. Additionally, other developers might need to work on the database, so you need to give them some clues about the purpose of the table.

   Currently, the table does not have any columns (that is, categories of information), so you need to add some.

3. On the first blank line of the Table Designer window, click in the Column Name cell.

4. Enter the following information in the cells of this first column description:

Datatype	Number
Size	Leave blank
Prec	Leave blank

Not Null	Leave blank
Unique	Leave blank

You now have finished creating your first column in your first table. But what do all these components mean? Many of them are *constraints*, limiting the type of information that can be stored in the column.

Table 2.3 explains the information entered for each column in the Table Editor window.

Table 2.3. Sections of the Table Editor window.

Component	Description
Column Name	The name of the column.
Datatype	The data type of any data entered in the column. Possible values include Varchar2, Number, Integer, Float, Date, Char, Long, Long Raw, and Row ID. Keep in mind that these are the data types applied to columns in the database, not controls (such as text fields) in the application. However, there is some correspondence: the data type Varchar2 in the database corresponds to the data type String in the application because both are used for a string of characters.
	As you remember from yesterday's lesson, when you select a data type, you limit (or *constrain*) the type of information the column can store. After you set the data type of a column to Number, it can only store numeric values of a particular type, not strings of text.
Size	Sets the maximum amount of memory set aside for values in this column. For Char and Varchar2 data types, the number entered for Size is the number of characters for any string stored in this column. For numeric data types, Size limits the precision of values.
Precision	Determines the precision of numeric values (that is, the number of digits past the decimal point). This component applies only to columns that have a data type of Float (a floating-point number).
Not Null	Indicates that every record must include some value for this column.
Unique	Indicates that every value entered in this column must be unique—no duplicate values in other records.

Why Do You Need All This?

If you're not familiar with relational databases, these parameters might seem to be a bit of overkill for you. These characteristics of databases, however, are crucial for maintaining information in a precise and efficient way. Think for a moment of the database as holding data in the same way that a warehouse holds goods. Each package corresponds to a record, in that it contains several components of particular types. When the warehouse adds objects to a package to ship to a customer, you want to be certain that exactly the right type of parts are added to each carton. Each component must be of the correct size and type. Additionally, you might want to make sure that every customer receives a particular item.

In the same way, the columns in your table indicate what type of information you can store. Just as with the warehouse, the database needs to know the type and size of each component. Although technically you can store numbers as String values, doing so is highly inefficient. Instead, you want to choose a numeric data type, of the right degree of numeric precision, for one type of information stored in the table. Additionally, you might want to make sure that every record (a type of informational "package") never has blank spots for particular components.

Primary Keys

In many tables, you need to specify a *primary key*, a unique identifier that every record must have. If you define a column as a primary key, then you are telling the database engine that you want a unique value in that column for every record in the table. In the PUBLISHERS table, you will be designating the PUBLISHER_ID column as the primary key.

In addition to enforcing the UNIQUE constraint, primary keys also apply the NOT NULL constraint. Therefore, whenever you enter a new publisher into the PUBLISHER table, you will need to enter a value for PUBLISHER_ID. Otherwise, the database engine will not enable you to add the new record to the PUBLISHERS table.

Adding this primary key ensures that the ID number you assign to each publisher record is unique. You could use the same technique when assigning employee ID numbers, customer ID numbers, or any other identifier you want to be unique to each record. A primary key also accelerates the database's capability to query records quickly from a table.

Usually, primary keys are numeric IDs. However, you could just as easily specify a column containing text strings (such as PUBLISHER_NAME) as the primary key.

Adding a Primary Key to PUBLISHERS

To add a primary key constraint to PUBLISHER_ID, follow these steps:

1. Open the Table Designer window for the PUBLISHERS table.
2. Click the Row Selector button next to the PUBLISHER_ID column definition. The column now appears highlighted (see Figure 2.9).
3. Click the Primary Key tool in the Table Designer window (see Figure 2.10).

Figure 2.9.
*Selecting the
PUBLISHER_ID column.*

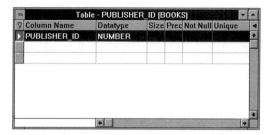

Figure 2.10.
Adding the primary key.

The primary
key tool

The primary key
set for the column

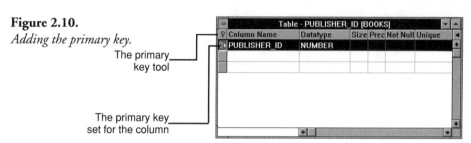

The Primary Key icon now appears next to the column definition for PUBLISHER_ID.

Note: You can add a primary key to only one column in a Blaze database. In other
database formats, however, a primary key can include multiple columns.

Finishing the Table

You are almost finished creating your first table, and you have some idea what the different
options are for each column in the table. Now that you have created the column that contains
the ID number for each publisher, you can add the next column containing the publisher's
name. Because the name is a string of text, this column will have the VARCHAR2 data type rather
than NUMBER.

To add the new column, follow these steps:

1. Click in the Column Name cell of the blank line beneath the description of the
   PUBLISHER_ID column.

2. Type PUBLISHER_NAME as the name of the new column.

3. Click the Datatype cell of the column to view the pop-up list of data types (see Figure
   2.11).

Figure 2.11.
Selecting a data type.

The list of column
data types

4. From this list, select VARCHAR2.

5. In the Size cell, type 72.

    As you might remember, the Size section of the Table Editor window specifies the amount of memory set aside for data in this column. In the case of strings of text (such as VARCHAR2 and CHAR data types), the number entered is the maximum number of characters that can be saved in this column. In entering 72, you are limiting the number of letters, numbers, and spaces in the name of a publisher to 72.

6. Click the Not Null cell.

    A check mark appears in this cell. Now, the user cannot save a new publisher record to the database without first entering a name in the PUBLISHER_NAME column.

7. Click the Unique cell.

It would be strange for two publishers to have the same name. If they were two branches of the same publishing house (such as fiction and non-fiction), you would want to distinguish them somehow in the name (such as Blake Publishing—Fiction). Therefore, you want to add this constraint to the PUBLISHER_NAME column.

That's all you need for this table. Later, you can add columns for other types of information, such as the address of the publisher or the name and phone of a publisher's representative. However, for your bookstore application, these two columns are enough.

To add the new table to the database, click the Save button on the Designer toolbar. The new table now appears in the Session window, the first object added to the database. However, the table is still empty. In the "Entering Records into the Table" section of this chapter, you will add some publisher records to it.

Working with Other Databases

Note that because Oracle Power Objects is designed to communicate with other types of databases, you use the same techniques to define an Oracle7 or SQL Server database. To save time, you can define and test tables and views in a Blaze database, and then quickly add them to an Oracle7 or SQL Server database by dragging them from the Blaze session window into the other database's session window (see Figure 2.12).

Figure 2.12.
Blaze and Oracle7 sessions.
By dragging the icon for
PUBLISHERS into the
Oracle7 session, you add the
table and its data to the
Oracle7 database.

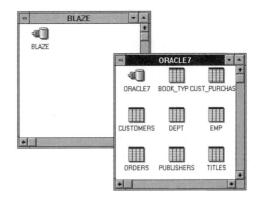

There are always differences between database formats, however. Before you migrate database objects between different database formats, you should review the information you have on these differences. The Oracle Power Objects documentation describes the differences between Blaze, Oracle7, and SQL Server.

DO	DON'T

DO normalize your tables.

DO add primary keys.

DO create numeric IDs for key columns.

DO build tables as you go.

DON'T normalize to the point of lunacy (a table defining TRUE and FALSE, or YES and NO).

DON'T add a primary key to a table where records do not need unique identifiers.

DON'T use a smaller numeric data type (Integer) when you need a larger one (Number) for a large number of records.

DON'T start with no data model at all.

Entering Records into the Table

Now that you have the receptacle for storing publisher records—the PUBLISHERS table—added to the database, you can enter publisher information directly into the Blaze database.

When you "run" a table, you see a spreadsheet-like view of the table, including all the columns and records (or rows) in it. This spreadsheet is called the *Table Editor window*, and is extremely useful when you need to quickly enter some test data into the database.

To enter publisher records, follow these steps:

1. Select the Table Designer window for the PUBLISHERS table.

2. Click the Run Table button. The Table Browser window appears (see Figure 2.13).

Figure 2.13.

The Table Browser window for PUBLISHERS.

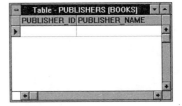

3. Click in the cell under the PUBLISHER_ID heading.

4. Type 1 in this cell.

5. Tab to the next cell and type Maximum Books.

You'll notice that as you type, a lock icon appears to the left of the new record (see Figure 2.14). Whenever you edit a new or existing record, the database locks it, preventing other users from editing the same record. This feature of Blaze and other databases prevents two users from overwriting each other's changes by accident.

Figure 2.14.

The lock icon.

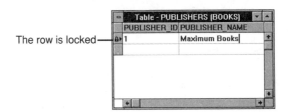

The row is locked

In addition, the Commit and Rollback buttons on the toolbar are no longer disabled (or dimmed). When you edit a new or existing record, the database does not actually write the changes to the table until it receives instructions to commit or roll back (that is, undo) these changes. When you're finished typing these new publisher records, you'll commit these additions to the PUBLISHER table.

6. Add the additional records shown in Table 2.4 to the PUBLISHERS table.

Table 2.4. Publisher records entered into the PUBLISHERS table.

PUBLISHER_ID	PUBLISHER_NAME
2	Enigma Books
3	Logos Press
4	Rollercoaster Books
5	Chatham House
6	Enderby Press

7. Click the Commit button.

The new publisher records are now added to the PUBLISHER table.

Using the Table Browser

The Table Browser lets you quickly enter test data, but you shouldn't use this technique to enter all the data for the final application. If there are any special relationships among data stored in separate tables, you must ensure that the relationships hold up.

For example, if you enter a publisher ID number for a book in a table that contains information on book titles, then you must first make sure that the publisher ID you enter actually exists in the PUBLISHERS table. Otherwise, you run the risk of entering an ID number for a nonexistent publisher. However, if you enter the same information through a form connected to the database, the application can automatically check to see if the publisher ID is valid.

This type of automated check is called a *lookup*, and is one of the types of operations that relational databases are designed to do. Again, the reason why they're called *relational* is because they're constructed to help intelligently relate information from a variety of sources. Creating the tables and "populating" them with data is only the first step in establishing these relationships, however.

Additionally, entering records through the Table Browser window can often be cumbersome when (as is often the case) a table contains a large number of columns. Again, it's preferable to enter the same information through a form, which can display the data through a series of text fields or other controls.

A Few More Words on Data Types

As you saw on Day 1, data types are important throughout a database application. Not only should you be careful about the data types you use in the "front end" of the application (that is, the forms and reports you use for editing data), you must be equally careful to define the right data type on the "back end," in the database itself. In fact, you should be doubly concerned about the data types you use in the database, because that is where the information is ultimately stored.

There are many reasons for being precise about data types. For one, data types have been designed to make working with particular kinds of data easy. Although String values can hold any type of character, they cannot be the subject of mathematical operations. Therefore, instead of storing some numeric information as a string, such as the number of copies of a particular book in stock, you want to store it as an integer or a number. The choice between these two data types shouldn't be arbitrary, however: integers are designed for smaller numbers, and numbers for larger ones. If you don't expect to have more than 500 copies of a particular book in stock, you should use the Integer data type for this column in a table, not Number.

The available data types are described in Table 2.5.

Table 2.5. Available data types.

Data type	Description
VARCHAR2	A string of characters. The size specified for this column is the maximum number of characters that can be stored in the column. If you enter fewer characters, the database allocates enough space to store the length string you have entered.
CHAR	A string of characters of a fixed length, as specified through the Size parameter of the column. If you enter fewer characters, the database pads out the remaining character with spaces.
DATE	A numeric representation of a particular date, including year, month, day, minute, and second. However, when you enter date information, you do not need to specify all of these components.
INTEGER	A numeric value between −32,768 and 32,767. The number does not include a decimal. Therefore, if you enter a decimal as part of a value, the database removes the decimal. If you enter 1.3, the database stores 1.
NUMBER	A numeric value between −2,147,483,648 and 2,147,483,647. Like Integer values, Number values do not include a decimal.
FLOAT	A floating-point decimal value.
LONG	A binary value, used to store a variety of different data formats. For example, graphics can be stored in a Long column.
RAW	Similar to Long.
LONG RAW	Similar to Long.
ROWID	A special data type used in some databases for maintaining the unique row number of a record.

Note that the data types appearing in the Table Editor window are a kind of "plain brown wrapper" version because they have to apply to several different database platforms. Not every database defines these data types in the same way. (Hence, one of many drives within the software industry for standards, so that everyone has the same definition of key concepts such as the Date data type.) When you copy table definitions between database platforms, Oracle Power Objects reinterprets the data type definitions for the new platform.

For example, when you copy a table containing Date values from your Blaze database to an Oracle7 database, the minimum date will be different in each database. In Blaze, the minimum date possible is January 1, 100 AD; in Oracle7, it is January 1, 4712 BC. Although this difference might not be important for your financial records, it will be for a historical database. Therefore, whenever you do "cross-platform" development (in this case, across database platforms), you must check the differences in data type definitions across these database engines.

A Few Words on Constraints

As discussed on Day 13, "Enforcing Business Rules," you can enforce many of the same constraints you added to the database through the application instead. For example, you can easily enforce the NOT NULL constraint through a form by adding method code to prevent the user from saving a record when a particular field is left blank.

The choice of where to enforce certain rules is one of the most important parts of development in a client-server environment. Although it might be possible to enforce the NOT NULL business rule through the application, it is generally better to do so through the database. This way, the user cannot leave that column blank, regardless of the application used to access the database. However, there are other business rules that, for other reasons, might be better enforced through the application. During these lessons, keep this question in mind: Where is the best place to perform these checks, to ensure the "integrity" of the data written to the database?

Adding Another Table

To practice your table-building skills, you will create a second table, ORDERS. This new table will contain information about books that customers have ordered. By necessity, ORDERS will have more columns than the PUBLISHERS table, as well as a wider variety of data types and constraints.

To create the new table, follow these steps:

1. Select the Session window for BOOKS.POS.
2. If the session is not connected, double-click the Connector icon.
3. Click the New Table button, or select New Table from the File menu.
   The Table Editor window appears.

4. Open the Property sheet for the new table and type ORDERS for its Name property.

5. Click in the Name cell in the blank row and type ORDER_ID.

6. Select Number for the column's data type.

7. Click the Row Selector button for this new row.

8. Click the Primary Key tool.

   The Primary Key icon appears next to the column.

9. Add the following columns to the table:

Name	Data type	Not Null
DATE_ENTERED	Date	Yes
DATE_RECEIVED	Date	
DATE_PURCHASED	Date	
CUSTOMER_ID	Number	Yes

10. Click Save.

The table now looks like the table shown in Figure 2.15.

Figure 2.15.

The completed ORDERS table.

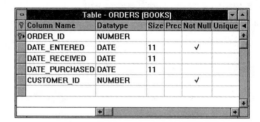

Following are a few important notes about this table:

☐ Clearly, these columns do not encompass every piece of information you might want to store about an order. For example, you might want to keep information on the employee who took the customer's order and entered it in the database. However, you can always add new columns to a table. Oracle Power Objects is designed to enable you to use this "build as you go" technique when you work with both the database and the application.

☐ The table stores a numeric ID number for the customer who placed the order. The information describing the customer—most importantly for a book order, the customer's name and phone number—is stored in another table, CUSTOMERS, that you will create in the next lesson. When you are reviewing an order, the database will need to perform a lookup into the CUSTOMERS table to get this information.

☐ The DATE_ENTERED column has the NOT NULL constraint applied to it so that a salesperson must enter the date the customer made the order before saving the new order to the database. This constraint ensures that no one forgets to include this information in the order.

Summary

2

For experienced users of relational databases and development tools, you have learned how easy it is to define databases and their objects in Oracle Power Objects. In addition, this chapter has given beginning developers a quick introduction to some of the critical concepts of relational databases: what they are, why they're designed the way they are, and what they can do. For the beginner, therefore, this chapter has covered a big piece of terrain, so you might want to review this chapter carefully before continuing to the next lesson.

The key points from this chapter include the following:

☐ Relational databases are designed to help view separate pieces of information in whatever relationship you want.

☐ You must enter a schema or user name, plus a password, to access a relational database.

☐ Relational databases store information in tables. Each column in a table represents a single category of information, such as the price of a book or its publisher.

☐ Each record (or row) in a table represents one entity, such as a book title or a publisher. A record can have values for each column in the table.

☐ Aside from the data type of the column, you might want to specify other important characteristics of the column, many of which limit the type of information that can be entered into it. For example, the NOT NULL constraint applied to a column ensures that all records in that table must have some value entered for that column.

☐ Many tables use primary keys to identify the columns used to uniquely identify each record.

☐ You use the Table Editor window to design a table.

☐ The Table Browser window enables the developer to add some initial data into the table, but the user will enter information through a form.

☐ Data types are as important in the database as they are in the application.

☐ Many constraints can be enforced, either in the application or the database; however, most constraints are best enforced in either the front end or the back end, but not both.

What Comes Next?

Tomorrow, you will begin using Oracle Power Objects to do some real relational work with the BOOKS database. Using views, you can easily relate information from separate tables through the database itself. In later lessons, you will relate information from separate tables through the application in a variety of ways.

Q&A

Q Do I need to add a primary key to every table?

A No. For example, a table containing a publisher's ID number and a book title might help identify all the titles by that publisher. In this case, you would not want to apply a primary key because you can have duplicate values in both columns. Each publisher will produce many books, and the same book (such as classic novels such as *The Three Musketeers* and *Dracula*) might be published by several different companies. Additionally, books by different authors might have the same title. Therefore, although you should use primary keys whenever possible, they are not a feature of every table.

Q How many columns should each table have?

A This question resembles one asked of Abraham Lincoln: "How long should a man's legs be?" His answer was, "Long enough to reach the ground." Similarly, a table should have enough columns to describe all the facets of something described in an individual record. When you create a table containing employee records, you first should think about all the kinds of information you want to store about each employee: name, salary, hire date, and so on. You should be careful not to duplicate the same data across tables, however.

If you store employee data in one table, you should not add the same type of information in another table. Because you can always relate (or join) information between tables, there's no reason to duplicate the information. In fact, it's important not to duplicate it because changes in one table (such as a salary increase) won't be reflected in the other.

Q How many tables should I have in my database?

A Again, enough to do the job. Developers describe the process of creating database objects as *designing their data model* because it's an important step worthy of such a lofty phrase. This process can be very complex, and is beyond the scope of this book to describe. Keep in mind, however, the cardinal rule of working with relational databases: If information looks as though it should be in a separate table, put it there! Breaking down information into distinct components and then defining tables to contain this information is called *normalization*, a key part of relational database design.

The BOOKS database, for example, will contain separate tables for publishers, titles, and book topics (mystery, children's literature, and so on). Theoretically, you could create one table containing all this information, but it would defeat the purpose of having a relational database (and create other problems as well). You could no longer enjoy the flexibility of viewing all titles for a publisher, or the publisher for each title. Additionally, you could not ensure that when a user entered a new title, the name of the publisher exactly matched what someone else typed for that same company. When it comes time to generate a report on sales by publisher, the same publisher might be falsely represented as several different companies, each with a slightly different spelling.

There are other reasons for normalizing that should become clear during later lessons.

Q **Can you define a primary key that uses more than one column?**

A The current version of Blaze does not enable you to define multicolumn primary keys (also called *multisegmented keys*). Other relational databases, such as Oracle7, have this feature. When you create a multisegmented key, the combination of values in primary key columns must be unique, not the value in a single column.

Workshop

The Workshop consists of quiz questions to help you solidify your understanding of the material covered today. Try and understand the quiz answers before you go on to tomorrow's lesson.

Quiz

1. What do the rows and columns of a table represent?
2. Why not use the String data type only, because you can enter any type of character in it?
3. What two constraints does a primary key add to a column?
4. What makes a relational database relational?
5. What are the three components of a connect string?

Quiz Answers

1. The columns represent the categories of information within a table, whereas the rows represent individual records. You specified two categories of information, publisher ID number and publisher name, when you created the publisher table, represented by two columns. Each publisher's record in the table includes a row of information, with data for the ID number and name in the appropriate columns.

2. Although the String data type can contain any type of character, it is not designed for the type of operations you perform on numeric, date, and other kinds of information. For example, the String data type does not enable you to take the square root of a number stored in a text string.

3. A primary key adds the NOT NULL and UNIQUE constraints to a column.

4. Because information is stored in tables independent of each other, relational databases enable you to relate this information in any way you want. As you will see in the next chapter, you can view titles by publisher or identify the publisher for each title simply by querying the data from the TITLES and PUBLISHERS tables.

5. The three components of a connect string are the schema or user name, password, and location of the database. In the case of remote servers, the address is the database's location on the network; in the case of Blaze databases, the location is its filename and directory.

Creating a View

Overview

Today, you learn about the following topics:

- ☐ Joins and queries
- ☐ Views as stored queries
- ☐ Single- and multitable views
- ☐ Why use views?
- ☐ Views in Oracle Power Objects
- ☐ The View Editor window
- ☐ Viewing data through a view

As you learned yesterday, relational databases are designed to provide easy and flexible ways to relate information stored in separate tables. This design enables you to ask the database a boundless number of questions, as long as you are careful to phrase these questions in terms the database can understand (through the SQL query language).

Do you want to look at all the books published by a particular author? The buying habits of particular customers? The sales performance of particular books? Relational databases can provide fast answers to these types of questions. In fact, your bookstore application will be designed to answer many of these exact questions.

In a client/server environment, you can pose the question from within an application or from within the database itself. However, when you are looking for answers that can come only from multiple tables, you face an initial challenge: how can you query records so that information from one table is grouped with relevant information from another table? For example, to get a listing of the publishing houses and the books they publish, you need to look at data stored in two separate tables: PUBLISHERS and TITLES, which is a new table added later in this chapter.

You can relate information from multiple tables (such as PUBLISHERS and TITLES) through a *view*, which is a special kind of database object designed for this task. A view can query columns from a single table or from multiple tables.

- ☐ In the case of a *single-table view*, you identify the columns queried to limit the range of data that can be queried from that table.
- ☐ In the case of a *multitable view*, you query information across multiple tables, in a way that provides a composite picture of something.

To return to the PUBLISHERS and TITLES example, the view can use a column that appears in both tables, PUBLISHER_ID, to provide information on all books produced by each publisher. By finding an ID number in TITLES that matches the current record in PUBLISH-ERS, the view can properly query these records together (see Figure 3.1).

Figure 3.1.
Relating PUBLISHERS and TITLES.

Column Name	Datatype
PUBLISHER_ID	NUMBER
PUBLISHER_NAME	VARCHAR2

The tables share a column, making it posible to relate records between them

Column Name	Datatype
TITLE_ID	NUMBER
TITLE_NAME	VARCHAR2
AUTHLNAME	VARCHAR2
AUTHFNAME	VARCHAR2
PUBLISHER_ID	NUMBER
PRICE	FLOAT
WS_PRICE	FLOAT
PROMOTION_PRICE	FLOAT
PRINTING	INTEGER
TYPE_ID	NUMBER

Views are designed to perform just this type of look-up into multiple tables. The view itself is not a table storing data. Instead, it is a piece of SQL code, stored in the database, that includes two important components:

☐ The columns to be queried from the base tables of the view

☐ The columns used to find matching values in separate tables

In the case of TITLES and PUBLISHERS, you program the view to use the PUBLISHER_ID columns in both tables to find matching values. This connection between complementary columns, called a *join*, is one of the most important features of a relational database.

When you query records through the view, it then returns information from all the columns specified. When there are matching values found in joined columns, such as TITLES.PUBLISHER_ID and PUBLISHERS.PUBLISHER_ID, the database can then provide related data from both tables.

Joins and Queries

As described in the previous lesson, you use the SQL language to query information from a relational database. The piece of SQL code that queries information (also called a SELECT statement because it always starts with the keyword SELECT) might look something like the following:

```
SELECT ENAME FROM EMPLOYEES WHERE ENAME LIKE 'SMITH'
```

or

```
SELECT ENAME FROM EMPLOYEES WHERE SAL > 20000
```

A view essentially is a SELECT statement stored in the database. Although the syntax of SQL is relatively simple to understand, writing the SELECT statement for a view can be a complicated affair. The following SQL code, for example, queries employee records by department. The tables DEPT and EMP (not used in this tutorial) mentioned in this query store departmental and employee records. The query also applies some conditions to the query: only show the names of employees earning more than $20,000 and working in a department that has an ID number that is greater than 20.

```
SELECT "EMP"."ENAME", "DEPT"."DNAME", "EMP"."SAL"
FROM "DEPT", "EMP"
WHERE  ( "DEPT"."DEPTNO" = "EMP"."DEPTNO" )
   AND  (  ( "EMP"."SAL" > 20000 )
   AND  ( "DEPT"."DEPTNO" > 20 )  )
```

As you can see, the query for this view is far more complicated than a simple SELECT statement. In addition to applying the conditions, the query uses a nested SELECT statement (essentially, a query within a query) to view all employees by department. A more complicated query like this can take time to write and debug. As the number of base tables and conditions increases, so does the time needed to create and test the query.

Fortunately, Oracle Power Objects provides a relatively simple way to define a query so that you do not have to write the SQL code yourself.

Before you use this feature, you first need to create another table for storing information about book titles. There is an obvious relationship between the records stored in this table, TITLES, and those stored in PUBLISHERS: every book has a publisher, and every publisher produces several books. In a later lesson, you will build forms to display PUBLISHERS and TITLES information both ways.

Adding a New Table to BOOKS.BLZ

The new table, TITLES, will have more columns than the PUBLISHERS table. TITLES will have a PUBLISHER_ID column for each book's record, so that you can join records from PUBLISHERS and TITLES. A different column, TYPE_ID, will provide the means for a query to find the type of book in a separate table, BOOK_TYPES, used to hold descriptions of all categories of books.

To create the new table, follow these steps:

1. From the Main window, open the BOOKS session.

2. Double-click the Connector icon to open a connection to the Blaze database.

3. Click the New Table button.

   A new table, with its property sheet, now appears. From Day 2, "Creating a Table," you should know how to define columns within the table, as well as give the table a descriptive name.

4. In the table's Property sheet, type TITLES as the name of the new table.

5. In the Table Editor window, add the columns shown in Table 3.1.

Table 3.1. The TITLES table.

Column	Data type	Size Precision
TITLE_ID	Number	
TITLE_NAME	String	200
AUTHLNAME	String	32
AUTHFNAME	String	32
PUBLISHER_ID	Number	
PRICE	Float	2
WS_PRICE	Float	2
PROMOTION_PRICE	Float	2
PRINTING	Integer	
TYPE_ID	Number	
ON_ORDER	Number	
IN_STOCK	Number	
ON_HOLD	Number	

6. Set `TITLE_ID` as the primary key.

The Table Editor window for TITLES should now look like Figure 3.2.

Figure 3.2.
The finished TITLES table.

Table - TITLES (BOOKS)					
Column Name	**Datatype**	**Size**	**Prec**	**Not Null**	**Unique**
TITLE_ID	NUMBER				
TITLE_NAME	VARCHAR2	200			
AUTHLNAME	VARCHAR2	32			
AUTHFNAME	VARCHAR2	32			
PUBLISHER_ID	NUMBER				
PRICE	FLOAT		2		
WS_PRICE	FLOAT		2		
PROMOTION_PRICE	FLOAT		2		
PRINTING	INTEGER				
TYPE_ID	NUMBER				
ON_ORDER	NUMBER				
IN_STOCK	NUMBER				
ON_HOLD	NUMBER				

As you might remember from the previous lesson, to designate a primary key, you select the desired column and click the Primary Key tool.

7. Click Save to add the new table to the database.

While you're here, you should add some sample data to the TITLES table. To do this, follow these steps:

1. With the Table Editor window for TITLES selected, click the Run Table button.

2. Enter into this table the data in Table 3.2.

   The Table Browser window for TITLES should now look like Figure 3.3.

Figure 3.3.

The Table Browser window for TITLES, with new records entered.

TITLE_ID	TITLE_NAME	AUTHLNAME	AUTHFNAME	PUBLISI
1	The Big Book of Computers	Grant	Tom	2
2	Just for Fun	Hartwell	Clive	3
3	Many Mysteries	Lumley	Agatha	1
4	Color Me Blue	Leavitt	Hanford	4
5	Fun for Everyone	Hartwell	Clive	3
6	Sleep No More	Black	Morton	1
7	Development Made Easy	Fortran	Pascal	2
8	A Boy's Life in New Zealand	MacAvoy	Gerald	6
9	Kiss Me Dead	Steele	Dirk	5
10	An English Garden	Throckmorton	Hilda	5

Table - TITLES (BOOKS)

3. Click the Commit button.

The new titles are now saved in the database.

Table 3.2. Data for the TITLES table.

BOOK _ID	TITLE_NAME	AUTHLNAME	AUTHFNAME	PUBLISHER _ID
1	The Big Book of Computers	Grant	Tom	2
2	Just for Fun	Hartwell	Clive	3
3	Many Mysteries	Lumley	Agatha	1
4	Color Me Blue	Leavitt	Hanford	4
5	Fun For Everyone	Hartwell	Clive	3
6	Sleep No More	Black	Morton	1
7	Development Made Easy	Fortran	Pascal	2
8	A Boy's Life in New Zealand	MacAvoy	Gerald	6
9	Kiss Me Dead	Steele	Dirk	5
10	An English Garden	Throckmorton	Hilda	6

The values in two columns might seem somewhat mysterious at this point. The PUBLISHER_ID column uses a numeric identifier for each publisher, instead of the name. Similarly, the SUBJECT_ID column uses a numeric value rather than a string to describe the type of book.

In both cases, the table uses the numeric ID rather than a text string for two major reasons:

☐ It's easier to find matching values in two separate tables when you compare number or integer values rather than strings. If someone mistypes the name of a publisher in the TITLES table, the maddeningly literal computer will not be able to find a matching value in the PUBLISHERS table. However, it's hard to mistype 1, 2, or 3.

☐ The database can compare the values in the two tables faster when they're numbers rather than strings of characters. When the database must compare "The Really Big Publishing Corporation," character by character, with another string, it by necessity must take more time than when it compares the value 5 in one table to the value 5 in another. Although this won't be a problem in your application because you're working with a small amount of data, applications that must access thousands of records in multiple tables can slow to a crawl when comparing large strings.

In the section "Adding More Tables to the Database," later in this lesson, you will create the BOOK_TYPES table so that you can get a description of each topic. First, however, you should get a brief grounding in some of the terminology used to describe the concepts you've just learned.

PRICE	WS_PRICE	TYPE_ID	PRINT-ING	PROMOTION_PRICE	ON_ORDER	IN_STOCK	ON_HOLD
29.99	15.99	2	1	5	20	2	
8.99	4.50	8	3		2	5	1
6.99	2.99	3	5		0	8	0
4.99	2.49	4	1		4	4	0
5.99	2.99	8	1		2	6	0
5.99	2.99	3	5		2	5	1
29.99	15.00	1	1		0	6	0
12.99	6.00	9	1		0	2	0
4.99	2.49	3	5	4.5	5	10	5
9.99	5.00	12	1	8.00	0	20	1

Joins and Lookups

Relational databases combine information in separate tables through *joins*. The join specifies the columns in separate tables used to compare values. For example, you can instruct the database to query the name of a publisher every time it queries a book record from the TITLES table. Therefore, in addition to the numeric PUBLISHER_ID, the query also then returns the name of the publisher (a text string) from the PUBLISHER_NAME column of the PUBLISHERS table. (See Figure 3.4.)

Figure 3.4.

Using the PUBLISHER_ID column to look up values in the PUBLISHERS table.

TITLES

Column Name	Datatype
TITLE_ID	NUMBER
TITLE_NAME	VARCHAR2
AUTHLNAME	VARCHAR2
AUTHFNAME	VARCHAR2
PUBLISHER_ID	NUMBER
PRICE	FLOAT
WS_PRICE	FLOAT
PROMOTION_PRICE	FLOAT
PRINTING	INTEGER
TYPE_ID	NUMBER

PUBLISHERS

Column Name	Datatype
PUBLISHER_ID	NUMBER
PUBLISHER_NAME	VARCHAR2

└ ─ ─ Joined by the PUBLISHER_ID column in both tables

When the database performs this type of operation, it looks up a value in a secondary table to match a value found in the main table. The view can perform any number of lookups, across several different tables. For example, in addition to the name of the publisher, the view also might look up the description of the book topic from the BOOK_TYPES table.

Note: The query does not automatically return all the columns in either table. When you write any query, you specify the columns returned from that table.

Creating Your First View

Now that you know how a view works, you are ready to add your first view to the BOOKS.BLZ database. Instead of writing the SQL code yourself, you will use a graphical tool, the View Editor window, to define the view. In this window (see Figure 3.5), you select the tables to use, choose the columns to display, and specify the joins between columns in separate tables. When you save the new view, Oracle Power Objects generates the SQL code for you and adds the new view to the database.

This window has the components described in Table 3.3.

Figure 3.5.
The View Editor window.

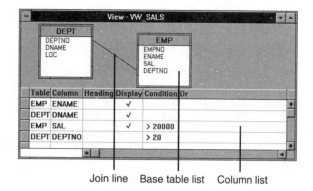

Join line   Base table list   Column list

Table 3.3. Components of the View Editor window.

Component	Description
Base table list	A window for each table (called a base table) included in the view. Within the window is a scrolling list of all the columns in that table, as well as the primary key icon, indicating which column is the primary key (if any).
Join lines	A line connecting columns between tables. These lines identify the columns used in the join as the primary and foreign keys.
Column list	A list of all columns appearing in the view. When the database queries records for the view, it returns data from all these columns, but not the other columns that might appear in the table. These columns can appear in one or more tables.

The column list includes some additional parameters for displaying and filtering records. We'll return to these parameters later.

You're now ready to create your first view, which will show all books by publisher.

The VW_TITLES View

To create the first view, VW_TITLES, follow these steps:

1. With the BOOKS Session window selected, click the New View button.
   The View Editor window appears.
2. In the Property sheet for this view, type VW_TITLES as the name of the new view.
3. From the Session window for BOOKS, drag the icon for the TITLES table into the Table List area of the View Editor window. The View Editor window now looks like Figure 3.6.

A small window displaying all the columns in TITLES now appears in the View Editor window.

Figure 3.6.
The View Editor window, with one table added.

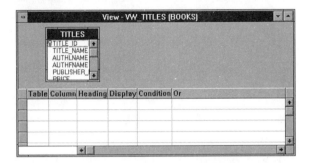

4. Again, from the Session window for BOOKS, drag the icon for the PUBLISHERS table into the same region of the View Editor window.

    The view now knows to query data from both tables. However, you have not yet identified the columns to display in the view (remember, views don't automatically display any columns), nor have you created the join between the two tables.

5. In the small window representing the TITLES table, scroll down until you find the PUBLISHER_ID column.

6. Click the PUBLISHER_ID column in TITLES and drag across the Table Editor window until you reach the PUBLISHER_ID column of the PUBLISHERS table (see Figure 3.7).

Figure 3.7.
The join line between PUBLISHERS and TITLES.

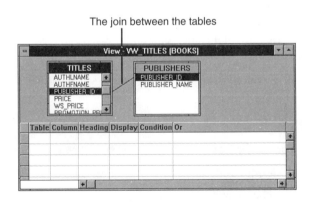

The join between the tables

As shown in Figure 3.7, a line appears, connecting these two matching columns. You now have specified the join, so that the database can query the correct record in the PUBLISHERS table to match a value in the PUBLISHER_ID column of the TITLES table.

The query does not yet query data from any columns, however.

7. Click the TITLE_NAME column of the TITLES table and drag it into the spread-sheet-like area at the bottom of the View Editor window.

   The TITLE_NAME column, as well as the name of its table, TITLES, now appears in the Column List area, as shown in Figure 3.8.

Figure 3.8.
TITLES added to the Column List area.

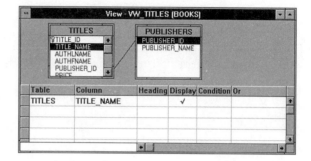

As you might remember, this region lists all the columns queried and displayed for the view. For this first view, you will be displaying the title of each book, followed by the name of its publisher. Now that you've added the book title, you can add the name of its publisher.

8. Click the PUBLISHER_NAME column of the PUBLISHERS table and drag it into the Column List area.

   Now that you have instructed the view to display both columns, you can run the view to see the values it queries.

9. Click Save.

   The new view now appears in the BOOKS database, with an icon appearing in the Session window for BOOKS.

10. Click the Run View button (see Figure 3.9).

Figure 3.9.
The new view in action.

TITLE_NAME	PUBLISHER_NAME
The Big Book of Computers	Enigma Books
Just for Fun	Logos Press
Many Mysteries	Maximum Books
Color Me Blue	Rollercoaster Books
Fun for Everyone	Logos Press
Sleep No More	Maximum Books
Development Made Easy	Enigma Books
A Boy's Life in New Zealand	Enderby Press
Kiss Me Dead	Chatham House
An English Garden	Chatham House

You now get a simple list of each book title and its corresponding publisher. Behind the scenes, the view first gets a record for a book title, and then performs a quick lookup into the PUBLISHERS table to get the publisher name that matches the publisher ID for that book.

11. Click Stop to stop running the view.

Changing the Headings

Presently, the headings that appear for each column are the actual column names; however, you might want something a little more readable. The Heading section of the Table Editor window enables you to change the headings for each column.

1. In the View Designer window for VW_TITLES, type `Book Title` in the Heading section for the TITLE_NAME column.

2. In the same section for the PUBLISHER_NAME column, type `Publisher Name`.

3. Click the Save button to save your changes.

4. Click the Run View button to run the view (see Figure 3.10).

Figure 3.10.

The view, with more readable headings.

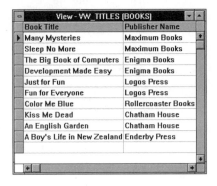

The same records appear. However, you have modified the headings to be somewhat more readable.

Adding a Condition to a View

Suppose that you wanted to query data on only those books that cost more than $7.00. Relational databases provide several ways for you to apply this condition when you are querying records. Views have their own method for applying such a condition (or filter).

To exclude books under $7.00, you first must add another column, PRICE, to the view. This column won't be displayed when you run the view, but the view will use it to apply the condition.

1. With the View Editor window open, double-click the PRICE column in the TITLES table.

   The PRICE column now appears in the Column List area. You can use this technique as well as the click-and-drag method to add columns to the view.

2. Click the Display cell for the PRICE column.

   The check mark in this cell disappears. This indicates that the view does not display values queried from this column.

3. In the Condition cell, enter the following:

   ```
   > 7.00
   ```

   The View Editor window now looks like Figure 3.11.

   This specifies the condition: don't query a record from the TITLES table unless its sale price is greater than $7.00.

Figure 3.11.
The view, with condition added.

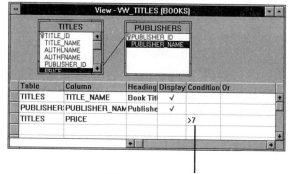

The condition added to the view

4. Click the Save button.

   The modifications to the view are now saved to the database.

5. Click the Run View button (see Figure 3.12).

Figure 3.12.
The new set of records queried by the view.

81

As shown in Figure 3.12, the view displays the same two columns of data, but fewer records appear. That's because only a few books in the TITLES table have cover prices greater than $7.00.

Conditions you enter for a view must follow the SQL syntax used by Oracle Power Objects. The online help for Oracle Power Objects provides a complete SQL language reference. In addition, the *Oracle Power Objects User's Guide* includes a chapter on SQL that explains the syntax and conventions of this language.

The SQL Code Behind the View

To give you some sense of how much Oracle Power Objects simplifies the task of creating views, following is the SQL code you would have to write to create the VW_TITLES view as it is currently defined:

```
SELECT "TITLES"."TITLE_NAME" "Book Title", "PUBLISHERS"."PUBLISHER_NAME"
"Publisher Name"  FROM "TITLES", "PUBLISHERS"
    WHERE  ( "TITLES"."PUBLISHER_ID" = "PUBLISHERS"."PUBLISHER_ID" )
    AND  ( "TITLES"."PRICE" > 7 )
```

Because Power Objects automates the task of generating this code, the process is much less error-prone and time-consuming than if you were to program the SQL yourself.

Limitations to Views

Before you stop running the view, try to select the blank line below the records displayed. Oracle Power Objects prevents you from entering a new record, beeping at you to indicate that you have committed an error.

What went wrong? In the case of views encompassing multiple tables, you cannot enter new records. That's because you are not trying to enter a single record—in fact, you're trying to insert a new record in each of the tables used in the view (in this case, PUBLISHERS and TITLES). Because the view might or might not include many columns that are primary keys or have the NOT NULL constraint applied to them, there is no way to ensure that a new record inserted into each table will have all values for these columns. Therefore, the database does not enable you to enter new records for a multitable view.

Other than browsing data, then, what use is a view?

Uses of Views

Although views have their limitations, they also are useful in the following circumstances:

☐ When an application needs fast access to information queried across multiple tables, and you do not have to edit the information. More often than not, the database can

sort and present this information faster than the client application. For performance reasons, therefore, you might want to use a view to browse this information.

For example, you might want to view records covering all the accounts payable transactions in a business day. This information can span tables involving vouchers, vendors, managers with approval powers, shipping and receiving, and a host of other information. Instead of querying all this data from each separate table, a view provides a faster, more compact presentation of this information.

☐ When you are designing a cross-table report. When you print a report, you often want to use descriptive information rather than a series of numeric codes. The easiest way to provide this information is to use a view as the source of the report.

For example, if you wanted to provide a simple listing of all titles carried by a bookstore, you could use the view you just designed, VW_TITLES, as the source of records for the report.

☐ When you want to limit the columns in a table a user can view. You can create single-table or multitable views that show the user only a subset of all columns in the table (or tables). If there is information in other columns that the user does not need to see, then the columns can be excluded from the view.

☐ When you want to simplify the information presented. Because the view can use only a subset of the columns from its base tables, you can weed out any information that is not needed for a particular purpose. For example, in the case of a one-table view designed to show sales performance, you can add to the view the total sales and number of customers for a particular salesperson, leaving out other information that might be stored in the SALESPERSON table.

To illustrate this, you can create your own one-table view using TITLES.

A Single-Table View

If you want to create a view for a report displaying the prices of each book, you could create a single-table view that included information from the columns storing the sales price, wholesale price, and promotion price. In the next exercise, you will create just such a view.

1. With the Session window for BOOKS selected, click the New View pushbutton.

2. In the Property sheet for this view, type VW_BOOK_PRICE as the name of the view.

3. Click the TITLES table and drag it into the Table List area of the View Editor window for VW_BOOK_PRICE.

4. In the window for the TITLES table that now appears in the Table List area, double-click each of the following columns to add them to the Column List area:

TITLE_NAME
PRICE

```
WS_PRICE
PROMOTION_PRICE
```

The View Editor window should look like Figure 3.13.

Figure 3.13.
The View Editor window for the new single-table view.

Table	Column	Headng	Display	Condition	Or
TITLES	TITLE_NAME		✓		
TITLES	PRICE		✓		
TITLES	WS_PRICE		✓		
TITLES	PROMOTION_PRICE		✓		

View - VW_BOOK_PRICE (BOOKS)

TITLES
TITLE_ID
TITLE_NAME
AUTHLNAME
AUTHFNAME
PUBLISHER_
PRICE

5. Click the Save button to add the new view to the database.

6. Click the Run View button to run the view (see Figure 3.14).

Figure 3.14.
A few columns from the TITLES table.

View - VW_BOOK_PRICE (BOOKS)

TITLE_NAME	PRICE	WS_PRICE	PROMOTION_PRICE
The Big Book of Computers	28.99	15.99	
Just for Fun	8.99	4.5	
Many Mysteries	6.99	2.99	
Color Me Blue	4.99	2.49	
Fun for Everyone	5.99	2.99	
Sleep No More	5.99	2.99	
Development Made Easy	29.99	15	
A Boy's Life in New Zealand	12.99	6	
Kiss Me Dead	4.99	2.49	4.5
An English Garden	9.99	5	8

As shown in Figure 3.14, you now see a simple listing of all titles, including pricing information for each one.

Entering Data Through a View

Another advantage of a single-table view is that you can use it to enter data into the table. This again illustrates how a view can cut down the complexity of a table: when you create a one-table view designed for data entry, you can include only those columns relevant to the type of data to be entered.

For example, you might design a view used to enter customer information, including the customer's name and phone number. Other information, such as the customer's buying habits, also might be stored in the same table. For the salesperson entering the new customer into the

database, however, this information is extraneous: all that matters when a customer is paying for a purchase is that person's name and phone number. Later, as that customer makes more purchases, you can track buying behavior through other columns in the table.

As discussed on Day 15, "Adding Security to Your Application," you can use a single-table view to hide sensitive information in a table. For example, if you want to give users access to the name and position of employees by querying this information from the EMPLOYEES table, you do not want to advertise their salaries. To avoid exposing private information, you can grant access to the table through a view that includes their names and positions, but excludes information from the column that stores their current salary.

You can use single-table views for data entry only under the following conditions:

- ☐ The view includes the primary key column
- ☐ The view includes all columns with the NOT NULL constraint
- ☐ No expressions appear in the Condition section of the Column List area

Adding More Tables to the Database

At this point, you should add a few more tables to the database that you'll need in later lessons. By now, you should not need detailed instructions on how to create a table, so this section gives you only the descriptions of each table. Do not forget to enter the name of the table through its Property sheet before you click the Save button.

The following are the tables to create:

Name: BOOK_TYPES

Purpose: Stores the description of book types (mysteries, biographies, and so on).

Column	Data type	Size	Constraints
TYPE_ID	Number		Primary Key
TYPE_DESC	Varchar	48	NOT NULL

Name: CUSTOMERS

Purpose: Stores information on customers.

Column	Data type	Size	Constraints
CUSTOMER_ID	Number		Primary Key
LNAME	Varchar	48	
ADDRESS1	Varchar	120	
ADDRESS2	Varchar	120	

continues

Column	Data type	Size	Constraints
CITY	Varchar	48	
STATE	Varchar	2	
ZIP	Varchar	10	
PHONE	Varchar	24	
MAILING_FLAG	Integer		

Name: CUST_PURCHASES

Purpose: Stores information tracking the types of books purchased by each customer.

Column	Data type	Size	Constraints
CUSTOMER_ID	Number		NOT NULL
TYPE_ID	Number		NOT NULL
NUM_BOUGHT	Integer		NOT NULL

A Few Words on Database Object Naming

As you might have noticed by now, these lessons ask you to follow some implicit naming conventions for database objects. All names are capitalized, and the same types of names (such as TYPES_ID and PUBLISHERS_ID) appear regularly.

Because of case sensitivity and other problems interpreting uppercase and lowercase letters, it is generally safest to keep the names of columns, tables, views, and other database components uppercase. If you then move tables and views among different database engines (for example, from Oracle7 to SQL Server), you do not have to worry about case-sensitivity problems.

The reason for using the same suffix on different column names (_ID, _DESC, and _FLAG) is to make it easier to remember the names of columns. If you use a different naming convention for every primary key column, you risk confusing yourself when you later need to remember the name of one of these columns. If you apply the same conventions regularly, however, it will be easy to guess what the primary key column in the PUBLISHERS table is likely to be: PUBLISHER_ID.

Populating the New Tables

Before continuing, you should add some sample data to the new tables. Open each table and click the Run Table button to once again open the Table Browser window. You then can begin entering the sample data. After you have entered new records, click the Commit button to save your changes to the database.

In the BOOK_TYPES table, enter the following data:

TYPE_ID	TYPE_DESC
1	Reference
2	Computer
3	Mystery
4	Science fiction
5	Literature
6	Science
7	History
8	Current affairs
9	Biography
10	Children's
11	General fiction
12	General non-fiction

In the CUSTOMERS table, add the following data:

CUSTOMER_ID	LNAME	FNAME	PHONE NUMBER
1	Gallup	Alicia	415-555-1044
2	Vogel	Karen	415-555-8911
3	Jenkins	Tanya	408-555-1111
4	Tribbensee	Bruce	415-555-7777
5	Krauel	Jennifer	415-555-9999
6	Simmons	Lance	510-555-2420
7	Edlund	Ben	415-555-8425

In the CUST_PURCHASES table, add the following data:

CUSTOMER_ID	TYPE_ID	NUM_BOUGHT
1	3	17
1	4	11
2	2	16
3	10	4
3	8	9
4	7	2

continues

CUSTOMER_ID	TYPE_ID	NUM_BOUGHT
4	8	3
5	4	21
5	12	9
6	3	8
6	1	1
7	4	12
7	10	2
7	5	4

The entries for the last table might seem cryptic because it uses two numeric IDs and a number to store the number of each type of book a customer purchases. When you build the next view, however, you will be able to view this information in a somewhat more meaningful format.

Adding Another View

This new view, VW_CUST_PREFS, will be later used in a report. If the store is planning a sale on computer books, it would be useful to know which customers buy computer books. The report based on this view will provide that information.

This view uses three base tables. CUST_PURCHASES is the focus of the view because it stores information describing which customers buy which types of books. It stores data on both the customer and the book types as ID numbers (data type Number), however. If a human being, not a computer, wants to review this information, then you want to provide the name of the customer, as well as the description of each type of book.

☐ To get the customer's name, this view must create a join between the CUSTOMER_ID columns in the CUSTOMERS and CUST_PURCHASES tables.

☐ To get a description of each book type, the view must create a join between the TYPE_ID columns in the CUST_PURCHASES and BOOK_TYPES tables.

To create the new view, follow these steps:

1. With the Session window for BOOKS selected, click the New View button, or select New View from the File menu.

2. In the Property sheet for the new view, type VW_CUST_PREFS (that is, view containing customer preferences) for the Name property of the view.

3. Select the BOOKS Session window again.

4. Click and drag the CUST_PURCHASES table from the Session window into the Table List area of the View Editor window.

5. Release the mouse button to drop the CUST_PURCHASES table into the view (see Figure 3.15).

Figure 3.15.

*The Table Editor window
so far.*

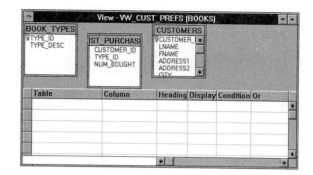

6. Use the same technique to add the CUSTOMERS and BOOK_TYPES table to the view.

7. Click the CUSTOMER_ID column of the CUSTOMERS table and drag it to the CUSTOMER_ID column of the CUST_PURCHASES table, releasing the mouse button when you reach the second column.

8. Click the TYPE_ID column of the BOOK_TYPES table and drag it to the TYPE_ID column of the CUST_PURCHASES table, releasing the mouse button when you reach the second column.

The view should now look like Figure 3.16.

Figure 3.16.

*The joins added to view
the view.*

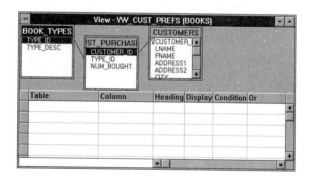

You now have the two joins needed to make this view work. The next step is to specify the columns to appear in the view.

9. Double-click the FNAME and LNAME columns of the CUSTOMERS table to add these columns to the view.

The names of these columns, as well as their base table (CUSTOMERS), now appears in the Column List area.

10. Double-click the TYPE_DESC column of the BOOK_TYPES table to add it to the view.

11. To add the final column, double-click the NUM_BOUGHT column of the CUST_PURCHASES table (see Figure 3.17).

Figure 3.17.
The final view.

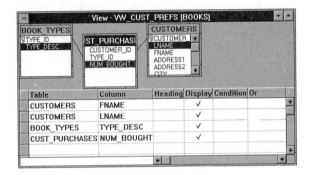

12. Click the Save button to save the new view to the database.

13. Click the Run View button to run the view (see Figure 3.18). You now can see how many books of each type every customer has purchased.

Figure 3.18.
Using the view to examine customer purchasing habits.

FNAME	LNAME	TYPE_DESC	NUM_BOUGHT
Alicia	Gallup	Mystery	17
Alicia	Gallup	Science fiction	11
Karen	Vogel	Computer	16
Tanya	Jenkins	Children's	4
Tanya	Jenkins	Current affairs	9
Bruce	Tribbensee	History	2
Bruce	Tribbensee	Current affairs	3
Jennifer	Krauel	Science fiction	21
Jennifer	Krauel	General non-fiction	9
Lance	Simmons	Mystery	8
Lance	Simmons	Reference	1
Ben	Edlund	Science fiction	12
Ben	Edlund	Children's	2
Ben	Edlund	Literature	4

Again, to give you some sense of how much SQL code Oracle Power Objects is generating behind the scenes for you, following is the SQL code behind this view:

```
SELECT "CUSTOMERS"."FNAME", "CUSTOMERS"."LNAME",
"BOOK_TYPES"."TYPE_DESC", "CUST_PURCHASES"."NUM_BOUGHT"  FROM
"BOOK_TYPES", "CUST_PURCHASES", "CUSTOMERS"
     WHERE  ( "CUSTOMERS"."CUSTOMER_ID" = "CUST_PURCHASES"."CUSTOMER_ID" )
     AND  ( "CUST_PURCHASES"."TYPE_ID" = "BOOK_TYPES"."TYPE_ID" )
```

Adding Conditions to a View

Suppose that you want to focus this listing to customers who have purchased more than a few books of a particular type. A customer who has purchased only one computer book will be only mildly interested in the sale; a customer who has purchased ten computer books, on the other hand, will be far more interested.

Therefore, you want to modify your view to display customers who have purchased more than five of a particular book type. You will add this restriction to your view in the following way:

1. With the View Editor window selected, click in the Conditions cell for the CUST_PURCHASES.NUM_BOUGHT column.

2. Type > 5 in this cell.

   The view now looks like Figure 3.19.

Figure 3.19.

The view, with a condition added.

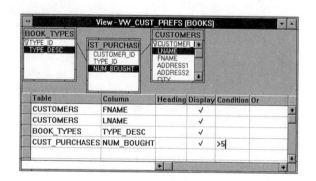

3. Click the Save button.

4. Click the Run View button (see Figure 3.20).

Figure 3.20.

Running the view with a condition applied.

You now see a much smaller number of customer purchase records—only those customers who purchase more than five of a particular kind of book.

However, the view currently shows all types of books, while you might be interested only in computer book purchases. How would you limit the view to customers who have purchased more than five computer books?

By entering ='Computer' in the BOOK_TYPES.BOOK_DESC column, you limit the records to computer books. However, there is a danger to this method: what if you mistype the name of the type of book? For example, what if the description is stored as *Computers* rather than *Computer*? Or what if someone changes the description of this class of book in the BOOK_TYPES table to *Computer books*?

There are two ways around this problem:

☐ In SQL, you can use wildcard characters. The percent sign (%) in SQL. In this case, you could enter ='Computer%' to catch the strings of *Computer*, *Computer*, and *Computer Books*. This solution would not work if someone changed the description to *Software*, however.

☐ A better way to specify the condition is to add the CUST_PURCHASES.TYPE_ID column to the view, but do not display it (that is, a check mark does not appear in the Display column for CUST_PURCHASES.TYPE_ID). You then can specify the numeric ID for computer books rather than the text string from BOOK_TYPES.TYPE_DESC. If anyone changes the description of the book from Computer to Software, the view will still work.

DO	DON'T
DO create views when needed.	
DO use single-table views to limit user access to data.	
DO specify conditions for views.	
DON'T create so many views that you cannot modify base tables without breaking several views.	
DON'T create a single-table view for every form and report.	
DON'T apply the condition to the wrong column (such as TYPE_DESC rather than TYPE_ID).	

This example should give you a bit more insight into the logic of relational database design.

For your reference, following is the SQL code behind the final view, with the two conditions added:

```
SELECT "CUSTOMERS"."FNAME", "CUSTOMERS"."LNAME", "BOOK_TYPES"."TYPE_DESC",
➥"CUST_PURCHASES"."NUM_BOUGHT"
  FROM "BOOK_TYPES", "CUST_PURCHASES", "CUSTOMERS"
```

```
WHERE  ( "CUST_PURCHASES"."TYPE_ID" = "BOOK_TYPES"."TYPE_ID" )
AND  ( ( "CUSTOMERS"."CUSTOMER_ID" = "CUST_PURCHASES"."CUSTOMER_ID" )
AND  ( ( "CUST_PURCHASES"."NUM_BOUGHT" > 5 )
AND  ( "BOOK_TYPES"."TYPE_ID" = 2 )  )  )
```

Designing Tables and Views

The following are some general tips on designing tables and views:

☐ Plan your tables and views before you create them. A little forethought in this area can save you a great deal of work. If you need to change a column, for example, you might discover that you will need to rebuild the table. Rebuilding the records stored in the table can be an enormous headache. Even if you do not have to take this extreme step, any modifications you make to a column can "break" views that use that column. Therefore, you should create a plan for the database (otherwise known as a *data model*) before you begin. The data model does not have to be 100 percent complete, but you should have some clear notion about the tables and views you will create.

☐ As mentioned earlier, whenever possible use a numeric data type for the columns to be joined.

☐ Use consistent naming for similar columns. When you built a view combining records from TITLES and PUBLISHERS, it was easy to identify the columns used for the join because they have the same name (PUBLISHER_ID).

☐ Use the appropriate data type. For example, if you use a Varchar data type for storing dates, you will not be able to use some of the date functions in Oracle Basic to format, compare, and edit date information.

☐ For numeric data types, use whatever type is sufficient for the job. If you do not expect the values to exceed 1,000, you should use an Integer, not a Number. A Number value requires more memory to store a value than does an integer, so you improve the efficiency of the database when you use an Integer instead.

☐ Before applying a condition to a view, think about the most efficient way to define it. An earlier example discussed how you should apply the condition to numeric values rather than strings whenever possible. This technique improves the performance of the view. Additionally, you should review the list of SQL operators in the online help to see if there are wildcard characters or other operators that might help you write the condition.

What Comes Next?

So far, the focus has been on the "back end" of the application, the database that stores information used by the Bookstore application. However, the user does not yet have the means to view and edit this information. Because you now have some tables and views, as well as some sample information, you can create your first form that reads from and writes to the database.

As with other techniques you have already learned, connecting a form to a table or view can be as simple as dragging and dropping some icon. In addition, this new form will have a great deal of the logic needed to make a client/server application work already built into it.

Q&A

Q **When different types of users all access the same table, should I create a view for each one?**

A Only if all of these users have other means than Oracle Power Objects to access the database. If, on the other hand, each class of user (manager, data entry clerk, sales person, accountant, and so on) can only view the data through a Power Objects application, then you can limit and tailor their perspectives on the data through the application. Creating a different view for each user makes it difficult to maintain the database.

Q **How often are views used as the record source for forms and reports?**

A More frequently for reports than forms. Because you cannot enter data through a multitable view (in practice, the most common form of view), these types of views are useful in forms only when the user is browsing data. However, because the user cannot interact with a report (except to print it), views are commonly used in reports. In fact, many views are designed explicitly for reporting. The second view you created, VW_CUST_PREFS, is a good example of such a view.

Q **How can I view the SQL code behind a view?**

A Blaze currently does not provide a tool for viewing the SQL code behind a view. Oracle7 and SQL Server, however, have utilities for interacting with the database (such as SQL*Plus for Oracle7 and SAF for SQL Server) that enable you to view the SQL code behind a view.

If you need to get the SQL text for a view in a Blaze database, you can use the SQLLOOKUP function (described on Day 6, "More About Recordsets") to get its text. The table in which the SQL code is stored is called ALL_VIEWS, and important columns are VIEW_NAME and SQL_TEXT. Therefore, to query the SQL code behind the view VW_MYVIEW, you would use the following syntax:

```
SELECT SQL_TEXT FROM ALL_VIEWS WHERE VIEW_NAME = 'VW_MYVIEW'
```

Because Oracle Power Objects provides a graphical view editor, you do not need to access the SQL code behind the view. If you are an experienced SQL programmer, and a pre-existing view does not work as expected, you might need to look at the SQL code behind the view. However, this is the exception that defines the rule: the other 99 percent of the time, you don't need to tinker with the SQL code to make the view work.

Workshop

The Workshop consists of quiz questions to help you solidify your understanding of the material covered. Try and understand the quiz answers before you go on to tomorrow's lesson.

Quiz

1. What is a join?
2. Because you query data through both a table and a view, what distinguishes the two?
3. What is one important use of a single-table view? Of a multitable view?
4. How do you limit the records queried to a view to those that meet some set of criteria?

Quiz Answers

1. A join defines a relationship between two tables whose records are being queried. The join does not exist before the query; instead, part of the query's SQL code defines how the two tables are connected. A join connects two columns of the same data type that might have matching values, such as the PUBLISHER_ID column that exists in both the PUBLISHERS and TITLES tables.

2. A table stores the records, whereas a view merely identifies a set of columns from one or more tables from which data will be queried. The view itself does not contain data; instead, it acts as a pointer to the tables where the data are stored.

3. You use a single-table view to limit the range of columns the user can see in a table, while still enabling that user to add, delete, and modify records in the table. A multitable view performs lookups into several tables to provide a composite picture of something. The lookups often return additional or explanatory information, such as the name of a publisher from the PUBLISHERS table that matches the PUBLISHER_ID of a book in the TITLES table.

4. You can enter conditions that apply to each column appearing in a view through the Conditions section of the Column List area.

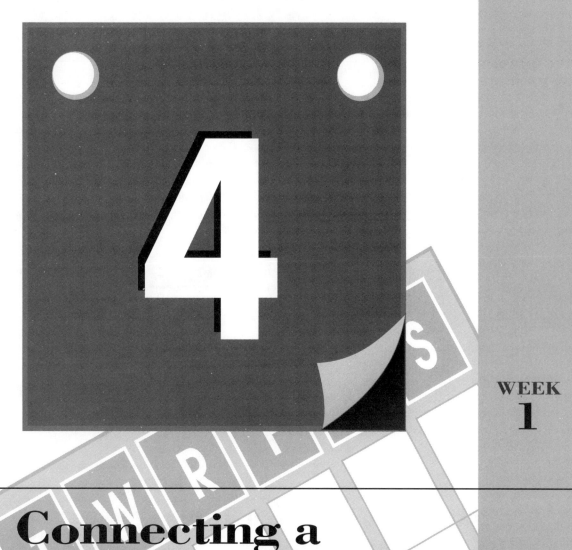

Connecting a Form to a Record Source

The strongest feature of Oracle Power Objects is its capability to enable you to work with both applications and databases within the same tool, using easy-to-use tools such as the View Editor window. Oracle Power Objects also simplifies the task of connecting (or binding) a form or report to the table or view from which it queries records. Normally, you must write extensive code to bind the container to a table or view; in Power Objects, you can accomplish the same task without writing a single line of code. Additionally, without adding any code, the application automatically monitors changes to the records viewed through the form, enforcing rules about this data and prompting the user when necessary.

In this lesson, you will learn the relatively simple techniques needed to bind forms to tables and views. Along the way, you will learn some important facts about the ways in which Oracle Power Objects applications follow the rules of client/server computing. You will also learn about the following:

☐ Binding forms to tables and views

☐ Binding controls to columns

☐ Drag-and-drop binding

☐ Testing bound forms

☐ The all-important properties for binding

☐ Forms, recordsets, and the database

☐ Manually binding containers and controls

☐ Scrollbars as record browsers

Binding a Form to a Table

In Oracle Power Objects, you can build a form connected to a table right away, so that you can view and edit information in the database (the core feature of a database application). After you build and test such a form, you will take stock of what you just did and how the new form works.

To create the new form, follow these steps.

1. In the Main window, double-click the icon for the BOOKS application to open its Application window (see Figure 4.1).

2. With the Application window selected, click the New Form button, or select New Form from the File menu.

   A new form now appears. As you remember from Day 1, "Your First Form," you should always give your form a descriptive name before you continue.

3. If the form's Property sheet is not open, click the Edit Properties button.

4. Type Publishers for the Label property.

Figure 4.1.
The Application window for BOOKS.POA.

5. Type `frmPublishers` for the Name property of the form, and then close the Property sheet.

6. Click Save to save your work in the new form. The form should now look like Figure 4.2.

Figure 4.2.
The form so far.

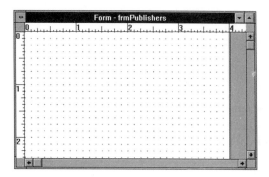

Presently, the form is not bound, meaning that it is not connected to a table. You're ready to change that situation right now.

To connect the new form to the PUBLISHERS table, follow these steps:

1. Select the Main window and double-click the icon for the BOOKS session.

   The Session window for BOOKS.POS now appears. Notice that the windows for the front end (the Bookstore application) and the back end (the database) coexist in the Oracle Power Objects desktop. As mentioned earlier today, this is another important feature of Oracle Power Objects: you use the same tool to work with both parts of a client/server database application, and you use many of the same techniques to work on both. For example, you define the name of a table and a form through the same interface, the Property sheet.

2. Double-click the Connector icon to open a connection to the BOOKS.BLZ Blaze database.

All the database objects created in earlier lessons now appear. At this point, you need to make sure that both the Session window and the new form are visible. If not, move things around until you can see at least part of the form. The Desktop should now look like Figure 4.3.

Figure 4.3.
The Application and Session windows.

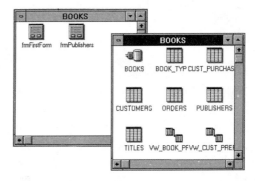

3. Click and drag the PUBLISHERS table icon until the cursor appears over part of the new form, frmPublishers. The form now looks like Figure 4.4.

Figure 4.4.
The form after dragging and dropping the icon for PUBLISHERS.

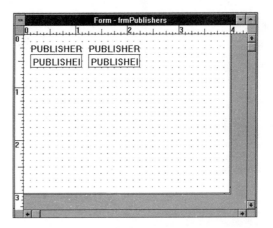

Two new text fields now appear on the form. The names appearing in these fields are the actual names of the fields, as defined through their Name property. However, this also is the name of the column in the PUBLISHERS table to which each field is bound. When you run the form, data from the PUBLISHER_ID column appear in the PUBLISHER_ID field, and data from the PUBLISHER_NAME column appear in the PUBLISHER_NAME field. In addition, two labels (or static text objects) displaying the names of these columns appear adjacent to these text fields.

If you were to run the form now, however, you could view only one record: the first one queried from the PUBLISHERS table. To browse among records, you need some kind of control—in this case, a scrollbar. By default, a scrollbar added to a bound form (one connected to a database) acts as a browsing tool, enabling the user to move back and forth through records.

4. In the Object palette, click the Horizontal Scrollbar drawing tool.

The cursor now changes, indicating that you will create a new scrollbar when you click the form.

5. Click somewhere on the form (but not on the text fields or static text objects).

A horizontal scrollbar now appears on the form, as shown in Figure 4.5.

Figure 4.5.
Adding the scrollbar to the form.

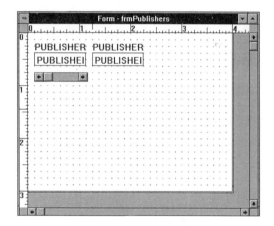

6. Click Save to save your work.

Testing the New Form

You now have completed all the steps to create a form bound to a table. It was a relatively painless process, a far cry from the large amount of code you might have to write to perform the binding in other tools.

At this point, you can see how the user will view data through this form. As you remember from Day 1, by clicking the Run Form button, you can run just this one form (not the rest of the application). Unlike the forms built in the first lesson, however, this form will have live data queried from the database displayed in it.

To test the new form, follow these steps:

1. With the new form selected, click the Run Form button (see Figure 4.6).

Figure 4.6.

Running the form.

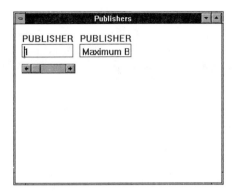

The form now appears as it will at runtime (that is, when the real application is running). A new toolbar appears: the standard toolbar that appears whenever you select a form in Oracle Power Objects (see Figure 4.7). This form contains several buttons for editing records. You will use all these controls during this lesson.

Figure 4.7.

The Form Runtime toolbar.

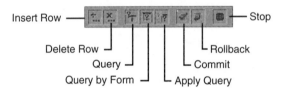

The record now displayed in the form is the first one queried from the database. However, the form also has queried all other records from the database—you just can't see them yet.

2. Click the right arrow of the scrollbar.

Another publisher record from the PUBLISHERS table now appears.

3. Continue clicking the scrollbar's right arrow.

Additional records appear until you reach the last one queried from the database. Then, if you click one more time, the two text fields appear blank. If you were to start typing in new values in these fields, you would be telling the application that you want to insert a new record into the PUBLISHERS table. In fact, that's what you'll do right now.

4. Click in the PUBLISHER_ID text field in the form and type 99.

5. Press the Tab key to move to the PUBLISHER_NAME text field.

At this point, you might notice that the Commit and Rollback buttons have been enabled (see Figure 4.8). When you typed a new value for PUBLISHER_ID, Oracle Power Objects recognized that you were entering changes to this table. As with the

Commit and Rollback buttons used when you entered new records directly into the PUBLISHERS table on Day 2, "Creating a Table," these two buttons enable you to save or undo your changes to the table.

Figure 4.8.

The enabled Commit and Rollback buttons.

The Commit and Rollback buttons are now enabled

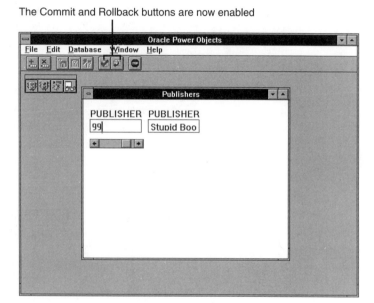

6. In the second text field, type Stupid Books.

7. Click the Commit button to save the new record.

8. Click the right and left arrows of the scrollbar to move among the records.

    The new publisher record for Stupid Books now appears next to the original records in the table. With a name like Stupid Books, however, you might guess that this record will not be a permanent addition to the PUBLISHERS table.

9. Use the scrollbar to move to the record for Stupid Books.

10. Click the Delete Row button to delete this record.

    Once again, the Commit and Rollback buttons are enabled. Like the creation of a new record, the deletion of a record is a change to the database that Oracle Power Objects recognizes. At this point, if you were to click the Rollback button, the new record would reappear. However, you're going to remove this record from the PUBLISHERS table.

11. Click the Commit button.

The record is now deleted from the database.

There is a new publisher you need to add to the table. To do so, you will be using a different technique for inserting a new record into the PUBLISHERS table.

To add the new record, follow these steps:

1. Click the Insert Row button to insert a new record.

   By now, you might have noticed that the terms *row* and *record* can be used interchangeably.

2. In the PUBLISHER_ID field, type 5.

3. Click the Commit button.

   Whoops! Oracle Power Objects is displaying an error message (see Figure 4.9). Your mistake was to leave the PUBLISHER_NAME text field blank, thereby violating the NOT NULL constraint applied to the PUBLISHER_NAME column in the database. This illustrates some of the automatic checks Oracle Power Objects applications can perform.

Figure 4.9.

The application realizes you left a NOT NULL column blank.

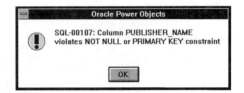

4. In the PUBLISHER_NAME field, type Smart Books.

5. Click the Commit button to save the new record to the database.

   At this point, you can requery the records for this form by clicking the Query button. In this form, clicking the Query button will have only one significant effect: the records will be reordered in ascending order of PUBLISHER_ID. Therefore, the record for Smart Books will appear last, just before the blank line. Essentially, the Query button requeries all records from the table to which the form is connected, which can be useful on forms more complex than this one.

   Don't touch the other two buttons on the toolbar: Query By Form (QBF) and Apply Criteria. You will learn how to use these buttons later in this lesson. However, there is one more step to take.

6. Click the Stop button to end your test of the form.

The form returns to design-time mode, and data queried from the database no longer appears in the form.

What Just Happened?

From the standpoint of the user, what just happened seems straightforward: you entered a new record, deleted it, and then entered and saved a second record. However, as a developer, you need a more complete picture of what transpired in your new form to use Oracle Power Objects effectively.

Sessions and Applications

When you run the form, it seems as though you have a direct window into the form, just as you did when you entered data into the database through the Table Browser window. In fact, that is not the case—there are two layers of other objects between the form and the database.

As discussed previously, the session regulates connections between the application and the database. The session can connect and disconnect from the database, depending on certain conditions. Unless the session is maintaining an open connection, you cannot read from or write to the database. The session also recognizes when you have entered changes (record insertions, deletions, or updates) that you have not yet committed or rolled back.

When you ran the new form, the application notified the session to open a connection to the database. When you stopped running the form, the session closed the connection. Every session has two methods, `Connect()` and `Disconnect()`, that the application automatically calls to perform these tasks. In addition, you can write method code that explicitly calls either of these methods when needed. For example, to close a connection to a database, switch to a different database, and then open a new connection, you would call both `Disconnect()` and `Connect()`.

Recordsets and Forms

Although the session is already familiar to you, the other object that lies between the application and the database is not. Every bound container, such as the form you just created, has a *recordset* associated with it. This special application object contains copies of all records queried from the form's associated table or view. Although the database takes care of the actual records stored in a table, the application maintains the recordset as a "local" copy of these records. Therefore, when you are viewing or editing records you are changing the contents of the recordset, not the table behind it.

Figure 4.10 shows you the relationship among a form, a recordset, and a table.

When you run the form, the application automatically creates the recordset for the form. Although there are ways of accessing the recordset directly through code, you do not have to write any code to create and maintain it.

Figure 4.10.
*A form, a recordset,
and a table.*

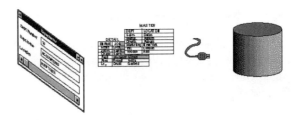

The recordset queries data from all the columns represented by bound controls on the form. Some columns, however, are not bound to controls; in this case, the recordset does not include a corresponding column for these records. For example, if you had a single control bound to PUBLISHER_ID, the recordset for the form would not have a column for PUBLISHER_NAME. There can be exceptions to this rule, as you shall see later in this lesson.

The reasons for having this additional object between the form and its associated table or view lie in the client/server design (also called a *program architecture*) of an Oracle Power Objects application. In a client/server database application, you want to free the database as much as possible, asking it to perform tasks only when necessary. This feature of client/server systems is called *distributed processing*: the database (or server) splits responsibilities with the application (or client). Figure 4.11 shows the different components of a database application created with Oracle Power Objects.

Figure 4.11.
*The program architecture of
a Power Objects application.*

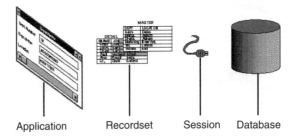

Application   Recordset   Session   Database

Because the application can maintain this local copy of the records, the database does not have to respond to every change to these records. Only when the user clicks the Commit button are changes actually written to the database.

Therefore, the database acts only when it receives the message from the client to save the new information. Before writing these changes to any tables, however, the database can perform some checks, such as checking to see that NOT NULL and UNIQUE constraints have not been violated.

With this in mind, you can see that an Oracle Power Objects application consists of four layers, not simply two. Three of these layers—the application, the recordset, and the session—are all part of the client portion of a client/server application. All three are objects with properties and methods that you can access through method code. The server, on the other hand, consists of the database itself.

Saving a Record to the Database

To illustrate this point, look at the record you added to the PUBLISHERS table in the last exercise. Although it looked as if you simply saved your changes to the database, the same way you might save a word processor document to disk, a great deal more actually happened. Following is a more accurate break-down of what occurred:

1. You began typing the new record. Oracle Power Objects then inserted a new row in the recordset associated with the frmPublishers form. As you typed, the new information became part of the recordset.

2. When you finished entering values for the new record, you clicked the Commit button. The application took this proposed addition to the frmPublishers table and passed it along to the session. At this point, the application might have performed some checks on the new information before enabling it to be sent to the database. These application-based checks, called *validations*, are the subject of Day 13, "Enforcing Business Rules."

3. As long as the changes did not cause the session to disconnect, the application passed these changes along to the database.

4. In the database, the database engine (the intelligence behind the database) received the message to enter a new record in the PUBLISHERS table. Before enabling the change, however, the database checked to see that information in the PUBLISHER_ID column adhered to the restrictions of a primary key value, and that the value in the PUBLISHER_NAME column was NOT NULL (that is, left without a value). If the new record met these criteria, then the database engine added the new record to the database table.

   Figure 4.12 shows how a change to a record passes through the different layers of an Oracle Power Objects application.

Figure 4.12.

The passage of a new record through the four application layers.

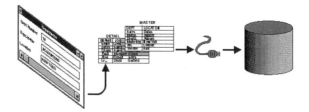

Constraints in the Application and the Database

As indicated, you as a developer can instruct the application to check information in both the application and the database. Day 2, "Creating a Table," called these checks *constraints*. You can apply the same terminology to checks enforced in the application, or use another term, *business rules*.

In a client/server environment, you can choose where to enforce a constraint. Frequently, for sake of efficiency, you perform the check before the record is sent to the database.

Suppose that you want to make sure that every book price entered in the database is a number greater than zero. Neither the application nor the database will perform this check unless you instruct one of them to do so. Ideally, you should perform this check within the application, before the database ever has a chance to see any new information. This reduces the workload on the database, which might have a great deal of processing already to do when handling requests from the application to query and modify records. Server overload can be a greater problem with remote databases such as Oracle7 or SQL Server, which simultaneously handle requests for data from a large number of users.

On the other hand, if you define the constraint in the database, you can be certain that it will be enforced centrally by the server, regardless of the client connected to it. Therefore, no matter what application is writing a new record to a table, the constraint will be in force.

In a client/server environment, you have some important choices to make about where you enforce a constraint. In later chapters, you will create some application-level constraints that enforce business rules before new data ever reaches the database.

Recordset-Related Properties

You now have some knowledge of the drag-and-drop techniques for binding forms to tables and views (also called *record sources*). In addition, you have learned about the program architecture of an Oracle Power Objects application, including forms, recordsets, sessions, and databases. Now, you can make sense of the properties that bind forms to record sources.

When you dragged the icon for the PUBLISHERS table, you set two key properties of the form. To view these properties, follow these steps:

1. Select the form frmPublishers.
2. If the form's Property sheet is not open, click the Edit Properties button.
3. Scroll down the list of properties and methods until you can view the RecSrcSession and RecordSource properties (see Figure 4.13).

Currently, the RecordSource property is set to PUBLISHERS, the name of the table to which this form is bound. You could enter a different table for the form by typing its name into the Property sheet in place of PUBLISHERS. Unless this new table had columns named PUBLISHER_ID and PUBLISHER_NAME, however, with the right data types, the form could no longer get records from the database.

Figure 4.13.

The RecordSource *and*
RecSrcSession *properties.*

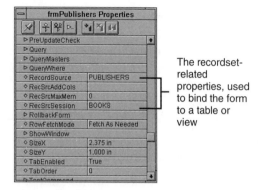

The recordset-
related
properties, used
to bind the form
to a table or
view

Additionally, the RecSrcSession property is set to BOOKS. This is the name of the session through which the form accesses the BOOKS.BLZ database. In some cases, you can actually leave the RecSrcSession property blank if you specify a default session for the application. You will do exactly that in a few moments, but first, Table 4.1 shows a summary of these two key properties.

Table 4.1. Recordset-related properties.

Property	Description
RecSrcSession	Specifies the session through which a database is accessed. The session itself contains information on the schema name or username, the password, and the location of the database. If you leave this property blank, the application attempts to use the session identified as the default session for the application (through the application's DefaultSession property).
RecordSource	Specifies the table or view to which the form is bound. The table must exist in the schema specified for the session. If the record source is a read-only view (such as in the case of a multitable view), the user will be able to view records through the form, but not edit them.

These two properties appear on other containers (reports, user-defined classes, embedded forms, and repeater displays) that you can bind to a table or view. Although these objects are in some cases very different from forms, you use the same techniques to bind them to a table that you used to bind the frmPublishers form to the PUBLISHERS table.

To recap the important points about binding forms to record sources:

☐ When you drag the icon for a table or view onto a form, it automatically creates text fields corresponding to the columns in this record source.

4

☐ The form is automatically bound to the record source through the RecordSource property.

☐ In addition, Oracle Power Objects automatically sets the RecSrcSession property of the form to the session through which the table or view is accessed.

Binding Controls to Columns

The RecordSource property identifies the table or view to which the form is bound. But how are the text fields connected to particular columns in the record source?

Not surprisingly, the answer lies in a property of the text fields.

1. Click the PUBLISHER_ID text field in the frmPublishers form to select it.

   As you might remember, the handles (small black rectangles) appear around the borders of an object when you select it. Keep in mind this graphical indicator of which object is selected as you work with objects on a form.

2. If the Property sheet for the text field is not open, click the Edit Properties button.

3. Scroll down the Property sheet until you can see the DataSource property.

   The value currently assigned to this property is PUBLISHER_ID. Binding a text field or other control to a column is as simple as typing in the name of the column for this property. If the form already has a record source assigned to it through the RecordSource property, however, Oracle Power Objects provides an additional shortcut for selecting the column in that table or view.

4. Click the label for the DataSource section of the Property sheet.

   A drop-down list of columns in the PUBLISHERS table now appears, as shown in Figure 4.14. If you click on PUBLISHER_NAME, the text field then will be bound to that column rather than PUBLISHER_ID. However, leave PUBLISHER_ID as the column specified for this control.

In the drop-down list, the =Derived option is a special case of the DataSource property, used to populate the control with the result of an expression. Derived values are discussed in a later lesson.

There is one final way to bind a control to a column, as illustrated in the next exercise:

1. Delete the PUBLISHER_NAME text field on the form.

   Don't worry—you will re-create and rebind it in a moment.

2. In the Object palette, select the Text Field drawing tool.

3. Click somewhere on the form.

   A new text field now appears. You might want to reposition and resize it to the location of the original PUBLISHER_ID field.

Figure 4.14.
*The list of columns to which
the control can be bound.*

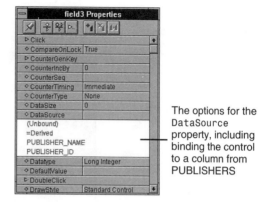

The options for the
DataSource
property, including
binding the control
to a column from
PUBLISHERS

4. Select the BOOKS Session window and double-click the icon for the PUBLISHERS table.

   The Table Editor window for this table now appears.

5. Click the Row Selector button for the PUBLISHER_NAME column.

   The column description for PUBLISHER_NAME now is highlighted, as shown in Figure 4.15.

Figure 4.15.
*The PUBLISHER_NAME
column selected.*

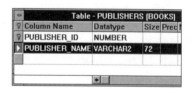

6. Click again on the row selector button for the PUBLISHER_NAME column and drag it onto the new text field.

7. Release the mouse button.

   The text appearing in the control now changes to PUBLISHER_NAME, indicating that the Name property of this text field has changed. You also rebound the control to the PUBLISHER_NAME column, as you will now confirm.

8. Select the text field and open its Property sheet.

9. Scroll down to the DataSource property.

As you can see, the control is now bound to the PUBLISHER_NAME column through this property. In addition, its Datatype property is now set to String, to match the data type of the column (VARCHAR2). Figure 4.16 shows the PUBLISHER_ID text field bound to the PUBLISHER_ID column.

Figure 4.16.

The form with the PUBLISHER_ID *text field re-created.*

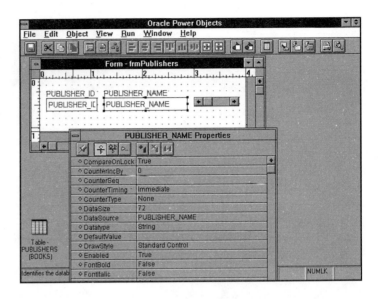

To recap:

- [ ] Controls are bound to columns through their DataSource property.
- [ ] Oracle Power Objects automatically sets the DataSource property of a control when you drag the icon for a table or view onto a form, automatically creating a text field corresponding to each column.
- [ ] Alternatively, you can drag a column description onto an existing control to bind it.
- [ ] When you use either drag-and-drop technique, Oracle Power Objects automatically sets the Datatype property.

Control and Database Data Types

Because previous chapters have discussed the importance of data types, you should understand how control data types "map" to column data types. In other words, what are the corresponding data types for controls and columns?

Table 4.2 summarizes how Oracle Power Objects maps data types for controls and columns. When you drag a column from a table onto a control, Oracle Power Objects looks at the data type of the column and then decides which is the appropriate data type for the control, according to the guidelines in Table 4.2.

Table 4.2. Data type equivalencies.

Controls	Blaze	Oracle7	SQL Server
Long	Integer	Long, Number	VarBinary
Double	Float	Float	Float
String	Varchar2	Varchar2	Varchar
Date	Date	Date	Date

All the data types for controls apply to data types in Oracle Basic. However, Oracle Basic has a wider range of data types, such as `Object`.

Another Way to Bind a Form

By dragging the icon for the PUBLISHERS table onto the form, you create text fields bound to all of the columns in the table. You might, however, want to create only a few such controls, especially when you have a large table with many columns. In these cases, you might want to create a form that displays information from only a small range of columns in the table.

To illustrate how to create bound controls representing a few columns in a table, you will create a new browser form for reviewing book titles. This new form, frmSeeBooks, will show data from only a few columns of the TITLES table.

To create the new form, follow these steps:

1. Select the Application window for BOOKS.POA.
2. Click the New Form button, or select New Form from the File menu.
3. If it does not appear already, open the Property sheet for the new form.
4. For the `Name` property of the form, type `frmSeeTitles`.
5. For the `Label` property of the new form, type `Review Book Titles`.

   Your new form is finished. Now you can add some controls bound to a subset of the columns in TITLES.
6. Select the Session window for BOOKS.POS. If the session is not currently connected, double-click the Connector icon.
7. Double-click the icon for the TITLES table to open the Table Editor window for this table.
8. Click the Row Selector button for the AUTHLNAME column.
9. Holding down the Ctrl key, click the Row Selector buttons for the TITLE_NAME and PRICE columns (see Figure 4.17).

> **Note:** Holding down the Ctrl key is a common way to make non-contiguous selections from spreadsheets, list boxes, and similar scrolling lists of items.

Figure 4.17.

Selecting three columns from the table.

Column Name	Datatype	Size
TITLE_ID	NUMBER	
TITLE_NAME	VARCHAR2	200
AUTHLNAME	VARCHAR2	32
AUTHFNAME	VARCHAR2	32
PUBLISHER_ID	NUMBER	
PRICE	FLOAT	126
WS_PRICE	FLOAT	126
PROMOTION_PRICE	FLOAT	126
PRINTING	INTEGER	
TYPE_ID	NUMBER	
ON_ORDER	NUMBER	
IN_STOCK	NUMBER	
ON_HOLD	NUMBER	

Table - TITLES (BOOKS)

10. Release the mouse button.

    The three columns remain selected (and highlighted).

11. Click again on the Row Selector buttons for one of these columns and hold down the mouse button.

12. Drag the cursor onto the new form, frmSeeTitles, and release the mouse button (see Figure 4.18).

Figure 4.18.

Three new text fields bound to the three selected columns.

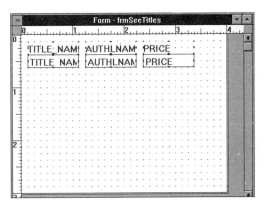

As shown in Figure 4.18, only three new text fields appear, one for each of the selected columns in TITLES.

114

Now that you have created three new bound controls, you need just a few more touches to test the newly bound form.

1. From the Object palette, select the horizontal scrollbar drawing tool and click the form.
2. Resize and reposition the text fields to make the form more readable.

   Most important, widen the TITLE_NAME field to display all the words in the title.
3. Click Save to save the new form in the application.
4. Click the Run Form button (see Figure 4.19).

Figure 4.19.
The final form.

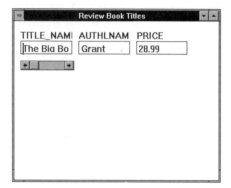

The form now appears as it will at runtime. You can use the scrollbar to move between the records. The two bound forms seen so far, however, have one disadvantage: you can view only one record at a time in each of them. In the next exercise, you will add a special type of bindable container, a repeater display, that enables you to view multiple records simultaneously.

DO	DON'T

DO use drag-and-drop binding to speed development.

DO drag columns onto existing controls to bind them.

DO set the RecSrcSession property when needed.

DON'T make every control a text field.

DON'T forget to use naming conventions to identify controls clearly by name and type.

DON'T manually enter the RecSrcSession property for every bound container if the application uses a single session already identified through the DefaultSession property.

A Different Type of Bound Container

As described earlier in this lesson, Oracle Power Objects provides several types of containers that can be bound to tables or views, which are described in Table 4.3.

Table 4.3. Types of containers.

Container	Description
Forms	Standard forms that can contain a variety of different objects. Forms show records one at a time.
Embedded forms	A form that can appear within another container. For example, you can add an embedded form to a form. Embedded forms also show records one at a time.
User-defined classes	A special type of bindable container that can be copied into other containers. Classes show records one at a time.
Repeater displays	A bindable container that displays the same set of controls and other objects for each record in the repeater display's recordset. The repeater display has a scrollbar for moving through the recordset. Therefore, unlike the previously described containers, repeater displays can display multiple records in a scrolling list.
Reports	A bindable container used to display records, but which does not enable the user to interact with the controls within the report. Reports are divided into several functional sections (Report Header, Page Footer, Detail), all of which can contain bound controls. Like repeater displays, reports are designed to display multiple records.

As the descriptions in Table 4.3 imply, some bindable containers (user-defined classes, repeater displays, and embedded forms) can appear within other containers. Other containers (forms and reports), however, never appear within other containers—hence, they are classified as *top-level containers.* You can continue adding containers within containers, like a series of Chinese boxes or matrushka dolls, if you want. The relationship between containers and the objects within them is called the object *containment hierarchy,* and appears throughout Oracle Power Objects.

For the sake of your form, however, you will add one additional container—a repeater display. Like the form, this container will be bound to the TITLES table and will display data from the AUTHLNAME, TITLE_NAME, and PRICE columns. Unlike a form, however, a repeater display is designed to show several records simultaneously.

Repeater displays have two components: the frame and the panel. The *frame* includes the border surrounding the container and the vertical scrollbar appearing on its left edge. The *panel* is a rectangle within the frame that can contain controls and static objects, such as the text fields you will soon add. For every record in the repeater display's recordset, one instance of the panel appears, capable of displaying data from that record.

Figure 4.20 shows the components of a repeater display.

Figure 4.20.

The anatomy of a repeater display.

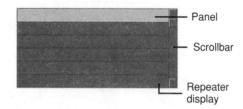

Panel

Scrollbar

Repeater display

Now that you understand the basics of repeater displays, you can create one yourself. First, however, you need to clean up your form to make room for the repeater display.

1. Select the frmSeeTitles form.
2. Click and drag across the face of the form until you select all the text fields and labels you added in the previous exercise. Once you have selected all the objects, release the mouse button.

    The fields and labels remain selected. This technique for selecting several objects at once is called *lassoing*.

3. Click the Cut button or press the Delete key to eliminate these objects from the form.
4. Open the form's Property sheet and delete the entries for the RecordSource and RecSrcSession properties.

Because the repeater display, not the form, will be bound to the TITLES table, there is no need to have a table and session specified for these two properties.

Now you can add the repeater display to the form by following these steps:

1. From the Object palette, select the Repeater Display drawing tool (see Figure 4.21).
2. Click in the upper-left corner of the form, but do not release the mouse button.
3. Drag the cursor across the face of the form until it reaches the lower-right corner.

    The repeater display now covers the entire form, as shown in Figure 4.22.

4. Select the Table Editor window for the TITLES table.

    This window should still be open, and the three columns (AUTHLNAME, TITLE_NAME, and PRICE) still selected. If not, you can click each column's Row Selector button while holding down the Ctrl key to select each column in turn.

Figure 4.21.

Selecting the Repeater Display drawing tool.

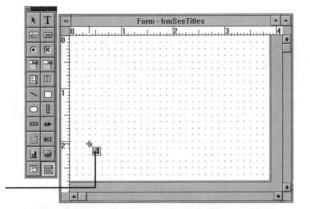

The Repeater Display drawing tool selected

Figure 4.22.

The new repeater display.

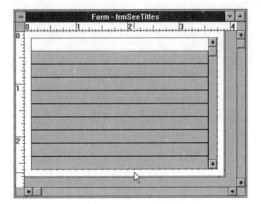

5. Click the row selector button for one of these columns and drag the cursor over the panel within the repeater display.

When the cursor is over the panel, the panel will be selected (see Figure 4.23).

Figure 4.23.

Dragging the columns into the repeater display panel.

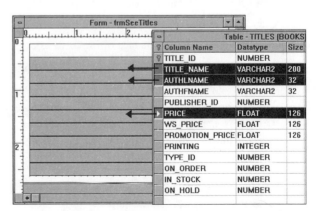

6. Release the mouse button.

   The same three text fields you added to the form now appear within the repeater display. These controls are bound to the appropriate columns in the TITLES table, and the repeater display itself is bound to the table. To confirm this fact, select the repeater display, open its Property sheet, and scroll down to the RecordSource property. The name of the TITLES table now appears in the RecordSource section of the Property sheet, indicating that the repeater display is bound to this table.

7. Click the Save button.

8. Click the Run Form button to test the form (see Figure 4.24).

   The form and its repeater display now appear as they will at runtime. You might notice that the repeater display has a blank line under the records queried from the table. You have seen this blank record before, when you scrolled past the last record in the frmPublishers form. If you start typing values into one of the text fields in this blank row, you are inserting a new book record into the repeater display's recordset (presumably to be later added to the table).

   If the repeater display were showing many more records than the ones here, then you could use the scrollbar to navigate among these records. However, because this table has only a few records right now, clicking the scrollbar does nothing.

9. Press Stop to end this exercise.

Improving the Form's Appearance

Because reading the title of each book is hard, you need to make some cosmetic changes to the text fields in this repeater display.

1. Place the cursor over one of the text fields and click the mouse.

   You might notice that the text field is not yet selected. Because the panel is contained within the repeater display frame, and the text field is contained within the panel, you need to click more than once to move down the object containment hierarchy to the text field.

2. Click twice more to select the text field.

3. Hold down the Shift key and click the other text fields within the repeater display.

> **Note:** This technique—holding down the Shift key and clicking several objects to select them as a group—is another way to select multiple objects in the Oracle Power Objects desktop.

4. Open the Property sheet for these text fields (see Figure 4.24).

Figure 4.24.

The text fields' shared Property sheet.

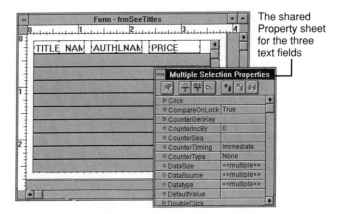

The shared Property sheet for the three text fields

The Property sheet can display the properties and methods of several selected objects at once. In these cases, the Property sheet shows only the properties and methods shared by all these objects. If the same value is assigned to a property shared by the selected objects, then the value appears in that section of the Property sheet. For example, the three text fields have their `FontBold` property set to `False`.

If the objects do not share the same value for a property, then << MULTIPLE >> appears as the setting for that property. For example, if you scroll down to the `Name` property, << MULTIPLE >> appears in this section of the Property sheet (because these fields all have different names).

At this point, you could set a property for all three text fields by entering the new value for the property. You use this technique to change the font settings for the text appearing within the controls.

5. Change the `FontName` property to `Arial`.

6. Change the `FontSize` property to `9` (that is, 9-point text).

7. Resize and reposition the text fields until the repeater display looks something similar to Figure 4.25.

   Before you run the repeater display, you will add a special control that helps you select a particular record. In addition, this control displays a lock icon whenever the record has been added or changed. You have seen this icon before, when you were editing records through the Table Browser window.

8. From the Object palette, select the Current Row Control drawing tool.

9. Click the left edge of the repeater display panel, where you just left some space when you moved the text fields in the repeater display.

   The new control, called the current row control, now appears next to the text fields (see Figure 4.26).

Figure 4.25.
A better-looking form.

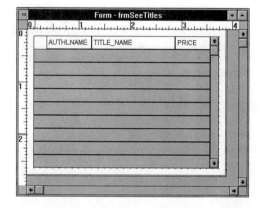

Figure 4.26.
The current row control added to the repeater display.

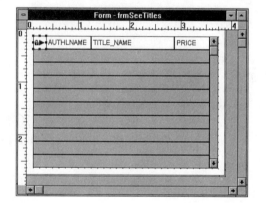

10. Click the Save button.
11. Click the Run Form button.

You now see a better version of the scrolling list of titles within the repeater display. You can click the current row control to select a particular record. When you make the selection, the current row control for that record turns black, to identify the selected record.

Views as Record Sources

Looking at this scrolling list of books, you might see another use for a repeater display in your Bookstore application: displaying the list of customer preferences you created through a view on Day 3. The VW_CUST_PREFS view queried records from the CUSTOMERS, CUST_PURCHASES, and BOOK_TYPES tables to show how many of each type of book customers had purchased.

Because Oracle Power Objects enable you to bind containers to either a table or a view, you can easily create a repeater display that uses this view as its record source. Instead of querying directly from the base tables, this repeater display will query records through a view as its record source.

The technique for binding the form to the view is the same as before:

☐ The container (in this case, a repeater display) is bound to the view through its RecordSource and RecSrcSession properties.

☐ The controls within the container are bound to columns in the view through their DataSource property.

Additionally, you can use the same drag-and-drop techniques to create bound controls (text fields) within the form or repeater display. First, however, you must create the new form and its repeater display.

1. Select the Application window for BOOKS.POA.
2. Click the New Form button, or select New Form from the File menu.

   A new form now appears.
3. Open the Property sheet for the new form.
4. Set the new form's Label propery to Customer Preferences and its Name property to frmCustPrefs.
5. From the Object palette, select the Repeater Display drawing tool.
6. Click and drag across the form to create the new repeater display.

Now that you have the form and its repeater display, you can add the bound controls.

1. Select the Session window for BOOKS.POS.
2. Open the View Editor window for the VW_CUSTPREFS view.
3. Delete the conditions you set for the view (NUM BOUGHT > 5, TYPE_ID = 2). You set these conditions on Day 3 when you were refining the view.
4. Click Save to save your changes to the view.
5. Holding down the Ctrl key, click the Row Selector icon for the CUSTOMERS.LNAME and BOOK_TYPES.TYPE_DESC columns in the Column List area (see Figure 4.27).
6. Click and drag these columns from the view into the repeater display in frmCustPrefs.

   Another set of text fields now appears in the repeater display.
7. Edit the font properties of the text fields to make their contents more readable (such as FontSize = 10, FontName = Arial).
8. Move and resize the text fields so that you can easily read their contents.

   Most significantly, make the TYPE_DESC field large enough to display the description of each type of book.

Figure 4.27.
Selecting the columns from the view.

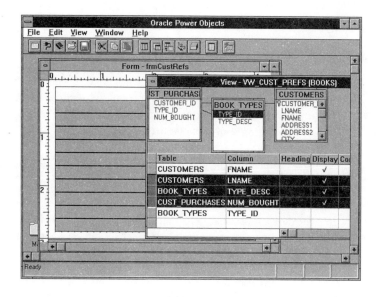

9. Click Save and then run the form (see Figure 4.28).

Figure 4.28.
The repeater display, bound to the view VW_CUST_PREFS.

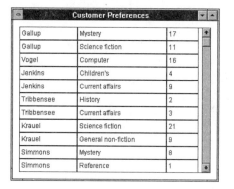

You now have a form that shows the same scrolling list of customer purchases that you saw when you ran the view on Day 3. Because the record source of this form is a multitable view, you cannot edit its contents. However, if you had added a single-table view to the repeater display, you might be able to edit records through this form.

Take a Breather

You have accomplished a great deal in this lesson. Each form you created and then bound to a table or view gave the user information queried from the database. You also chose two different ways of presenting the same information: either one record at a time or several records simultaneously. Finally, you used a view to give the user meaningful information queried from several tables. Time for congratulations!

What you have not done yet, however, is use method code to manipulate records. All your work so far has been code-free: rather than entering Basic code that queried and manipulated records, you used drag-and-drop binding techniques as well as the Property sheet. In the next exercise, you will be coding some changes to a form's recordset.

Working with Recordsets

As indicated earlier in today's lesson, forms and other containers do not provide a direct window into the database. Instead, a form maintains local copies of records queried from a table or view, called a *recordset object*. The recordset behaves in many ways like an actual table:

- [ ] The recordset has columns and rows.
- [ ] The recordset has the same constraints applied to each column as in the table (NOT NULL, UNIQUE, or PRIMARY KEY).
- [ ] The recordset maintains a pointer to the current record. If you perform any operations on a record by calling a method of the recordset, the application takes this action on the current record.

The recordset always has a column corresponding to the primary key column for the table, whether or not there is a control on the form (or other container) connected to that primary key column. You cannot see this column because there is no control bound to it. The hidden column exists as part of the recordset, making it available for *programmatic manipulation* (that is, changes made through code). You can specify additional hidden columns to add to the recordset through the RecSrcAddCols property.

Recordset Methods

Unlike a table or view, a recordset is an application object, with its own set of standard methods. These methods are designed for viewing and editing data, moving the pointer within the recordset, and evaluating characteristics of the recordset object (such as the number of records in it). In the next exercise, you will call a method of this object that inserts a new row into the recordset.

Table 4.4 indicates the standard methods of recordsets.

Table 4.4. Standard methods of recordset objects.

Method	Description
DeleteRow()	Deletes the current row
GetColCount()	Returns the number of columns in a recordset
GetColName()	Returns the name of a column, specified by its column number (a Long value)
GetColNum()	Returns the number of a column, specified by its name (a String value)
GetColVal()	Returns the value stored in the specified column of the current record
GetRowCount()	Returns the number of rows in the recordset
GetCurRow()	Returns the number of the current row
GetSession()	Returns a reference to the recordset's session
InsertRow()	Inserts a new row
LockRow()	Locks the currently selected row
SetColVal()	Assigns a value to the specified column of the current record
SetCurRow()	Moves the pointer in the recordset to the specified record number

Referencing the Recordset Object

Before you can call one of these methods, you need to get a reference to the recordset. GetRecordset() is a standard method of all bindable containers that returns such a reference to the recordset associated with a particular container. To get the reference, you use the following syntax:

```
container_name.GetRecordset()
```

Because the method returns a reference, you can assign this reference to a variable of type Object (a special data type designed for object references). For example, the following code assigns a reference to a form's recordset to a variable:

```
DIM vObj AS Recordset
vObj = frmPublishers.GetRecordset()
vObj.SetCurRow(1)
```

The final line uses the object reference to call one of the methods of a recordset, SetCurRow().

Alternatively, you can call a method of a recordset from within the same line of code that returns the object reference. Many developers prefer this technique because it makes the code more compact and easy to maintain. The following is the syntax for this type of call to the method of a recordset:

```
container_name.GetRecordset.method_name()
```

If you want to insert a row into a form's recordset, you might write the following code:

```
frmPublishers.GetRecordset.InsertRow()
```

This is precisely the code you will write in this exercise. Here, you will add two pushbuttons to the frmPublishers form that deletes or inserts a record, depending on the button you click.

1. Select the Application window for BOOKS.POA and double-click the icon for frmPublishers.

2. When the form appears, select the Pushbutton tool from the Object palette and click the form.

   A new pushbutton appears in the form.

3. Repeat step 2 to add another pushbutton.

4. Change the Label property of one pushbutton to Insert, and to Delete for the other.

5. Position the two pushbuttons in the form so that it looks something similar to Figure 4.29.

Figure 4.29.

The two pushbuttons added to the form.

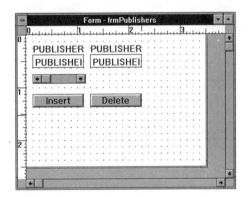

6. Open the Property sheet for the Insert button.

7. Click the Click() section to open the Code Editor window for this method (see Figure 4.30).

8. Add the following method code to the method:

   ```
   frmPublisher.GetRecordset.InsertRow()
   ```

9. Select the other pushbutton, open the Code Editor window for its Click() method, and enter the following code:

   ```
   frmPublisher.GetRecordset.DeleteRow()
   ```

10. Click Save to save your work.

Figure 4.30.
*The Code Editor window
for* Click().

You are now ready to test the form.

1. Click the Run Form button to view the form in Run Time mode (that is, how it will appear to the user).

2. Click the Insert button.

    The two text fields now appear blank, indicating that you have inserted a new record into the form's recordset. In addition, the Commit and Rollback buttons are now enabled.

3. Type 88 for the publisher ID number and Temporary Books for its name.

4. Click the Commit button.

    The new record has now been copied from the recordset into the PUBLISHERS table. To confirm this, click the Query button and then scroll among the publisher records. The new record for Temporary Books appears as the last record (because its publisher ID number is the highest).

5. Select the record for Temporary Books and click the Delete pushbutton.

    The new record is now deleted from the recordset. You now need to save this change to the PUBLISHERS table.

6. Click Commit to instruct the database to delete the record from the PUBLISHERS table.

7. Click the Stop button to end your test of this form.

Although it might not be obvious right now, there are many uses for these recordset methods. For example, if you maintain a recordset hidden from the user, you must use the GetColVal() method to read a value from the recordset. One such hidden recordset might be the usernames and passwords for all users, read from the database once for the sake of efficiency. To see if a password is valid, you then call the GetColVal() of this hidden recordset to perform the check.

Scrollbars as Record Browsers

While you are looking at the frmPublishers form, it is a good time to make two parenthetical observations. First, the scrollbar automatically knew how to scroll among records in this form—you did not have to add any method code to make it work. By default, when you add a scrollbar to a bound container such as a form, the scrollbar acts as a browser control for the container. Keeping with its code-light design, Oracle Power Objects automatically sets a few properties of the scrollbar to make it an effective browser (see Table 4.5).

Table 4.5. Scrollbar properties.

Property	Description
ScrollObj	Identifies by name the container whose recordset the scrollbar can be used to browse. The default setting for this property is Container, specifying the container in which the scrollbar appears as the one browsed by using this control.
ScrollPos	Specifies the current position of the scrollbar. When the scrollbar acts as a browser, the value assigned to ScrollPos is the number of the current record.
ScrollMax	Defines the maximum value for the ScrollPos property of the scrollbar. For a scrollbar acting as a browser, this value is set to the number of records in the recordset.
ScrollMin	Defines the minimum value for the ScrollPos property. For browser scrollbars, this value is set by default to 1.

Creating a 3-D Look and Feel

The other parenthetical comment about this form has to do with its aesthetics. Many applications now use a 3-D look and feel that looks as though the controls are embossed in the surface of a metal background. If you look at the dialog boxes appearing in Microsoft Word 6.0, for example, you will see an example of this new interface convention in practice.

You can apply this look and feel to Oracle Power Objects applications as well. To illustrate, you will change the appearance of the frmPublishers form from two-dimensional to three.

1. In the form frmPublishers, select the form itself and open its Property sheet.
2. In the ColorFill section, select light gray as the new color for the form's background.
3. Hold down the Shift key and click the two text fields.
4. In the combined Property sheet for these two controls, click the DrawStyle section.

A drop-down list of two selections, Standard Control and 3D Control, now appears (see Figure 4.31).

Figure 4.31.
The DrawStyle *property.*

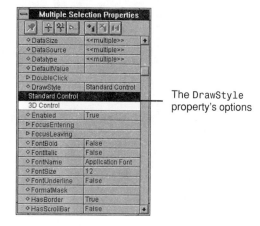

The DrawStyle property's options

5. Select 3D Control as the new setting for this property.

The two text fields now appear embossed within the form.

Summary

Today, you have learned the basics of the core feature of Oracle Power Objects, its capability to connect application objects to database objects quickly and easily. The following list recaps the key points:

☐ An Oracle Power Objects application has four layers: the application, the recordset objects behind bound containers, the session, and the database.

☐ There are several types of bindable containers, including forms, reports, user-defined classes, embedded forms, and repeater displays. Although these containers have different appearances and uses, you use the same techniques to bind each one to a record source.

☐ You use the RecordSource property of the container to specify the table or view that acts as the record source. Additionally, you can specify the session through which this database object is accessed through the container's RecSrcSession property. However, if you do not set this latter property, the container uses whatever default session is defined for the application through its DefaultSession property.

☐ The DataSource property of a control (such as a text field) specifies the column in the record source to which the control is bound.

☐ You can use several drag-and-drop techniques to bind a container to a record source:

☐ By dragging the icon for the table or view from the Session window onto a form, Oracle Power Objects creates a text field bound to each column in the record source and automatically sets the RecordSource and RecSrcSession properties of the form.

☐ By selecting a range of columns from a table or view and then dragging them onto the form, Oracle Power Objects creates a text field bound to each of these columns and again sets the RecordSource and RecSrcSession properties of the form.

☐ By dragging a column from the table or view onto an existing control, you set the control's DataSource property to bind it to that column. Additionally, the control's Name property is changed to the name of the column.

☐ When you run a bound container, the application creates an associated recordset object, containing records queried from the table or view. There is a column in the recordset for each column bound to a control. If there is no control bound to the primary key column, the application also creates a column in the recordset matching this column.

☐ By calling the standard methods of a recordset, you can evaluate and change its contents.

☐ You can use a scrollbar as an object for browsing records through a form.

☐ You can use the DrawStyle and ColorFill properties of objects to create a brushed, 3-D look and feel in your application.

What Comes Next?

Now that you have learned the basics of binding containers to record sources, you can begin relating the data displayed in separate containers. You already know how to relate data in separate tables through a view; the next step is to learn how to perform the same kind of task through the application.

Q&A

Q What is the best method for binding controls?

A It depends on your approach to development. If you like creating the user interface first, and then connecting the controls to columns, you should drag the columns one-by-one onto the controls to which they are bound. The risk of using this method, however, is that the drag-and-drop action changes the Name property of the control to match the name of the column. This change breaks any method code that identifies these controls by name.

If you are more concerned with testing the data as viewed and edited through the form, then you might consider dragging the entire table or individual columns onto the form, creating a text field bound to each column. You then can modify these text fields as needed, or replace some of them with other controls (check boxes, radio buttons, pop-up lists, and so on). If, during your initial testing, you add some method code to one of these text fields, you should be careful to copy the code to a text file before replacing it with a different control.

Q Should I always perform a check on a record before sending it to the database?

A As discussed earlier, you might want to enforce some constraints through the database if you want to ensure central enforcement of a business rule. In addition, because server machines often have more processing power than client systems, you might want to shift some of the more processing-intensive constraints to the server. If the server is already heavily in use, however, you might want to continue to enforce many constraints in the application.

In some cases, the application obviously is the place to enforce the constraint. There are some checks the server is not as well equipped to handle as the application is, such as comparing the values in two different columns. If you want to ensure that the due date for an invoice always comes after the entry date, you should perform this check through method code, using a standard method discussed in length on Day 13.

The equivalent action taken by the server would require writing special server-based SQL code, called a stored procedure or a trigger, that would then need to inform the application why the record was not saved. This can be complex, particularly when you need to instruct the application to interpret this message and respond accordingly.

Q Because you cannot edit records through a multitable view, when, if ever, should I use them as a record source?

A Because views can quickly combine information from multiple tables, they are useful when you want to browse a composite picture assembled from multiple tables, but you do not want to edit them through that form. If, for example, you want to view all books with their publisher and topic information, you might make a view combining information from the TITLES, BOOK_TYPES, and PUBLISHERS tables the record source for a form.

Alternatively, you can bind embedded forms and repeater displays to views to add information about whatever is displayed on the main form. When you look through customer purchases, for example, you can add a scrolling list of books they purchased, with topic and publisher data included, in a repeater display. Creating this type of relationship between bound containers and their recordsets is the topic of tomorrow's lesson.

Workshop

The Workshop contains quiz questions to help you solidify your understanding of the material covered in today's lesson. Try and understand the quiz answers before you go on to tomorrow's lesson.

Quiz

1. What are the two key properties for binding a container to a record source? Which one can you leave blank, and under what conditions?

2. If you change a value in a form's recordset, what happens to the corresponding record in the database?

3. If you were to add text fields connected to everything but the primary key column in a table, how would you then insert primary key values into this column?

4. How would you bind a check box to a column in a table?

Quiz Answers

1. The two important properties are RecordSource, which specifies the table or view from which records are queried, and RecSrcSession, which specifies the session through which the table or view is accessed. You can leave the RecSrcSession property blank if the application has a default session assigned to it through the application's DefaultSession property.

2. Nothing, until the user commits the change to the database. (Incidentally, you can write method code that automatically commits such changes.)

3. The only way to avoid problems created by the lack of values for the primary key is to add the primary key column to the form's recordset. You can do this by specifying the name of the primary key column in the RecSrcAddCols property, indicating that you want this column queried in addition to those bound to controls on the form. You also will have to enter a primary key value for each new record by calling one of the standard recordset methods, SetColVal().

4. You have three options: (1) drag the column from the Table or View editor window onto the check box; (2) select the column from the drop-down list that appears when you click the name of the DataSource property in the Property sheet; or (3) type in the name of the column for the check box's DataSource property.

Master-Detail Relationships

Overview

Today, you learn about the following topics:

- [ ] One-to-many and one-to-one relationships
- [ ] The master-detail properties of containers
- [ ] Alternative ways to show master-detail relationships
- [ ] Master-detail-detail relationships

When you request information from a relational database, you often want to query related information stored in separate tables. As you learned on Days 2 and 3, relational databases provide a great deal of flexibility in defining relationships among records in different tables. All you need to define the relationship is the ability to find matching values in a column in each table.

For example, if you want to find the name of a publisher to match the PUBLISHER_ID number stored in the TITLES table, you join the PUBLISHER_ID column with its namesake in the PUBLISHERS table. The two columns do not have to have the same name, just the same data type and some matching values.

The chief disadvantage of views, however, is that you cannot edit the contents of a multitable view. Unfortunately, there are many occasions when you want to edit records from both related tables. For example, financial databases store invoices in one table, and line items for each invoice in another table. When you create a new invoice, you also want to enter line items to the invoice. Multitable views cannot give you this capability, so you must look elsewhere for the means to edit related records in multiple tables.

Theoretically, the application should enable you to perform this task. If you had a form that included records from both tables (one table holding general information for each invoice, and another storing line items from the invoices), you could enter both sets of records simultaneously. The application would need some way to maintain the join for these records, so that the line items appearing in the form matched the invoice currently being edited.

Oracle Power Objects provides a simple way of joining records from different tables. By now, with your familiarity with the object-oriented, code-light design of Oracle Power Objects, you should not be surprised to learn that you create this relationship through a set of properties.

One-to-One and One-to-Many Relationships

When you look for the publisher of a book, you find only one matching record in the PUBLISHERS table for the PUBLISHER_ID value. This situation is called a *one-to-one* relationship: For each value in one table, there will be only one matching value in another table.

When you created the CUST_PURCHASES table on Day 3, however, you entered data that indicated that some customers have purchased books in several topic areas. When you queried records through the view VW_CUSTPREFS, some customers appeared more than once. This situation is known as a *one-to-many* relationship: For any value in a column in one table, you might find many matching values in the corresponding column in another table.

In both cases, however, one table is driving the relationship. In the case of TITLES and PUBLISHERS, the TITLES table is the main table. For each record in TITLES, the join finds one corresponding value in PUBLISHERS, because each publisher has a unique ID number. The one-to-one join between these tables is sometimes called a *lookup*: The application looks up the single value in the secondary table (such as the publisher's name) that matches a value in the primary table (in this example, the PUBLISHER_ID value). Figure 5.1 illustrates this lookup.

Figure 5.1.

Titles and their publishers.

TITLES

Column Name	Datatype
TITLE_ID	NUMBER
TITLE_NAME	VARCHAR2
AUTHLNAME	VARCHAR2
AUTHFNAME	VARCHAR2
PUBLISHER_ID	NUMBER
PRICE	FLOAT
WS_PRICE	FLOAT
PROMOTION_PRICE	FLOAT
PRINTING	INTEGER
TYPE_ID	NUMBER

PUBLISHERS

Column Name	Datatype
PUBLISHER_ID	NUMBER
PUBLISHER_NAME	VARCHAR2

For each book's PUBLISHER_ID value, you can look for a matching value in PUBLISHERS

However, if the PUBLISHERS table were driving the relationship, you would create a one-to-many relationship. For each publisher, you would find several books published by that author in the TITLES table. Figure 5.2 shows the same two tables, but in a one-to-many relationship: for each publisher, you can look up all associated titles by checking for matching PUBLISHER_ID values.

Figure 5.2.

Publishers and their titles.

PUBLISHERS

Column Name	Datatype
PUBLISHER_ID	NUMBER
PUBLISHER_NAME	VARCHAR2

For each publisher, you can look for all books with a matching value for PUBLISHER_ID

TITLES

Column Name	Datatype
TITLE_ID	NUMBER
TITLE_NAME	VARCHAR2
AUTHLNAME	VARCHAR2
AUTHFNAME	VARCHAR2
PUBLISHER_ID	NUMBER
PRICE	FLOAT
WS_PRICE	FLOAT
PROMOTION_PRICE	FLOAT
PRINTING	INTEGER
TYPE_ID	NUMBER

5

These examples show the flexibility of relational databases and the ease with which you can ask a variety of questions about the data stored in them. By specifying a join between two tables, or among several tables, you can look at related information from almost any angle.

As you've observed, when you create a join there is a primary table that drives the relationship and a secondary table from which matching records can also be queried. For example, when you started with the PUBLISHERS table, you found several matching records in TITLES. When you started with TITLES, you found one matching record in PUBLISHERS. This association between two tables, in which one table drives the join, is called a *master-detail relationship*.

Masters and Details

In relational database parlance, the main table used to drive the one-to-one or one-to-many relationship is called the *master*, and the secondary table is called the *detail*. For every record in the master, there can be one, several, or no records in the detail table. For example, for every invoice, there can be one or several line items. For every customer, there can be outstanding book orders, or none at all.

The column in the master table (sometimes also called the *main table*) used to define its part of the join is called the *primary key*. Its counterpart in the detail table is called the *foreign key*. For the master-detail relationship to work, the two columns must be the same data type, and must have matching values.

These relationships, however, do not define themselves. In the database, the means by which you joined tables was a view. In the application, you must also find some mechanism for relating master and detail records.

Many tools require you to write the code that creates and regulates this relationship. You would have to include the following components:

- [ ] The SQL code that queries the records from the master and detail tables.
- [ ] Additional code that populates controls on the form with the results of this query.
- [ ] Still more code to maintain the relationship when the user deletes a master record with associated details, or changes the primary key value of a record. If you just delete the master record, you will "orphan" a number of records in the detail table. Similarly, if you change the primary key value, any associated records would remain in the master and detail tables, but there would be no way to query master and detail records together because the primary and foreign key values no longer match.

As you can imagine, you might have to write a great deal of code to create and maintain the master-detail relationship. In Oracle Power Objects, however, you can define a master-detail relationship without any code at all. This feature vastly simplifies the process of developing database applications, which rely heavily on creating master-detail relationships.

Master-Detail in Oracle Power Objects

In Oracle Power Objects, you define the master-detail relationship through four properties of the container that displays the detail records. In fact, 99 percent of the time, you need to set only three of these properties, specifying the following information:

- ☐ The column in the master recordset used as the primary key
- ☐ The column in the detail recordset used as the foreign key
- ☐ The container bound to the master record source (a table or view)

> **Note:** The fourth property, LinkPrimaryKey, is used infrequently to determine where the primary key lies, in the master or detail recordset. Because the primary key is in the master recordset the vast majority of times, you do not need to worry about this fourth property in this lesson.

Creating the complete master-detail relationship therefore requires three steps.

1. Bind one container to the master table or view.
2. Bind the other container to the detail record source.
3. Set the properties of the second container to define the master-detail relationship.

Creating a Master-Detail Form

In this exercise, you will create a new form for viewing publishers and books. The main form will display information on each publisher, while the repeater display will show all the books printed by each publisher.

1. Select the Application window for BOOKS.POA.
2. Press the New Form pushbutton, or select the File | New Form menu command.
3. Open the Property sheet for this form and enter Publishers and Books for its Label property.
4. Enter frmPubsBooks for the form's Name property.
5. Open the Session window for the BOOKS.POS session and double-click the Connector icon.
6. Drag the icon for the PUBLISHERS table onto the form. The form now looks like Figure 5.3.

   What happened when you performed the last step should come as no surprise by now.

5

Figure 5.3.

The new form, bound to PUBLISHERS.

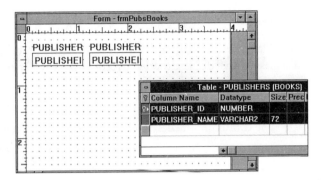

Oracle Power Objects creates a text field bound to every column in the table. Additionally, the form now has its `RecordSource` property set to PUBLISHERS, and its `RecSrcSession` property set to BOOKS.

7. Move the two fields and their labels to the top of the form, so that it looks something like Figure 5.4.

Figure 5.4.

Positioning the bound text fields.

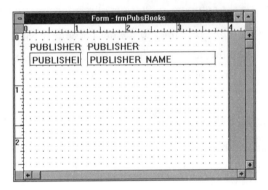

8. After clicking somewhere on the form to select it, select the Repeater Display drawing tool from the Object palette.

9. Click and drag the Repeater Display drawing tool across the lower half of the form to add a repeater display, as shown in Figure 5.5.

   The next step is to bind this new container to the TITLES table and add some bound controls.

10. In the Session window for BOOKS.POS, double-click the icon for the TITLES table.

11. In the Table Editor window for TITLES, click the Row Selector buttons for AUTHLNAME, TITLE_NAME, and PRICE while holding down the Ctrl key.

Figure 5.5.

A new repeater display.

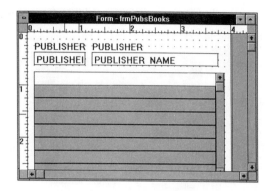

12. Click the Row Selector button of one of these columns and drag the column into the repeater display.

    Text fields bound to AUTHLNAME, TITLE_NAME, and PRICE now appear in the repeater display.

13. Make any necessary modifications to the repeater display and its contents to make the information appear as readable as possible (see Figure 5.6).

Figure 5.6.

A more readable repeater display.

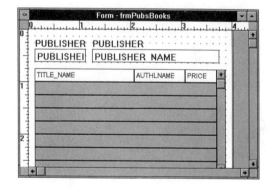

14. In the Object palette, select the Horizontal Scrollbar control.

15. Click the form somewhere outside the repeater display to add a scrollbar.

16. Press the Save button.

17. Press the Run Form button to test the form.

As you scroll around the publisher records, the contents of the repeater display do not change. Instead, as shown in Figure 5.7, the repeater display shows all titles from the TITLES table rather than the book titles belonging to the currently selected publisher. What gives?

Figure 5.7.

Not quite master-detail yet.

Publishers and Books		
PUBLISHER PUBLISHER		
1	Maximum Books	
The Big Book of Computers	Grant	28.99
Just for Fun	Hartwell	8.99
Many Mysteries	Lumley	6.99
Color Me Blue	Leavitt	4.99
Fun for Everyone	Hartwell	5.99
Sleep No More	Black	5.99
Development Made Easy	Fortran	29.99
A Boy's Life in New Zealand	MacAvoy	12.99

The master-detail relationship has not yet been defined. Although data from both tables appear in the form and in the repeater display, the application has no idea what columns to use as the primary and foreign keys. Nor does it understand which container, the form or the repeater display, has the records from the master recordset. Therefore, to define the master-detail relationship you need to set three properties of the container displaying the detail records (that is, the repeater display).

1. Press the Stop button to return to Design Time mode.

2. Select the repeater display and open its Property sheet.

   Be careful to select the repeater display *frame*, not the repeater display panel or some control within the panel.

3. Scroll down to the section of the Property sheet containing the properties `LinkMasterColumn`, `LinkDetailColumn`, and `LinkMasterForm`.

4. For the `LinkMasterColumn` property, enter `PUBLISHER_ID`.

   You have now specified the primary key, the column in the master recordset used in the join.

5. For the `LinkDetailColumn` property, enter `PUBLISHER_ID`.

   The application now knows which column in the detail recordset is the foreign key.

6. For the `LinkMasterForm` property, enter `frmPubsBooks`.

   This property specifies the container that holds the master records—in this case, the main form in which the repeater display appears.

7. Press Save, and then run the form.

8. While the form is running, use the scrollbar to move through the publisher records.

As shown in Figure 5.8, the form now behaves as expected: Whenever a new publisher record appears on the form, all of the books published by that company appear in the repeater display. When you move to the next publisher record, a different set of matching book titles appears.

Figure 5.8.

The completed master-detail form.

You might note that, in the repeater display, you did not have to add a text field bound to the foreign key, the PUBLISHER_ID column. When establishing master-detail relationships, you do not need to have controls bound to a key column on either the master or the detail containers. As long as you specify the primary and foreign key columns through the LinkMasterColumn and LinkDetailColumn properties, the application will query values from these columns and perform the join.

Behind the Scenes: The Record Manager

Although the forms have two separate recordsets, something in the application is synchronizing master and detail records. That something is the Record Manager, a hidden portion of Oracle Power Objects that, as its name implies, takes care of recordsets behind the scenes.

Through the Record Manager, Oracle Power Objects automates many recordset-related tasks that you might otherwise have to code yourself. For example:

- ☐ How does the application know to display only those detail records associated with the master records?

- ☐ How does it know that the user has inserted, deleted, or modified a record?

- ☐ If the user rolls back changes to a recordset, how does the application remember the initial status of the recordset?

- ☐ If the user deletes a master record, how does the application know whether to delete its associated detail records or "orphan" them?

The Record Manager, an intrinsic part of any Oracle Power Objects application, takes care of all these tasks. By setting the LinkMasterForm, LinkMasterColumn, and LinkDetailColumn

properties, you gave the Record Manager everything it needed to know to keep master and detail records in sync. In addition, the Record Manager also takes care of another important area of responsibility, *referential integrity.*

Referential Integrity

As implied earlier, the application might do one of three things when the user attempts to delete a master record:

1. Refuse the deletion. In many cases, you might want to prevent the user from deleting a master record until all detail records are deleted. For example, in the case of PUBLISHERS and TITLES, you might not want to let the user delete a publisher's record from PUBLISHERS until all the corresponding books in TITLES have been deleted first.

2. Delete the detail records. In this case, the deletion "cascades" from the master recordset to the detail recordset. You might choose this option if you delete a book order (the master record), in which case you would want to delete all the books included in the order (the detail records).

3. Orphan the detail records. If you think it is important to delete a master record but to leave the detail records alone, you choose this option. For example, if you eliminate a job classification (the master record), but you do not want to delete the employee records matching that classification (the detail records), you would choose to orphan the details.

The same questions arise when you modify the primary key value of a master record. The application uses values in the primary key column to search for matching values in the foreign key column. Therefore, if you change the value for ORDER_ID in a book order, the application might not be able to find the correct books for that order. Only the ORDER_ID value in the master record might be changed; ORDER_ID in the detail records would remain set to the original value.

The problems that arise when deleting or modifying master and detail records are issues of *referential integrity.* When you work with master and detail records, you want to ensure that the application can properly cross-reference primary key and foreign key values, to preserve the integrity of the database. If you create a mess of the database by mistakenly deleting or orphaning detail records, you compromise the database's integrity.

Referential Integrity Properties

When you defined the master-detail relationship between the recordsets of the form and the repeater display, you set three properties of the repeater display. To specify the rules of referential

integrity that the Record Manager must enforce, you once again set two properties of the repeater display: `LinkMasterDel` and `LinkMasterUpd`. As their names imply, the former concerns what happens when the user deletes a master record, and the latter determines what happens when the user modifies the primary key value of a master record.

The three settings for `LinkMasterDel` are listed in Table 5.1.

Table 5.1. Settings for `LinkMasterDel`.

Setting	Description
`Refuse if children present`	Prevents the user from deleting the master record as long as there are associated detail records.
`Delete cascade`	Deletes the detail records when the master record is deleted.
`Orphan details`	Deletes only the master record.

`LinkMasterUpd` has three similar settings, shown in Table 5.2.

Table 5.2. Settings for `LinkMasterUpd`.

Setting	Description
`Refuse if children present`	Prevents the user from updating the master record as long as there are detail records.
`Update cascade`	Modifies the foreign key values of all detail records to match the new primary key value of the master record.
`Orphan details`	Allows the change to the primary key value, but does not update foreign key values.

In effect, each setting represents a different level of referential integrity. At the lowest level, you allow detail records to be orphaned. At the highest level, you prevent the user from deleting a master record before deliberately deleting each detail record.

To illustrate referential integrity in action, you will experiment with the `LinkMasterUpd` property in the next exercise.

1. If it is not open already, double-click the icon for the form frmPubsBooks in the BOOKS Application window.

2. Open the Property sheet for the form by pressing the Edit Properties button.

   At this point, the Property sheet for the form should appear. Remember that the name of the currently selected object always appears in the title bar of the Property sheet. If you accidentally selected an object within the form, click some area of the form not occupied by another object to select the form.

3. Scroll down the Property sheet until you find the LinkMasterUpd property.

4. Click the name of this property in the Property sheet.

A drop-down list of settings now appears (see Figure 5.9).

Figure 5.9.

Settings for LinkMasterUpd.

Settings for the
LinkMasterUpd
property

5. From this list, select Refuse if Children Present.

6. Save and run the form.

Now that the application has a live connection to the database, you can test what happens when you change a primary key value.

7. Select the PUBLISHER_ID text field.

8. Delete the old PUBLISHER_ID value for the current record and enter 99.

9. Press Commit.

An error message appears, as shown in Figure 5.10.

Figure 5.10.

The error message.

The application prevents you from making this change, so that master and detail records will remain synchronized. If you were to delete the books published by this company, however, the application would have allowed the change. Because no detail records were present, the Refuse if Children Present setting for the LinkMasterUpd property would have been irrelevant.

Next, you can test what happens with a different setting for LinkMasterUpd.

1. Press Stop to return to Design Time mode.
2. Once again, click the LinkMasterUpd section of the form's Property sheet.
3. From the drop-down list, select Orphan details.
4. Save and run the form.
5. Select the PUBLISHER_ID text field and enter 99.
6. Press Commit.

    The detail records disappear from the repeater display (see Figure 5.11). They have not been deleted from the database, however; instead, they have been *orphaned.* Because the primary key value (PUBLISHER_ID) is now set to 99, and the foreign key values are still set to 1, the master-detail relationship is broken. Fortunately, you can fix this situation easily.

Figure 5.11.
The detail records disappear.

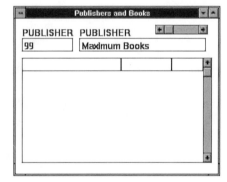

7. Change the PUBLISHER_ID value to 1.
8. Press Commit.

As soon as the primary key value is changed, the application sees that there are matching detail records. The records for books produced by that publisher reappear in the repeater display (see Figure 5.12).

Figure 5.12.

The detail records reappear.

You now can perform the final test of the LinkMasterUpd property.

1. Stop running the form and return to Design Time mode.

2. In the Property sheet for the form, change the setting for LinkMasterUpd to Update cascade.

3. Save and run the form.

4. Select the PUBLISHER_ID value for the first record that appears and change it to 99.

5. Press Commit.

Nothing changes in the form, except the PUBLISHER_ID value. No error message appeared, and the detail records did not disappear. Why not?

Because LinkMasterUpd is set to Update cascade, the application changed the foreign key values of the detail records to match the new primary key value. If you were to view the book data directly through the Table Browser window, you would see that these records in the TITLES table have their PUBLISHER_ID value changed to 99, as shown in Figure 5.13.

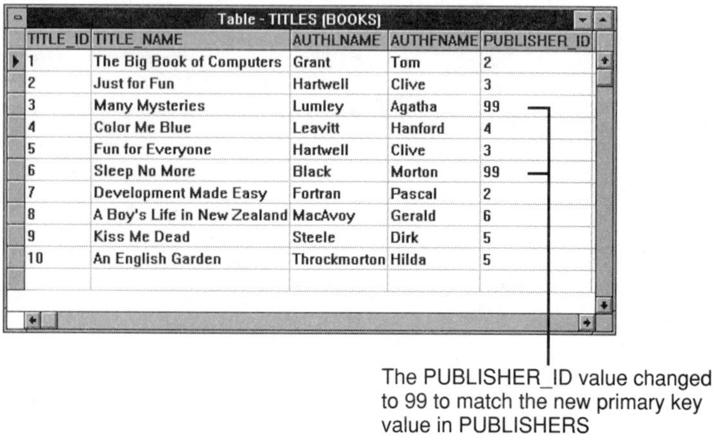

Figure 5.13.

The Table Browser window, with newly revised TITLES records.

The PUBLISHER_ID value changed to 99 to match the new primary key value in PUBLISHERS

Based on your experience, you should be able to guess what would happen if you changed the settings for the related property `LinkMasterDel`, and then tried to delete a publisher record. The settings and their effects are shown in Table 5.3.

Table 5.3. The effects of the `LinkMasterDel` settings.

Setting	Effect
`Refuse if children present`	You would not be able to delete the publisher record.
`Delete cascade`	The application would delete the publisher record as well as all associated book records.
`Orphan details`	The application would delete the publisher record, but leave the book records alone.

Another Type of Integrity

There is another type of integrity in relational databases: *entity integrity*. The purpose of specifying a primary key is to ensure that some column acts as a unique identifier for each record, and that this column is never left null. For example, every publisher needs a publisher ID number. If this value is left blank, a publisher record effectively has no identity distinct from other records. Only if you add a primary key to PUBLISHER_ID can you guarantee that each publisher record will have a unique identity (in this case, an ID number).

Other Ways of Showing Master-Detail Relationships

Now that you have some familiarity with master-detail relationships and referential integrity in Oracle Power Objects, you can begin to experiment with alternative ways of displaying these relationships in your application. Although many forms have master records in the form and detail records in a repeater display, this is by no means the only way to depict a master-detail relationship.

Remember that Oracle Power Objects is designed to give you a great deal of flexibility in how you define objects, while letting you use the same techniques no matter what you build. Because any container can be bound to any table or view, you can make any bound container the master and any other bound container the detail. As long as you set the necessary three properties of the detail container (`LinkMasterForm`, `LinkMasterColumn`, and `LinkMasterColumn`), you can create the relationship between recordsets.

To illustrate this point, you will build a form that displays a one-to-one relationship. For every book title, there is only one publisher. Therefore, you will create a new form with a repeater display containing a scrolling list of titles. The text fields bound to the PUBLISHER_ID and PUBLISHER_NAME will appear on the form itself, not in the repeater display. In this case, the book titles in the repeater display will be the master recordset, and will therefore drive the relationship. When you select a book title, its appropriate publisher record will appear on the form.

1. With the Application window for BOOKS.POS selected, press the New Form button, or select the File | New Form menu command.

2. Open the Property sheet for the form.

3. In the Property sheet, give the new form a name of frmMD2, and a label of Publishers by Title.

4. From the Object palette, select the Repeater Display drawing tool and create a repeater display in the top half of the form.

5. Open the repeater display's Property sheet and set the Name property to repTitles.

6. Select the Session window for the BOOKS session and double-click the icon for the TITLES table.

7. From the Table Editor window, select the TITLE_NAME column and drag it into the repeater display (see Figure 5.14).

Figure 5.14.

Binding the repeater display to TITLES.

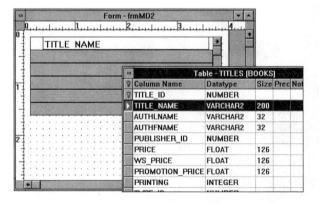

The repeater display is now bound to TITLES, and a text field bound to the TITLE_NAME column appears.

8. Resize the text field so that it stretches across almost the entire width of the repeater display panel, except for the left side.

9. From the Object palette, select the Current Row Control drawing tool and click the repeater display panel.

Your form should now look something like Figure 5.15.

Figure 5.15.

The form so far.

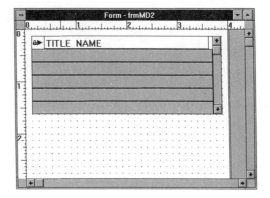

10. From the BOOKS Session window, click the icon for the PUBLISHERS table and drag it onto the form (but not into the repeater display).

The two familiar text fields bound to PUBLISHER_ID and PUBLISHER_NAME now appear, and the form is bound to PUBLISHERS.

11. Select the form and open its Property sheet.

12. Set `LinkMasterForm` to `repTitles`, `LinkMasterColumn` to `PUBLISHER_ID`, and `LinkDetailColumn` to `PUBLISHER_ID`.

13. Save and run the form.

14. Click the Current Row Control within the repeater display to select different book titles.

As you do this, the publisher of the selected book appears in the form, as shown in Figure 5.16. The way you presented a master-detail relationship in the first form is now reversed: The repeater display is the master, and the form is the detail.

You would use this technique when you want to focus on editing the detail records. In this form, you do not edit the book titles, but you can edit information about the publisher. This type of form is particularly useful when the master-detail relationship is a one-to-one relationship, and the detail records have a large number of columns that need to be displayed. For example, if you added a large amount of information about publishers (address, rep's name and phone number, and so on), you might want to create a form like this one to view and edit publisher records, selected by the books they produce.

Figure 5.16.

The new form in action.

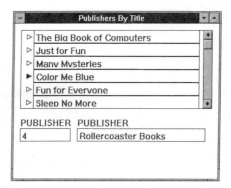

Master-Detail Across Forms

What do you do, however, if you want to edit the other columns in TITLES that do not appear in the repeater display? In this case, you want to split the master and detail recordsets into two separate forms. In the next exercise, you will separate publisher and title records into two separate forms, one for TITLES and one for PUBLISHERS. While perusing publisher information, you can then press a button that opens a second form displaying all the titles manufactured by that company.

1. In the BOOKS application, add a new form.
2. In the form's Property sheet, assign it a name of `frmMD3a` and a label of `Publishers`.
3. From the session window for BOOKS.POS, click and drag the icon for the PUB-LISHERS table onto the form.

   No need to explain what happens next—by now, you are very familiar with drag-and-drop binding in Oracle Power Objects.

4. From the Object palette, select the Pushbutton drawing tool.
5. Click just below the two new text fields to add a new pushbutton.
6. In the Property sheet for the pushbutton, assign it the label `Titles`.
7. From the Object palette, select the Horizontal Scrollbar drawing tool.
8. Click the form to add the scrollbar.

   At this point, you might also want to resize and reposition the controls within the form to make it more visually appealing. Once you are finished, you can then add the code that opens the second form when you press the pushbutton.

9. With the pushbutton selected, click the `Click()` method in the control's Property sheet.
10. Enter the following method code:

    ```
    frmMD3b.OpenWindow()
    ```

11. Save your new form.

This form will hold the master records for publishers. The next step is to create the form holding the detail records.

1. With the Application window selected, press the New Form button, or select File | New Form.

2. Open the Property sheet for the new form and give it a name of frmMD3b and a label of Titles.

3. Using the correct tool from the Object palette, create a new repeater display that covers the entire face of the new form.

4. In the Session window for books, double-click the icon for the TITLES table.

5. Select the columns AUTHLNAME and TITLE_NAME from this table and drag them into the repeater display panel.

   As expected, two new text fields appear within the repeater display. You might want to reposition and resize these controls to make their contents more readable.

6. Select the repeater display and open its Property sheet.

7. Set the LinkMasterForm property to frmMD3a, LinkMasterColumn to PUBLISHER_ID, and LinkDetailColumn to PUBLISHER_ID.

8. Save your new form. The form now looks like Figure 5.17.

Figure 5.17.
The detail form with all controls added.

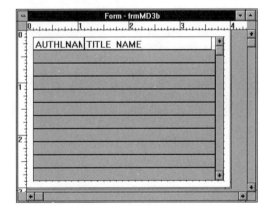

At this point, you need to make a minor modification to the application to test these two forms. If you run one of these forms, Oracle Power Objects does not also run the other form. Therefore, if you clicked the Titles pushbutton on the first form, Oracle Power Objects could not then open the other form. To test more than one form, you need to run the application, not just one form.

Unfortunately, when you run the application, it does not know which form to open unless you give it explicit instructions. Fortunately, this task is easy to complete.

1. Select the Application window for BOOKS.POA.

2. Open its Property sheet.

   As you might remember from Day 1, "Your First Form," applications are objects, with their own set of standard properties and methods. You need to find the property that determines what happens when the application launches, and add to it the code that opens the first of your two forms.

3. Click the OnLoad() section of the Property sheet.

   Both this method and Initialize() execute whenever the application launches.

4. In the Code Editor window for OnLoad(), enter the following method code:

   ```
   frmMD3a.OpenWindow()
   ```

   Essentially, you have told the application to open the first of your two new forms whenever the application launches. You are now ready to test the forms.

5. Press the Run Application button.

6. In the form that appears, press the Titles pushbutton.

   The detail form now appears. At this point, you should move the two forms so that you can view them side by side, as shown in Figure 5.18.

Figure 5.18.

The master and detail forms at runtime.

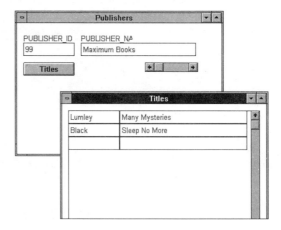

7. Use the scrollbar to move between publisher records.

Every time you view a different publisher, a different set of titles published by that company appears in the repeater display.

Master with Two Details

It's conceivable that records from one table can act as the masters for records from multiple detail tables. You might want to edit all these sets of records on the same form. For example, if you are editing a salesperson's employment history, you might find that events are stored in one table, and records of monthly commissions are stored in another table. Both sets of records could be details for the master employee record, including the employee's name, Social Security number, home address, and other general information.

In the Bookstore application, however, you will create a different example of this type of form. In the new form, you will make the different types of books the master recordset. Two repeater displays will contain the detail records:

☐ The list of book titles that match the current book type

☐ The customers who have purchased this type of book

There are many possible uses for such a form. For example, if you are planning a sale on a different type of book each month, you might want to see which books fall under each category, and how many customers might be interested in buying more of such books.

To create this form, you use the same techniques you did when you created the first master-detail form in this lesson, with a repeater display acting as the detail. To make the form work, you need only set the same group of properties to define the master-detail relationship on both repeater displays.

1. In the Application window for BOOKS.POA, create a new form.

2. Open the Property sheet for the form and assign it a name of frmMD4, and a label of Book Types, Titles, and Customers.

3. Open the Session window for BOOKS.POS and find the icon for the BOOK_TYPES table.

4. Drag the icon onto the form.

   As you should know by now, Oracle Power Objects then creates two text fields—one bound to TYPE_ID and the other bound to TYPE_DESC. In addition, the form's RecordSource property is now set to BOOK_TYPES.

5. Position the two text fields and their labels to appear in the upper-left corner of the form.

6. From the Object palette, select the Horizontal Scrollbar tool and click the form.

7. Move the scrollbar so that it appears in the upper-right portion of the form.

8. Click the border of the form and make it large enough to contain two repeater displays (see Figure 5.19).

5

Figure 5.19.
The form so far.

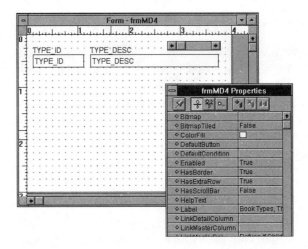

The repeater displays do not have to be very wide—just large enough so that a single column's worth of information can be displayed on each one.

9. From the Object palette, select the Repeater Display drawing tool.

   Click and drag across the lower-left side of the form.

10. Repeat the previous step to create another repeater display on the lower-right side of the form.

11. Select the Static Text drawing tool from the repeater display and click just above one of the repeater displays.

12. Click in the new static text object until the text is highlighted, and then type `Titles`.

13. Create another static text object above the repeater display on the right, and then change its text to `Customers`. The form should now look something like Figure 5.20.

14. From the Session window for BOOKS.POS, open the Table Editor window for TITLES.

   By now, you know that to open the window containing the table's description, you double-click the icon for the table.

15. Press the Row Selector button for the TITLES column.

   This column's description should now be highlighted.

16. Click and drag the TITLES column into the left repeater display.

   A single text field, bound to the TITLES column of the TITLES table, now appears within the repeater display panel.

17. Open the Table Editor window for the CUST_PURCHASES table.

Figure 5.20.

The form, with two repeater displays.

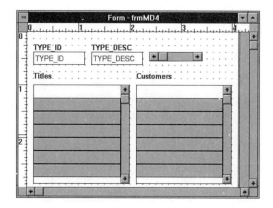

18. Holding down the Ctrl key, click the Row Selector button for the CUSTOMER_ID column.

19. Click and drag this column into the right repeater display.

A text field bound to CUSTOMERS.LNAME now appears in the other repeater display. Because both repeater displays are now also bound to the TITLES and CUSTOMERS tables, the application will query records for these two containers when you run the form. The form does not, however, show the customer's name, only that person's unique ID number.

The final step for creating this master-detail relationship is to set the relevant properties of the two repeater displays.

1. Select the left repeater display.

   As always when working with a repeater display, be careful that you do not accidentally select the repeater panel or a control within the panel.

2. Open the Property sheet for the repeater display until you find the `LinkMasterForm`, `LinkMasterColumn`, and `LinkDetailColumn` properties.

3. Set `LinkMasterForm` to `frmMD4`, `LinkMasterColumn` to `TYPE_ID`, and `LinkDetailColumn` to `TYPE_ID`, as shown in Figure 5.21.

4. Select the other repeater display and open its Property sheet.

5. Assign the same values for the three master-detail properties as you did for the first repeater display.

   By setting these properties, you have identified one primary key, TYPE_ID, in the main form. Additionally, you have designated two foreign keys, which are named TYPE_ID in both cases (although they appear in separate tables).

Figure 5.21.
Setting the three properties.

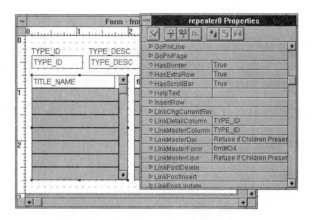

6. Add a current row control to both repeater displays.

7. Save and run your form. It should appear as shown in Figure 5.22.

8. Use the scrollbar to navigate among different book types.

Figure 5.22.
The completed form at runtime.

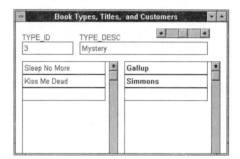

As you move to the description of each new type of book, one repeater display shows all the titles that fall under that topic. In addition, the other repeater display shows all customers who have purchased that type of book.

A Tabbed Form

Increasingly, applications use tabbed forms as an interface device. In this GUI design, a form contains what appears to be a set of folders, each with a tab projecting from one edge (usually the top). When the user clicks one of the tabs, a different folder opens, displaying its own set of controls (see Figure 5.23).

Figure 5.23.
A standard tabbed form.

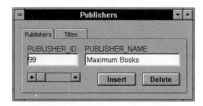

Although Oracle Power Objects includes the type of 3-D controls that appear on tabbed forms, it does not have an actual tab control. It is possible to simulate a tabbed form in several different ways; in fact, one of the sample applications provided with Oracle Power Objects uses simulated tab controls.

For the sake of the next exercise, you will use pushbuttons to act as the tabs. In this form, the folder for the master records appears when you press one pushbutton, and the folder for the details appears when you press the other.

This form uses two embedded forms to display the master and detail records. When you press a pushbutton, one of these embedded forms becomes visible, and the other becomes invisible. Once again, the container bound to the PUBLISHERS table will act as the master, while the container bound to TITLES will be the detail.

When an object's `Visible` property is set to `False`, the user cannot move the focus into the object. Therefore, you do not have to worry about the user inadvertently tabbing or clicking into a control on an invisible embedded form.

To create this tabbed form, follow these steps:

1. In the Application window for BOOKS.POA, create a new form.
2. When the form appears, open its Property sheet and enter `frmMD5` for its `Name` property, and `Publishers and Titles` for its `Label` property.
3. While in the Property sheet, change the `ColorFill` property to light gray.
4. From the Object palette, select the Pushbutton drawing tool.
5. Click the upper-left corner of the form to add a new pushbutton.
6. Repeat the process to create a second pushbutton to the immediate right of the first.

   You might have to move the second pushbutton to get it flush against the first one (see Figure 5.24).
7. In the Property sheet for the left pushbutton, change its `Label` property to `Publishers`.

   Alternatively, you can click the pushbutton to highlight the text within it, and then type the new label directly into the control.

Figure 5.24.

Positioning the two pushbuttons.

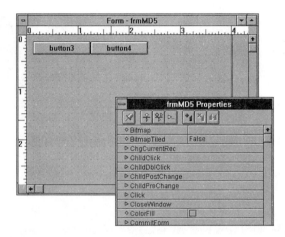

8. In the Property sheet for the right pushbutton, change its Label property to Titles.

9. From the Object palette, select the Embedded Form tool.

10. Click and drag across the form until the embedded form looks something like Figure 5.25.

Figure 5.25.

The new embedded form.

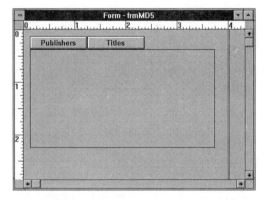

11. Open the Property sheet for the embedded form and set its Name property to embPublishers.

12. Also in the Property sheet, change the setting for the Transparent property to True. Now, the color of the form shows through the background of the embedded form.

13. With the embedded form still selected, press the Copy button, or select Edit | Copy.

14. Click the form to deselect the embedded form and press the Paste button. A copy of the embedded form now appears on the form (see Figure 5.26).

Figure 5.26.

Two embedded forms within the "tabbed" form.

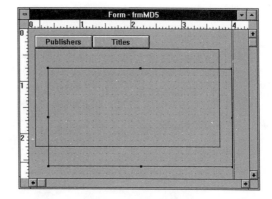

15. Open the Property sheet for the second embedded form and change its name to `embTitles`.

16. With the second embedded form still selected, choose the Repeater Display control and click within this embedded form.

17. Size the repeater display to fill the embedded form, embTitles. The form should now look like Figure 5.27.

Figure 5.27.

The repeater display added to an embedded form.

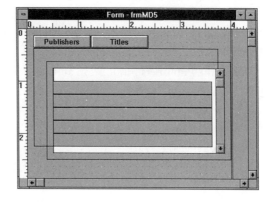

18. Open the Session window for BOOKS.POS and find the icon for the TITLES table.

19. Double-click this icon to open the Table Editor window for TITLES.

20. Select the TITLES table and drag it into the repeater display panel.

21. Select the first embedded form, embPublishers.

22. In the session window for BOOKS.POS, locate the PUBLISHERS table.

23. Click and drag this icon into the embedded form, embPublishers.

    The form should now look like Figure 5.28.

24. Select the repeater display and set its `LinkMasterForm` property to `embPublishers`, `LinkMasterColumn` to `PUBLISHER_ID`, and `LinkMasterColumn` to `PUBLISHER_ID`.

Figure 5.28.

The tabbed form so far.

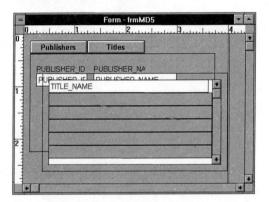

At this point, you have done everything needed to bind the containers and create a master-detail relationship between two containers, an embedded form, and a repeater display. However, you do not yet have the means to create tabbing behavior. You will add some method code to the two pushbuttons to control which embedded form becomes visible when the user presses each pushbutton.

1. Select the Publishers pushbutton and open its Property sheet.

2. Click the section for the `Click()` method in the Property sheet to open the Code Editor window.

3. Enter the following method code:
   ```
   embPublishers.Visible = TRUE
   embTitles.Visible = FALSE
   ```

4. With the Property sheet still open, select the other pushbutton.

   The Property sheet now displays the properties and methods of the second pushbutton.

5. Open the Code Editor window for `Click()` and enter the following:
   ```
   embPublishers.Visible = FALSE
   embTitles.Visible = TRUE
   ```

6. Select the embedded form, embTitles, (the second one you created) and through the Property sheet, change its `Visible` property to `False`.

   This step is needed to make the second embedded form invisible when you first open the form.

7. Move this embedded form so that it covers its cousin, embPublishers.

   Now, when you press one of the pushbuttons, it will appear as if you are selecting a different folder. What actually happens is that one embedded form becomes invisible, while another of the same dimensions becomes visible in the exact position of the first.

8. From the Object palette, select the Horizontal Scrollbar tool and add it to the right of the two pushbuttons.

   The final form should now look like Figure 5.29.

Figure 5.29.
The "tabbed" form,
nearly complete.

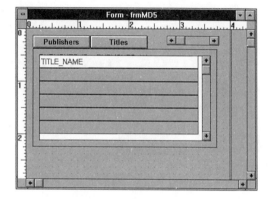

9. Select the scrollbar and open its Property sheet.

10. For the ScrollObj property, enter embPublishers.

    This last step is needed to link the scrollbar to the embedded form as a browsing tool. Otherwise, by default, the scrollbar would be linked to the form, which currently is not bound to any table or view.

11. Save and run the form.

The form at runtime looks like Figure 5.30. Using the scrollbar, you can scroll between publisher records. When a new publisher appears in the tabbed form, press the Detail button. All of the books published by that company now appear in the repeater display. You can continue to switch between publisher and title information, using the scrollbar to continue browsing these master and detail records.

Although some work was required to give this form a tabbing effect, establishing the master-detail relationship was one of the easiest steps. The only unusual aspect of setting up this relationship was that you bound an embedded form to a repeater display in another embedded form. No matter what containers you used in any of these exercises, however, you applied the same technique for creating a master-detail relationship.

Figure 5.30.
*The "tabbed" form
at runtime.*

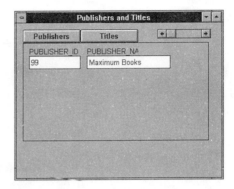

A Few Words on Object Naming

You might be puzzled by the choice of names for the two embedded forms in this exercise. Why not just name the forms Titles and Publishers, instead of adding the emb prefix?

The names given to these two embedded forms illustrate some of the important object-naming conventions in Oracle Power Objects and similar tools. The reason for the prefix is to prevent confusion about the nature of the object. When you see the prefix emb, you always know that the object is an embedded form, not a repeater display, user-defined class, form, or other kind of object.

These conventions are especially useful when you write method code. Because you can modify properties and call methods through method code, you must be careful which object owns these properties and methods. If you change a property on the wrong object, you can create some serious bugs in your application. For clarity, therefore, following object naming conventions is a must.

> **Note:** The appendices include the list of object naming conventions used in this book. These are the same conventions outlined in Appendix A of the *Oracle Power Objects User's Guide*, "Coding Standards."

Master-Detail-Detail Relationships

The final type of master-detail relationship you'll learn today is a master-detail-detail relationship. Here, there are two levels of master-detail relationships: The detail records in one level of this scheme act as the master records for the next level.

For example, suppose you tracked your book sales more carefully, so that you knew the exact books purchased by each customer. You could then create a master-detail-detail relationship in the following way:

- ☐ The BOOK_TYPES recordset could be the master, while the TITLES records could be the detail. In this case, when you queried a book type, you could also see a list of all books fitting that classification (computer, mystery, children's, and so on).

- ☐ The TITLES table could then act as a master to the records of each customer purchase. For each book, you could view the names of all customers who had purchased that book.

The relationship between the three tables is shown in Figure 5.31.

Figure 5.31.

Two levels of master-detail relationships.

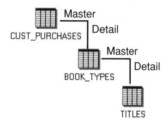

This type of multilevel master-detail relationship, also called a *drill-down*, is quite common in all sorts of applications. For example, all departments have employees, and all employees have significant events in their history at the company. In this case, department records are the masters to the employee records, which in turn are the masters to the employee history records. For every department record, there are many corresponding employee records; for every employee, there can be many employee history records. You can probably imagine many similar relationships: For every academic program, there are many students majoring in it; for every student, there are records for all the courses that person took while enrolled at the university.

Theoretically, the master-detail relationship could continue down many further levels, as long as there is a logical relationship between each master and detail recordset. However, for the sake of this exercise, we will keep the number of master-detail relationships to two.

In this new form, you will display master records on the form and detail records in two repeater displays. On the main form, you will show the names of all customers. In the first repeater display, you will show a list of all types of books purchased by that customer. In the second repeater display, you will show the titles matching each book type purchased by the customer. In this case, the customer records are the master, and the book types purchased by that customer are the detail. Each book type, then, is the master to the books that fall under that topic category.

Once again, you will be creating an aid for the manager thinking about how to market books. If there are some preferred customers in the store, the manager might review the types of books that person regularly purchases. With this information in hand, the manager can determine which new books might interest that customer.

1. In the Application window, create a new form.

2. Open the form's Property sheet and give it the name `frmMD6`, and the label `Possible Customer Purchases`.

3. In the Session window for the BOOKS.POS session, double-click the CUSTOMERS table to open its Table Editor window.

4. In this window, select the columns FNAME, LNAME, and PHONE.

5. Click and drag these columns onto the form.

6. Move the text fields and labels as close to the upper edge of the form as possible.

7. In the upper-right corner of the form, add a scrollbar.

8. From the Object palette, select the Repeater Display drawing tool and create a repeater display covering the lower-left half of the form.

9. Add another repeater display to the lower-right half of the form.

10. In the Session window, open the Table Editor window for CUST_PURCHASES.

11. Select the TYPE_ID and NUM_BOUGHT columns and drag them into the left repeater display.

12. From the Object palette, select the Current Row Control tool and add a current row control to the left side of the repeater display panel, next to the text field you just created.

    You might need to reposition and resize the text field and current row control to make best use of the available space. Eventually, the form should look like Figure 5.32.

Figure 5.32.
The drill-down form, with repeaters.

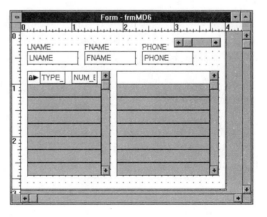

13. In the Session window, open the Table Editor window for TITLES.

14. Select the TITLE_NAME column, and drag it into the right repeater display.

15. Size the new text field (bound to the TITLE_NAME column) so that it fills the repeater display panel.

16. Select the left repeater display and open its Property sheet.

17. Set its Name property to repTypes, LinkMasterForm to frmMD6, LinkMasterColumn to CUSTOMER_ID, and LinkDetailColumn to CUSTOMER_ID.

18. Select the other repeater display, open its Property sheet, and enter the following changes to its properties:

19. Save and run the form. The form at runtime looks like Figure 5.33.

Figure 5.33.

The drill-down format at runtime.

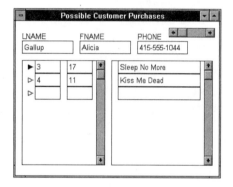

20. Click the current row pointer for each book type.

    A different set of matching titles appears in the other repeater display.

21. Use the scrollbar to move to a different customer record, and again click the current row control for each type of book (now displayed by type ID number) purchased by that customer.

    As before, all titles matching the currently selected book type appear in the other repeater display.

22. Press Stop to end this exercise.

Summary

This lesson has covered a great deal of territory and shown some of the more powerful features of Oracle Power Objects. In the process of building several master-detail forms, you learned the methods for creating joins between separate recordsets. In addition, you saw how the potent combination of relational database technology and Power Objects makes it possible to view the same information from a wide variety of vantage points. Using these techniques, you have already squeezed a lot of mileage out of a mere four tables!

To summarize the main points of this lesson:

☐ Each bound container has its own recordset, a set of rows queried from a table or view.

☐ If two bound containers' recordsets have matching values in two columns, then you can create a master-detail relationship between the two recordsets. For every master record queried, the application also queries matching detail records.

☐ The two columns used to create the join are the primary key in the master recordset and the foreign key in the detail recordset.

☐ To establish the master-detail relationship, you set three properties of the container displaying detail records: `LinkMasterForm`, `LinkMasterColumn`, and `LinkDetailColumn`.

☐ You can use a variety of different containers for displaying master and detail records. Although it is common to display the master records on the main form, it is by no means the only technique. The detail container can be a repeater display or an embedded form within the main form, the main form itself, or a separate form altogether.

☐ In addition, it is possible to create multiple levels of master-detail relationships, with the detail recordset in one relationship acting as the master for another.

What Comes Next?

On Day 6, "More About Recordsets," you will continue to learn how to work with recordsets in Oracle Power Objects. For example, through a shared recordset, you can synchronize records in two separate containers. The more you understand about working with recordsets—arguably, the heart of a database application—the more success you can achieve with Oracle Power Objects.

Q&A

Q What other properties or methods are relevant to master-detail relationships?

A The most significant is `LinkPrimaryKey`, which specifies the location of the primary key column. For the vast majority of cases, the primary key (which drives the join between master and detail recordsets) will appear on the master recordset. However, on a few rare occasions, you will want to specify the primary key as appearing in the detail recordset.

There are several methods that execute when the application queries, deletes, inserts, or updates master records. A large part of the Property sheet for bindable containers is taken up with these methods (such as LinkPreInsert(), LinkChgCurrentRec(), and the like). Unfortunately, you will find very few occasions for using these methods. However, if you encounter a situation in which you need to intercept some unusual circumstance involving master-detail relationships, you might need to use one of these methods.

Q **What if I need to look up only a single value in a foreign table? For example, what if I want to just get the matching PUBLISHER_NAME value for a title's PUBLISHER_ID?**

A In these cases, creating an embedded form or repeater display for a single column's worth of detail information seems like overkill. In these cases, you should add a text field or other control that uses the SQLLOOKUP function to populate the control. SQLLOOKUP performs a lookup into a foreign table, using a SQL query that you code. This technique saves you the headache of creating an additional container for each lookup into a foreign table for a single column's worth of information.

Workshop

The Workshop consists of quiz questions to help you solidify your understanding of the material covered and an exercise to give you experience in using what you've learned. Try and understand the quiz and exercise answers before you go on to tomorrow's lesson.

Quiz

1. What is a primary key? What is a foreign key?
2. To create a master-detail relationship between records displayed in two different containers, you must set three properties of which container?
3. What is a drill-down form?
4. How many levels of master-detail relationships are possible?

Exercise

Create a form with the master recordset, PUBLISHERS, appearing on the main form, and records from the detail recordset, TITLES, appearing in an embedded form. Design the form so that all of the information about each book can appear within the embedded form, and that the user can browse all of the titles from each publisher.

Quiz Answers

1. The primary key is the column in the master recordset used in the join, whereas the foreign key is the corresponding column in the detail recordset. For every value in the primary key column, you can request for the database all records with the same value in the foreign key column.

2. The three critical properties are `LinkMasterForm`, `LinkMasterColumn`, and `LinkDetailColumn`, all of which are set on the container displaying the detail records.

3. A form that displays multiple levels of master-detail relationships.

4. Theoretically, any number. As long as you are able to identify primary and foreign keys in separate recordsets, you can continue establishing master-detail relationships.

More About
Recordsets

Overview

As you can see from the previous two lessons, Oracle Power Objects is designed to simplify many common database-related tasks. Using some drag-and-drop features, you can bind a form and its controls to a record source without having to write a single line of code. By setting three properties, you can create a master-detail relationship between bound containers, and the application even takes care of enforcing referential integrity among the master and detail recordsets. Not surprisingly, Oracle Power Objects provides many more ways to work with recordsets.

Because recordsets are objects, you can manipulate them in ways you might not have imagined. As you have already seen, you can call standard methods of a recordset to view and modify its contents. In this chapter, you will work with recordsets in two new ways:

- [ ] Share the same recordset between two bindable containers
- [ ] Create new recordsets that are not connected to any container, but which you can access through method code

You will also learn about the following topics:

- [ ] Sharing recordsets between containers
- [ ] Building browser and "further information" forms
- [ ] Stand-alone recordsets
- [ ] The `SQLLOOKUP` function
- [ ] List controls

Shared Recordsets

Suppose that you have a large number of records (over 100 or more) in a form's recordsets. Using a scrollbar to navigate among these records can be tedious. As the number of records increases, the usefulness of the scrollbar as a recordset browsing tool declines further.

To make matters worse, you cannot see the contents of the next record as you scroll through the recordset. Often, you might want to find a particular record (a book, a customer, and so on), but you have to scroll through many, perhaps hundreds, of records to find the right one.

To address this problem, you might replace the scrollbar with a dialog box that displays a scrolling list of all records. The list need only include one or two values, not every column in the recordset. In the case of book records from the TITLES table, for example, you might display only the author's last name (`AUTHLNAME`) and the title (`TITLE_NAME`).

Now when you scroll through the list of records, you see only the names of books and their authors, which makes it much easier to find a particular title. Once you select a book from this list, the original form should then display its entire record, including information from the rest of the columns in the recordset. The form should look like Figure 6.1.

Figure 6.1.
The Browse Titles form.

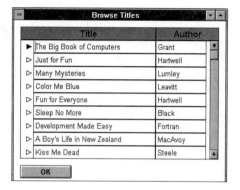

As useful as this dialog box might be, it poses one development challenge: How do you make the record in the form match the one selected from the scrolling list?

Using Code to Select a Record

At first glance, without knowing anything more about Oracle Power Objects, you might guess that you need to write code that does the following:

1. Evaluates which record is selected in the scrolling list.
2. Displays the matching record in the form.

In other words, when you select a title from the scrolling list, you then want to move the pointer in the form's recordset to that book's record. The pointer indicates which record in the recordset is currently selected. In a form, the record that has the pointer is the one displayed in the form. In a repeater display, the record with the pointer is the one currently selected (and perhaps being edited).

As you might remember from Day 4, "Connecting a Form to a Record Source," the current row pointer (the small triangle) that you added to a repeater display turns black when you select another record. In other words, the current row pointer indicates the position of the cursor within the recordset.

A recordset has a method, SetCurRow(), that can move the pointer to a particular record. However, Oracle Power Objects provides a far more elegant way of accomplishing your goal.

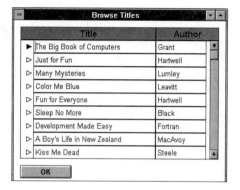

Creating a Shared Recordset

In Oracle Power Objects, two containers can share the same recordset. Any changes made to the recordset through one container are immediately reflected in the other container. These changes include all recordset-related operations, including

☐ Moving the pointer to a record

☐ Inserting, deleting, or modifying a record

☐ Changing the status of a record (for example, locking it)

Therefore, if two containers have the same recordset, you can use one container to select a record, and the other to edit it. The moment you select a record in the browser dialog box, you can then switch to the form to edit the complete record. This is the technique you will use to create the Titles Browser form.

1. Open the Application window for BOOKS.POA.

2. Press New Form, or select the File | New Form... menu command.

3. Open the Property sheet for the new form and enter frmBooks for its Name property and Books for its Label property.

4. Open the Session window for BOOKS.POS and double-click the Connector icon.

5. Click and drag the icon for the TITLES table onto the new form frmBooks.

   Text fields bound to each column in the TITLES table appear in the form.

6. Resize and reposition these text fields and their labels so that the form looks something like Figure 6.2.

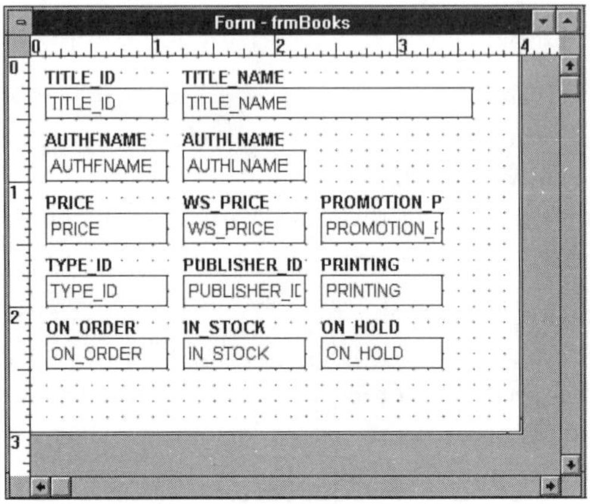

Figure 6.2.

The frmBooks form, bound to TITLES.

7. From the Object palette, select the Horizontal Scrollbar drawing tool and add a scrollbar to the form.

   Although the scrollbar will no longer be the only recordset browsing tool, it is still a useful feature of the form.

8. From the Object palette, select the Pushbutton tool and add a pushbutton beneath the text fields on the form.

9. Click the text within the pushbutton and type Browse.

   As you might remember, this technique is a shortcut for changing the Label property of a control. Alternatively, you can open the Property sheet for the pushbutton and enter Browse for its Label property.

10. Save your form before continuing. The form should now look something like Figure 6.3.

Figure 6.3.

The frmBooks form, with the scrollbar and pushbutton added.

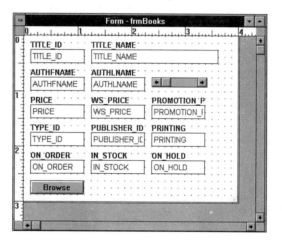

The next step is to create the browser form.

1. Select the Application window for BOOKS.POA again.

2. Add a new form to the application.

   By now, you should know how to create a form without detailed prompting.

3. Open the new form's Property sheet and enter frmBrowseTitles for its name, and Browse Titles for its label.

4. From the Object palette, select the Repeater Display drawing tool.

5. Click and drag across the form until the new repeater display covers nearly all of the form. Be sure to leave room above and below the repeater display, however, to add other objects.

6. Select the Session window for TITLES and double-click the icon for the TITLES table.

7. In the Table Editor window for TITLES, select the columns AUTHLNAME and TITLE_NAME.

8. Drag the selected columns into the repeater display panel.

   As before, Oracle Power Objects creates two text fields, each bound to one of the columns selected from TITLES.

9. Change the FontSize property of the two text fields to 9, and the HasBorder property to False.

10. Resize and reposition the two text fields so that the TITLE_NAME column fills two-thirds of the repeater display panel, and the AUTHLNAME field fills the remaining one-third. Leave some room on the left side of the panel for a current row control.

11. From the Object palette, select the Current Row Control tool and add a current row control in the panel. The repeater display should now look like Figure 6.4.

Figure 6.4.

The frmBooks form, bound to TITLES.

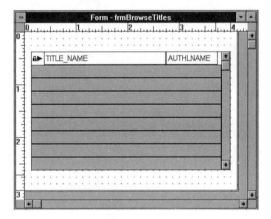

Now that you have created the repeater display, you should add some labels to identify the two columns of data displayed within it.

1. From the Object palette, select the Rectangle drawing tool and add a rectangle above the left half of the repeater display.

2. Size the rectangle so that it extends from the left edge of the repeater display to the right edge of the text field TITLE_NAME within it.

3. Open the rectangle's Property sheet and set its ColorFill property to dark gray. The rectangle should look like Figure 6.5.

Figure 6.5.
The rectangle added above the repeater display.

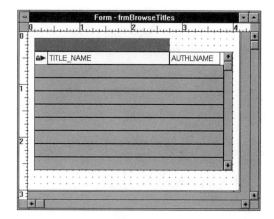

4. With the rectangle still selected, use the Static Text Object drawing tool from the Object palette to create a new label within the rectangle.

   Because rectangles, like forms and repeater displays, are containers, the new static text object is now contained within the rectangle.

5. Size the new static text object so that it completely fills the rectangle.

6. Click the text within the static text object and type Title.

   The form should now look like Figure 6.6.

Figure 6.6.
A label added above the repeater display.

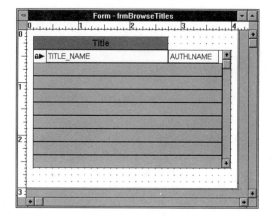

7. Repeat the process to create another label covering the rest of the top edge of the repeater display. Type Author for the new label.

8. Select the Pushbutton tool and add a pushbutton below the repeater display.

9. Click in the text within the repeater display and type OK.

Again, you can accomplish the same goal by entering OK for the pushbutton's Label property through its Property sheet.

10. Press Save to save the new form.

You now have two forms, both bound to the TITLES table. (Actually, the repeater display in the second form is bound to TITLES—the form itself is unbound.) How then do you share recordsets between these forms?

Shared Recordsets and the *RecordSource* Property

Select the repeater display and open its Property sheet. If you look at its RecordSource property, you should not be surprised that it is now set to TITLES, the name of the table to which this container is bound. To share the recordset, you replace the current setting with a reference to another container bound to the same record source, using the following syntax:

```
=container_name
```

To share a recordset between the repeater display and the frmBooks form, you need only enter the following for the repeater display's RecordSource property:

```
=frmBooks
```

Therefore, to finish this exercise, complete the following steps:

1. Select the repeater display and open its Property sheet.

2. Delete the current setting for the repeater display's RecordSource, TITLES, and enter =frmBooks.

3. Select the OK pushbutton on the same form.

4. In the Property sheet, open the Code editor window for the pushbutton's Click() method.

5. Enter the following code in Click() (see Figure 6.7):

   ```
   self.GetContainer.CloseWindow()
   ```

   This code uses the self keyword to refer to the object that has a method which is being called—in this case, the pushbutton. The GetContainer() method returns a reference to the container in which the pushbutton appears—the form. GetContainer() is a generic method used to "return an object reference" to an object's container. Finally, the code calls the CloseWindow() method of the form to close the Browse Titles form.

Figure 6.7.

Code entered for the pushbutton's Click() *method.*

6. Switch to the other form, frmBooks, and select the Browse pushbutton on this form.

7. Open the Code Editor window for the Click() method of this pushbutton and enter the following code:

```
frmBrowseTitles.OpenWindow()
```

This code opens the browser form when the user presses the button.

So far, so good: You push the button on the Books form, and the browser form opens. Once you have selected a record from the repeater display, you can close the browser by pressing the other pushbutton. The only step remaining is to add the code to the application that opens the Books form when the application launches.

8. Select the Application window for BOOKS.POA.

9. In the application's Property sheet, open the Code Editor window for the OnLoad() method.

You see some code left over from an earlier exercise.

10. Delete the leftover code and enter the following:

```
frmBooks.OpenWindow()
```

11. Save and run the application.

Remember, you press the Run Application button, not the Run Form button, to test the application. The Books form, frmBooks, now appears.

12. Press the Browse button to open the browser form. You can now use the Browser form to scroll through records (see Figure 6.8).

13. Scroll through the repeater display, clicking the current row control for each book's record.

As you select records in the repeater display, the same record appears in the other form. When you click a book's record within the repeater display, you are moving the pointer within the recordset to that record. This exercise illustrates how important it is to keep in mind that the recordset exists as an object within the application, separate from the table from which it queries records.

6

Figure 6.8.

*Both the Books and Browse
Titles forms open together.*

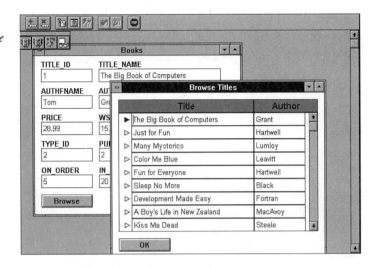

Figure 6.9.

*The two forms and their
shared recordset.*

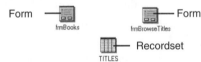

To further illustrate how useful this feature can be, you can now enter a new record through one form, and it will appear in the other form.

1. Press OK on the Browse Titles form.

   Because of the code you added to the `Click()` method of this pushbutton, the browser form now closes.

2. Press the Insert Record button to add a new title.

   Alternatively, you could scroll past the last record queried from TITLES to the blank row. When you begin typing values in this blank row, the application understands that you intend to insert a new record into the form's recordset.

3. Enter the values from Table 6.1 for the new book.

Table 6.1. Information describing the new book.

Column	Value
TITLE_ID	11
TITLE_NAME	Science Fiction: Beyond the Golden Age
AUTHLNAME	Pettigrew
AUTHFNAME	Rowan

Column	Value
PUBLISHER_ID	1
PRICE	5.99
WS_PRICE	2.99
PROMOTION_PRICE	4.50
PRINTING	1
TYPE_ID	4
ON_ORDER	10
IN_STOCK	11
ON_HOLD	6

4. Press the Commit button to add the new record to TITLES.

5. Press the Query button to re-query the form's recordset.

   Although this last step is not strictly necessary, it re-sorts all the book records so that they appear in order of their TITLE_ID values.

6. Press the Browse button.

   The Browse Titles form now reappears.

7. Scroll to the end of the book list until you find the new book you just entered. The new book now appears in the scrolling list (see Figure 6.10).

Figure 6.10.

The new book, Science Fiction: Beyond the Golden Age, appears in the browser form.

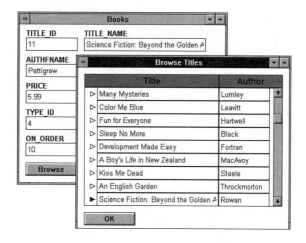

Once again, a shared recordset simplifies an important development task!

Entering Conditions Through the Browser

As a record navigator, the Browse Titles form is certainly superior to a scrollbar. It still has one important limitation, however: If the TITLES table has a large number of records (say, over 500), it is inconvenient to scroll through the list to find a single title. If the user has some idea of the author's name or the title, the form should provide a way to narrow the list down to a more manageable number.

To put this idea in the framework of Oracle Power Objects, what you want to do is apply a condition to the query that populates a form's recordset. Whenever the application queries a table or view for records, you want to specify a condition that limits the records queried to only those that meet the condition.

You give the user this option by adding a text field to the browser form. After you enter a condition in this field (using SQL syntax), the application requeries the shared recordset. Only the records meeting the condition will appear in the browser, and by extension in the Books form as well.

1. Select the form frmBrowseTitles.
2. From the Object palette, select the Text Field drawing tool and add a text field to the form, below the repeater display and to the right of the pushbutton.
3. Resize and reposition the text field so that the form looks like Figure 6.11.

Figure 6.11.
The new text field appearing on the form.

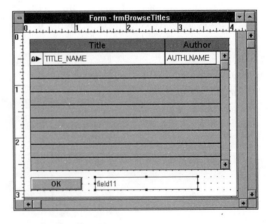

4. Open the text field's Property sheet.
5. Change the text field's `Datatype` property to `String`, and its `DataSize` property to `120`.

   You now have a text field in which you can type a string specifying the condition. The string's maximum length is 120 characters.
6. In the Property sheet, change the text field's name to `fldCondition`.

This step gives the text field a descriptive name, which you will use in method code later in this exercise.

At this point, you want to add the method code that requeries the recordset of two forms, applying the condition typed into this field, as soon as the user finishes typing. In other words, you need a method that executes whenever the value of the text field changes (when the user types a new condition).

As you've already learned, Oracle Power Objects provides a wide array of methods that are triggered by particular events. When you press a button, you trigger its `Click()` method. Similarly, when the user enters a new value and presses Enter, the `PostChange()` method executes. This is just the method you need!

7. With the text field still selected, scroll down its Property sheet until you find the `PostChange()` method.

8. Open the Code Editor window for `PostChange()` and enter the following method code:

```
Inherited.PostChange()
frmBooks.QueryWhere(self.Value)
```

As you'll explore later, this code triggers a method, `QueryWhere()`, that requeries the form while applying the condition entered in the text field. What if you want to requery all the records, effectively removing the condition?

When you press theQuery button on the Form Run Time toolbar, the application requeries all records for the form's recordset. A new user might not understand this, however, and might look for something on the form to clear the condition entered in the field. To avoid this confusion, you will add a button that clears the condition entered in the text field and requeries the form.

1. From the Object palette, select the Pushbutton tool and add a new pushbutton to the form, to the immediate right of the text field (see Figure 6.12).

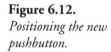

Figure 6.12.
Positioning the new pushbutton.

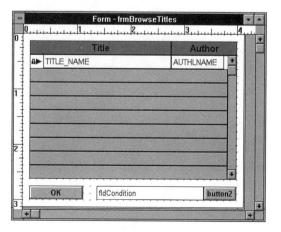

2. Click the text within the pushbutton until it is highlighted, and type Clear as the new label.

3. Open the pushbutton's Property sheet and add the following method code to its Click() method:

```
fldCondition.Value = ""
frmBooks.Query()
```

The first line clears the condition entered in the text field by assigning an empty string (denoted by double quotation marks, with nothing between them). The second line calls the Query() method on the form to requery the form without applying any condition.

4. Save and run the form.

5. In the Books form, press the Browse button.

The browser form now appears, with the new text field and pushbutton added. It's time to enter a condition.

6. In the condition field, type PRICE > 10.

Effectively, you are instructing the application to limit the records queried to books with prices greater than $10.00. SQL does not understand the dollar sign, and ignores the decimal if you enter a round number.

7. Press Enter.

The application now requeries the shared recordset, applying the condition. Only books that cost more than $10 appear in the list, as shown in Figure 6.13.

Figure 6.13.

The new condition applied to the shared recordset.

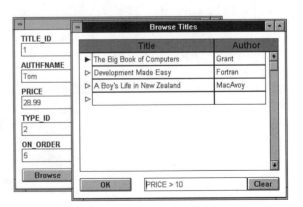

8. In the text field, type ON_ORDER > 0 and press Enter (see Figure 6.14).

Figure 6.14.
A different condition applied.

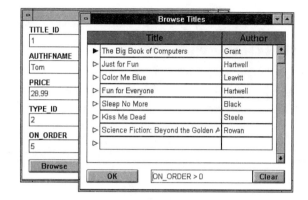

After the application requeries the recordset, only titles on order appear in the list.

9. In the text field, type TYPE_ID = 3 OR TYPE_ID = 4 and press Enter.

The TYPE_ID values 3 and 4 indicate mystery and science fiction novels, respectively. The OR operator instructs the database to query records that fulfill either condition (TYPE_ID of 3 *or* 4). By entering this condition, the list displays only the mystery and science fiction titles stored in the TITLES table (see Figure 6.15).

Figure 6.15.
A third condition applied to the list of titles.

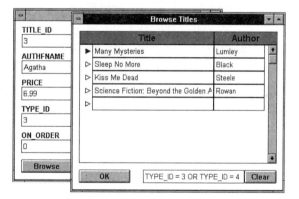

10. Press the Clear pushbutton.

The list once again displays all the records from the TITLES table.

11. Press Stop to end this exercise.

The *Query()* and *QueryWhere()* Methods

As shown in this exercise, Oracle Power Objects has two methods that query records, `Query()` and `QueryWhere()`. Both are standard methods of bindable containers (forms, reports, repeater displays, embedded forms, and user-defined classes), but they have different uses.

☐ The `Query()` method takes no arguments. When called, this method requeries the entire recordset for a container. `Query()` is called when you first open the container, and when you press the Query button on the Form Run Time toolbar.

☐ The `QueryWhere()` method takes a single argument, a string that defines the condition to apply to the query. This condition must follow SQL syntax. `QueryWhere()` is not automatically triggered—you must call it through method code.

To show you how to use `QueryWhere()`, the following is the method code that should appear in the `PostChange()` method of the text field `fldCondition`:

```
Inherited.PostChange()
frmBooks.QueryWhere(self.Value)
```

The first line calls the default processing for `PostChange()`, which otherwise does not execute. (As discussed on Day 1, "Your First Form," method code suppresses default processing unless you add the `Inherited.method_name` statement to your code.)

The second line uses the value entered in the text field to specify the argument passed to the `QueryWhere()` method. Because the text field has a data type of `String`, the statement `self.Value` refers to the string entered into the text field as its new value. The method code calls the `QueryWhere()` method on the Books form; however, because the two forms share a recordset, the new contents of the recordset are displayed in both the Books form and the Browse Titles form.

Before leaving this discussion of `Query()` and `QueryWhere()`, you should know that all bindable containers also have another relevant property, `DefaultCondition`. When you design a form or other container, you can enter the same kind of condition that you pass as an argument to `QueryWhere()`. When the `Query()` method executes on the container, the application automatically applies the condition specified in `DefaultCondition` to the query. If you call the `QueryWhere()` method on the same container, the condition passed as an argument to the method replaces the one defined in the `DefaultCondition` property.

Now that you know how `Query()`, `QueryWhere()`, and `DefaultCondition` work, here are some tips:

☐ If you want to define a condition that applies whenever you open or requery a form, specify it through the `DefaultCondition` property. For example, if you design a form for viewing all books on order, you would assign this condition (`ON_HOLD = TRUE`) to the form's `DefaultCondition` property.

☐ If you want to redefine a condition while the application is running, you should build the necessary string and pass it to the QueryWhere() method. The condition field you added to the browser form provides a good example of this technique.

Creating a "Further Information" Form

The previous exercise used a shared recordset to give the user an improved way to select a record. This exercise shows a different use for a shared recordset: If there is not enough room to display all the information you would like on a form, you can create two forms that share the same recordset. The second form displays the information that does not fit on the first form.

Specifically, you will return to a form you created on Day 5, "Master-Detail Relationships." The first master-detail form you created, frmPubsBooks, displayed publisher records on the form and title records in a repeater display. Given the limited space of the repeater, you could display only the author's last name, the title, and the price for each book. In this lesson, you will use a shared recordset to gain quick access to additional information about each book.

1. In the Application window for BOOKS.POA, double-click the icon for the form frmPubsBooks.

2. After this form appears, resize and reposition the three text fields in the repeater display to make room for a small pushbutton on the right side of the repeater display panel.

3. Using the Pushbutton tool from the Object palette, add a pushbutton to the space you just made in the repeater display panel.

4. Change the label in the pushbutton to More....

   The form should now look like Figure 6.16.

Figure 6.16.

The More... pushbutton added to the form.

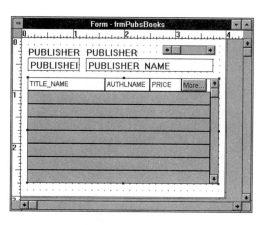

5. Open the Property sheet for the new pushbutton and enter the following code in its `Click()` method:

   ```
   frmMoreBooks.OpenWindow()
   ```

   This code will open a form that displays complete information on each book. The next step is to create this secondary form.

6. Select the Application window and create a new form.

7. In the form's Property sheet, change its name to `frmMoreBooks`, and its label to `Further Book Information`.

8. From the Session window for BOOKS.POS, click and drag the icon for the TITLES table onto the form.

   Again, Oracle Power Objects creates a text field bound to each column in the table. Now, both the repeater display in the form frmPubsBooks and this new form are bound to the TITLES table. Unfortunately, this is not what you want. You want the two containers to share the same recordset, not query records for two separate recordsets (one for the form, one for the repeater display). The fact that both containers use the same table is not helpful; you want the secondary form to display the record for the book selected in the repeater display. Therefore, you need to edit the `RecordSource` property of the new form to create the shared recordset.

9. Select the form frmMoreBooks and enter `=frmPubsBooks.repBooks` for its `RecordSource` property.

10. In the form frmPubsBooks, change the name of its repeater display to `repBooks`.

11. Save both forms before continuing.

12. Select the application and open its Property sheet.

13. Delete the code left over from the last exercise and enter the following:

    ```
    frmPubsBooks.OpenWindow()
    ```

    Again, this code is necessary to tell the application which form to open when it launches.

14. Save and run the application.

15. Select a book from within the repeater display and press the More... pushbutton. The Further Book Information form now appears, as shown in Figure 6.17.

The Further Book Information form now appears, displaying information from all the columns for the selected book.

Figure 6.17.
The Further Book Information form appears after you press the pushbutton.

Further Book Information		
TITLE_ID	TITLE_NAME	AUTHLNAME
3	Many Mysterie:	Lumley
AUTHFNAME	PUBLISHER_ID	PRICE
Agatha	99	6.99
WS_PRICE	PROMOTION_PI	PRINTING
2.99		3
TYPE_ID	ON_ORDER	IN_STOCK
3	0	8
ON_HOLD		

Stand-Alone Recordsets

So far, all of the recordsets used in these lessons have been connected to a form, a repeater display, or an embedded form. In some cases, you want to maintain a recordset that the user can never view or edit, but which maintains information needed in the application.

Although it might seem strange at first to create these free-floating recordsets, remember that you are developing applications for a client/server environment in which performance and security are important considerations. A stand-alone recordset can address both needs.

Because a stand-alone recordset is invisible to the user, you can use it to store confidential information that the application needs, but that should remain hidden from the user. For example, you can create a stand-alone recordset that queries all usernames and passwords from the database. When a user tries to log in to an application, the application can search the contents of the recordset to see if the user and password are valid.

Because the stand-alone recordset keeps records in memory, you can use the recordset's contents when you need to make regular lookups for a value, instead of constantly requerying the database for the same information. If you need to keep information on the types of books available, but the user will never edit the BOOK_TYPES table, you might create a stand-alone recordset containing the subject classifications for books. Whenever the application needs a description of a particular book topic, it can search the stand-alone recordset for this information.

6

Two Types of Stand-Alone Recordsets

Oracle Power Objects gives you two options for creating and maintaining this recordset:

☐ A hidden form—Using the techniques you already know, you can create a form bound to the table or view you want to populate the recordset. You can hide this form, keeping it in memory but making it invisible to the form.

Whenever you make a reference to an object in method code, you load that object into memory. You do not display it to the user, however, unless you call its `OpenWindow()` method (or the `OpenWindow()` method of the form in which it appears).

In the case of a bound form, the application queries its recordset when it opens and hides the form. Both the form and its recordset remain in memory, making it possible to read values from bound controls or from the recordset through method code. The form can be relatively simple, like the one shown in Figure 6.18.

Figure 6.18.

A hidden form whose recordset is available for lookups.

☐ A stand-alone recordset—Through method code, you can create a recordset that has no association with a bound container. Usually, you add the necessary method code to the `OnLoad()` method of the application or a form so that the stand-alone recordset appears at the same time the application launches or a form opens.

Stand-alone recordsets can be bound to a table or a view, in which case the application queries values from the record source to populate the recordset. Optionally, you can populate the recordset entirely through method code, creating each record and assigning values to each of its columns.

Creating Stand-Alone Recordsets

Whatever type of stand-alone recordset you use, the important Oracle Basic commands for creating and deleting the recordset are, respectively, NEW and DELETE. When you create the new recordset object, you use a different keyword for bound and unbound recordsets.

To create a bound recordset, you use the following syntax:

```
NEW DBRECORDSET(session_name)
```

The *session_name* parameter identifies the session through which the recordset will access its record source. This syntax can take other optional parameters, but for the sake of simplicity, you can ignore them for now.

After you create the stand-alone recordset with the NEW command, you specify the query that populates it with records. SetQuery() is a standard method of stand-alone recordsets. SetQuery() uses the following syntax to perform the query:

```
recordset.SetQuery(query_string, updatable)
```

The *updatable* parameter is a Boolean value (TRUE or FALSE) indicating whether you can update the contents of the recordset. If you want to be able to insert, delete, or update records and save these changes to the database, you set this parameter to TRUE.

The *query_string* parameter is a string value that specifies the SQL query used to populate the recordset. For example, to populate a stand-alone with data from the BOOK_TYPES table, you would use the following SELECT statement as the query string:

```
SELECT TYPE_ID, TYPE_DESC FROM BOOK_TYPES
```

 Note: You cannot use the asterisk (*) to select all columns in this query. Instead, you must specify each column by name.

Using an Unbound Stand-Alone Recordset

In this lesson, you'll give the database a little rest and create an unbound recordset to do the job of looking up the description of each type of book. When you type a value for the TYPE_ID column in a form bound to TITLES, the application will look into the stand-alone recordset for a matching value and return the description for this type of book. The description appears in a text field on the form.

You need to go through the following process to create the recordset:

1. Create the stand-alone recordset.
2. Add columns to it.
3. Populate the recordset with data.

Then, when the user types in a value for TYPE_ID, the application

☐ Looks into the stand-alone recordset for a matching value

☐ Displays this value in a text field

With this in mind, you are ready to create a new form, frmLookup, to simplify lookups. Follow these steps:

1. In the Application window, create a new form.
2. In the form's Property sheet, enter frmLookup for its name, and Look Up Descriptions as its label.
3. In the Session window for BOOKS.POS, open the Table Editor window for TITLES.
4. Select the columns TITLE and TYPE_ID from the table and drag them onto the form.

5. Add a horizontal scrollbar to the form.

6. Resize and position the controls until the form looks something like Figure 6.19.

Figure 6.19.

The form frmLookup, bound to TITLES.

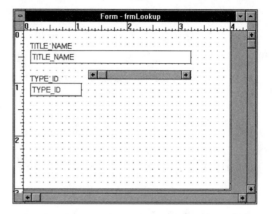

7. Add a text field in the position indicated in Figure 6.20.

   This new text field will display a description of a book category to match the numeric value entered for TYPE_ID.

Figure 6.20.

The new text field added.

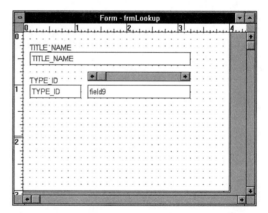

8. In the text field's Property sheet, change the control's Datatype to String, and its DataSize to 48.

   This step allows the text field to display strings up to 48 characters long—enough to show the description of each book type.

9. Change the text field's Name to fldTypeDesc.

The next step is to add the method code that creates the stand-alone recordset, populates it with book type records, and performs the lookup. Ideally, you want this code to execute whenever a new value appears in the TYPE_ID field. Whether you type in a new TYPE_ID value, or the value changes when you scroll to a new record, the application performs the lookup into the recordset for the correct description.

You will add the necessary code to the text field's PostChange() method, which executes whenever a value in the text field changes.

1. Open the Code Editor window for the TYPE_DESC field's PostChange() method.

2. Enter the following code (get ready to type!):

```
Inherited.PostChange()
' Create the new recordset
DIM vRec AS Object
vRec = NEW RECORDSET

' Add columns to the recordset, checking
' to see if there's a matching description
vRec.AddColumn("TYPE_ID", RecDty_Long)
vRec.AddColumn("TYPE_DESC", RecDty_String)
IF self.Value = vRec.GetColVal("TYPE_ID") THEN
   fldTypeDesc.Value = vRec.GetColVal("TYPE_DESC")
END IF

' Populate the recordset with data
vRec.InsertRow()
vRec.SetColVal("TYPE_ID", 1)
vRec.SetColVal("TYPE_DESC", "Reference")
IF self.Value = vRec.GetColVal("TYPE_ID") THEN
   fldTypeDesc.Value = vRec.GetColVal("TYPE_DESC")
END IF

vRec.InsertRow()
vRec.SetColVal("TYPE_ID", 2)
vRec.SetColVal("TYPE_DESC", "Computer")
IF self.Value = vRec.GetColVal("TYPE_ID") THEN
   fldTypeDesc.Value = vRec.GetColVal("TYPE_DESC")
END IF

vRec.InsertRow()
vRec.SetColVal("TYPE_ID", 3)
vRec.SetColVal("TYPE_DESC", "Mystery")
IF self.Value = vRec.GetColVal("TYPE_ID") THEN
   fldTypeDesc.Value = vRec.GetColVal("TYPE_DESC")
END IF

vRec.InsertRow()
vRec.SetColVal("TYPE_ID", 10)
vRec.SetColVal("TYPE_DESC", "Children's")
IF self.Value = vRec.GetColVal("TYPE_ID") THEN
   fldTypeDesc.Value = vRec.GetColVal("TYPE_DESC")
END IF
```

```
vRec.InsertRow()
vRec.SetColVal("TYPE_ID", 11)
vRec.SetColVal("TYPE_DESC", "General fiction")
IF self.Value = vRec.GetColVal("TYPE_ID") THEN
   fldTypeDesc.Value = vRec.GetColVal("TYPE_DESC")
END IF

vRec.InsertRow()
vRec.SetColVal("TYPE_ID", 12)
vRec.SetColVal("TYPE_DESC", "General non-fiction")
IF self.Value = vRec.GetColVal("TYPE_ID") THEN
   fldTypeDesc.Value = vRec.GetColVal("TYPE_DESC")
END IF
```

3. Save and run the form.

The code works for the most part: As you scroll through the records from TITLES, a description of each book's topic appears in the lookup field. Even though the code works, however, it does nearly everything wrong.

Why This Is the Wrong Approach

Stand-alone recordsets have their uses. Unfortunately, this example shows how to do everything wrong. Although the rest of the book so far has given you positive examples, this exercise teaches you some important principles by way of negative example:

☐ The application has to re-create the recordset object every time a TYPE_ID value changes. Effectively, every time you scroll to a different record, or when you type a new value yourself, the application creates the recordset and checks for a matching value. This is an inefficient approach that threatens to slow down the application.

☐ The values in this recordset are hard-coded. If the descriptions of books in the TITLES table change, or if they expand to include new categories, these changes don't appear in the stand-alone recordset. The lookup field will display the revised descriptions only if you go through the effort of recoding this method, and then recompiling the application.

☐ The code repeats itself. Several times, you entered the same code for checking to see if the value in the TYPE_ID field matches the TYPE_ID value in the recordset. Not only is it tedious to retype this code, it's potentially dangerous. If the code does not work, you then have to fix it everywhere it is repeated. The greater the redundancy, the more likely it is you'll miss one instance of the code you need to fix.

You can remedy this situation somewhat by following good coding practices. For example, you can write code that is less redundant, so that you can define a procedure in only one place and then reuse it anywhere you want. Reusable code makes maintaining the procedure easier: by modifying it once, the fix appears wherever you use the code.

Oracle Power Objects provides some other ways around the problems posed by bad code. For example, you can use the SQLLOOKUP function to perform the lookup, instead of going through the unnecessary agony of coding the stand-alone recordset. In fact, to perform the lookup, you will use SQLLOOKUP to help define a property. Therefore, you will not have to write any code at all to add the same (if not better) lookup feature to the form.

The *SQLLOOKUP()* Function

SQLLOOKUP is one of the most widely used tools for looking up values, and it's the preferred technique for finding a single matching value to explain something else appearing on a form (a common occurrence in database applications). In the case of your new form, you need only perform a quick lookup to find a description of a book's topic. Creating a master-detail container just to show the description looked up from BOOK_TYPES would be overkill, to say the least.

This Oracle Basic function takes one argument, a SQL query (a string). When it executes, SQLLOOKUP returns a value queried from the table specified in the query string.

For example, to find the description of a book classification from BOOK_TYPES, you would pass a SELECT statement that would query the database for the TYPE_DESC value that matches a particular TYPE_ID.

```
SELECT TYPE_DESC FROM BOOK_TYPES WHERE TYPE_ID = 1
```

In this case, the query would return the string "Reference"—the TYPE_DESC value that matches a TYPE_ID of 1.

You will add the SQLLOOKUP function to the DataSource property of the field fldTypeDesc. Think about this approach and you'll see it makes sense: You are specifying where the control gets its data. Instead of binding the control to a column in the form's record source, you are looking up a value in a different table or view.

1. With the TYPE_ID text field selected, open the PostChange() Code Editor window.

2. Delete all the code you entered in the previous exercise.

   If you leave any code here, it will continue to execute when TYPE_ID values change, interfering with the alternative lookup method you are about to use. Be sure to delete every bit of text from this method, so that the application can use the default processing for PostChange().

3. Select the text field fldTypeDesc.

4. In the field's Property sheet, enter the following for its DataSource property:
   ```
   =SQLLOOKUP(BOOKS, "SELECT TYPE_DESC FROM BOOK_TYPES
   ➥WHERE TYPE_ID = " & STR(TYPE_ID.Value))
   ```
   The DataSource section of the Property sheet should now look like Figure 6.21.

6

Figure 6.21.

The SQLLOOKUP *statement entered for the field's* DataSource *property.*

SQLLOOKUP uses the TYPE_ID's Value property as part of the query string. (The Basic command STR changes the numeric TYPE_ID value to a string, so that you can add it to the rest of the query string.) Therefore, if the value in the TYPE_ID field were currently 1, SQLLOOKUP would build and use the following query string:

```
SELECT TYPE_DESC FROM BOOK_TYPES WHERE TYPE_ID = 1
```

5. Save and run the form.

The form appears as in Figure 6.22, displaying the description of books as queried through SQLLOOKUP.

Figure 6.22.

The same lookup, accomplished with much less work.

Find the Book Type
TITLE_NAME
The Big Book of Computers
TYPE_ID
2   Computer

Now, when you scroll through the TITLES records, the correct description of each type of book appears in the text field.

More About *SQLLOOKUP*

To get a bit more practice working with SQLLOOKUP, you will add some publisher information to the form.

1. Open the Table Editor window for TITLES.
2. Click and drag the PUBLISHER_ID column onto the form.

3. Position the new text field so that the form looks like Figure 6.23.

Figure 6.23.
The PUBLISHER_ID text field added to the form.

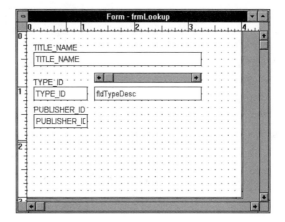

4. Create a new text field, sizing and positioning it so that the form appears like Figure 6.24.

Figure 6.24.
Adding the second lookup field.

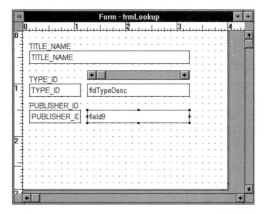

5. Change the text field's Name property to fldPubName, its Datatype property to String, and its DataSize property to 48.

6. For the new text field's DataSource property, enter the following:
```
=SQLLOOKUP("SELECT PUBLISHER_NAME FROM PUBLISHERS WHERE PUBLISHER_ID = " &
➥STR(PUBLISHER_ID.Value))
```

7. Save and run the form. The form now displays two fields with explanatory information provided by SQLLOOKUP (see Figure 6.25).

Figure 6.25.
Two lookup fields at work on the form.

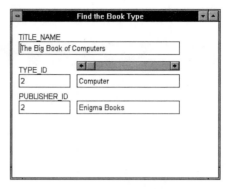

A Short Word on Derived Values

Until this point, you were familiar with one way to automatically provide a value for a field, by binding it to a column in a table or view. When the application queried a record, it displayed in the control whatever value it found in the associated column. Your experience with SQLLOOKUP suggests a new way to give a value to a control: through an expression.

Some expressions are simple calculations: You can display the sum of two numbers (for example, the values displayed in the text fields named fldOne and fldTwo) in a text field by defining the necessary calculation as its DataSource, as shown in Figure 6.26.

Figure 6.26.
Summing values for display in a field.

Similarly, you can combine (or concatenate) two strings, such as the first and last names of a customer, for display in the control (see Figure 6.27). You can define the field's DataSource property as the expression that combines the two strings.

To use Oracle Power Objects terminology, a *derived value* uses an expression to provide a value to a control. The derived value is defined through an expression entered for the control's DataSource property.

When you used SQLLOOKUP in the last exercise, you defined a derived value for the text field's DataSource property. Instead of a numeric calculation or a string operation, however, you used a different kind of expression to query a value.

Figure 6.27.
Concatenating strings for display in a field.

▷ Click	
◇ CompareOnLock	True
▷ CounterGenKey	
◇ CounterIncBy	0
◇ CounterSeq	
◇ CounterTiming	Immediate
◇ CounterType	None
◇ DataSize	0
◇ DataSource	=fldFirstName & " " & fldLastName
◇ Datatype	Long Integer
◇ DefaultValue	
▷ DoubleClick	

Limitations of *SQLLOOKUP*

In contrast to your stand-alone recordset experience, using SQLLOOKUP might seem like deliverance. As useful as SQLLOOKUP can be, however, it has its limitations:

☐ The application must perform a lookup into the database every time the primary key value for the lookup changes. When you move to a new record, the application must immediately perform a lookup into the PUBLISHERS and BOOK_TYPES tables to find the publisher's name and the book topic's description. Therefore, SQLLOOKUP can be a performance-killer, especially when you are performing several lookups on the same form.

☐ You cannot select the descriptive value. Usually, if you are entering a publisher for a book, you want to enter the publisher's name, not its numeric ID. Just entering 1 is probably meaningless, unless you have memorized the PUBLISHERS table. The name Magnum Books, however, is perfectly understandable.

In the form created in the last exercise, you must type the numeric publisher ID, and then see which name appears. Needless to say, this trial-and-error method is much less efficient than selecting the publisher by name instead of by ID number.

List Controls

To avoid these problems, you can substitute the lookup fields with a list control. These special bindable controls present a list of values from which the user can make a selection. The list usually provides descriptive text rather than a numeric ID, making it easier to find the right selection. List controls provide a more "human-friendly" technique for selecting publishers or titles.

To avoid SQLLOOKUP's performance shortcomings, list controls query the foreign table for values as soon as their form is opened. A list control that replaced the text field fldTypeDesc would query the BOOK_TYPES table when the form opened, instead of every time the value for TYPE_ID changed.

It should come as no surprise, then, that you will replace some of the text fields on the lookup form with list controls. The three types of list controls are shown in Figure 6.28 and described in Table 6.2.

Figure 6.28.

The three types of list controls.

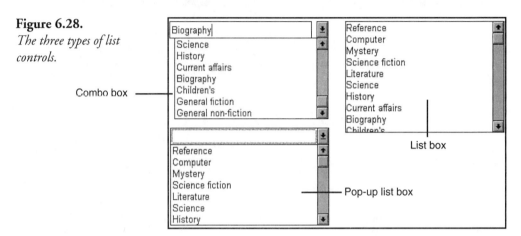

Combo box

List box

Pop-up list box

Table 6.2. List controls.

Control	Description
Pop-up list	Provides a list of values from which the user can make a selection. The list does not appear until you click the pop-up list control. You use this type of list control when you want to prevent the user from selecting a value from a limited list of options.
Combo box	A list control that includes both a drop-down list and a text box. You can select an item from the list or type your own value into the text box. A combo box is useful when you want to give users a list of suggested values, but also let them enter their own values.
List box	A box that includes a scrolling list of values from which the user can make a selection. Like a pop-up list, the user cannot select a value other than an item on the list.

Identifying a List Control's Record Source

As you've learned, list controls enable you to show a list of descriptive values, instead of less understandable codes. You have two ways of determining the values displayed in the list:

☐ By hard-coding them. When you set the property that determines the list to be displayed, you specify all the items yourself.

☐ By querying them from a table. Alternatively, you can look up the descriptive text in another table. In the lookup form you created, you would instruct the list control to look in the PUBLISHERS table to find the name of a publishing house.

Two Types of Values for List Controls

Because a pop-up list bound to PUBLISHER_ID performs a lookup into the PUBLISHERS table to find a publisher's name, you can see that the pop-up list has two values: the actual value of the control, and the text it displays. When you select the name of a publisher (a *display value*), you set the pop-up list's Value property to the publisher's ID number (the *internal value*). There is often this kind of difference between display values and internal values in the case of both list boxes and pop-up lists.

Although this arrangement might seem confusing at first, the design of a list control is in fact quite intuitive.

☐ The pop-up list of publishers must be bound to the PUBLISHER_ID column.

☐ Because this column has a numeric data type (Number), the control's internal value must also be numeric.

☐ However, the control needs to display all the names of publishers queried from the PUBLISHERS table. Although the user might select the display value of Magnum Books, the control's Value is in fact set to 1.

Just remember that the display value exists only to make it easy for the user to understand the selection. Although the user selects the name of the publisher, the control might actually store the numeric publisher ID instead.

Creating a Pop-up List

To illustrate these points, you will replace the lookup fields on the form with pop-up lists.

1. On the form, delete the fields fldPubs, fldTypeDesc, TYPE_ID, and PUBLISHER_ID, as well as their associated labels.

2. Select the Pop-up List drawing tool from the Object palette and click the form.

   A pop-up list now appears on the form (see Figure 6.29).

3. Repeat the process to create a second pop-up list.

4. Move the pop-up lists until the form looks like Figure 6.30.

5. Select the top pop-up list and open its Property sheet.

6. Enter Publishers for its Label property.

7. Click the DataSource property so that the drop-down list of choices appears (see Figure 6.31).

Figure 6.29.
The new pop-up list.

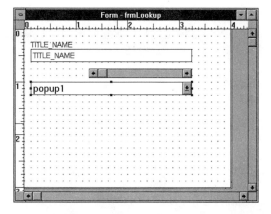

Figure 6.30.
*The two pop-up lists,
repositioned on the form.*

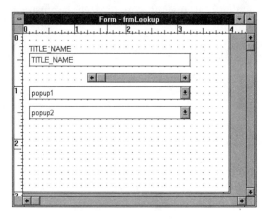

Figure 6.31.
*Selecting a column for the
DataSource property.*

As before, this list includes the columns in TITLES to which you can bind the pop-up list. Because this list will display the names of all publishers, you will select PUBLISHER_ID.

8. From this list, select PUBLISHER_ID.

   Next, you will use the Translation property to determine the internal and display values of the control.

9. For the Translation property, enter the following (see Figure 6.32):

   ```
   = PUBLISHERS.PUBLISHER_NAME = PUBLISHER_ID
   ```

   This string tells the application how to perform the lookup. Effectively, this syntax tells the application, "For every value you find in the PUBLISHER_ID column, display the publisher's name in the list."

   For a full description of this syntax, see the Oracle Power Objects online help topic for the Translation property.

Figure 6.32.

Entering the Translation property.

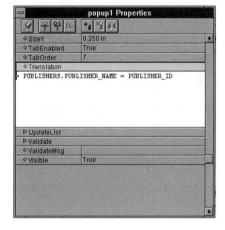

10. Select the other pop-up list and change its Label to Topic.

11. For the same pop-up list, select TYPE_ID for its DataSource, and set its Translation property to the following:

    ```
    = BOOK_TYPES.TYPE_DESC = TYPE_ID
    ```

    To interpret this string: "For every TYPE_ID value you find in the BOOK_TYPES table, display the associated descriptive text from TYPE_DESC."

12. Save and run the form.

    Now, when you move among the TITLES records, you will see the value in the list control change.

13. Click the Publishers pop-up list. You can now see a list of book publishers, as shown in Figure 6.33.

201

Figure 6.33.

The pop-up list of publishers.

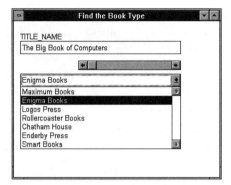

14. Click one of the publishers in the list.

    The Commit and Rollback buttons are now enabled, signaling that you have made a change to this record. Remember that you are in fact changing a numeric publisher ID, even though you selected the name of a publisher.

15. Press the Rollback button to undo the change.

16. Press Stop to end this exercise.

Hard-Coding a List

As indicated earlier, you can hard-code the contents of a list rather than querying the list from a table. If there is no table to help populate a list control, you must hard-code the values.

To illustrate this technique, you will add a pop-up list that lets the user select the number of the printing for a book. There is no table defining printings; instead, the book's printing (that is, its first edition, 1) is simply stored as an integer value for each book. For the first printing, the value appears as 1 in the PRINTING column of TITLES. You might want to show the value as First, instead of 1, however, to make the value slightly more readable and understandable.

1. In the frmLookup form, add a new pop-up list beneath the other two.

2. For the DataSource property of the new pop-up list, select PRINTING.

3. For the Translation property of the control, enter the following:

   ```
   "First" = 1
   "Second" = 2
   "Third" = 3
   "Fourth" = 4
   "Fifth" = 5
   "Sixth" = 6
   "Seventh" = 7
   ```

   The Translation section of the Property sheet should now look like Figure 6.34.

Figure 6.34.
*The hard-coded values for
the* Translation *property.*

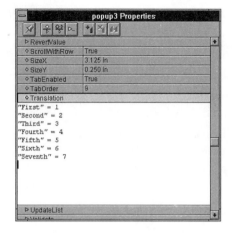

4. Save and run the form.
5. Select the new pop-up list.

You can now see the hard-coded list of printings (see Figure 6.35). If you were to select First from this list, the control would store the value as 1. Remember, because the PRINTING column uses the integer data type (Integer), you need to store the value as a number (1), not as a string (First).

Figure 6.35.
*The hard-coded list of
possible printings for a book.*

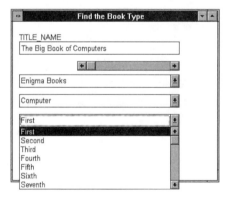

More on List Controls

A few quick words on list controls before ending this lesson:

☐ Whereas pop-up lists and list boxes define the contents of the list through their Translation properties, combo boxes have a different property, ValueList, to perform the same task. ValueList uses a slightly different approach, as described in the Oracle Power Objects online help.

203

☐ When you read values for a list from a table, you can use one of two syntaxes:

`= record_source.display_column = actual_column`

or

`= SELECT display_column, actual_column FROM record_source`

In the second case, you are using SQL syntax to query the values, so you can apply conditions (`WHERE, ORDER BY, GROUP BY`) to the query.

To populate the list displaying publishers, therefore, you could use either of the following settings for the `Value` property:

`= PUBLISHERS.PUBLISHER_NAME = PUBLISHER_ID`

or

`= SELECT PUBLISHER_NAME, PUBLISHER_ID FROM PUBLISHERS`

☐ When you hard-code the contents of the list, you use the following syntax:

`display_value = internal_value`

Summary

Today's lesson has shown you several new ways to work with recordsets.

☐ Two or more containers can share the same recordset. When you enter a change through one container, the new value for a bound control appears immediately in all the other controls.

☐ Shared recordsets make it easier to create browser forms, "further information" forms, and other means for organizing information.

☐ You can create stand-alone recordsets not associated with any container. You can populate these recordsets through a query or entirely through code.

☐ Stand-alone recordsets are useful when you want to maintain information that the user does not need to see, but that the application needs to use regularly.

☐ You can use the SQLLOOKUP function to look up values in a table. This feature is especially useful when you want to present explanatory text to match some numeric value appearing in a form. For example, in one of the exercises in this lesson, you used SQLLOOKUP to search for the name of a publisher in the PUBLISHERS table that matched the publisher ID for a book.

☐ List controls provide this same explanatory information, but they also make it easier for the user to select a new value. Although the user might select some explanatory text, such as the name of the publisher, the control might store a different value, such as a numeric value in the PUBLISHER_ID column.

What Comes Next?

Although forms are an important part of any application, so are reports. When you design a report in Oracle Power Objects, you use the same techniques to bind the form to a table or view, create master and detail sections, and use some of the other recordset-related tricks you have learned in the last three lessons. However, reports have their own peculiarities, especially when it comes to designing the different sections of a report. The next lesson walks you through both simple and sophisticated report design, but much of this work will seem like familiar territory to you already.

Q&A

Q How many lookups should a form have?

A As many as needed to explain information on the form. Remember, however, that if you use SQLLOOKUP to provide this information, performance suffers if you have a large number of controls using SQLLOOKUP to find descriptive information across several tables. However, users might be willing to sacrifice a little speed in order to view information about book types, customer names, and other types of information commonly looked up.

Q Is there any reason to use a bound stand-alone recordset for lookups?

A If you want to provide a highly secure way of storing sensitive information in your application, then a stand-alone recordset is a good place to put it. However, looking up values in a stand-alone recordset can be slow if the recordset is large, because you need to run some Basic code to iterate through all the records in the stand-alone recordset (somewhat slower than using SQLLOOKUP and other techniques). Therefore, you should use a stand-alone recordset for lookups if (1) the recordset is not too large, and (2) the application needs to perform the lookup infrequently.

Workshop

The Workshop consists of quiz questions to help you solidify your understanding of the material covered and an exercise to give you experience in using what you've learned. Try and understand the quiz answers and the exercise before you go on to tomorrow's lesson.

Quiz

1. If you want to create a form for viewing titles, not for editing them, what are the best options for displaying the name of a book's publisher?

2. If you have two embedded forms on a tabbed form, both showing values from the same table, what is the simplest way to synchronize records between them?

3. If you wanted to maintain a copy of the usernames and passwords queried from the USERS table in a database, what would be the safest way to store this information in an application?

Exercise

Create a form with a repeater display showing each customer's name, and the number of each type of book purchased by that person. The repeater display should be bound to the CUST_PURCHASES table, and the main form should be bound to the CUSTOMERS table.

Quiz Answers

1. You can use a list control to interpret the numeric publisher ID and display the publisher's name instead. If the user will not be editing any data in this form, however, you might choose to add a text field that uses SQLLOOKUP to find the publisher's name.

   In the latter case, you could move the SQLLOOKUP field over the PUBLISHER_ID field, to display only the name of the publisher.

2. The easiest way to synchronize these records is to bind one embedded form to a table. Next, set the other embedded form's RecordSource property to share the first embedded form's recordset. When you switch between embedded forms, the same record is selected for both of them, because they share a recordset.

3. You might create a stand-alone recordset storing this information in USER_ID and PASSWORD columns. When the user enters a name and password, the application could then use this hidden recordset for verification.

7

Reports

Overview

Today, you learn about the following topics:

- ☐ Reports in Oracle Power Objects
- ☐ The sections of a report
- ☐ Binding a report to a table or a view
- ☐ Views and lookups in reports
- ☐ Organizing information in a report
- ☐ Adding conditions to a report
- ☐ Creating a master-detail report
- ☐ Adding a chart to a report
- ☐ Displaying graphics in reports
- ☐ Tips on report design

Sometimes, you want to view data, but you don't want to edit it. For example, you might want to print a list of all the books carried in the bookstore for later reference (when you're not working on the computer). If a customer calls and asks about new books, it would be useful to have this information available to any employee, in readable format.

To provide this information, you want to create reports. Like a form, you bind a report to a table or view so that you can view information stored in the database. Unlike a form, you can view records, but you cannot edit them. Reports are designed to display any amount of information, large or small, in an intelligible, readable format. Figure 7.1 shows a sample Oracle Power Objects report.

Figure 7.1.

A sample Oracle Power Objects report.

Product Report
MoonLight Products 🌙	***Product Catalog***
"Everything under the Moon"	*Wednesday, September 27, 1995*

Welcome to the MoonLight Products catalog!
We carry a select assortment of fine candles, lamps, and other illumination devices - in fact, everything you need to enhance a moonlit night.

Battery-Operated Lights	Price
Large Flashlight	$12.20
Small Flashlight	$9.00

Electric Lamps and Lanterns	Price
Floodlamp	$50.00
Brass Table Lamp	$72.00
Multi-Color Holiday Lights, 15 feet	$15.00

In many tools, the report designer is an afterthought, or might not be provided at all. To create a report with such tools, you must use a report writer that is completely separate from the development tool used to create the application. Not only must you link two separate entities (the application and the report) that were created with two different tools, but you also must use two different techniques to create applications and reports.

In reality, forms and reports are equal in importance, because you need both of them to effectively "leverage" information from the database. Your CEO wants not only to make sure that financial transactions are entered promptly and accurately by employees, she also wants to see a comprehensive, readable balance sheet!

I'm happy to report that the report writer function is an intrinsic part of Oracle Power Objects, not a separate piece independent from the rest of the application development environment.

Although the Oracle Power Objects report writer does not have as many features as some other tools, it does let you create reports with a minimum of fuss. You have already mastered the techniques for binding forms to a table or a view, and you can use the same techniques for binding reports. And once you use some of the powerful shortcuts in Oracle Power Objects for performing this task, you can focus your attention on how well the report presents information to the reader.

To get a better sense of how reports work in Oracle Power Objects, let's create a new one.

1. Select the Application window for BOOKS.POA.
2. Press the New Report button, or select the File | New Report... menu command.

A new report now appears, as shown in Figure 7.2. Although you have not yet added anything to the report, it is already separated into several bands. Unlike forms, reports are divided into several functionally distinct sections, each with a different job to perform. These sections are described in Table 7.1.

Figure 7.2.
A new Oracle Power Objects report.

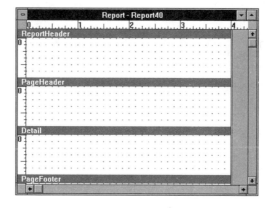

Table 7.1. The sections of a report.

Section	Purpose
Report Header	Contains whatever you want to display at the beginning of a report. For example, you would place the title of the report in this section, as well as any global information (such as the date the report was printed).
Page Header	Contains objects you want to display at the top of each page. For example, the page header might include the page number, the date the report was printed, and the title of the report.
Detail	Contains the main body of the report, including controls (generally, text fields) displaying information queried from the database. For example, if you want to display a list of all the books carried by the bookstore, this information would appear in the Detail section of the report. (Although this section is called Detail, it does not have any relevance to the master-detail relationships discussed in earlier lessons.)
Page Footer	Contains objects displayed at the bottom of each page.
Report Footer	Contains objects displayed at the end of the report.

Reports can also contain two other, optional sections: the *group header* and the *group footer*. These sections help organize the information in a report. For example, you would add these sections so that you could print a listing of books grouped by publisher. We'll leave discussion of these additional sections aside, however, until you have mastered the techniques for creating a simple report.

You can resize each section in your report, making them larger or smaller to accommodate whatever objects you place in them. For example, if you have a lot of data to display in the Detail section, you might want to increase its size. Alternatively, if you want to display only the page number of a report in the report footer, you could economize on space by shortening the height of this section. You can give any section an effective height of zero, so that it does not display at all. During the next exercise, you will resize some sections of the report to improve its appearance.

Creating a New Report

In this exercise, you will take a "blank slate" report and fill it with a listing of all the books carried by the bookstore.

1. Open the Session window for BOOKS.POS and open a connection to the database.

2. Open the Table Editor window for the TITLES table.

3. Select the TITLE_NAME, AUTHLNAME, PRICE, and PUBLISHER_ID columns from the Table Editor window and move them into the Detail section of the report.

   As expected, four text fields, each bound to one of the four selected columns, now appear on the form.

4. Select the report and open its Property sheet.

5. Change the name of the report to rptTitles and its label to Book Inventory Report.

   At this point, you have a fully functional report, a fact you can demonstrate by running the form.

6. Save and run the report.

Figure 7.3 shows how the report appears, including all the records queried from the TITLES table.

Figure 7.3.
The new report
at runtime.

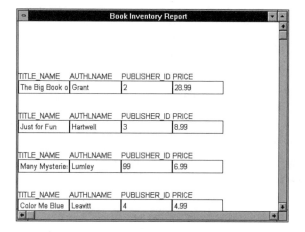

As you can see, the Detail section of the report repeats once for each record (that is, each book) queried from the TITLES table. That's exactly what this section of the report is supposed to do: display the same controls and static objects once for each record. In effect, the Detail section behaves like a repeater display, except that the Detail section doesn't limit how many records can be displayed at a time. (As you remember, in cases when several records were displayed in a repeater display, you had to scroll up and down to see all of them. By contrast, the Detail section does not have a lower "edge"—it just keeps repeating for every record queried.)

Improving the Appearance of the Report

Truth be told, this is not a very attractive report. Clearly you can change it to make it easier on the eye (and easier to read). For example, you might do the following:

- ☐ Resize the text fields (especially the one bound to TITLE_NAME) to make their contents more readable.
- ☐ Position the text fields so that each record appears as a row of text fields across the page.
- ☐ Place the headings for each column above their corresponding text fields.
- ☐ Change the font to make it more attractive.
- ☐ Remove the border surrounding each text field.

These are exactly the changes you will make in the next part of this exercise. Because aesthetics, readability, and organization are crucial features of a report, you will need to make similar changes in any report you create.

To make the changes,

1. Press Stop.

   The report returns to design mode.

2. Move the static text objects into the Page Header section of the report.

   If you place the labels here, they will appear at the top of each page of the report. Eventually, you will reposition and resize these labels and the text fields so that the correct label appears above its corresponding text field.

3. Stretch the report so that it is about 25 percent wider than before.

   This step is necessary so that you can display all of the text in each field when they are placed side by side.

4. Widen the TITLE_NAME text field so that it can display all the text in each book's title.

5. Move the four text fields to the top of the Detail section, so that they appear in the following order, from left to right: AUTHLNAME, TITLE_NAME, PRICE, PUBLISHER_ID.

6. Move the static text objects to the top of the Page Header section, positioning them so that each one appears above its matching text field.

   For example, the static text object that reads PRICE should appear above the PRICE text field.

7. Click and drag across the Page Header section so that you select all of the static text objects.

8. In the shared Property sheet for these objects, change their FontName property to Arial, their FontSize property to 12, and their FontBold property to True.

9. Select the text fields and change their `FontName` property to `Arial`, their `FontSize` property to `10`, and their `HasBorder` property to `False`.

   The last change is needed to remove the border surrounding the text field, making the report a great deal more readable and attractive.

10. Click the caption for the Detail section of the report.

    A line appears across the title of this section, indicating that you have selected this section of the report (see Figure 7.4).

Figure 7.4.
Selecting the Detail section of the report.

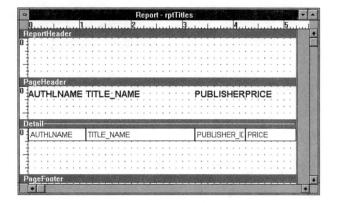

11. Without releasing the mouse button, drag this bar until it is flush against the bottom of the static text labels in the Page Header section.

12. Repeat this process with the Page Footer section, so that this bar is flush against the bottom of the text fields in the Detail section.

13. Repeat the process of dragging the title bar of each section until the Report Header, Page Footer, and Report Footer sections each have effective heights of 0.

> **Note:** When the title bar for one section is flush against another, then you have given one section a height of 0.

The report should now look like Figure 7.5.

14. Save and run the report.

You now see a much better-looking report. By placing the labels in the Page Header section, you need display them only once. This technique works when you have columns of information displayed in this fashion, with one record taking up only a single line across the page. As you shall see, other reports require different ways of labeling information.

Figure 7.5.
The final report.

```
┌─────────────────────────────── Report - rptTitles ──────────────▼│▲│
│  0........1........2........3........4........5.. │▲
│  ReportHeader                                                     │ │
│  PageHeader                                                       │ │
│ 0├ AUTHLNAME  ┌TITLE NAME ········ ·····┌PUBLISHER ID PRICE ······│ │
│  Detail                                                           │ │
│ 0├ AUTHLNAME    TITLE_NAME              PUBLISHER_ID   PRICE       │ │
│  PageFooter                                                       │ │
│  ReportFooter                                                     │ │
│ 0│                                                                │ │
│  │                                                                │ │
│  │                                                                │ │
│ 1│                                                                │ │
│  │                                                                │▼│
│ ◄│─────────────────────────────────────────────────────────────►│
└─────────────────────────────────────────────────────────────────┘
```

Using *SQLLOOKUP* in a Report

Although the report is much more readable than it was in its first incarnation, it has one significant flaw: Publishers are identified only by their ID numbers. Because the whole point of a report is to provide the reader with useful, comprehensible information, this numeric ID is much less useful than the name of the publisher.

As you saw on Day 6, "More About Recordsets," one way to get around this problem on forms is to create a lookup field. After you add a text field, you change its DataSource property to the SQLLOOKUP function, specifying the query string for looking up a single value. The query string must have the following components:

- ☐ The table and column used for the lookup
- ☐ The control in the form or report that holds the primary key value

In this case, the primary key is PUBLISHER_ID. The application should then look up the matching PUBLISHER_NAME value in the PUBLISHERS table.

To display the name of a publisher, instead of its numeric ID, follow these steps:

1. Add a new text field to the Detail section of the report.
2. Move the text field to cover the PUBLISHER_ID field.
3. Change the new text field's Datatype to String, its DataSize to 72, its FontName to Arial, its FontSize to 10, and its HasBorder to False.

   The text field now has the same appearance as the others appearing in the Detail section.

4. For the DataSource property of this new text field, enter
   ```
   =SQLLOOKUP(BOOKS, "SELECT PUBLISHER_NAME FROM PUBLISHERS
   ➥WHERE PUBLISHER_ID = " & STR(PUBLISHER_ID.Value))
   ```
5. Save and run the form.

The original control displaying the PUBLISHER_ID value is still part of the report. Its sole function now, however, is to provide the primary key value needed to look up the publisher's name, a more meaningful piece of information for the reader.

Reports using SQLLOOKUP don't suffer from the same performance problems as forms. As you learned yesterday, when you add a lookup field to a form, the application needs to perform a lookup every time the control containing the primary key value changes. If you scroll to a new record, or enter a new PUBLISHER_ID value for a book, the application stops to perform the lookup. Although it might have taken an extra moment to open the report this time, the delay was not as noticeable as when you were browsing records through a form using SQLLOOKUP.

Limitations of *SQLLOOKUP* in Reports

Although the decrease in performance might not be noticeable in a simple application like yours, it will be very noticeable in reports that access large numbers of records, or that use several lookup fields in the same report. In the former case, the application needs to look up a value in a larger set of records (perhaps numbering in the thousands), requiring greater time for the lookup. In the latter case, the application needs to perform several lookups for each record. In either case, SQLLOOKUP can seriously slow an application's performance when you generate a report with a large number of lookups.

There is an additional reason to avoid using SQLLOOKUP in a report: It might require some debugging if you make a mistake in the query string. For example, if you type the name of a table or column incorrectly, the lookup will fail. Unfortunately, there is no shortcut for debugging the query string in such a case: If you enter the wrong name for a column (for example, PUBLISHER_DESC instead of PUBLISHER_NAME), you must go back to the table description to find the actual name of the column.

For this reason, reports often use a different vehicle for performing lookups: views.

Views in Reports

To recap, a *view* is a database object that helps query columns from one or more tables. In the case of multitable views, the database can perform any number of lookups to find related data from separate tables. The chief disadvantage of multitable views as record sources for forms is that they query data but do not enable the user to edit it. Although you can look at information about books and their publishers through a view, you cannot use the view to enter new information.

Because reports only display data, a view is perfectly designed for performing cross-table lookups. Instead of creating lookup fields, you instead substitute a multitable view as the report's record source. The view can then look up data from several different tables, so that you can easily

display descriptive information in the report. In the case of your first report, if you substitute a view as its record source you can display a publisher's name instead of the publisher's ID number with a minimum of effort.

Because you can easily use a view in place of a table as a report's record source, databases often include views designed solely for reporting. In the case of the Bookstore application, however, you have already created a view that displays descriptive information about books, VW_TITLES. In the next exercise, you will make this view the record source for the report, to simplify the task of performing the necessary lookups.

Substituting a View as the Report's Record Source

First, you'll make some modifications to the view itself, so that it can display both the publisher's name and the type of book. The modified view will then query related information from three tables, TITLES, PUBLISHERS, and BOOK_TYPES. Before you begin, you might want to review Day 3, "Creating a View."

1. Open the Session window for BOOKS.POS and double-click the icon for VW_TITLES.

2. Click and drag the icon for the BOOK_TYPES table into the View Editor window.

3. Create a join between the TYPE_ID columns in both the TITLES and BOOK_TYPES tables.

4. Modify the contents of the Column List area so that the following columns appear in the view: TITLES.AUTHLNAME, TITLES.TITLE_NAME, BOOK_TYPES.TYPE_DESC, and PUBLISHERS.PUBLISHER_NAME.

5. Delete the headings for any of the columns in the view.

6. Save the modified view.

7. Select the report rptTitles and delete the text fields and static objects you added earlier.

8. From the View Editor window for VW_TITLES, drag all of the columns from the Column List area into the report's Detail section.

   Because you are now binding the report to a different record source, Oracle Power Objects asks if you want to make this change. Press OK to continue, and the application creates the now-familiar collection of text fields and their labels.

9. Repeat the same set of modifications to the text fields and static text objects to make them more readable. Additionally, change the label that reads Price to Type.

   The modified report should look like Figure 7.6.

Figure 7.6.

The same report, but with a view as its record source.

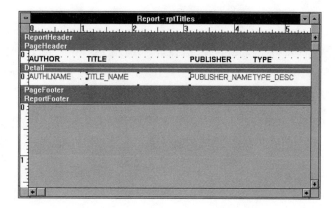

10. Save and run the report.

The new report provides the same information its earlier incarnation did—actually, slightly more, because you added the description of each book's topic. The work involved was much easier than coding the SQL string for SQLLOOKUP, and far more idiot-proof because Oracle Power Objects writes all the SQL code behind the view for you.

Adding More Columns to a Report

Thus far, layout has not been much of a challenge for your report. Because you can fit all of the text fields in a single row across the page, you can create a report that displays information as large tables, with labels appearing above each column of information. Unfortunately, many reports have too many columns to fit in a single row, so you need to find some other ways to make the information in the report just as readable.

In the next exercise, you will add some more columns to the view and then display this extra information in the report. Because the extra columns won't fit in a single row, you must make some important modifications to the report's design. In this case, the emphasis will be on the pricing information about a book, so you will change the layout to emphasize the different prices (retail, wholesale, and promotional) for each book.

1. Open the View editor window for VW_TITLES and add the following columns from the TITLES table to the Column List area: WS_PRICE and PROMOTION_PRICE.

2. Save the view.

3. Widen the Detail section of the report to add space for some new text fields.

4. Drag the columns PRICE, WS_PRICE, and PROMOTION_PRICE from the View Editor window into the report's Detail section.

5. Change the appearance of the new text fields to match the other text fields in the Detail section.

6. Change the following properties of the static text objects labeling the two new fields: FontName to Arial, FontSize to 10, and FontBold to True. In addition, change their Label properties to read Price, Wholesale, and Promotion.

7. Position the three text fields displaying price information and their corresponding labels so that the report looks like Figure 7.7.

Figure 7.7.
The modified report, with pricing information appearing beneath the description of each book.

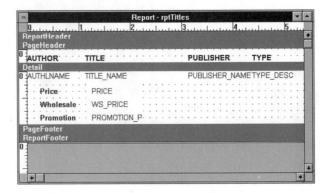

8. Change the TextJustVert property of these same fields and static text objects to Center.

9. Change the height of the Detail section so that there is only a small amount of space between the PROMOTION_PRICE field and the bottom of the section.

   This small amount of white space will act as a separator between each book in the report.

10. Save and run the report.

Although the new report doesn't display the entire record on one line, it is still easy to read. The general description of the book appears at the top, and the pricing information just beneath it, slightly indented. If you want a report that helps you quickly scan through books and their prices, this layout fills the bill.

DO	DON'T

DO create multiline reports when needed.

DO use views as the record source for reports.

DON'T leave out white space that helps visually organize and separate information.

DON'T add information to the view that you don't need. Every report needs a focus, so you should resist the temptation to add any piece of information that might be relevant, from across several base tables used in the view.

Organizing Information in a Report

As attractive as this report is, it does not sort the book titles according to any criteria. What if you want to view the titles alphabetically by author? Or by publisher?

With forms, the primary key value orders records by default. When you browsed books, for example, the records appeared in ascending order based on the values in the TITLE_ID column, the primary key for the TITLES table.

Alternatively, in the case of forms, you can sort records by column values by setting the OrderBy property of the form (or some other bindable container within the form). If you want to view records in alphabetical order by the author's last name, for example, you would set the OrderBy property of the form to AUTHLNAME.

Reports, however, do not have an OrderBy property. This is not an oversight. Reports have built-in functionality for sorting records: *report groups*.

Report Groups

A report group is a way of organizing records by a particular column. If you want to view books by publisher, for example, you would create a report group based on the PUBLISHER_ID values of records in the TITLES table. The report would first display all the books belonging to a particular publisher (specified by PUBLISHER_ID), before printing another set of books belonging to a different publisher.

You could sort records just as easily by category, by creating a report group based on the TYPE_ID column. The report would then display all the books that fall within a particular category (such as all children's books) before printing all the books belonging to a different topic category.

As you might imagine, report groups provide a great deal of flexibility in organizing the information in a report. By specifying any column within a report's record source as the basis of a report group, you can sort the records according to that column.

In fact, as you shall see later, you can use multiple report groups to sort records according to several criteria. For example, you can sort books by publisher with one report group, and then add another report group to separate all the different types of books belonging to each publishing house. By nesting report groups in this fashion, you see all the reference books published by an author, and then all non-fiction books, and so on.

When you create a report group, you want to give the reader some clue as to how the information is being sorted. Ideally, you would like to create a header for each section, so that when you move to a new value for the report group column (for example, a new PUBLISHER_ID value), the report displays a new heading, or footer, or some other indicator. In Oracle Power Objects reports,

every report group adds a Group Header and Group Footer section to a report, so that you can place these indicators in the body of the report. Figure 7.8 shows the placement of group headers and footers in a report.

Figure 7.8.

Group Header and Group Footer sections added to a report.

Group Header and Footer added when you create a report group

For example, if you sort books by publisher, you might want to print the publisher's name as the header for each new grouping of books within the report (see Figure 7.9). You would do this by adding a text field to the Group Header section to display the name of the publisher. Before showing all books published by Chatham House, the report could then display the publisher's name, Chatham House, above these books.

Figure 7.9.

Sorting records by publisher in an Oracle Power Objects report.

If this seems slightly confusing at first, don't worry. Like many features of Oracle Power Objects, the theory sounds more complicated than the practice. In the next exercise, you will create a report group that sorts books by publishers, exactly as described here. As you will see, working with report groups in this fashion is much easier than you might expect, providing you with powerful and easy-to-use tools for designing reports.

Working with Report Groups

In this first exercise, you will create a report group to sort books by publisher. Before the books belonging to a particular publisher are printed, the publisher's name will appear as a header for the new section of the report.

1. Select the report rptTitles.
2. From the Object palette, select the Report Group tool.
3. Click anywhere on the report.

   Two new sections appear, the Group Header and the Group Footer. You'll add the name of the publisher to the Group Header section, and resize the Group Footer until it disappears from the report.

4. Select the Group Header section and open its Property sheet.
5. For the GroupCol property, enter PUBLISHER_NAME.

   This property identifies the column used to sort records in a report group. If you had wanted to sort titles by topic, you would have entered the name of the TYPE_ID column as the setting for this property.

6. Drag the PUBLISHER_NAME text field from the Detail section into the Group Header.
7. Click and drag the right edge of this text field to about 50 percent of its width.
8. Change the FontSize property of the PUBLISHER_NAME field to 18.
9. Resize the Group Header section until its lower edge is flush against the bottom of the PUBLISHER_NAME field.

   This step avoids leaving the publisher's name floating too far above the list of books published by that company.

10. Resize the Group Footer so that it has an effective height of zero.
11. Delete the labels (that is, the static text objects) from the Page Header section of the report, and then resize this section to give it a height of zero.
12. Select the report and change its title to Publishers and Books.
13. Save and run the report.

Now, instead of just a list of titles, you can view all the books published by each company, as shown in Figure 7.10.

Figure 7.10.

The Publishers and Books report, using a report group to sort book records.

Publishers and Books		
Chatham House		
Steele	Kiss Me Dead	Mystery
Price	4.99	
Wholesale	2.49	
Promotion	4.5	
Throckmorton	An English Garden	Reference
Price	9.99	
Wholesale	5	
Promotion	8	
Enderby Press		
MacAvoy	A Boy's Life in New Zealand	General non-fiction
Price	12.99	
Wholesale	6	

Using Nested Report Groups

As described earlier, you can apply multiple sorting criteria by nesting report groups. In the next exercise, you will modify the existing report so that it sorts by publisher first, and then by book category.

To create nested report groups, you continue to add new report groups to the report. The first one you create identifies the first column to sort by, the second report group identifies the next column to sort by, and so on. Theoretically, you can have any number of nested report groups. Practically, it's rare to find more than four or five groups within the same report.

With this information in mind, you're ready to create your first nested report group.

1. If the report rptTitles is still running, press the Stop button.

2. Add a new report group to rptTitles.

   The name of the new report group's Group Header section is GroupHeader2, to signify that it was the second one added. Similarly, the new Group Footer section is GroupFooter2.

3. Select GroupHeader2 and change its GroupCol property to TYPE_DESC.

   This step tells the application to use the TYPE_DESC column as the sorting criterion for this report group. The report still sorts first by PUBLISHER_NAME, however.

4. Move the TYPE_DESC field from the Detail section into the new GroupHeader2 section.

5. Change the field's FontSize property to 12 and its FontBold property to True.

6. Resize the second Group Footer so that it has a height of zero.

7. Resize the second Group Header so that its bottom edge is flush against the bottom of the TYPE_DESC field.

8. Save and run the report.

The report now sorts books by two criteria, publisher and topic (see Figure 7.11).

Figure 7.11.
Two levels of report groups in the report.

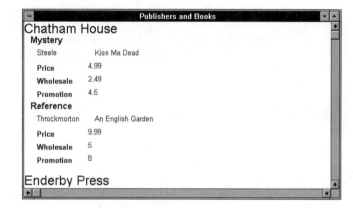

At this point, you might add yet another sorting criterion: author, price, or whatever. Although another level of report group nesting might be overkill for this report, many other reports can easily use several levels of report groups. A listing of employees, for example, might sort by department, manager, job, and salary level.

Tips for Using Report Groups

Although report groups can be powerful tools, you can easily misuse them. The following are some tips for working with report groups:

☐ Report groups often contain lookup fields, because the columns used for sorting records often require lookups into other tables for descriptive information. If you had used the TITLES table for this report's record source, the report would have used the PUBLISHER_ID column to sort by publisher and the TYPE_ID column to sort by category. You would then have to create lookup fields to get the names of publishers, and the description of each book category.

Therefore, if you plan to create a report that requires a large number of lookups, you should design a view to be used as the report's record source. This will reduce the hassle of trying to create a large number of SQLLOOKUP fields to display descriptive information in the report.

7

☐ Don't pack too many controls into a Group Header or Group Footer section if you plan to nest report groups. You can easily create a lot of visual confusion by having multiple report groups displaying a large number of fields.

☐ To clarify the separation between report groups, you might use a line, or indent the second level of the report group. In the report you created, you would then indent the controls displaying the type of book published by each other. You can also use a larger font for controls in the top-level report group.

☐ If you are nesting report groups, don't improvise. Think about the order in which you want to add new report groups to specify additional levels of sort criteria. Moving around nested report groups is not easy, so a little forethought can save you a lot of work later.

Adding a Chart to a Report

Frequently, a chart in a report can help explain what mere words cannot. Oracle Power Objects has a special chart control that you can add to a form or a report. When applied properly, the chart can use information queried from the database to depict information relevant to the entire report, or just one part of it. For example, you can create a chart that displays the number of employees in each salary range throughout the entire company, or on a department-by-department basis.

In many respects, the chart acts like a bindable container, but it is in fact a bindable control. Like a form or a report, a chart control has RecordSource and RecSrcSession properties. Unlike a form or report, however, a chart control cannot contain other objects.

Not surprisingly, chart controls have several additional properties that determine the contents and appearance of the chart. These properties will make more sense after a brief overview of the steps needed to create a chart control.

1. Choose a drawing tool from the Object palette to create a new chart control.

2. Select a chart style (pie chart, bar graph, and so on).

3. Specify the table or view that provides the data for the chart.

4. Specify the columns in the record source to be depicted in the chart. At least one of the columns must use a numeric data type (Number or Long).

5. Choose the legend or labels to display in the chart.

Adding the Chart

With these steps in mind, you're ready to create your first chart, which you will add to the report you've been developing. The chart will display the number of books published by each company, so it will appear in the report header for publisher information. Before you can create this chart, however, you must first add a column to the PUBLISHERS table.

1. Open the Session window for BOOKS.POS and open the Table Editor window for PUBLISHERS.
2. Click in the Column Name cell for the blank row appearing at the bottom.
3. Enter NUM_BOOKS as the name of the column.
4. Select Integer as its Datatype.
5. Save the modified table, and run it.

    The Table Browser window appears, through which you can enter values for this new column.

6. Enter the following values for NUM_BOOKS:

PUBLISHER_NAME	NUM_BOOKS
Maximum Books	1
Enigma Books	1
Logos Press	1
Rollercoaster Books	1
Chatham House	2
Enderby Press	1
Smart Books	0

7. Press Commit to commit the changes to the database.

The table now includes information about the number of books published by each publisher. You can add a chart displaying this information to the report.

1. Select the report rptTitles.
2. Expand the Report Footer section.
3. Select the Chart Control drawing tool from the Object palette and add a chart to the right side of the Report Header section.

    The report should now look like Figure 7.12.

4. Open the chart control's Property sheet and enter BOOKS for RecSrcSession, and PUBLISHERS for RecordSource.

    The chart can now find the data it needs.

Figure 7.12.
The new chart added to the report.

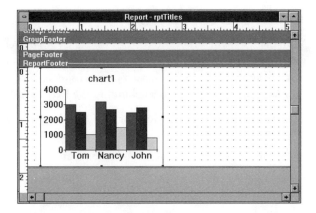

5. Scroll up until you find the chart-related properties of the control, near the top of the list in the Property sheet.

6. From the drop-down list of styles appearing for the ChartStyle property, select Horizontal Bar.

7. Enter PUBLISHER_NAME for the ChartXCol property of the control.

   This property specifies which column to use for plotting the x-axis of the chart.

8. Enter NUM_BOOKS for the ChartYCols property.

   This property specifies which columns will form the y-axis of the chart. In the case of a vertical or horizontal bar chart, the control will display a bar for each column. For example, if you were displaying both salary and commission information in a bar graph, the chart would display two bars (one for salary, the other for commission) for every employee.

 Note: All of the columns used in ChartYCols must have a numeric data type (Number or Long).

9. Save and run the report.

10. Scroll down to the end of the report.

The graph now shows the number of books published by each company, a useful piece of information if you are investigating which company's titles are the better sellers in the store.

Using Another Chart Style

This graph could just as easily be a pie chart instead of a bar graph. All you need to change is the ChartStyle property. Although there is no x-axis in a pie chart, you nonetheless need to specify the categories of information to be charted: the names of employees, the titles of books, the names of publishers, and so on. To create a pie chart, therefore, you do not need to change the ChartXCol property, which is currently set to PUBLISHER_NAME.

Every chart also needs some numeric values to plot the height of the bar, or the width of a slice of the pie chart. In a chart control, you specify one or more columns of numeric information through the ChartYCols property. Again, you do not need to change the setting for this property, which is now NUM_BOOKS. Figure 7.13 shows how the same values queried from the NUM_BOOKS column are displayed in different types of charts.

Figure 7.13.

The same numeric values from the NUM_BOOKS column determine the height of a bar or the width of a slice of a pie chart.

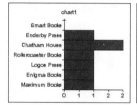 

Labeling a Chart

To make the chart more readable, however, you need to make some alterations. Specifically, after you convert the chart format to a pie chart, you will add a caption and some labels to identify the different sections of the chart.

1. Stop running the report and open the Property sheet for the chart control.
2. For the ChartStyle property, select Pie.

   The chart control now displays a pie chart instead of a bar graph. Next, you will add a caption to explain what the chart depicts.
3. For the Label property, enter Number of Books Published.
4. For the ChartLabelStyle, select Names.

   Now, when you run the chart, the name of each publisher, queried from the PUBLISHER_NAME column, labels each slice of the pie chart.
5. Save and run the report.

The chart control should now look like Figure 7.14.

Figure 7.14.
The new pie chart.

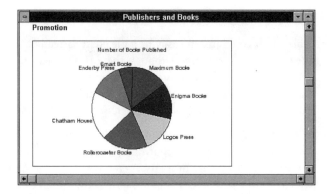

Alternatively, you can show a legend for the chart, instead of labels next to each section of the pie. If you were to set the `ChartShowLegend` property to `True`, the chart would display a legend for all columns plotted in the y-axis. For example, if you displayed both the salary and commission for each employee in a bar graph, the legend would show the colors used for the bars depicting salary and commission. Figure 7.15 shows a legend in a chart.

Figure 7.15.
A legend in place of labels.

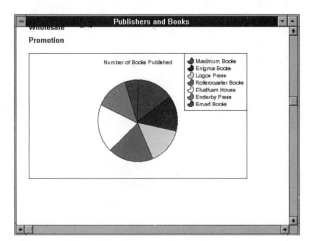

Chart Control Properties

Now that you have worked with chart controls, the properties specific to this type of object should make more sense. The properties in Table 7.2 appear only on chart controls, where they determine the chart's appearance.

Table 7.2. Properties of chart controls.

Property	Description
ChartStyle	Determines the style of chart displayed in the control (vertical bar, horizontal bar, pie, or line).
ChartXCol	Specifies the column used for plotting the x-axis. In other words, this property determines the number of records displayed in the chart. You must set this property for all charts, including pie charts (even though they do not display an x-axis).
ChartYCols	Specifies one or more columns used for plotting the y-axis. You must set this property for all charts, including pie charts (which can only use one y-axis value). The columns designated for this property must use numeric values.
ChartRowCount	Sets the maximum number of records displayed in the chart. The column used to query these records is specified through the ChartXCol property.
ChartAutoFormat	Determines whether the application automatically sizes the y-axis for bar and line charts. If set to True, the maximum value in the y-axis is the maximum value found for all records. If set to False, you must set the maximum and minimum values for the y-axis through the ChartMinVal and ChartMaxVal properties.
ChartMinVal	Determines the minimum value for the y-axis for a chart. By default, this is set to zero. If the ChartAutoFormat property is set to True, the application overrides the setting for ChartMinVal, using 0 if there is no value found in a record less than zero.
ChartMaxVal	Determines the maximum value for the y-axis. The setting for this property is ignored unless the ChartAutoFormat property is set to False.
ChartShowLegend	Determines whether or not a chart displays a legend.
ChartLegendHAlign	Determines the corner, right or left, in which the legend will appear.
ChartLegendVAlign	Determines the corner, top or bottom, in which the legend will appear.
ChartLineStyle	Specifies the style of lines displayed in a chart.
ChartShowGrid	Determines whether the chart displays a grid.
ChartPieCircle	Determines whether a pie chart appears as a circle (True) or as an oval (False).
ChartGap	In a bar chart, specifies the number of pixels between bars representing different records. For example, if you set this property to 4, a

continues

Table 7.2. continued

Property	Description
	gap of four pixels would appear between the pairs of bars depicting salary and commission for each employee.
ChartOverlap	Determines the number of pixels of overlap for bars in a bar chart, if there are multiple columns specified in the ChartYCols property. For example, if this property were set to 4, the bar depicting salary for an employee would overlap the bar depicting commission by four pixels.
ChartStacked	Specifies whether you want multiple bars in a bar chart to be sandwiched together in one large bar, or kept as separate but adjacent bars.

Although this might seem like a large, confusing array of properties, remember that not all will apply to every chart. Table 7.3 summarizes some of the important properties needed to create each type of chart.

Table 7.3. Chart styles and their properties.

Chart Type	Necessary Properties	Description
Vertical and horizontal bar	ChartXCol	Defines the x-axis. For each record, the chart plots one region on the x-axis.
	ChartYCols	Specifies the columns to be displayed as bars along the y-axis. For each column specified, a separate bar is displayed for each record. You can determine the spacing and positioning of the bars through the ChartGap, ChartOverlap, and ChartStacked properties.
	Other	You can use the ChartShowLegend, ChartLabelStyle, and associated properties to display labels or legends for each column depicted in the chart. The ChartRowCount property can limit the number of records to the maximum that can be shown along the space allotted within the control to the x-axis. The ChartShowGrid property specifies the type of grid to display within the chart.

Chart Type	Necessary Properties	Description
Pie	ChartXCol	Indicates the columns used to query records for the chart. Each record is depicted as a "slice" of the pie.
	ChartYCols	Specifies the column used to size each slice of the pie. You can use only one column for ChartYCols in a pie chart.
	ChartPieCircle	Determines whether the pie appears as a flat circle or as an oval (a circular pie tilted slightly to appear three-dimensional).
	Other	Again, you can use various properties to determine how to add labels or a legend to the pie chart.
Line	ChartXCol	Defines the x-axis. For each record, the chart plots one point on the x-axis.
	ChartYCols	Specifies the columns to be displayed as separate lines in the chart. For each column specified, a new line appears in the chart.
	Other	Various properties define the labels or legend, and ChartShowGrid specifies the type of grid to display.

Later, you will add another chart to a report. However, that's enough on charts for now—it's time to move on to techniques for designing more sophisticated reports.

Master-Detail Reports

So far, you have used SQLLOOKUP and views to perform lookups into foreign tables. However, in many cases, you might want a third option. As noted earlier, SQLLOOKUP requires that you code a SQL query string, a technique prone to human error. In addition, if you want to add several lookup fields to a report, you need to write a query string for each lookup field's DataSource property. The more SQLLOOKUP fields, the more time you will spend decoding your own query strings.

Although views are a more error-proof solution, they add to the overhead of maintaining the database. Because views do not automatically change to reflect modifications to their base tables, older views might no longer work. In addition, every view you add to the database increases the general clutter of what might be a database already crowded with tables, sequences, synonyms, indexes, and other views.

7

Master-Detail Reports and Lookups

When you created a master-detail form on Day 5, "Master-Detail Relationships," you learned how to query related data from multiple tables with a minimum of fuss. In reports, you frequently want the same type of shortcut to perform a large number of lookups. For example, if you print a report listing all books in stock, you might want to print the name, address, and phone number of the publisher of each book. Instead of creating several lookup fields, or designing a view for this purpose, you can use the techniques you learned to create a master-detail form and apply them to a report.

Creating a Master-Detail Report

As before, you will add a container to hold detail reports (in this case, an embedded form) to another container (a report). Once again, the application needs three pieces of information to create the master-detail relationship, as specified through three properties:

☐ The name of the primary key column in the master recordset (`LinkColumn`)

☐ The name of the foreign key column in the detail recordset (`LinkDetailColumn`)

☐ The name of the form bound to the master record source (`LinkMasterForm`)

The primary and foreign keys are easy to set up. After you add the embedded form, you specify the column names for the primary and foreign keys. The tricky part is knowing the container to specify for the `LinkMasterForm` property.

At first glance, you might guess that the container in question is the report itself. Consider for a moment, however, how a master-detail relationship should work: For every master record, you should display one or more detail records. As the application moves the pointer to a different master record, it should then display a different detail record.

Defining the report as the container for `LinkMasterForm` would be a mistake, albeit an understandable one. The report never has a single record displayed at a time; in fact, it's designed to display many records simultaneously. Instead, you need to use a section of the report that displays only one record at a time: either the Group Header section or the Group Footer section.

Using Report Groups as the Master

When you created a report group, you needed to set the `GroupCol` property of the Group Header section. This property specified the column used for sorting records. For example, when you specified `PUBLISHER_ID` as the column for `GroupCol`, the report sorted all books by their publishers. The column specified for `GroupCol`, therefore, makes an ideal primary key; for each new value in the GroupCol column, the report moves to a new unique key value.

Therefore, you will create a new report for displaying customer purchases, using the techniques for creating a master-detail report. The report, which will show how many books of each type a customer has purchased, might help a bookstore plan a sale targeting its best customers.

The report will have the following components:

- [ ] Records in the Detail section queried from CUST_PURCHASES
- [ ] A report group based on the CUSTOMER_ID column
- [ ] An embedded form displaying the customer's name and phone number

The embedded form will appear in the Group Header, which will act as the master container in the master-detail relationship.

1. With the Application window for BOOKS.POA selected, create a new report.

2. Give the new report a name of `rptCustPurchases` and a label of `Customer Purchases`.

3. Open the Session window for BOOKS.POS and drag the icon for `CUST_PURCHASES` into the Detail section of the report.

   The three text fields that appear—bound to `CUSTOMER_ID`, `TYPE_ID`, and `NUM_BOUGHT`—don't communicate very much to the reader. The report needs some explanatory information for the codes in `TYPE_ID` and `CUSTOMER_ID`.

   The information about each customer (name and phone number) will appear in the Group Header, yet to be added. At this point, however, you can add a field that displays a description of each book type.

4. Add a new text field to the Detail section.

5. Change the `Datatype` property of the text field to `String` and its `DataSize` property to `64`.

6. For the `DataSource` property of this new lookup field, enter

   ```
   =SQLLOOKUP(BOOKS, "SELECT TYPE_DESC FROM BOOK_TYPES
   ➥WHERE TYPE_ID = " & STR(TYPE_ID.Value))
   ```

   The new text field can now look up the description of a book topic that matches the numeric ID displayed in the `TYPE_ID` field.

7. From the Object palette, select the Report Group drawing tool and click the report.

   New Group Header and Group Footer sections appear in the report.

8. Move the `CUSTOMER_ID` text field into the new Group Header section, and set the `GroupCol` property of the Group Header to `CUSTOMER_ID`.

9. Using the Embedded Form drawing tool from the Object palette, add an embedded form to the Group Header.

10. In the BOOKS session window, double-click the CUSTOMERS table to open its Table Editor window.

11. In the Table Editor window, select the columns FNAME, LNAME, and PHONE.

12. Drag these columns into the embedded form.

13. Move and resize various objects within the report so that it looks like Figure 7.16.

Figure 7.16.

The new report, with the completed Detail and Group Header sections.

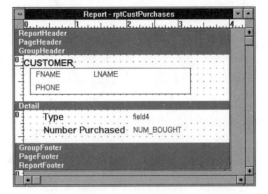

As you can see in the Detail section, the TYPE_ID field is covered by the lookup field. Because the reader only cares about the description of each book category, you can hide the TYPE_ID field. For the same reason, the CUSTOMER_ID field in the Group Header is covered by the embedded form.

Now that you have finished designing the appearance of the report, you can set the master-detail relationship between the customer records in the embedded form and the customer purchase records in the report.

14. Select the embedded form and set the following properties:

Property	Setting
LinkColumn	CUSTOMER_ID
LinkDetailColumn	CUSTOMER_ID
LinkMasterForm	GroupHeader

15. Save and run the report (see Figure 7.17).

The new report now presents an easy way to examine customer buying habits.

16. Press Stop.

DO	DON'T

DO create master-detail reports to simplify lookups.

DO add explanatory information to reports.

DO add charts and graphics to illustrate key points in the report.

DO use the Group Header section to sort records.

DON'T create a master-detail relationship when you need to query only one or two columns of information. In these cases, SQLLOOKUP is easier to use.

DON'T add so much explanatory information that it obscures the topic of the report. Reports can provide too much information or too little.

DON'T display so many graphics that it takes too long to run the report.

DON'T add so many levels of report groups that keeping track of the different sections of the report becomes hard. In cases where you have a large number of records to display, having several report groups can slow report generation.

Figure 7.17.
The completed Customer Purchases report.

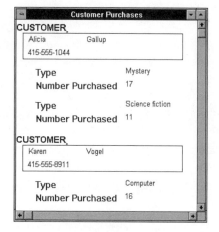

Filtering Records in a Report

An important part of report design is determining the type of information displayed in the report, and how it appears to the reader. Instead of incomprehensible ID numbers, for example, you might prefer to show descriptions of what these numbers mean. When you create a Group Header, you need to set it off somehow from the Detail section, so that the reader can tell easily where one group of records ends and another begins.

Another important consideration is the amount of information displayed in the report. The reports you created query all the records from a table or view, which in the case of these reports did not present much of a problem.

However, what if the table has a very large number of records, and you want to view only a small number of them? For example, if the TITLES table had thousands of books, how would you create a report that displayed only the computer books?

Clearly, you need some way to filter records in a report. There are two ways to apply a condition to a form's recordset:

☐ By setting the `DefaultCondition` property. The setting for this property is the `WHERE` clause specifying the condition (for example, `PRICE > 10`, or `AUTHLNAME='Smith'`).

☐ By calling the `QueryWhere()` method. This method requeries the container's recordset, applying the condition passed to the method as an argument.

Unlike forms, reports do not have a `QueryWhere()` method, but they do have a `DefaultCondition` property. You can set a condition when you design the report so that it queries only some of the records from a table or view. In addition, through method code, you can specify a new condition for `DefaultCondition` at runtime.

In the next exercise, you will create a form through which you enter a condition to be applied to a report. After you enter a valid condition through a text field, the application opens the report, applying the condition to its recordset.

1. Add a new form to the BOOKS.POA application.

2. Give the report a `Name` of `frmReportFilter` and a `Label` of `Apply Conditions`.

3. Add a text field to the form with a `Name` of `fldCondition`, a `Datatype` of `String`, and a `DataSize` of `128`.

4. Add a pushbutton to the form with a `Label` of `View Report`.

5. In the `Click()` method of the report, enter

```
' Apply the new condition to the report
rptTitles.DefaultCondition = fldCondition.Value
' Display the report.
rptTitles.OpenWindow()
```

6. Resize and reposition the form and its objects so that it looks like Figure 7.18.

Figure 7.18.
The Apply Conditions form.

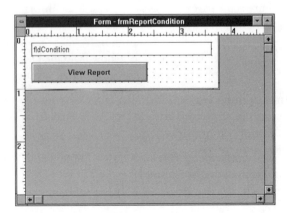

7. In the application's `OnLoad()` method, delete any leftover code and enter

    `frmReportCondition.OpenWindow()`

8. Save and run the application.

    The filter form appears, ready for you to enter a condition and open the report.

9. In the text field, enter `PRICE > 7`.

    This condition tells the application to query only those books that cost more than $7.00.

10. Press the View Report pushbutton.

    As expected, the report now shows books with a price of more than $7.00.

11. Close the report and select the Apply Conditions form.

12. In the text field, enter `PUBLISHER_NAME = 'Enigma Books'`.

13. Press the View Reports pushbutton.

    The report appears again, this time displaying only those titles published by Enigma Books.

14. Press Stop to end this exercise.

Tips on Report Design

Before you finish this lesson, here are some tips on designing reports:

☐ To display the page number of a report, add a text field to the Page Header or Page Footer section of the report. The field must have the `Datatype` integer, and the following setting for its `DataSource` property:

`=PAGENUM()`

☐ Use fonts that might be available on a wide range of systems, such as Arial and Courier.

☐ Use bitmaps and picture controls sparingly in reports, because displaying these graphics can slow down the process of printing the report.

☐ Repeater displays are rarely useful in a report. The scrollbar is meaningless because the user cannot do anything with it. Worse, if the repeater display has a large number of records in its recordset, it will be unable to show many of them.

☐ Similarly, many other controls are not appropriate for reports, because the user cannot push, press, select, or otherwise interact with them. The following controls, therefore, are not recommended for use in a report: pushbuttons, combo boxes, list boxes, pop-up lists, radio buttons (and their associated radio button frames), OLE controls, scrollbars, and current row pointers.

7

☐ Except in rare instances, text fields in a report will have their `HasBorder` property set to `False`. Otherwise, the report appears as an odd grid of rectangles of varying widths, all in different positions and not always justified.

☐ Using lines, rectangles, and ovals, you can create reports that mimic printed forms. For example, you can create a report that looks like a purchase order and displays a single record from the tables containing the information about a particular book. You can make the report accessible from the form used to enter the information for the purchase order, by pressing a pushbutton or some other control that opens the report. To limit the report to the purchase order displayed in the form, use some unique identifier (such as the purchase order number) as part of a query string applied to the `DefaultCondition` property. The user can then print a hard copy of the purchase order.

Summary

Today you learned about the following features of reports:

☐ Reports are bindable containers that, like forms, have `RecordSource` and `RecSrcSession` properties.

☐ To bind a report to a record source, you can use the same drag-and-drop techniques for binding a form.

☐ Unlike a form, a report is divided into several functionally distinct sections.

☐ Controls placed in the Detail section repeat once for each record displayed in the report.

☐ A report group organizes information in a report. When you add a report group, the report then includes new Group Header and Group Footer sections.

☐ To make a report group work, you must select a column in the report's record source to use for sorting records. You identify this column through the `GroupCol` property of the Group Header section.

☐ To apply multiple sorting criteria, you create nested report groups within the same report.

☐ To display information looked up from foreign tables, you can create a view as the form's record source, or you can add lookup fields (that is, text fields that use a `SQLLOOKUP` query as their record source).

☐ Reports can display master-detail relationships. The detail container must appear in either the Group Header or the Group Footer section, and it must identify the Group Header or Group Footer in its `LinkMasterForm` property.

☐ Charts are common features of reports. Oracle Power Objects reports use a chart control for displaying bar graphs, pie charts, and line graphs.

☐ You can use the `DefaultCondition` property to filter the records displayed in a report.

What Comes Next?

When you used SQLLOOKUP to create a lookup field, you discovered that you can use an expression as a control's DataSource. In this case, the expression defined a query. The expression could define just as easily a calculation whose result becomes the value displayed in the control. This kind of calculation, called a *derived value*, is one of the most widely used features of Oracle Power Objects. Tomorrow you will learn the many ways in which you can use derived values, as well as some new techniques for formatting information displayed in a control.

Q&A

Q Can you create multiple levels of master-detail relationships in a report?

A Yes, but only by adding multiple embedded forms in the same group header or footer area. One embedded form is the master, while the other is its detail. Unfortunately, this technique limits you to a one-to-one master-detail relationship between the two embedded forms.

Q Can I apply conditions to a report before I run it?

A Yes, by setting the report's DefaultCondition property before you open the report. This approach lets you apply conditions entered by the user or set by the application.

Q How can I make a chart apply only to a particular group of records?

A Because chart controls have the master-detail properties shared with bound containers (LinkMasterForm, LinkMasterColumn, and LinkDetailColumn), you can make the chart a detail of a report group in which the chart appears. You would enter GroupHeader (or some other name of the report group) for LinkMasterForm, and the primary and foreign key columns for LinkMasterColumn and LinkDetailColumn, respectively.

Workshop

The Workshop consists of quiz question to help you solidify your understanding of the material covered and exercises to give you experience in using what you've learned. Try and understand the quiz and exercises before you go on to tomorrow's lesson.

Quiz

1. What section of the report repeats once per record? Once per value found in a particular column?

2. When you create a master-detail report, what column do you specify for the LinkColumn property of the container displaying detail records? For example, which column did you specify for the embedded form added to the rptTitles report?

3. How many columns must you use in a graph?

4. When you need to perform a lookup in a report, what is the chief disadvantage of using SQLLOOKUP? Of using a specially designed view as the report's record source?

5. How would you create a report that printed only one record?

Exercise

Create a graph in the Group Header section of rptTitles that repeats each time a new publisher is displayed. The graph should apply to only the currently displayed publisher, not to all the publishers described in the PUBLISHERS table.

To complete this exercise, you need to use the LinkColumn, LinkDetailColumn, and LinkMasterForm properties of the chart control.

Quiz Answers

1. The Detail section repeats once per record. The Group Header and Group Footer sections repeat once per value found in the column specified in that section's GroupCol property. For example, if you make PUBLISHER_ID the column used for GroupCol, the Group Header and Group Footer sections repeat once for every value found in that column. Keep in mind, however, that this value might be found in several records. For example, several books might share the same publisher, but the Group Header and Group Footer sections will repeat once per unique PUBLISHER_ID value found in the TITLES table.

2. You need to use the same column specified for the GroupCol property of the report group in which the chart appears.

3. At least two. One column must always be specified for the ChartXCol property, and at least one for the ChartYCols property.

4. When you write the query string for SQLLOOKUP, you can mistype some element of the query, which then causes the entire query to fail. You must then debug the query instead of moving on to the next development task. Although views are less prone to human error, they add to the overhead of maintaining the database. Additionally, they are vulnerable to being "broken" when the base tables behind the view change.

5. By setting the report's DefaultCondition property to a query string that is assured to return only a single record. Normally, you accomplish this task by using some unique identifier of the record (such as the value in its primary key column) as part of the query condition.

Derived Values

Overview

Today, you learn about the following topics:

- [ ] Derived value calculations
- [ ] Derived values and strings
- [ ] Derived values and dates
- [ ] Aggregate functions
- [ ] Limitations of derived values
- [ ] Format masks

Frequently, you want to display the result of a calculation in a form or report. For example, you would need a calculation to show the user

- [ ] The number of days between the entry date and ship date for an order
- [ ] The dollar amount of a discount, calculated from the percentage off the normal retail price
- [ ] The dollar amount in sales tax for a purchase
- [ ] The total value of all line items in an invoice
- [ ] The percentage of customers that buy computer books
- [ ] The full name of a customer, combined from the text fields displaying the person's last and first name

At first glance, where you perform this calculation in Oracle Power Objects might not be obvious. Should you perform the calculation in a method? Several methods execute when the value in a control changes, so perhaps this is the place. Part of the method code could set the value of a text field or some other control, based on the new value.

However, although several such methods exist (for example, PostChange() and Validate()), methods are not the right place to perform the calculation. The answer lies in the DataSource property of a control.

SQLLOOKUP as an Expression

As you have seen already, you can use the DataSource property to define the contents of a field as the result of an expression. When you created a lookup field, the control used the SQLLOOKUP function to query a value from a table. For example, to show the name of a book's publisher, you entered a SQLLOOKUP statement that queried the value from the PUBLISHERS.PUBLISHER_NAME column to match the title's PUBLISHER_ID value. This statement looked like this:

```
=SQLLOOKUP(BOOKS, "SELECT PUBLISHER_NAME FROM PUBLISHERS
➥WHERE PUBLISHER_ID = " & PUBLISHER_ID.Value)
```

Although you might not think of this SQLLOOKUP statement as an expression, in fact it is. Generally speaking, an *expression* is any type of calculation that returns a value, so a SQLLOOKUP statement certainly qualifies.

When you enter any expression as the DataSource property of a control, you are using a *derived value*. Instead of querying a value from a column in a table or a view or relying on the user to enter a value, a control derives its value from the contents of other controls. To put this concept in terms that better fit Oracle Power Objects, the Value property of the control depends on the Value property of other controls, and the calculation that derives this value is defined in the control's DataSource property. (See Figure 8.1.)

Figure 8.1.

A control uses the Value *property of two other controls to set its own* Value *property.*

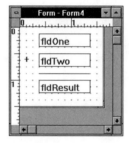

When you look at the DataSource property of a control, you can see that it includes the following options:

- ☐ =Derived, the result of a derived value calculation.
- ☐ The name of a column to which the control is bound. The list in the DataSource property includes all columns in the table or view to which the container is bound.
- ☐ Unbound, meaning that the control's value is neither queried from a column, nor calculated according to a derived value expression.

If you create a new text field through the Object palette, its default setting for DataSource is Unbound. As described in detail on Day 4, "Connecting a Form to a Record Source," you can use several drag-and-drop techniques to bind a control to a column, or you can type in the name of the column for its DataSource property.

If you enter any statement beginning with an equal sign (=), the application interprets it as a derived value calculation. The expression can be simple, such as adding the Value property of two different fields. Or it can be complex, involving several numeric operations and the contents of many different controls. Additionally, as you shall see in an exercise near the end of this lesson, you can use the settings for properties other than Value in a derived value calculation.

To illustrate all of these facets of derived values, you will create a form for entering book orders. The form will have the following components:

☐ The main form, displaying global information about the order (an order number, date entered, date received, and so on)

☐ A repeater display showing all the books ordered

☐ An embedded form displaying customer information

Before you can build this form, you need to perform a little housework on the application and the database. By now, you have created a large number of forms for all the exercises in previous lessons, and it's time to start deleting those that will not be part of the final application. In addition, you must create the tables to store data about book orders. Because the form will be displaying a master-detail relationship between the order (master) and its line items (details), you will be creating two tables.

Before you delete all these forms, you should make a backup copy of BOOKS.POA. This copy will keep all the forms intact for your reference, so that you can return to them when you want to see how to perform some development tasks illustrated in an earlier lesson.

Deleting Forms from the Application

To remove the excess forms from the application, follow these steps:

1. Open the Application window and select the form frmFirstForm.

2. Press the Cut button.

   A dialog box appears, warning you that the action you are about to take (deleting the form from the application) is irreversible.

3. Press OK to delete the form.

4. In addition, delete the following forms from the application:

   frmPublishers
   frmLookup
   frmMD2
   frmMD3a
   frmMD3b
   frmMD4
   frmMD5
   frmMD6
   frmReportCondition

Now the application should run faster, because it does not have to load the extra forms into memory.

Creating the Tables for Book Orders

8

Next, you will create the tables needed for storing information about book orders. To relate information in these tables for the master-detail relationship, an ORDER_ID column will appear in both tables.

1. Select the Session window for BOOKS.POS and open a connection to the database.

2. Create a new table and name it ORDERS.

3. Add the following columns to the ORDERS table:

Name	Data type	Size	Not Null
ORDER_ID	Number		
CUSTOMER_ID	Number		Yes
DATE_ENTERED	Date		Yes
DATE_RECEIVED	Date		
DATE_PURCHASED	Date		
RECEIVED_FLAG	Number		
PURCHASED_FLAG			
EMPLOYEE_ID	Number		Yes
NOTES	Varchar2	1000	

4. Set ORDER_ID as the primary key for this table.

5. Press Save to save this table to the database.

   The new table, ORDERS, now appears in the BOOKS session as part of the database.

6. Create a new table and name it ORDERS_ITEMS.

7. Add the following columns to the ORDERS_ITEMS table:

Name	Data type	Precision
ORDER_ID	Number	
TITLE_ID	Number	
QUANTITY	Number	
DISCOUNT	Float	2

   In this case, you do not want to set one of the columns (namely, ORDER_ID) as the primary key for the table. Because an order can include multiple books, you do not want to apply the UNIQUE constraint to the ORDER_ID column, which is part of a primary key's definition.

8. Save the new table to the database.

At this point, it would be easier to enter the data for an order through the form you will build, instead of entering test data through the Table Browser window. Therefore, you'll leave the session for a moment while you build the new form for entering book orders.

The Book Orders Form

This new form will make it easy for any employee to enter a book order for a customer. In addition to displaying both the order and its line items in a master-detail relationship, the form will have the following features:

☐ The employee must enter the date the customer made the order. If for some reason an impatient customer calls to complain that he is still waiting for his book order, you need to have this information handy.

☐ The employee must enter an employee ID number. Whenever an employee enters an order, you want her to identify herself for the sake of accountability within the store.

☐ When you enter a book for the order, you should also be able to apply a discount to that title. If you want to reward a customer for repeat business, or if you want to apply a sale price for the book, you should be able to enter a discount for each book in the order.

☐ The form should show the total cost of all books entered in the order.

☐ The employee should be able to check to see if a book is in stock.

☐ The form will display the customer's name, address, and phone number.

☐ The form will show whether all the books in the order are currently in stock, so that an employee can call the customer to say that the order is ready.

Several of these tasks demand that you use derived values. Other features of the form depend on techniques that you already know, such as performing a lookup or creating a master-detail relationship.

Creating the Book Orders Form

To create the form, follow these steps:

1. Add a new form to the BOOKS.POA application.

2. Name the form `frmBookOrders`, and give it the label of `Book Orders`.

3. In the session window for BOOKS.POA, open the Table Editor window for ORDERS.

4. Select the ORDER_ID, CUSTOMER_ID, DATE_ENTERED, DATE_RECEIVED, DATE_PURCHASED, EMPLOYEE_ID, and NOTES columns from the table and drag them onto the form.

5. Change the `FontName` for the new text fields and static text objects to `Arial` and their `FontSize` to `10`.

6. Move the text fields so that they occupy the upper half of the form.

7. In the Property sheet for the NOTES text field, change the settings for the MultiLine and HasScrollbar properties to True.

   This change enables the user to enter multiple lines of text in this field, and then scroll up and down through the text.

8. Resize the NOTES text field to give it more height.

9. Add a scrollbar to the form.

   The form should now look something like Figure 8.2.

   Now it's time to add the repeater display that will contain the books in each order.

Figure 8.2.

The ORDERS form so far.

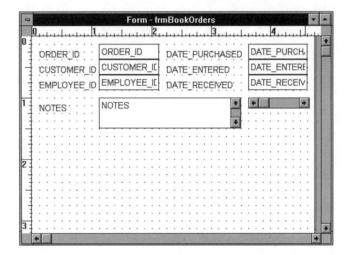

10. Add a repeater display that covers the center third of the form, and give it the name repTitles.

    Be sure to leave the bottom third of the form empty for the moment.

11. In the Session window, open the Table Editor window for ORDERS_ITEMS.

12. Click and drag all of the columns from this table except ORDER_ID into the repeater display panel.

13. While the four new text fields are still selected, change their FontName property to Arial and FontSize to 9.

    Although the repeater display now has all the columns from the ORDERS_ITEMS table, it displays the ID number for a book instead of its descriptive name. However, the user needs to see the title instead, so you'll now add a lookup field.

14. Add a text field to the repeater display and change its appearance to match the other fields.

15. Change this text field's `Name` property to `fldTitleName`, its `Datatype` property to `String`, its `DataSize` property to `128`, and its `DataSource` property to the following derived value expression:

```
=SQLLOOKUP(BOOKS, "SELECT TITLE_NAME FROM TITLES
➥WHERE TITLE_ID = " & STR(TITLE_ID.Value))
```

16. Position the new text field so that it is adjacent to the `TITLE_NAME` text field and occupies about one-third of the repeater display.

17. Select the repeater display and set the following properties to establish the master-detail relationship between the form and the repeater display:

Property	Setting
LinkColumn	ORDER_ID
LinkDetailColumn	ORDER_ID
LinkMasterForm	frmBookOrders

18. Change the repeater display's `HasExtraRow` property to `False`.

    This step removes the blank row used to enter new records. In a moment, you will add two pushbuttons for adding and deleting books from an order.

19. Add a current row pointer to the left side of the repeater display.

20. Change the `DISCOUNT` field's `DefaultValue` property to `0`.

    This step ensures that any book added to the order has a default discount of zero (`0`) percent, instead of `NULL`. Similarly, you need to make sure that when you add a new book, the initial quantity ordered is 1.

21. Change the `QUANTITY` field's `DefaultValue` property to `1`.

22. Set the `DefaultValue` property of `TITLE_ID` to `1` as well.

23. Save the form.

At this point, you could run the form, but it needs some additions to make it possible for the user to enter orders. The repeater display still does not show how much each book costs, or the adjusted price for each book if a discount is applied to it. Additionally, you need to add the pushbuttons for adding and deleting books from the order.

1. In the repeater display, add two new text fields and change their appearance to match that of the other fields in the same container.

   One of these text fields will perform a lookup to determine the price of a book, whereas the other will show the adjusted price, factoring in the number of copies ordered and the discount applied.

2. Change the `Datatype` property of these new fields to `Double`.

   This is the correct data type to use when you display numeric values with decimals.

3. Change the name of one of the new text fields to `fldPrice` and the other's to `fldTotalCost`.

4. Select `fldPrice` and enter the following expression for its `DataSource` property:

```
=SQLLOOKUP(BOOKS, "SELECT PRICE FROM TITLES
➥WHERE TITLE_ID = " & STR(TITLE_ID.Value))
```

The text field now looks up the price for each book entered in the order.

5. Select `fldTotalCost` and enter the following expression for its `DataSource` property:

```
=fldPrice.Value * QUANTITY.Value * (1-(DISCOUNT.Value)
```

You have now entered your first derived value calculation that wasn't a `SQLLOOKUP` statement, so let's pause for a moment to consider what it means.

The expression takes the value of three text fields in the repeater display—`fldPrice`, `QUANTITY`, and `DISCOUNT`—and uses them to determine the price for a particular title. Because a customer might order more than one copy of the same book, the value in the `QUANTITY` field appears as part of the calculation. Additionally, an employee might need to enter a discount for that title while taking the order, so the value in the `DISCOUNT` field is also included. This value is subtracted from one (1) so that the discount is figured properly: if the customer receives a 20-percent discount, the cost of the book should be multiplied by 80 percent.

Note that in this expression, you could have left out the `.Value` section of each field's name. By default, when you identify a control as part of a derived value calculation, Oracle Power Objects assumes that you want to use the `Value` property in the calculation, not some other property of the control. Therefore, you could have entered the following for the `DataSource` property of the control and achieved the same result:

```
=fldPrice * QUANTITY * (1-DISCOUNT)
```

6. Resize and reposition the controls in the repeater display to make them as readable as possible.

7. Add some static text labels just above the repeater display to label each text field within the repeater display.

At this point, the form should look like Figure 8.3.

8. Add two pushbuttons just below the repeater display, one labeled Add and the other Delete.

9. In the `Click()` method of the Add pushbutton, enter the following method code:

```
repTitles.InsertRow()
```

10. In the `Click()` method of the Delete pushbutton, enter the following method code:

```
repTitles.DeleteRow()
```

11. Save and run the form.

Figure 8.3.

The Book Orders form, with the finished repeater display.

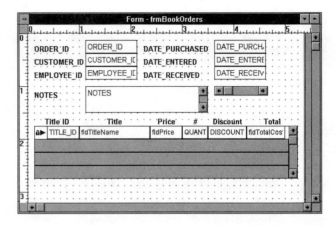

12. Enter the following for your first book order:

Control	Value
ORDER_ID	1
DATE_ENTERED	(Today's date, such as 1/1/96)
EMPLOYEE_ID	1
CUSTOMER_ID	1

13. Press the Add pushbutton to add a new book.

14. For the ID number of the book, enter 2.

As shown in Figure 8.4, the application now uses two derived values to display the title of the book and its price. Note that the initial discount is 0, and the initial quantity is 1. As you might remember, you set the DefaultValue of these two text fields to display these values when you added a new book to the order.

Figure 8.4.

Derived values in action on the Book Orders form.

15. In the QUANTITY field, enter 2.

Because you are now ordering two books instead of one, the adjusted price for this title changes. Figure 8.5 shows the adjustment to the price, based on the new quantity.

Figure 8.5.

The new adjusted price for the book.

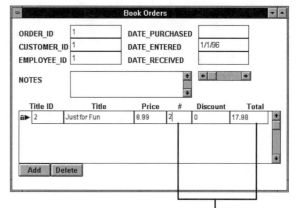

The application recalculates the total cost, based on a new quantity

Assume that the store is having a sale, and that you're applying a 10-percent discount to every order.

16. In the DISCOUNT field, enter 0.1.

Again, the application recalculates the adjusted cost of this book within the order.

17. Press Commit to save the order to the database.

18. Press Stop to end this exercise.

Right now, this form displays only one numeric calculation as a derived value. As you add new features to this form, it will use several additional derived values to display the number of books in the order, the total cost of the order, the full name of the customer, and the number of days since the order was placed.

Dealing with Null Values in Expressions

During the last exercise, you spent some effort making sure that a value appeared in two text fields whenever you added a book to an order. In the case of the DISCOUNT field, you assigned an initial value of zero. Why, you might ask, did you do this?

NULL Is Not Zero

As mentioned on Day 1, "Your First Form," the absence of a value for a property is not denoted by zero for numeric values, or by an empty string (denoted as "") for strings. Instead, the absence of a value is NULL, a special kind of data type in Oracle Power Objects and similar products.

When a variable or property has a null value (a common way of saying "the absence of a value," if a little confusing), it behaves differently than if it had a non-null value. Most importantly, if a null value appears within an expression, the entire expression evaluates as NULL. Therefore, if you multiply 10 times NULL, the result is NULL. In other words, null values propagate through an expression to make the result NULL—hence the term *null propagation*.

Null Propagation and Derived Values

When you work with any kind of expression, therefore, whether it appears in method code or in code for a derived value, you must be careful to handle the special case of null values. When you add a new record, all of the controls have the value of NULL until you enter a value, or the application itself enters a value from some source (for example, by querying one from a column).

If you had not assigned default values to the controls in the repeater display, for example, the adjusted cost of a book would initially be NULL. Because the DISCOUNT field would not have a value unless you typed one in, as would the QUANTITY field, the derived value calculation for the adjusted price of each book would be NULL.

The *NVL* Function

Setting a default value for a control through its DefaultValue property is one way to avoid having null values. Alternatively, you can use an Oracle Basic function, NVL, to replace a null value within an expression with some other value. The NVL function has the following syntax:

```
NVL(value_source , replacement_value)
```

The *value_source* argument is the name of the property or variable being tested for a null value. If the *value_source* is NULL, the application replaces the NULL value with whatever value is assigned as the *replacement_value*.

For example, to substitute a value of 0 for a variable's NULL value, you might enter the following:

```
vResult = NVL(vSource,0)
```

where *vSource* is the variable whose value is currently NULL.

Similarly, to handle the case when a control's Value property is NULL, you might enter this code:

```
vResult = NVL(fldOne.Value,0)
```

The *ISNULL* Function

Another way to handle nulls is to test for them, and then write the code that responds when a null value is found. For example, instead of entering a default value for the EMPLOYEE_ID field when the application discovers that it is NULL, you might want to prompt the user to enter a value. In this case, you need to use a command that tests for NULL, but does not replace the NULL value automatically (as NVL does).

In Oracle Basic, the ISNULL function takes a single argument, the name of a property or variable. If the value is currently NULL, ISNULL returns True; otherwise, ISNULL returns False.

For example, the following method code checks to see if the value of a control is currently NULL. If so, it prompts the user to enter a value.

```
IF ISNULL (fldQuantity.Value) THEN
    MSGBOX "You must enter a quantity for each title ordered")
END IF
```

The Three Ways to Handle Nulls

To summarize, there are three ways to handle NULL values:

- [ ] The DefaultValue property. By defining a default value through this property, the application always assigns that value to a control whenever you open the form or create a new record. If the user deletes the value from the control, however, the new value will be NULL.

- [ ] The NVL function. If the value of a variable or property appearing in an expression might be NULL, you can use the NVL function to assign a substitute value.

- [ ] The ISNULL function. This function simply tests to see if a variable or property's current value is NULL. Unlike NVL, ISNULL lets you take more action than substituting a non-null value for a null one.

Derived Values and Strings

In the previous example, you used a derived value to calculate a simple numeric value: the adjusted cost of a book, taking into account the number of copies ordered and the discount applied. In this exercise, you will use a derived value to join (or *concatenate*) two strings, the first and last names of a customer. This technique will let you display the customer's full name in a single field.

First, you must add an embedded form to display customer information in the Book Orders form.

1. Remove the `Notes` field from the form, as well as its label.

2. Add a new embedded form in the space previously occupied by the `Notes` field.

3. Open the Table Editor window for the CUSTOMERS table.

4. Select the columns LASTNAME, FIRSTNAME, and PHONE from this table and drag them into the embedded form.

5. Add a new text field to the form, with a `Datatype` of `String` and a `DataSize` of `72`. Also, give this text field the `Name` `fldFullName`.

6. Change the `DataSource` value of the new text field to the following derived value expression:

   `=NVL(FNAME,"") & " " & NVL(LNAME,"")`

   This derived value takes both the first and last names of a customer, displayed in separate fields, and combines them into a single string (separated by a space).

7. Select all of the text fields and static objects in the embedded form and change their `FontSize` to `9` and their `FontName` to `Arial`.

8. In addition, change the `ReadOnly` property of these fields to `False`.

   This step prevents the user from editing the contents of these text fields.

9. Delete the labels for the LASTNAME and FIRSTNAME text fields.

10. Position and size the text field `fldFullName` so that it covers the LASTNAME and FIRSTNAME fields.

    After some minor modifications to the size and position of the embedded form, the Book Orders form should now look like Figure 8.6.

Figure 8.6.

The new embedded form displaying customer information.

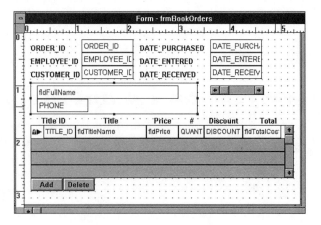

11. Set the necessary properties of the embedded form to create a master-detail relationship between the embedded form and frmBookOrders.

    Given your experience with master-detail relationships, this should present little challenge. The LinkMasterForm property must be set to frmBookOrders, LinkColumn to CUSTOMER_ID, and LinkDetailColumn to CUSTOMER_ID. Additionally, the LinkMasterUpd property must be set to Orphan details.

12. Save and run the form.

13. Enter 2 in the CUSTOMER_ID field.

    The form now displays a different customer's full name and phone number.

14. Press Commit to save the change to the CUSTOMER_ID value.

15. Press Stop.

Before moving on to the next exercise, you will make one final change to the derived value in fldFullName. If someone accidentally adds spaces to the first or last name, the full name displayed in fldFullName might look slightly peculiar. For example, extra spaces after the first name might make a larger gap between the two names in the fldFullName field. Therefore, to finish this exercise, you will add another Oracle Basic command, RTRIM, to the derived value. RTRIM removes any extra spaces that appear at the end of a string.

1. Select the text field fldFullName and open its Property sheet.

2. Enter the following expression for its DataSource property:

   ```
   =RTRIM(NVL(FIRSTNAME,"")) & " " & RTRIM(NVL(LASTNAME,""))
   ```

3. Save and run the form.

The form looks the same as it did before. However, you have added one more check within the derived value to ensure that the customer's name displays properly. This exercise shows that you can use a wide range of Oracle Basic commands and functions as part of derived value expressions, no matter what the data type of the control.

To illustrate this principle further, you will now add a new text field to the form that displays the number of days since the order was placed.

Derived Values and Dates

Dates are a special kind of data type. If you were to look at the actual value stored for a date, you would see a number that includes a decimal value. When you view the date through a control, however, it takes a standard date format, such as 01/01/96. How does this work?

When you designate a column in a table or a control on a form as having the Date data type, the application automatically interprets the decimal date value and displays it in a meaningful fashion. As a developer, you never need to see the decimal value or worry about what it means. The most important fact about date values is that, because they are represented numerically "behind the scenes," you can add and subtract them.

In this exercise, you will use a derived value calculation to subtract from today's date the date an order was placed, and then display the difference as the number of days since the order was made. Once again, this derived value calculation will appear in the DataSource property of a control, in this case with the data type of Date.

1. Add a new static text object in the upper section of the form.

2. Change this text object's label to Days Since Order.

3. Add a new text field to the form in the same area as the new label.

4. Change the text field's Name property to fldDaysSince and its Datatype property to Long.

5. For the DataSource property of this new text field, enter the following:

   = NOW - (DATE_ENTERED.Value)

   This expression uses the Oracle Basic function NOW, which returns today's date.

6. Change the appearance of the new label and field to match the other objects on the form.

7. Save and run the report.

8. In the DATE_ENTERED field, enter a date from one or two weeks ago.

   The number of days that have passed since that date now appears in the new text field.

9. In the same field, enter a date from the previous month.

   The new text field immediately recalculates the number of days that have passed since the order was entered.

10. Press Commit to save the new value for DATE_ENTERED.

11. Press Stop to end this exercise.

Performing Aggregate Calculations

So far, you have used derived values to provide three pieces of information: the adjusted cost of a book, the full name of a customer, and the number of days since the order was placed. Looking at this form, however, there still are several important pieces of information missing.

☐ The number of books in the order

☐ The total cost of all books ordered

☐ The total price to be paid, including sales tax and shipping charges

Obviously, you need to use a derived value to display this information. The situation is a little different from your earlier experiences with derived values, however. To calculate these values, you need to look at all instances of a control within the repeater display, and display the result on the form. In other words, you must perform a calculation that uses the aggregate of every time a control appears within the repeater display, instead of a single instance. For example, to get the total cost of all books in the order, you must add all of the adjusted prices from the fldTotalCost field within the repeater display.

When you perform an aggregate calculation, there is one important rule: You use a control in one container as the source of an aggregate calculation. For example, the fldTotalCost field in the repeater display has the data you need to determine the total cost of all books in an order. To perform the aggregate calculation, the derived value calculation must appear in a container outside the repeater display. In other words, the control that uses an aggregate calculation cannot appear within the same container as the control whose values are being aggregated. Therefore, you could not perform the derived value calculation in a control within the repeater display, but you could use a control on the form.

The only other piece of information you need to know is the list of aggregate functions shown in Table 8.1.

Table 8.1. Aggregate value functions.

Function	Description
SUM( )	Sums values
AVG( )	Averages values
MIN( )	Returns the minimum value
MAX( )	Returns the maximum value
STDEV( )	Returns the standard deviation of all values
COUNT( )	Returns the number of items

With this information in mind, you're ready to add some new text fields to the form to display the number of books ordered, the total price, and the cost with tax.

1. Add six new text fields to the form, below the repeater display and near the right edge of the form. Stack these three text fields vertically, one above the other.

   You might need to add some height to the form to make enough space for this stack of text fields.

2. Change the font used in these text fields to match the appearance of other text fields on the form.

3. Change the name of the top text field to fldCount and its Datatype to Long integer.

4. For the `DataSource` property of this control, enter the following derived value expression:

   `=SUM(repTitles.QUANTITY)`

   At runtime, the text field will display the total number of books in the order.

5. To the left of this text field, add a static text object with the label `Number of books in order`. Modify its font properties so that it matches the appearance of other labels on the form.

6. Change the name of the next control to `fldSubTotal` and its data type to `Double`.

7. For the `DataSource` property of `fldSubTotal`, enter

   `=SUM(repTitles.fldTotalCost)`

8. To the left of this text field, add another static text object with a label of `Total Book Price`.

9. Name the next control `fldCredit`, set its data type to `Double`, and enter `0` as its `DefaultValue` property.

   This field lets you enter a dollar value for any store credit (exchange, gift certificate, and so on) owed to a customer.

10. Add a static text object to label this control `Credit`.

11. Name the next text field `fldSalesTax`, and give it a data type of `Double`.

12. For the `DataSource` property of this control, enter

    `=(fldSubTotal.Value-fldCredit.Value) * 0.075`

    At this point, you are hard-coding the sales tax. Obviously, this is a bad idea for a real application, because sales tax rates can change. We'll leave that issue aside for the moment to keep this exercise simple.

13. Add another static text object to label this control `Sales Tax`.

14. Name the fifth field `fldShipping`, and give it a data type of `Double`.

    You enter shipping charges in this field if the order must be mailed to a customer.

15. Label this control `Shipping Fees`.

16. For the final control, give it the name `fldTotal` and the data type `Double`.

17. Label this control `Total Cost`.

    At this point, your form should look like Figure 8.7.

18. Enter the proper derived value expression for the `DataSource` property of this control.

    What would this expression be? By now, you should be able to enter it yourself. Before copying the text of the derived value expression below, try entering your own.

Figure 8.7.
The Book Orders form, with several new derived value fields added.

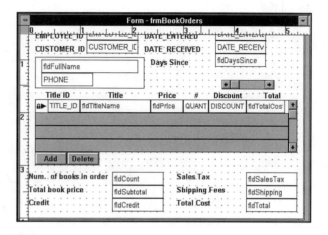

The expression should read something like this:

```
=fldSubTotal + fldSalesTax + fldShipping - fldCredit
```

In this case, because of the length of the expression the `Value` property is not added to the name of each text field involved in the calculation. Remember that if you omit the name of a property used as part of a derived value calculation, Oracle Power Objects assumes that you wish to use the `Value` property. If you were to add the reference to `Value`, the expression would read like this:

```
=fldSubTotal.Value + fldTax.Value + fldShipping.Value - fldCredit.Value
```

19. Set the `DefaultValue` property of `fldShipping` and `fldCredit` to `0`.

20. Save and run the form.

The form now displays all the pricing information for an order, as shown in Figure 8.8. Experiment by entering a new order, but be sure to give it an order ID number of 2.

Figure 8.8.
The Book Orders form at runtime, displaying the total cost of all books, any discount applied, the sales tax charged, and the final price.

ORDER_ID	1	DATE_PURCHASED	
EMPLOYEE_ID	1	DATE_ENTERED	1/1/95
CUSTOMER_ID	2	DATE_RECEIVED	
Karen Vogel		Days Since	267
415-555-8911			

Title ID	Title	Price	#	Discount	Total
▷ 2	Just for Fun	8.99	2	0.1	16.18

Add   Delete

Num. of books in order	2	Sales Tax	1.2
Total book price	16	Shipping Fees	0
Credit	0	Total Cost	17.2

DO use derived values to provide sums, averages, and other important information at a glance.

DO use derived values to help display strings in a more readable format. Combining the city, state, and zip code into a single field in a report is a good example of this technique.

DON'T crowd the form with information that the user does not always need to see. Many times, you can create a pop-up dialog box that includes the result of derived value calculations, such as the average price of books in a purchase.

DON'T include derived value fields on a form for their own sake. The application needs to perform the same set of calculations every time you scroll among records, so you can slow performance by adding too many derived value fields to a form.

Some More Facts About Derived Values

The following sections describe some important facts about derived values and controls.

Derived Values Make Controls Read-Only

While the form is still running, click the Sales Tax field. As you can see, this field is read-only—you cannot enter your own value for the sales tax applied to an order. Any control that uses a derived value calculation for its DataSource property is read-only, regardless of the settings for its ReadOnly and Enabled properties. In this case, keeping the Sales Tax field read-only makes sense; you do not want your employees to enter the wrong amount of sales tax for an order.

However, what should you do if you want the user to be able to enter a different value, or use the result of some automatic calculation? For example, if you take an order from an out-of-state customer, you should not apply the state or local sales tax to the transaction.

In these cases, you would have to perform the calculation through some means other than a derived value expression in the control's DataSource property. You have two options:

☐ When you change the value in a control that is part of the expression, you can perform the calculation through method code. You assign the result of this expression to the Value property of a control. The two methods that trigger as soon as a control's value changes are PostChange() and Validate(), both of which can be home to the method code that performs the calculation.

☐ You can add a pushbutton or other control that triggers the method code that performs the calculation. For example, you might add a pushbutton next to the Sales Tax field that, when pressed, calculates the sales tax. However, if you did not push this button, you could then enter the sales tax yourself.

In the next exercise, you will create just such a pushbutton, to give you some additional options for charging sales tax.

Controls Using Derived Values Are Not Bound

The choices for the DataSource property are mutually exclusive: Either you bind the control to a column in a table or view or you use a derived value as its DataSource. If you want to include a column in the ORDERS table for the total cost of an order, you could not connect this column to the same text field that calculates the total cost.

In one sense, this is not a problem. Adding a TOTAL_PRICE column to the ORDERS table breaks one of the cardinal rules of relational database design: Don't duplicate information across tables. The ORDERS_ITEMS table already contains the total cost of an order; all you need to do to calculate this figure is to look at the line items in the ORDERS_ITEMS table that share the same ORDER_ID value.

Performing such an operation can be a complicated process. If you want to generate a report on all orders entered in a particular business day, querying this information across several tables might be a tricky enterprise. As you remember, each book had an adjusted price, based on the number of copies ordered and the discount applied. In addition, the retail price of each book is stored in TITLES, a separate table from ORDERS_ITEMS altogether. Performing the necessary queries across ORDERS, ORDERS_ITEMS, and TITLES might be time-consuming, as would be all the calculations needed for each order. Because of the extra computing this would require, your report might take some time to generate and print if you were generating a report for a large bookstore or a chain of bookstores, with hundreds or thousands of orders involving many more thousands of books.

Denormalizing Databases

For this reason, database applications occasionally break with the perfect orthodoxy of relational database design to improve actual performance. By adding a TOTAL_COST column to the ORDERS table, you would speed report generation. However, because you are deliberately duplicating information across tables (a process called *denormalization*), you must build in extra safeguards to ensure that the values in ORDERS.TOTAL_COST are updated whenever the line items in individual orders change. If a customer cancels part of an order, you must recalculate the total

cost of the order and assign the new value to `ORDERS.TOTAL_COST` immediately, or else the ORDERS and ORDERS_ITEMS tables will be slightly out of sync.

Because of these limitations of a completely normalized database, many developers would rather sacrifice some performance to remain faithful to proper relational database design. Your application might not be the only one to access the tables in the database, so these other applications are unlikely to have the same safeguards.

A separate inventory management application, for example, might not have the mechanism for updating the ORDERS.TOTAL_PRICE column every time it removes from all orders a title that has been discontinued or is out of print. The book will disappear from an order, but the total price of the order stored in ORDERS.TOTAL_PRICE won't be changed. As a result, you would be charging customers for books that were removed from their orders—and they're unlikely to be understanding about a "computer error" excuse. Because the database is potentially open to many users and many applications, you always want to guard against these sources of error.

Some Final Changes to the Book Orders Form

As mentioned earlier, the Book Orders form does not let you enter the amount or type of tax; it simply calculates according to a fixed rate of 7.5 percent. There are cases, however, when you want to be able to select different sales tax amounts for local and out-of-state customers. To give you this option, you will add a new dialog box for selecting the tax rate applied to a purchase.

At this point, you might just add some control that lets you choose between the local 7.5 percent sales tax for local customers, and no tax at all for out-of-state mail order customers. You could create a pop-up list, list box, or radio button group for making this selection. This technique has one significant disadvantage, however: What happens if the tax rate changes? If you hard-code the tax rate through the derived value calculation you entered, or through the `Translation` property of a pop-up list or list box, or through radio buttons, you will have to change these settings and recompile the application every time the tax rate changes.

A better option would be to define sales tax rates in a table, which you could later update as the rates change. This new table will become the basis for a new dialog box that you will create for selecting the sales tax rate for an order.

1. Add a new table named SALES_TAX to the database.

   The table should have the following columns:

Name	Data type	Size	Precision
TAX_ID	Number		
TAX_DESC	Varchar2	64	
TAX_AMOUNT	Float	4	

2. Set the TAX_ID column as the primary key for the table.

3. Save and run the table.

4. Through the Table Browser window, enter the following records:

TAX_ID	TAX_DESC	TAX_AMOUNT
1	Local	.0750
2	Out of state	0

5. Press Commit to save these two new tax types, and then press Stop.

The next step is to create the dialog box for entering the tax type.

1. In the BOOKS.POA application, create a new form, named frmChooseTax, and give it the label Select Sales Tax.

2. Add a repeater display to the form and name it repRates.

3. In the Table Editor window for SALES_TAX, select the columns TAX_DESC and TAX_RATE and drag them into the repeater display.

4. Add another text field to the repeater display with a data type of Double.

5. For this new text field's DataSource property, enter

   =(frmBookOrders.fldSubTotal - frmBookOrders.fldCredit) * TAX_AMOUNT

   This calculation takes the total price of all books, subtracts the amount of store credit owed to the customer, and multiplies this figure by the sales tax rate. This field lets you see how much the tax will be as you select a tax rate from this dialog box.

   This calculation demonstrates an important principle: As long as you can have object references to controls, you can use them in a derived value calculation, even if they appear in different forms altogether.

6. Add a current row control to the left side of the repeater display panel containing the three new text fields.

7. Change the text field's font properties to match other controls in the application.

8. Add two pushbuttons to the bottom of the dialog box.

9. Label one pushbutton OK and the other one Cancel.
   The form should now look like Figure 8.9.

Figure 8.9.

The new dialog box for selecting tax rates.

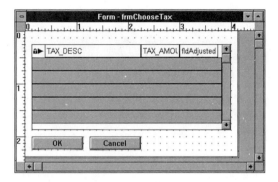

10. In the `Click()` method of the OK button, enter

```
Sub Click()
' Use the value for the currently selected tax rate
' to determine the sales tax for the book order
DIM vRate AS Float   'The tax rate

' Get the tax rate from the repeater display
vRate = repRates.GetRecordSet.GetColVal("TAX_AMOUNT")

' Set the value of the fldSalesTax field on the
' Book Orders form
frmBookOrders.fldSalesTax.Value = (frmBookOrders.fldSubTotal.Value -
➥frmBookOrders.fldCredit.Value) * vRate

' Close the dialog by calling the default
' behavior for Click()
Inherited.Click()
```

11. In the `Click()` method of the Cancel button, enter

```
Sub Click()
' Close the dialog by calling the default
' behavior for Click()
Inherited.Click()
```

12. Save the form.

13. Add a new pushbutton next to the text field `fldSalesTax` on the Book Orders form, adjacent to the right edge of the field.

14. Give the new pushbutton the following properties:

Property	Setting
SizeX	0.25 in
SizeY	0.25 in
FontName	Arial
FontSize	10
FontBold	True
Label	?

15. In the `Click()` method of this new pushbutton, enter

    ```
    Sub Click()
    ' Open frmChooseTax as a modal dialog
    frmChooseTax.OpenModal(0)
    ```

16. Delete the derived value expression you entered in the `DataSource` property for the text field `fldSalesTax`.

17. For the new `DataSource` property of this control, enter `TAX_RATE`.

    TAX_RATE is the name of a new column you will add to the ORDERS table.

18. For the `DefaultValue` property of this text field, enter `0`.

19. Add the new column, TAX_RATE, to the ORDERS table. This column should have a data type of `Double` and a precision of `4`.

20. Save the change to the table, and then return to the application.

21. Enter the code needed to open the Book Orders form when you run the application.

    As you should know by now, you need to run the application to test multiple forms—in this case, the Book Orders form and the Select Tax Type dialog box. The following is the code necessary to do this:

    ```
    Sub OnLoad()
    frmBookOrders.OpenWindow()
    ```

22. Save and run the application.

23. After the Book Orders form appears, press the pushbutton next to the field to open the Select Tax Type dialog box.

    The dialog box appears. Because of the derived value calculation you entered for one text field, the total tax applied to the book order appears for both types of sales tax rates.

24. In this dialog box, select the `Local` tax rate.

25. Press OK to close the dialog box.

    The application recalculates the tax rate. It also refigures the total cost of the book order. Because the `Sales Tax` field is now bound to a column in the ORDERS table, you need to save the new tax rate as part of the record.

26. Press Commit to save the modified order.

27. Press Stop to end this exercise.

Determining how Information Is Displayed

Before you finish today's lesson, you will make one more change to the Book Orders form. Currently, the data displayed in this form appear somewhat plain—currency values do not have a dollar sign, tax rates do not appear as percentages, and dates use a very terse format (1/1/96 rather than January 1, 1996).

Although changing the date format is not urgent, altering the appearance of tax and discount rates is. Beginning users of the Bookstore application might be confused when they see "0.05" as a discount instead of "5 percent." Clearly, you need some way to change the way information is displayed within a control.

In Oracle Power Objects, text fields and combo boxes have the FormatMask property for determining the display format for data. Based on the data type of information displayed in a control, you can select a predefined format mask, or you can enter your own.

To illustrate this point, select the DATE_ENTERED field on the Book Orders form and open its Property sheet. If you click the name of the FormatMask property, a drop-down list of date formats appears as in Figure 8.10.

Figure 8.10.

Format mask options for the DATE_ENTERED field.

All of these formats apply to dates alone. If you select a control with a different data type, you would see a different list of predefined format masks.

Select the fldCredit field, open its Property sheet, and click FormatMask again. Because fldCredit has its Datatype property set to Double, a different list of format masks appears, appropriate to Double values instead of Dates (see Figure 8.11).

Figure 8.11.

Format mask options for the field fldCredit.

For any text field, you can type in your own format mask definition for this property, instead of selecting one of the predefined types. You enter a mask as a string of format characters, such as

`dd-mm-yy, hh-mm-ss`

This format mask displays a date and time in the following way:

01-01-96, 11:34:05

Although defining your own format mask is often useful, for this exercise, you will apply predefined format masks to the controls on the Book Orders form. If you want to see a complete description of format mask characters, consult the topic "Format Mask Characters" in the Oracle Power Objects online help.

The predefined format masks by data type include the following:

Data type	Format Mask	Description	Example
`Long integer,` `float`	General number	Standard number, without formatting.	10000
	Currency	Number with currency symbol, comma separators, and two decimals.	$10,000.00
	Fixed	Number with two decimal places.	10000.00
	Percent	Moves decimal two places to the left and displays % symbol.	13.5%
	Scientific	Displays number with exponent.	1E+5
	Yes/No	Displays 0 as No, all other values as Yes.	Yes
	True/False	Displays 0 as False, all other values as True.	True
	On/Off	Displays 0 as Off, all other values as On	On

Data type	Format Mask	Description	Example
String	All caps	Displays text in all caps.	ORACLE POWER OBJECTS
	Init cap	Displays first letter of each word as a capital.	Oracle Power Objects
	All lowercase	Displays all letters as lowercase.	oracle power objects
Date	General date	Displays m/d/y h:m:s.	1/1/96 11:31:06
	Long date	Displays full text of date.	January 1, 1996
	Short date	Displays date as d-m-y.	01-January -96
	Long time	Displays hour, minute, and seconds.	11:31:06 AM
	Medium time	Displays hour and minute.	11:31 AM
	Short time	Displays hour and minute without AM/PM notation.	11:31

DO   DON'T

DO test for nulls when needed in your method code.

DO write derived values expressions to anticipate nulls.

DON'T worry about nulls if they won't affect the outcome of the expression. In some cases, you might want to allow null propagation (that is, a null value in the expression causes the result of the expression to be NULL).

DON'T create such complicated derived value expressions that it is impossible to type them into the DataSource property. By the time you have added NVL statements to the expression, you might have entered a very long string for the DataSource property. To break up a long expression, you can always create invisible fields to handle small parts of the calculation.

Working with Format Masks

You can now add some format masks to the Book Orders form.

1. Select the DATE_ENTERED, DATE_RECEIVED, and DATE_PURCHASED text fields and open their shared Property sheet.

2. For their FormatMask property, select Short Date.

3. Select the text fields fldSubTotal, fldSalesTax, and fldTotalCost, and change their data type to Currency.

4. In the repeater display, select the DISCOUNT field and change its FormatMask to Percent.

5. In the form, select the field fldSalesTax and change its FormatMask to Percent.

6. In the repeater display, change the FormatMask for the fldPrice and fldTotalCost text fields to Currency.

7. Save and run the form.

   As shown in Figure 8.12, the fields displaying date, currency, and percentage information now use more familiar formats.

8. Change the discount for a title to 0.2 and press Enter.

Although you entered 0.2, the application displays the discount as 20%. This is how the format mask should work: The control stores the value as 0.2, but displays it as 20%. As with list controls, the display value of a control might not match the internal value.

Figure 8.12.
The new format masks applied to the Book Orders form.

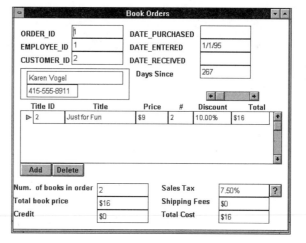

Limitations on Format Masks

A format mask determines how information is displayed; it does not restrict what information you can enter. Although you might like to force the user to enter data in a particular format, format masks cannot enforce these rules. Instead, you can use the data validation methods, `Validate()` and `ValidateRow()`, to enforce formats.

Unfortunately, this requires a fair amount of coding, and not the most interesting kind of coding. Essentially, you must write a procedure that breaks down the text or number entered into a field, determines whether all the pieces appear in the correct format, and then prompts the user if necessary to re-enter the value. Fortunately, future releases of Oracle Power Objects will include input masks that will constrain what values the user can enter.

DO	DON'T

DO use format masks to clarify currency, date, and time information.

DO use format masks to help format text and numbers.

DON'T override the international settings for your system (PC or Macintosh). Unless you want to restrict currency, date, and time information to a particular format, you should use the format mask characters that apply the settings entered for the environment through the Control Panel.

DON'T use format masks if they will confuse the user about the text being entered. For example, if you use a mask that formats text to be displayed in all caps, you have only changed its display value. The actual text stored in the control may include lowercase characters, but it won't appear this way to the user.

Summary

Today you learned the following points about derived values and format masks:

☐ You can set the value in a control by using a derived value expression. You enter this expression as the setting for the control's `DataSource` property, instead of binding the control to a column (or leaving the control unbound).

☐ The choice between settings for the `DataSource` property are mutually exclusive. Either a control can use a derived value, or it can query values from a column in its container's record source.

☐ The derived value expression can use Oracle Basic operators, commands, and functions. For example, you can use the `NOW` function to set the value of a field to today's date, or the `AVG` function to display the average of all values displayed in a text field.

8

- [ ] The expression can use the Value of a control as part of the calculation. If you do not enter the .Value suffix after the name of the control, the application assumes that you are referring to that property.

- [ ] Controls that use derived values are read-only.

- [ ] If you use an aggregate function as part of a derived value calculation, the control displaying the result of the calculation must appear in a different container than the controls used as part of the calculation.

- [ ] A format mask determines how values are displayed in a control.

- [ ] You can use a predefined format mask, appropriate to the data type of the control, or you can define your own.

What Comes Next?

Tomorrow you will learn how to give your users the ability to move between different forms. In addition to a navigator form that lets you open a form by pressing a button, you will also create menus to open these forms. One menu will let you enter "transaction" forms, such as the Book Order form. The other new menu will open "maintenance" forms, used to add new records to commonly used tables, such as CUSTOMERS, PUBLISHERS, and TITLES.

Q&A

Q Based on the following quiz question #1, if I want to show an average salary on a form that displays individual employee salaries, how can I do it?

A Because you cannot include the text field displaying average salaries on the same form as the text field displaying each employee's salary, you have a bit of a challenge to show these two figures side-by-side. There are several ways around this problem, however:

- [ ] You can put the employee records in an embedded form or repeater display, and then show the average salary on the main form.

- [ ] You can create a column in another table to hold the average salary figure. Unfortunately, this technique requires that you duplicate information (employee salaries, expressed singly or as a company average) across tables, which is not recommended in relational databases.

- [ ] You can show the average salary in a dialog box that can be opened from the main form.

One solution that you might have considered was placing another container with the average salary figure within the form. Unfortunately, this technique does not work. Because the application creates an instance of every control on the form for every record in its recordset, it also creates one copy of the embedded form or repeater display for every record. Therefore, the extra container is part of the relationship between instances of controls and records. Oracle Power Objects cannot then use an aggregate function when the container is part of this relationship.

Q **Can I use multiple aggregate functions in the same derived value calculation?**

A Certainly, as long as you follow the rules for aggregate functions. In fact, the aggregate values for different functions can come from separate containers. For example, the result of the derived value calculation could be the sum of values displayed in two different repeater displays.

Q **How do I make it possible for a format mask to use the international settings for the environment? For example, if I want to apply a format mask that uses the settings in Microsoft Windows Control Panel for currency and date formats, how do I do this in Oracle Power Objects?**

A If you look at the list of format mask characters in the online help, you will see that several are designed to read these settings from the environment. For example, the format mask *dddd* displays the date according to the format set in the Control Panel.

Workshop

The Workshop consists of quiz questions to help you solidify your understanding of the material covered and exercises to give you experience in using what you've learned.

Quiz

1. Suppose you want to display an employee's salary and the average salary for all employees in the same form. Is this possible, using the AVG function?

2. Why should you not use the String data type for a text field for displaying dates, if you want to apply a format mask to the field?

3. How would you design a form to keep track of the customer with the largest number of books in an order?

4. Suppose you wanted to charge customers a shipping fee for orders, based on the weight of the books in the order. The rate is 10 cents per pound, plus an additional $2 flat fee. Assuming the weight of each book were part of its record, how would you then write a derived value expression to perform this calculation?

Exercises

1. Add a text field that displays the number of books in the order. You need to use the SUM function to add the number of books displayed in the repeater display.

2. Add another text field that displays the average cost of all books in the order. You need to use the text field you created in the first exercise as part of the expression.

Quiz Answers

1. No, because the text field displaying the average must appear on a different container than the form that has the control displaying salaries. Because AVG is an aggregate function, you cannot use it within the same form as the SALARY field.

2. Because format masks are designed for one data type alone. If you want to use format masks designed to display dates in different formats, you can apply them to fields with the data type Date, but not String.

3. You could add a text field to the Book Orders form that displayed the sum of the QUANTITY field for each order, if you wanted to track by the number of copies, or COUNT if you wanted to track by the number of titles. As you scrolled through orders, you would see the number of copies or titles in each order. Then, if you wanted to show the name of the customer with the largest number of copies or titles in an order, you would use the MAX function to determine the maximum number of copies or titles. (The text field displaying this information, however, would have to appear in a separate form, because MAX is an aggregate function applied to the Book Orders form.) You could then use this information to display a list of the customer(s) with that number of books or titles in an order.

4. Assuming that the weight of each book appeared in a text field named fldWeight in the repeater display, the derived value calculation would look like this:

```
=(fldWeight * .1) + 2
```

Menus and Toolbars

Overview

Today, you learn about the following topics:

- ☐ Creating a navigator dialog box
- ☐ Defining a menu bar
- ☐ Associating a menu bar with a form or a report
- ☐ Using the `DoCommand()` and `TestCommand()` methods
- ☐ Defining what happens when you select a menu command
- ☐ Toolbars and status lines
- ☐ Creating a custom toolbar

So far, you have created several forms and reports separately from one another. When you develop any application, however, the forms and reports are not really separate—instead, they are part of a larger whole, the application itself.

When you run the application, you need to provide the user with the means to reach all of the forms and reports. As yet, the Bookstore application does not have that means. The best vehicle you have for running a form is adding method code to the application's `OnLoad()` method, which opens a particular form when the application launches. Obviously, you need to do better than this when you are developing a real application.

In any application created with Oracle Power Objects, you have essentially two options for helping the user "navigate" to forms and reports:

- ☐ Navigation dialog boxes: You can create a form that includes several pushbuttons for opening other forms. These forms can lead to other forms. For example, the Book Orders form created on Day 8, "Derived Values," opens another form for selecting the type of sales tax applied to an order. In effect, you create a chain of forms, each one leading to another, when you use this method.

- ☐ Menus: Instead of a chain of forms, you create menu commands that open forms. For example, later in this lesson, you will add a new menu, Setup, that includes all the maintenance forms in the Bookstore application. In this menu, the Setup | Publishers menu command opens a form used to view and edit publisher records. Not every form needs to be accessible from a dialog box. For example, the Sales Tax dialog box you created yesterday is used only when entering an order, so it is only opened through a pushbutton on the Book Orders form. However, you should be able to open most forms through a menu command.

In Oracle Power Objects, menus have inherent properties and methods, much like other objects. Unlike most other objects, however, you do not use a graphical designer to create

menus. Instead, you write method code that creates a menu, defines all the menu commands within it, and associates the menu with the application, a form, or a report.

In other words, it's time to limber up your fingers, because you will be writing a great deal more method code than you have in earlier lessons. In fact, several objects, including menus, toolbars, and status lines (described later in this chapter) require some amount of coding to create. However, you'll start with a more familiar and somewhat easier technique by creating a navigator form that lets you open the main forms and reports in the application.

Creating a Navigator Dialog Box

By now, the steps needed to create a dialog box with pushbuttons that open other forms should be relatively easy. All you need to do is add the necessary method code for opening the form to the Click() method, using the OpenWindow() method.

1. In the application BOOKS.POA, create a new form.
2. Name the form frmMain and the label Main Menu.
3. Add four pushbuttons to the left side of the form, and stack them vertically.
4. Delete the Label from all four pushbuttons.
5. Size the pushbuttons so that they are 0.375 inches wide by 0.375 inches high.

   You can accomplish this step by clicking and dragging the border of each pushbutton, or by manually setting the SizeX and SizeY properties of the pushbuttons.

6. Add four static text objects to the right side of the form, aligned with the four pushbuttons.
7. Change the FontName property of the pushbuttons to Arial, FontBold to True, and FontSize to 14.
8. From top to bottom, the Label properties of the four static text objects should read as follows:

   Book Orders

   Publishers

   Titles

   Customers

9. Add the following method code to the Click() method of the top pushbutton, after the Sub Click() line:

   ```
   frmBookOrders.OpenWindow()
   ```

10. Add the following method code to the Click() method of the second pushbutton (do not type the Sub Click() line):

    ```
    Sub Click()
    frmPubsBooks.OpenWindow()
    ```

11. Enter this method code for the third pushbutton:
    ```
    Sub Click()
    frmBooks.OpenWindow()
    ```

12. Add the final method code to the fourth pushbutton's `Click()` method:
    ```
    Sub Click()
    frmCustomers.OpenWindow()
    ```

13. Change the form's `WindowStyle` property to `Fixed-size Document`.

    This change removes the resizable window from the border of the form. In addition, the form will not have buttons for minimizing and maximizing the form appearing on its toolbar. Because frmMainMenu is the navigator form in the application, you want to keep it visible at all times. In addition, this window style distinguishes this form, designed for navigation among other parts of the application, from other forms that are designed for data entry.

    The completed Main Menu form should now look like Figure 9.1.

Figure 9.1.

The Main Menu form.

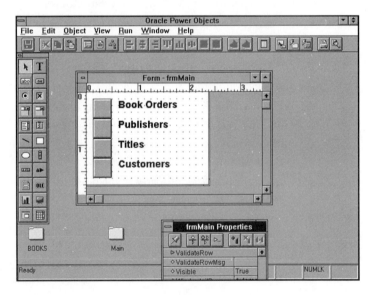

14. Add the following method code to the application's `OnLoad()` method:
    ```
    Click()
    frmMainMenu.OpenWindow()
    ```

15. Save and run the application.

    The Main Menu appears, giving you the ability to open the other forms in the application.

16. Press the Publishers pushbutton.

    An old friend, the frmPubsBooks form, now appears.

17. Select the Main Menu form and press the Titles pushbutton.

    The frmBrowseTitles form now appears. As you might remember, this form opens another dialog box used to browse the list of titles and select one to view.

18. Press the Browse button on this form.

    As shown in Figure 9.2, the application now opens the browser dialog box for selecting a title. This step shows that you can design your application to open one form from another, in a continuing chain of forms.

Figure 9.2.
Forms opened from the Main Menu form, and the browser form opened from frmBooks.

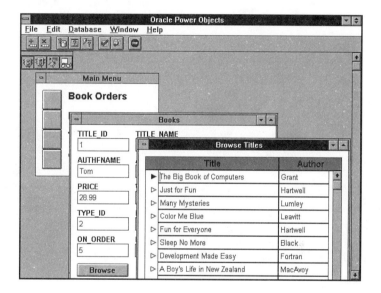

19. Press Stop to end this exercise.

Shortcomings of Navigator Forms

Although navigator forms like frmMainMenu are easy to design, they have some significant shortcomings. For example:

☐ Already, you are experiencing clutter in the application interface. When you are opening dialog boxes, reports, and other forms from one form, the interface quickly becomes visually "busy." The navigator dialog box adds to this clutter, because it must always be open.

☐ Adding another form complicates the task of switching among forms. When you have Main Menu and several other forms open simultaneously, selecting one of these forms becomes that much trickier.

☐ If by accident you close the Main Menu form, you no longer have the means to navigate to other forms. Worse, if the Main Menu form is the only one open and you close it, the application shuts down. When you close the last form in an application, the LastWindowClosed() method is triggered, which, as part of its default processing, terminates the application.

For these reasons, many developers prefer to use menus to open forms. In the next exercise, you will create a custom menu and add it to the standard menu bar appearing near the top of the application window.

The Components of a Menu Bar

What we normally call a menu actually consists of three different components, as shown in Figure 9.3.

Figure 9.3.

The components of a menu.

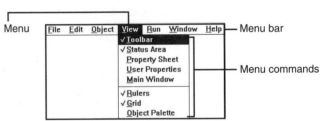

☐ The *menu bar*—The bar that stretches across the application window.

☐ A *menu*—A heading that appears on the menu bar. For example, the File and Edit menus are a standard feature of Windows and Macintosh applications. When you click the name of the menu, all the menu commands appear.

☐ A *menu command*—Entries within a menu that, when selected, perform an action. For example, the File | Exit command closes the application, and the Edit | Copy command copies whatever information is currently selected within the application. Menu commands often have keyboard accelerators, combinations of keys (such as Ctrl+C for Edit | Copy) that perform the same task as a menu command.

The menu bar, therefore, is the object that includes the menus and menu commands. You must create a new menu bar, and then add the menus and commands to it.

Default Menu Bars

Without writing any code, a default menu bar appears in any Oracle Power Objects application. In Windows, this menu bar includes several standard menus, including File, Edit, Window, and Help. The first three menus are fully functional in an Oracle Power Objects application; the last menu, Help, only opens an online help file if you write the method code that performs this task. Even though the Help menu does not do anything by default, it would look odd if it were not part of the menu bar, given that the vast majority of applications include this menu. In Oracle Power Objects, these menu headings comprise the *system default menu bar*, shown in Figure 9.4.

Figure 9.4.
The system default menu bar.

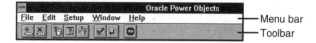

Additionally, Oracle Power Objects applications have another menu, Database, that lets you perform database-related tasks when you select a bound form. The Database menu, added to the system default menu, forms the default menu bar. The Database menu appears between the Edit and Window menus on the menu bar.

Custom Menu Bars

You can replace the default menu bar with a custom menu bar of your own. Custom menu bars can (and, more often than not, do) use the default menu bar as a template, adding new items to it or deleting default items from it. You create custom menu bars entirely through method code. Your definition of a menu bar must include all the menus and menu commands appearing on it, as well as the actions taken when a user selects a particular menu command.

After you create a menu, you can make it appear throughout the application, or only when a particular form or report is selected. This latter option is a common feature of Windows and Macintosh applications. For example, when you select the Book Orders form, you might want some special menu options to appear. You might want to quickly check the storewide promotions, check the customer's account status, or view that person's purchasing habits. To provide access to this information, you can design a special menu, Customer, that appears only when the Book Orders form is the active window. The menu commands on this new menu would open the forms needed to review customer information. If you were to select a different form, the Customer menu would then disappear.

Alternatively, you could add items to an existing menu, instead of creating an entirely new menu. When the Book Orders form is selected, new menu commands might appear on the Edit menu. When you select a different menu, these items would disappear.

Creating a Custom Menu Bar

Because creating a menu bar is more complicated than other tasks you have learned so far, here is a quick summary of the steps you'll need to perform:

1. Enter the method code that creates a new menu bar as an object. In this code, the statement NEW MenuBar creates the menu bar. The menu bar is the skeleton on which you will add the menus.

2. Decide whether to use one of the default menu bars as the basis for the custom menu bar. If you call either the SysDefaultMenuBar() or the DefaultMenuBar() method, the application automatically adds all the standard menus for the system default menu or the default menu, respectively. These methods save you a great deal of coding: Rather than defining what the standard menus do, you can define them by calling a single method of the menu bar.

3. Define any new menus added to the menu bar. The NEW Menu statement creates a new menu. Like menu bars, menus are separate objects within the application. You cannot display a menu, however, unless you associate it with a menu bar during a later step.

4. Define any new menu commands. You use one of two methods, AppendMenuItem() or InsertMenuItem(), to add a menu command.

5. Add the new menu to the menu bar. You use one of two methods, AppendMenu() and InsertMenu().

6. Write the method code needed to define what each menu command does when it is selected. The method code appears in two methods, TestCommand() and DoCommand(). Briefly, TestCommand() determines whether the user has selected a menu item, and DoCommand() defines what happens as a result of that selection.

7. Associate the menu bar with the application, a form, or a report. Up to this point, the application understands the different components of the menu bar, but it does not know when to display the custom menu bar. This final step determines when the menu bar appears in the application.

As you might imagine, creating menu bars requires no small amount of coding, compared to the scant method code you have written so far in the application. Moreover, it is not immediately obvious which method should contain this method code.

Where Does the Code Go?

The application needs to know the components of a menu bar as soon as the user launches the application or selects a form. Therefore, the method code that creates a menu bar might appear in the OnLoad() method of either the application, a form, or a report. As you learned in earlier lessons, the OnLoad() method executes whenever the application loads an item into memory, such as when you open a form. In addition, the application itself has an `OnLoad()` method that is triggered when you launch the application.

Indeed, `OnLoad()` is the place to put method code for menu bars that appear throughout an application. However, if you want to define a menu bar that appears only when you select a particular form or report, you would use that form or report's `InitializeWindow()` method instead. As part of its default behavior, `InitializeWindow()` displays the default menu bar. You can replace this default processing, however, with the code that defines a custom menu bar associated with that form or report.

As mentioned earlier, the method code that determines what happens when the user selects a menu command appears in two methods of the application, `TestCommand()` and `DoCommand()`. The code in `TestCommand()` sets the appearance and behavior of menu commands when you open a menu, whereas `TestCommand()` determines what happens when you select a menu command.

Creating a Setup Menu

In this exercise, you will create your first custom menu, Setup. In the Bookstore application, the Setup menu will give you the ability to open all the "setup" forms used to define records used throughout the application. Because you have used PUBLISHERS and TITLES repeatedly in this application, there will be two menu items under Setup to open the forms displaying records from these tables. In addition, you will add another menu command, Setup | Employees, that will display records from a new table, EMPLOYEES.

Adding Two New Setup Forms

Before continuing, you should quickly create two new forms. The first, frmCustomers, should have text fields bound to each column in CUSTOMERS. Because you are creating menu commands that open setup forms for every major table in the database, you need to add a form that displays customer records.

The second form, frmBookTypes, should be bound to the BOOK_TYPES table in the same fashion.

Steps for Creating a Menu Bar

Because you must replace an existing menu bar with a custom one to add a new menu, one of the first steps in creating the Setup menu will be to create a menu bar.

The way menus work in Oracle Power Objects, however, requires that you take another step first. Because all menu commands are identified by ID numbers, you must find a way to keep these numbers unique. If you accidentally assign the same ID number to two menu commands,

Menus and Toolbars

you can make your application behave in unpredictable ways. Therefore, the first step in defining the menu commands will be to assign application-level constants as their ID numbers. Because the constants will be defined at an application level, you will not be tempted to assign new numbers at the form level when you create a menu bar that appears only when that form is selected.

During the process of assigning the ID numbers for the Setup menu, you will also define some for a second menu, Orders, that you will create later.

1. Select the BOOKS.POA application and open its Property sheet.

2. Open the Code Editor window for (Declarations).

   You use this section of the application's Property sheet to make application-level declarations. If you want to define a global variable, a constant, or an externally defined function (which you'll learn on Day 11), you would add the necessary declaration in this section of the Property sheet.

3. Enter the following method code to define the constants used for new menu commands:

```
(Declarations)
' Declare the base value for all menu IDs
CONST cMenuNum = 1000

'Assign menu IDs for commands in the Setup menu
CONST cTitles = cMenuNum + 1
CONST cPublishers = cMenuNum + 2
CONST cBookTypes = cMenuNum + 3
CONST cEmployees = cMenuNum + 4

'Assign menu IDs for commands in the Sales menu
CONST cOrders = cMenuNum + 10
CONST cCustomers = cMenuNum + 11
CONST cCustPurchases = cMenuNum + 12
```

   Now that you have the ID numbers assigned to the menu commands, the next step is to define the new menu bar.

4. Enter the following code in the application's OnLoad() method:

```
Sub OnLoad()
' Define the new menu bar and menu as objects
DIM mbrNewBar AS Object
DIM mnuSetup AS Object
mbrNewBar = NEW MenuBar
mnuSetup = NEW Menu

' Add the standard menus and menu commands to the
' new menu bar
mbrNewBar.SysDefaultMenuBar()

'Create the Setup menu
mnuSetup.Label = "&Setup"
mnuSetup.AppendMenuItem("&Titles", cTitles, 0, "^t")
```

```
mnuSetup.AppendMenuItem("&Publishers", cPublishers, 0, NULL)
mnuSetup.AppendMenuItem("&Book Types", cBookTypes, 0, NULL)
mnuSetup.AppendMenuItem("&Employees", cEmployees, 0, NULL)

' Add the Setup menu to the menu bar
mbrNewBar.InsertMenu(4, mnuSetup)
```

You have now defined a menu and a menu bar, added menu commands to the menu, and added the menu to the menu bar as the fourth item. The final step is to replace the default menu bar with the custom one when a form is selected.

Remember, you can associate a particular custom menu bar with any number of forms or reports. In this case, you want the new menu bar to appear no matter which form is selected, so you will add the necessary code to associate the menu bar with every form.

The best time to create this association between the menu bar and the forms is when the application launches. Therefore, you need to add the following method code to the end of the application's `OnLoad()` method:

```
Sub OnLoad()
' Associate the menu bar with all menus in the application
frmBookOrders.SetMenu(mbrNewBar)
frmBooks.SetMenu(mbrNewBar)
frmCustomers.SetMenu(mbrNewBar)
frmPubsBooks.SetMenu(mbrNewBar)
frmBookTypes.SetMenu(mbrNewBar)

' Open the Book Orders form
frmBookOrders.OpenWindow()
```

The final part of the code opens the Book Orders form when the application launches. The Setup menu will look like Figure 9.5.

Figure 9.5.

The new Setup menu.

Right now, the menu commands do nothing when you select them. The next step is to add code to the `DoCommand()` method that opens the correct form when a menu command is selected. As described earlier, the application passes the menu command's ID number (a constant) to both methods `TestCommand()` and `DoCommand()` when you select that menu item. The code you add to either method then specifies what action to take.

The code within both `TestCommand()` and `DoCommand()` normally performs this check with a SELECT CASE statement. In Oracle Basic, SELECT CASE uses a particular value to take one of several possible actions. (For more information on the syntax for SELECT CASE, consult the Oracle Power Objects online help.) In this case, you use SELECT CASE to test the value of the menu ID number passed to `DoCommand()` as the argument cmdCode.

Because DoCommand() is a function, you need to specify a return value. Normally, you return the constant TRUE to indicate that you want the application to continue.

1. Open the DoCommand() method for the application.

2. In DoCommand(), enter the following code:

```
Function DoCommand(cmdCode as Long) as Long
' Test for the constant assigned to each menu command.
' Depending on the constant, open the correct form.
SELECT CASE cmdCode
CASE cTitles
  frmBooks.OpenWindow()
  DoCommand = TRUE
CASE cPublishers
  frmPubsBooks.OpenWindow()
CASE cBookTypes
  frmBookTypes.OpenWindow()
END SELECT
```

In this code, the CASE ELSE statement handles any value not covered by other CASE statements.

3. Save and run the application.

Because you have added code to DoCommand(), selecting an item from the Setup menu will actually do something now.

4. Select the Setup | Titles menu command.

The frmBooks form now appears.

5. Close both forms.

The application now stops running.

A Word on Closing Down Applications

Whenever you close the last form or report in an application, the application quits. The method LastWindowClose(), called when the last form or report closes, terminates the application as part of its default processing.

Many GUI applications do not quit when you close the last window, so this feature of Oracle Power Objects applications might come as a surprise for your users. For example, you can run Microsoft Word without having any documents open. If your application quits as soon as you close the final form, you might be surprised, if not dismayed, that you have to launch the application again.

More significantly for this lesson, however, this feature complicates the task of maintaining a custom menu that opens forms and reports. Because menu bars must be associated with forms or reports, the menu bar disappears as soon as the form or report is closed. If you somehow prevent the application from terminating when the last form or report is closed, you will no

longer have access to the custom menu bar. Essentially, you will be stuck without any way to open a form or report, so you might as well close the application.

> **Note:** When you close the last window in an application, the `LastWindowClosed()` method executes. As part of its default processing, `LastWindowClosed()` terminates the application.

How then can you circumvent this problem? One solution is to create a form that always appears in the application, but which the user cannot close.

You can rule out immediately two techniques for doing this: Although you might try to set a form's `Visible` property to `FALSE`, in fact a form cannot be rendered invisible in this fashion. (If you try, all of the objects on the form become invisible!)

Likewise, if you call the `HideWindow()` method of a form, the form is hidden but still held in memory. Unfortunately, you cannot select a hidden form, so you cannot display the custom menu bar by selecting this form.

The best solution is a bit unattractive, but it works: By moving a form beyond the boundaries of the application window, it remains open within the application but beyond your ability to reach it. If you close every other form in the application, you automatically select this other form, somewhere in the Outer Mongolia of the application interface. If the custom menu bar is associated with this form, it appears regardless of whether you have closed every other form. You can still close the application by selecting the File | Exit menu command (File | Quit on the Macintosh).

The form that will serve this purpose in the Bookstore application is a splash screen.

Adding a Splash Screen

In many GUI applications, a form appears briefly when you first open the application. Generally, this form shows the name of the application, some version information, and perhaps a graphic.

As with many splash screens, the one you will add to the Bookstore application will have a pushbutton that makes the form disappear when pressed. However, in this case, the pushbutton will simply move the form to an inaccessible location, instead of removing it from the application.

1. Add a new form to the BOOKS.POA application, frmSplash.
2. Add a static text object to the form, giving it a label of `The Bookstore Companion`.

   You now have an official name for your application!

3. Set the following other properties of the static text object:

Property	Setting
FontName	Arial
FontSize	18
FontBold	True
TextJustHoriz	Center
TextJustVert	Center

4. Add a pushbutton to the form with the label OK.

5. Enter the following method code in the pushbutton's Click() method:

```
Sub Click()
frmSplash.WinPositionX = 1000
frmSplash.WinPositionY = 1000
```

The WinPositionX and WinPositionY properties specify the vertical and horizontal position of the form. This position is measured from the top of the area beneath the toolbar for WinPositionY, and from the left of the application for WinPositionX. By setting both values to 1000, you move the form far beyond the lower-right corner of the application (see Figure 9.6).

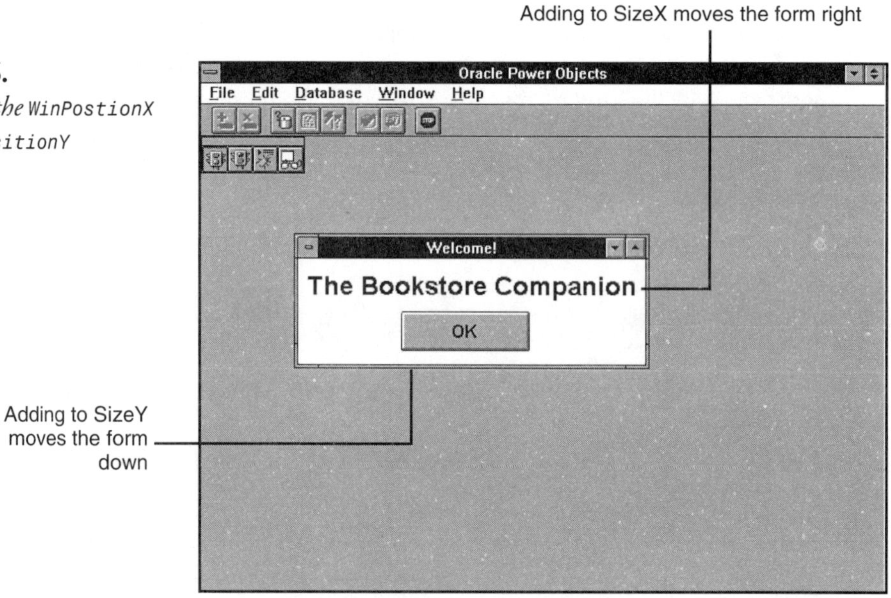

Figure 9.6.

Changing the WinPostionX *and* WinPositionY *properties.*

Adding to SizeX moves the form right

Adding to SizeY moves the form down

6. Resize and reposition the objects in this dialog box so that it looks like Figure 9.7.

Figure 9.7.
How the splash screen should look.

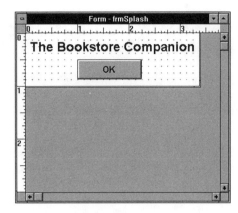

7. Change the splash screen's WindowStyle property to Standard Dialog.

   This window style prevents the user from minimizing or maximizing the form or closing it by pressing the system button. Without these options, the user knows to press the pushbutton to remove the form (or in this case, move it out of sight).

8. Delete the following lines from the application's OnLoad() method:

   ```
   ' Open the Book Orders form
   frmBookOrders.OpenWindow()
   ```

   Originally, the code you just deleted opened the Book Orders form whenever the application launched. Now, you will open the splash screen instead.

9. At the end of the code appearing in the application's OnLoad() method, add the following as the last lines of code:

   ```
   ' Open the splash screen
   frmSplash.OpenWindow()
   ' Associate the menu bar with the splash screen
   frmSplash.SetMenu(mbrNewBar)
   ```

   This final step associates the new menu bar with the splash screen.

10. Save and run the application.

    The splash screen now appears as the first form in the application.

11. Press the OK button in the dialog box.

    The dialog box disappears. The Setup menu remains, however, because the form is actually still open but moved out of sight.

Adding Employee Information to the Application

Because you have a menu command for opening an employee information form, it's time to add employee information to the application. The EMPLOYEES table will contain records for each employee, and the frmEmployees form will display these records in the application.

The EMPLOYEES table will be very important when you learn about security in an Oracle Power Objects application during Day 15's lesson. For now, the form displaying each employee's information will be available to anyone—not a feature you want to leave in the final application!

1. In the BOOKS.POS session, add a table to the database named EMPLOYEES.
2. Add to EMPLOYEES the columns described in Table 9.1.

Table 9.1. Columns in the EMPLOYEES table.

Column	Data Type	Size	Precision	Not Null	Unique
EMPLOYEE_ID	Number				
EMPLOYEE_LNAME	VARCHAR2	32	N/A	Yes	
EMPLOYEE_FNAME	VARCHART2	32	N/A	Yes	
SALARY	FLOAT	N/A	2	N/A	
ALIAS	VARCHAR2	12	N/A	N/A	
PASSWORD	VARCHAR2	12	N/A	N/A	
MANAGER	NUMBER	N/A	N/A	N/A	

3. Set EMPLOYEE_ID as the primary key for this table.
4. Save and run the table.
5. Enter in the table the new records described in Table 9.2.

Table 9.2. Employee records in the EMPLOYEES table.

EMPLOYEE_ID	EMPLOYEE_LNAME	EMPLOYEE_FNAME	SALARY	ALIAS	PASSWORD	MANAGER
1	Boss	Jane	40000	jboss	daboss	-1
2	Supervisor	Joe	38000	jsupervisor	silicon	-1
3	Bond	Victor	24000	vbond	antwerp	0
4	Sanchez	Julie	24000	jsanchez	oreo	0
5	Hu	Karen	28000	khu	bugs	0

6. Press Commit to save these records to the EMPLOYEES table.

7. Press Stop to close the Table Browser window.

8. In the application, create a new form with the name frmEmployees and the label Employees.

9. Drag the icon for the EMPLOYEES table from the database onto the form.

10. Add a scrollbar for browsing employee records.

11. Save the new form.

12. Open the Property sheet for the application and make the following addition to the method code in DoCommand(). The added lines are marked in bold.

```
Function DoCommand(cmdCode as Long) as Long
' Test for the constant assigned to each menu command.
' Depending on the constant, open the correct form.
SELECT CASE cmdCode
CASE cTitles
  frmBooks.OpenWindow()
  DoCommand = TRUE
CASE cPublishers
  frmPubsBooks.OpenWindow()
CASE cBookTypes
  frmBookTypes.OpenWindow()
CASE cEmployees
  frmEmployees.OpenWindow()
END SELECT
```

The added code opens the new form, frmEmployees, when you select the Setup | Employees menu command.

13. Save and run the application.

14. Select the Setup | Employees menu command.

The new form now appears in the application.

15. Press Stop to end this exercise.

The Sales Menu

Now that you are accustomed to working with menu bars and menus, you should feel comfortable adding a second menu to your custom menu bar. This new menu, Sales, will contain several menu commands related to selling books. For example, the Sales | Orders command will open the frmBookOrders form, and the Sales | Customers command will open the frmCustomers form.

You have already defined constants for the menu commands that will appear in the Sales menu. Before beginning this exercise, review the code you entered in the (Declarations) window of the application's Property sheet to see these constants.

Where to Place This Menu

The new Sales menu will appear immediately before the Setup menu. Many GUI designers prefer to place menus in an order reflecting the frequency with which the user selects commands from that menu. More frequently used menus appear on the left, whereas less frequently used menus appear on the right. In all cases, the menus should appear between the standard Edit and Window menus. In the case of an Oracle Power Objects application, you should also place menus to the right of the Database menu, which is standard in all applications.

During a business day, you will be accessing the Sales menu more frequently than the Setup menu. You will be placing orders more often than entering new publisher records, so the menu that opens the Book Orders form should appear before the menu used to set up publisher records. Therefore, the Sales menu should appear first, as the user reads across the menu bar from left to right.

Other GUI gurus advocate a different approach: The setup data should appear before the operations that depend on this information. Using this approach, you would place the Setup menu before the Sales menu, so that your users know that you must enter publisher and title information before selling any books.

In this application, you will take the first approach. In your own applications, follow your own instincts. Whatever rule you apply for positioning menus, apply it consistently so that users will know what to expect.

Adding the Sales Menu

To create the Sales menu, follow these steps:

1. Open the Property sheet for the application.

2. In the Code Editor window for `OnLoad()`, make the following additions (the added code appears in bold):

```
' Define the new menu bar and menus as objects
DIM mbrNewBar AS Object
DIM mnuSetup AS Object
DIM mnuSales AS Object
mbrNewBar = NEW MenuBar
mnuSetup = NEW Menu
mnuSales = NEW Menu

' Add the standard menus and menu commands to the
' new menu bar
mbrNewBar.SysDefaultMenuBar()

' Create the Setup menu
mnuSetup.Label = "&Setup"
mnuSetup.AppendMenuItem("&Titles", cTitles, 0, "^t")
```

```
mnuSetup.AppendMenuItem("&Publishers", cPublishers, 0, NULL)
mnuSetup.AppendMenuItem("&Book Types", cBookTypes, 0, NULL)
mnuSetup.AppendMenuItem("&Employees", cEmployees, 0, NULL)

' Create the Sales menu
mnuSales.Label = "S&ales"
mnuSales.AppendMenuItem("&Orders", cOrders, 0, NULL)
mnuSales.AppendMenuItem("&Customers", cCustomers, 0, NULL)

' Add the Setup menu to the menu bar
mbrNewBar.InsertMenu(4, mnuSetup)

' Add the Sales menu to the menu bar
mbrNewBar.InsertMenu(4, mnuSales)

' Associate the menu bar with all menus in the application
frmBookOrders.SetMenu(mbrNewBar)
frmBooks.SetMenu(mbrNewBar)
frmCustomers.SetMenu(mbrNewBar)
frmPubsBooks.SetMenu(mbrNewBar)
frmCustPurchases.SetMenu(mbrNewBar)
frmBokTypes.SetMenu(mbrNewBar)

' Associate the menu bar with the splash screen
frmSplash.SetMenu(mbrNewBar)

' Open the splash screen
frmSplash.OpenWindow()
```

3. Add the following bold code to the application's `DoCommand()` method:

```
Function DoCommand(cmdCode as Long) as Long
' Test for the constant assigned to each menu command.
' Depending on the constant, open the correct form.
SELECT CASE cmdCode
CASE cTitles
  frmBooks.OpenWindow()
  DoCommand = TRUE
CASE cPublishers
  frmPubsBooks.OpenWindow()
CASE cBookTypes
  frmBookTypes.OpenWindow()
CASE cEmployees
  frmEmployees.OpenWindow()
CASE cOrders
  frmBookOrders.OpenWindow()
CASE cCustomers
  frmCustomers.OpenWindow()
END SELECT
```

4. Save and run the application.

   The new menu now appears on the menu bar (see Figure 9.8).

5. After dismissing the splash screen, select the Sales | Orders menu command.

   As expected, the Book Orders form now appears.

6. Press Stop to end this exercise.

Figure 9.8.
The Sales menu added to the menu bar.

Oracle Power Objects
File Edit Setup Sales Window Help
            Orders
            Customers

Additional Features of Menus

So far, the two menus you have created are relatively simple. They do not yet have many of the common features of menus, including

- ☐ Separators, which are horizontal lines separating menu commands
- ☐ Check marks
- ☐ Disabled menu commands, which appear grayed to indicate that you cannot select that item
- ☐ Accelerators, keyboard shortcuts that automatically select a menu option

Begin with two of the simpler additions to the menu, separators and accelerators.

Adding a Separator

Of all the additions to your new menus, separator lines are the easiest to implement. Essentially, the separator line is a row of hyphens (-) that together form a line across the menu. The user cannot select this row of hyphens—they serve only to separate menu commands.

You should use separators to define the boundaries between groups of related menu commands. For example, the Edit menu in an Oracle Power Objects application has the separator shown in Figure 9.9.

Figure 9.9.
The Edit menu, with its separator.

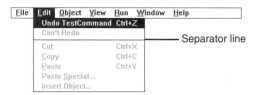

This separator groups the copy, cut, and paste commands on one side of the line, and the commands related to undoing an operation on the other side of the line.

In the Bookstore application, you will add a separator line to the Setup menu that separates the Setup | Employees menu command from other commands. Because the ability to view employee records should be limited to managers only, the line will serve to remind the user that the Setup | Employees menu command is different from other commands in this respect.

The `AppendMenuItem()` method, which adds menu commands to a menu, is already configured to add separator lines. Whenever you specify the text of a new menu item as a single hyphen, `AppendMenuItem()` understands that you wish to create a separator line.

1. Open the Property sheet for the application.

2. Add the following bold line to the `OnLoad()` method.

   The following code excerpt does not have the complete method code from `OnLoad()`, only the portion that defines the items in the Setup menu.

```
Sub OnLoad()
' Create the Setup menu
mnuSetup.Label = "&Setup"
mnuSetup.AppendMenuItem("&Titles", cTitles, 0, "^t")
mnuSetup.AppendMenuItem("&Publishers", cPublishers, 0, NULL)
mnuSetup.AppendMenuItem("&Book Types", cBookTypes, 0, NULL)
mnuSetup.AppendMenuItem("-", NULL, NULL, NULL)
mnuSetup.AppendMenuItem("&Employees", cEmployees, 0, NULL)
```

3. Save your changes to the application.

Now, if you were to run the application, the separator line would appear in the Setup menu. However, before you test the menu bar further, you will add some keyboard accelerators to it.

Adding an Accelerator

If you expect that the user will select a particular menu command frequently, consider assigning a keyboard accelerator to it. The accelerator can be a single key (normally one of the function keys, such as F10), or a key combination (such as Ctrl+T).

In Microsoft Windows, some keyboard accelerators are standard across many applications. For example, the Ctrl+C combination copies whatever is selected, mimicking what the menu command Edit | Copy does. Similarly, on the Macintosh, the command key often is part of an accelerator, such as Command+C to copy a selected item.

In the Bookstore application, you should expect users to frequently open the Book Orders form. Therefore, add a keyboard accelerator that opens the Book Orders form whenever the user types the combination of the Ctrl and R keys. This new accelerator will do exactly what the Sales | Orders menu command does, and the accelerator will appear next to that menu command as a reminder.

You might have noticed that you already added a keyboard accelerator to one menu, Setup | Titles. When you type the Ctrl+T combination, the application opens the frmBooks form (see Figure 9.10).

In addition, you have created some keyboard shortcuts when you designed all your menu commands. A shortcut uses the Alt key plus another key to first select a menu, and then another combination of Alt and another key to select a command within that menu. The additional key in both cases is denoted by an underline character somewhere within the label for the menu or menu command. (See Figure 9.11.)

Figure 9.10.

The accelerator for opening the Titles form, as it appears in the Setup menu.

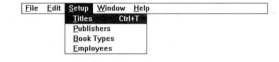

Figure 9.11.

Keyboard shortcuts in the Setup menu.

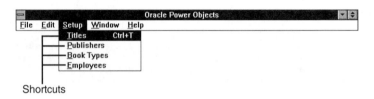

When you assign a label to a menu or a menu command, you specify the shortcut key by adding an ampersand (&) before the letter you want to act as a shortcut. When you assigned the Label property to the Sales menu, for example, you entered the following method code:

```
mnuSales.Label = "&Sales"
```

Similarly, when you created the Sales | Orders menu command, you entered the following:

```
mnuSales.AppendMenuItem("&Orders", cOrders, 0, NULL)
```

In both cases, the ampersand precedes the character that acts as the shortcut, and which is underlined to indicate its role.

Because you have already added shortcuts for each of the new menu commands, you will add a new keyboard accelerator in this exercise.

1. Open the Code Editor window for the application's OnLoad() method.
2. Make the following change (in bold) to the section that defines the menu commands in the Sales menu:

```
Sub OnLoad()
' Create the Sales menu
mnuSales.Label = "&Sales"
mnuSales.AppendMenuItem("&Orders", cOrders, 0, "F5")
mnuSales.AppendMenuItem("&Customers", cCustomers, 0, "F6")
mnuSales.AppendMenuItem("&Purchases", cCustPurchases, 0, NULL)
```

In other words, you are assigning the function keys F5 and F6 to two of the menu commands.

3. Save and run the application.

4. Select the Setup menu to view the new separator line.

5. Select the Sales menu to view the new keyboard accelerators, shown in Figure 9.12.

Figure 9.12.

The new accelerators in the Sales menu.

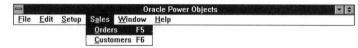

6. Press Stop to end this exercise.

As you can tell, the keyboard accelerator assigned to a menu command is the last argument passed to the AppendMenuItem() method. If you do not want to assign any accelerator, pass the constant NULL as this argument. If you want a keyboard accelerator, you can use the characters described in Table 9.3 to denote the accelerator.

Table 9.3. Keyboard accelerator characters.

Character	Description
character	Any alphanumeric character appearing on the keyboard.
function_key	Any of the function keys appearing at the top of the keyboard (for example, F1).
^	A symbol denoting the Ctrl key (or the Command key on the Macintosh).
+	A symbol denoting the Shift key.

Therefore, if you wanted to assign the accelerator combination of Ctrl, Shift, and A to a menu command, you would enter something like this:

```
mnuTest.AppendMenuItem("&Bogus", NULL, NULL, "^+A")
```

Disabling Menu Commands

Frequently, applications disable menu commands when selecting them is not appropriate. If no text is highlighted (that is, selected for copying) in your word processor document, the Edit | Copy command should be disabled. Similarly, if a form is not bound to a record source, the items in the Database menu of an Oracle Power Objects application are disabled.

If you want to disable a menu command, you must write the method code that performs this task. Where do you put this code?

You have already worked with the DoCommand() method, which defines what actions the application will take when you select a menu command. A similar method, TestCommand(), determines the status of each menu command. Like DoCommand(), TestCommand() takes as its argument the ID number of the menu command in question. The code you add to TestCommand() should use this ID number to identify the menu command, and then perform whatever change you wish to make to it.

Although DoCommand() executes when you select a menu command, you trigger TestCommand() when you "pull down" a menu to view it. At that moment, the application needs to determine the status of each menu command (checked or unchecked, enabled or disabled), so it triggers TestCommand() to perform the check.

Unlike DoCommand(), the return value of TestCommand() can take several forms. In each case, you want to define a return value that determines the status of a particular menu command. The constants for each return value are summarized in Table 9.4.

Table 9.4. Return values for `TestCommand()`.

Constant	Description
TestCommand_Disabled	Disables the menu command.
TestCommand_Enabled	Enables the menu command.
TestCommand_Checked	Adds a check mark next to the menu command, which also appears enabled. If you want to remove the check mark, use the constant TestCommand_Enabled instead.
TestCommand_Disabled_Checked	Adds a check mark next to the menu command, which appears disabled. If you want to remove the check mark, use the constant TestCommand_Disabled instead.

In this exercise, you will write method code that disables the Sales | Orders menu command if the Book Orders form is already open. When the form closes, the application re-enables the menu command, so that you can select it to open the Book Orders form again.

This exercise involves this process:

☐ Define a global variable used to store information about whether the Book Orders form is open or not.

☐ Add the code to the OpenWindow() and CloseWindow() methods of the form to change the value assigned to the global variable. This way, you can change the value of the global variable whenever the form opens or closes.

☐ Add the code to TestCommand() to enable or disable the menu command.

Here are the steps you follow:

1. Open the application's Property sheet.

2. In the `(Declarations)` section, add the following line of method code:

   ```
   (Declarations)
   GLOBAL gFormOpen AS Long
   ```

   This is the global variable that will track whether the Book Orders form is open or not.

3. In the `OnLoad()` method, add the following line:

   ```
   Sub OnLoad()
   gFormOpen = FALSE
   ```

   This step assigns an initial value (that is, initializes) the global variable `gFormOpen`. If you do not initialize the variable, its beginning value will be `NULL`. As you know from previous lessons, you should often be careful to avoid leaving the value of many variables and property as `NULL`.

4. In the `TestCommand()` method of the application, enter the following method code:

   ```
   Function TestCommand(cmdCode As Long) As Long
   SELECT CASE cmdCode
   CASE cOrders
      ' Based on the status of the global variable gFormOpen,
      ' enable or disable the menu command.
      IF gFormOpen = FALSE THEN
         TestCommand = TestCommand_Enabled
      ELSE
         TestCommand = TestCommand_Disabled
      END IF
   END SELECT
   ```

5. Open the Property sheet for the frmBookOrders form.

6. Add the following code to its `OpenWindow()` method:

   ```
   Sub OpenWindow()
   ' Allow the default processing needed to open the window
   Inherited.OpenWindow()

   ' Assign a new value to the global variable
   gFormOpen = TRUE
   ```

7. Add the following code to its `CloseWindow()` method:

   ```
   Sub CloseWindow()
   ' Allow the default processing needed to close the window
   gFormOpen = FALSE

   ' Assign a new value to the global variable
   Inherited.CloseWindow()
   ```

8. Save and run the application.

9. Select Sales | Orders.

   The Book Orders form now appears.

10. Select the Sales menu again.

The Sales | Orders menu command is now disabled, as shown in Figure 9.13, because the Book Orders form is open.

Figure 9.13.
The disabled menu command Sales | Orders.

11. Press Stop to end the exercise.

Adding a Check Mark

Actually, disabling the menu command is unnecessary. If you select the Sales | Orders menu command after you have opened the form, you simply select the form again. There's no need to worry that you will open a second copy of the form.

However, it might be useful to add a check mark to the menu command if the form is already open. When you have several forms open simultaneously, figuring out quickly which forms are open can be difficult. By adding the check mark to the menu when the form is opened, you can tell easily whether you have opened the form.

To add a check mark instead of disabling the menu code, you need only change the method code in the TestCommand() method.

1. Change the method code in the application's TestCommand() method to read as follows:

```
Function TestCommand(cmdCode As Long) As Long
SELECT CASE cmdCode
CASE cOrders
   ' Based on the status of the global variable gFormOpen,
   ' enable or disable the menu command.
   IF gFormOpen = FALSE THEN
      TestCommand = TestCommand_Enabled
   ELSE
      TestCommand = TestCommand_Checked
   END IF
END SELECT
```

2. Save and run the application.

3. Select Sales | Orders to open the Book Orders form.

4. Select the Sales menu again.

The Sales | Orders command is now checked to indicate that you have opened the form already (see Figure 9.14).

5. Press Stop to end this exercise.

Figure 9.14.

The check mark appearing next to the Sales | Orders menu command.

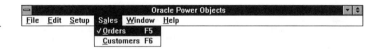

Menu-Related Properties and Methods

This chapter has taken a different approach toward explaining some of the standard Oracle Power Objects methods. Instead of reading a detailed description of each property before using it, you leaped into writing method code using several fairly complex properties.

Menus require a fair amount of coding, and the reasons behind some of the steps are not immediately obvious. Additionally, some of the options for designing menu bars, menus, and menu commands might not be clear until you have seen a completed menu in operation. For these reasons, this chapter has postponed the description of the menu-related properties until well after you have had some experience designing menus.

This lesson has not used all of the menu-related methods. Most significantly, you have not seen how you can access the contents of both the standard menus as well as the ones you define. In one of the last exercises in this chapter, you will remove the Help menu, a standard part of any menu bar, from your custom menu bar. Before continuing, however, Table 9.5 briefly reviews the menu-related properties and methods. For a complete description of the syntax for each method, including their arguments and return values, consult the Oracle Power Objects online help.

Table 9.5. Menu-related properties and methods.

Property/Method	Applies To	Description
Label	Menu	Defines the text appearing at the top of the menu.
SysDefaultMenuBar()	Menu bars	Adds the standard menus to the menu bar.
AppendMenu()		Adds a new menu to a menu bar after all existing menus appearing on the menu bar.
InsertMenu()		Adds a menu at the specified position. The leftmost menu is counted as one, and other menus are counted from left to right.
DeleteAllMenus()		Removes all menus from the menu bar.
RemoveMenu()		Deletes the specified method from the menu bar.

continues

Table 9.5. continued

Property/Method	Applies To	Description
GetMenu()		Returns a reference to a particular menu. Because menus are objects, the return value of this method has the Object data type.
GetMenuCount()		Returns the number of menus appearing in the menu bar.
AppendMenuItem()	Menus	Adds a new menu command after all other menu commands.
InsertMenuItem()		Inserts a new menu command at the indicated position.
GetMenuItem()		Returns information about some aspect of the specified menu command.
SetMenuItem()		Sets the value for some component of the specified menu.
GetItemCount()		Returns the number of menu commands in a menu.
DeleteMenuItem()		Deletes the specified menu command.
InitializeWindow()	Form or report	Called to set the default menu bar, toolbar, and status line for a form or report.
DefaultMenuBar()		Associates the default menu bar with a form or report.
GetMenuBar()		Returns a reference to the menu bar (type Object) associated with a form or report.
SetMenuBar()		Associates a menu bar with a form or report.
DoCommand()	Application	Performs an action based on the menu selected.
TestCommand()		Sets the status of a menu command.

There are quite a few methods! However, the number of methods is also a measure of the quantity of options you have available when you work with menus. To illustrate this point, you will use some of these methods to remove the Help menu from the custom menu bar. Because your application will not have an online help file explaining how to use it, leaving the Help menu can serve only to frustrate users expecting to access online help through it.

Removing a Menu

To remove the Help menu, follow these steps:

1. Open the Code Editor window for the application's OnLoad() method.

2. Add the following highlighted lines to the method code in OnLoad().

   Again, the following excerpt shows only some of the method code appearing in the OnLoad() method.

```
Sub OnLoad()
mbrNewBar(4, mnuSetup)
mbrNewBar(4, mnuSales)

' Get the position of the Help menu (always the
' last item on the menu bar)
DIM vMenuNum AS Long
vMenuNum = mbrNewBar.GetMenuCount()

' Delete the Help menu
mbrNewBar.RemoveMenu(vMenuNum)
```

3. Save and run the application.

   The menu bar now appears as in Figure 9.15, but without the Help menu.

Figure 9.15.
The menu bar after the Help menu has been removed.

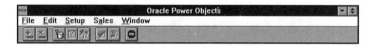

4. Press Stop to end this exercise.

Working with Standard Menus

As you can see from this exercise, you can work with both standard menus as well as custom ones you design yourself. Each menu command in the standard menus (File, Edit, and so on) has its own menu ID number, to which a constant is already assigned. When you write method code in the DoCommand() method that mimics what a standard menu command does, you use the appropriate constant in your code. For example, if you were to test to see whether the user is trying to close the application, you would use the constant CMD_QUIT.

The *Oracle Power Objects User's Guide* has a list of all the constants available to you, including those predefined for standard menu commands. These menu-related constants include the following:

CMD_ABOUT	CMD_HELPONHELP	CMD_PRINTPREVIEW
CMD_APPQUERY	CMD_INSERTOBJECT	CMD_PRINTSETUP
CMD_CLEAR	CMD_INSERTROW	CMD_QBF
CMD_CLOSE	CMD_NEW	CMD_QBFRUN
CMD_COMMIT	CMD_NEWWINDOW	CMD_QUIT
CMD_COPY	CMD_NEXTPAGE	CMD_REDO
CMD_CUT	CMD_OPENB	CMD_ROLLBACK
CMD_DELETEROW	CMD_PASTE	CMD_RUNSTOP
CMD_FIRSTUSERCOMMAND	CMD_PASTESPECIAL	CMD_SAVE
CMD_FULLPAGE	CMD_PREVPAGE	CMD_SAVEAS
CMD_HELP	CMD_PRINT	CMD_UNDO

That's plenty of work for one day! To create a new menu bar, you have had to write the largest amount of code so far. Although the various methods required to create a menu bar seemed arcane at first, by now the logic of their design should make greater sense. However, before you end today's lesson, you should be aware of two other kinds of objects that you design in the same fashion as you created a custom menu bar.

Toolbars and Status Lines

In Oracle Power Objects, a toolbar always appears near the top of the application window, just below the menu bar. The toolbar displays several buttons that provide shortcuts for commonly used menu commands, such as Commit, Roll Back, Insert Row, and Query.

Additionally, a status line appears at the bottom of the application. As its name implies, the status line displays information about the status of the application, as well as help text for each control.

The toolbar changes, depending on whether you select a form or report. When you select a form, buttons appropriate to editing a form (such as Rollback and Insert Row) appear on the toolbar. When you select a report, a different set of buttons, appropriate for viewing and printing reports, appears instead. Because different types of toolbars can appear depending on what you select, one is called the Form Run Time toolbar, and the other the Report Run Time toolbar.

You create toolbars and status lines in the same fashion as you created a menu bar: by adding method code to the application's OnLoad() method. In addition, because you perform actions through a toolbar, you need to somehow define what happens when you press a button. Not surprisingly, you add code to the TestCommand() method to define what happens when you press a particular button.

On Day 11, you will create a new toolbar including a few new buttons. For now, you need to review what you have learned about working with menus.

Summary

Today, you learned the following:

- ☐ Menus and menu bars are objects that you define completely through code.
- ☐ After you create a new menu bar, you need to add menus to it.
- ☐ The method `SysDefaultMenuBar()` adds the default menus to a menu bar.
- ☐ Menus consist of menu commands, which you can add using the `AddMenuItem()` or `InsertMenuItem()` methods.
- ☐ After you create menus, you must add them to the menu bar.
- ☐ After completely defining the menu bar and its associated menus, you must associate the menu bar with forms and reports.
- ☐ Menus often use keyboard accelerators for commonly used menu commands.
- ☐ To determine what happens when you select a menu command, you add code to the `DoCommand()` method.
- ☐ To determine the status of a menu command, you add code to the `TestCommand()` method.
- ☐ Using the menu-related methods, you can manipulate both standard and custom menus.
- ☐ Status lines and toolbars are defined through many of the same means used to create menu bars.

What Comes Next?

Tomorrow, you will begin to reach beyond the built-in functionality of an Oracle Power Objects application, and begin to use the capabilities of the application environment. Although you can define many procedures within Oracle Power Objects, other procedures can be defined through dynamic link libraries, separate from the application entirely. In Microsoft Windows, you can use many built-in procedures to perform tasks by calling these procedures from within your Oracle Power Objects application. This capability of Oracle Power Objects adds *extensibility*, your ability to use code written by other developers.

Q&A

Q How do I make a menu bar appear only when the user selects a particular form?

A In many cases, you will want particular menus or menu commands to appear only when a particular form is selected. To do this, associate the menu bar with that form alone.

DAY

9

Menus and Toolbars

Q How can I disable or check a standard menu command, such as Edit | Paste?

A By adding code to `TestCommand()` that tests for the constant assigned to that menu command, and then disables or checks that menu item. In the case of Edit | Paste, you would use the constant `CMD_PASTE`.

Workshop

The Workshop consists of quiz questions to help you solidify your understanding of the material covered. Try and understand the quiz answers before you go on to tomorrow's lesson.

Quiz

1. If you create a new menu and it does not appear on your menu bar, what might be the problem?

2. Are menu commands objects?

3. If you want to disable a menu command if the user has not yet committed changes to a record, where do you add the necessary code?

4. How would you create a new menu command that copied what a standard menu command does? For example, how would you create a new menu command that commits changes to a record in the same fashion that the Database | Commit menu command does?

Quiz Answers

1. There are two potential problems. First, you might not have successfully associated a custom menu bar with a form, using the `SetMenuBar()` method. Second, you might not have properly associated the menu with the custom menu bar, using the `AppendMenu()` or `InsertMenu()` methods.

2. No. Menu bars are objects, but menu commands are not. Menu commands are components of a menu object that you add using the `AppendMenuItem()` or `InsertMenuItem()` method.

3. Because you are determining the status of a menu command, the code must appear in the `TestCommand()` method.

4. When you create the new menu command, you would assign it the same constant as the standard menu command. In the case of `Commit`, you would use the constant `CMD_COMMIT` when you create the new menu command through the `AppendMenuItem()` or `InsertMenuItem()` method.

10

Dynamic Link Libraries

Overview

Today, you learn about the following topics:

- [ ] Dynamic link libraries (DLLs)
- [ ] Declaring DLL procedures
- [ ] Calling DLL procedures
- [ ] Inherent Windows procedures
- [ ] Playing sounds in Windows
- [ ] Launching other applications from an Oracle Power Objects application
- [ ] Working with Windows configuration (.INI) files
- [ ] Creating custom toolbars

Developers writing applications in the C or C++ programming languages often define procedures in libraries separate from the actual executable application. By keeping these procedures separate from the .EXE file, the developer can easily fix or improve upon these procedures without having to recompile the entire application.

These storehouses of compiled procedures are called *dynamic link libraries* (or *DLLs*). DLLs are compiled like .EXE files, so you cannot view the actual code behind these procedures, but you can call them to perform tasks for you. As long as you know the components of a procedure, you can call it from within your own application. The full description of the procedure is called an *Advanced Programming Interface* (API). As long as you declare the API in your application, telling it what to expect, you can call the procedure.

DLL procedures can be very useful because they often perform tasks more efficiently than you could through method code. Furthermore, many are already designed to handle some sophisticated tasks. This is particularly true when you try to work with the application's environment, such as trying to take advantage of the multimedia capabilities of Windows.

Today, you will call several DLL procedures to perform tasks within the Bookstore application. In the process, you will learn how you can use DLLs to extend your application, taking advantage of the work done by other developers.

Note: This chapter covers features available in Microsoft Windows only. Macintosh users still need to build some of the forms used in this lesson, because they are used in later lessons. However, you cannot add the functionality of these forms to a Macintosh version of the Bookstore application.

Types of DLLs

When you are developing applications for Microsoft Windows, there are two kinds of DLLs you can work with:

☐ Windows DLLs—Windows depends on several core DLLs to run. Because Microsoft has made the APIs for various Windows procedures public, you can work directly with the Windows environment by calling these DLLs. For example, some of these procedures return information about the Windows environment, such as the amount of available memory and the "handle" (a unique identifier) for various applications and forms currently displayed in Windows. Others determine how Windows displays graphics and plays sounds.

The more proficient you become in developing Windows applications, the more you will use the native Windows APIs for performing many tasks. The Windows DLLs provide many important shortcuts, and they let you work on elements of the Windows environment directly (controlling the way Windows displays graphics, for example, rather than relying on some secondary tool to help you). However, before you can use these procedures effectively, you must understand some important facts about DLLs, as outlined in this chapter.

☐ Third-party DLLs—Many programmers publish the APIs for DLLs that they develop, so that other developers can use them. Some DLLs are designed to be independent of any single application, to stand as generic libraries of procedures. For example, many graphics applications use generic DLLs designed for displaying pictures in various formats (JPG, GIF, TIFF, and so on). As long as you know the API, you can call a procedure from one of these DLLs.

During the exercises in today's lesson, you will be using several Microsoft Windows DLLs to

☐ Display the amount of free memory
☐ Display the amount of free system resources
☐ Display the system time
☐ Play a sound file
☐ Run another Windows application

Although you will be working with Windows procedures only, the techniques you learn will apply when you call any DLL procedure.

Declaring a DLL Procedure

Before you can use any DLL procedure, you must first declare it. Because computers are precise creatures, they need to know everything about a procedure before you can use it in your application. A DLL procedure has several components that you must determine before you can call the procedure:

☐ The procedure's name.

☐ The name of the library in which the procedure is defined. The term *library* in this case means the name of the DLL—not the Oracle Power Objects library, which is a repository of reusable application objects. To access the DLL, it must be in the path, or you must add its directory as part of its filename.

☐ Whether or not the DLL has a return value. If the procedure has a return value, it is a function. If it does not, it is a subroutine. The syntax for declaring functions and subroutines is slightly different.

☐ The arguments passed to the procedure. The description of each argument includes its name and its data type. In addition, the description of the argument includes information about whether you are passing the argument by value or by reference (you'll learn this more in a later section, "Passing Arguments").

☐ The return value, if any, of the procedure. You declare a return value by identifying its data type.

For example, to declare a hypothetical DLL procedure, you might enter

```
DECLARE SUB MySub LIB "MYLIB.DLL" (arg1 AS Long, arg2 AS Variant)
```

In this case, you are declaring a DLL procedure without a return value. You know this by looking at the type of procedure (SUB, short for subroutine). Also, after the argument list, there is no mention of a return value's data type.

The procedure is defined in the library MYLIB.DLL. As this declaration also indicates, the procedure has two arguments, one with the data type Long, and the other with the data type Variant.

In contrast, if this procedure were a function, its declaration might look like this:

```
DECLARE FUNCTION MySub LIB "MYLIB.DLL" (arg1 AS Long, arg2 AS Variant) AS Long
```

The procedure has many of the same characteristics as when you declared it as a subroutine. In this case, however, the keyword FUNCTION declares the procedure as a function. In addition, after the argument list, you have declared the data type of this procedure's return value as Long.

Right now, you pass both arguments to the function by reference. If you were to pass one of the arguments by value, you would enter the following change:

```
DECLARE FUNCTION MySub LIB "MYLIB.DLL" (ByVal arg1 AS Long,
➥arg2 AS Variant) AS Long
```

As you can see, the ByVal keyword indicates that you must pass the argument by value instead of by reference. If you are not yet familiar with this terminology, don't worry—this lesson covers in detail the options and requirements for passing arguments.

> **Note:** If the DLL is not in the same directory as the application, or it is not in the path defined for the environment, then you need to add the directory in which it is located to its filename in this declaration. For example, if MYLIB.DLL were in the C:\MYDIR directory, you would enter C:\MYDIR\MYLIB.DLL in the function declaration. Obviously, hard coding the path in this fashion is a bad idea because you cannot ensure that your users will keep the DLL in the specified directory, or even on that drive.

Syntax for Declaring DLL Procedures

The general syntax for declaring a DLL subroutine, therefore, is

```
DECLARE SUB Sub_Name LIB "Library_Name" (arguments)
```

And the syntax for declaring DLL functions is

```
DECLARE FUNCTION Func_Name LIB "Library_Name" (arguments) AS return_datatype
```

Regardless of whether you are declaring a Windows procedure or a procedure defined in a different DLL, the syntax is the same. The only important difference in DLL procedure declarations is between subroutine and function declarations.

Where Do I Declare the Procedure?

As you might have already guessed, you declare DLL procedures in the (Declarations) section of the application's Property sheet. As is true of other things you declare here, a procedure declaration becomes global to the application, meaning that you can call the procedure from any form or report.

You now know of three things you can declare in the (Declarations) section, all of which become global to the application.

☐ Global variables. For example, you declared a global variable to track whether the Book Orders form was currently open.

☐ Constants. When you assigned unique ID numbers to menu commands, you declared constants for each of them.

☐ DLL procedures. Later, you will be adding some of these DLL procedure declarations to the application's Property sheet.

Passing Arguments

As mentioned earlier, you can pass arguments either by value or by reference. When you use a DLL procedure, you do not have any choice in the matter; this aspect of the procedure has already been defined. However, you need to know the difference between these ways of passing an argument to know what you can and cannot do with these values.

When you pass an argument by *reference*, the procedure can change that value. For example, if you passed the ColorFill property of a form by reference, theoretically the procedure could change the value assigned to that property, thereby changing the color of the form.

The documentation covering a DLL procedure should describe whatever changes the procedure makes to values passed by reference. In some cases, nothing happens to the value; in others, the procedure always changes the value passed to the procedure. Not surprisingly, then, you need to read the description of a DLL procedure carefully, so that you will not be caught unaware by some unexpected change to a value passed to a procedure.

When you pass an argument by *value*, you pass only the value, not a reference to the variable or property that has that value. Therefore, the procedure can use this value, but it cannot assign a new value to its source (the variable or property).

Developers design arguments to be passed by value when there are clear risks presented if you change the value. For example, when you pass the name of a user as an argument to a procedure that checks usernames and passwords, you do not want to change that value within the procedure. Similarly, if you are simply checking to see if a file exists in a particular directory, you do not want the procedure that performs this check to attempt to change the name of the file.

As mentioned earlier, procedures assume that you are passing a value by reference unless you precede the argument's name with the ByVal keyword.

Capturing Return Values

Another important rule to remember when you use DLL procedures is that, in the case of functions, you must "capture" the return value. Some functions are designed to return a desired value, such as the system date and time, or the result of a complex tax calculation. Other return values simply indicate whether the function executed correctly. In either case, as long as there is a return value, you must capture it by assigning it to a variable or property.

To use one of the examples just cited, if you wanted to call a function to perform a tax calculation, you might capture the value in two ways:

```
fldTotalTax.Value = CalcTax(fldIncome.Value, fldDependents.Value)
```

In this case, the Value property of a text field captures the return value of the function CalcTax. Alternatively, you could capture the return value in a variable:

```
vTotalTax = CalcTax(fldIncome.Value, fldDependents.Value)
```

Again, either technique is fine as long as you capture the value. Otherwise, your application will stop running as soon as the function returns an uncaptured value. Although this information is not important when you declare a function, it will be when you call it.

Using Your First DLL Procedure

To demonstrate how to use DLL procedures, you will call a Windows procedure to display the amount of free memory available. This information will appear in the application's splash screen, immediately visible when you launch the application.

Using this procedure is a three-part process:

- ☐ Declaring the Windows-based procedure
- ☐ Calling the procedure when you open the form
- ☐ Displaying the return value (the amount of free memory) in a text field in the splash screen

With this in mind, you're ready to use your first DLL procedure:

1. Open the (Declarations) section of the application's Property sheet.

2. Add the following line to this section:

   ```
   Declare Function GetFreeSpace Lib "Kernel" (ByVal wFlags As Integer) As Long
   ```

   The Windows procedure GetFreeSpace returns the number of bytes of free memory currently available. The procedure is defined in the library Kernel, and it takes a single argument. When you call GetFreeSpace, in Windows 3.1 the procedure ignores any parameter passed as the wFlags argument. Therefore, you can call this procedure without passing any argument. This situation is unusual, the exception that defines the rule of passing arguments to DLL procedures.

3. Open the form frmSplash.

4. Add a new text field to the lower-right section of the form, and give it the name fldFreeMemory.

5. Change the text field's data type to String, its data size to 32, its HasBorder property to False, and its ReadOnly property to True.

Dynamic Link Libraries

6. Add a static text object to the left of the new text field, and give it the following label:

```
Free Windows memory =.
```

7. Change the following properties of the two new objects:

Property	Setting
FontSize	9
FontName	Arial
FontBold	False

8. Add the following code to the form's OnLoad() method:

```
Sub OnLoad()
DIM vMem AS Long          'The amount of free memory
DIM vMemStr AS String     ' A string that will display the
                          ' amount of free memory available
' Call the Windows procedure GetFreeMem
vMem = GetFreeSpace(0)
' Calculate the number of kilobytes free by dividing this figure by 1000
vMem = vMem/1000
' Build the string to display in the text field
vMemStr = STR(vMem) & " KB"
' Display the amount of free memory in the text field
fldFreeMemory.Value = vMemStr
```

9. Save and run the form.

The form now appears as in Figure 10.1.

Figure 10.1.
The amount of free memory available, displayed in the application's splash screen.

The amount of free memory now appears in the text field, giving the user some crucial information about likely system performance when running the application.

10. Press Stop to end this exercise.

Calling Another Windows DLL Procedure

To give you some more practice calling procedures, you will add another text field to the splash screen that displays the percentage of system resources that are free while running the application. To get this information, you will call another Windows procedure,

314

`GetFreeSystemResources`. This procedure takes a single argument, a flag for the type of free resources you wish to measure. In this case, you want to know the total amount of system resources available.

1. Open the `(Declarations)` section of the application's Property sheet.

2. Add the following procedure declaration:

```
Declare Function GetFreeSystemResources Lib "User"
➥(ByVal fuSysResource As Integer) As Integer
```

3. Add a new text field beneath the one you created in the last exercise, `fldFreeMemory`.

4. Give this new text field the following properties:

Property	Setting
Name	fldFreeResources
Datatype	Double
FormatMask	Percent
FontSize	9
FontName	Arial
HasBorder	False
ReadOnly	True

5. Add the label `Free resources =` next to the new text field.

6. Open the Property sheet for the form frmSplash.

7. Add the following code to the form's `OnLoad()` method:

```
Sub OnLoad()
DIM vMem AS Long 'The amount of free memory
DIM vMemStr AS String     ' A string that will display the
     ' amount of free memory available
' Call the Windows procedure GetFreeMem
vMem = GetFreeMem

' Calculate the number of kilobytes free by dividing this figure by 1000
vMem = vMem/1000

' Build the string to display in the text field
vStr = STR(vMem) & " KB"

' Display the amount of free memory in the text field
fldFreeMemory.Value = vStr

' Call the Windows procedure GetFreeSystemResources
' to display the percentage of system resources free in
' the text field fldFreeResources
DIM vRes AS Double
vRes = GetFreeSystemResources(0)
fldFreeResources.Value = (vRes/100)
```

10

8. Save and run the form.

   The percentage of free system resources now appears in the new text field (see Figure 10.2). The actual percentage is stored as a decimal value, but displayed as a percentage because of the format mask you applied to this text field.

Figure 10.2.

Displaying the percent of system resources free when you launch the application.

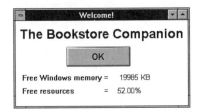

9. Press Stop to end this exercise.

As you can see, calling Windows DLL procedures can be relatively easy. Both `GetFreeSpace` and `GetFreeSystemResources` are relatively simple procedures, with few or no arguments. Other Windows procedures are more complex, as you shall see in later exercises.

Where to Get Windows API Information

Obviously, I did not recall the exact API for each of these Windows procedures off the top of my head. There are many excellent Windows API references available that describe the entire range of available procedures in depth. In fact, several of these references describe the undocumented APIs that Microsoft originally did not make available to Windows developers outside of Microsoft itself.

Additionally, many Windows development books cover particular categories of Windows APIs in even greater detail. For example, if you want to develop games for Windows, you might purchase one of many books covering this topic. These books focus on the Windows APIs covering graphics and sound, providing important tips and tricks in this area.

Playing a Sound File

If you want to play sounds through your application, the easiest technique is to use Microsoft Windows' built-in capability for playing .WAV files. As long as you have a sound driver loaded in Windows, you can play sounds through your PC speaker or sound card.

If your system is not currently configured to play sounds, and you do not have a sound card, you can use the sound driver SPEAKER.DRV to play sounds through the PC speaker. Although many Windows installations do not include this driver, you can get a copy from many

commercial online services and Internet sites. Because the next two exercises involve playing sound files, you might want to track down a copy of SPEAKER.DRV if your system is not configured to play sounds.

The *sndPlaySound* Procedure

Once you have a sound driver installed, you can call the Windows procedure sndPlaySound to play a particular .WAV file. Windows comes with three .WAV files installed: CHORD.WAV, TADA.WAV, and CHIMES.WAV. PC users have recorded thousands of other .WAV files, including sound effects, movie and TV clips, music, historical speeches, and other types of sound excerpts.

In the Bookstore application, you want to play a sound when the application starts. To do so, you need to call the sndPlaySound procedure when either the application loads into memory or the splash screen is first displayed. Because you have already added a lot of code to the application's OnLoad() method, you'll instead add the call to sndPlaySound() to the frmSplash form's OnLoad() method.

To use sndPlaySound, you have to make the following declaration:

```
DECLARE FUNCTION sndPlaySound LIB "MMSYSTEM" (ByVal WaveFile As String,
➥ByVal Flag As Integer) As Integer
```

The argument WaveFile is the name of the .WAV file you wish to play. If the file is not in the WINDOWS directory, you need to specify its path as part of its name (for example, C:\BOOKS\KABOOM.WAV).

The second argument, Flag, determines how Windows plays the sound file. The values for this argument include those shown in Table 10.1.

Table 10.1. Constants for the sndPlaySound procedure.

Constant	Description
0	Windows plays the sound synchronously, meaning that Windows cannot do anything else until the .WAV file finishes playing.
1	Windows plays the sound asynchronously, meaning that if you are playing the sound through a sound card, you can perform other tasks while the .WAV file is playing.
2	If Windows cannot find the specified sound file, it plays nothing but does not return an error.
3	Windows plays the sound in a continuous loop until you stop it.
4	Windows will play the sound as long as it is not already playing. If Windows is already playing the .WAV file, it does not play the sound, and sndPlaySound returns FALSE.

When you call `sndPlaySound`, you want to play the sound asynchronously, so the `Flag` argument will be 1. Because it's a good startup sound, the application will play the sound file TADA.WAV when it opens.

Playing a .WAV File

To play the TADA.WAV sound file when the application launches, follow these steps:

1. In the `(Declarations)` section of the application's Property sheet, add the following function declaration:

   ```
   (Declarations)
   DECLARE FUNCTION sndPlaySound LIB "MMSYSTEM" (ByVal WaveFile
   ➥As String, ByVal Flag As Integer) As Integer
   ```

2. In the `OnLoad()` method of frmSplash, add the following line of code:

   ```
   Sub OnLoad()
   x = sndPlaySound("TADA.WAV", 1)
   ```

   Because `sndPlaySound` is a function, you must capture its return value somehow. In this case, you are capturing it in the variable *x*, which has an undeclared data type. Any undeclared variable has the data type `Variant`. Because a variant can initially capture any data type, you can use this undeclared variable to capture the integer value returned from `sndPlaySound`. As soon as you use an undeclared variable, its data type is fixed, so *x* has the data type `Integer` when it captures the return value.

   You often use this technique when you need a variable only for a moment. In this case, adding a `DIM` statement is a piece of unnecessary code, because you need the variable only briefly to capture a return value.

> **Note:** Once again, you need to make sure that the application can find a file referenced in the code. In this case, you need to make sure that TADA.WAV is in the system's path or the application directory.

3. Save and run the application.

   The application now plays the familiar *Tada!* music when you launch the Bookstore application.

Another Way to Play Sound Files

The procedure `sndPlaySound` plays a specific .WAV file. However, Windows can also play a sound file in response to a particular event. If you try to page down past the bottom of a document in Microsoft Word, for example, Word will play a beep to tell you that you just made a mistake. Word is designed to play whatever sound file is designated as Window's default beep. Just as easily, any application you design can use the default beep, or sounds associated with other standard Windows events (for example, Exclamation, Critical Stop, or Question).

Windows stores the description of each system event and the sound attached to it in the WIN.INI file, a system configuration file for Windows. If you view WIN.INI (located in the WINDOWS\SYSTEM directory) in Notepad, Write, or some other word processor, you can find something like the following entry within the file:

```
[Sounds]
SystemDefault=ding.wav, Default Beep
SystemExclamation=chord.wav, Exclamation
SystemStart=chimes.wav, Windows Start
SystemExit=chimes.wav, Windows Exit
SystemHand=chord.wav, Critical Stop
SystemQuestion=chord.wav, Question
SystemAsterisk=chord.wav, Asterisk
```

This part of WIN.INI defines each system event and indicates the sound to play when it occurs. In the sample WIN.INI excerpt shown here, when Windows receives notification that it should play the Default Beep (denoted as `SystemDefault`), it plays the sound file DING.WAV.

Not surprisingly, Windows has a procedure that you can call to play a sound associated with a system event. In the next exercise, the Bookstore application will play the sound associated with the Question event when you try to delete a record.

The *MessageBeep* Procedure

The procedure that you will call in this exercise is `MessageBeep`, which has the following API:

```
DECLARE SUB MessageBeep Lib "User" (ByVal BeepType As Integer)
```

The procedure's sole argument, `BeepType`, specifies the event that has the associated .WAV file you want to play. Windows has several numeric constants already defined for standard Windows, as described in Table 10.2.

Table 10.2. Constants for `BeepType`.

Constant	Description
MB_DEFBEEP	The Default Beep (`SystemDefault`) event.
MB_ICONASTERISK	The Asterisk (`SystemAsterisk`) event.
MB_ICONEXCLAMATION	The Exclamation (`SystemExclamation`) event.
MB_ICONHAND	The Critical Stop (`SystemHand`) event.
MB_ICONQUESTION	The Question (`SystemQuestion`) event.

Remember, because this procedure is a subroutine, you do not have to capture a return value as you did when you called sndPlaySound.

Playing an Event Sound

Follow these steps to play the sound assigned to the Question event when you try to delete a record:

1. In the (Declarations) section of the application's Property sheet, add the following line to declare the MessageBeep procedure:

   ```
   DECLARE SUB MessageBeep Lib "User" (ByVal BeepType As Integer)
   ```

2. Open the Property sheet for the form frmTitles.

3. In the Code Editor window for DeleteRow(), enter the following:

   ```
   Sub DeleteRow()
   ' Play the sound for a question
   MessageBeep(-1)

   ' Display a message box asking if the user wants to
   ' delete the record. If the answer is Yes, allow the
   ' deletion by calling the default processing for DeleteRow()
   IF MSGBOX("Do you want to delete this record?", 4,
   ➥"Deleting a record") <> 7 Then
      ' Go ahead with the deletion by calling the method's
      ' default processing
      Inherited.DeleteRow()
   END IF
   ```

   This code uses the MSGBOX function to display two buttons, Yes and No. The argument -1 instructs MessageBeep to play the standard beep.

   If the user presses the No button, the MSGBOX function returns 7. If the user presses Yes, the value returned is 6.

4. Save and run the form.

5. Press the Delete button on the toolbar.

   The message box you just defined now appears (see Figure 10.3). More significantly for this exercise, Windows plays the sound associated with the Question event.

Figure 10.3.

The message box asking whether you want to delete a record.

6. Press No to prevent the deletion.

7. Press Stop to end the exercise.

When you learned how to use MessageBeep, you had your first glimpse into the system configuration file WIN.INI. In the next exercise, you will use similar configuration files to set some characteristics of the Bookstore application.

DO	**DON'T**

DO use Windows procedures when appropriate.

DO write your own procedures when needed.

DO use Windows procedures to work directly with Windows.

DON'T use a Windows procedure when you can write a simpler version yourself.

DON'T write complex procedures that duplicate the well-tested Windows API procedures, unless absolutely necessary.

DON'T use the Windows APIs that control the fundamentals of the Windows environment, such as memory management, until you are very familiar with the Windows environment.

Working With an .INI File

The next exercise is more complex than earlier efforts with Windows DLL procedures, but it represents one of the most common tasks in Windows. You often want to store system configuration information about an application so that the user does not need to keep entering the same preferences, username, and other information every time the application launches.

The traditional way to store this information is by writing it to an .INI file. Windows already has two .INI files, SYSTEM.INI and WIN.INI, that store information about Windows environment settings. For example, when you choose a different default printer for your Windows applications, the information about this printer is stored in one of these .INI files.

To see how an .INI file is organized, run the SYSEDIT.EXE program from Windows. This application displays four different system configuration files, two for DOS (AUTOEXEC.BAT and CONFIG.SYS) and two for Windows (WIN.INI and SYSTEM.INI). Although SYSEDIT.EXE is not documented in many Windows references (including those released from Microsoft), it is a handy tool for changing system settings.

1. In the Windows Program Manager, select File | Run.

2. In the dialog box that appears, enter SYSEDIT as the command-line argument.

3. Press OK.

The System Configuration Editor, SYSEDIT.EXE, now appears, as shown in Figure 10.4.

Figure 10.4.

The SYSEDIT.EXE tool.

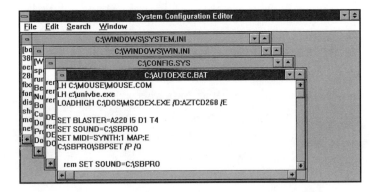

4. Select the window displaying the contents of the WIN.INI file, as shown in Figure 10.5.

Figure 10.5.

The WIN.INI file displayed.

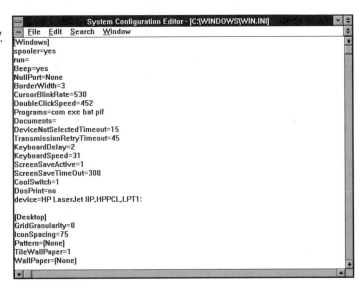

As you can see from the figure, Windows stores information about system settings in the following format:

```
[Section_Heading]

setting = value
```

The section heading divides Windows settings into functional groups. For example, the [fonts] section stores information about installed fonts. Each entry under a heading represents something about Windows that you have to set. In the case of fonts, each line under [fonts] specifies the name of a font, as well as the file in which the font is defined.

Whether you are storing information about the color palette used in Windows, or default settings for Microsoft Word, all .INI files use this same format. The reason for consistency has less to do with applying specific conventions for system or application settings, and more to do with two Windows procedures that read these settings from configuration (.INI) files.

The first procedure, GetProfileString, reads a setting from the WIN.INI file. Two of several arguments are the section in which the setting appears and the name of the setting. For example, if you wanted to read the setting for the graphic displayed as the background for Windows, you would look for the WallPaper= setting under the [Desktop] section of WIN.INI.

The second procedure, GetPrivateProfileString, reads these settings from a different .INI file than WIN.INI. These files are normally stored in the C:\WINDOWS\SYSTEM directory. Frequently, each Windows application installed will have its own .INI file in this directory. In fact, the Oracle Power Objects designer has its own .INI file, PWROBJX.INI, that stores the name and directory for each application, session, and library displayed in the Main window.

Where Should I Store Configuration Information?

Clearly, you have to make a choice where to write your configuration information for an application, either in WIN.INI or some other .INI file. (Because SYSTEM.INI stores information about Windows settings only, you should not write application configuration information in this file.)

There are pros and cons to either choice:

☐ If you add new configuration information to WIN.INI, you add to the clutter in this file. On the other hand, the risk of your users accidentally deleting this file is small, because most savvy Windows users know that you should never delete this core configuration file.

☐ If you create your own .INI file, it adds to the general clutter of the WINDOWS\SYSTEM directory. However, it does not add yet another set of entries to the already crowded WIN.INI file.

For this exercise, you'll use the second option, creating your own .INI file to save configuration information about the Bookstore application.

1. In Windows, open the Notepad.

   You can access the Notepad by double-clicking the icon for this application in the Accessories program group. Alternatively, you can choose the Program Manager's File | Run menu command, and then enter NOTEPAD for the command line.

2. In the Notepad, enter

   ```
   [UserInfo]
   ScreenName=Jane
   UserName=jboss
   ```

   As you might remember from Day 9, jboss is the username for one of the bookstore managers. You entered the information for Jane Boss in the employees table.

3. Save the new text file as BOOKS.INI in the C:\WINDOWS\SYSTEM directory.

You now have saved a plain text file as the new configuration file for the bookstore application. The next step is to instruct your application to read this information from the new .INI file.

Before you continue, however, you should review the syntax for the GetPrivateProfileString procedure. Here is the full declaration of this function:

```
Declare Function GetPrivateProfileString Lib "Kernel" (ByVal
➡lpApplicationName As String, lpKeyName As Any, ByVal
➡lpDefault As String, ByVal lpReturnedString As String,
➡ByVal nSize As Integer, ByVal lpFileName As String) As Integer
```

Table 10.3 summarizes the arguments passed to GetPrivateProfileString.

Table 10.3. Arguments for GetPrivateProfileString.

Argument	Description
lpApplicationName	The name of the section in the .INI file to be read. You do not need to add the brackets, because they're assumed. In the case of BOOKS.INI, you'll be reading the "UserInfo" section. The quotation marks are required, as is the capitalization.
lpKeyName	The name of the setting to be read. In this exercise, you'll be reading the "ScreenName" entry in BOOKS.INI (quotation marks required).
lpDefault	Assigns a default value to the entry if there is none. You cannot leave this argument null, so you'll display "USER" as the user's name if there isn't an entry for UserName= in the BOOKS.INI file.
lpReturnedString	Names the variable that will receive the setting being read. In this case, you'll read the string into a variable named vUserName, so you'll enter vUserName for this argument.

Argument	Description
nSize	Specifies the number of bytes set aside in memory for this variable. In this exercise, you don't expect the number of characters to be very large, so you'll assign the value 16 to this parameter.
lpFileName	The filename of the application configuration file being read (.INI). In this case, the filename will be "BOOKS.INI" (quotation marks required).

GetPrivateProfileString has several more arguments than the Windows procedures used in previous lessons. By reviewing the argument list, however, you can see that the procedure is not as complex as it might seem at first.

Now that you understand the arguments for this procedure, you're ready to use it within the application.

1. Add a text field at the bottom of the form frmSplash.

   This new text field will display the user's name in the splash screen when the application is launched.

2. Set the following properties of the new text field:

Property	Setting
Name	fldUserName
Datatype	String
DataSize	64
FontName	Arial
FontSize	9
HasBorder	False

3. Save the form.

4. In the (Declarations) section of the application's Property sheet, enter

   ```
   (Declarations)
   Declare Function GetPrivateProfileString Lib "Kernel" (ByVal
   ➥lpApplicationName As String, lpKeyName As Variant, ByVal
   ➥lpDefault As String, ByVal lpReturnedString As String,
   ➥ByVal nSize As Integer, ByVal lpFileName As String) As Integer
   ```

   You must enter this as a single line of text. If you want to view all the text for the declaration at once, you can use the ampersand (&) to break the declaration into multiple lines. For example, if you used ampersand symbols, you might enter the declaration as follows:

```
Declare Function GetPrivateProfileString Lib "Kernel" &
  (ByVal lpApplicationName As String, lpKeyName As Any, &
  ByVal lpDefault As String, ByVal lpReturnedString As &
  String, ByVal nSize As Integer, ByVal lpFileName As &
  String) As Integer
```

Using the ampersand as a string concatenation symbol is the only way to enter the declaration in multiple lines of text.

5. In the `OnLoad()` section of the form `frmSplash`, add the following after the existing code in the method:

```
Sub OnLoad()
DIM vStr AS String
DIM x AS Long

' Initialize vStr
vStr = STRING(255, "")

x = GetPrivateProfileString("UserInfo","UserName", "USER",
➥vStr, LEN(vStr), "BOOKS.INI")
fldUserName.Value = "Welcome, " & vStr
```

6. Save and run the form.

The username read from the BOOKS.INI file now appears in the splash screen.

You can use another procedure, `WritePrivateProfileString`, to write a new value to some element of an .INI file. In a later exercise, when you create a system configuration dialog box, you will be adding new entries to BOOKS.INI.

DO	DON'T

DO use .INI files to store configuration settings.

DO add entries for significant configuration options.

DO add configuration information to WIN.INI, if you prefer.

DON'T store sensitive information in an .INI file, because all you need is a text editor to read it.

DON'T add every imaginable configuration option, because you have to write the code to read and set each one.

DON'T add entries to SYSTEM.INI, the other Windows configuration file. SYSTEM.INI is designed for the most basic environment settings, not for application configuration information.

Launching Another Application

In many cases, you want to launch one application from another. For example, if you are reviewing financial information, you might quickly want to perform some calculation. Therefore, it would be helpful to open the Windows calculator or a spreadsheet program from within your application, instead of switching back to the Program Manager to launch the secondary application.

This feature is especially useful when you need to launch several small applications, such as Calculator, from within a primary application. When you are using a desktop publishing package, for example, you might often like to be able to open simple graphics or text editors from within the desktop publishing application.

Similarly, in BOOKS.POA, you might want to open another application. Any number of possible applications come to mind:

10

- [ ] A calculator, to check figures in an order
- [ ] A word processor, to write a letter to a customer or publisher
- [ ] A desktop publishing application, to design a flyer announcing a sale or promotion
- [ ] An Internet browser, so that you can find information on books, authors, or genres

One can think of so many different applications to launch, that it would be useful to have the ability to launch any program from within BOOKS.POA. Therefore, in this exercise, you will create a new form used to launch other Windows applications. Method code within this form will call a Windows procedure, WinExec, to launch the application.

The *WinExec* Procedure

WinExec is a relatively simple procedure, with just two arguments.

```
DECLARE FUNCTION WinExec Lib "Kernel" (ByVal lpCmdLine As String,
➥ByVal nCmdShow As Integer) As Integer
```

The first argument, lpCmdLine, is the name of the application and its directory. In the case of applications already in the path set when you start up your computer, you can simply enter the name of the application. For example, if you wanted to run Microsoft Excel, the first argument to WinExec might be "C:\EXCEL\EXCEL.EXE."

The second argument, nCmdShow, determines the state of the application's window when the application launches. Some of the options for this argument are included in Table 10.4.

Table 10.4. Options for the `WinExec` argument `nCmdShow`.

Value	Description
0	Hides the application's window when it is launched.
4	Maximizes the application window.
5	Minimizes the application window to an icon.

There are other possible values to pass as this argument, but for the moment you'll just use these.

Using *WinExec* in Your Application

`WinExec` makes opening another application trivial, as you will see in this exercise. In the Bookstore application, you will be able to open a form that lets you launch a secondary application. To open the form, you double-click anywhere within the Book Orders form.

1. Add the following procedure declaration to the (Declarations) section of the application's Property sheet:

```
(Declarations)
DECLARE FUNCTION WinExec Lib "Kernel" (ByVal lpCmdLine As
➥String, ByVal nCmdShow As Integer) As Integer
```

2. Create a new form named `frmLaunch`, with the label `Run Application`.

3. Add a radio button frame to the form, and name it `rbfAppID`.

4. Change this radio button frame's label to `Select Application`.

5. Inside the radio button frame, add four new radio buttons, stacked vertically.

   Make sure that the radio button frame is selected when you create the radio buttons, so that the buttons are contained within the frame.

6. Change the top radio button's `Label` property to `Calculator` and its `ValueOn` property to `1`.

7. Change the next radio button's `Label` property to `Write` and its `ValueOn` property to `2`.

8. Change the next radio button's `Label` property to `Notepad` and its `ValueOn` property to `3`.

9. Change the bottom radio button's `Label` property to `Other` and its `ValueOn` property to `4`.

10. Within the radio button frame, and next to the Other radio button, add a text field.

11. Change the text field's `Name` to `fldRunApp`, its `Datatype` to `String`, and its `DataSize` to `120`.

    Before continuing, you might want to change the fonts used in this form to match the appearance of the rest of the application.

12. Add a pushbutton to the bottom of the form, beneath the radio button frame.

13. Change the pushbutton's Label to OK, and add the following code to its Click() method:

```
Sub Click()
Inherited.Click()

DIM x AS Integer
' Based on the radio button selected, run an application
SELECT CASE rbfAppID.Value
CASE 1
  x = WinExec("CALC.EXE", 9)
CASE 2
  x = WinExec("WRITE.EXE", 9)
CASE 3
  x = WinExec("NOTEPAD.EXE", 9)
CASE 4
  ' Get the command line argument for the application to run
  ' from the text field, and then pass this argument to WinExec
  DIM vCmdLine AS String
  vCmdLine = fldRunApp.Value
  x = WinExec(vCmdLine, 9)
  ' If the system cannot find the application, or it
  ' runs out of memory, display an error message
  IF x < 32 THEN
    SELECT CASE x
        CASE 0
        MSGBOX "Insufficient memory"
      CASE 3
        MSGBOX vCmdLine & " not found"
      CASE 4
        MSGBOX vCmdLine & " not found"
      CASE ELSE
        MSGBOX "Error running application " & vCmdLine
    END SELECT
  END IF
END SELECT
```

14. Add the following method code to the PostChange() method of the text field:

```
Sub PostChange()
Inherited.PostChange()
IF (NOT ISNULL(self.Value)) OR (self.Value <> "") THEN
  rbfAppID.Value = 4
END IF
```

This piece of code selects the Other radio button whenever you change the value in the text field, unless the value in the text field is an empty string or NULL.

15. Add a second pushbutton to the bottom of the form, with the Label property of Cancel.

16. Make sure that the IsDismissBtn property of both pushbuttons is set to True.

The form should now look like Figure 10.6.

Figure 10.6.

The Run Application form.

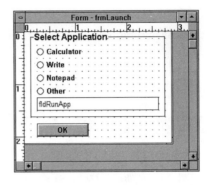

17. Open the Property sheet for the Book Orders form (frmBookOrders).

18. Add the following method code to the `ChildDblClick()` method of the Book Orders form:

```
Sub ChildDblClick(child As Object)
Inherited.ChildDblClick(child)
frmLaunch.OpenModal(0)
```

The `ChildDblClick()` method executes whenever you double-click any item within the form. Therefore, this method code opens the form frmLaunch as a modal dialog box whenever you double-click any object within the form.

19. Add the following method code to the `DoubleClick()` method of the form:

```
Function DoubleClick() As Long
Inherited.DoubleClick()
frmLaunch.OpenModal(0)
```

This additional code covers cases in which the user clicks the form, not on an object within the form. You can now open the frmLaunch form by double-clicking anywhere within the form.

20. Save and run the application.

21. Open the Book Orders form by selecting Sales | Orders.

22. Double-click somewhere on the form (but not within a text field).

The Run Application form appears.

23. In the radio button frame, select the button for Calculator and press OK.

The dialog box disappears, and Windows launches the CALC.EXE application.

24. Double-click the Book Orders form again to re-open the Run Application form.

25. In the text field, type `C:\WINDOWS\WRITE.EXE` and press Return.

The fourth radio button, Other, is now selected.

26. Press the OK pushbutton.

    The application you specified by name, WRITE.EXE, now launches.

27. Re-open the Run Application dialog box and enter the following in the text field:
    `C:\FOO\FOO.EXE.`

    This should be a nonexistent application in a nonexistent directory.

28. Press OK.

    The dialog box disappears, and the application displays an error message.

29. Press Stop to end this exercise.

The easiest part of this exercise was calling `WinExec`. You spent most of your time designing the user interface—the proper balance of effort when using Oracle Power Objects. Because you can draw on the Windows procedures with the same ease as you used drag-and-drop techniques to bind a form to a table, you can spend less time on making the application work, and more time focused on how you want the application to behave.

Adding a Custom Toolbar

As indicated in the previous lesson, creating a toolbar is not very different from creating a custom menu bar and menus. In both cases, you write similar scripts to define the object (a menu bar and a toolbar). Additionally, you use the `TestCommand()` and `DoCommand()` methods to determine the state of the object, and what happens when the user selects some component of it (either a menu command or a button).

In this exercise, you will create a new toolbar button to open the Run Application form. Toolbar buttons generally provide a shortcut for frequently performed tasks, so a button that opens the Run Application button seems like a good candidate for a custom toolbar.

When you created a menu bar, you first wrote the code, and then learned more about the methods called in the code. You will use the same approach in this exercise, so get ready to dive right into some coding.

1. In the `(Declarations)` section of the application's Property sheet, enter the following bold method code:

   ```
   (Declarations)
   ' Declare the base value for all menu IDs
   CONST cMenuNum = 1000

   'Assign menu IDs for commands in the Setup menu
   CONST cTitles = cMenuNum + 1
   CONST cPublishers = cMenuNum + 2
   CONST cBookTypes = cMenuNum + 3
   CONST cEmployees = cMenuNum + 4
   ```

```
'Assign menu IDs for commands in the Sales menu
CONST cOrders = cMenuNum + 10
CONST cCustomers = cMenuNum + 11
CONST cCustPurchases = cMenuNum + 12

'Assign IDs for additional toolbar buttons
CONST cButtons = 2000
CONST cRunApp = cButtons + 1
```

This new entry begins numbering toolbar buttons at 2001. You are using a different range of IDs for toolbar buttons, to avoid accidental overlaps. Because you don't know how many custom menu commands you will add in the final application, it's safer to maintain a large gap between the ID numbers for menu commands and toolbar buttons.

2. Add the following to the code already appearing in the application's OnLoad() method:

```
Sub OnLoad()
' Create a new custom toolbar
DIM tbrNewToolbar AS Object
tbrNewToolbar = NEW Toolbar

' Add the standard buttons to the toolbar
frmBookOrders.DefaultToolbar(tbrNewToolbar)

' Add a new button to the toolbar. When pressed, this
' button will open the Run Application form.
tbrNewToolbar.TBAppendButton(0, NULL, ToolbarStyle_Separator, 0)
tbrNewToolbar.TBAppendButton(cRunApp, NULL, ToolbarStyle_PushBtn, 0)

' Associate the new toolbar with the Book Orders form
frmBookOrders.SetToolbar(tbrNewToolbar)
```

In this code, the first call to TBAppendButton() creates a space between the standard toolbar buttons and the new button created with the second TBAppendButton() statement.

3. Add the following bold method code to the DoCommand() method:

```
Function DoCommand(cmdCode as Long) as Long
' Test for the constant assigned to each menu command.
' Depending on the constant, open the correct form.
SELECT CASE cmdCode
CASE cTitles
  frmTitles.OpenWindow()
  DoCommand = TRUE
CASE cPublishers
  frmPubsBooks.OpenWindow()
CASE cBookTypes
  frmBookTypes.OpenWindow()
CASE cEmployees
  frmEmployees.OpenWindow()
CASE cOrders
  frmBookOrders.OpenWindow()
```

```
   CASE cCustomers
     frmCustomers.OpenWindow()
   cCustPurchases
     frmCustPurchases.OpenWindow()
   CASE cRunApp
     frmLaunch.OpenWindow()
   END SELECT
```

4. Add the following bold lines to `TestCommand()`:

```
   Function TestCommand(cmdCode As Long) As Long
   SELECT CASE cmdCode
   CASE cOrders
     ' Based on the status of the global variable gFormOpen,
     ' enable or disable the menu command.
     IF gFormOpen = FALSE THEN
        TestCommand = TestCommand_Enabled
     ELSE
        TestCommand = TestCommand_Checked
     END IF
   CASE cRunApp
     'Make sure the button is always enabled
        TestCommand = TestCommand_Enabled
   END SELECT
```

   Save and run the application.

5. Select Sales | Orders to open the Book Orders form.

   When the Book Orders form appears, a new button appears on the toolbar.

6. Press the new button on the toolbar.

   The Run Application form opens.

7. Select the Write radio button on this dialog box and press OK.

   The dialog box disappears, and Windows launches the Write application.

8. Press Stop to end this exercise.

Adding a custom toolbar is a relatively simple task, involving less code than you wrote for the menu bar. The custom toolbar's only deficiency is the lack of a graphic on the new toolbar button. Obviously, you need some type of icon to indicate what the button does when pressed. In tomorrow's lesson, you will display an imported bitmap on this toolbar.

Toolbar-Related Methods

Based on your experience with menus and menu bars, the logic behind the methods used to create and manipulate custom toolbars will seem familiar. Table 10.5 is a summary of the toolbar-related methods.

Table 10.5. Toolbar-related methods.

Method	Applies To	Description
TBAppendButton()	Toolbars	Adds a toolbar button to the right of all other buttons.
TBInsertButton()		Adds a toolbar button at the specified position.
TBGetButton()		Returns an object reference to a toolbar button.
TBSetButton()		Modifies some characteristic of a toolbar button.
TBDeleteButton()		Deletes a toolbar button from a specified position on the toolbar.
ClearToolbar()		Deletes all buttons from a toolbar.
GetToolbar()	Forms and reports	Returns an object reference to the toolbar associated with that form or report.
SetToolbar()		Assigns a toolbar to a form or report.

Again, for the complete syntax for each toolbar method, consult the Oracle Power Objects online help.

Summary

Today, you learned the following points about DLL procedures:

- ☐ You can call procedures defined in both the Windows DLLs and "third-party" DLLs.

- ☐ As long as you know the API for a DLL procedure, you can use the procedure.

- ☐ Before you can use a DLL procedure, however, you must declare it in your application. The declaration includes all the important aspects of the procedure's API, including its name, the DLL in which it is defined, its return value, and its argument list.

- ☐ Arguments can be passed to the DLL by reference or by value. When you pass by reference, the procedure can change the value assigned to the property or method from which the value was read. When you pass by value, the procedure cannot change the value assigned to the property or method. To pass an argument by value, you use the ByVal keyword.

☐ Data types are again important, this time for arguments and return values.

☐ When a procedure has a return value, you must capture this value in a variable or a property.

☐ The Windows environment has many built-in DLL procedures that you can use to directly manipulate the Windows environment.

☐ Using some of these built-in procedures, you can read information from application configuration (.INI) files.

☐ You design toolbars in many of the same ways that you create menus and menu bars.

What Comes Next?

Tomorrow will tie up several loose ends in the Bookstore application. First, you will add graphics to several forms and reports. In several places, you have left out a graphic where one might have been useful. Most obviously, you needed to add an icon to the toolbar button created in today's lesson. Therefore, the next lesson will illustrate several options for showing graphics in an Oracle Power Objects application.

In addition, you will create a form through which the user can enter preferences about the application, such as the standard background color for forms. The application will store this information in the BOOKS.INI file. Building on what you learned about .INI files in today's lesson, you will read and write entries in BOOKS.INI.

Q&A

Q How can I write my own DLLs?

A You must understand the C or C++ programming languages to write DLLs, and you must have a compiler. Once you have written the procedures, you can compile them into a .DLL file and call the procedures from other applications. Whether you are designing a DLL for your own use, or to be used by other developers, you should always carefully and thoroughly document the API for each DLL procedure. Otherwise, you might forget how the DLL works, and other developers will be equally confused.

Q What rule of thumb should I follow about creating a new .INI file or adding new entries to WIN.INI?

A It's primarily a matter of taste. However, over the last few years, an increasing number of developers have created their own application-specific .INI files, rather than adding new entries in WIN.INI.

Q I've looked at a Windows API reference, and I'm a little confused about what some of the descriptions mean. Where can I get more information?

A API references are often written with different types of developers in mind. Before you buy an API "Bible," you should peruse it carefully to make sure that it has the information you need. Windows API guides are often written for advanced Windows developers, or for programmers working on particular types of applications. Therefore, you must be careful to get the right type of reference for yourself.

Workshop

The Workshop consists of quiz questions to help you solidify your understanding of the material covered in today's lesson. Try and understand the quiz questions before you go on to tomorrow's lesson.

Quiz

1. What is missing from the following DLL procedure declaration?

```
DECLARE FUNCTION GetWindowHandle (By Val vWindowName As String,
➥vFlag As Integer) AS Integer
```

2. Suppose you are designing a DLL procedure of your own that will perform complex scientific calculations based on values entered into text fields. If you want to display the results in another text field, how should you declare the function?

3. Suppose that you press a toolbar button you created, and it does something completely unexpected, such as closing the application. What was your mistake?

Quiz Answers

1. The API declaration does not include the name of the .DLL file in which the procedure is stored.

2. Any values read from these fields should be passed as arguments by value, so that you do not change these values in mid-calculation. As the complexity of an expression increases, so does the risk of mishap. When you pass by value, you make each value "tamper-proof." The result should be the appropriate data type, and the text field displaying the result should have a matching data type.

3. You accidentally assigned a numeric ID to the toolbar button that duplicates the ID for a menu command.

Graphics and
Other Matters

Overview

Today, you learn about the following topics:

- ☐ Importing bitmaps as application resources
- ☐ Adding bitmaps to application objects
- ☐ Using picture controls
- ☐ Storing graphics in the database
- ☐ Adding a graphic to a toolbar button
- ☐ Creating a system configuration dialog box
- ☐ Writing entries to an .INI file
- ☐ Remembering the position of a form
- ☐ Tips on graphics and .INI files

Although many business applications use very few graphics, finding one that uses no graphics at all is rare. Graphics have several important uses, from providing visual cues about the purpose of a pushbutton, to displaying the corporate logo on a report. Even smaller companies, such as the hypothetical bookstore that might use BOOKS.POA, have some graphics needs in their applications. Without an icon, the custom toolbar button that you created yesterday is a complete mystery to the new user of the Bookstore application.

Oracle Power Objects provides several options for displaying graphics in an application:

- ☐ Imported bitmaps. You can import a bitmap into an Oracle Power Objects application as a resource. Once imported, you can display the graphic in several places within the application, such as the background of a form or the face of a toolbar button.
- ☐ Picture controls. Oracle Power Objects has a control designed to display a bitmap. The control is bindable, so you can use it to store pictures in a database table.
- ☐ OLE controls. You can use several kinds of OLE controls to display and edit graphics within an Oracle Power Objects application.
- ☐ OCX controls. Similarly, you can use a custom control (OCX format) to display and edit graphics.

You learn how to use OLE and OCX controls on Day 17, "Working with OLE Objects." Today you will focus on imported graphics and the picture control.

In addition, today you will tie up some loose ends in the Bookstore application. Most significantly, you will be able to specify whether you want the company logo displayed in the background of forms. You will set this and other options through a system configuration dialog box that reads from and writes to an .INI file.

Imported Bitmaps

When you import a bitmap into an application, you copy the information from the .BMP file in which the graphic was originally defined. The picture then becomes an application resource, stored within an application and available for use in other application objects. When you import the bitmap, it appears within the Application window with the forms and reports you created in earlier lessons (see Figure 11.1).

Figure 11.1.
Bitmap resources in the
Application window.

At this point, you can view the bitmap resource, but you cannot edit it. By double-clicking the icon for the bitmap, you open a window in which you can see the bitmap (see Figure 11.2).

Figure 11.2.
Viewing the bitmap.

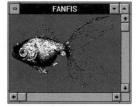

To display the bitmap within a form or report, or in some object appearing within that container, you need only drag the icon for the bitmap into the object. You will use this technique in a later exercise, when you add the corporate logo to one of your forms.

Drawing the Corporate Logo

At this point, you are ready to design a logo for the bookstore. Be creative, and don't worry about your artistic skills. This is an exercise for your own edification, after all, and not an art contest!

There are only three guidelines you need to follow when you design the logo:

☐ The graphic must be 1-inch by 1-inch in size.

☐ The graphic must have something to do with a bookstore.

☐ The graphic must limit itself to a 256-color palette. Imported bitmaps in Oracle Power Objects cannot use more than 256 colors.

The 256-Color Limitation

If you create a graphic with more colors, it might look extremely strange after you import it, because the application will substitute colors from the 256-color palette for colors it does not recognize. The easiest way to limit the palette is to select a 256-color graphics driver for Windows through the Windows Setup program.

The Size Limitation

You can draw your logo using the Microsoft Windows built-in graphics editor, Paintbrush. To specify the size of the graphic, select Options | Image Attributes, and open a dialog box in which you can set the size of the image (see Figure 11.3).

Figure 11.3.
The Image Attributes dialog box.

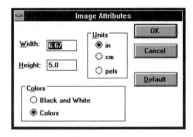

Once you have finished drawing the logo, save it as LOGO.BMP in the C:\BOOKS directory (in which you are storing all the files that comprise your application). When you save the graphic, be sure to use the Windows bitmap (.BMP) format, not another format like .JPG, .GIF, or .PCX. Oracle Power Objects can import .BMP files only, not graphics in other formats.

Importing the Corporate Logo

When you have finished your brief foray into the art world and saved the .BMP file, you are ready to import the logo into your application as a resource.

1. Open the Application window for BOOKS.POS.
2. Select the File | Import BMP menu command.
3. In the dialog box that appears, select LOGO.BMP in the C:\BOOKS directory.
4. Press OK to import the bitmap.

   The bitmap now appears as a resource in the Application window. By default, its name is the same as its filename (without the extension), LOGO.

5. Double-click the icon for the LOGO bitmap resource.

You can now see that the bitmap resource imported into BOOKS.POA is identical to the .BMP file you drew earlier. However, keep in mind that this is a copy of that graphic. At this point, if you were to edit LOGO.BMP in Paintbrush, the changes would not appear in the imported bitmap.

Adding the Corporate Logo to a Form

Importing the bitmap was easy—in fact, you probably spent far more time drawing the logo. Adding the bitmap to a form is just as simple.

1. Open the form frmSplash.
2. Drag the icon for the LOGO bitmap resource onto the form.
3. The bitmap now appears in the background of the form (see Figure 11.4).

Figure 11.4.

The logo appearing on the form.

4. Open the Property sheet for the form and locate the Bitmap property.

   As you can see, dragging the bitmap onto the form automatically set the Bitmap property to LOGO (the name of the bitmap resource). If you had another bitmap imported into the application, you could display the second bitmap instead by entering its name in place of LOGO.

5. Change the form's `BitmapTiled` property to `True`.

The logo is now tiled across the entire background of the form.

6. Save and run the form (see Figure 11.5).

Figure 11.5.

The splash screen at runtime, with the company logo tiled across its background.

Well, no one will ever have to guess what company uses this application! Clearly, tiling the corporate logo across the form is a bit of overkill, so you'll use the logo in a more limited fashion in the next exercise.

Displaying the Logo in an Embedded Form

Rather than creating the visual confusion of a logo tiled across the face of the form, you might instead display the logo in a corner of the form.

Both forms and embedded forms have a `Bitmap` property, so you could add the LOGO bitmap to an embedded form within the Book Orders form. The whole purpose of the embedded form would be to act as the frame for displaying this bitmap.

1. Delete the current setting for the `Bitmap` property of the splash screen.

When you delete the word LOGO from this property, the bitmap disappears from the background of the form.

2. Add about one inch to the width of the form.

3. Add an embedded form to the right side of the form.

4. Change the `Name` of this embedded form to `embLogo`, its `SizeX` property to `1 in`, and its `SizeY` property to `1 in`.

`SizeX` and `SizeY` determine the width and height of a form. You can enter the value for these properties as inches by adding `in` after the numeric value. For example, to enter a value of one inch, you would type `1 in` as the value for `SizeX` and `SizeY`.

5. For the `Bitmap` property of the form, enter `LOGO`.

   The LOGO bitmap now appears within the embedded form. Because the bitmap and the embedded form have the same width and height (2 inches), the bitmap fills the entire container.

6. Widen the form to give some added space on the right side for the logo.

7. Move the objects within the form to suit your aesthetic sensibilities.

8. Save and run the form.

The company logo is now limited to the upper-right corner of the Book Orders form, instead of being tiled several times across the form.

To give you a preview of things to come, you could have added the bitmap to another type of container, a user-defined class, that can be displayed on the form in the same fashion as the embedded form. As you shall see when you replace the embedded form with the class, you can more easily update the logo on all forms where it is used when you display it in a class. However, that's a matter for a later lesson.

Working with Picture Controls

Right now, the same graphic appears, regardless of the record currently displayed in the Book Orders form. What would you do if you wanted to display a different graphic for each form?

For example, suppose your employee files included a photograph of each bookstore employee. As long as you have a scanner, you can create a digitized version of the photo, and then save it as a bitmap. Obviously, you should be able to display each employee's picture as you scroll through employee records. Importing a bitmap does not give you that capability—ideally, you would like to have the picture saved in the EMPLOYEES table as part of each employee's record.

Oracle Power Objects includes a picture control to give you this capability. Because the picture control is bindable, you can use it to store picture data in a table. Therefore, displaying a photograph for each employee is a snap: Simply add the picture control to a form already bound to the EMPLOYEES table, and then use the column storing the picture data as the control's `DataSource`.

Storing Graphics in the Database

The column that stores any graphics data must use the `Long Raw` data type, and the graphic itself must use the .BMP format. You use the `Long Raw` data type for other types of multimedia data, such as sound and video. In a later lesson, when you store OLE multimedia data in the database, the column that stores this information will use the `Long Raw` data type.

Adding a Picture Control to Your Application

Because you don't necessarily have a set of digitized photographs handy, use different graphics to illustrate how to use a picture control. Instead of employee photos, you'll add some company logos to the PUBLISHERS table.

1. Open the Session window for BOOKS.POS and open a connection to the database.
2. Open the Table Editor window for PUBLISHERS.
3. Add a column named PIC_LOGO to the table, and give it the Long Raw data type.
4. Save the new table description to the database.

At this point, you cannot add the data for the picture through the Table Browser window. We'll quickly add a picture control to the form frmPubsBooks, however, so that you can add a logo to each company record.

For the sake of simplicity, use some of the wallpaper bitmaps provided with Windows as the "logos" for each company. If you would prefer for aesthetic reasons to design your own logo for each publisher, go ahead! The standard wallpaper bitmaps will suffice, however, to show how to paste graphic information into a picture control, and then save the graphics to the database as part of the publisher records.

1. Open the form frmPubsBooks.
2. From the Object palette, select the Picture Control drawing tool.
3. Draw a picture control somewhere in the top half of the form.

   You'll have to move and resize the repeater display to make the room needed for the picture control.
4. Change the SizeX and SizeY properties of the picture control to 1.5 in.

   The picture control is sized to hold some of the larger Windows wallpaper bitmaps. Most will easily fit.
5. Set the DataSource property of the picture control to PIC_LOGO.
6. Save and run the form.

   The picture control now appears on the form, but currently it does not display any graphics. In the next few steps, you will add some pictures to the PUBLISHERS table.
7. Run the Paintbrush application from the Accessories program group in Windows.

   The icon for Paintbrush is normally displayed in the Accessories group. If it is not, you can run the application by selecting File | Run in the Program Manager, and then entering PBRUSH.EXE as the command-line argument.
8. In Paintbrush, open the bitmap ARCHES.BMP in the C:\WINDOWS directory.

If you do not have this .BMP file on your system, you can substitute another bitmap for it.

9. Use the Pick tool to select the entire bitmap (see Figure 11.6).

    The Pick tool in Paintbrush lets you click and drag across a region of a graphic to select this area. In this case, you want to select the entire graphic, so you should click in one corner and drag the cursor to the diagonally opposite corner.

Figure 11.6.
The Pick tool in Paintbrush.

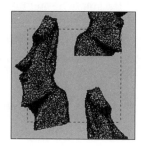

10. Select Edit | Copy.
11. Return to Oracle Power Objects and click the picture control in the form.

    The outline of the picture control should turn solid black to indicate that you have selected it.

12. Select Edit | Paste.

    The graphic you copied from Paintbrush now appears in the picture control (see Figure 11.7).

Figure 11.7.
The ARCHES graphic appearing in the picture control.

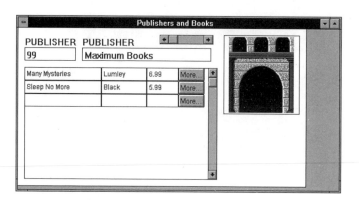

13. In Paintbrush, open a different bitmap in the Windows directory.

    Which bitmap you select does not matter. In fact, you could use a logo you drew and saved as a .BMP file.

14. In Oracle Power Objects, move to a different publisher record.

15. Paste the second bitmap into the picture control.

16. Repeat this process until you have a bitmap pasted into the picture control for every publisher record.

17. Press the Commit button to save these graphics in the PUBLISHERS database.

    As shown in this exercise, you have to paste a graphic into the picture control. If you want to edit the graphic, you must then copy the contents of the picture control, and then paste the graphic into Paintbrush or some other graphics editor. After you make your changes, you paste the modified graphic back into the picture tool.

18. Select the picture tool while it is displaying one of the graphics you just added to the PUBLISHERS table.

19. Select Edit | Copy.

    You have now copied the graphic into the Windows clipboard, just as you did when you copied graphics from Paintbrush into Oracle Power Objects.

20. In Paintbrush, select File | New.

21. Paste the graphic into Paintbrush.

22. Make some modification to the picture.

    Write your name on it, draw a happy face—do whatever you like.

23. Using the Pick tool, reselect the entire graphic and then choose Edit | Copy.

24. In Oracle Power Objects, paste the modified graphic into the picture control.

25. Press Commit to save the new graphic in the table.

26. Press Stop to end this exercise.

DO	DON'T

DO use the picture control to display graphics.

DO store graphics as part of records.

DO store color as well as black-and-white pictures.

DON'T display too many graphics at once, so that the application does not have to query a large number of graphics simultaneously.

DON'T add graphics for their own sake. Bitmaps can require a large amount of disk space to store, and they slow down application performance.

DON'T try to display photo-realistic graphics through the picture control. As mentioned earlier, the picture control has a limited palette—only 256 colors.

A Development Challenge

This lesson has given you some experience working with a picture tool. With your knowledge of Oracle Power Objects in general, you should be able to guess the solution to the following development puzzle.

How Do I Search for a Graphic?

To search for a graphic, run the form frmPubsBooks again, and then press the QBF button on the Form Run Time toolbar. A copy of the form appears, in which you can enter conditions to apply to the form's recordset. After typing in a valid condition, you can press the Do QBF button to re-query the form while applying the condition.

Searching for a particular publisher by ID or name is very easy. If you were looking for Logos Books, you would enter =`'Logos Books'` in the QBF form. But how would you look for a publisher, if all you know is its logo?

The QBF form does not provide you with this capability. Because there is no way to search all the data for the graphic as a condition, you cannot use the QBF form to search publisher records for a particular corporate logo.

Think for a moment before looking at the solution. In an earlier lesson, you already learned how to give the user quick access to a particular record; the only trick is knowing how to search by graphic.

The Solution

When you were adding features to the frmTitles form, you created a special browser dialog box that displayed a scrolling list of titles. Because this dialog box and the form shared the same recordset, the form showed all the information from whatever title you selected in the browser form. The repeater display in this browser dialog box gave you the ability to quickly move the pointer in the form's recordset to a different book, instead of scrolling through each title one at a time.

When you are looking for a particular logo, you are faced with essentially the same challenge. In this case, however, you are looking for a picture instead of the name of a book. You can use the same technique to meet this development challenge, by creating a special graphics browser form.

1. Add a new form to the BOOKS.POA application. Give this form the name frmPicBrowser and the label Find a Picture.

2. Add a repeater display to this new form.

   The repeater display should cover the entire form except for a small area at the bottom.

3. Resize the repeater display so that it is at least three inches wide.

4. Resize the repeater display panel so that it is 1.5 inches high (that is, its SizeY property is set to 1.5 in) and approximately 1.5 inches wide (SizeX = 1.5).

   The repeater display panel is now tiled both vertically and horizontally. This will give you the ability to view several graphics simultaneously.

5. Set the RecordSource property of the repeater display to =frmPubsBooks.

   The repeater display now shares a recordset with frmPubsBooks.

6. Add a picture control to the repeater display.

7. Resize the picture display so that it is 2-inches wide by 2-inches high.

8. For the DataSource property of the picture control, enter PIC_LOGO.

   The picture control is now bound to the column in PUBLISHERS that stores graphics.

9. Add a pushbutton labeled OK to the bottom of the form.

10. Make sure that the pushbutton's IsDismissBtn property is set to True.

    The form should now look like Figure 11.8.

Figure 11.8.

The new dialog box for browsing corporate logos.

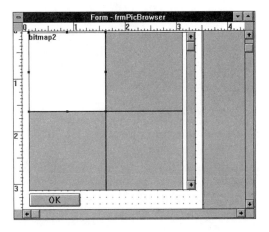

11. In the form frmPubsBooks, add a pushbutton with the label Select Graphic beneath the picture control.

12. In the Click() method of this pushbutton, add the following method code:

```
Sub Click()
frmPicBrowser.OpenModal(0)
```

13. Save and run the application.

14. From the application menu, select Setup | Publishers.

15. Press the Select Graphic pushbutton.

    The new browser dialog box appears, displaying a few of the logos stored in the PUBLISHERS table.

16. Click one of these logos.

    You select the picture control, which in turn moves the pointer in the shared recordset. The form frmPubsBooks now displays the publisher whose logo you just selected.

17. Press OK to close the dialog box.

18. Press Stop to end this exercise.

One of the most important features of Oracle Power Objects is its consistency: Whatever the development task, the same principles and techniques apply. As this exercise showed, handling graphics was much like handling other types of data. If you wanted to give the user the ability to scan through all the publisher logos, you created a browser much like the earlier browser form you built.

By now, these exercises should be giving you the mindset necessary for working with Oracle Power Objects, and with object-oriented, client/server development tools in general. The next development puzzle for you to solve should not give you much trouble.

Another Development Puzzle

Suppose you want to display the graphics for a publisher in the frmTitles form. For each book that you view through this form, you also want to see the logo for that book's publisher. What is the easiest way to display the logo that should appear with each book?

Again, think for a moment about some of the earlier lessons, and the type of relationship between the records in TITLES and PUBLISHERS. Once you have decided upon a solution, read the next section.

The Solution to the Second Puzzle

To solve this puzzle, you need to perform a lookup into the PUBLISHERS table to find the logo that belongs to a book's publisher. This situation suggests that you should use the SQLLOOKUP function as a picture control's DataSource. Even though the return value is a graphic (data that uses the Long Raw format), the SQLLOOKUP should work in the same fashion it did earlier.

Unfortunately, SQLLOOKUP has problems returning Long Raw data. Additionally, this solution suffers from the same weaknesses as earlier efforts with SQLLOOKUP: You can make a mistake in the query string for the lookup, and performance can be slow. Fortunately, there is a better solution, one that should be extremely familiar after your experience creating master-detail relationships.

If you display the picture control within an embedded form, you can create a master-detail relationship between the embedded form and the form. The record source for the form frmTitles is the TITLES table; the embedded form's record source should be the PUBLISHERS table. By setting the master-detail properties of the embedded form, you can then query a publisher record that matches the title displayed on the form. In this case, the primary key would be TITLES.PUBLISHER_ID, and the detail would be PUBLISHERS.PUBLISHER_ID.

After you establish the master-detail relationship, you can query data from any column in the PUBLISHERS table, including PIC_LOGO (the column containing the logo). The master-detail relationship then ensures that the logo matches the publisher of the book.

Adding the Embedded Form

To add the embedded form that displays the appropriate publisher logo for each book, follow these steps:

1. Open the form frmTitles and make room near the PUBLISHER_ID text field.
2. Add an embedded form in this section of the form.
3. Set the embedded form's SizeX and SizeY properties to 2 in.

    Again, you want to create a container for the picture control that is just large enough to display a 2-inch by 2-inch graphic.

4. Set the following properties of the embedded form:

Property	Setting
RecordSource	PUBLISHERS
RecSrcSession	BOOKS
LinkMasterForm	frmTitles
LinkColumn	PUBLISHER_ID
LinkDetailColumn	PUBLISHER_ID

5. Add a picture control to the embedded form.
6. Resize the picture control so that it fills the entire embedded form.
7. Set the DataSource property of the embedded form to PIC_LOGO.
8. Save and run the form.

    As shown in Figure 11.9, the form now shows the logo for each publisher.

The correct logo now appears for each book's publisher. Browse through the titles displayed in this form to see a different logo displayed for each publisher.

Thus far, you have seen how to add a graphic in the background of a form, and how to display graphics in the bindable picture control. In the next exercise, you will add a graphic to a third part of your application, in the toolbar button you created yesterday.

Figure 11.9.
The logo appearing for each book's publisher.

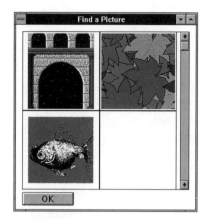

Adding a Graphic to a Toolbar Button

Before you can add a graphic to a toolbar button, you must first import the graphic as a bitmap resource into your application. When you call the `TBAppendButton()` or `TBInsertButton()` method to create a new toolbar button, the name of the graphic to display is one of the arguments passed to this method.

Because you did not have a graphic available in the last lesson, you passed NULL as the argument specifying the new toolbar button's graphic. In this lesson, you will draw the new icon and then add it to the button.

Toolbar buttons have a very limited space in which to display a graphic, so you will have to limit the size of your bitmap to 16-by-16 pixels. If you were to make a larger graphic, the application would simply crop everything but a 16-by-16 pixel area.

1. Launch Paintbrush (or some other graphics editor).
2. Set the size of the graphic to 16-by-16 pixels.
3. Draw the icon for running a Windows application.

   Remember, the toolbar button you added opens a form from which you can launch another Windows application. Therefore, you should create an icon that evokes the idea of launching an application. My personal preference is a lightning bolt; no doubt you can think of other ideas yourself.

4. Save the graphic as `C:\BOOKS\RUNAPP.BMP` and switch to Oracle Power Objects.
5. Select the Application window for BOOKS.POA.
6. Select File | Import BMP.
7. Import the bitmap RUNAPP.BMP into your application.

   An icon for RUNAPP now appears, indicating that you have successfully imported the graphic.

8. Open the Code Editor window for the application's `OnLoad()` method and make the following bold modification:

```
Sub OnLoad()
' Add a new button to the toolbar. When pressed, this
' button will open the Run Application form.
tbrNewToolbar.TBAppendButton(0, NULL, ToolbarStyle_Separator, 0)
tbrNewToolbar.TBAppendButton(cRunApp, "RUNAPP", ToolbarStyle_PushBtn, 0)
```

The code now passes the name of the bitmap RUNAPP to `TBAppendButton()` when it creates a new toolbar button. The second argument of `TBAppendButton()` is the name of a bitmap resource to display on the button.

9. Save and run the application.

10. Select Sales | Orders to open the Book Orders form.

The custom toolbar now appears. The button that in the previous lesson appeared blank now displays the graphic you just created. The users of this application now have a visual clue about the purpose of the button.

11. Press Stop to end this exercise.

Graphics in Pushbuttons

What if you want to display the graphic on a pushbutton within a form? The technique is the same as for displaying a graphic as the background for a form: By dragging the icon for the bitmap resource from the Application window onto the pushbutton, Oracle Power Objects automatically displays the graphic on the face of the pushbutton. The pushbutton's `Bitmap` property is set to the name of the bitmap resource, and the graphic replaces whatever label previously appeared on the pushbutton.

A Few Additional Words on Graphics

Graphics are a necessity in most applications, even aesthetically modest ones (like the Bookstore application). Here are some additional tips on using graphics in your applications:

☐ Remember to use no more than 256 colors. Not only does Oracle Power Objects not support a larger palette, but many older client systems might not display 256 or more colors. You do not want to add graphics to your application that end up looking splotchy and ugly on many PCs.

☐ Similarly, you should give some thought to how your graphics will look when they are displayed on a monochrome (black-and-white) monitor. Although most desktop systems by now have color monitors, a few do not. You also need to take into account the laptop computers that are limited to 640 × 480 displays.

- Although this lesson has focused on adding graphics to forms, reports are also a common place to display bitmaps. You want to be careful not to add too many graphics to reports, however, because bitmaps slow down the task of printing the report.

- When you are designing graphics for toolbar buttons or form backgrounds, take time to consider what kind of icon would immediately suggest the purpose of the pushbutton to the majority of users.

- In general, simplicity is best. Don't become so enamored with adding graphics that your application becomes a visual jungle of icons for the user. Graphics are striking, naturally attracting the eye to them. Be judicious in using them, so that you focus your user's attention on important details. The graphics should be designed so that these details become immediately clear to the user.

Creating a System Configuration Dialog Box

On Day 10, "Dynamic Link Libraries," you read some system configuration information, the name of the user, from an .INI file. In this exercise, you will create a dialog box that lets the user save preferences about the application, including whether you want to display a graphic as the background of every form. To add this functionality to your application, you need to be able to write to an .INI file, as well as read from it. Toward this end, you will use another Windows procedure to add or change entries in the BOOKS.INI file you created in the last lesson.

The *WritePrivateProfileString* Procedure

The code you will write for the system preferences dialog box will call the `WritePrivateProfileString` procedure, a Windows API function designed to work in tandem with `GetPrivateProfileString`. When you call `WritePrivateProfileString`, the procedure writes a new setting in the .INI file. For example, on Day 10, you could have added code that wrote a new user name in BOOKS.INI.

If `WritePrivateProfileString` does not find the specified entry, it automatically adds it. In the next exercise, you will specify a value for some new application settings, such as whether you want to display a graphic as a form's background. These settings do not appear in BOOKS.INI yet, so `WritePrivateProfileString` will add them.

`WritePrivateProfile` string has the following API declaration, which is described in the following list:

```
DECLARE FUNCTION WritePrivateProfileString Lib "Kernel"
➥(ByVal lpApplicationName As String, lpKeyName As Any, lpString As Any,
➥ByVal lplFileName As String) As Integer
```

Argument	Description
lpApplicationName	The name of a section in the .INI file. Although the section heading is surrounded by brackets ([ ]) in the .INI file, you do not add these brackets to the name of the section when passing it as an argument.
lpKeyName	The name of the entry in the .INI file whose value you will set. The procedure looks for this setting under the section heading specified in the previous argument.
lpString	The new value for the setting.
lplFileName	The filename of the .INI file. If the .INI file is not in the path, then you need to specify its directory as part of the filename.

In the next exercise, you will use WritePrivateProfileString to add the following section to BOOKS.INI:

```
[Graphics]
FormBackground=TRUE
```

1. Add the following line to the (Declarations) section of the Bookstore application's Property sheet:

   ```
   DECLARE FUNCTION WritePrivateProfileString Lib "Kernel" (ByVal
   ➥lpApplicationName As String, lpKeyName As Any, lpString
   ➥As Any, ByVal lplFileName As String) As Integer
   ```

2. In BOOKS.POA, create a new form, frmPreferences, and change the Label property to User Preferences.

3. Add a check box to the form, chkGraphics, and change the Label property to Show Graphics in Forms.

4. Set the DefaultValue property of the check box to 0.

5. Set the ValueOn property of this check box to -1, and its ValueOff property to 0.

   The values -1 and 0 are the values used for the constants TRUE and FALSE, respectively. The ValueOn property determines the value of the check box when it is checked; the ValueOff property determines its value when unchecked. Therefore, if a check appears in the check box, its value is -1 (or TRUE).

6. Add a pushbutton with the Label property OK to the bottom of the form.

7. In the Click() method of the form, add

   ```
   Sub Click()
   DIM x AS Long
   DIM vGraphics AS Long
   ```

```
' Read the value in the check box
vGraphics = chkGraphics.Value

' Write the value to the appropriate section of BOOKS.INI
x = WritePrivateProfileString("Graphics", "FormBackground",
➥vGraphics, "BOOKS.INI")

' If WritePrivateProfileString returns 0, then it can't find
' BOOKS.INI. The following code informs the user of this fact.
IF x = 0 THEN
  MSGBOX "Configuration file BOOKS.INI not found"
END IF

' Close the form
frmPreferences.CloseWindow()
```

Now that you have defined the User Preferences form, you need to add a menu command that opens this form. First, you will assign a constant for the new menu command.

8. Change the section of the application's OnLoad() method that defines the Setup menu to read as follows:

```
(Declarations)
' Declare the base value for all menu IDs
CONST cMenuNum = 1000

'Assign menu IDs for commands in the Setup menu
CONST cTitles = cMenuNum + 1
CONST cPublishers = cMenuNum + 2
CONST cBookTypes = cMenuNum + 3
CONST cEmployees = cMenuNum + 4
CONST cPreferences = cMenuNum + 5
```

Next, you need to add the code to DoCommand() that defines what happens when you select the menu.

9. Add the following bold lines to the DoCommand() method:

```
Function DoCommand(cmdLine As Long) As Long
' Test for the constant assigned to each menu command.
' Depending on the constant, open the correct form.
SELECT CASE cmdCode
CASE cTitles
  frmTitles.OpenWindow()
  DoCommand = TRUE
CASE cPublishers
  frmPubsBooks.OpenWindow()
CASE cBookTypes
  frmBookTypes.OpenWindow()
CASE cEmployees
  frmEmployees.OpenWindow()
CASE cPreferences
  ➥frmPreferences.OpenWindow()
```

11

```
CASE cOrders
  frmBookOrders.OpenWindow()
CASE cCustomers
  frmCustomers.OpenWindow()
cCustPurchases
  frmCustPurchases.OpenWindow()
CASE cRunApp
  frmLaunch.OpenWindow()
CASE cPreferences
  frmPreferences.OpenWindow()
END SELECT
```

Finally, you need to add the menu command to the Setup menu.

10. Add the following bold code to the section of the form's OnLoad() method that defines the Setup menu:

```
Sub OnLoad()
mnuSetup.Label = "&Setup"
mnuSetup.AppendMenuItem("&Titles", cTitles, 0, "^t")
mnuSetup.AppendMenuItem("&Publishers", cPublishers, 0, NULL)
mnuSetup.AppendMenuItem("&Book Types", cBookTypes, 0, NULL)
mnuSetup.AppendMenuItem("-", NULL, NULL, NULL)
mnuSetup.AppendMenuItem("&Employees", cEmployees, 0, NULL)
mnuSetup.AppendMenuItem("-", NULL, NULL, NULL)
mnuSetup.AppendMenuItem("&Preferences", cPreferences, 0, NULL)
```

11. After all the code appearing in the OnLoad() method, add the following:

```
Sub OnLoad()
' If the FormBackground entry in the .INI file is set to TRUE,
' then add a graphic to all the forms in the application.
DIM vPictureSet AS Long
DIM vTempString AS Long
DIM x AS Long
' Get the setting for the FormBackgound entry, which will
' be either -1 (TRUE) or 0 (FALSE)
x = GetPrivateProfileString("Graphics", vTempString, 8,
➥"FormBackground", "BOOKS.INI")
vPictureSet = VAL(vTempString)

' Get the first form in the application and add the
' logo to it
DIM vForm AS Object
vForm = Application.GetFirstForm()
IF vForm <> 0 THEN
  vForm.Bitmap = "LOGO"
  vForm.BitmapTiled = TRUE

' Use the GetNextForm() method to cycle through
' all forms in the application, displaying the
' graphic on each one
 DO
 vForm = Application.GetNextForm(vForm)
   IF ISNULL(vForm) THEN
      EXIT
```

```
    ELSE
        vForm.Bitmap = "LOGO"
        vForm.BitmapTiled = TRUE
    LOOP
END IF
```

12. Add the same code from the previous step to the Click() method of the OK pushbutton on the Preferences dialog box, just before the code that closes the form.

    Adding the code here instructs the application to add the logo to the background of all forms as soon as the user checks the box and closes the Preferences dialog box.

13. Save and run the application.

14. Open the Book Orders form, and then open the Preferences form.

15. Check the Show Graphics in Forms check box, and then press OK to close the form.

    The background of the Book Orders form changes to show the logo.

16. Select Setup | Employees to open the form frmEmployees.

    The logo also appears on the background of this form.

17. Open the Preferences dialog box and uncheck the Show Graphics in Forms check box.

18. Press OK to close the Preferences form.

    The logo now disappears from frmEmployees and all other forms in the application.

19. Press Stop to end this exercise.

The method code in this exercise used the GetFirstForm() and GetNextForm() methods to cycle through all the forms in the application.

Using the same approach, you can add other system configuration options to the Preferences dialog box. Using similar code, you could reset the font used throughout the application, change the background color of forms, or define other global characteristics of the application. In the next exercise, you will store the position of a form in the .INI file, so that it appears in the same location when you re-open it.

Remembering a Form's Position and Window Size

One important use of .INI files is storing information about the position and size of a window. Users often like the application to "remember" where a form appeared, so that it reappears in that portion of the interface when you reopen the form.

Now that you have had experience using the GetPrivateProfileString and WritePrivateProfileString procedures, storing this information in BOOKS.INI should be simple. In fact, you might want to try to do this exercise on your own before following the step-by-step instructions.

Each form has two properties, PositionX and PositionY, that determine where the form appears in the application window. When you close the form, you can store this information in the BOOK.INI file. When you reopen the form, the application can read these settings from BOOKS.INI, and then apply them to determine the position of the form.

If you are trying to perform this exercise on your own, remember that every form has two methods, OpenWindow() and CloseWindow(), that execute when you open and close the form.

1. In the CloseWindow() method of the form frmTitles, enter the following method code:

```
Sub CloseWindow()
' Store the X and Y position of the form in BOOKS.INI
DIM vPosX AS Long
DIM vPosY AS Long
DIM x AS Long
vPosX = self.PositionX
vPosY = self.PositionY
x = WritePrivateProfileString("frmTitles","PositionX", vPosX, "BOOKS.INI")
x = WritePrivateProfileString("frmTitles, "PositionY", vPosY, "BOOKS.INI")

' Close the form
Inherited.CloseWindow()
```

This method code adds two entries under the heading [frmTitles] that store the horizontal and vertical position of the form.

2. In the OpenWindow() method of the form, enter

```
Sub OnLoad()
' Open the form
Inherited.OpenWindow()

' Determine the position of the form
Sub OnLoad()
DIM vPosX AS Long
DIM vPosY AS Long
vPosX = GetPrivateProfileString("frmTitles","PositionX", 0,
➥vPosX, 255, "BOOKS.INI")
vPosY = GetPrivateProfileString("frmTitles","PositionY", 0,
➥vPosY, 255, "BOOKS.INI")
self.PositionX = VAL(vPosX)
self.PositionY = VAL(vPosY)
```

3. Save and run the application.

4. Select Setup | Titles to open the Employees form.

5. Move the form to a different part of the application window.

6. Close the form.

At this point, the application writes the position of the form to BOOKS.INI.

7. Select Setup | Titles again.

The form appears in the same position as when you closed it.

8. Press Stop to end this exercise.

The Crowded *OnLoad()* Method

As a result of the last few days, the application's OnLoad() method is filling up with code. This situation is fairly common, because you often need to set many aspects of the application (forms, reports, toolbars, menus, global variables, and so on) as soon as the application launches. The more you do at startup, the more code you add to OnLoad().

If the Code Editor window had some text search capabilities, this might be less of a problem. Because you cannot search for text within a method, however, you need to scroll through many lines of code in OnLoad() to find a particular entry. Overcrowding the OnLoad() method quickly becomes a headache for you as the developer.

The solution to this problem is a few lessons away, but it is worth mentioning here. Much of the code in OnLoad() consists of functionally distinct procedures: create a new menu bar; read entries in the .INI file and then apply these system configuration settings; open a particular form at startup. Although they share the need to execute when the application launches, they should be separate methods.

In Oracle Power Objects, you can create your own methods and then add them to objects. To resolve this code-crowding problem in OnLoad(), you could create a different user-defined method for each procedure, add the method to the application, and then copy the code for that procedure into the new method. To execute the procedure at startup, all you need is a single line of code in the OnLoad() method that calls the new user-defined method.

When Not to Store Information in an .INI File

Windows .INI files are excellent places to store application and system configuration information. When you use the GetPrivateProfileString and WritePrivateProfileString procedures, you have some quick shortcuts at your disposal for reading and writing settings for your own application.

The information you have stored in BOOKS.INI has been relatively harmless—the name of a user, an indicator whether you want to display the corporate logo in forms, and the position of a form when closed. However, other sorts of information should never appear in an .INI file, especially when they could endanger system security.

For example, although it is safe to save a username in an .INI file, you should never store a password in the file. If someone wanted to impersonate another user, all the malefactor would need to do is read the password from BOOKS.INI. Because .INI files are simple text files, all they would need is a text editor (Notepad would suffice) to get someone's password.

> **Note:** You can save an encrypted string to an .INI file, but you must use a DLL or an application to help encrypt and decrypt this string.

Follow these guidelines when you store information in an .INI file:

☐ Never use the .INI file to store information that might compromise system security.

☐ When designing the name for a section or an entry, always use a name that makes it immediately clear what kind of information it stores. Other developers might need to determine what the setting does, and you might forget what a particular entry was supposed to do. Therefore, naming an entry something like *WinPositionX* instead of *Parameter1* is always a good idea.

☐ Always store the .INI file in the WINDOWS\SYSTEM directory. This directory is always in the path where you install Windows, so it is the safest place to place an .INI file. For this reason, the WINDOWS\SYSTEM directory is the standard location for .INI files.

Summary

Today you learned about the following points:

☐ You have several options for displaying graphics in an Oracle Power Objects application.

☐ Once you import a graphic as an application resource, you can display it as the background of a form, an embedded form, a pushbutton, or a user-defined class. The `Bitmap` and `BitmapTiled` properties determine which bitmap is displayed, and whether it is tiled across the object.

☐ You can also display imported bitmaps in toolbar buttons. One of the arguments passed to `TBAppendButton()` and `TBInsertButton()` is the name of the bitmap resource. You should always display a bitmap on a toolbar button to give the user a visual clue to the purpose of the button.

☐ Oracle Power Objects has a picture control used to display graphics. This control is bindable, so you can use it to store graphics in a database table.

☐ You can write to .INI files as easily as you can read from them, using another Windows API, `WritePrivateProfileString`. By creating a Preferences dialog box, you can write application configuration settings entered by the user to an .INI file.

What Comes Next?

The first few days of this book focused on the basics of using Oracle Power Objects. In the last few lessons, you have been learning how to use Oracle Power Objects to address some common development challenges, such as storing application configuration information in an .INI file. The remaining lessons in this book will give more of the latter kind of information. Now that you have mastered many of the fundamentals of Oracle Power Objects, you can begin tackling common development tasks.

Tomorrow's lesson combines both types of lessons. You will learn how to add new types of database objects, such as sequences and indexes, to your database. Additionally, you will see how to use some of these database objects to handle some development challenges. For example, you will use a sequence to create a unique ID for each record in each table.

Q&A

Q How would I display on a single form all of the graphics from a table?

A The most obvious method is to use a repeater display. However, there are some cases in which you don't want to scroll vertically to see all the graphics. In these cases, you need to spread the graphics horizontally as well as vertically across the form.

You can use either embedded forms or user-defined classes to display each graphic. In advance, you need to know how many records are in the table, so that you can add a class or embedded form to display each one. Unfortunately, because the current version of Oracle Power Objects does not let you create objects on the fly, you cannot add new picture controls (and their containers) at runtime for additional graphics found in the table.

Q Is there any way to make larger buttons on a toolbar?

A The 16-by-16 pixel size of the toolbar buttons is standard for Windows applications. In some cases, developers want to create larger buttons, in part to accommodate larger graphics. Although you cannot design larger toolbar buttons, you can create a form that acts as a floating palette, with nothing but pushbuttons in it. You can size these pushbuttons to fit the graphics you wish to display.

Workshop

The Workshop consists of quiz questions to help you solidify your understanding of the material covered and exercises to give you experience in using what you've learned. Try to understand the quiz answers and the exercise before you go on to tomorrow's lesson.

Quiz

1. Suppose you copy a bitmap into a picture control and save it to a table. When you requery the form and display the bitmap, many of the colors have changed. What happened?

2. How would you write code to copy graphics between picture controls?

Exercises

1. Add an icon to the pushbutton in frmPubsBooks that opens the logo browser form.

2. Add a new toolbar button to tbrNewBar that opens the Book Orders form, and add an icon to this button.

3. Create toolbar buttons that copy and paste the contents of a picture control. (Hint: You need to write code that emulates the Edit | Copy and Edit | Paste menu commands.)

Quiz Answers

1. The graphic uses more than 256 colors, and the picture control supports only 256 colors.

2. You would use the same technique for copying values between any two controls. The code would look something like this:

```
picDestination. Value = picSource. Value
```

Although the value of the control is a graphic, it is nonetheless the current setting of the picture control's Value property. Therefore, copying a picture is no harder than copying string, numeric, or date information between controls.

Advanced
Database Objects

Overview

Application developers face several challenges while working with database records and the values within them. For example:

☐ How do you generate a unique primary key value for each record?

☐ How do you query and sort records efficiently, especially when you are working with large recordsets?

☐ How do you give users access to the database without giving everyone access to every table and view?

Relational databases have several features to address these challenges, as described in today's lesson. Today, you will learn about the following:

☐ Sequences

☐ Sequences and counter fields

☐ Other ways to generate unique IDs

☐ Locking a table

☐ Multipart keys

☐ Indexes

☐ Indexes and system performance

☐ Synonyms

☐ The SYS/SYS schema in Blaze databases

Generating Unique ID Numbers

As you learned on Day 3, "Creating a View," there are several good reasons for using numeric ID numbers to uniquely identify each record. For example, when you are performing a join between master and detail recordsets, you need two identical values. Maintaining identical numeric IDs as primary and foreign key values is easier than maintaining two strings with the same information. Additional spaces, slight misspellings of names, and other variations between strings can make it impossible to be certain that two string values are the same.

For this reason, you gave each publisher, book, book type, order, customer, and employee a unique ID number. Generating new ID numbers, so that new records get a new ID quickly and easily, is an important part of your application.

Numeric IDs have one pitfall: How do you make sure that each ID number you enter is unique? For example, suppose that you had an unexpectedly busy day for book orders, and your employees were working hard to enter these orders as quickly as possible. What prevents two clerks from accidentally entering the same ID number for an order? If this were to happen, the second order entered might overwrite the first, so you would lose one of your sales (and possibly a customer!).

Sequences and ID Numbers

Clearly, you need some way to automate the task of assigning ID numbers, to shield the process from human error. The designers of many relational database engines anticipated this need and created a special database object, a *sequence*, to automatically generate unique ID numbers for records. In this lesson, you will create several new sequences, and then call on them to generate a unique ID whenever you add a new record.

Sorting Records

Whatever means you use for generating ID numbers, your application also needs to sort records according to these and other values. When you assign a primary key, you are specifying a sort criterion:

- [ ] For numeric IDs, sort in ascending order.
- [ ] For strings, sort in alphabetical order.
- [ ] For dates, sort in ascending order.

In addition, your application and the database engine behind it have sorted records on other occasions. For example:

- [ ] When you specified a new setting for the OrderBy property of a form, you indicated the column used to sort records. For example, if you wanted to sort orders by the dates on which customers placed them, you would specify the column DATE_ENTERED as the setting for the OrderBy property.

  Because you can change the setting for the OrderBy property at runtime, your application can re-sort records for the user. When you created a browser dialog box for books and their authors, you could easily sort records in this dialog box by author or by title by changing the setting for the OrderBy property.

- [ ] When you specify a master-detail relationship between recordsets, you sort the detail records according to their foreign key value. Because you can set up the master-detail relationship in nearly any way imaginable, as long as you have matching primary and foreign key values, you should expect the data in your tables to be consistently re-sorted. As long as new ways to define joins exist, expect that applications and users will take advantage of this flexibility in defining relationships among records.

Within the database, these records might not be sorted according to any of these criteria. Whatever way you sort records that you query from the database, the records as they are physically written on disk might not follow any sorting criteria you could recognize. Therefore, when you query records, the database engine must first read the records from disk, and then order them according to whatever sorting criteria is defined within the database itself (such as a primary key). When the database passes these records to the client, the application might sort them again, according to a new set of criteria (such as those specified in the OrderBy property).

Although smaller database applications might not experience problems while juggling and sorting these records, larger ones will. When the system needs to sort and re-sort hundreds or thousands of records, performance might suffer. Relational databases need some mechanism to shorten the time spent sorting records.

Indexes, Querying, and Sorting

Not surprisingly, they have such a mechanism, an *index*. As its name implies, an index provides the database engine with a quick pointer to where it can find records. The index uses one or more columns to help query records, anticipating the columns someone might use to sort records. For example, because you often want to view orders by the date they were entered, you could create an index designed to help query ORDERS records according to the values in the DATE_ENTERED column.

During Days 2 and 3, you learned that a good relational database is designed with some degree of disregard for how it might be used. Through the process of normalization, you break down the information into the smallest possible logical units (publishers, customers, books, and so on), each of which then becomes a table. The goal here is not necessarily to create what you might think is the best database design for your application, but an organization of information that's versatile enough to be usable by many different applications. Because an order entry application might not access information the same way the inventory application does, you need to keep the database highly normalized.

In contrast, indexes are designed with far less disregard for the applications that use them. You create an index to anticipate how an application might need to sort information. Usually, the application in question is the one you're in the midst of developing, not some abstract, hypothetical application. Indexes, then, are database objects firmly rooted in the applications you design, not in the orthodoxy of how to design a good relational database.

Providing Access to Objects

Last of all, you need to provide the means for users to access database objects in different schemas. For example, the database administrator might want to give users the ability to view the table that stores a list of all the tables in the database. Although you do not want employees to edit the records in this table, it might be useful for them to see this information. Tables containing lists of database objects and their descriptions are often called the *data dictionary*, because they define the contents of the database.

Another reason to create an alias for an object in a different schema is security. In the Bookstore application, you will eventually build a login form for entering a username and password when the application launches. The table containing this information, however, should exist in a schema that is accessible only by a very small number of users—primarily, managers and the system administrator. If you make the table containing usernames and passwords part of the schema used by all employees, you run the risk of giving a large amount of highly sensitive information to any clever, enterprising employee.

However, if you keep the table containing usernames and passwords in a highly guarded schema, how do you get the necessary information for the login form? The answer is to create a *synonym*, an alias for a database object in a different schema. The user can access the username and password table only through this alias, not directly through the schema in which this table exists. There might be other equally sensitive tables in that schema, but the alias gives access to only one of them. If you want to protect system security, therefore, synonyms give you an important alternative to giving users access to all database objects in all schemas.

Three New Database Objects

As you just learned, there are three important types of database objects beyond tables and views:

12

- [ ] *Sequences* that generate unique ID numbers
- [ ] *Indexes* that provide quick roadmaps for where to find records, accelerating the process of querying and sorting records
- [ ] *Synonyms* that give limited access to database objects in different schemas

Not every database platform supports all of these objects. For example, SQL Server databases do not have sequences. If not all, then most of these objects are found in any relational database. Without them, relational databases would be crippled, or require so many "hacks" to duplicate what sequences, indexes, and synonyms do that the database could become worthless.

Working with Sequences

As described earlier, a sequence automatically generates a new number every time you use it. The sequence adds one to the last number it generated, not to the largest value in a table. Sequences can therefore be a headache if you are not careful about how you use them.

Each sequence has the following characteristics:

☐ *A name.* As with any database object, the name must be unique, and you should use some naming convention. In the upcoming exercises, you will use the prefix SEQ_ in every sequence name.

☐ *A beginning number.* If your database is a blank slate, you should use 1 as the starting number. When you insert your first record into a table that has a primary key value which is generated by a sequence, the first ID number will then be 1. However, if you are working with an existing database, the beginning ID number will be higher.

☐ *An increment.* This value specifies the amount to add whenever you ask the sequence for a new number. Normally, the increment is one, although you can specify any increment you wish.

☐ *A maximum value.* This optional feature of a sequence specifies the largest value the sequence can generate.

☐ *A minimum value.* Additionally, you can specify a lower bound for numbers generated by the sequence.

☐ *A flag for whether sequence-generated values cycle back to the minimum value.* Once the sequence reaches the maximum value (either explicitly defined for the sequence, or imposed by the limits of the data type used for a column), the sequence can return to the minimum value (normally 1) when you ask it to generate a new ID number.

In relational databases that support sequences, you can create a sequence through SQL code, using the CREATE SEQUENCE command and specifying the characteristics of the sequence. Instead of writing SQL code, you can create a new sequence through Oracle Power Objects.

Creating a Sequence

The first sequence you will create will generate new ID numbers for the PUBLISHER_ID column in the PUBLISHERS table. The first step is to create the sequence itself.

1. Open the Session window for BOOKS.POS and open a connection to the database.

2. Press the New Sequence button, or select the File | New Sequence menu command.

   The Create Sequence dialog box appears, as shown in Figure 12.1. As you can see, it includes controls for specifying all the characteristics of a sequence.

3. For the name of the new sequence, enter SEQ_PUBLISHER_ID.

   As mentioned earlier, use a naming convention for sequences that includes the prefix SEQ_, followed by the name of the column for which it will generate new IDs.

4. For the starting value, enter 10.

   The first number generated by the sequence will be 10.

5. For the increment, enter 1.

Figure 12.1.

The Create Sequence dialog box.

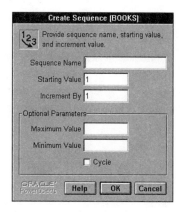

6. Skip the Optional Parameters section of this dialog box.

   Because you will not be entering thousands of publisher records in the PUBLISHERS table, you do not need to worry about setting an upper bound for numbers generated by this sequence. However, if you were dealing with a sequence that you planned to use in a table with a very large number of records, you would need to give some thought to this feature of the sequence, if the ID numbers threatened to exceed the maximum value allowed for that column's data type.

   However, you rarely set the upper bound of a sequence except when you are generating a counter. For example, you might want to limit the number of line items in an invoice to 10, in which case you could use a sequence to keep track of the number of line items added.

7. Leave the Cycle check box unchecked.

8. Press OK.

   The new sequence now appears as part of the database.

9. Repeat the process for creating a new sequence, specifying the same parameters for the following sequences:

Name	*Purpose*
SEQ_EMPLOYEE_ID	Used to generate new employee IDs.
SEQ_CUSTOMER_ID	Used to generate new customer IDs.
SEQ_TYPE_ID	Used to generate new book type IDs.

10. Create another sequence, SEQ_TITLE_ID, with a starting value of 20.

    Because you might have entered more than 10 books in the TITLES table, you want to start with an ID number larger than 10. During development, you always want to give yourself some margin of error.

11. Select the View | Refresh menu command.

Oracle Power Objects now updates the list of objects in the BOOKS.BLZ database, displaying them in alphabetical order (see Figure 12.2). All of the sequences now appear in the same part of the Session window—an added benefit of beginning the name of each sequence with the prefix SEQ_.

Figure 12.2.
The updated Session window for BOOKS.BLZ.

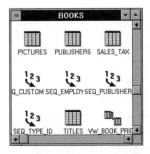

However, if you wanted to view sequences next to each table for which they generate ID numbers, you would add _SEQ as a suffix, instead of a prefix. Following this convention, the sequence, PUBLISHER_ID_SEQ, would appear next to the PUBLISHERS table in the Session window. Either technique is fine, as long as you apply it consistently.

As you can also see from Figure 12.2, when you give database objects long names (more than 12 or 15 characters), the names begin to overlap in the Session window. Unfortunately, there is no way to space them out, so you should keep database object names as short as possible without sacrificing readability. As you will see later, the naming convention you use for sequences will be important when the application requests a new ID number from a sequence.

When Do I Generate a Sequence?

Right now, you have new sequences, but there is no obvious way to associate them with a particular table. Sure, you used a naming convention to indicate which table the sequence is designed for, but how to you ask the sequence to generate a new number?

Again, Oracle Power Objects provides a relatively simple way of accomplishing this task. Through several properties of a text field, you can request a new ID number from the sequence whenever you insert a new record through a form.

Creating a Counter Field

When you use a text field to automatically generate new ID numbers, the text field becomes a counter field. For example, in the next exercise, the PUBLISHER_ID text field in the frmPubsBooks form will become a counter field that uses the sequence SEQ_PUBLISHER_ID to generate new

ID numbers. Whenever you enter a new publisher record through this form, the application asks the sequence for a new ID number, which then appears in the text field.

Before continuing, you should know that requesting an ID from a sequence is one of three ways a counter field can generate a new ID number. In later exercises, you will experiment with other ways to generate new ID numbers through a counter field.

If you want to use a sequence as the source of an ID number, you must set two properties of the text field to the settings in Table 12.1.

Table 12.1. Setting properties for sequence-generated IDs.

Property	Description	Setting
CounterType	Specifies whether the text field generates new ID numbers and, if so, the technique used.	Sequence
CounterSeq	Indicates the column that will receive the new ID number.	The name of the column.

Once you set these properties, the application requests a new value from the sequence whenever you insert a record through the form.

1. Open the form frmPubsBooks.
2. Remove the picture control and the Select Graphic button from the form.
3. Resize the form so that there is only a small gap between the right edge of the repeater display and the right edge of the form.

    Because you have removed the picture control, you do not need the extra space.

4. Select the text field PUBLISHER_ID and open its Property sheet.
5. Set the text field's CounterType property to Sequence.

    The application knows that you want a sequence to be the source of new ID numbers.

6. Set the CounterSeq property to SEQ_PUBLISHER_ID.

    In this step, you have specified the name of the sequence that will generate new ID numbers. Here is where the naming convention comes into play: Because the sequence's name includes the name of the column for which it is designed to generate values, it's easy to remember the sequence name when you enter it in the CounterSeq property.

7. Set the ReadOnly property of the text field to True.

    Now, the user cannot enter a value in this field. The only time new values will appear is when you insert a new record into the form's recordset, at which point the new PUBLISHER_ID value automatically appears.

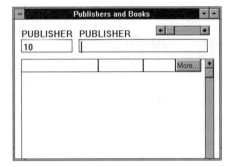
8. Save and run the form.

9. Press the Insert button, or select Database | Insert Row.

A new record now appears in the form (see Figure 12.3). Unlike other times when you entered a new record through a form, a primary key value already appears in the appropriate text field (in this case, PUBLISHER_ID). Because you set the starting value for numbers generated through SEQ_PUBLISHER_ID to 10, this is the value that appears in PUBLISHER_ID.

Figure 12.3.

*A new publisher record,
with a PUBLISHER_ID value
automatically generated
through a sequence.*

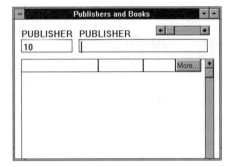

10. Enter Laumer Books as the name of the new publishing company.

11. Press Commit to save the new record.

12. Create a new record.

The next value generated by the sequence, 11, appears in the text field.

13. Enter Leiber Press as the name of the publishing house, and then press Commit to save the new publisher record.

14. Press Stop to end this exercise.

DO	DON'T
DO add sequences that apply to tables with records already in them. **DO** create sequences with increments larger than 1. **DON'T** make the starting value of a sequence 1, if the sequence will apply to a table that already contains records. In this case, you need to look at the appropriate column in that table to find the maximum value already stored there, and then set the sequence to a larger number than that. **DON'T** create increments so large that you quickly exhaust the maximum value for a column's data type.	

DON'T increment sequences by 1 if you believe that users will need to insert records "between" other records. For example, you might develop a sequence for generating ID numbers for cars, and then later insert new records describing the same car, but sold with different sets of options. In this case, you want each version of the same car to have an ID number close to the standard version of the car.

Counters, Sequences, and Primary Keys

As you might guess from the previous exercise, as well as the discussion of sequences, you commonly use sequences to generate primary key values. By using a sequence, you avoid the problem of having two users accidentally enter the same primary key value for a new record. For example, as long as you keep the ReadOnly property set to TRUE, and the counter field properly set up to use SEQ_PUBLISHER_ID to generate values, users cannot accidentally enter the same publisher ID for different publishers. The only source of new publisher ID values is the sequence SEQ_PUBLISHER_ID.

In some applications, you might use a sequence for columns other than the primary key. For example, you might want to keep track of the number of times customers have placed orders. Because you can delete orders from the ORDERS table, the number of orders appearing in the table might not equal the total number of orders that employees have entered. In this case, you can use a sequence to generate a new ID number every time someone enters a new order. This value can appear as part of the order, or be stored elsewhere in the database. By comparing the number of orders entered with the number still in the database, you can estimate the number of canceled orders, giving you a better sense of the store's capability to fulfill orders.

Another hypothetical use for a sequence is to help reward every hundredth customer added to the database. In this case, you would design a sequence that had a maximum value of 100, and then cycled back to 1 after it reached this value. Therefore, whenever you entered a new customer into the system, you could check to see if the sequence returned 100. This value then indicates that the customer was the 100th, 200th, or some other hundredth added to the CUSTOMERS table, and therefore deserving of a special discount.

Generating primary key values might be the predominant use of sequences, but it is not the only one, as demonstrated in the next two exercises.

12

Why Not Use a Sequence?

Because you have enjoyed some success in using a sequence to generate primary key values, you might ask yourself, why use any other method?

The most obvious reason for not using sequences is when your database does not support them. As noted earlier, SQL Server does not support sequences, nor do other database formats that might be supported in future releases of Oracle Power Objects. (However, both Oracle7 and Blaze support sequences.)

Finally, sequences are less useful if you need to generate IDs within different ranges, instead of in a strictly consecutive fashion. Suppose you assign ranges of ID numbers for titles. For example, every computer book would fall into the 1000-1999 range, while mysteries would be assigned to 4000-4999. In these cases, a single sequence could not generate a new title ID for a book and make it fall into the appropriate range. Instead, the sequence would continue producing consecutive values, with complete disregard for whatever equivalent to the Dewey decimal system you concocted for your bookstore. (You might also use multiple sequences to generate the ID numbers, each sequence corresponding to a different range of topic values.)

Alternatives to Sequences

In these and other cases, you have two alternatives to sequences for generating unique ID numbers.

☐ Look for the maximum value for the ID within the table. Oracle Power Objects provides an automated mechanism for looking into the database to determine the highest value in a particular column. Using this technique, you could look into the PUBLISHER_ID column, find the highest value for this primary key, and then add 1 to it for a new record.

☐ Create and assign the ID number through method code. In this case, you write method code to generate the new ID number. This code might perform a lookup into a table as part of this process.

Both of these approaches have their strengths and weaknesses, as you will see in the next two exercises.

Finding the Maximum Value for an ID Number

To demonstrate how to find the maximum value for an ID number and then increment it by one, you will use a different setting for the CounterType property. Once you have set CounterType to the somewhat cryptic Table, MAX()+CounterIncBy, the application knows to generate a new ID number for the counter field.

The second piece of information the application needs is the increment between the largest ID number found and the new one generated. Another property, CounterIncBy, specifies the amount of the increment.

You will use this technique to generate new ID numbers for customers.

1. Open the form frmCustomers.
2. Select the CUSTOMER_ID text field and open its Property sheet.
3. Select MAX()+CounterIncBy as the setting for the CounterType property.
4. Enter 1 for the CounterIncBy property.
5. Set the ReadOnly property of the text field to True.

   Again, you want the process of generating ID numbers to be completely automated, so you are making it impossible for the user to edit the CUSTOMER_ID field.

6. Save the form.
7. In the Session window for BOOKS.POS, open the Table Editor for the CUSTOMERS table.
8. Run the table to view the records in it.

   As you scan through the records in the Table Browser window, you can see that the largest value currently shown for CUSTOMER_ID is 7 (see Figure 12.4).

Figure 12.4.
The current values for CUSTOMER_ID.

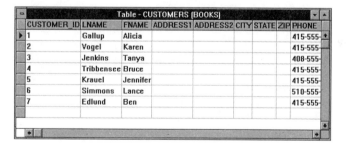

9. Stop running the form and return to the form frmCustomers.
10. Run the form, and then insert a new record.

    When the new record appears, the application assigns the value 8 to the CUSTOMER_ID field, as shown in Figure 12.5.

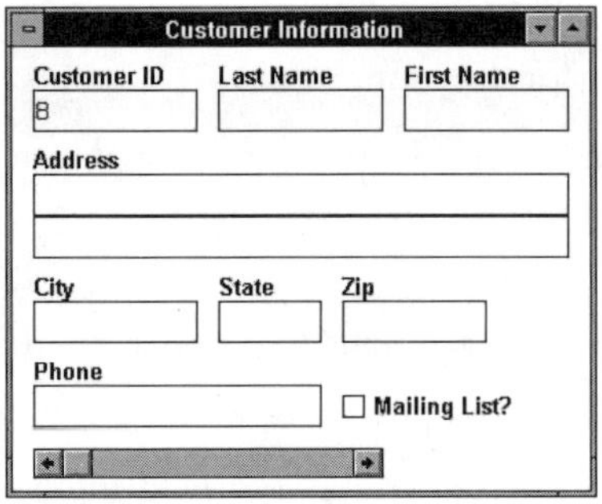

Figure 12.5.

Using the
`Table,MAX()+CounterIncBy`
method for generating a new
CUSTOMER_ID value.

11. Press Rollback, or select the Database | Roll Back menu command, to eliminate the new record.

12. Press Stop to end this exercise.

This technique for generating a unique ID was just as easy as using a sequence to do the same job. What are the pros and cons of this approach?

Pros of Using the *Table,Max()+CounterIncBy* Technique

One benefit of using this approach is that there will be no gaps between ID numbers. When you created a sequence for generating PUBLISHER_ID values, the sequence started numbering IDs at 10. However, there is a gap between this value and the highest existing customer ID, 7. The sequence failed to plug this hole in your numbering scheme for customer IDs.

Second, the act of rolling back the insertion of a new record has no effect on the sequence. Whenever you ask a sequence for a number, regardless of what you do with it, the sequence sets its internal counter to the next value, according to whatever increment you set for the sequence.

Suppose the last customer ID value generated by a sequence is 100. You roll back that insertion, however, so that no new customer record with a customer ID of 100 appears in the database. You then insert a new record, and the sequence gives you a value of 101 for its customer ID. When you commit this new record to the database, no customer record will have 100 as its customer ID—although there will be IDs numbered 99 and 101!

Most of the time, this situation won't be a problem. There are those rare occasions, however, when you want to ensure that there are no gaps in your numbering scheme.

Cons of Using the *Table,Max()+CounterIncBy* Technique

As useful as this technique might seem, it has a big deficiency if several users are entering records at the same time. If you insert a new record into your application's CUSTOMERS recordset, the database has no idea what you're doing until you commit the new customer record. However, your application will generate the new ID number (say, 100) without any obvious problems.

Meanwhile, while you're talking with the customer or doing something else, another employee might be creating another customer record through her copy of the Bookstore application. Because you have not committed the new customer record to the database, she will get the same new ID number, 100.

Within a few minutes, both of you will have committed two different customer records with the same ID number. The database will store only one of these, because CUSTOMER_ID is the primary key value for the CUSTOMERS table. Therefore, the second employee to commit a customer record overwrites the first person's work!

Clearly, the Table,Max()+CounterIncBy technique does not work well in multiuser systems—a deficiency that is also shared by the next approach.

Generating ID Numbers Through Method Code

12

As mentioned earlier, a sequence cannot generate unique ID numbers within separate ranges. In this case, you need to write some code to generate the ID number.

In this exercise, you will write some method code that generates a new TITLE_ID value, depending on the type of book. First, you must add two columns to the BOOK_TYPES table to store the range of IDs for each book type.

1. Open the Session window for BOOKS.POS.

2. Open the Table Editor window for the BOOK_TYPES table.

3. Add a new column to the table, ID_LBOUND.

    This column will store the lower bound of ID numbers for this type of book.

4. Set the column's Datatype property to Number, and check the Not Null section.

    You want to make sure that each type of book has an ID range assigned to it, so you want to enforce the NOT NULL constraint on this column.

5. Add a second column, ID_UBOUND, with the same data type and NOT NULL constraint.

This column specifies the upper bound for TITLE_ID values for each book type.

6. Save and run the table.

Now that you have added the columns, you want to enter the range of TITLE_ID values for each type of book.

7. Enter in this table the data from Table 12.2.

Table 12.2. ID number ranges added to the BOOK_TYPES table.

TYPE_DESC	ID_LBOUND	ID_UBOUND
Reference	10000	19999
Computer	20000	29999
Mystery	30000	39999
Science fiction	40000	49999
Literature	50000	59999
Science	60000	69999
History	70000	79999
Current affairs	80000	89999
Biography	90000	99999
Children's	10000	10999
General fiction	11000	11999
General non-fiction	12000	12999

Use fairly large numbers because you do not know how many books will ultimately appear in the database. You don't want to provide too few available ID numbers. If the store expands to the point where you need to store hundreds of thousands of title records, you want enough room within these ranges to accommodate all these books.

8. Press Commit, and then stop running the table.

You're finished defining the range of ID numbers for each type of book. Now you're ready to create a new kind of counter field that uses this information to assign TITLE_ID values that fit into the correct range, according to the type of book.

1. Open the form frmBooks and select the pop-up list labeled Topic.

2. In the PostChange() method of this control, add the following:

```
Sub PostChange()
' Allow the change to the control's value
Inherited.PostChange()
```

```
' Check to see if the new value for this control is not null,
' and if the record is new. In the case of a new record, the
' method GetRowStat returns 5. If the new record passes these tests,
' generate a new ID number.
IF NOT ISNULL (self.Value) AND (self.GetContainer.GetRecordset.GetRowStat
➥= 5) THEN
    DIM vLower AS Long
    DIM vUpper AS Long
    DIM vNewVal AS Long

    ' Get the upper and lower bounds for TITLE_IDs falling under this book type
    vUpper = SQLLOOKUP(BOOKS, "select ID_UBOUND from BOOK_TYPES
➥where TYPE_ID = " & STR(self.Value))
    vLower = SQLLOOKUP(BOOKS, "select ID_LBOUND from BOOK_TYPES
➥where TYPE_ID = " & STR(self.Value))

    ' Look up the maximum value in the TITLES table for title IDs
      ➥within the specified range.
    ' If there are no IDs in this range, use the lower bound value.
    vNewVal = NVL((SQLLOOKUP("select MAX(TITLE_ID) from TITLES
➥where TITLE_ID <= " & STR(vUpper) & " AND TITLE_ID >= " &
➥STR(vLower)) + 1),vLower)

' Assign the new
    TITLE_ID.Value = vNewVal

END IF
```

This code reads the upper and lower bounds for TITLE_ID values, as defined in the new columns you added to the BOOK_TYPES table. Once the code reads these values, it uses them to find the largest TITLE_ID value that falls between these ranges, and then adds 1 to that value. If there are no title IDs in this range, the code uses the lower bound value.

3. Select the TITLE_ID text field and change its ReadOnly property to TRUE.

4. Save and run the form.

5. Insert a new record, and then select Mystery as the topic for the book.

   The application now assigns 30000 as the new ID number for this book record. Because there are no titles with a TITLE_ID between 30000 and 39999 (the range of IDs for mysteries), the code uses the lowest ID value possible, 30000, for this type of book.

6. Press Rollback to undo the insertion.

7. Press Stop to end this exercise.

As you can see, generating ID numbers through code can demand a significant amount of programming. However, this technique affords you the greatest amount of flexibility when assigning new ID numbers.

12

The *CounterGenKey()* Method

Although this exercise showed how to generate unique IDs through method code, it did not use the method designed for this purpose, CounterGenKey(). Because you did not set the TITLE_ID text field as a counter field (its CounterType is still set to None), the field had no way to generate a new ID on its own. Because the new ID number was dependent on the value entered for TYPE_ID, the application did not assign a new TITLE_ID value until you selected the topic of the book.

However, if you had set the CounterType property to User Generated, you could have placed the code that generated the new TITLE_ID in the CounterGenKey() method. (The name of this setting is a little misleading: The user in this case is you, the developer, not the person using your finished application.) CounterGenKey() executes when you insert a new record, as long as the text field's CounterType property is set to User Generated.

Generating ID Numbers Through Code: Pros and Cons

Although this technique makes it possible to generate IDs in ways that sequences cannot, it does have its weaknesses. As with the Table,MAX()+CounterIncBy technique, you cannot be sure that another user has generated the same ID number through a different copy of the application.

There is a severe measure you can take to prevent this problem: lock the table into which you are inserting a new record. Unfortunately, this technique completely prevents other users from entering new records until you commit yours. Even in a small setting, like a bookstore, this measure can be highly annoying (and potentially more trouble than it's worth, as the size of the organization increases).

Locking a Table

If, however, you wanted to lock the table, you would need to use the LOCK TABLE and UNLOCK TABLE commands in SQL. To lock a table, you would use the following syntax:

```
LOCK TABLE table_name IN mode_name MODE
```

In this syntax, the mode specifies the degree of lock. You can use the LOCK TABLE command to lock a single row, or you can lock the entire table. If, for example, you wanted to lock the entire PUBLISHERS table, you would enter the following SQL statement:

```
LOCK TABLE PUBLISHERS IN EXCLUSIVE MODE
```

The online help topic for LOCK TABLE describes all of the modes and the syntax to use them.

Once you have committed the new record, you use the LOCK TABLE command again to give other users the ability to write records to the table. The ROW SHARE mode releases the lock completely. Therefore, to "unlock" the PUBLISHERS table, you would enter the following SQL statement:

```
LOCK TABLE PUBLISHERS IN ROW SHARE MODE
```

However, it remains to be seen how to pass these SQL commands to your database. Your method code is written in Oracle Basic, with a little SQL occasionally added for database-related tasks.

Fortunately, Oracle Basic includes the EXEC SQL command, which lets you pass a SQL statement to the database. If you wanted to lock and unlock the table, you would use EXEC SQL to pass these instructions to the database.

The next exercise illustrates how to lock a table in the Bookstore application. Because the Blaze database BOOKS.BLZ is single-user, there's no need to do this—only one user (yourself) can access the database at any time. However, if you were to then copy the database objects from BOOKS.BLZ into an Oracle7 or SQL Server database, this measure would be necessary to prevent different users from accidentally generating the same ID number.

1. Open the form frmCustomers.

2. Add the following method code to the InsertRow() method:

```
Sub InsertRow()
Inherited.InsertRow()
EXEC SQL LOCK TABLE CUSTOMERS IN EXCLUSIVE MODE
MSGBOX "Table CUSTOMERS locked until you commit or roll back"
```

This message tells the user not to dally—other people might need access to the CUSTOMERS table.

3. In the CommitForm() method, enter

```
Sub CommitForm()
Inherited.CommitForm()
EXEC SQL LOCK TABLE CUSTOMERS IN ROW SHARE MODE
MSGBOX "Table CUSTOMERS now unlocked"
```

The CommitForm() method executes whenever you commit the changes you have entered in a form. In this case, the code first commits the changes by calling the default processing for the method, and then unlocks the table and informs the user.

4. In the RollbackForm() method of the same form, enter

```
Sub RollbackForm()
Inherited.CommitForm()
EXEC SQL LOCK TABLE CUSTOMERS IN ROW SHARE MODE
MSGBOX "Table CUSTOMERS now unlocked"
```

5. Save and run the form.

6. Insert a new customer record.

The message box telling you that the table is locked now appears.

12

7. Roll back the new record.

   Another message box informs you that the lock has been removed.

8. Press Stop to end this exercise.

As you can see, EXEC SQL is a highly useful Oracle Basic command, as long as you know SQL. EXEC SQL will appear again in some later exercises.

The Bottom Line on Counter Fields

As illustrated in these exercises, you have three options for generating unique ID numbers in a counter field. Each of these techniques corresponds to a different setting for the text field's CounterType property.

- ☐ Sequence-generated. The counter field requests new ID numbers from a sequence. To use this technique, set CounterType to Sequence.
- ☐ Table-generated. The application reads the maximum value from a column in a table, and then adds some increment to this value (usually 1). To use this technique, set CounterType to Table,MAX()+CounterIncBy.
- ☐ Code-generated. Method code added to CounterGenKey() generates the new value. To use this technique, set CounterType to User Generated. Alternatively, you can enter the necessary code in a different method, as when you added code to the PostChange() method of a pop-up list.

Now that you are familiar with sequences (and some alternatives to them), it's time to learn about another new database object: the index.

Working with Indexes

As mentioned earlier today, indexes speed up queries by providing pointers to different records. Indexes use one or more columns as pointers, anticipating the columns that you might use to sort these records. For example, if you expect that your application will frequently sort customer records by ZIP code, you create an index that uses the ZIP column of CUSTOMERS to order records queried from this table. Even more frequently, you will sort customer records by name, in which case you would use the LNAME column for sorting.

Because relational databases make it easy to query records from the same table in many different ways, each table often has several indexes designed for it. Each index corresponds to a different type of query, such as viewing customer records by the customer's last name, ID number, zip code, city, or phone number.

In many respects, indexes are some of the easiest database objects to create and use. Unlike sequences, indexes require no additional work on the front end. Once you have defined the index, it automatically speeds queries for a particular table from any source.

The parameters you need to define for an index are also relatively simple.

☐ The name of the index.

☐ The table with which the index is associated, and whose records the index will help query.

☐ The columns in that table used to help index records. If you use multiple columns, you separate their names with commas.

In the next exercise, you will create several indexes. Later, when you open some of the main forms in the application, you might notice that the application queries records for these forms significantly faster than before. You can thank the sequences for this improvement in performance!

Adding Indexes to BOOKS.BLZ

To add some new indexes, follow these steps:

1. Open the Session window for BOOKS.BLZ.

2. Press the New Index button, or select File | New Index.

   The Create Index dialog box now appears (see Figure 12.6). As indicated, it has fields for the name of the index, the table to which it applies, and the columns in that table used to index records.

3. For the name of the new index, enter IDX_CUST_LNAME.

   As the name indicates, this index will use the last name of each customer (stored in the CUSTOMER.LNAME column) to index records in the CUSTOMERS table.

4. For the name of the table, enter CUSTOMERS.

5. For the columns to index, enter LNAME.

6. Press OK, and then select View | Refresh.

   The new index now appears in the database, as shown in Figure 12.7.

7. Create a new index, named IDX_RPTCUSTPURCHASES.

   In this case, the index's name indicates that it is designed to help query records for a report, rptCustPurchase. This report uses the column CUSTOMER_ID to sort records from the CUST_PURCHASES table. Because this is not a primary key in the table, the index will help sort the records for this report.

8. For the name of the table, enter CUST_PURCHASES, and enter CUSTOMER_ID as the column used for indexing.

9. Press OK to create the new index.

10. Create a new index, IDX_TITLES.

    As its name implies, this index will apply to the TITLES table.

12

Figure 12.6.

The Create Index dialog box.

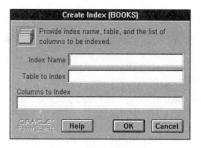

Figure 12.7.

The index IDX_CUST_LNAME added to the BOOKS.BLZ database.

11. For the table, enter TITLES.

12. For the columns used to index, enter TITLE_ID.

13. Press OK to create the index.

14. Open the Application window for BOOKS.POA, and then open the form frmPubsBooks.

    This form displays publishers and books in a master-detail relationship. Because it uses the TYPE_ID value to sort records, the index should decrease the time needed to query records for the report.

15. Run the report.

    You might notice some difference in the time needed to run the rptTitles report. If you were running this report against a table with thousands of book records, the difference would be very noticeable.

16. Press Stop to end this exercise.

Some Tips on Indexes

Because you can conceivably apply any number of indexes to the tables in your database, you need some guidelines for when to add indexes.

- [ ] If a column is frequently used as a foreign key, but does not have the primary key restraint applied to it, then you should create an index that uses the foreign key column. For this reason, the TITLES.TYPE_ID column is a natural candidate for an index, as are TITLES.PUBLISHER_ID, ORDERS.CUSTOMER_ID, and ORDER_ITEMS.TITLE_ID.

- [ ] If you frequently reorder records that are displayed in a form according to a particular column, you should create an index that uses that column. For example, if you created a browser form that could re-sort records according to different columns, you should create an index that includes all of these columns. In other words, if you reset the OrderBy property of a form at runtime, you should create sequences that use whatever columns might be used as the setting for this property.

- [ ] Blaze databases do not yet support multicolumn indexes. If you are using a Blaze database to prototype an application for later deployment on Oracle7 or SQL Server, this is not much of a problem. Indexes are often the last database objects you add, because their only purpose is to enhance performance. You can add the multicolumn indexes to the remote server after you migrate the other database objects from your Blaze prototyping database.

- [ ] If a report group uses a column for its GroupCol property that is not the primary key for the table, then you should create an index that uses the GroupCol column. For example, because the report rptTitles used the TYPE_ID column for the GroupCol property of a report group, you needed an index on this column to help sort records in the report. If you had nested report groups, you would add the GroupCol column from each report group to the index.

12

DO	DON'T

DO create indexes for columns that you think might be used not only by your application, but other applications that need to sort records according to particular columns.

DON'T add too many indexes to the database. Indexes can fill a great deal of disk space, adding a great deal to the overhead needed to maintain the database on the server.

DON'T try to anticipate every possible column that someone might use for sorting records. Most columns that deserve an index should be obvious. In cases where you're not as sure, don't create the index. Indexes are easy to add to the database later, as needed.

Providing Aliases for Database Objects

The last kind of database object you'll use in this lesson is a *synonym*. As its name implies, a synonym provides an alias for another object. If you use the name of the synonym instead of the object, you still get full access. For example, if you use the name of a synonym for a table in a SELECT statement, you can still query records from the table.

Then why create the synonym? In Oracle Power Objects, there are two instances in which a synonym can be useful:

☐ To provide a shorthand for an object with an extremely long name. As you can tell from the lessons so far, you want to give objects meaningful names. However, some of these names can get very long; the index you created in an earlier exercise, IDX_RPTCUSTPURCHASES, is a prime example.

☐ To give access to a database object in a different schema. In some cases, you want to let users view and edit data from a different schema, without giving them direct access to the schema itself. For example, if you have a schema containing tables full of private or sensitive information, you can create synonyms for these tables. Users can view the data in these tables through the synonym, without being given access to the other tables and views in this schema. In these cases, you would create a *public synonym* that gives access to the same object across all schemas.

Once you create the synonym, you can use it throughout the application, including:

☐ In method code. For example, instead of specifying the name of a table in a SQLLOOKUP statement, you can use the synonym instead.

☐ In property settings. For example, if you create a synonym for a table or a view, you can enter the name of the synonym in the RecordSource property of a form, report, or other bindable container.

In the next exercise, you will create a synonym for the PUBLISHERS table, and then replace the table name with the synonym's name as the RecordSource for a form. Because none of your tables have overly long names, you're selecting PUBLISHERS as the subject of a synonym.

Creating a Synonym for PUBLISHERS

To create the synonym, follow these steps:

1. In the Session window for BOOKS.POS, press the New Synonym button, or select File | New Synonym.

The Create Synonym dialog box appears, as shown in Figure 12.8.

Figure 12.8.
The Create Synonym dialog box.

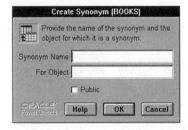

2. For the name of the synonym, enter SN_PB.

   You're keeping the synonym's name as short as possible without being totally cryptic.

3. For the name of the object, enter PUBLISHERS.

4. Leave the Public check box unchecked.

   If you were creating a public synonym, you would check this box.

5. Press OK.

The new synonym appears in the Session window as part of the database.

Using a Synonym As a Record Source

The next step is to substitute the new synonym as the setting for the RecordSource property of a form.

1. Open the form frmPubsBooks.

2. For the RecordSource property of the form, enter SN_PB.

3. Save and run the form.

The form runs just as it did before, except that you are using the name of a synonym for PUBLISHERS, instead of the name of the table itself, as the setting for the RecordSource property.

Limitations on Synonyms in Blaze

Although this exercise shows how you can create synonyms for objects within the same schema, it does not show you how to create public synonyms. Unfortunately, the current version of Blaze does not support public synonyms—not a terrible defect, because you cannot add new schemas to a Blaze database.

Blaze databases actually do have more than one schema, however. So far, you have been accessing objects in the DBA schema. Every Blaze database also has another schema, SYS, that contains tables describing every object in the database. Although providing access to some of these objects through a synonym might be an interesting experiment, Blaze's lack of support for public synonyms makes this impossible.

Fortunately, there is a way around this problem, by creating a brand new session that connects to the SYS schema instead of to the DBA schema.

The SYS Schema in Blaze

As mentioned on Day 2, "Creating a Table," you use the DBA schema by default when you open a connection to a Blaze database. This schema includes all of the objects that you added to the BOOKS.BLZ database.

In contrast, the SYS schema includes several tables storing the descriptions of all the objects in both the DBA and SYS schemas. For example, the table ALL_OBJECTS stores descriptions of all the tables, views, sequences, indexes, and synonyms in the database. Additionally, the database includes a view, ALL_TABLES, that uses ALL_OBJECTS as a base table for displaying a list of all tables in the database. The SYS schema includes several such tables and views, as you'll see in an upcoming exercise.

These descriptions of various database objects, maintained in SYS schema, are collectively called the *data dictionary*. This information is invisible to ordinary users so that they cannot accidentally cause catastrophic damage to the database by changing the descriptions of objects through these tables. The data dictionary is a crucial component of the database, hence it is kept out of sight.

At times, however, developers and system administrators need to look at the data dictionary. If users cannot access a table, you can look at its description in ALL_TABLES to see if there is some problem with this table's definition.

Accessing the SYS Schema

To view the data dictionary objects in the SYS schema, you need to either change the connect string of an existing session or create a brand-new session. You'll use the latter approach in this next exercise.

1. Press the New Session button, or select File | New Session.

2. In the dialog box that appears, select Blaze as the database type, and enter the following connect string:

```
sys/sys@c:\books\books.blz
```

3. Press OK to continue.

   The dialog box for entering the filename and directory for the new session file object appears.

4. Name the session ADMIN.POS, and save it in the C:\BOOKS directory.

   After you press OK, the session window for ADMIN.POS appears.

5. Select the icon for the BOOKS session in the Main window and press Cut.

   You need to temporarily remove this icon from the Main window, because Oracle Power Objects maintains a connection to it as long as it's in this window.

6. Double-click the connector icon in ADMIN.POS to open a connection through this session.

   As shown in Figure 12.9, several tables and views now appear. These are all standard data dictionary objects within the SYS/SYS session—no other objects will ever appear in this schema.

Figure 12.9.

Data dictionary objects in the SYS schema.

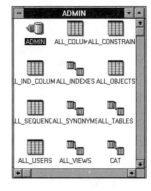

7. Open the View Editor window for ALL_TABLES, and then run the view.

   As shown in Figure 12.10, you can now see how a Blaze database stores the descriptions of tables. ALL_TABLES is a single-table view, using ALL_OBJECTS as its base table.

8. Stop running this view, and then open and run the ALL_COLUMNS table.

   You now see the structure of the ALL_COLUMNS table, as shown in Figure 12.11.

9. Stop running this table.

Figure 12.10.
Table descriptions in ALL_TABLES.

View - ALL_TABLES (ADMIN)

SCHEMA	TABLE_NAME	NUMCOLS
SYS	ALL_OBJECTS	8
SYS	ALL_COLUMNS	12
SYS	ALL_USERS	3
SYS	DUAL	1
SYS	ALL_IND_COLUMNS	5
SYS	ALL_SEQUENCES	8
SYS	ALL_CONSTRAINTS	2
SYS	VERSION	2
dba	PUBLISHERS	4
dba	ORDERS	10
dba	TITLES	13
dba	BOOK_TYPES	4
dba	CUSTOMERS	10
dba	CUST_PURCHASES	3
dba	PICTURES	2

Figure 12.11.
The ALL_COLUMNS table, listing all columns in all tables.

Table - ALL_IND_COLUMNS (ADMIN)

TABLE_ID	COL_NUM	COMPKEY_ORDER	INDEX_SCHEMA	INDEX_NAME
00000000.00010064	0	0	INDEX	1
00000000.00010066	0	0	INDEX	2
00000000.00010068	0	0	INDEX	3
00000000.0001006A	0	0	INDEX	4
00000000.0001006C	0	0	INDEX	5
00000000.0001006E	0	0	INDEX	6
00000000.00010070	0	0	INDEX	7
00000000.00010070	1	0	INDEX	8
00000000.0001007A	0	0	INDEX	9
00000000.0001007C	0	0	INDEX	10
00000000.000100CF	0	0	INDEX	12

An Important Warning

Although you can view descriptions of objects through these tables and views, you should never edit database object descriptions through the SYS schema. Even the slightest error can cause serious harm to your database and application, so you should let the database manage itself.

It is important at times, however, to see whether a problem exists with a database object. For example, if you run into difficulties creating a master-detail relationship, you might need to ensure that the source of the problem is not one of the tables. A database administrator's view into the Blaze database, designed to make it impossible to edit the data dictionary tables, can be extremely useful in these cases.

Creating Database Administrator Forms

In this exercise, you will create a form designed to view table definitions, including a list of all the columns in a table. You will add menu commands for opening these forms to the Setup menu.

In a real application, you would definitely want to deny most users access to these forms. Primarily, you want to keep the exact names of database objects a privileged secret, to make it harder for enterprising employees to "hack into" parts of the database they should never see. On Day 15, you will remove all access to these menu commands from the Setup menu if the user is not a database administrator.

1. In the BOOKS.POA application, create a new form named frmAllTables. Give this form the Label property of View Tables.

2. Add a repeater display named repTables to the upper half of the form.

   This repeater display will display a scrolling list of all tables in the database, but not those in the SYS schema.

3. In the Session window for ADMIN.POA, open the Table Editor window for ALL_OBJECTS.

4. Drag the description of the NAME column into the new repeater display.

   The repeater display now displays a list of all objects from all schemas. You want to limit this list, however, to tables that are not part of the data dictionary. Therefore, you need to specify a condition for querying records from the ALL_OBJECTS table.

5. Select the repeater display and enter the following setting for its DefaultCondition property:

   TYPE = 'TABLE' AND SCHEMA != 'SYS'

6. Add a current row pointer to the left side of the repeater display panel.

   You're finished designing the repeater display for showing a list of table names. Now you will add a second repeater display for displaying descriptions of all the columns in that table. Because the currently selected table in the first repeater display determines the list of columns in the second repeater display, you need to create a master-detail relationship between these containers.

7. Create a new repeater display named repColumns.

12

8. Open the Table Editor window for the ALL_COLUMNS table.

9. Click and drag the COL_NAME, TYPE, SIZE, NOT_NULL, and UNIQUE columns into the second repeater display.

   The repeater display will now display the name and data type of each column, as well as the constraints applied to them.

10. For the DataSource property of the UNIQUE text field, enter "UNIQUE".

   Because UNIQUE is a reserved word in Oracle Power Objects, you need to surround the name of this column with quotation marks. Otherwise, Oracle Power Objects would display an error message when you tried to run the form.

11. For the DataSource property of the SIZE text field, enter "SIZE".

12. Change the FontSize for each of these text fields to 9, and the FontName to Arial.

   You might also set these text fields' HasBorder property to False, to make the repeater slightly more readable.

   The form should now look like Figure 12.12.

Figure 12.12.
The View Tables form.

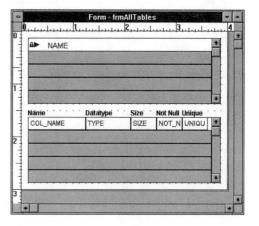

13. Set the following properties of the repeater display repColumns to establish a master-detail relationship:

Property	Setting
LinkMasterForm	repTables
LinkColumn	ID
LinkMasterColumn	ID

14. Set the `ReadOnly` property of every text field in this form to `True`.

    This step prevents users from trying to edit table names or column descriptions through the two repeater displays.

    At this point, you might also add labels above the text fields in repColumns to describe each of them (for example, Name, Not Null, and so on).

15. Save and run the form.

    The completed form now appears, with scrolling lists of tables and columns. As you select a different table from the upper repeater display, the description of the columns in that table appears in the lower list.

16. Press Stop to end this exercise.

You also need to restore the BOOKS session to the Main window:

1. In the Main window, select File | Open.

2. Select the session BOOKS.POS in the C:\BOOKS directory and press OK.

To make the View Tables form part of your application, you now need to add some menu commands to the Setup menu.

1. Add the following bold line to the (Declarations) section of the application's Property sheet:

```
(Declarations)
' Declare the base value for all menu IDs
CONST cMenuNum = 1000

'Assign menu IDs for commands in the Setup menu
CONST cTitles = cMenuNum + 1
CONST cPublishers = cMenuNum + 2
CONST cBookTypes = cMenuNum + 3
CONST cEmployees = cMenuNum + 4
CONST cDBAdmin = cMenuNum + 5

'Assign menu IDs for commands in the Sales menu
CONST cOrders = cMenuNum + 10
CONST cCustomers = cMenuNum + 11
CONST cCustPurchases = cMenuNum + 12

'Assign IDs for additional toolbar buttons
CONST cButtons = 2000
CONST cRunApp = cButtons + 1
```

2. Add the following bold line to the section of the application's `OnLoad()` method that defines the menu commands on the Setup menu:

12

```
Sub OnLoad()
' Create the Setup menu
mnuSetup.Label = "&Setup"
mnuSetup.AppendMenuItem("&Titles", cTitles, 0, "^t")
mnuSetup.AppendMenuItem("&Publishers", cPublishers, 0, NULL)
mnuSetup.AppendMenuItem("&Book Types", cBookTypes, 0, NULL)
mnuSetup.AppendMenuItem("&Employees", cEmployees, 0, NULL)
mnuSetup.AppendMenuItem("-", NULL, NULL, NULL)
mnuSetup.AppendMenuItem("&Database", cDBAdmin, 0, NULL)
```

3. Add the following bold lines to the end of the SELECT CASE statement in the application's DoCommand() method:

```
Function DoCommand(cmdCode As Long) As Long
.
.
.
cCustPurchases
   frmCustPurchases.OpenWindow()
CASE cRunApp
   frmLaunch.OpenWindow()
CASE cDBAdmin
   ' Since Blaze can't accommodate multiple connections, close any connection to
   ' the DBA session in BOOKS.BLZ
   DIM vSess AS Object
   vSess = frmPubsBooks.GetRecordset.GetSession()
   vSess.CommitWork()
   vSess.Disconnect()

   ' Now open the database administration form
   frmAllTables.OpenWindow()
END SELECT
```

Using Multiple Sessions in the Same Application

As demonstrated in the exercises that use the SYS schema to view data dictionary objects, you can use several sessions in the same application. All of these sessions can connect to several different schemas, including those in separate databases.

Connecting to several schemas in several databases is as easy as creating a session for each schema. This feature of Oracle Power Objects is extremely powerful in larger systems that use multiple servers with even more schemas.

For example, you might maintain information about products in one schema, and orders in another. Although these two types of information might coexist in the same database, you might maintain them in separate schemas so that the order entry staff would have a separate domain for order information in the database, while the inventory staff would maintain their own set of data about products. By defining two separate schemas, each group in the company would "own" a different type of information.

However, when you design an order entry form, you would need to query information about orders and products. The form itself, used for entering an order, might query records from tables appearing in the ORDERS schema, while an embedded form displaying product information would use the PRODUCTS schema.

As you can see, not only can you use several schemas for the same information, but information accessed through different schemas can appear within the same form. Accessing different schemas is as simple as setting up a session object for each of them, and then identifying each schema through the RecSrcSession property of bindable containers.

Summary

Today, you learned about the following topics:

- ☐ Sequences can automatically generate consecutive numbers.
- ☐ A counter field is a text field designed to generate unique ID numbers.
- ☐ You select the source of a counter field's IDs through the CounterType property.
- ☐ You can use a sequence as the source of a counter field's IDs.
- ☐ Alternatively, a counter field can add 1 to the largest value found in a column, or it can generate a new value through method code (normally using the CounterGenKey() method).
- ☐ An index decreases the time needed to query records from a table.
- ☐ Indexes often use columns that are primary or foreign keys in joins.
- ☐ A synonym provides access to a database object through an alias.
- ☐ A public synonym gives other schemas access to an object.
- ☐ The SYS schema of a Blaze database contains data dictionary tables, describing all the objects in the database.
- ☐ Applications frequently use multiple schemas, even on the same form.

12

What Comes Next?

By this point in your experience with Oracle Power Objects, you are thinking of both the application and the database as a unified whole—the two halves of a database application. In this lesson, you created new database objects, such as sequences, and used them to add new features to the application. In addition, you learned how to control the way users view data and navigate among forms and reports in the application.

In the next lesson, you will again put all the pieces of the database application together, to control how users edit records and save them to the database. You have already defined some rules in

the database itself: The values in some columns cannot be null, while others must be unique. On Day 13, "Enforcing Business Rules," you will be enforcing new and more complex business rules through the front end of the application.

Q&A

Q How many indexes should I add to a table?

A No more than needed. If a table already has a primary key, you already have a way to index records. However, if values from a column in this table frequently appear as primary or foreign keys, you should create an index on this column as well. You should be careful not to add too many indexes to the database, however, because they can take up a significant amount of room to maintain them.

The only reason not to create an index is to keep the number of objects in the database to the smallest number necessary.

Q How many synonyms should I create?

A In this case, you have two criteria to apply. First, how many database objects need a synonym to act as a useful shorthand? And second, how many database objects need to be made available across all schemas?

Q Suppose I don't want to use a sequence for generating IDs, but I also don't want to lock the table. Is there any other way to handle this situation?

A There are several ways around this problem. One relatively simple solution is to create a table, ID_VALUES, with three columns, TABLE_NAME, COLUMN_NAME, and LAST_ID. This table would store the name of a table, a column in that table for which you regularly generate new ID numbers, and the last ID number generated for that column. Instead of reading values from the column that will store the new ID number, you read the last ID number generated for that column from the LAST_ID column in ID_VALUES. As soon as you generate a new ID number, you store this value in ID_VALUES.LAST_ID. Other users running the same application also look to this table for new IDs, which are added to the table immediately after they are generated.

Workshop

The Workshop consists of quiz questions to help you solidify your understanding of the material covered and exercises to give you experience in using what you've learned. Try and understand the quiz answers and the exercises before you go on to tomorrow's lesson.

Quiz

1. If you add code to the CounterGenKey() method to generate unique ID numbers, and these new IDs do not appear when you insert new records, what could be the source of the problem?

2. Suppose you wanted to design an order entry form that numbers each new order by a multiple of 10. Additionally, each line item has its own sub-ID, which is the order's ID number plus the number of the item (for example, 11 for the first item, 12 for the second, and so on). How would you create these features?

3. In an earlier exercise, you created a report, rptCustPurchases, to show the buying habits of your customers. The report used the CUST_PURCHASES table as its RecordSource. In addition, it displayed customer information in an embedded form, with records queried from the CUSTOMERS table to match the current CUSTOMER_ID. In addition, the report uses SQLLOOKUP to display a description of each type of book purchased by a customer, information queried from the BOOK_TYPES table. What kind of index might you create to speed the querying of records for this report?

Exercise

Design a form that displays the name of each view in a Blaze database, along with the SQL query that defines it. (Hint: The view-related database objects in the SYS schema include a column named SQL_TEXT that stores the SQL query behind a view.)

Quiz Answers

1. Either you do not have the CounterType property set to User Generated, or there is something wrong with your method code in CounterGenKey().

2. The counter field on the main form would use a sequence for generating new IDs. When you create this sequence, you would define the interval between each new ID number as 10, and the starting value as 10.

   To create the sub-ID for each line item, you would write method code to generate the new ID number, based on the order's ID number. In this case, you would want to add the code to the CounterGenKey() method of whatever text field displayed the sub-ID for line items.

3. This report has two primary keys, CUSTOMER_ID and TYPE_ID, used to look up descriptions of customers and book categories. Therefore, the index should be based on the CUST_PURCHASES table, and it should include both of these columns, if you are using Oracle7 or SQL Server. (In the case of a Blaze database, use the CUSTOMER_ID column alone.) Because the CUST_PURCHASES table has no primary key (which would help index records), you are not adding any redundancy by including these columns in the index.

Enforcing Business Rules

Overview

Today, you learn about the following topics:

- ☐ Business rules in an organization
- ☐ Business rules in a client/server application
- ☐ When and where to enforce business rules in an application
- ☐ The `Validate()` method
- ☐ The `ValidateRow()` method
- ☐ The `CommitWork()` method
- ☐ Other methods available for enforcing business rules
- ☐ Properties related to business rules

Long before computers were invented, organizations had rules about storing, viewing, and editing information. To follow the tax code, companies have needed to maintain certain kinds of information on income, and when required, to provide this information in a particular format to the tax authorities. To keep personal information about employees private, firms have kept the information out of other employees' hands by locking it in a locked filing cabinet. When employees took orders over the phone, their managers trained them to ask a particular set of questions about the order ("Do we have your phone number and address on file?" and "Did you know about our sale?") and then record that information thoroughly and accurately.

Because computers automate the way you store and view data, they also need to automate the rules governing how you store, view, and edit this information. Instead of keeping employee records under lock and key, however, you design security measures in the database (password protection, encryption, and so on) to keep this information private. Instead of having your sales manager stand behind an employee to make sure a phone order is entered properly, the order entry application can perform these checks itself. Instead of trusting an employee to identify himself as the person who took the order (an important measure for tracking accountability if there is an error in fulfilling that order), the application can automatically enter that employee's ID number as part of the new record in the ORDERS table.

Not surprisingly, organizations are very excited about applications that enforce these types of business rules without human intervention. Conversely, these same organizations are very skeptical of applications that cannot automate these checks. Enforcing business rules through an application is therefore one of the most important tasks facing you as an application developer.

Development Tools and Business Rules

Your development tools need to make it easy for you to add these business rules. In addition, in a client/server application, you need the means to assign the enforcement of these rules to either the client (the application) or the server (the database), depending on which seems to be the more appropriate or efficient place to perform the check.

Oracle Power Objects gives you several options for deciding where to enforce a business rule and how to do so. When you defined some database constraints (NOT NULL, UNIQUE), you already defined some business rules. The NOT NULL constraint is functionally equivalent to the business directive "Do not leave this section of the form blank." Similarly, the UNIQUE constraint is akin to saying "Do not duplicate information (customer name, employee Social Security number, book title, and so on) from other records."

However, these constraints handle only a small portion of a much larger universe of business rules that you need to enforce through an application. For example, some of these rules are listed here:

☐ How do you ensure that the entry date for an order is the earliest date appearing in that record? Obviously, you don't want your orders to have entry dates later than the date they were fulfilled.

☐ How do you make sure that an employee reviews a customer's purchase history while entering an order, so that she can apprise customers of any sales on books they regularly buy?

☐ How do you make sure that a single order does not exceed a particular dollar amount?

Clearly, the kind of constraints you define in the definition of a column (data type, size, precision, NOT NULL, and UNIQUE) cannot handle these types of business rules. Instead, you need to make the application responsible for enforcing these rules. In Oracle Power Objects, you generally define the means for enforcing rules through several standard methods. Some of these are familiar, like PostChange(), whereas others are new to you.

13

Rules in a Client/Server Application

Whether you enforce a rule in the application or the database depends on the type of rule, some simple guidelines include the following:

☐ If a rule can be defined as a constraint within a column (for example, NOT NULL), you should define the constraint within the database.

Using this technique, you can be confident that the rule will be enforced, no matter what application accesses the table.

For example, if you want to make sure that every order record includes the date it was entered, you would apply the NOT NULL constraint to the DATE_ENTERED column of the ORDERS table. After applying this constraint, you could not forget to enforce this rule—no matter what form you designed for entering orders, the database would enforce the rule. Additionally, if other applications tried to access the ORDERS table, the same rule would apply to them automatically.

☐ If you want to enforce a rule at the moment the user enters a new record, you should enforce the rule within the application.

To use an earlier example, suppose you want your employees to tell customers about sales while they are taking the customer's orders. In this case, it's not appropriate to wait until the order is finished—you want to tell the customer about any books they might want to add to the order before it has been completed. In this case, you would enforce the business rule through the application, not the database.

☐ If the business rule requires that you use values from several different controls, or from different tables, you should enforce the rule through the application.

As mentioned earlier, you never want the fulfillment date of an order to be earlier than the entry date. Unless your employees are gifted with psychic powers, there is no rational explanation for why they fulfilled the order before the customer ever called to make the order. In this case, you want to compare the values displayed in two different text fields, DATE_ENTERED and DATE_RECEIVED, to make sure that these two dates appear in the proper order.

☐ If the business rule involves restricting access to information, you can enforce the rule in either the database or the application, depending on the capabilities of the database itself.

For example, suppose you want to keep the store budget confidential. You don't necessarily want an employee to see how much the store spends in salaries, advertising, and taxes; nor do you need to advertise the current profitability of the bookstore to everyone. Although you might want to make some of this information available to employees in a monthly or quarterly report, you don't need to give them access to all the budget and finances all the time.

If your database supports multiple schemas and public synonyms, you store the budget information in a separate schema. You can provide some of the information from the budget's schema to employees through a synonym for a table or view in that schema. If you want to maintain all the store information in the same schema (or if you have to, because of your database engine's limitations), you can show only some of the information in the table by creating a single-table view that includes only a small subset of all the columns in the base table.

However, in many cases, it might be simpler to limit access to information through the application. By assigning different privileges to users, you can limit the forms and reports accessed through the application. As discussed on Day 12, the average employee should not see the data dictionary information from the SYS schema, but the database administrator should. To enforce this rule, you need only make it impossible for anyone but the database administrator to open this form.

Server-Based Procedures

So far, these guidelines are fairly straightforward. However, there is an added consideration that we cannot address in this sample application. In many cases, you can enforce business rules through server-based procedures, pieces of SQL code stored in the server. When a particular event occurs (such as deleting a record), or you explicitly call the procedure, it then executes to enforce the rule.

Unfortunately, Blaze databases do not have this capability. These server-based procedures, called *triggers* and *stored procedures*, are common features of high-end relational databases like SQL Server and Oracle7.

Enforcing a Simple Business Rule

As you might remember, the Book Orders form included a field for entering a discount for each title ordered. There's a small problem with this field, however, as you'll see in this exercise.

1. Open and run the form `frmBookOrders`.

   The Book Orders form appears, as shown in Figure 13.1, displaying the order you entered a few lessons ago.

2. For the first book's discount, enter `-0.5`.

   Oops! From a business perspective, you should not be able to enter a negative discount (thereby charging the customer more for a book), but nothing in the application prevents you from doing so. This text field has an additional problem.

3. Enter `50` for the discount.

   Even worse! As you can see in Figure 13.2, now you are giving the customer a 5000 percent discount, instead of 50 percent. Clearly, this is an error an employee could easily commit, because a new user of the Bookstore application might not know that you must enter a percentage as a decimal.

   Obviously, the application needs to limit the range of values that you can enter for the discount—or for nearly any field on this form, as you shall see.

4. Enter `-15` for the quantity of books ordered.

5. Enter `-100` for the customer credit.

   These values make little sense for the bookstore, but the application does not know this fact. Clearly, to enforce some common-sense business rules for the bookstore, this form needs some built-in logic to limit the range of values that you can enter in these fields.

6. Press Rollback and then Stop to end this exercise.

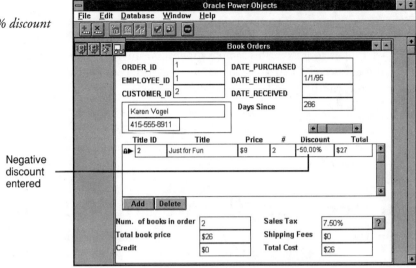
Figure 13.1.

Entering a –50% discount for a book.

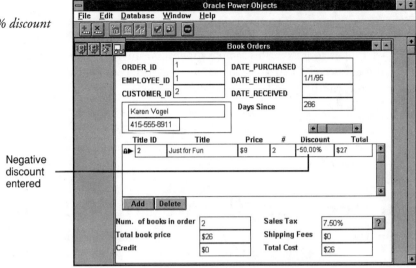

Negative discount entered

Figure 13.2.

Entering 50 for the discount, instead of 0.5.

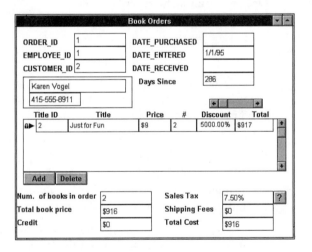

The question remains, however, how you can enforce these rules. Text fields (as well as other controls) have a method, PostChange(), triggered when the control's value changes. PostChange() seems like a good candidate for containing the code that enforces the business rule: as soon as the value for a discount, quantity, or credit changes, the method executes and performs the check.

However, Oracle Power Objects provides a better method for enforcing the business rule: the Validate() method. This method also appears in all controls that have a value, and it too executes whenever that value changes. Unlike PostChange(), Validate() has some additional features that help you perform more sophisticated checks on what the user has entered.

The *Validate()* Method

The Validate() method of a control executes whenever the control's value changes and one of the following events occurs:

- [ ] The user presses Enter
- [ ] The user tabs to another control
- [ ] The user tries to commit the modified record

Unlike PostChange(), Validate() has an argument and a return value, both of which are designed to help perform a check and then enforce a rule (otherwise known as *performing a validation*). The Validate() method's syntax looks like this:

```
Function Validate(newval as Variant) As Long
```

The argument *newval* is the new value that you entered in the control. Because it is data type Variant, the *newval* argument can be of any data type.

The return value for Validate() determines whether the application lets you keep the new value. The method code you write should make this determination. If you want to allow the change, you instruct Validate() to return TRUE. If the new value fails to meet whatever test you have defined in your method code, Validate() should return FALSE. (The constant TRUE is defined as -1, and FALSE as 0.)

Using *Validate()*

To show this method in operation, follow these steps:

1. Select the text field QUANTITY within the repeater display in frmBookOrders.

2. Open the text field's Property sheet, and then open the Code Editor window for the Validate() method.

3. Enter the following method code:

```
Function Validate (newval As Variant) As Long
' Test to see if the quantity entered is greater than 0.
' If so, allow the new value for QUANTITY
IF newval > 0 THEN
  Validate = TRUE
  Inherited.Validate(newval)
ELSE
  Validate = FALSE
END IF
```

4. Enter the following for the `ValidationMsg` property:

   `The quantity must be greater than zero`

   The `ValidationMsg` property defines the message that the application displays in a message box when `Validate()` returns `FALSE`.

5. Save and run the form.

6. Enter `0` in the `QUANTITY` text field and press Enter.

7. The error message you defined for the `ValidationMsg` property appears in a message box, as shown in Figure 13.3.

Figure 13.3.

The error message that appears when `Validate()` *returns* `FALSE`.

8. Press OK to dismiss this dialog box.

   The value you just entered remains in the control.

9. Enter `-10` for the quantity and press Enter.

   The same error message appears.

10. Press OK, and then press the Open Debug Window button from the Debug palette.

    The Debugger now appears, as shown in Figure 13.4.

Figure 13.4.

The Debugger displaying the properties and methods of the `QUANTITY` *text field.*

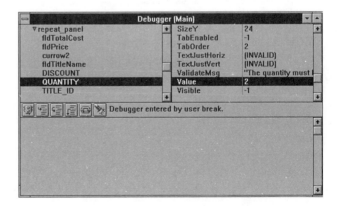

11. In the Object list in the Debugger, select the QUANTITY field.

    To do this, you must navigate down the hierarchy of objects within the Object list. From the form frmBookOrders, you must select the repeater display repTitles, then repeat_panel, and finally the text field QUANTITY.

12. Scroll down the Property/Method list until you find the `Value` property.

Although you entered `-10` for the quantity, the actual value of the control is `2`. When `Validate()` returned `FALSE`, the application did not change the internal value of the control. Only the display value changed to `-10` (the number you entered). In some instances, the display and internal values of controls might differ (especially in the case of list controls); this is one such case.

13. Press Continue on the Debug palette to continue running the form.

14. Press Rollback and then Stop to end the exercise.

The *RevertValue()* Method

Why does the display value remain the same after the validation fails? In many cases, you want to continue displaying whatever the user entered. For example, if you need to enter a long string of characters (such as an ISBN number for a book, or a Social Security number for an employee), you do not want to force your user to begin typing from scratch when the validation fails. In many cases, all the user needs to do is change one or two characters—a much less frustrating task than retyping the entire string.

If you want to remove the value entered, you can call the `RevertValue()` method to make the control's display value match its internal value.

1. Open the Code Editor window for the text field QUANTITY's `Validate()` method.

2. Enter the following bold line of code:

```
Function Validate (newval As Variant) As Long
' Test to see if the quantity entered is greater than 0.
' If so, allow the new value for QUANTITY
IF newval > 0 THEN
  Validate = TRUE
  Inherited.Validate(newval)
ELSE
  Validate = FALSE
  self.RevertValue()
END IF
```

3. Save and run the form.

4. Enter `-10` in the QUANTITY field and press Enter.

5. After dismissing the error dialog box, look at the value displayed in the QUANTITY field.

Instead of displaying the value you just entered, the text field displays its internal value (the original value for the control).

6. Press Rollback and Stop to end the exercise.

13

Whether to call `RevertValue()` when a validation fails is a matter for your own discretion. Frequently, it's less confusing for the user when the original value reappears in the control. On the other hand, as described earlier, you often do not want to force the user to retype a long string of characters.

Adding Validation Checks to Other Controls

Now that you understand how `Validate()`, `ValidationMsg`, and `RevertValue()` work, you can add some code to the `Validate()` method of other controls in the Book Orders form.

1. Select the DISCOUNT text field and open its Property sheet.

2. Add the following method code to this control's `Validate()` method:

```
Function Validate (newval As Variant) As Long
' Check to see if the discount entered is
' between 0.0 and 1.0. Allow a discount of 1.0
' in cases when the customer will receive a free
' copy of a book.
IF newval >= 0 AND newval <= 1.0 THEN
  Validate = TRUE
  Inherited.Validate(newval)
ELSE
  Validate = FALSE
  self.RevertValue()
END IF
```

3. For the DISCOUNT field's `ValidationMsg` property, enter the following:

```
You must enter a discount as a decimal value between 0.0 and 1.0
```

Next, you will make sure that the credit owed to a customer is never a negative number, and that the credit does not exceed the total amount of the order.

4. Select the field `fldCredit` and enter the following code in its `Validate()` method:

```
Function Validate (newval As Variant) As Long
' If the credit is less than zero, the validation fails
IF newval < 0 THEN
    self.ValidationMsg = "You cannot enter a credit less than zero"
    Validate = FALSE
    self.RevertValue()
' If the credit exceeds the amount of the order, the validation fails
ELSEIF newval > fldSubtotal.Value
    self.ValidationMsg = "The discount cannot exceed the total
    ➥amount of the order"
    Validate = FALSE
    self.RevertValue()
ELSE
    Validate = TRUE
    Inherited.Validate(newval)
END IF
```

In this case, the method code in `Validate()` is setting the `ValidationMsg` property. Because there are two possible reasons why the validation might fail, you cannot have a single setting for the `ValidationMsg` property. Therefore, instead of setting `ValidationMsg` through the Property sheet, you set this property through the code in `Validate()`, depending on why the validation failed.

Next, you will make sure that the value in `DATE_ENTERED` is never later than today.

5. Select the `DATE_ENTERED` field and enter the following code in its `Validate()` method:

```
Function Validate (newval As Variant) As Long
' If the date in this field is later than today's date, as
' returned by the NOW function, then the validation fails
IF newval > NOW THEN
   Validate = FALSE
   self.RevertValue()
ELSE
   Validate = TRUE
   Inherited.Validate(newval)
END IF
```

6. Enter the following for the `DATE_ENTERED` field's `ValidationMsg` property:

```
The entry date cannot be after today's date
```

Next, you will make sure that the customer ID number entered for the order exists in the `CUSTOMERS` table.

7. Select the `CUSTOMER_ID` field and enter the following code in its `Validate()` method:

```
Function Validate (newval As Variant) As Long
IF NOT ISNULL (SQLLOOKUP(BOOKS, "select CUSTOMER_ID from CUSTOMERS
➥where CUSTOMER_ID = " & STR(newval))) THEN
   Validate = TRUE
   Inherited.Validate(newval)
END IF
```

In this case you do not have to enter a section defining what to do if the validation fails. Part of the default processing for `Validate()` is to return `TRUE`. As you should know by now, any code added to a method suppresses its default processing, unless you explicitly call the default processing with the `Inherited.method_name()` statement. Here, the code calls the default processing only if the value entered passes the check.

The validation requires the application to look in the CUSTOMERS table to see if the value entered exists in the CUSTOMERS.CUSTOMER_ID column. If it does not, `SQLLOOKUP` will return `NULL`, indicating that a matching `CUSTOMER_ID` value does not exist in that column.

In a moment, you will use the same technique to make sure that a `TITLE_ID` value exists in the TITLES table.

8. For the `ValidationMsg` property of CUSTOMER_ID, enter the following:

```
That customer ID does not exist in the database
```

13

9. In the `Validate()` method of the text field `TITLE_ID`, enter the following:

```
Function Validate (newval As Variant) As Long
IF NOT ISNULL(SQLLOOKUP(BOOKS, "select TITLE_ID from TITLES
➥where TITLE_ID = " & STR(newval))) THEN
   Validate = TRUE
   Inherited.Validate(newval)
END IF
```

10. For the `ValidationMsg` property of `TITLE_ID`, enter this line:

    ```
    That title ID does not exist in the database
    ```

11. Add the necessary method code to the `fldShipping` field's `Validate()` method to prevent the user from entering a negative value for shipping fees.

    By now, you should be able to write the code yourself. Be sure to add an error message to `ValidationMsg`.

12. Save and run the form.

    Now you can test the validation routines you have entered in this exercise.

13. For CUSTOMER_ID, enter `99` and press Enter.

    The application now checks to see if the customer ID 99 exists in the database. Because it does not, `Validate()` returns `FALSE`, and the application displays the appropriate error message.

14. In the `DATE_ENTERED` field, enter `9/9/99`.

    Again, the validation fails.

15. For a book discount, enter `50`.

    The application now corrects the error you made earlier. Because of the code you added to this text field's `Validate()` method, you must enter the discount as a decimal between 0.0 and 1.0.

16. Press Rollback and Stop to end this exercise.

Duplicating Database Constraints

Open the Table Editor window for ORDERS. This table already has three columns that have NOT NULL constraints explicitly applied to them: DATE_ENTERED, CUSTOMER_ID, and EMPLOYEE_ID. Additionally, because ORDER_ID is the primary key, the NOT NULL constraint is also applied to this column.

At this point, you might conclude that, because these constraints are already defined in the database, there is no need to duplicate them in the application. The point of these constraints is to ensure that you cannot save an order to the database without entering the ID number for the employee taking the order, the ID of the customer, and the date the customer called. If this job is already done in the database, why bother enforcing the same business rules in the application?

In the current incarnation of the application, this assumption is correct. If you were running the Bookstore application on a single PC, with a Blaze database as the back end, there is no compelling reason to have the application share responsibility for enforcing the same rules about entering information for an order.

Giving the Server Some Relief

Now imagine a larger bookstore with several client systems communicating with a remote database. In this case, you might need to consider how much of a processing burden the server is shouldering. If the database is already handling a large number of requests for information, generating reports with large numbers of records, and enforcing business rules through server-based procedures, then at times the processing load might get a bit heavy for a low-end server.

In this case, you might consider having the application perform some of the same checks on column values that the database already does. For example, you can use the Validate() method to test whether the value of the DATE_ENTERED field is NULL (generally because the user left it blank). By testing for a NULL value through the text field's Validate() method, you relieve the server of some of the burden of performing this check.

Getting Immediate Feedback

Additionally, the user gets immediate feedback before trying to save the new record to the database. If you are enforcing several business rules through the application and the database, the user generally prefers to know which business rules haven't been satisfied before trying to commit the record.

For example, suppose a new and somewhat careless employee leaves the DATE_ENTERED, CUSTOMER_ID, and EMPLOYEE_ID fields blank. The employee won't discover her mistake until she tries to commit the new order to the database and receives a series of somewhat cryptic error messages, shown in Figures 13.5 and 13.6.

Figure 13.5.
The first error dialog box viewed when the DATE_ENTERED field is left blank.

Figure 13.6.
The second error dialog box, with some hard-to-decipher text.

If the employee then enters today's date for DATE_ENTERED and tries again to commit the new record, another pair of error messages will appear because the CUSTOMER_ID field has been left blank.

Obviously, it would be more efficient to have the application check to see if fields have been left blank before passing the new record on to the database. The application can perform some of these checks as the user types, triggering the Validate() method.

Therefore, you need to add some additional lines to the code you entered for the Validate() method of these text fields.

Checking for Nulls Through *Validate()*

To duplicate the NOT NULL constraint in the Book Orders form, follow these steps:

1. Change the code appearing in the Validate() method of the text field CUSTOMER_ID:

```
Function Validate (newval As Variant) As Long
' First, check for null
IF NOT ISNULL(newval) THEN
   ' Then check to see if the record exists in the database
   IF (SQLLOOKUP(BOOKS, "select CUSTOMER_ID from CUSTOMERS
   ➥where CUSTOMER_ID = " & STR(newval))) THEN
      Validate = TRUE
      Inherited.Validate(newval)
   ELSE
      self.ValidateMsg = "That customer ID is not in the database"
      Validate = FALSE
   END IF
ELSE
   self.ValidateMsg = "You must enter a customer ID number"
END IF
```

2. Edit the code in the DATE_ENTERED field's Validate() method to read as follows:

```
Function Validate (newval As Variant) As Long
' If the date in this field is later than today's date, as
' returned by the NOW function, then the validation fails.
IF newval > NOW THEN
   self.ValidationMsg = "The entry date cannot be after today's date"
   Validate = FALSE
   self.RevertValue()

' Additionally, if newval is null, the validation also fails.
ELSEIF ISNULL(newval) THEN
   self.ValidationMsg = "You must enter the order's entry date"
   Validate = FALSE
   self.RevertValue()

' Otherwise, the validation succeeds
ELSE
   Validate = TRUE
   Inherited.Validate(newval)
END IF
```

3. Add the following code to the EMPLOYEE_ID field's Validate() method:

```
Function Validate (newval As Variant) As Long
' See if the field has been left blank
IF ISNULL(newval) THEN
  self.ValidationMsg = "You must enter an employee ID"
  Validate = FALSE

' Additionally, check to make sure that the employee ID exists
' in the EMPLOYEES.EMPLOYEE_ID column
ELSEIF ISNULL(SQLLOOKUP(BOOKS, "select EMPLOYEE_ID from EMPLOYEES
➥where EMPLOYEE_ID = " & STR(newval))) THEN
  self.ValidationMsg = "That is not a valid employee ID"
  Validate = FALSE

' Otherwise, allow the new EMPLOYEE_ID
ELSE
  Validate = TRUE
  Inherited.Validate(newval)
END IF
```

   Again, you want to determine whether the ID number entered exists in a table, as well as check to see if the user left this field blank.

4. Save and run the form.

5. Create a new order by pressing the Insert Row button or selecting Database | Insert Row.

6. Tab through the text fields on the form.

   As you reach the DATE_ENTERED, CUSTOMER_ID, and EMPLOYEE_ID text fields, the application informs you immediately that you cannot leave these fields blank.

7. Press Rollback to remove the new record from the Book Order form's recordset.

8. Press Stop to end this exercise.

DO   **DON'T**

DO use Validate() to perform several checks on whatever value the user entered.

DO use the RevertValue() method in cases where you don't need to continue displaying the value the user entered.

DON'T forget to test the code you enter in Validate(). If you enter several checks, it's easy to accidentally set up conditions that are impossible to fulfill.

DON'T forget to allow for NULL when you evaluate the value entered in the control.

DON'T write a single message for ValidateRowMsg if you plan to perform multiple checks on the value entered. Rarely can you write a message clear enough to handle several cases. Normally, such generic messages are vague to the point of not being useful.

> **DON'T** use RevertValue() if the user needs to refer to whatever value she entered in the field. For example, if the user enters a 32-digit transaction code incorrectly, you don't want to delete the whole string of numbers and characters; all you need to do is explain the mistake the user made in entering this code.

Another Level of Validation

So far, you have been performing tests that involve the values in single controls. In the previous exercises, you checked to see if DATE_ENTERED's value was left blank, or if the value in the DISCOUNT field fell within a particular range.

Many business rules require that you look at values in several controls, not just one. Often, the values are all part of the same record, but in other cases, they can involve many different recordsets.

For example, suppose you want to enforce a business rule that prevents employees from entering orders for customers that still owe a large outstanding balance. In this case, you would need to take the customer ID entered for an order and use this value to look in the CUSTOMERS table to see what that person's current balance was.

To use another example, there is an implied sequence among the DATE_ENTERED, DATE_RECEIVED, and DATE_PURCHASED values in an order. The customer cannot have made the order after it was received, so you should never have a DATE_ENTERED value later than the DATE_RECEIVED or DATE_PURCHASED.

The *ValidateRow()* Method

In these cases, you might say that you are looking at larger facets of the entire record, instead of the value in a single column or control. Therefore, the method you use to enforce these business rules is ValidateRow(), to indicate that you are performing a check on the status of the entire row. Because records are displayed in bindable containers such as forms, embedded forms, and repeater displays, ValidateRow() is a method of these containers.

ValidateRow() executes whenever the user or the application tries to commit a record, or when the user tries to navigate to a different record. Therefore, you cannot save your changes to the database or leave a record that you have edited without triggering ValidateRow().

The structure of ValidateRow() is similar in some respects to Validate():

```
Function ValidateRow(rownum As Integer) As Long
```

`ValidateRow()` returns TRUE or FALSE, just as `Validate()` does. However, `ValidateRow()`'s single argument, *rownum*, is the row number of the record.

The *rownum* Argument and Its Uses

Every record has a row number within the recordset. The first record queried has a row number of 1, the second 2, and so on. Although these values are not stored within a column in the recordset, the application nonetheless maintains a row number for every row in a recordset.

Therefore, when you add code to `ValidateRow()`, you can use the *rownum* argument to work directly with that row in the recordset. Several of the recordset-related methods, such as `SetCurRow()` and `SetColVal()`, depend on knowing the row number to make changes to the recordset or read values from it. For example, if you want to read values from adjacent rows, you can use *rownum* when you call `SetCurRow()` to move the pointer to the record immediately before or after the current row in the recordset.

The *ValidateRowMsg* Property

Just as `Validate()` has a corresponding property, `ValidationMsg`, that defines the error message displayed when a value does not conform to a particular business rule, `ValidateRow()` has its `ValidateRowMsg`. Whenever `ValidateRow()` returns FALSE, Oracle Power Objects displays in a message box the text defined for `ValidateRowMsg`.

As with `ValidationMsg`, you can enter the text for `ValidateRowMsg` through the Property sheet, or you can change it at runtime through method code.

The *RevertRow()* Method

In the previous exercise, you used the `RevertValue()` method to erase the value just entered in a control and replace it with the original value displayed. When you entered a negative credit, for example, the method code in `Validate()` called `RevertValue()` to show the original value appearing in the CREDIT field.

Similarly, the `RevertRow()` method replaces all the values you changed in a form, embedded form, or repeater display with the original values displayed in this container. In later exercises, you will call `RevertRow()` to undo all the changes in a book order that violated one of the bookstore's business rules.

13

Making Sense of Dates in a Book Order

As mentioned earlier, you want to make sure that the dates entered in a book order follow a logical sequence. In this exercise, you add method code to the ValidateRow() method that enforces this business rule.

1. Open the Property sheet for the Book Orders form, frmBookOrders.

2. In the ValidateRow() method, enter the following method code:

```
Function ValidateRow(rownum As Integer) As Long
' Determine whether the DATE_ENTERED value precedes the
' DATE_RECEIVED and DATE_PURCHASED
IF DATE_ENTERED.Value > DATE_RECEIVED.Value THEN
self.ValidateRowMsg = "The entry date cannot be later than the date
➥received"
  ValidateRow = FALSE
ELSEIF DATE_ENTERED.Value > DATE_PURCHASED.Value THEN
    self.ValidateRowMsg = "The entry date cannot be later than the date the
    ➥customer paid for the order"
ValidateRow = FALSE
ELSE
  ValidateRow = TRUE
  Inherited.ValidateRow(rownum)
END IF
```

3. Save and run the form.

4. For the DATE_ENTERED value in the record displayed, enter a date three weeks from today.

5. For the DATE_RECEIVED, enter today's date.

6. Press Commit.

   The application displays an error message, as shown in Figure 13.7, telling you that you have entered some dates that don't make sense.

Figure 13.7.

The error message appearing when the receipt date precedes the entry date.

7. Enter today's date for the new DATE_ENTERED value.

   At this point, the application would accept these dates, if you were to commit the changes to the database.

8. For the DATE_PURCHASED, enter yesterday's date, and then press Commit.

Again, you get an error message, as shown in Figure 13.8, and the application refuses to commit your changes.

Figure 13.8.

The error message that appears when the entry date for a order is later than the date the customer paid for that order.

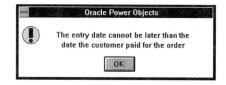

9. Change the DATE_PURCHASED field to tomorrow's date.

10. Press Commit to save the changes, and then press Stop to end the exercise.

Using ValidateRow() is as simple as using Validate(): enter the code that performs the check, indicating the conditions under which the validation fails or succeeds. For occasions when the validation fails, you also define the message explaining why the values entered for a record do not conform to a business rule.

Performing Additional Checks on Dates

The kind of check you perform through the code you entered in ValidateRow() is relatively simple—perhaps too simple. It looks a little strange to have the order entered, fulfilled, and paid for on the same day. However, according to the code, this situation is perfectly permissible.

At times an order might have a turnaround this quick. If you get an order to a supplier early in the day, perhaps you could receive the books in the afternoon. That evening the customer could arrive at the store and pay for her purchase.

Although possible, this scenario is certainly unusual enough to ask for confirmation before letting someone enter the same date for DATE_ENTERED, DATE_RECEIVED, and DATE_PURCHASED. Follow these steps to add some additional code to the Book Orders form's ValidateRow() method to ask for this confirmation:

1. Open the Code Editor window for the ValidateRow() method of frmBookOrders.

2. Add the following bold lines to the method code in ValidateRow():

```
Function ValidateRow(rownum As Integer) As Long
' Determine whether the DATE_ENTERED value precedes the
' DATE_RECEIVED and DATE_PURCHASED
IF DATE_ENTERED.Value < DATE_RECEIVED.Value THEN
  self.ValidateRowMsg = "The entry date cannot be later than the date
  ➡received"
  ValidateRow = FALSE
ELSEIF DATE_ENTERED.Value < DATE_PURCHASED.Value THEN
  self.ValidateRowMsg = "The entry date cannot be later than the date
  ➡the customer paid for the order"
```

13

```
ValidateRow = FALSE
ELSEIF DATE_ENTERED.Value = DATE_PURCHASED.Value THEN
   IF MSGBOX("The date purchased and date entered are the same.
   ➡Proceed?", 52, "Question") = 7 THEN
     self.ValidateRowMsg = "Dates not valid"
     ValidateRow = FALSE
   ELSE
     ValidateRow = TRUE
     Inherited.ValidateRow(rownum)
   END IF
ELSEIF DATE_ENTERED.Value = DATE_RECEIVED.Value THEN
   IF MSGBOX("The date received and date entered are the same.
   ➡Proceed?", 52, "Question") = 7 THEN
self.ValidateRowMsg = "Dates not valid"
     ValidateRow = FALSE
   ELSE
     ValidateRow = TRUE
     Inherited.ValidateRow(rownum)
   END IF
ELSE
  ValidateRow = TRUE
  Inherited.ValidateRow(rownum)
END IF
```

The code uses several values to determine the contents of a message box and evaluate which button the user presses to dismiss it. The second parameter of MSGBOX is a numeric value that defines the icon displayed in the message box and the buttons appearing in it. In this case, the value 52 is the sum of two values: 4, to display Yes and No buttons; and 48, to display an exclamation icon. In addition, the return value of 7 from the MSGBOX function indicates that the user pressed the No button.

For more information, consult the topic on MSGBOX in the Oracle Power Objects online help.

3. Save and run the form.

4. Enter today's date for all three date fields in the form, and then press Commit.

The application then displays the first message box, shown in Figure 13.9, asking you to confirm that the order's purchase date and entry dates should be the same.

Figure 13.9.

The message box asking for confirmation.

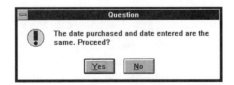

5. Press the Yes button in this dialog box.

The second message box appears, asking again for confirmation.

6. Press No.

The application now displays the error message defined for when the validation fails because the entry date and purchase date should not be identical.

7. Press Rollback to undo your changes, and then press Stop to end this exercise.

Applying Business Rules to Titles

To give you some more practice with ValidateRow(), you will apply some business rules in the form used to enter books, frmBooks. In this exercise, you will apply the following rules to frmBooks:

☐ A book's promotion price must always be less than its retail price and more than its wholesale price.

☐ The wholesale price cannot exceed its retail price.

☐ Additionally, the book's wholesale price cannot be more than 75 percent of its retail price. If the wholesale price exceeds 75 percent, the application asks whether you want to adjust the retail price so that the wholesale price is 75 percent of the new retail price.

☐ Any time a validation fails, the form should display the original values appearing in the text fields.

This time, you should try to enter the necessary code to ValidateRow() on your own.

The Solution

Although your code might vary slightly, it should look like Listing 13.1.

Listing 13.1. The necessary code.

```
Function ValidateRow(rownum As Integer) As Long
' Is the promotion price less than the retail price?
IF PROMOTION_PRICE.Value >= PRICE.Value THEN
  self.ValidateRowMsg = "The promotion price must be less
  ➥than the retail price"
  ValidateRow = FALSE
  self.RevertRow()

' Is the promotion price greater than the wholesale price?
ELSEIF PROMOTION_PRICE.Value < WS_PRICE.Value THEN
  self.ValidateRowMsg = "The promotion price must be greater
  ➥than the wholesale price"
  ValidateRow = FALSE
  self.RevertRow()

' Is the wholesale price less than the retail price?
ELSEIF WS_PRICE.Value > PRICE.Value THEN
```

continues

13

Listing 13.1. continued

```
   self.ValidateRowMsg = "The wholesale price cannot exceed the retail price"
   ValidateRow = FALSE
   self.RevertRow()

' Is the wholesale price 75% of the retail price?
ELSEIF WS_PRICE > (PRICE.Value * 0.75) THEN
   ' If not, do you want to adjust the retail price?
   IF MSGBOX("Do you want to adjust the retail price?", 52, "Question") = 7 THEN
     self.ValidateRowMsg = "Reverting to original wholesale price"
     ValidateRow = FALSE
   ELSE
     PRICE.Value = WS_PRICE.Value / 0.75
     ValidateRow = TRUE
     Inherited.ValidateRow(rownum)
   END IF

ELSE
 ValidateRow = TRUE
 Inherited.ValidateRow(rownum)
END IF
```

The Structure of Code in *ValidateRow()*

As you can see, the code in ValidateRow() consists of a series of conditional statements. Because you are performing different kinds of checks, the code takes the form of an extended IF..ELSEIF...ELSE...ENDIF statement. Following every IF or ELSEIF is a new type of test: Is the wholesale price smaller than the retail price? Is the retail price larger than the promotion price?

Although this structure lets you perform several different tests, it can get confusing when you actually write the code. Every IF or ELSEIF needs to be followed by an END IF statement, which is easy to miss when you are nesting one or more IF statements inside one another.

This situation makes commenting your code especially important. The comments in Listing 13.1 not only explain the nature of each test, but also indicate when one test ends and another begins. Equally important is indenting each new level of IF...END IF statement when you nest one test inside another.

Testing Values in Other Tables

So far, every test has been in a single table. However, you can access information from other tables to your validation, using a variety of different means.

Checking on Customer Balances

In this first exercise, you prevent your employees from entering new orders for customers with large outstanding balances (more than $100). First, you need to add a column in the CUSTOMERS table to hold the amount owed by that customer.

1. Add the following columns to the CUSTOMERS table:

Parameter	Setting
Name	BALANCE_DUE
Datatype	Float
Precision	2

2. Save and run the table.

   Enter a balance due for the following customers:

Name	BALANCE_DUE
Gallup	$15.99
Vogel	$121.11

3. Commit these changes to the database.

4. Open the Book Orders form, frmBookOrders.

5. Add the following bold lines to the ValidateRow() method:

```
Function ValidateRow(rownum As Integer) As Long
' Determine whether the DATE_ENTERED value precedes the
' DATE_RECEIVED and DATE_PURCHASED
IF DATE_ENTERED.Value < DATE_RECEIVED.Value THEN
   self.ValidateRowMsg = "The entry date cannot be later than the date
   ➥received"
   ValidateRow = FALSE
ELSEIF DATE_ENTERED.Value < DATE_PURCHASED.Value THEN
    self.ValidateRowMsg = "The entry date cannot be later than the date
    ➥the customer paid for the order"
ValidateRow = FALSE
ELSEIF DATE_ENTERED.Value = DATE_PURCHASED.Value THEN
   IF MSGBOX("The date purchased and date entered are the same.
   ➥Proceed?", 52, "Question") = 7 THEN
self.ValidateRowMsg = "Dates not valid"
      ValidateRow = FALSE
   END IF
ELSEIF DATE_ENTERED.Value = DATE_RECEIVED.Value THEN
   IF MSGBOX("The date received and date entered are the same.
   ➥Proceed?", 52, "Question") = 7 THEN
self.ValidateRowMsg = "Dates not valid"
      ValidateRow = FALSE
   ELSE
      ValidateRow = TRUE
      Inherited.ValidateRow(rownum)
   END IF
```

13

```
ELSEIF SQLLOOKUP(BOOKS, "select BALANCE_DUE from CUSTOMERS
➥where CUSTOMER_ID = " & STR(CUSTOMER_ID.Value)) > 100 THEN
    self.ValidateRowMsg = "Customer balance due exceeds $100"
    ValidateRow = FALSE
ELSE
    ValidateRow = TRUE
    Inherited.ValidateRow(rownum)
END IF
```

6. Save and run the form.

7. Insert a new order record.

8. Enter 2 for the customer ID.

   A customer with an outstanding balance, Karen Vogel, appears in the form.

9. Add some books in the order.

10. Press Commit to save the new order.

    The application now looks in the CUSTOMERS table to see if the customer owes more than $100. Because this customer does, you cannot enter this order.

11. Change the customer ID to 1.

    This customer has a smaller outstanding balance, $15.99—well under the $100.00 limit.

12. Press Commit to save the new order.

    This time, the application accepts the new order.

13. Press Stop to end this exercise.

This exercise was fairly easy—all you needed to do was perform a quick lookup into CUSTOMERS to read the value in the BALANCE_DUE column for this customer. Because you should feel comfortable working with ValidateRow() by now, you should be able to finish the next exercise with few problems.

Limiting the Number of Titles in an Order

Once again, you should try to complete this exercise yourself before looking at the solution.

Companies often impose limits on the number of items in an order or its total dollar amount. For smaller bookstores that have to be careful about ordering too many books that remain on the shelves unsold, placing such limits on an order makes perfect sense. You can easily automate enforcement of this rule in the book orders form.

In this case, add code to the ValidateRow() method that prevents an employee from entering an order with more than 10 titles in it.

If you have trouble with this exercise, you should look at the list of aggregate functions for a hint.

The Solution

The highlighted lines in Listing 13.2 limit the number of titles in an order to 10.

Listing 13.2. The solution for the second puzzle.

```
Function ValidateRow(rownum As Integer) As Long
' Determine whether the DATE_ENTERED value precedes the
' DATE_RECEIVED and DATE_PURCHASED
IF DATE_ENTERED.Value < DATE_RECEIVED.Value THEN
   ValidateRowMsg = "The entry date cannot be later than the date received"
   ValidateRow = FALSE
ELSEIF DATE_ENTERED.Value < DATE_PURCHASED.Value THEN
   ValidateRowMsg = "The entry date cannot be later than the date
➡the customer paid for the order"
   ValidateRow = FALSE
ELSEIF DATE_ENTERED.Value = DATE_PURCHASED.Value THEN
   IF MSGBOX("The date purchased and date entered are the same.
➡Proceed?", 52, "Question") = 7 THEN
ValidateRowMsg = "Dates not valid"
      ValidateRow = FALSE
   END IF
ELSEIF DATE_ENTERED.Value = DATE_RECEIVED.Value THEN
   IF MSGBOX("The date received and date entered are the same.
➡Proceed?", 52, "Question") = 7 THEN
ValidateRowMsg = "Dates not valid"
      ValidateRow = FALSE
   ELSE
      ValidateRow = TRUE
      Inherited.ValidateRow(rownum)
   END IF
ELSEIF SQLLOOKUP(BOOKS, "select BALANCE_DUE from CUSTOMERS
➡where CUSTOMER_ID = " & STR(CUSTOMER_ID.Value)) > 100 THEN
self.ValidateRowMsg = "Customer balance due exceeds $100"
   ValidateRow = FALSE
ELSEIF COUNT(repTitles.TITLE_ID) > 10 THEN
   self.ValidateRowMsg = "More than 10 titles in an order"
   ValidateRow = FALSE
ELSE
   ValidateRow = TRUE
   Inherited.ValidateRow(rownum)
END IF
```

The only trick to this test is counting the number of line items in the order. The aggregate function COUNT returns the number of times a control is repeated within a container. Because a control repeats once per record in a container's recordset, you can use COUNT to determine the number of line items in the repeater display.

Alternatively, you could have used the GetRowCount() method to return the number of records in the repeater display's recordset. In this case, the code fragment would have looked like this:

```
ELSEIF repTitles.GetRecordset.GetRowCount > 10 THEN
   self.ValidateRowMsg = "More than 10 titles in an order"
   ValidateRow = FALSE
```

13

Hardcoded Business Rules: A Bad Idea

In the previous exercises, you defined the business rule exclusively through the method code in ValidateRow(). However, hardcoding some of the elements of these rules can be a bad idea.

For example, suppose you want to increase the maximum number of line items permitted in a book order or lower the maximum balance due a customer can have before refusing further orders from that person. Currently, you would need to recode some sections of ValidateRow() to change these limits, and then recompile the application.

Although this code served to teach you how to use ValidateRow(), it does not represent how you should design a real application. Whenever you implement a business rule in an application, you should ask yourself the following questions:

"Is this rule likely to change?" "If so, how can the application accommodate the change?"

In many cases, business rules are not likely to change. You never want to enter a negative discount or leave the customer ID blank in an order. In other cases, you might want to modify the business rule and then adjust the way the application enforces it.

Your options for building this flexibility into your application include the following:

☐ Add entries to the .INI file. You can store some of the settings for business rules in an application's .INI file. By entering a new setting through a preferences dialog box, you can then modify how the application enforces the rule.

This approach has two chief disadvantages. First, you might not want to give users the ability to change these settings themselves to circumvent a rule. When you rely on an .INI file for defining the terms of a business rule, users can enter new terms through a preferences dialog box or simply change the .INI file through a text editor.

The second problem with this approach is consistency. If you make a store-wide change about the maximum number of line items in an order, you want this change to appear in every copy of the application running on every PC in the store. However, unless you check the .INI file settings personally, you cannot be confident that every application has made the change.

☐ Store the entries in a Blaze database. Unlike an .INI file, a Blaze database is fairly "hack-proof": you cannot use a text editor to change a setting stored within it, and you can deny access to this database through the application. However, you once again face the consistency problem: you have to make sure that every PC in the store has an updated copy of the Blaze database that stores these settings.

☐ Define the terms of business rules in a table on a remote server. If your organization is using Oracle7 or SQL Server, you can store the settings for various business rules in a special table designed for this purpose.

Using this technique, you can be sure that any changes to the terms of a business rule apply to every copy of the Bookstore application. When an application needs to know the maximum number of titles in an order, it can read this information from the table. You can place this table in the same schema as other database objects used by the Bookstore application, or if security is a concern, you can place it in a separate, protected schema.

Other Methods Used to Enforce Business Rules

`Validate()` and `ValidateRow()` can shoulder the burden for enforcing the majority of business rules in your application. In some cases, you might want to use a different method.

The list of standard methods in Oracle Power Objects is very large and somewhat intimidating to the beginning developer. However, this plenitude of methods gives you a great deal of flexibility in determining where and how you enforce business rules.

Some of the methods commonly used to house method code that enforces business rules are shown in Table 13.1.

Table 13.1. Methods commonly used to apply business rules.

Method	Applies To	Description
PreChange()	Controls	Triggered when the user begins editing a control, or before the application changes its value.
PostChange()	Controls	Triggered after the value of a control changes.
ChgCurrentRec()	Containers	Triggered when the pointer moves to a different record in a recordset.
InsertRow()	Containers	Triggered when the user or the application inserts a new row.
DeleteRow()	Containers	Triggered when the user or the application deletes a row.
CommitForm()	Containers	Triggered to commit all work in all sessions represented on a form.
PreDeleteCheck()	Containers	Triggered before you delete a record.
PreInsertCheck()	Containers	Triggered before you insert a record.
PreUpdateCheck()	Containers	Triggered before you update a record.
CommitWork()	Sessions	Triggered to instruct a session to commit all work pending in it.

13

425

In addition to performing an action, these methods are designed to let you trap a particular event, such as deleting a row or changing the Value property of a control. Before the event occurs (deleting the record, changing the Value property, and so on), you can perform a check in the code you add to the method to see if the user is adhering to the business rule.

For example, if you want to prevent an employee from deleting the record of any customer who has an outstanding balance, you would add the code within the DeleteRow() method to trap the event from deleting that customer from the database. Before allowing the deletion, your code would first check to see if the customer has an outstanding balance.

Therefore, the job of enforcing business rules extends far beyond what the Validate() and ValidateRow() methods can do. In the next exercise, you use a different method, CommitWork(), to apply a rule: before you save a new order to the database, you must first open a form displaying books currently on sale. Therefore, you can be sure that your employees have not forgotten to mention a sale before finishing an order (thus missing a chance to sell one or two extra books within the order).

DO	DON'T

DO use methods other than Validate() and ValidateRow() to enforce business rules.

DO use ChgCurrentRec() to prevent the user from scrolling to another record until making some necessary correction.

DO use CommitWork() and CommitForm() to make the session a checkpoint for validating entries.

DON'T use PostChange() in place of Validate() if you need to check the value entered in a control. Unlike Validate(), PostChange() does not provide the new value as an argument, nor does it display the error message entered for the ValidationMsg property.

DON'T use PreUpdate(), PreDelete(), or PreInsert() to perform checks. These methods execute after the application has allowed the change to a record, not before. If you want to intercept an insertion, deletion, or update, use PreInsertCheck(), PreDeleteCheck(), or PreUpdateCheck().

DON'T add code to the CommitWork() method of a session that deletes all of the transactions waiting to be flushed to the database, if one of them has a problem. Remember that the session can have multiple transactions pending at any time, so calling the RollbackWork() method rolls back all of them.

Informing the Customer About a Sale

All the components needed to add this feature to the Bookstore application are present, except for the form that displays all books on sale.

1. Add a new form, frmBookSales, to the application, with the label Book Sales.

2. Add a repeater display to the form.

3. Open the TITLES table and select the columns TITLE_NAME, PROMOTION_PRICE, TYPE_ID, and PRICE.

4. Drag the four selected columns into the repeater display.

   At this point, you might also change the appearance of the text fields in the repeater display to make them more readable.

5. Add a lookup field to the form to display the description of a book's type, as read from the BOOK_TYPES table.

   This new text field should cover the TYPE_ID field, so that the employee sees the description of a book's topic, not the ID number for that topic. The DataSource property of the control should read something like this:

   ```
   =SQLLOOKUP(BOOKS, "SELECT TYPE_DESC FROM BOOK_TYPES
   ➥WHERE TYPE_ID = " & STR(TYPE_ID.Value))
   ```

6. Add static text objects above the repeater display to label the four columns.

   The form should now look something like Figure 13.10.

Figure 13.10.
The Book Sales form.

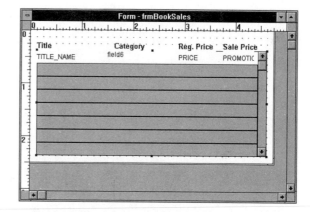

The repeater display now shows all books. However, you want to show only those books that are currently on sale (that is, their PROMOTION_PRICE is not NULL).

7. Open the Property sheet for the repeater display and enter the following setting for its `DefaultCondition` property:

   `NVL(PROMOTION_PRICE, 0) > 0`

   Because customers generally order the same types of books (computer references, mysteries, biographies, and so on), the scrolling list of books on sale should be sorted by category.

8. In the Property sheet for the repeater display, enter `TYPE_ID` for its `OrderBy` property.

9. Add a pushbutton to the bottom of the form, with the label `OK`.

10. In the `Click()` method of this pushbutton, enter the code needed to close this form. By now, writing this single line of code should be old hat.

    `frmBookSales.CloseWindow()`

11. Save the form.

    Next, you need to add the means to open the Book Sales form. For now, you can settle for a pushbutton on the Book Orders form, instead of a new menu command.

12. Add a pushbutton with the label Sales to the Book Orders form.

13. Enter the method code needed to open the Book Sales form when the user presses this pushbutton.

14. Save the changes to the Book Orders form.

Before continuing, consider the business rule you wish to enforce: If an employee has entered a new order, you want to make sure that the employee opens the Book Sales form before saving the new order to the database. To add this feature to the Book Orders form, where should you place the necessary code, and what else might you need?

You need some way to determine whether the user has opened the Book Sales form while entering a new order. You might use a global variable to store a value (`TRUE` or `FALSE`), indicating whether the user has opened the Book Orders form. To assign `TRUE` or `FALSE` to this variable, you need to add code to the `InsertRow()` method of the Book Orders form, and to the `OpenWindow()` method of the Book Sales form.

☐ When the user enters a new record, the code in the Book Orders form's `InsertRow()` method sets the value of the global variable to `FALSE`. This indicates that a new order is being entered but the Book Sales form has not yet been entered.

☐ When the user opens the Book Sales form, code in its `OpenWindow()` method sets the global variable to `TRUE`.

However, what you are really interested in preventing is the user saving a new order before entering the form. Therefore, you need to add some additional code to the `CommitWork()` method of the Book Orders form, triggered when the user tries to save a new record, that automatically opens the Book Sales form if it hasn't been opened already.

1. In the `(Declarations)` section of the application's Property sheet, add the following line:

```
GLOBAL gOpenSales AS Long
```

   This global variable stores information about whether the Book Sales form has been opened.

2. In the `InsertRow()` method of the Book Orders form, `frmBookOrders`, enter the following code:

```
Sub InsertRow()
Inherited.InsertRow()
gOpenSales = FALSE
```

3. In the `OpenWindow()` method of the Book Sales form, `frmBookSales`, enter the following method code:

```
Sub OpenWindow()
Inherited.OpenWindow()
gOpenSales = TRUE
```

   So far, so good. When you create a new order, `gOpenSales` equals `FALSE`. As soon as you open the Book Sales form, `gOpenSales` equals `TRUE`. All you need is the code to open the form when the user tries to save a new order and `gOpenSales` still equals `FALSE` (because the Book Sales form hasn't been opened yet).

4. In the `CommitForm()` method of the Book Orders form, enter the following:

```
Sub CommitWork()
IF gOpenSales = FALSE THEN
  frmBookSales.OpenWindow()
ELSE
  Inherited.CommitForm()
END IF
```

5. Save and run the application.

6. Open the Book Orders form and enter a new order.

7. Press Commit to save the new order to the database.

   Because of the code you entered in this exercise, the Book Sales form automatically opens. Before your employee finishes a new order, she can tell the customer about any sales on books that fall within the same topic as titles in the order.

8. Press Rollback and then Stop to end this exercise.

In this exercise, more effort went into explaining the business rule than entering the code that enforced it. This fact demonstrates what makes Oracle Power Objects an extremely versatile development tool: the focus of your work is the rule itself, not writing dozens of lines of code to enforce it.

13

Summary

Today you learned the following:

- [ ] Applications use a variety of mechanisms to enforce business rules.
- [ ] A great deal of application development requires making choices about whether to enforce these rules on the client or the server.
- [ ] In many cases, you enforce rules on the client to give the user immediate feedback about the reasons why certain changes have been refused.
- [ ] In Oracle Power Objects, the `Validate()` and `ValidateRow()` methods are important vehicles for enforcing business rules.
- [ ] The code added to these methods consists of a variety of conditional statements, using the `IF...END IF` format or `SELECT CASE..END SELECT`.
- [ ] In addition, you can use a variety of other methods that trap particular events or user actions to enforce business rules.

What Comes Next?

Many business rules involve who can view and edit information. Not everyone should see employee salaries, a class of information that should be reserved to managers within the organization. Additionally, you might want to restrict some kinds of actions to keep everyone honest. For example, to create a paper trail (or its electronic equivalent), you might want to stamp every book order with the ID number of the employee who took the order. In this case, you can ensure accountability if problems emerge later.

Both of these cases illustrate the importance of system security, which involves both restrictions and accountability. Security is itself a special class of business rule—one that can make or break the success of an application. (Many large companies reject certain database engines or applications in large part because of their lack of confidence in the degree of security they provide.)

However, to implement many security measures, you need to understand how to use some additional features of Oracle Power Objects. In particular, once you know how to create user-defined methods and properties, many security-related development tasks become much easier. Therefore, before the lesson on security, tomorrow you learn some new features of Oracle Power Objects, including user-defined methods and properties.

Q&A

Q **Does performing frequent validations have any effect on performance?**

A Unless the code that performs the check involves a great deal of processing (large numbers of lookups into the database, very complex and lengthy calculations, and so on), the frequency of a validation does not decrease system performance.

Q **Should you enforce business rules immediately, before letting the user edit or add another record, or should you allow changes to queue up before performing one large pass on all of them before committing these changes to the database?**

A Generally, you want to give immediate feedback to the user. Instead of sorting through a multitude of possible problems when committing a batch of changes, users generally want to deal with any problems immediately, on a record-by-record basis. The process is much less confusing and tedious this way.

However, there are occasions when you want to delay performing a check. If you have some means of turning a particular constraint off, you might want to do so once for a batch of records, instead of doing it every time you add, delete, or modify a record. For example, there might be occasions when you want to leave a customer's phone number blank. If you are quickly entering a large number of names and addresses for a mass mailing, you don't want to wait to get everyone's phone number before saving these records. However, when you are taking an order from a new customer, you definitely want that person's phone number in the database.

In this case, because the constraint is optional, you definitely want to enforce it through the client instead of the server. (You cannot turn the NOT NULL constraint off once you define it for a column.) If you design a special form for quick entry of customer information, you might also want to delay enforcement of the NOT NULL rule until after you have entered a number of records. Then, before you commit these records, you can place a check in a check box or signal in some other way that you do not want to enforce this rule temporarily. For the sake of the business process, you would then enforce the rule (or give the option of not doing so) only after you have entered several new records.

Workshop

The Workshop consists of quiz questions to help you solidify your understanding of the material covered and exercises to give you experience in using what you've learned. Try and understand the quiz and exercise answers before you go on to tomorrow's lesson.

13

Quiz

1. Suppose you enter code in the Validate() method and you cannot enter any new values in a control without the validation failing. What has happened?

2. If you wanted to prevent an employee from creating a new order for customers with large outstanding balances due, where would you put the necessary method code to perform the check as quickly as possible?

3. If you wanted to perform a global check on the status of a database before allowing any new records to be added to it, where would you put the code to perform this check?

Exercise

In the final exercise in this chapter, modify the Book Orders form so that the only books on sale that appear in the Book Sales form share a TYPE_ID with titles already entered in the order.

Quiz Answers

1. Either you have defined conditions in your method code that are impossible to meet, or you have forgotten to instruct the Validate() method to return TRUE when particular methods have been met.

2. You would add the code to the InsertRow() method. Before calling the default processing for InsertRow(), adding a new order record to the Book Order form's recordset, you would perform a lookup into the CUSTOMERS table to see which customers have outstanding balances. Only after you received confirmation from the user that the customer was not on this list would you allow the new order to be created.

3. Because the CommitWork() method of a session commits all changes entered in the application to the database, you would place the necessary code in this method. Only after you checked on the database would you let the session pass along the new records to the database, by calling the default processing for this method.

User-Defined
Properties and
Methods

Overview

Today, you learn about the following topics:

- ☐ Creating user-defined properties
- ☐ Creating the API for user-defined methods
- ☐ Adding user-defined methods and properties to objects
- ☐ Adding code to user-defined methods
- ☐ User-defined properties and global variables
- ☐ User-defined methods and generic procedures
- ☐ Managing the bookstore inventory through user-defined methods
- ☐ Compartmentalizing procedures in user-defined methods

Thus far in this book, you have worked exclusively with standard properties and methods—those that are already predefined for various objects. For example, you have used the `RecordSource` property to bind a container to a table or view, and you have added code to the `Validate()` method to prevent the user from leaving a text field blank.

If you look at the list of standard properties and methods in the appendix of the *Oracle Power Objects User's Guide*, you are immediately struck by how comprehensive this list is. The designers of Oracle Power Objects have provided you with a cornucopia of properties and methods that cover nearly every contingency, from determining the background color of a form (the `ColorFill` property) to moving the pointer within a recordset (the `SetCurRow()` method).

However comprehensive a list might be, it cannot cover every conceivable situation. Your need for properties and methods is largely determined by the type of applications you write, and no set of properties and methods can anticipate all your specific needs.

Handling the Bookstore's Inventory

To illustrate this point, consider what you need to do to properly handle the inventory of the bookstore. If you look at the TITLES table, you see that it has three columns used to track the number and status of books: IN_STOCK, ON_HOLD, and ON_ORDER. When you sell books, take customer orders, or order new titles, you want the application to update these values accordingly. But where should you put the method code to perform this operation?

Although you might think of several possible candidates (such as `CommitWork()`, `ValidateRow()`, and others), what you really need is a set of procedures dedicated to the task of managing the inventory. When a customer orders a book in stock, you need to place that book on hold (and

tell an employee to take it off the shelf). If the book is not in stock, you need to order it from your distributor.

Similarly, when you sell a book, you need to make sure it is not on hold, and then adjust the IN_STOCK value for that title. When you order new titles, you need to adjust values in the ON_ORDER column. When the books arrive from the distributor, you need to adjust the values in both IN_STOCK and ON_ORDER (because the books are now in the store and no longer on order).

The Need for Your Own Methods

Rather than add a large (and potentially unwieldy) amount of code in a single method to handle all these tasks, you might instead create a separate procedure for each one. When you need to make an adjustment to the inventory, you call the appropriate procedure, which then changes values in the TITLES table accordingly.

Although you might let the user simply enter new values for the ON_HOLD, ON_ORDER, and IN_STOCK columns through a form, you want to automate this process as much as possible to reduce or eliminate the possibility of human error. Someone selling a book might forget to see if a copy is on hold and then accidentally sell a book that should have been set aside for another customer. When you receive new titles from the distributor, you might forget to reduce the amount of each title on order while changing the number in stock.

The Need for Your Own Properties

Therefore, what you need are methods dedicated to handling these inventory-related tasks for a bookstore. On other occasions, you might also need to define your own properties to handle other situations in the Bookstore application not adequately covered by the standard properties. When you checked to see if an employee had opened the Book Sales form before completing an order, you were in fact evaluating a characteristic of the form itself—whether it had been opened since the employee started entering a new order.

In other words, you needed a property of the form to store information about whether the form had been opened, but instead you kept this information in a global variable. The technique you used in the last exercise therefore broke one of the key tenets of object-oriented development: if a piece of information describes some characteristic of an object, it should be stored in a property of that object.

Because you were limited to the standard properties, you were compelled to use a global variable to store this information. However, in this lesson, you rectify that situation by adding a new property to the Book Sales form.

User-Defined Properties and Methods

In Oracle Power Objects, you create new properties and methods through roughly the same technique. You define the basic characteristics of both properties and methods through the same datasheet, the User Properties window, shown in Figure 14.1.

Figure 14.1.
The User Properties window.

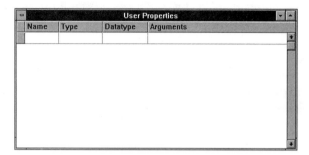

The name is slightly misleading, because you define both properties and methods through this window.

The sections of the User Properties window are shown in Table 14.1.

Table 14.1. The User Properties window.

Section	Description
Name	Determines the name of the property or method.
Type	Defines an entry as a property, subroutine (a method without a return value), or function (a method with a return value).
Datatype	The data type of a property or the return value of a method (if defined as a function).
Arguments	The arguments passed to a method. The declaration of each argument must include its data type. Additionally, if you want to pass an argument by value, you must use the ByVal keyword or surround the argument with parentheses.

As you can see, you use most of the datasheet to define both properties and methods. The description of a property is complete: to use it, all you need to do is add it to an object.

However, in the case of methods, you cannot define one of the most important features of the method through the User Properties window. After you add a user-defined method to an object, you must then enter the code that defines what the method does when called. This extra step poses a small problem for maintaining user-defined methods, as you will see in a later exercise.

Adding User-Defined Properties and Methods to Objects

After you have created a new user-defined property, you add it to an object simply by dragging the description of the property from the User Properties window onto an object, as shown in Figure 14.2. While you are clicking and dragging, the selection rectangles appear over objects that the cursor passes over. When you release the mouse button, Oracle Power Objects adds the new property to the selected object.

Figure 14.2.
Dragging a user-defined property from the User Properties window onto an object.

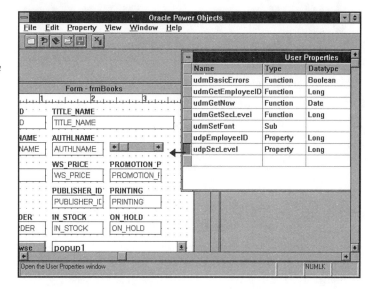

The technique is the same for user-defined methods. In fact, it's familiar to you from earlier lessons, when you dragged the description of a column from the Table Editor window onto a form or control. This feature once again illustrates that, in Oracle Power Objects, you use the same techniques to handle many different development tasks, limiting the number of things you need to learn in order to use this tool effectively.

Alternatively, you can drop the new property or method onto an object's Property sheet. This technique is particularly useful in cases when an object is hard to select, such as a text field hidden behind another object, or a particularly small control.

Where Can You Add Properties and Methods?

You can add new properties and methods to any objects in the front end of the application, including applications and sessions themselves. For example, if you wanted to store information

14

on the current version of an application, you might add a property to the application for this purpose. If you wanted to define a new method for cleaning up the database, you might add this method to the session.

Most commonly, you will be adding properties and methods to objects within an application. In the first exercise in this lesson, you add the property to the Book Orders form that replaces the need to maintain the global variable gOpenSales, which is used to keep track of whether the Book Sales form has been opened since you started entering a new order.

Adding a New Property to the Book Sales Form

The first step in this exercise is defining the new property in the User Properties window:

1. Select the View | User Properties menu command.
2. Enter the following characteristics of the new property:

Entry	Value
Name	udpWasOpened
Type	Property
Datatype	Boolean

We chose the Boolean data type because it is designed to store TRUE or FALSE values. The actual values are numeric: the constant TRUE is defined as -1, and FALSE as 0.

The User Properties window should now look like Figure 14.3.

Figure 14.3.

The User Properties window, after adding the new property udpWasOpened.

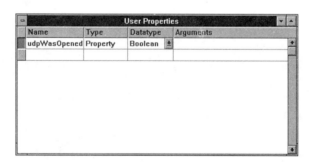

Now that you have defined the property, you can add it to an object.

3. Open the Book Sales form and then open its Property sheet.

   To avoid accidentally dragging the new property onto an object within the form, drag it into the form's Property sheet instead of the form itself.

4. In the User Properties window, click the row selector button for udpWasOpened.

   The description of the new property is now highlighted.

5. With the mouse button still pressed, drag the property onto the form's Property sheet. The new property is now part of frmBookSales, as shown in Figure 14.4.

Figure 14.4.

The new property added to the frmBookSales *Property sheet.*

6. Set udpProperty to FALSE.

   Now that you have added the new property, the global variable gOpenSales is now superfluous. Because you should never leave something in an application that you know you will not use, the next step is to replace references to gOpenSales with the new property, udpWasOpened.

7. Open the Property sheet for the Book Orders form, frmBookOrders, and make the following change to the method code appearing in InsertRow():

   ```
   Sub InsertRow()
   Inherited.InsertRow()
   udpWasOpened = FALSE
   ```

   Now, when you enter a new order, the initial value for the Book Sales form's property udpWasOpened is FALSE (0). The code inserts a new row and then indicates by assigning this value to udpWasOpened that the Book Sales form has not been opened yet.

8. In the CommitWork() method of the Book Orders form, enter the following change:

   ```
   Sub CommitWork()
   IF udpWasOpened = FALSE THEN
     frmBookSales.OpenWindow()
   ELSE
     Inherited.CommitWork()
   END IF
   ```

9. In the method code appearing in the Book Sales form's OpenWindow() method, make the following change:

   ```
   Sub OpenWindow()
   Inherited.OpenWindow()
   udpWasOpened = TRUE
   ```

10. In the (Declarations) section of the application's Property sheet, remove the line that declares the global variable gOpenSales.

11. Save and run the application.

The application should now behave the same, referencing a user-defined property instead of the global variable. If you create a new order and try to save it without first opening the Book Sales form, the application automatically opens the second form.

12. Enter a new order and try to commit it.

At this point, the application evaluates the current setting for the Book Order form's new udpWasOpened property and discovers it to be FALSE. When it opens the new form, the OpenWindow() method sets this property to TRUE.

13. Roll back the new order and press Stop.

As you can see, the user-defined property does everything the global variable did. In addition, applying a new property to the form to store some information about it better fits the object-oriented development model.

User-Defined Properties and the Property Sheet

The Property sheet has a few buttons for working with user-defined properties and methods, shown in Figure 14.5.

Figure 14.5.

Property sheet buttons for user-defined properties.

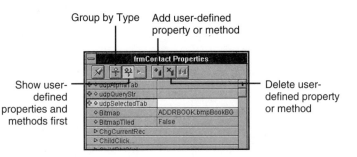

Button	Description
Group by Type	Displays user-defined methods and properties at the top of the scrolling list in the Property sheet.
Show User-Defined Methods and Properties First	Displays all user-defined properties and methods before standard ones in the Property sheet.
Add User Property	Opens the User Properties window, from which you can add a new user-defined property or method.
Delete User Property	Deletes the currently selected user-defined property or method.

Because this chapter focuses on user-defined properties and methods, you use the Group by Type button to keep these new properties and methods at the top of the Property sheet.

1. Open the Property sheet for the Book Sales form.

2. Press the Group by Type button in the Property sheet.

The new property, udpWasOpened, now appears at the top of the Property sheet. As long as you keep this copy of the Property sheet open, user-defined properties and methods added to any selected object appear at the top of the list.

Tracking the Number of Orders Entered

To give you some more experience working with user-defined properties, you will create a new property to keep track of the number of orders you have entered since you opened the Book Orders form.

1. Open the User Properties window.

2. In the blank row, add the following new properties:

Entry	Value
Name	udpNumOrders
Type	Property
Datatype	Long

3. Add the new property to the Book Orders form, frmBookOrders.

   Remember that to add the new property you can click and drag it from the User Properties window onto the form or its Property sheet.

   The new property now appears at the top of the form's Property sheet, as shown in Figure 14.6.

Figure 14.6.

The property udpNumOrders added to the Book Orders form.

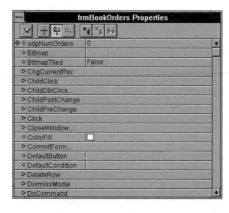

> **Note:** The plus icon indicates that this is a user-defined property. The same icon appears next to the names of user-defined methods as well.

4. Set this property to 0.

   When you first open this form, you want this property set to zero, indicating that you have not yet entered new orders. To change the setting for this property every time you create a new order, you need to add some code to the InsertRow() method.

5. Add the following bold code to the form's InsertRow() method:

```
Sub InsertRow()
Inherited.InsertRow()
self.udpWasOpened = FALSE

' Add one to the number of orders entered since you opened the form
self.udpNumOrders = self.udpNumOrders + 1

' Display the number of orders entered so far
DIM vMsg AS String
SELECT CASE udpNumOrders
  CASE 1
    vMsg = "1st"
  CASE 2
    vMsg = "2nd"
  CASE 3
    vMsg = "3rd"
  CASE ELSE
    vMsg = STR(self.udpNumOrders) & "th"
END SELECT

MSGBOX "This is the " & vMsg" & " order entered"
```

Figure 14.7.

The application tells you this is the first order entered.

6. Save and run the application, and then select Sales | Orders.

7. Enter a new order.

   Because of the code you added to InsertRow(), the application tells you that this is the first order you have entered (see Figure 14.7).

8. Press OK to dismiss the message box.

9. Press Rollback and Stop to end this exercise.

Avoiding Resetting the Property

Supposedly, you want to keep track of the number of orders entered through a particular copy of the application in the same day. However, if you close and reopen the Book Orders form, the property udpNumOrders will be reset to zero. How do you then avoid losing this information every time the user closes the form?

You have two options:

☐ You can store the information in a global variable. No matter how many times the user opens and closes the form, the information is still available in the application. However, this solution breaks the object-oriented paradigm. Because the number of orders entered through a form is properly a characteristic of that form, the information should be stored in a property of the form.

☐ You can make it appear that the form has closed, when in fact it is merely hidden. If you call the HideWindow() method, the form becomes invisible, but the application keeps it in memory. Because the form never closes, the setting for udpNumOrders never reverts to zero. Although this solution cleaves to the object-oriented model better, it requires a little extra coding to make it work. (See the "Exercises" section of this chapter for the additional steps this approach demands.) In addition, this approach can degrade system performance by keeping a form with a potentially large recordset in memory at all times, even when you're not using it.

As this exercise shows, you should definitely apply user-defined properties whenever appropriate, but you need to exercise some thought about how to use them.

A Note on Property Naming Conventions

In the last two exercises, you applied the prefix udp to both new properties, udpNumOrders and udpWasOpened. This prefix helps identify the property as user-defined, instead of a standard property. This naming convention is suggested in the coding standards in the *Oracle Power Objects User's Guide*.

Although developers vary in their opinions of the usefulness of this convention, the prefix udp is especially useful for new users of Oracle Power Objects:

☐ Because there are a large number of standard methods, it is easy to accidentally give a user-defined property the same name as a standard property. This is the most important reason to apply this naming convention.

☐ In addition, if you do not keep the Group by Type button depressed in the Property sheet, all the user-defined properties will appear in the same part of the alphabetized list of properties and methods.

☐ Finally, this naming convention makes it easier to identify user-defined properties that you reference in your method code.

14

In later exercises in this chapter, you will apply a similar prefix, udm, to all user-defined methods.

Creating a Point-of-Sale Form

In the next few exercises, you add some new user-defined methods to the Bookstore application to make adjustments to the store's inventory. As described earlier, you need to define procedures to perform the following tasks:

- [ ] When you sell a book, you need to ensure that it is not already on hold for someone else.
- [ ] After you sell the book, you need to subtract a copy from the number in stock.
- [ ] When customers order books, you need to put copies in stock on hold.
- [ ] If there are not sufficient copies in stock to fulfill an order, you need to order new copies from the distributor.
- [ ] When new copies of a book arrive, you need to add them to the amount in stock and subtract them from the amount on order.
- [ ] If the customer is buying books that were on order, the application needs to record that the order has been purchased.

Each of these tasks is handled by a separate user-defined method, added to different forms in the application.

Before continuing, however, you need to add some new forms to the application and some new objects to the database.

The PURCHASES and PURCHASES_ITEMS Tables

Specifically, you need to add some features to the application to control and record customer purchases within the store. For example, before allowing a purchase, you need to make sure that book is not on hold for someone else. Similarly, as the stock of a particular book decreases, you need to order new copies.

To handle customer purchases, you need two tables: PURCHASES and PURCHASES_ITEMS. The first table records information about the purchase—a unique ID number, the employee who took the purchase, the customer who bought the books, and the date of this transaction. In addition, the PURCHASES order needs some reference to the ORDERS table, in case a customer is picking up some books ordered earlier. The second table stores all the books in each order. If the customer is receiving a discount for a book, the application can read the discount from an order, a sales price from the TITLES table, or some other discount entered on the spot.

Obviously, records in the two tables form a master-detail relationship when presented in the application. PURCHASES acts as the master table, driving which records are then queried from PURCHASES_ITEMS, the detail table.

To create these two tables, follow these steps:

1. Open the Session window for BOOKS.POS and open a connection to the database.
2. Add a new table named PURCHASES, with the following columns:

Name	Data Type	NOT NULL
PURCHASE_ID	Number	No
CUSTOMER_ID	Number	Yes
DATE_PURCHASED	Date	Yes
ORDER_ID	Number	No
EMPLOYEE_ID	Number	Yes

3. Set PURCHASE_ID as the primary key for this table.
4. Save the PURCHASES table to the database.
5. Create another table, PURCHASES_ITEMS, with the following columns:

Name	Data Type	Precision	NOT NULL
PURCHASE_ID	Number		Yes
TITLE_ID	Number		Yes
NUM_COPIES	Number		Yes
DISCOUNT	Float	2	Yes

6. Save this second table to the database.

   Because you need to generate unique values for PURCHASE_ID every time you enter a new purchase, you'll add a sequence designed to create these ID numbers.

7. Create a new sequence named SEQ_PURCHASE_ID, with a starting value of 1 and an increment of 1.

   In addition, you want to create an index to help query records from the PURCHASES_ITEMS table.

8. Create a new index, IDX_PURCHASES_ITEMS, that uses the PURCHASE_ID column in the PURCHASES_ITEMS table.

You now have all the database objects you need to record purchases. Next, you need to create a form to record new purchases.

1. In the BOOKS.POA application, create a new form named frmPurchases, with the label Book Purchases.
2. Drag the icon for the PURCHASES table into the upper half of this form.

   The lower half of the form is reserved for a repeater display for showing all the books in an order.

14

3. Add a scrollbar to the upper section of the form.

4. Add a repeater display named repTitles to the lower half of the form.

5. Drag the icon for the PURCHASES_ITEMS table into the new repeater display. Several new text fields now appear in the repeater display.

6. Set the DefaultValue property of the TITLE_ID text field to 1, DISCOUNT to 0, and NUM_COPIES to 1.

7. Inside the repeater display, add an embedded form named embTitles.

   This embedded form will hold price information about books, queried from the TITLES table. To give fast access to prices, set this embedded form as a detail of the repeater display, using TITLE_ID as the primary and foreign keys.

8. Set the HasBorder property of this embedded form to FALSE and its ReadOnly property to TRUE.

9. Set the following properties of the embedded form to establish a master-detail relationship:

Property	Setting
LinkMasterForm	repTitles
LinkColumn	TITLE_ID
LinkDetailColumn	TITLE_ID

10. Drag the PRICE and TITLE_NAME columns from the TITLES display into the repeater display.

11. Inside the repeater display (but not within the embedded form), add another text field, fldAdjPrice, with the data type Double.

12. Set the DataSource property of fldAdjPrice to the following:

    ```
    =(1-NVL((DISCOUNT.Value), 0)) * embTitles.fldPrice.Value
    ```

13. Add a current row control to the left side of the repeater display panel.

    Before finishing with the repeater display, you need to enter settings for the properties that establish a master-detail relationship between records from the PURCHASES and PURCHASES_ITEMS tables.

14. Open the Property sheet for the repeater display and enter the following settings:

Property	Setting
LinkMasterForm	frmPurchases
LinkColumn	PURCHASE_ID
LinkDetailColumn	PURCHASE_ID

At the bottom of the form, you need to add fields for displaying the amount of sales tax applied, the total discount applied, and the total amount of the purchase.

15. Add four new text fields—fldSubTotal, fldTaxRate, and fldTotal, and fldTax—to the bottom of the form, beneath the repeater display. All of these text fields must have the data type Float.

16. Set the DataSource property of fldSubTotal to the following:

    ```
    =SUM(repTitles.fldAdjPrice.Value)
    ```

17. Set the DataSource property of the fldTaxRate field to the following:

    ```
    =SQLLOOKUP(BOOKS, "Select TAX_AMOUNT FROM SALES_TAX WHERE TAX_ID = 1")
    ```

    This field now reads the local sales tax figure from the SALES_TAX table. As you learned on Day 13, you do not want to hard code the sales tax amount, because this amount can change.

18. Set the Visible property of this text field to FALSE.

    This field queries the tax rate for you, so you don't need to display it. However, you use this rate in the next calculation.

19. Set the DataSource property of the fldTax field to the following:

    ```
    =fldSubtotal * fldTaxRate
    ```

20. Set the DataSource property of the fldTotal field to the following derived value:

    ```
    =fldSubTotal + fldTax
    ```

21. Set the DefaultValue property of the DISCOUNT field to 0.

22. Add static text objects to label the different components of the form, and then change the size, position, and appearance of the objects within this form so that it looks something like Figure 14.8.

Figure 14.8.
The Purchases form.

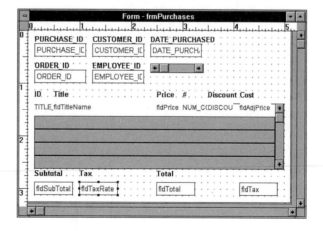

Next, you want to set up the PURCHASE_ID field as a counter field that uses the new sequence you added to the database.

23. Open the Property sheet for the PURCHASE_ID text field.

24. Enter the following settings for its counter-related properties:

Property	Setting
CounterType	Sequence
CounterSeq	SEQ_PURCHASE_ID

25. Save the form.

26. Add a new menu command, Sales | Purchases, to open the Book Purchases form.

    By now, you should be experienced enough with menus to add this new item to the Sales menu. Remember that you must define a constant for the menu command and then pass this constant to the code in DoCommand(). In turn, you need to modify the code in DoCommand() to open the Book Orders form when you select the Sales | Purchases menu command.

27. Save the application.

You should congratulate yourself at this point: consider how little time it took you to assemble a form with this much functionality. As good as this form is, however, it's missing some important features.

DO	DON'T

DO add user-defined properties in place of global variables.

DO add user-defined properties to the application, if they describe features of that application.

DO add user-defined properties to objects within forms. Although most of the examples in this chapter discuss user-defined properties applied to the application and forms, there are many situations in which you might want to add properties to other types of objects.

DON'T create user-defined properties if they do not describe some aspect of an object.

DON'T add a user-defined property to the application for every application configuration option. If it's easier to keep this information in an .INI file or in a Blaze database, then don't define these features as new user-defined properties.

DON'T add several related user-defined properties to the same object if it's possible to compact them into a single property. As discussed on Day 20, you can pack several pieces of information into the same string of characters or the same integer. You can often improve system performance by compacting information in a single property in this fashion.

Adding Your First User-Defined Method

To learn how to work with user-defined methods, you will start by defining a relatively simple method that adds some information to new purchases. The method, `udmGetNow()`, returns today's date (and the current time, if you want that information). You can use a method like this in several places, whenever you insert a new record that needs to record an entry date (such as an order).

The method takes no arguments, but it does have a return value (today's date).

1. Open the User Properties window.
2. Add the following entries:

Section	Setting
Name	udmGetNow
Type	Function
Value	Date

3. Open the Property sheet for the application.
4. Press the Row Selector button next to `udmGetNow()` to select this method.
5. Click and drag the description of the new method from the User Properties window onto the application's Property sheet.
6. Open the Code Editor window for the `udmGetNow()` method.

   The user-defined method looks like any other method, except for the small icon (a plus sign) indicating that it is not a standard method (see Figure 14.9).

Figure 14.9.

The Code Editor window for udmGetNow().

However, unlike standard methods, `udmGetNow()` has no default processing. You must define everything that this method does through your own code.

7. Enter the following code:

```
Function udmGetNow() As Date
' Get the current date
udmGetNow = NOW
```

The function calls the Oracle Basic `NOW` function to get the current date.

8. Open the Property sheet for the new Book Purchases form, `frmPurchases`.

9. Open the Code Editor window for the form's `InsertRow()` method and add the following code:

```
Sub InsertRow()
Inherited.InsertRow()
DATE_PURCHASED.Value = Application.udmGetNow()
```

10. Save and run the form.

11. Insert a new purchase.

Today's date now automatically appears in the `DATE_ENTERED` field.

12. Press Rollback and Stop to end this exercise.

This method demonstrated how to work with user-defined methods, but it actually did very little. In the next exercise, you create another method that does something much more useful.

Displaying an Order

What happens when a customer picks up an order? When you enter a purchase, you should make some notation about the order it might be fulfilling. In addition, you should check to make sure that all the items in the order are part of the purchase.

The easiest way to handle this situation is to add a new method, `udmShowOrder`, that opens the Book Orders form and displays the information about an order whenever you enter a value for the ORDER_ID column as part of a purchase. As soon as you enter the ORDER_ID, the application opens `frmBookOrders` and shows you the order.

1. Open the User Properties window.

2. Add the following new entry:

Section	Setting
Name	udmShowOrder
Type	Sub
Arguments	ByVal vOrderID As Long

Because the method is a subroutine and therefore has no return value, you leave the `Datatype` section blank.

3. Press the Row Selector button for the new method, `udmShowOrder`.

4. Drag the method onto the text field `ORDER_ID` in the Book Purchases form.

5. Open the Property sheet for this text field and scroll down the list of properties and methods until you find `udmAddOrderItems`.

6. Open the Code Editor window for this method.

7. Enter the following method code in `udmAddOrderItems`:

```
Sub udmShowOrder(ByVal vOrderID As Long)
' Check to see if the ORDER_ID is valid
IF SQLLOOKUP(BOOKS, "SELECT ORDER_ID FROM ORDERS
➥WHERE ORDER_ID = " & STR(vOrderID)) THEN

  ' Show the Book Orders form
  fldBookOrders.OpenWindow()

  ' Move the pointer in the Book Orders form to the matching order
  DIM vRecs AS Object           ' The form's recordset
  DIM vNumRecs AS Long          ' The number of records in this recordset
  DIM vCUrRow AS Long           ' The current row
  vRecs = frmBookOrders.GetRecordset()
  vNumRecs = vRecs.GetRowCount()
  vCurRow = 1

  DO
    vRecs.SetCurRow(vCurRow)
    IF vRecs.GetColVal("ORDER_ID") = vOrderID THEN
      EXIT DO
    ELSE
      vCurRow = vCurRow + 1
    END IF
  LOOP

ELSE
  ' ORDER_ID not found in the ORDERS table
  MSGBOX ("Order not found", 48, "Error")
END IF
```

Although this method has quite a few lines of code, its logic is fairly simple:

☐ Find the order with a matching value for `ORDER_ID`.

☐ Open the Book Orders form.

☐ Move the pointer in the Book Orders form's recordset until you find the matching `ORDER_ID` value.

All that's left is to call this method whenever someone enters a new value in the `ORDER_ID` field.

8. Open the Property sheet for the `ORDER_ID` field and enter the following method code in its `PostChange()` method:

```
Sub PostChange()
Inherited.PostChange()
```

14

```
IF NOT ISNULL(self.Value) THEN
  self.udmShowOrder(self.Value)
END IF
```

9. Save and run the application.

10. Select the Sales | Purchases menu command.

    If you have designed the new menu command correctly, the Book Purchases form should open.

11. Press the Insert Row button to enter a new purchase.

    Because PURCHASE_ID is a counter field that uses the sequence SEQ_PURCHASE_ID, the application automatically sets ORDER_ID to 1.

12. Enter CUSTOMER_ID as 1, and EMPLOYEE_ID as 1.

13. For ORDER_ID, enter 1.

    Because there is an order with an ID number of 1, the application opens the Book Orders form and displays that order, as shown in Figure 14.10.

Figure 14.10.
Opening the Book Orders form.

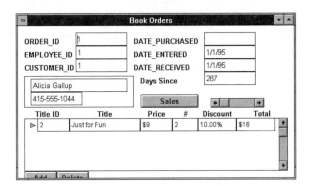

Because you need to add some other procedures to the form, you don't need to save this new record to the database.

14. Press Rollback and then Stop to end this exercise.

Checking on the Status of Books

Before you sell a book, you want to make sure it is not on hold for someone. You need to add a new procedure, udmGetBookStatus, to make this determination. This method is a function that returns TRUE if you can sell the book or FALSE if it is on hold.

1. Open the User Properties window and add the following entries:

Section	Setting
Name	udmGetBookStatus
Type	Function
Datatype	Boolean
Arguments	ByVal vTitleID As Long, ByVal vQuantity As Long

2. Add this new method to the text field TITLE_ID in the Book Purchases form.

3. Open the Property sheet for the TITLE_ID field and scroll down until you find udmGetBookStatus.

4. Enter the following code to this method:

```
Function udmGetBookStatus(ByVal vTitleID As Long,
➥ByVal vQuantity As Long) As Boolean
' See if all of the copies of this book
' in stock are on hold. If so, then refuse to
' add the new book to the order
DIM vOnHold As Long
DIm vInStock As Long
vOnHold = SQLLOOKUP("SELECT ON_HOLD FROM TITLES
➥WHERE TITLE_ID = " & STR(vTitleID))
vInStock = SQLLOOKUP("SELECT IN_STOCK FROM TITLES
➥WHERE TITLE_ID = " & STR(vTitleID))

' Add the number of copies on hold to the number in the purchase
' to see if it's possible to sell the book
IF vQuantity > (vInStock - vOnHold) THEN
    udmGetBookStatus = FALSE
ELSEIF vQuantity > vInStock THEN
    udmGetBookStatus = FALSE
ELSE
    udmGetBookStatus = TRUE
END IF
```

Now, call udmGetBookStatus within the Validate() method of TITLE_ID to determine whether the application lets you add a particular book to the order.

5. In the TITLE_ID field's Validate() method, enter the following:

```
Function Validate(newval As Variant) As Long
IF self.udmGetBookStatus(newval) THEN
    Validate = TRUE
    Inherited.Validate(newval)
ELSE
    Validate = FALSE
END IF
```

6. For the ValidateMsg property of this control, enter Number of books exceeds the amount available.

14

Your work is finished. You might want to test the new method by entering a purchase with 18 copies of the book with the TITLE_ID of 1.

Removing Sold Books from the Inventory

Next, you add a method that subtracts the number of books sold from the number in stock.

1. Open the User Properties window and add the following new entry:

Section	Setting
Name	udmSubtractBooksSold
Type	Sub
Arguments	ByVal vQuantity As Long

The two arguments include the TITLE_ID value of a book and the number of copies sold.

2. Add the new method to the embedded form embTitles within the repeater display.

3. Click and drag the ON_HOLD, IN_STOCK, and ON_ORDER columns from the TITLES table into the embedded form.

4. Hide the new text fields behind the PRICE and TITLE_NAME fields, so that only these two are visible within the embedded form.

   You can use the Bring to Front and Send to Back buttons to hide some of these text fields behind the others.

   Adding these new controls bound to columns in TITLES gives you access to additional information about each title without having to display the number in stock, on hold, or on order.

5. Open the Property sheet for the embedded form and add the following code to the udmSubtractBooksSold() method:

```
Sub udmSubtractBooksSold(ByVal vQuantity As Long)
' Subtract the number of copies sold from the number in stock
IN_STOCK.Value = IN_STOCK.Value - vQuantity
```

6. Add the following lines to the Validate() method of the QUANTITY text field in the repeater display:

```
Function Validate(newval As Variant) as Long
IF self.udmGetBookStatus(newval) THEN
    Validate = TRUE
    Inherited.Validate(newval)
    ' Subtract the number of copies sold from IN_STOCK
    embTitles.udmSubtractBooksSold(newval)
ELSE
    Validate = FALSE
END IF
```

7. Save and run the form.

8. Enter a new purchase with a single book.

9. Commit the new purchase to the database and press Stop to end the exercise.

Although you cannot see it, the application subtracts one copy of that book from TITLES.IN_STOCK.

Placing Books on Hold

The next user-defined method, udmPutBooksOnHold, takes any books entered in an order and places them on hold. This time, the method is added to the Book Orders form instead of the Book Sales form.

First, you need an easy reference to the TITLES table. You use the same invisible embedded form, bound to TITLES, to provide this reference.

1. Copy the embedded form embTitles from the Book Purchases form.

2. Paste the embedded form in the repeater display in frmBookOrders.

   Because the two forms have repeater displays named repTitles, both of which have text fields bound to the TITLE_ID column, you do not need to make any changes to this embedded form to maintain a master-detail relationship between line items in the order and books in the embedded form.

   However, you do need to make one change: the embedded form should be invisible.

3. Set the Visible property of the embedded form to FALSE.

4. Open the User Properties window and add the following entries:

Section	Setting
Name	udmSubtractBooksOrdered
Type	Sub
Arguments	ByVal vQuantity As Long

5. Add the new user-defined method to the repeater display repTitles in the Book Orders form.

6. Open the Code Editor window for this new method and enter the following code:

```
Sub udmSubtractBooksOrdered(ByVal vQuantity As Long)
' Add the new books to the number on order, or place some
' in stock on hold
IF vQuantity > IN_STOCK.Value THEN
  ON_ORDER.Value = ON_ORDER.Value + vQuantity
ELSE
  ON_HOLD = ON_HOLD + vQuantity
END IF
```

Finally, you need to call this method whenever you save an order to the database.

7. Add the following code to the `Validate()` method of the `QUANTITY` field:

```
Function Validate (newval AS Variant) As Long)
IF newval > 0 THEN
  Validate = TRUE
  Inherited.Validate()
  embTitles.udmSubtractBooksOrdered(newval)
ELSE
  Validate = FALSE
  self.RevertValue()
END IF
```

At this point, if you entered a new order, the application would make the necessary adjustments to the ON_HOLD column, as well as ON_ORDER if there are not enough books available to fulfill the order.

Fulfilling an Order

If a customer buys books that she ordered, you need to mark that order as fulfilled by adding today's date to the DATE_PURCHASED column of the ORDERS table.

1. Add a small embedded form, embOrders, to the Book Purchases form.

2. Drag the DATE_PURCHASED and PURCHASED_FLAG columns from the ORDERS table into this embedded form.

   The embedded form is now bound to the ORDERS table, and it has a single text field bound to the DATE_PURCHASED column. Next, you need to establish a master-detail relationship between the main form and the embedded form.

3. Enter the following master-detail properties of the embedded form:

Property	Setting
LinkMasterForm	frmPurchases
LinkColumn	ORDER_ID
LinkDetailColumn	ORDER_ID

4. Set the embedded form's `Visible` property to `FALSE`.

   Next, you need to create a new method for updating the ORDERS table to indicate that an order has been purchased.

5. Add the following entry to the User Properties window:

Section	Setting
Name	udmFulfillOrder
Type	Sub
Arguments	ByVal vDate As Date

6. Add the new method to the embedded form.

7. Open the embedded form's Property sheet and enter the following code to `udmFulFillOrder`:

```
Sub udmFillOrder()
' Mark the order as purchased
PURCHASED_FLAG.Value = TRUE

' Enter today's date as the date purchased
DATE_PURCHASED.Value = vDate
```

8. Add the following code to the `PostChange()` method of the `ORDER_ID` field:

```
Sub PostChange()
Inherited.PostChange()
IF NOT ISNULL(self.Value) THEN
  IF ISNULL(DATE_PURCHASED.Value) THEN
   DATE_PURCHASED.VAlue = NOW
  END IF
  embOrders.udmFillOrder(DATE_PURCHASED.Value)
END IF
```

9. Save and run the application.

10. Open the Purchases form and enter a new purchase. For the ORDER_ID, enter 1.

    Although you cannot see it, the application has noted that this order has been fulfilled by entering values in the DATE_PURCHASED and PURCHASED_FLAG columns.

11. Commit the new purchase.

12. Close the Book Purchases form and open the Book Orders form.

    As you can see in Figure 14.11, the DATE_PURCHASED value has been updated to show that the customer bought the items from the order.

Figure 14.11.

The DATE_PURCHASED field now has a value, based on the day the customer bought these books.

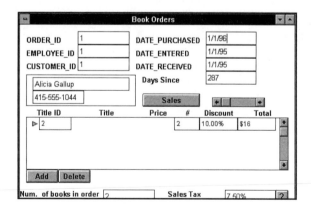

13. Press Stop to end this exercise.

Applying the Sale Price to Titles

In this last exercise, you use the sale price for a book instead of the normal retail price, if there is a sale price entered in the TITLES table.

To add this feature, you need to make the adjustment immediately after the user enters a title ID in the repeater display in frmPurchases. The value in the text field used to display prices then depends on whether there is a promotion price entered for that book.

1. Add the TITLES.PROMOTION_PRICE text field to the embedded form within the repeater display.

2. Position the PROMOTION_PRICE field directly over the PRICE field.

3. Set the Visible property of PROMOTION_PRICE to FALSE.

4. Add a new field, fldPrice, in the same position. Give this field a data type of Double and the same font characteristics as other controls.

5. Create a new user-defined method with the following features:

Section	Setting
Name	udmSetPrice
Type	Function
Datatype	Double

6. Add the new property to the TITLE_NAME text field inside the embedded form.

7. Enter the following code in the udmSetPrice() method:

```
Function udmSetPrice() As Double
IF NOT ISNULL(PROMOTION_PRICE.Value) THEN
   udmSetPrice = PROMOTION_PRICE.Value
ELSE
   udmSetPrice = PRICE.Value
END IF
```

8. Add the following method code to the TITLE_NAME field's PostChange() method:

```
Sub PostChange()
Inherited.PostChange()
IF NOT ISNULL (self.Value) THEN
  fldPrice.Value = self.udmSetPrice()
END IF
```

9. Change the DataSource property of the text field fldAdjPrice in the repeater display to read as follows:

```
=(1-NVL(DISCOUNT.Value), 0)) * embTitles.fldPrice.Value * NUM_COPIES.Value
```

10. Save and run the form.

To test this new form, create a new purchase and enter some new books in it. As you enter new TITLE_ID values for each book in the purchase, the application checks to see if a book is on sale before determining its price.

Creating Generic Procedures

In the last exercise, you created a user-defined method that could be used in a variety of settings. For example, if you wanted to view the current price of all books in stock, you could create a form that calls the udmSetPrice() method to display the amount customers would pay for each book. Using this information, you could fairly estimate your cash flow from various types of books and then decide whether your sale prices for books need some adjustment.

Whenever possible, you want to design user-defined methods to be as generic as this. When you put hard work into coding a new procedure, you want to put that work to use as often as possible. Before you add code to a new method, you should ask yourself, "Where else might I use this procedure?" Even if the answer is not immediately obvious, you should design the method to be reusable.

Tips on Generic Procedures

To make a method useful across a wide range of situations, you should do the following:

☐ If you are using the procedure to assign a new value to a variable or property, you should not make reference to whatever will receive the value within the code itself. You should always use the return value of a method to set a new value, instead of setting it within the method itself.

☐ Avoid making reference to specific objects within the code whenever possible. Instead of reading a value from within the method code, you should pass that value as an argument. For example, the following method is very poorly designed, because it can average the values from only two specific text fields:

```
Function udmAverage() As Double
udmAverage = (Field1.Value + Field2.Value) / 2
```

Instead, the method should receive the values from these fields as arguments, so that you can call udmAverage to average numbers appearing in any two fields:

```
Function udmAverage(ByVal vFirst As Double, ByVal vSecond As Double) As
➥Double
udmAverage = (vFirst + vSecond) / 2
```

☐ If you need to make reference to an object within a method, pass that object as an argument. For example, the following user-defined method passes an object's recordset as an argument:

```
' Get an object reference to the form's recordset
DIM vObj AS Object
vObj = self.GetRecordset

' Use the object reference as an argument to a method that
' deletes all rows from the recordset
udmDeleteAllRows(vObj)
```

14

The declaration for the method might look like this:

```
Sub udmDeleteAllRows(vObj As Object)
```

DO	**DON'T**

DO add user-defined methods that call each other in sequence. When you have some action that can be broken down into several steps, you can implement these steps into separate methods, each of which calls the next in sequence. This technique might make it easier to maintain the code.

DO add user-defined methods to objects other than the application and forms. As with properties, there are many cases in which you want to add new methods to objects within forms. In addition, user-defined methods commonly appear within user-defined classes (discussed on Day 16), because these classes add the same new functionality throughout an application. Some of this functionality might depend on methods you add to this special kind of object.

DON'T write user-defined methods that duplicate what standard methods already do. You can always add code to the standard method to modify or supplement its default processing.

DON'T write user-defined methods that duplicate the environment's API procedures. If there is a Windows or Macintosh procedure that you can call instead of a user-defined method, use the API procedure. These system procedures have already been debugged, and frequently they can execute faster that Oracle Basic method code.

Where Do I Put the Code?

If you successfully write a generic procedure used in several different places, an important question arises: Where should I put the code that defines what the method does?

Adding the same code to every instance of a user-defined method is a bad idea. If you modify the code in one instance, you must make the same change in every instance. Remembering all the places where you added a method can be quite a mental feat, and copying the same new text in several places is an inefficient use of your time as a developer.

Instead, you should add the method to a single object and then add the code to this single instance. When you need to call the method, you call it from that object. For example, if you write a generic tax calculation method, udmCalcTax(), you can add the method to the application. To call the procedure from anywhere in the application, you use the following syntax:

```
Application.udmCalcTax()
```

The application is the logical home for generic procedures. Unfortunately, adding a few dozen procedures to the application's Property sheet can make it difficult to find some of its standard properties and methods.

If you want to find a different home for these generic procedures, you can create a form that you never plan to show in the application, named something easy to remember, such as frmProcs. Because properties and methods are global to the application, you can call the method using the syntax `frmProcs.method_name()`.

Writing the API for User-Defined Methods

Wherever you place a user-defined method, you need to keep track of its features: its arguments, return values, objects to which you have added it, and a description of what the method does. In effect, you need to write your own API documentation, for your own reference as well as that of other developers. A few weeks after you finish your application, when you need to find a procedure and debug it to fix some unexpected problem, you need to find the procedure quickly and understand its design. If other developers become responsible for maintaining the application, they need this documentation even more.

Appendix A, "User-Defined Property and Method Worksheet," includes worksheets for keeping track of user-defined properties and methods. These worksheets are designed to help you document the API for a user-defined method, as well as maintain a development history of the changes you have made to this procedure. The short amount of time spent filling out this information for each important user-defined method can save you a great deal of trouble when you return to the application to perform some maintenance.

Compartmentalizing Procedures

Here is a final piece of advice on user-defined methods: Keep tasks compartmentalized in separate procedures. Every user-defined method should perform one task and no other.

Although several different changes occurred to the inventory whenever you entered an order or a purchase, you encapsulated each type of change in a separate method. When you needed to make a change, such as subtracting a copy of a book sold in a purchase from the TITLES.IN_STOCK column, you called the method designed specifically for that task.

Very often, it's difficult to adhere to this maxim, because within one task you need to perform another task. For example, suppose you want to add a menu command that deletes all old purchases from the database. Before you start deleting records, the application needs some

14

assurance that you are authorized to make this significant change to the database. The two tasks are related but distinct: see if the user has the authority to delete old purchase records; and then go ahead with the deletions.

In this case, you can create two different methods for these tasks, one of which calls the other. Within the method code for `udmDeleteOldPurchases()`, you can call another user-defined method, `udmCheckUserPrivileges()`.

Keeping each task compartmentalized in a single method makes it easier to write and maintain methods. However, as the number of methods increases, you need to document the API for each method, to make it easier for you to call them without having to track them down in the application. (Now, in which form did I define that method?)

Summary

Today you learned the following points:

- [ ] You can add user-defined properties and methods to objects in the front end of an application, including both applications and sessions themselves.

- [ ] Before adding it to an object, you must first declare a new user-defined property or method in the User Properties window.

- [ ] After making this declaration, you drag the description of the property or method onto the object or the object's Property sheet.

- [ ] When you add a user-defined property or method, it appears on an object's Property sheet along with the standard properties and methods.

- [ ] User-defined properties can use any valid Oracle Power Objects data type, including `Object`.

- [ ] You should create a user-defined property to replace any global variable that refers to the characteristic of an object.

- [ ] User-defined methods can be defined as both functions and subroutines, and they can take arguments by value or by reference.

- [ ] Whenever possible, you should design a user-defined method to be generic, so that you can use it in a variety of circumstances.

- [ ] You should compartmentalize tasks in your user-defined methods.

- [ ] You should also carefully document each user-defined method you create.

What Comes Next?

Now that you have mastered user-defined methods and properties, you can use this knowledge to address some of the challenges of system security. A good database application not only gives quick access to data, but it also knows when to restrict this access. Using a combination of techniques learned today and earlier, you're now ready to create not just a powerful application, but a secure one.

Q&A

Q Can you create too many user-defined methods and properties?

A Actually, no. Because you add a property to define a characteristic of an object not covered by the standard properties, it's fairly easy to remember the purpose of a property, as long as you name it meaningfully or you document it.

The same principle applies to methods. However, the special concern about user-defined methods is remembering where you added the method. Unless you know the name of the object, you cannot call the method or edit the code appearing in it. Once again, it's vitally important to document user-defined methods.

Q How do I debug user-defined methods that call one another?

A In the Debugger, you can use the Call Chain feature to track how one method calls another. In addition, if you set a breakpoint, you can step line-by-line through the execution of any method. These features should help you debug the highly compartmentalized methods I urge you to design.

Workshop

The Workshop consists of quiz questions to help you solidify your understanding of the material covered and exercises to give you experience in using what you've learned. Try and understand the quiz and exercise answers before you go on to tomorrow's lesson.

Quiz

1. If you want to keep track of the form from which the user opened a dialog box, what is the best way to do this?

2. If you design a user-defined method that returns TRUE or FALSE, what should be the data type of its return value?

3. Suppose you pass the ColorFill property to a user-defined method, but the code within the method cannot change this property. What might be the problem?

Exercises

1. Add a new user-defined property, udpIsOpen, to replace the global variable gFormOpen, which is used to track whether the Book Orders form is open. After adding the new method to Book Orders, modify the method code in the form's OpenWindow() and CloseWindow() methods, as well as the method code in the application's TestCommand() method, to use this new property in place of the global variable.

2. In the Book Purchase form, add a method that fills in the appropriate value for CUSTOMER_ID when you select an ORDER_ID.

3. Fix the following problem with udmGetBookStatus: What if all the copies of a book are on hold, but some of those copies are on hold for a customer picking up the order? Currently, if the number in stock does not exceed the number on hold, you cannot sell a book, even if one or more of these copies is on hold for the customer picking up his order. You therefore need to change this method to let a customer purchase copies that are on hold if the customer is picking up books in an order. (Hint: The key to fixing this method is to test for NULL in the ORDER_ID field.)

Quiz Answers

1. You can add a new property with the data type Object that identifies the form.

2. The data type should be numeric, and because you want to use the smallest amount of memory necessary to store a value, Integer is your best choice. Because the constant TRUE is defined as -1, this value never exceeds the range for Integer.

3. You might have passed the argument by value, instead of by reference, in which case you cannot change the setting for the property.

Adding Security to
Your Application

Overview

Security is one of the most important considerations for real-world business applications. When you implement a new set of applications to help automate common tasks such as entering an order, or you start storing company information such as employee salaries and Social Security numbers in the database, you want to make sure that information is protected from deliberate or accidental tampering. For example:

☐ Although employees should be able to enter new purchases and orders in the database, they should not see information on other employees' salaries, commissions, and bonuses that might be stored in the same database.

☐ If you are trying to keep careful track of your inventory, you need to add an employee ID number to every purchase and order.

☐ To prevent users from knowing that they can access particular kinds of information through the application, you can hide the fact that particular forms are part of the application.

☐ To give employees the ability to view some kinds of information without editing it, you grant them restricted privileges that do not include adding, deleting, or modifying records.

☐ To ensure that someone using an application is a valid employee, you ask for a username and password before giving the user access to the rest of the application.

Security therefore involves restricting access to both information in the database and portions of the application. In addition, security requires a certain degree of accountability, providing a paper trail (electronic, in the case of applications) recording who made what decisions.

Today, you learn about the following topics:

☐ Security and business rules

☐ Security in a client/server environment

☐ Security in the database

☐ Security in the application

☐ Creating a login form

☐ Restricting access to forms

☐ Disabling menu commands

☐ Removing menu commands

☐ Creating an approval system

Security and Business Rules

Essentially, security is a subset of the universe of business rules. Part of the standard operating procedures of any organization is the list of privileges and restrictions assigned to each employee.

15

For example, although employees can handle many day-to-day tasks, other responsibilities are reserved for managers. Similarly, some employees in the MIS department are responsible for maintaining the computer network, which involves privileges about company computers not granted to other people in the organization.

Relational databases, PC- and Macintosh-based applications, and computer networks give people quick access to the information they need to do their jobs. In fact, enthusiasts of advances in computer technology often say that these advances empower employees and force companies to rethink the entire way they do business.

As important as it is to give users information, it is equally important to define and enforce rules that limit their access to information. You already have some experience enforcing other types of business rules. In this lesson, you use this knowledge to add security features to the Bookstore application.

Security in a Client/Server Environment

Client/server applications give you a wide range of choices for enforcing business rules. As seen in earlier lessons, you can define some restrictions within the database itself: for example, the NOT NULL constraint on a column forces the user to enter a value in this column, whereas the UNIQUE constraint ensures that each value entered is different from all others in that column.

Just as easily, you can define and enforce these restrictions within the application itself. You can enforce a rule from the moment the user types a new value in a text field to the time when the user tries to commit the new record to the database. Each layer of the application can be part of enforcing the rule—from the control on a form, to the form itself, to the recordset behind the form, to the session used to mediate data flow between the recordset and the database, to the database itself.

Because you can view security as another type of business rule (albeit an acutely important one), you can enjoy the same flexibility in determining where you enforce security-related rules. For example, if you want to restrict some users to viewing data, without giving them the ability to edit it, you can enforce this restriction at several levels:

☐ You can prevent the user from editing a control by setting its ReadOnly property to TRUE or its Disabled property to TRUE.

☐ Alternatively, you can write code in the Validate() method that returns FALSE if a particular class of user tries to change a value.

In these two cases, you are enforcing the business rule at the level of a control. For example, to prevent a clerk from changing a customer's outstanding balance, you can disable the text field in which this value appears, or you can write code that returns FALSE for Validate() whenever a clerk tries to edit this control.

Additionally, you can enforce this rule at the level of the form:

☐ You can prevent the user from committing changes to the database by adding code to the CommitForm() method that blocks changes entered by particular types of users.

☐ You can achieve the same result by removing the Commit button from the toolbar and disabling or removing the Database | Commit menu command.

Suppose instead that you want the session to be the checkpoint for enforcing these restrictions. You apply the same approach here:

☐ You can prevent the session from passing changes along to the database by adding code to the session's CommitWork() method.

Additionally, in databases that support multiple schemas, you can restrict a user's privileges within the database:

☐ When you define a schema, you can grant database access privileges to it. Because the user accesses database objects through a schema, you can deny anyone using that schema the ability to use the INSERT, DELETE, and UPDATE commands in SQL needed to edit records.

Once again, your choice of where in a database application to enforce a rule is largely determined by the nature of the rule itself, plus a dash of personal preference as the developer. If you want to define a security restriction that must be enforced rigorously, no matter how the user accesses the database, you want to enforce the restriction within the database itself, if possible. Therefore, if you want to globally enforce a restriction on how certain classes of users can edit customer records, you should define a special schema for that class of employee that limits what these users can do with records in the CUSTOMERS table.

On the other hand, if you want to respond immediately to the user, you should enforce the restriction through the application. If you want the application to close down after several failed attempts to enter a valid username and password (and possibly alert the system administrator about this situation), you should add this feature to the application.

Security in the Database

Although you cannot add new schemas to Blaze databases, you have already seen one schema, SYS, that is fairly restricted. By default, if you log in to a Blaze database without specifying the correct username and password for SYS, you open a connection to the database through the DBA schema. Only if you know the right connect string for SYS can you get access to the data dictionary tables.

Although this restriction exists largely to prevent inexperienced users from causing irreparable damage to the database, there are additional security reasons for denying access to SYS.

In many cases, you might not want employees to know all the information you keep in a database. Although this might sound sinister on the face of it, in fact there are many benign circumstances in which you might not want to advertise that you maintain certain kinds of information. For example, suppose you keep information on each customer's credit rating and history in the database. Although you might need this information when you are deciding whether to reward certain good customers by giving them a special discount, a customer's credit situation should not be available to any employee with a burning curiosity about the finances of people who frequent the store. To protect the customer's privacy, you need to restrict access to this information.

You can enforce security in the database in several ways:

☐ By requiring the user to enter a valid username and password before accessing the database

☐ By giving the user access to database objects through a schema that limits this access

☐ By granting restricted privileges to insert, delete, update, or view records

☐ By giving users access to records through views that restrict the range of columns queried for each record

☐ By writing server-enforced procedures (stored procedures and triggers) that help enforce security rules

Security in the Application

As shown on Day 13, "Enforcing Business Rules," you can replicate many server-enforced rules in the application. For example, in one exercise, you enforced the NOT NULL constraint through the Validate() method of a text field, as well as in the description of the column to which that control was bound. Therefore, most of the security measures enforced through the database can be replicated in some way in the application.

In addition, there is another wide range of security measures you can add to an application that restrict what users can do with forms and reports. At the simplest level, you can prevent certain users from opening forms and reports containing sensitive information. In addition, you can prevent users from opening the application altogether if they cannot fill in the correct username and password in a login screen.

Therefore, applications provide the greatest flexibility in enforcing security restrictions. The two weaknesses of relying on the application for applying these rules are as follows:

☐ You must ensure that every copy of the application is updated to the current version, so that any new restrictions you add are included on everyone's PC or Macintosh.

☐ You always must be concerned that, in the case of remote databases, enterprising users can circumvent the application altogether and access database objects through other tools.

Because you have already defined most of the constraints in the database that you will add, you will start adding security to the Bookstore application through the front end.

Creating a Login Form

Nearly every application that provides access to a database requests a username and password through a login form. Although you can often log in after you open the application (but before you access the database), many applications require you to log in as you launch the application.

In the sample Bookstore application, you use the latter approach. The login form appears immediately after you launch the application, and until you enter a valid username and password, you cannot access the rest of the application.

On Day 13, you created the EMPLOYEES table, which included ALIAS and PASSWORD columns. The login form queries information from this table to determine if a username and password are valid.

Follow these steps to create the login form:

1. Create a new form, frmLogin, with the label Enter Username and Password.
2. Add two text fields, fldUserName and fldPassword.
3. Give both text fields the data type String and a data size of 16.
4. Add two text labels with the labels Username and Password to the left of the text fields.
5. Add a pushbutton labeled OK to the bottom of the form.
6. Resize and reposition objects in the form until it looks like Figure 15.1.

Figure 15.1.
The login form.

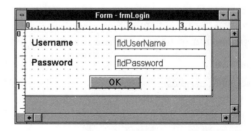

7. In the Click() method of the pushbutton, under the Sub Click() line, enter the following code:

```
DIM vUsername AS String
DIM vUserExists As Long

' Assign a value to vUserName, based on the contents of fldUsername
vUserName = NVL(fldUsername.Value, "")
```

```
' Use vUserName to determine if the alias exists in EMPLOYEES
IF SQLLOOKUP(BOOKS, "SELECT ALIAS FROM EMPLOYEES WHERE ALIAS =
➥'" & vUserName & "'") THEN
   vUserExists = TRUE
   ' Check to see if the password fits the username
   IF SQLLOOKUP(BOOKS, "SELECT PASSWORD FROM EMPLOYEES
   ➥WHERE ALIAS = '" & vUserName.Value & "'") = fldPassword THEN
' Close the form
     Inherited.Click()
   ELSE
   MSGBOX "Incorrect password"
   END IF

' The username doesn't exist in EMPLOYEES
ELSE
    vUserExists = FALSE
    MSGBOX "That username is not valid"
END IF
```

The final step in designing the login form is to open it at start-up as a modal form, preventing the user from accessing any other part of the application until he or she enters a valid username and password.

Note: You might have been puzzled about why the code calls the default processing for Click() instead of calling the CloseWindow() method. Because you will be calling the OpenModal() method to open frmLogin as a modal form, you can close the form simply by clicking a pushbutton that has a IsDismissBtn property which is set to TRUE. However, the application won't close the modal form unless you call the default processing for Click(), which tells the application that you pressed the pushbutton.

8. Add the following as the last line of code appearing in the application's OnLoad() method:

```
Sub OnLoad()
frmLogin.OpenModal(0)
```

9. Save and run the application.

The splash screen momentarily appears, only to be quickly covered by the login form.

10. Enter FNORD as the username, FNORD as the password, and press OK.

The application tells you that FNORD is not a known user (see Figure 15.2). Therefore, you need to change the username.

11. Enter jboss as the username and press OK.

This time, the application found the username in the ALIAS column of TABLES. However, the password is wrong (see Figure 15.3).

Figure 15.2.

The error message displayed when the user enters a name not found in the database.

Figure 15.3.

The error message displayed when the user enters the wrong password for jboss.

12. Enter daboss for the password and press OK.

The login form now disappears, and you can access the rest of the application.

13. Press Stop to end this exercise.

Limiting the Number of Attempts to Log In

The new login screen prevents you from entering the wrong username and password. However, it lacks a common feature of login forms: instead of limiting you to a certain number of tries, the login form lets you try to guess the correct username and password any number of times.

Giving the user a limitless number of tries is bad for two reasons. First, you do not want to keep the application open if the user has exhausted all the possible username/password combinations he can remember. Second, you want to make it clear that if you cannot remember your password, you should contact the system administrator for help (or you should stop trying to guess someone else's password).

To limit the number of login attempts, follow these steps:

1. Open the Property sheet for the OK pushbutton's Click() method and add the following modifications (in bold) to your code:

```
Sub Click()
DIM vUsername AS String
DIM vUserExists AS Integer
STATIC vWrongTries AS Integer

' Assign a value to vUserName, based on the contents of fldUsername
vUserName = NVL(fldUsername.Value, "")

' Use vUserName to determine if the alias exists in EMPLOYEES
IF SQLLOOKUP(BOOKS, "SELECT ALIAS FROM EMPLOYEES
➥WHERE ALIAS = '" & vUserName & "'") THEN
  vUserExists = TRUE
  ' Check to see if the password fits the username
  IF SQLLOOKUP(BOOKS, "SELECT PASSWORD FROM EMPLOYEES
```

```
➡WHERE ALIAS = '" & vUserName.Value & "'") = fldPassword THEN
   ' Close the form
   Inherited.Click()
ELSE
 MSGBOX "Incorrect password"
 vWrongTries = vWrongTries + 1
END IF

' The username doesn't exist in EMPLOYEES
ELSE
   vUserExists = FALSE
   MSGBOX "That username is not valid"
   vWrongTries = vWrongTries + 1
END IF

' After 5 failed attempts to log into the application,
' close it down
IF vWrongTries = 5 THEN
  frmSplash.CloseWindow()
  Inherited.Click()
END IF
```

If you declare a variable using the STATIC command, the application remembers the value assigned to that variable the last time you called the method. In this case, the method code in Click() keeps track of the number of times the user has failed to log in.

2. Save and run the application.

3. For username and password, enter Julius and Caesar.

4. Press OK five times.

Every time you enter an invalid username and password, the variable vWrongTries is incremented by one. After the fifth try, the Bookstore application shuts down.

Alerting the Database Administrator

If someone continues to enter the wrong username or password, you might want to alert the database administrator to this fact. Whether you have a highly forgetful user or someone is trying to get access to the application through someone else's account, you need to store some kind of notification that a particular username and password combination is becoming a problem.

You store this information in the EMPLOYEES table:

1. Add the following columns to the EMPLOYEES table:

Name	Data Type
NUM_HACKS	Number
LAST_HACKED	Date

NUM_HACKS stores the number of times someone tried to unsuccessfully log in to an account as a particular user. LAST_HACKED contains the most recent date someone made a failed attempt to log in as that person.

2. Save the modified EMPLOYEES table to the database.

3. Add an embedded form to the login form, frmLogin.

   Because the embedded form is invisible, you don't need to worry about its exact size and position.

4. Give the embedded form the name embEmployees and set its Invisible property to TRUE.

5. From the Table Editor window for EMPLOYEES, drag the columns ALIAS, NUM_HACKS, and LAST_HACKED onto the form.

6. Add the following bold method code to the Click() method of the OK pushbutton:

```
Sub Click()
DIM vUsername AS String
DIM vUserExists AS Integer
STATIC vWrongTries AS Integer

' Assign a value to vUserName, based on the contents of fldUsername
vUserName = NVL(fldUsername.Value, "")

' Use vUserName to determine if the alias exists in EMPLOYEES
IF SQLLOOKUP(BOOKS, "SELECT ALIAS FROM EMPLOYEES
➥WHERE ALIAS = '" & vUserName & "'") THEN
  vUserExists = TRUE
  ' Check to see if the password fits the username
  IF SQLLOOKUP(BOOKS, "SELECT PASSWORD FROM EMPLOYEES
  ➥WHERE ALIAS = '" & vUserName.Value & "'") = fldPassword THEN
    ' Close the form
    Inherited.Click()
  ELSE
   MSGBOX "Incorrect password"
   vWrongTries = vWrongTries + 1
  END IF

' The username doesn't exist in EMPLOYEES
ELSE
   vUserExists = FALSE
   MSGBOX "That username is not valid"
   vWrongTries = vWrongTries + 1
END IF

' After 5 failed attempts to log into the application,
' close it down
IF vWrongTries = 5 THEN
  IF vUserExists = TRUE THEN
    ' Move the pointer to the correct employee record
    DIM vRecs AS Object
    vRecs = embEmployees.GetRecordset()
    DO
```

```
      FOR x = 1 to Recs.GetRowCount()
        vObj.SetCurRow(x)
        IF vObj.GetColVal("ALIAS") = fldUsername.Value THEN
          EXIT DO
        END IF
    LOOP

    ' Add one to the number of times this account has potentially
    ' been hacked by another user, and record today's date
    embEmployees.NUM_HACKS.Value = NVL(embEmployees.NUM_HACKS.Value, 0) + 1
    embEmployees.LAST_HACKED.Value = NOW
    embEmployees.CommitForm()
  END IF
  frmSplash.CloseWindow()
  Inherited.Click()
END IF
```

7. Save and run the application.

8. Enter jboss for the username, blort as the password, and then press OK five times.

   The application shuts down. However, before it closed, it recorded that someone failed today to log in as jboss.

9. Open the Table Editor window for EMPLOYEES and run it.

   As you can see in Figure 15.4, the record for jboss now includes information about your unsuccessful attempt to log in to the application under this name.

Figure 15.4.

The application recorded the unsuccessful login attempt in the database.

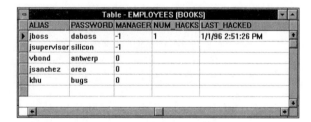

ALIAS	PASSWORD	MANAGER	NUM_HACKS	LAST_HACKED
jboss	daboss	-1	1	1/1/96 2:51:26 PM
jsupervisor	silicon	-1		
vbond	antwerp	0		
jsanchez	oreo	0		
khu	bugs	0		

10. Press Stop to end this exercise.

Reviewing Unsuccessful Login Attempts

In the next exercise, you create a form used by the database administrator to review all incidents in which users have made failed attempts to log in to the application. The form has the following components:

☐ A repeater display showing a scrolling list of all users who have failed to log in

☐ An embedded form showing all the information about a user selected from the scrolling list

To open this form, you enter a special username and password combination reserved for the database administrator. When the application sees this name and password, the only form that opens is the new form for reviewing failed login attempts. Using this form, the administrator can make adjustments to the EMPLOYEE table as needed.

Right now, you have all the skills needed to implement this feature. You might want to attempt to create this form yourself before reviewing the following suggested solution.

Creating the Employee Account Usage Form

Before you can add the new form, you need to consider how to store the special username/ password combination for the database administrator (DBA). You have the following options:

- [ ] Hard code the username and password into the application. The weakness of this approach is obvious: If another employee learns the database administrator's password, the DBA needs to change it.

- [ ] Store the DBA's username and password in the EMPLOYEES table. Because this table is part of the schema used by other employees, maintaining this information in EMPLOYEES exposes it to the view of other users.

- [ ] Instead of accessing the EMPLOYEES table directly, replace it with a single-table view that uses EMPLOYEES as its base table but excludes the DBA's record from the list. By using this view as a form or report's RecordSource, no employee records viewed through the application would include the database administrator. Unfortunately, in many cases you want to include this record, such as in a report displaying employee salaries and bonuses.

- [ ] Encrypt the password before storing it. Using an encryption algorithm defined in the application or in a DLL, you can encrypt any text the user enters as a password, and then compare this encrypted text with the encrypted password stored in the database.

- [ ] Place the information in a different schema. This is the best solution, because it gives you both the ability to change the password when necessary and the security of a protected schema.

Although you cannot create a new schema in a Blaze database, you can create a separate database to store a special table, DBA_INFO, containing the DBA's special username/password combination for opening database maintenance forms like the one you'll create in this exercise. The DBA will also have a regular username and password stored in the EMPLOYEES table for logging in to the application.

Follow these steps to create a separate database:

1. Select File | New Blaze Database to create a new Blaze database.
2. Give this new database the filename BLORT.MSD and save it in the C:\BOOKS directory.

   The filename is sufficiently ambiguous to conceal the purpose of the file. In fact, without the .BLZ extension, it's hard to determine what type of file this is.
3. Create a new session, DBA.POS, with the connect string C:\BOOKS\BLORT.MSD.
4. Double-click the connector icon in DBA.POS.
5. Add a new table, named DBA_INFO, to this schema, with the following columns:

Name	Data Type	Size	Not Null
USERNAME	VARCHAR2	16	Yes
PASSWORD	VARCHAR2	16	Yes

6. Save and run the table.
7. In the Table Browser window, enter Alexander for the USERNAME and Macedon for the PASSWORD.
8. Press Commit, and then stop running the table.

Later, you will use this information to open the new Employee Account Usage form if the user enters the special username/password combination for the DBA. First, however, you need to create the form.

1. Create a new form, frmDBA, with the label Employee Account Usage.
2. Add a repeater display, named repUsers, to the top half of this form.
3. Click and drag the following columns from the EMPLOYEES table into the repeater display: EMPLOYEE_LNAME, ALIAS, PASSWORD, NUM_HACKS, and LAST_HACKS.
4. Add a current row control to the left side of the repeater display's panel.
5. Open the Property sheet for the repeater display and enter the following for its DefaultCondition property:

   NUM_HACKS > 0

   The repeater display now queries only those employee records where someone has unsuccessfully attempted to log in as that person.
6. Add an embedded form to the bottom of the repeater display and give it the name embUsers.
7. Click and drag the following columns from the EMPLOYEES table into the embedded form: EMPLOYEE_ID, EMPLOYEE_LNAME, EMPLOYEE_FNAME, and MANAGER.

You want to synchronize the records in both the repeater display and the embedded form. When you select an employee record in the repeater display, information about that person appears in the embedded form. You use a shared recordset to create this feature.

8. Enter the following as the `RecordSource` property of the embedded form:

   ```
   =repUsers
   ```

9. Add a button with the label `Done` to the bottom of the form.

10. Add the following code to this button:

    ```
    Sub Click()
    self.GetContainer.CloseWindow()
    ```

11. Change the appearance of objects in the form until it looks like Figure 15.5.

Figure 15.5.

The Employee Account Usage form.

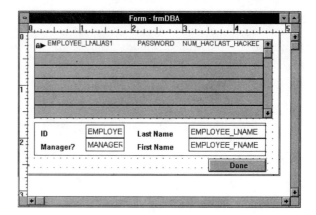

The final step in this exercise is to add the method code that opens this form if you enter the correct username/password combination for the database administrator.

12. Open the form frmlogin.

13. In the `Click()` method of the pushbutton, add the following bold lines of method code:

    ```
    Sub Click()
    DIM vUsername AS String
    DIM vUserExists AS Integer
    STATIC vWrongTries AS Integer

    ' Assign a value to vUserName, based on the contents of fldUsername
    vUserName = NVL(fldUsername.Value, "")

    ' Open the DBA administrator form, if the right
    ' user/name password combo appears
    IF SQLLOOKUP(DBA, "SELECT PASSWORD FROM DBA_INFO
    ➡WHERE USERNAME = '" & vUsername & "'") = fldPassword.Value THEN
    ```

```
frmDBA.OpenWindow()
  Inherited.Click()

ELSE
' Use vUserName to determine if the alias exists in EMPLOYEES
  .
  .
  .
END IF
```

The bulk of the code in the `Click()` method has been omitted. The additional method code adds another `IF...END IF` block to determine whether the application needs to open the special DBA form if the user enters the correct username/password combination. Don't forget to add the final `END IF` as the last line of code now appearing in this method. Note that you could just as easily use a `SELECT CASE` statement to test the values entered for the username, instead of nested `IF...END IF` statements.

14. Save and run the application.

15. In the login form, enter `Alexander` as the username and `Macedon` as the password.

    Be sure to use the proper capitalization, because the values searched are case-sensitive.

    The Employee Account Usage form appears, as shown in Figure 15.6. Because only one user, jboss, has failed to log in to the application, that person's record is the only one appearing in this form.

Figure 15.6.

The Employee Account Usage form at runtime, with a problem account displayed.

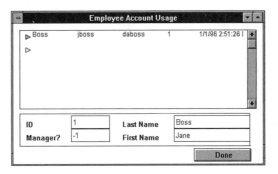

Because you have full access to the EMPLOYEES table at this point, you can change the user's password.

16. Enter `Hannibal` as the new password and press Commit.

    If you suspect that another employee was trying to log in as jboss, you have blocked their further access to the account, if they were lucky enough to guess jboss's password after the first failed attempt. If you were really the DBA, you would need to tell jboss her new password, so that she could get access to the application.

17. Close this form and the splash screen.

When you close the last form, the application closes.

Restricting Access to Forms

Many forms in the Bookstore application should not be opened by anyone. The most obvious example is frmEmployees, which shows every employee's salary, username, and password. This information should be viewed only by store managers, not by everyone.

There are several ways to restrict access to the information displayed on these forms:

- ☐ Make invisible the controls displaying sensitive information.
- ☐ Create two different versions of the same form, one with a more limited range of information displayed.
- ☐ Prevent some users from opening certain forms.
- ☐ Disable the menu commands that open these forms.
- ☐ Remove the menu commands that open these forms.

In all cases, the information displayed depends on the type of employee that has launched the application. In many respects, this piece of information is a property of the application: Who is currently using it? Therefore, before showing the variety of different means for restricting access to a form, you will create a new user-defined property that defines the type of user currently running the Bookstore application.

Adding the New Property

Before you add the new property, you will add another column to the EMPLOYEES table: SEC_LEVEL. Although EMPLOYEES already has a column indicating whether someone is a manager, there are good reasons to distinguish different levels of access, even among all the managers in the store. Although the store manager should know the salary every manager makes, the assistant manager does not need to know how much the store manager earns. Similarly, the DBA might need a special level of access reserved for maintaining the database.

To add a security rating to the description of each employee, as well as to a form, follow these steps:

1. Open the Table Editor window for EMPLOYEES.
2. Add the following new column:

Name	Data Type	Not Null
SEC_LEVEL	Integer	Yes

3. Save the modified table to the database.
4. Run the table and add the following information to the employee records:

EMPLOYEE_ID	SEC_LEVEL
1	50
2	40
3	10
4	10
5	10

5. Add the following new record to employees:

Column	Setting
EMPLOYEE_ID	6
EMPLOYEE_LNAME	Shreeves
EMPLOYEE_FNAME	Sally
SALARY	2600
ALIAS	sshreeves
PASSWORD	cello
MANAGER	0
SEC_LEVEL	99

You have now defined the security level for each employee. Average employees have a security rating of 10; the assistant manager has a rating of 40; and the store manager has one of 50. Additionally, the new employee, the system administrator, has a special rating of 99.

Now that you have added the necessary information to the EMPLOYEES table, you are ready to create the new property of an application that stores the user's security level.

1. Open the User Properties window and add the following entry:

Section	Setting
Name	udpSecLevel
Type	Property
Data type	Long

2. Open the Property sheet for the application.

3. Drag the description of the new property onto the application's Property sheet.

   The new property is now added to the application, as shown in Figure 15.7.

4. Set the property udpSecLevel to 10.

   This step ensures that if for some reason you forget to assign a value to this property, whoever logs into the application is treated as an average employee with a security level of 10.

5. Save the application.

Figure 15.7.

The user-defined property
udpSecLevel *added to the*
application.

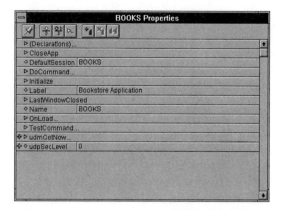

The next step is to look up a user's security level when the application launches and assign that number to the udpSecLevel property.

Because this is a self-contained procedure, you create a new user-defined method to handle this task.

6. Add the following entry to the User Properties window:

Section	Setting
Name	udmGetSecLevel
Type	Function
Data type	Long
Arguments	ByVal vUserName As String

The function takes the employee's username as an argument and returns that person's security level.

7. Add the new property to the application.

8. Open the Code Editor window for udmGetSecLevel and add the following method code:

```
Function udmGetSecLevel (ByVal vUserName As String) As Integer
udmGetSecLevel = SQLLOOKUP(BOOKS, "SELECT SEC_LEVEL FROM EMPLOYEES
➥WHERE ALIAS = '" & vUserName & "'")
```

Next, you need to call udmGetSecLevel on application startup, to assign its return value (the user's security rating) to the property udpSecLevel.

9. Open the login form, frmLogin.

10. Add the following bold code to the Click() method of the OK pushbutton:

```
Sub Click()
DIM vUsername AS String
DIM vUserExists AS Integer
STATIC vWrongTries AS Integer
```

```
' Assign a value to vUserName, based on the contents of fldUsername
vUserName = NVL(fldUsername.Value, "")

' Open the DBA administrator form, if the right
' user/name password combo appears
IF SQLLOOKUP(ADMIN, "SELECT PASSWORD FROM DBA_INFO
➥WHERE USERNAME = '" & vUsername & "'") = fldPassword.Value THEN
   frmDBA.OpenWindow()
   ' Assign the DBA's security level to the udpSecLevel property
   Application.udpSecLevel = Application.udmGetSecLevel(vUserName)
   Inherited.Click()

ELSE
' Use vUserName to determine if the alias exists in EMPLOYEES
IF SQLLOOKUP("SELECT ALIAS FROM EMPLOYEES
➥WHERE ALIAS = " & vUserName) THEN
  vUserExists = TRUE
  ' Check to see if the password fits the username
  IF SQLLOOKUP("SELECT PASSWORD FROM EMPLOYEES
  ➥WHERE ALIAS = " & fldUsername.Value) = fldPassword.Value THEN
' Assign the user's security level to the udpSecLevel property
    Application.udpSecLevel = Application.udmGetSecLevel(vUserName)
    ' Close the form
    Inherited.Click()

       .
       .
       .
```

(The remaining code in `Click()` has been omitted.)

11. Save the application.

The Bookstore application now keeps track of the security rating of any user who logs in to the application. As discussed earlier, there are several ways to use this information to restrict access to forms or some of the information displayed on a form.

DO	**DON'T**

DO make the user log in again if the application has been left idle for some interval. You want to prevent situations in which the user leaves the application running and untended, allowing other people to use it.

DO make sure that you record unsuccessful attempts to log into the application. Someone in the company needs to be alerted if users are trying to "hack into" the application using someone else's name.

DO record successful efforts to log into the application, as well as when the user closed the application. If you record only unsuccessful efforts to log into the application, you'll only catch the less skilled hackers. However, you might find information

> on successful efforts to log into the application even more informative: why did this person log in at 2 a.m.? And why did he log in simultaneously from two different copies of the application?
>
> **DON'T** be afraid to force the user to close the application before logging in under a different name. Closing down the application first is a good way of ensuring that all transactions are committed or rolled back before starting another session under a different username.
>
> **DON'T** store too much information about the user in an .INI file. You might not want to store an employee's username in a file, because preventing someone from knowing this alias is the first step toward preventing unauthorized access.

Hiding Information on a Form

First, you will use an employee's security rating to determine whether several text fields appear on a form.

1. Open the form frmEmployees.
2. From the Table Editor window for EMPLOYEES, drag the columns SEC_LEVEL, NUM_HACKS, and LAST_HACKED onto the form.
3. Change the appearance of these new text fields so that they match the other fields on the form.
4. Open the Code Editor window for the form's OnLoad() method and add the following code beneath the Sub OnLoad() line:

```
SELECT CASE Application.udpSecLevel
    ' First, the average employee
    CASE 10
        SEC_LEVEL.Visible = FALSE
        NUM_HACKS.Visible = FALSE
        LAST_HACKED.Visible = FALSE
        ALIAS1.Visible = FALSE
        PASSWORD.Visible = FALSE
        SALARY.Visible = FALSE
    ' Second, the assistant manager
    CASE 40
        ALIAS1.Visible = FALSE
        PASSWORD.Visible = FALSE
        SALARY.Visible = FALSE
    ' Third, the database administrator
    CASE 99
        SALARY.Visible = FALSE
    ' Finally, the store manager
    CASE ELSE
        MSGBOX "Welcome, store manager"
END SELECT
```

5. Save and run the application.

6. In the login form, enter vbond as the username and antwerp as the password.

   You are now logged in to the application as Victor Bond, a store clerk.

7. Select the Setup | Employees menu command.

   The Employees form appears, as shown in Figure 15.8, but several controls are invisible.

Figure 15.8.
The form frmEmployees, with several fields now invisible because of the user's security rating.

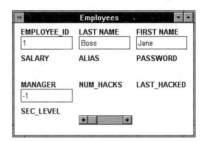

If you fine-tuned this form, you would also remove the labels for the invisible fields.

8. Press Stop to end this exercise.

Preventing the User from Opening a Form

One alternative way to restrict access to information is to prevent the user from opening a form altogether. In the next exercise, you add some simple method code that verifies that the user has a high enough security rating before opening a form.

1. Open the form frmAllTables and its Property sheet.

2. Add the following method code to the form's OpenWindow() method:

```
Sub OpenWindow()
' Check if the user is the store manager or DBA
' before opening the form
IF Application.udpSecLevel >= 50 THEN
    Inherited.OpenWindow()
ELSE
    MSGBOX ("You are not authorized to open this form",
    ➡16, "Unauthorized Access")
END IF
```

3. Save and run the application.

4. Log in to the application with the username vbond and the password antwerp.

5. Select Setup | Database.

The application prevents you from opening the form and displays an error message, as shown in Figure 15.9.

Figure 15.9.

The user cannot open the form frmAllTables.

6. After dismissing the message box, press Stop to end this exercise.

Disabling a Menu Command

Although this technique works, it is not the standard behavior for a Windows or Macintosh application. Normally, when you should not be able to select a menu command, the application disables (or grays) that command. This approach prevents the user from trying to open the form at all, because the menu command itself cannot be selected.

To disable the Setup | Database menu command, you need to add some code to the TestCommand() method. As described on Day 9, TestCommand() determines the status of menu commands when you select the menu in which they appear.

1. Open the Property sheet for the application.

2. Add the following bold code to TestCommand():

```
Function TestCommand(cmdCode As Long) As Long
SELECT CASE cmdCode
CASE cOrders
    ' Based on the status of the global variable gFormOpen,
    ' enable or disable the menu command.
    IF gFormOpen = FALSE THEN
       TestCommand = TestCommand_Enabled
    ELSE
       TestCommand = TestCommand_Disabled
    END IF

CASE cDBAdmin
    ' Based on the user's security level, enable or disable
    ' the Setup¦Database menu command
    IF Application.udpSecLevel >= 50 THEN
       TestCommand = TestCommand_Enabled
    ELSE
       TestCommand = TestCommand_Disabled
    END IF

END SELECT
```

3. Save and run the application.

4. Once again, log in to the application as vbond/antwerp.

5. Select the Setup menu.

The Setup | Database menu command now appears grayed, as shown in Figure 15.10.

Figure 15.10.
Disabling the Setup |
Database menu command.

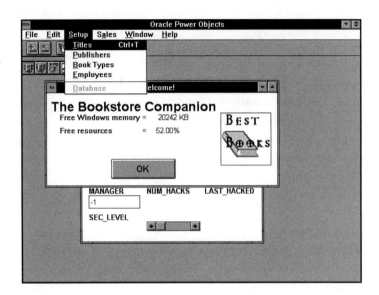

6. Press Stop to end this exercise.

Removing a Menu Command

The safest measure for preventing user access to a form is to remove the menu command that opens it. The same principle applies when you open a form through a pushbutton—if you remove the pushbutton you remove the temptation to open the form.

This technique is especially useful when you don't want users to know that a particular form even exists. In the case of frmAllTables, you might want to conceal the fact from most users that a database administration form is available through the Bookstore application. The surest measure is to remove the Setup | Database menu command, which requires a little extra code in the application's OnLoad() method.

1. Open the application's Property sheet.

2. Add the following bold code to the section of the menu bar that defines the Setup menu:

```
Sub OnLoad()
' Create the Setup menu
mnuSetup.Label = "&Setup"
mnuSetup.AppendMenuItem("&Titles", cTitles, 0, "^t")
```

```
mnuSetup.AppendMenuItem("&Publishers", cPublishers, 0, NULL)
mnuSetup.AppendMenuItem("&Book Types", cBookTypes, 0, NULL)
mnuSetup.AppendMenuItem("&Employees", cEmployees, 0, NULL)
mnuSetup.AppendMenuItem("-", NULL, NULL, NULL)
mnuSetup.AppendMenuItem("&Preferences", cPreferences, 0, NULL)
IF Application.udpSecLevel >= 50 THEN
    mnuSetup.AppendMenuItem("-", NULL, NULL, NULL)
    mnuSetup.AppendMenuItem("&Database", cDBAdmin, 0, NULL)
END IF
```

3. Save and run the application.

4. After logging in to the application as vbond/antwerp, select the Setup menu.

   The Setup | Database menu command does not appear on the menu.

   If, on the other hand, you logged in as the store manager or the database administrator, this menu command would appear on the Setup menu.

5. Press Stop to end the exercise.

Although this technique works to demonstrate a principle, in an actual application you would need to write code that removes the menu command on a form-by-form basis. This code would appear in the form's InitializeWindow() method, which controls the appearance of menu bars, toolbars, and status lines associated with that form. In this demonstration, the menu command disappears regardless of the type of user, because the OnLoad() method code is called before the user logs in.

DO	DON'T

DO remove menu commands instead of disabling them. Often, the text of a menu command says something about the type of information stored in the database. For sensitive information, removing the related menu command is the safest step.

DO separate extremely sensitive information in a separate application when this is a more efficient technique. Instead of implementing elaborate security measures within a single application, such as disabling menu commands and preventing access to forms to some users, you can create a separate application for viewing and editing sensitive information.

DON'T get too clever when removing or disabling menu commands. Unless you extensively test your application, you might accidentally make it impossible for any user to open a form or access a key menu command because of some unforseen situation not handled by the security measures you added to your application.

DON'T simply hide fields containing sensitive information. It's usually pretty obvious to the user that some key piece of information is missing from a form, which then suggests the question, "What might this information be?"

Creating a Paper Trail

As discussed earlier in this lesson, security has as much to do with accountability as restrictions. You already have one piece of accountability built into the Bookstore application: whenever you enter a new order or purchase, you must enter an employee ID as well. Because the EMPLOYEE_ID columns in the PURCHASES and ORDERS tables have the NOT NULL constraint applied to them, you cannot save a purchase or an order unless you enter a value for EMPLOYEE_ID.

However, the database does not demand that you enter your own ID, or even a valid ID. You can enter any number you want and the database is content that the NOT NULL constraint has been fulfilled.

Obviously, from the standpoint of the bookstore, this situation isn't acceptable. You need some way to automate the paper trail, so that the application automatically enters the correct EMPLOYEE_ID value for whatever employee is currently logged into the application.

1. Open the User Properties window and add the following entries:

Name	Type	Data Type	Arguments
udpEmployeeID	Property	Long	
udmGetEmployeeID	Function	Long	ByVal vUserName As String

2. Add both `udpEmployeeID` and `udmGetEmployeeID` to the application.

   Again, rather than leaving this property NULL, you assign a value of 0 to it in case you somehow forgot to read the user's ID at application startup or there is something wrong with the code you wrote to perform this task.

3. Open the Code Editor window for the application's new `udmGetEmployeeID()` method and enter the following method code:

```
Function udmGetSecLevel (ByVal vUserName As String) As Integer
udmGetEmployeeID = SQLLOOKUP(BOOKS, "SELECT EMPLOYEE_ID FROM EMPLOYEES
➥WHERE ALIAS = '" & vUserName & "'")
```

4. Open the login form frmLogin.

5. Add the following bold lines to the code appearing in the pushbutton's `Click()` method:

```
Sub Click()
DIM vUsername AS String
DIM vUserExists AS Integer
STATIC vWrongTries AS Integer

' Assign a value to vUserName, based on the contents of fldUsername
vUserName = NVL(fldUsername.Value, "")

' Open the DBA administrator form,
```

```
➥if the right user/name password combo appears
IF SQLLOOKUP(ADMIN, "SELECT PASSWORD FROM DBA_INFO
➥WHERE USERNAME = '" & vUsername & "'") = fldPassword.Value THEN
frmDBA.OpenWindow()
   ' Assign the DBA's security level to the udpSecLevel property
   Application.udpSecLevel = Application.udmGetSecLevel(vUserName)
   ' Assign the DBA's employee ID to the udpEmployeeID property
   Application.udpEmployeeID = udmGetEmployeeID(vUserName)
   Inherited.Click()

ELSE
' Use vUserName to determine if the alias exists in EMPLOYEES
IF SQLLOOKUP("SELECT ALIAS FROM EMPLOYEES WHERE ALIAS = " & vUserName) THEN
   vUserExists = TRUE
   ' Check to see if the password fits the username
   IF SQLLOOKUP("SELECT PASSWORD FROM EMPLOYEES
   ➥WHERE ALIAS = " & fldUsername.Value) = fldPassword.Value THEN
      ' Close the form
      ' Assign the user's security level to the udpSecLevel property
   Application.udpSecLevel = Application.udmGetSecLevel(vUserName)
   ' Assign the employee's ID number to the udpEmployeeID property
   Application.udpEmployeeID = udmGetEmployeeID(vUserName)
      Inherited.Click()
   .
   .
   .
```

(Once again, the remaining code in `Click()` has been omitted.)

Now that the application automatically stores the user's employee ID as a property of the application, you can enter this value whenever the user enters a new purchase or order.

6. Open the Book Orders form, frmOrders.

7. Set the `ReadOnly` property of the text field `EMPLOYEE_ID` to `TRUE`.

   Now, the user cannot change the value appearing in this field.

8. In the `InsertRow()` method of the form, add the following bold lines of method code:

```
Sub InsertRow()
Inherited.InsertRow()
udpWasOpened = FALSE

' Assign the employee's ID number to the record
EMPLOYEE_ID.Value = Application.udpEmployeeID

' Add 1 to the number of orders entered since you opened the form
self.udpNumOrders = self.udpNumOrders + 1

' Display the number of orders entered so far
DIM vMsg AS String
SELECT CASE udpNumOrders
   CASE 1
      vMsg = "1st"
   CASE 2
      vMsg = "2nd"
```

```
    CASE 3
      vMsg = "3rd"
    CASE ELSE
      vMsg = STR(udpNumOrders) & "th"
  END SELECT

  MSGBOX "This is the " & vMsg" & " order entered"
```

9. Open the Book Purchases form, frmPurchases.

10. Again, set the ReadOnly property of the EMPLOYEE_ID field to TRUE and enter the following lines of code to the form's InsertRow() method:

```
Sub InsertRow()
Inherited.InsertRow()

' Assign the employee's ID number to the record
EMPLOYEE_ID.Value = Application.udpEmployeeID
```

11. Save and run the application.

12. Log in as vbond/antwerp.

13. Select Sales | Purchases to enter a new purchase.

    When you create the new purchase record, the application automatically enters your employee ID, as shown in Figure 15.11.

Figure 15.11.

The application enters the employee's ID number.

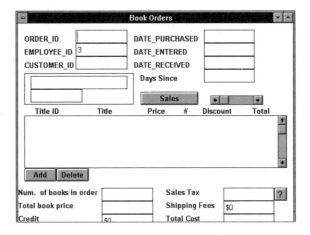

Because you set the ReadOnly property of the EMPLOYEE_ID field to TRUE, you cannot change the ID number entered in this control. Therefore, the application makes it impossible for you to misrepresent who you are when you enter a new purchase or order.

14. Press Rollback and Stop to end this exercise.

Creating an Approval System

In the final exercise in today's lesson, you will add an approval system. Many applications put financial transactions or some other business decision on hold until a manager or another user gives permission to go ahead.

In the Bookstore application, you prevented users from entering orders for customers with large outstanding balances owed. However, you might want to waive this restriction in some cases if a manager decides it's okay to go ahead with the order. Therefore, you will add a new approval system that temporarily puts orders on hold for customers with outstanding balances until a manager approves them.

As with other exercises, the first step here is to add another column to a table. The ORDERS table needs a new column indicating whether an order is on hold. Later, you can build in the features of the application that enter data into this column.

1. Open the Table Editor window for ORDERS.

2. Add the following new column to the table:

    Name   `ON_HOLD`
    Data type   `Integer`

3. Save the modified table to the database.

    Next, you add a check box to the Book Orders form that displays whether an order is on hold.

4. Open the Book Orders form, frmBookOrders, and add a check box to it.

    The exact location of the check box isn't important, as long as it's outside the repeater display containing the line items of the order.

5. Name the check box `chkOnHold` and enter `ON_HOLD` as its `DataSource`.

6. Set the `ValueOn` property of the check box to `-1` and its `ValueOff` property to `0`.

    As you know, these values correspond to the constants `TRUE` and `FALSE`.

7. Set the `ReadOnly` property of the check box to `TRUE` and its `DefaultValue` to `0`.

    Now employees can see that an order is on hold if the check box is checked. They cannot change the status of the order, however, because the `ReadOnly` property is set to `TRUE`.

8. Give the check box the label `On Hold?`.

    Right now, code added to the form's `ValidateRow()` method makes it impossible to save the new order. You need to automatically set the value of the new check box to `TRUE` whenever the user tries to enter an order for a customer with an outstanding balance.

9. Enter the following bold changes to the form's `ValidateRow()` method:

```
Function ValidateRow(rownum As Integer) As Long
' Determine whether the DATE_ENTERED value precedes the
' DATE_RECEIVED and DATE_PURCHASED
IF DATE_ENTERED.Value < DATE_RECEIVED.Value THEN
   self.ValidateRowMsg = "The entry date cannot be later than
   ➥the date received"
   ValidateRow = FALSE
ELSEIF DATE_ENTERED.Value < DATE_PURCHASED.Value THEN
   self.ValidateRowMsg = "The entry date cannot be later than
   ➥the date the customer paid for the order"
ValidateRow = FALSE
ELSEIF DATE_ENTERED.Value = DATE_PURCHASED.Value THEN
   IF MSGBOX("The date purchased and date entered are the same.
   ➥Proceed?", 52, "Question") = 7 THEN
self.ValidateRowMsg = "Dates not valid"
   ValidateRow = FALSE
   END IF
ELSEIF DATE_ENTERED.Value = DATE_RECEIVED.Value THEN
   IF MSGBOX("The date received and date entered are the same.
   ➥Proceed?", 52, "Question") = 7 THEN
self.ValidateRowMsg = "Dates not valid"
   ValidateRow = FALSE
   ELSE
   ValidateRow = TRUE
   Inherited.ValidateRow(rownum)
   END IF
ELSEIF SQLLOOKUP(BOOKS, "select BALANCE_DUE from CUSTOMERS
➥where CUSTOMER_ID = " & STR(CUSTOMER_ID.Value)) > 0 THEN
' Get the amount owed
   DIM vMsg AS String

   ' Place the order on hold
   chkOnHold = -1
   ' Tell the user that the order is on hold
   vMsg = STR(SQLLOOKUP(""select BALANCE_DUE from CUSTOMERS
   ➥where CUSTOMER_ID = " & STR(CUSTOMER_ID.Value))
   MSGBOX ("This order is on hold because the customer owes
   ➥an outstanding balance of $" & vMsg

   ValidateRow = TRUE
   Inherited.ValidateRow(rownum)
ELSE
  ValidateRow = TRUE
  Inherited.ValidateRow(rownum)
END IF
```

10. Save and run the form.

11. Create a new order and enter 1 for the CUSTOMER_ID.

12. After entering the line items and other information in the form, press Commit.

   As shown in Figure 15.12, the application now tells you that the order has been placed on hold, and the On Hold? check box is now checked.

Figure 15.12.

*The application places
an order on hold for a
customer with an out-
standing balance.*

13. After dismissing the message box, press Stop.

Creating the Review Form

The next step is to create a manager review form to release orders that are on hold. You'll disable
this form whenever someone other than a manager logs in to the application.

First, you need to add the menu command that creates the menu command and disables it when
appropriate.

1. In the (Declarations) section of the application's Property sheet, add the following
   bold line to the section that assigns constants to menu commands:

```
(Declarations)
' Declare the base value for all menu IDs
CONST cMenuNum = 1000

'Assign menu IDs for commands in the Setup menu
CONST cTitles = cMenuNum + 1
CONST cPublishers = cMenuNum + 2
CONST cBookTypes = cMenuNum + 3
CONST cEmployees = cMenuNum + 4
CONST cDBAdmin = cMenuNum + 5

'Assign menu IDs for commands in the Sales menu
CONST cOrders = cMenuNum + 10
CONST cCustomers = cMenuNum + 11
CONST cCustPurchases = cMenuNum + 12
CONST cOrderReview = cMenuNum + 13
```

2. Add the following bold lines to the section of the application's OnLoad() method that
   defines the Sales menu of the custom menu bar:

```
Function DoCommand(cmdCode as Long) as Long
' Test for the constant assigned to each menu command.
' Depending on the constant, open the correct form.
SELECT CASE cmdCode
CASE cTitles
  frmTitles.OpenWindow()
  DoCommand = TRUE
CASE cPublishers
  frmPubsBooks.OpenWindow()
CASE cBookTypes
  frmBookTypes.OpenWindow()
CASE cEmployees
  frmEmployees.OpenWindow()
```

```
   CASE cOrders
     frmBookOrders.OpenWindow()
   CASE cCustomers
     frmCustomers.OpenWindow()
   cCustPurchases
     frmCustPurchases.OpenWindow()
   CASE cRunApp
     frmLaunch.OpenWindow()
   CASE cOrderReview
     frmOrderReview.OpenWindow()
   END SELECT
```

3. Add the following bold line to the section of the application's OnLoad() method that defines the Sales menu:

```
Sub OnLoad()
' Create the Sales menu
mnuSales.Label = "S&ales"
mnuSales.AppendMenuItem("&Orders", cOrders, 0, NULL)
mnuSales.AppendMenuItem("&Review Orders", cOrderReview, 0 NULL)
mnuSales.AppendMenuItem("&Customers", cCustomers, 0, NULL)
```

4. Add the following bold code to the TestCommand() method:

```
Function TestCommand(cmdCode As Long) As Long
SELECT CASE cmdCode
CASE cOrders
   ' Based on the status of the global variable gFormOpen,
   ' enable or disable the menu command.
   IF gFormOpen = FALSE THEN
      TestCommand = TestCommand_Enabled
   ELSE
      TestCommand = TestCommand_Disabled
   END IF

CASE cDBAdmin
   ' Based on the user's security level, enable or disable
   ' the Setup¦Database menu command
   IF Application.udpSecLevel >= 50 THEN
      TestCommand = TestCommand_Enabled
   ELSE
      TestCommand = TestCommand_Disabled
   END IF

CASE cOrderReview
   ' If the user is not a manager (security level 40 or higher),
   ' disable the Sales¦Review Orders menu command
   IF Application.udpSecLevel >= 40 THEN
      TestCommand = TestCommand_Enabled
   ELSE
      TestCommand = TestCommand_Disabled
   END IF

END SELECT
```

5. Create a new form, named frmOrderReview, with the label Review Orders on Hold.

6. Add a repeater display to the form.

7. Drag the ORDER_ID and CUSTOMER_ID columns from the ORDERS table into the repeater display.

8. Add a lookup field to the repeater display that shows the customer's last name.

   The entry in the `DataSource` property that performs the lookup should look like this:

   ```
   =SQLLOOKUP(BOOKS, "SELECT LNAME FROM CUSTOMERS WHERE
   ➥CUSTOMER_ID = " & STR(CUSTOMER_ID.Value))
   ```

9. Add a check box to the form with the following attributes:

Property	Setting
Name	chkOnHold
Label	(None—delete whatever label appears)
DataSource	ON_HOLD
ValueOn	-1
ValueOff	0

10. Add a current row control to the left side of the repeater display panel.

    At this point, you might also want to add a field that displays the total dollar amount of the order. However, the ORDERS table does not include a column with this information. When you created the Book Orders form, you displayed the total cost of the order through a derived value. The actual total cost depended on values that appear in the ORDER_ITEMS and TITLES table (such as TITLES.PRICE and ORDER_ITEMS.DISCOUNT), not in ORDERS.

    Displaying the total amount of the order at this point requires more work than it is worth. This situation illustrates why in some cases developers denormalize tables: if you had stored the total amount of an order in a column of the ORDERS table, displaying an order's cost would be simple. However, this step would break with the orthodoxy of relational database design, in which all information is carefully normalized.

11. In the repeater display's Property sheet, enter the following for the `DefaultValue` property:

    ```
    NVL(ON_HOLD, 0) != 0
    ```

12. Save and run the form.

    The form appears with a single order on hold—the one you entered a few moments ago. You will now release this order.

13. Click in the check box for the order so that the x disappears.

14. Press Commit to save this change.

    The record is no longer on hold.

15. Press Stop to end this exercise.

Other Security Options

Tomorrow, we return to some security issues, but armed with a different type of tool, user-defined classes. For the time being, here are some additional tips about security in an Oracle Power Objects application:

☐ If you want to store application configuration information that you do not want users to easily edit, you should consider storing this information in a Blaze database. You can easily create a table containing a record for each configuration option, instead of an .INI file or some other format that the user can easily read and modify. Remember that Blaze databases do not need to have the extension .BLZ in their filenames, so you can add a different filename extension to hide their purpose.

☐ Synonyms provide another layer of protection against access to tables and views.

☐ A stand-alone recordset can store sensitive information without ever risking displaying it on a form. By querying records into a stand-alone recordset, the information remains in the application but no form or report ever displays it. If you want to maintain the usernames and passwords for all employees, you can then read them from this recordset.

☐ Be judicious when using redundant checks. You enjoy another level of certainty that security rules are being enforced if you add the necessary code several places in the application. For example, a restriction you add to ValidateRow() might also appear in the form's CommitForm() method or a session's CommitWork() method. However, whenever you create redundant checks, you must apply any changes to these procedures in every part of the application that performs these checks.

☐ Build some flexibility into your security options. In the previous exercises, you hard coded the security level needed to access forms. However, if you decided to change this rule or assign a new range of security IDs to employees, you would need to change this code and recompile the application. You might save some of these definitions of security ratings and privileges in a Blaze database, or a protected schema, so that you can redefine them when necessary.

Summary

Today you learned the following points on system security:

☐ You can enforce security through both the application and the database.

☐ Because security concerns are a type of business rule, you can apply many of the same techniques for enforcing business rules to the task of maintaining system security.

☐ In the database, you can protect information through views, synonyms, and protected schemas.

☐ In the application, you can protect information through a variety of means, from hiding controls to disabling menu commands.

☐ Enforcing security rules through the database affords you the greatest consistency and thoroughness, whereas the application affords you the greatest flexibility in enforcing these restrictions.

☐ You need to maintain information about the type of user currently logged in to the application, so that you can restrict that person's ability to view and edit data accordingly.

☐ Security also involves creating a paper trail and enforcing an approval system for many types of business activities.

What Comes Next?

In several lessons, you added features to the application that were reusable. For example, in today's lesson you added a user-defined property, `udpSecLevel`, that you used in several different ways to restrict a user's access to information. In yesterday's lesson, you wrote user-defined methods that were deliberately generic, so that you could call each of them under a variety of circumstances.

Tomorrow, you work with reusable objects that you can add repeatedly to different parts of the application. As you have already seen, you frequently add the same sets of objects, such as OK and Cancel buttons, throughout the forms and reports you design. User-defined classes give you the ability to define these objects in one place and then use them in as many other places as you like.

Q&A

Q How do I create a protected schema if the only database I plan to use is Blaze?

A Because you should not add further database objects to the SYS schema, you have only one option available: create another Blaze database for storing the protected information. Because Oracle Power Objects applications can access data through any number of sessions, you need only define a new session for the second Blaze database to give your application access to this information. As shown in an exercise in this chapter, it's a good idea to name this file something ambiguous, without the .BLZ extension.

A Blaze database is also a good place to store system configuration options that you do not want to place in an .INI file, for the sake of privacy or some other reason.

Q Is there an easy way to alert the DBA immediately that someone might be trying to circumvent system security rules?

15

A If the DBA is logged in with another copy of the application or some other Oracle Power Objects application connected to the same database, you can use a stored procedure or a trigger (a server-based procedure) to alert the DBA. One of the exercises in Day 20 involves writing just such a stored procedure.

Workshop

The Workshop consists of quiz questions to help you solidify your understanding of the material covered and exercises to give you experience in using what you've learned. Try and understand the quiz and exercises before you go on to tomorrow's lesson.

Quiz

1. Where is the best place to enforce a rule that prevents anyone but managers from changing the DATE_ENTERED value for an order?
2. How can you prevent employees from deleting records, using the user-defined property udpSecLevel?

Exercise

Add a button to the frmDBA form that opens the form frmAllTables, used to review the table descriptions stored in the ALL_TABLES view and ALL_COLUMNS table in the SYS schema. Because only the database administrator should be able to open frmDBA (used to review instances when users have unsuccessfully tried to log in to the application), you ensure that only the DBA can view the additional information from the data dictionary tables viewed through frmAllTables.

Quiz Answers

1. You would enter the code in the Validate() method of the DATE_ENTERED field. If someone who was not a manager tried to edit the value, the Validate() method would return FALSE, preventing the change.
2. To prevent anyone but managers from deleting records, you would add code to the DeleteRow() method of forms that did not let the application delete a record unless the value in udpSecLevel was in the appropriate range (40 or higher).

User-Defined
Classes

Overview

In a small way, you have already learned the value of creating reusable application components. For example, methods written to be generic save you the trouble of rewriting the same code several times. A method that returns the system date and time could be useful in several different forms or reports, so you want to define this method once and then call it from several different places.

Today you learn about the following topics:

- [ ] Reusable components of an application
- [ ] User-defined classes
- [ ] The object inheritance hierarchy
- [ ] Creating a logo class
- [ ] Creating OK and Cancel buttons
- [ ] The object containment hierarchy
- [ ] Binding a class to a table or view
- [ ] Creating a customer information class
- [ ] Creating a VCR control class for recordset browsing
- [ ] Libraries and classes

The Importance of Reusability

Reusability is one of the most important features of Oracle Power Objects, as shown in Day 14's lesson on user-defined properties and methods. Not only does creating a generic method make it easier to use the procedure, it also simplifies the task of maintaining it. If you discover a bug in the code, you can modify the code once, in the one object that contains this method. When you have modified the code, the improvement appears every time you call it from anywhere within the application.

Similarly, the user-defined property udpSecLevel gave you a single point of reference for a user's security level that you then used in several different ways. When creating user-defined properties and methods, you saw the immediate rewards of designing them to be reusable.

Reusable Objects

The same rule might apply to application objects you create. For example, several forms in the Bookstore application have OK buttons, or the combination of OK and Cancel buttons. These two buttons always do the same thing:

☐ When you press the OK button, the form closes and the application applies any changes entered in the form.

☐ When you press the Cancel button, the form also closes, but the application ignores any changes you entered in the form.

This behavior is standard to any GUI application. However, it seems like a waste of time to re-create the same two pushbuttons on dozens of forms.

User-Defined Classes As Reusable Objects

Fortunately, with user-defined classes, Oracle Power Objects provides a powerful solution to this problem. When you create a class, you add a template for a collection of objects that you can copy throughout the application. Therefore, instead of developing a new set of OK and Cancel buttons for every form, you can define these buttons once, and then copy them wherever you want to use them. Classes are highly maintainable because Oracle Power Objects applies any changes you make to the class to all copies of that class that you add to forms and reports.

Although this description might sound fairly abstract, you will quickly learn to appreciate the practical applications of user-defined classes.

Classes, Instances, and Inheritance

Because object-oriented developers share a common lexicon to describe the functions of reusable objects such as user-defined classes, review this terminology before continuing.

Instances and Instantiation

When you create a copy of a class, you are *instantiating* the class, or creating an *instance* of that class. The class itself never appears within a form or report; only an instance of the class appears. After you create the class containing OK and Cancel buttons, you will add instances of this class on several forms. Because the class itself acts as a template defining the instances, you often hear the term *master class definition* to refer to a user-defined class.

You can edit an instance of the class, adding or changing the settings for properties and rewriting the code that appears in methods. However, editing an instance affects the way it inherits changes.

Inheritance

As mentioned earlier, when you make a change to a class, the change is immediately reflected in all instances of the class. If you decide to add a third pushbutton to the OK/Cancel class, all

instances of this class automatically include the new pushbutton. If you change the text on any of these pushbuttons, the instances of this class inherit this change.

Inheritance, the capability to propagate changes from the class to its instances, is the most important feature of a user-defined class. Inheritance makes it possible to centralize the definition of many application objects in a class, instead of working with several identical but otherwise unrelated objects. Instead of adding the same code to the OK and Cancel buttons' Click() method, you would add this code to the pushbuttons in the master class definition. Whenever you add an instance of this class to a form, the instance already includes the code in the pushbutton's Click() method. Later, if you decide to change this code, the instances automatically inherit the change.

The same principle applies to properties. If you change the background color (ColorFill) of a user-defined class, all of its instances inherit the same change.

Breaking Inheritance

However, if you edit a property or method in the instance of a class, that property or method no longer inherits changes to the master class definition. If you change the label of a pushbutton in an instance, the instance no longer inherits changes to the Label property of the pushbutton made in the master class definition. Inheritance is therefore broken until you explicitly tell the object to re-inherit the setting for that property from the class.

Although it might sound as though you never want to break inheritance, in many cases it is a necessary step—particularly when you are working with relatively trivial properties. You should not touch the Click() method of the pushbuttons in the OK and Cancel classes, but you easily could slightly resize and reposition these pushbuttons to better fit within the available space on a form. These properties of the pushbuttons are far less important than the method code that defines what happens when the user presses each of these buttons.

Subclasses

You can make a new user-defined class based on another class. In this case, you are not creating an instance, but the new class (or *subclass*) inherits changes to the original class.

In this sense, the subclass is more like a younger, impressionable sibling of a class than like its child. You can create instances of the subclass in the same fashion that you add instances of the original class to forms and reports. Both the subclass and its instances inherit changes to the master class, as long as you have not broken inheritance in some way.

The Chain of Inheritance

Because inheritance can have several levels, you often hear of the *chain of inheritance*. When you enter a change to a user-defined class, the subclass inherits the change, as does the instance of the subclass. If you break inheritance in the subclass, you have broken the chain of inheritance for a particular property or method. The changes to that property or method no longer propagate to the subclass's instance.

This process implies a hierarchical relationship among the different elements of the chain of inheritance. In the previous example, the first class sits at the top of this hierarchy. Changes to this object propagate downward to the subclass and the instance, which sits at the bottom of the hierarchy. For this reason, the Oracle Power Objects documentation often uses the term *object inheritance hierarchy* as a synonym for the chain of inheritance.

16

The Flexibility of User-Defined Classes

Clearly, user-defined classes give you a great deal of flexibility. You can create subclasses, or even add one class to another class. In both cases, the secondary class inherits changes to the first. You can choose to leave the chain of inheritance untouched, or you can prevent certain changes from propagating. As with other objects, you can add new properties and methods to user-defined classes.

Classes are powerful tools, especially because they are bindable containers such as forms, reports, embedded forms, and repeater displays. Although the significance of this fact might not be immediately apparent, you will see the usefulness of bound classes later in this lesson.

Before reaching this degree of sophistication in your use of classes, you need to start with a more simple class.

Creating a Logo Class

As shown on Day 11, "Graphics and Other Matters," you can easily add a logo to forms or reports. Adding the logo to the background of one of these containers was not very aesthetically appealing: Tiled across the form or report, the logo created a visual mess. Therefore, you added an embedded form, and then made a bitmap its background.

Previously, if you wanted to add the same logo to several forms, the process was fairly tedious. Adding the new logo to other forms was the easy part, requiring only a simple copy-and-paste operation. However, if you changed the graphic somehow, you then had to add the same bitmap several times—once for each copy of the embedded form you created.

As you will see, using a class in place of the embedded form makes this task much simpler.

1. Open the Application window for BOOKS.POA.

2. Press the New Class pushbutton, or select File | New Class.

   A new user-defined class appears. It looks much like a form, and in fact it shares many of the same properties of a form.

3. Open the Property sheet for the new class.

   As you can see, many familiar properties and methods (`Click()`, `ColorFill`, `PositionX`, `RecordSource`, and `Validate()`) appear in the class's Property sheet. For the moment, however, you're interested only in the `Bitmap` property.

4. For the `Bitmap` property, enter `Logo`.

As you might remember from Day 11, the `Bitmap` property identifies the imported bitmap resource to display as the background of an object. Whatever bitmap you created as the company logo now appears in the user-defined class.

Next, you need to size this class so that the bitmap fits exactly within its borders.

1. Set both the `SizeX` and `SizeY` properties of the user-defined class to `1 in`.

2. You should always apply a descriptive name to the object. Therefore, set the `Name` property to `clsLogo`.

3. Save the new class.

   The user-defined class now appears in the Application window for BOOKS.POA (see Figure 16.1).

Figure 16.1.
The new class added to the application.

Next, you can add the new logo to some forms.

1. Open the login form, frmLogin.

2. Click and drag the icon for the class clsLogo from the application window onto the form.

   Clicking and dragging creates an instance of the class on the form, as shown in Figure 16.2.

Figure 16.2.
*The new class added
to the form.*

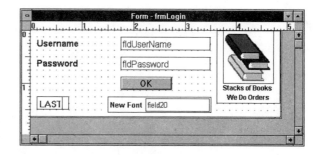

Because you have not edited any properties of the instance, it inherits any changes you make to the master class definition. To illustrate this, add a label to the logo.

3. Select the user-defined class and add a new static text object to it.

4. Set the following properties of the static text object:

Property	Setting
Label	Stacks of Books
FontName	Arial
FontSize	9

As you change each property of the class, the instance automatically inherits each of these changes.

The logo class now displays the name of the bookstore, Stacks of Books. However, depending on the graphic you designed for the bookstore's logo, the label might be hard to read if it is superimposed over the logo.

Classes Within Classes

As mentioned earlier, you can add one user-defined class to another. To learn how to use this feature of classes, add the logo class to a second class. The label will appear within this second class, but it won't be superimposed on the logo.

1. Create a new class named clsLogo2.

2. Click and drag the icon for clsLogo into the new class.

   You have now added an instance of clsLogo to clsLogo2, as shown in Figure 16.3.

3. Select the window for clsLogo. (Be sure to select the master class definition for clsLogo, not its instance.)

4. Click the label you just added and select Edit | Cut.

   When you remove the label from the master class definition, it also disappears from all instances. Take a moment before continuing to look at the instances of clsLogo within the form frmLogin and the class clsLogo2 to confirm this.

Figure 16.3.

The clsLogo class appearing within another class.

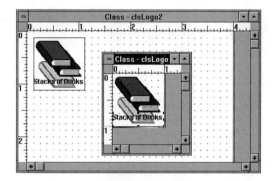

5. Select the window for clsLogo2, and then select Edit | Paste.

   You have now added the label to the second class.

6. Add a second static text object to the class with the label Established 1996.

7. Set the font properties of the new label to match the other static text object, and set both of their TextJustHoriz properties to Center.

8. Resize and reposition the objects within clsLogo2, as well as the borders of the class, to look like those shown in Figure 16.4.

Figure 16.4.

The finished class clsLogo2, containing two labels and the class clsLogo.

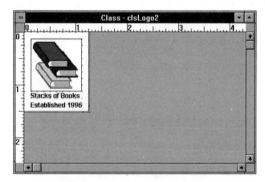

9. Delete the instance of clsLogo from the form frmLogin and replace it with an instance of clsLogo2.

   Because this logo class looks pretty good, you can add it to some other forms to stamp the store's trademark on the application.

10. Add instances of clsLogo2 to the upper-right corner of frmBookOrders, frmPurchases, frmEmployees, and frmPubsBooks.

    You might need to move objects to accommodate the new logo within these forms.

    Perhaps, at this point, you want to change the motto appearing beneath the name of the bookstore. Replacing the motto across the application is now as simple as typing in a new label in one of the static text objects in clsLogo2.

11. Change the label that reads `Established 1996` to `We Do Orders`.

    If you look at the forms in which you added an instance of the class, you can see that all of these instances immediately inherit this change.

12. Save your changes to the application.

Creating OK and Cancel Buttons

As discussed earlier, a set of OK and Cancel buttons is a prime candidate for a user-defined class. These two buttons are common fixtures in every dialog box, as well as in a large number of forms. In the case of forms bound to a table, the OK button might stand for *Close the form and commit*, whereas the Cancel button might stand for *Close the form and rollback*.

In this exercise, you will create a set of OK and Cancel buttons that have this behavior. To start, the two pushbuttons will simply close the form.

1. Create a new class named `clsOKCancel`.

2. Add two pushbuttons with the labels OK and Cancel.

3. Add the following method code to the `Click()` method of the OK pushbutton:

```
Sub Click()
' If the form is modal, close the form, let the application
' hide the form by calling the default processing for Click()
IF self.IsDismissBtn = TRUE THEN
  Inherited.Click()
ELSE
  Self.GetTopContainer.HideWindow()
END IF
```

    The method `GetTopContainer()` returns an object reference to the form or report in which a class appears. You will learn about this and similar methods later today, in the section "The Object Containment Hierarchy."

4. Add the following method code to the `Click()` method of the Cancel pushbutton:

```
Sub Click()
Self.GetTopContainer.CloseWindow()
```

The difference between the code in these two pushbuttons is subtle, but important. If you open a dialog box used for setting application preferences or some other application-level feature, you often want to make it easy for the application to find this information. Opening a form modally (the standard way to open a dialog box) by calling the `OpenModal()` method causes the dialog box to be hidden, not closed, if you press a pushbutton on the form. The only requirement is that the pushbutton has its `IsDismissBtn` property set to `TRUE`, and the default processing for the pushbutton's `Click()` method has not been suppressed by code added to the method.

In the case of an OK pushbutton, you want to keep the dialog box in memory but hidden from the user. The application can then refer to the new values you entered in controls in the dialog box without having to keep the dialog box displayed. For example, if you add a check box for an application preferences dialog box that determines whether you want a 3-D look and feel on

your form, the application can check the value of this check box (probably either TRUE or FALSE) whenever it opens a new form. The application can then apply this preference to any form it opens.

On the other hand, the Cancel button simply closes the dialog box. Therefore, any changes you entered in the dialog box do not remain in memory—which is exactly what you expect to happen. The normal behavior of Cancel buttons is to undo any changes entered in a form, which in this case means that the application closes the form and "forgets" anything you entered in it.

To finish the class, follow these steps:

1. Set the HasBorder property of the class to FALSE.

   Unless there is some need to attract attention to the objects within a class by drawing a rectangle around them, you should remove the border surrounding the class. Without this border, the instance looks like any other part of the form.

2. Resize and reposition the class and the objects within it until it matches Figure 16.5.

3. Press Save.

Figure 16.5.

The class clsOKCancel.

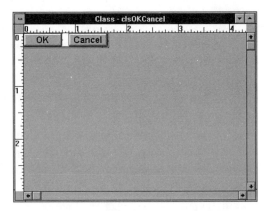

Once again, the new class is added to the Application window for BOOKS.POA.

In the next part of this exercise, you will add this class to the splash screen. The Cancel button might be redundant on this form, because you only need a button to close the splash screen.

However, as you remember from Day 9, "Menus and Toolbars," this form remains in the application so that your custom menu bar remains visible. In addition, if you close this form before opening another form or report, the application closes. Because the splash screen would be the only form open, closing it would call the LastWindowClosed() method, which would shut down the application.

Therefore, in this form, pressing OK keeps the application running, whereas pressing Cancel closes it.

1. Open the splash screen form, frmSplash.

2. Select the OK pushbutton and open its Property sheet.

3. Open the Code Editor window for the pushbutton's Click() method, select all of the code, and then select Edit | Copy.

4. Delete the OK pushbutton from the bottom of the form.

5. Drag the icon for clsOKCancel from the Application window onto the form.

   An instance of the class now appears on the form.

6. Move the instance to the area previously occupied by the OK pushbutton you just deleted.

7. In the instance, open the Code Editor window for the OK pushbutton's Click() method.

   Although you added code to this pushbutton in the master class definition, no code appears here. This might seem strange, but consider that the whole point of a class is to define the properties and methods of objects within the class in one place—the master class definition itself. Therefore, if you want to adjust this code, you should do so in the master class definition, not in the instance.

   However, any code you add here replaces the code you added to the Click() method in the master class definition. This is exactly what you want to do. Instead of closing and hiding the splash screen, you want to move it out of sight.

8. Select Edit | Paste.

You now have pasted the original code from the first OK pushbutton's Click() method into its replacement. In addition, the triangle next to the name of the Click() method is now filled in (see Figure 16.6).

Figure 16.6.

The new code added to the Click() method of the OK pushbutton.

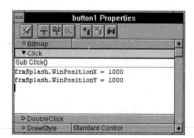

The filled-in triangle for the property indicates that you have modified this method in the instance. This graphical cue tells you that, if you modify the code in the Click() method in the master class, this instance will no longer inherit that change.

If you were to change the setting for a property in an instance, the diamond next to the property's name would also be filled in to indicate that you have overridden the setting for this property

inherited from the master class. Once again, if you modify the setting for that property in the class, the instance will not inherit the change.

1. Save and run the application.

2. Log in as vbond/antwerp.

   After you finish logging in as user vbond and press OK, the splash screen appears, showing the two pushbuttons within the class instance (see Figure 16.7).

Figure 16.7.
The new splash screen,
displaying OK and
Cancel pushbuttons.

3. Press the Cancel pushbutton.

The code in the button closes the form, which in turn causes the application to close.

Adding More Features to clsOKCancel

As described earlier, you might want to add the OK and Cancel pushbuttons to a bound form, so that you could commit or roll back changes to the form's recordset. To add this feature, you need to expand the code in the OK and Cancel buttons' Click() methods to perform two tasks:

☐ Make sure that the form has a recordset.

☐ If it does, commit or roll back all changes to that recordset.

To add an instance of the class to a form, follow these steps:

1. In the class clsOKCancel, open the Code Editor window for the OK pushbutton's Click() method and add the following lines beneath the Sub Click() line:

```
IF NOT ISNULL(self.GetTopContainer.GetRecordset) THEN
  self.GetTopContainer.CommitForm()
  MSGBOX ("Changes saved", 64, "Committed")
END IF

' If the form is modal, close the form, let the application
' hide the form by calling the default processing for Click()
IF self.IsDismissBtn = TRUE THEN
  Inherited.Click()
ELSE
  self.GetTopContainer().HideWindow()
END IF
```

2. Change the code for the Cancel pushbutton's `Click()` method to read as follows:

```
Sub Click()
IF NOT ISNULL(self.GetTopContainer.GetRecordset) THEN
  self.GetTopContainer.RollbackForm()
  MSGBOX ("Changes deleted", 64, "Rolled back")
END IF
Self.GetTopContainer.CloseWindow()
```

3. Save the changes to the class.

4. Open the form frmPurchases and add an instance of clsOKCancel to the bottom of the form.

   Again, you might need to move some objects to provide space for the instance.

5. Save and run the form.

6. Enter a new purchase in the form.

   As you fill out the text fields, remember the business rules enforced in this form.

7. Press the OK pushbutton.

A message box appears, telling you that the changes have been committed to the database. In addition, after you close the message box, the form also closes.

If the form did not have a recordset, the code you added would not have been called. Therefore, your OK and Cancel pushbutton class is designed to work on both bound and unbound forms.

DO	DON'T

DO create subclasses when you need to make slight variations to a class, but you want several copies of this variant to appear throughout the application.

DO create classes when you have the same sets of controls appearing throughout an application.

DO create classes when you are adding information from the same tables in several forms. Because classes are bindable containers, you can use them to represent the same set of information repeated in several forms, such as customer data.

DON'T create too many subclasses. Your application might suffer a loss of performance if it needs to resolve too many levels of the object inheritance hierarchy.

DON'T change the setting for a property or method in an instance unless you absolutely need to make the change. Remember that you need to explicitly instruct an instance of a class to re-inherit property or method settings if you have overridden these settings in the instance.

DON'T forget to keep some record of instances of a class where you have overridden some important property or method setting.

The Object Containment Hierarchy

In this and other lessons, you have written method code that refers to containers and their recordsets. For example, in the previous exercises, the code appearing in the Click() method of the OK pushbutton called the GetTopContainer() method to return an object reference to the form in which a pushbutton appeared.

Being able to get references to containers and the objects within them is an important part of Oracle Power Objects development. Several methods are designed to give you the answer to questions such as the following:

☐ What is the container in which an object appears?

☐ What is the form in which an object appears? This is a slightly different question than the first, because an object can appear within a container that itself appears within a form. For example, a text field might appear within an embedded form, which itself appears within the form.

☐ What objects appear within a container?

☐ What forms and reports are contained within the application?

In other words, these methods help you discover what containers include which objects within your application. Calling these methods gives you a quick way to find all the objects within a form, or the form containing a particular object. The application itself is a container that holds all of the objects within that application.

Again, you have discovered a hierarchical relationship: The application contains a form, which in turn contains a repeater display. Within the repeater display is a panel that itself contains text fields and other objects. Because there are obvious levels to this relationship, you can use the term *object containment hierarchy* to describe it. The standard methods related to containment, such as GetTopContainer(), let you get references up and down this hierarchy.

The standard methods used to get these references include those shown in Table 16.1.

Table 16.1. Object containment methods.

Method	Applies To	Description
GetContainer()	Controls, embedded forms, repeater displays, classes, and static objects	Returns a reference to the container in which the object appears.
GetTopContainer()	Controls, embedded forms, repeater displays, classes, and static objects	Returns an object reference to the form or report (such as the top-level container) in which the object appears.

Method	Applies To	Description
FirstChild()	Containers	Returns a reference to an object within the container.
NextControl()	Containers	Returns a reference to another object within that container. You cannot call NextControl() before you call FirstChild(). If you call NextControl() repeatedly, you will return a reference to each object within the container.
GetFirstForm()	Applications	Returns a reference to a form in the application.
GetFormByName()	Applications	Returns a reference to a form or report, identified by name as an argument passed to this method.
GetNextForm()	Applications	Returns a reference to another form or report in the application.

In addition, there are two related methods that return references to recordsets and sessions:

Method	Applies To	Description
GetRecordset	Bindable containers	Returns a reference to the container's recordset.
GetSession	Recordsets	Returns a reference to the session through which the recordset accesses database objects.

Finally, Oracle Power Objects has some object identifiers for getting references to members of a containment hierarchy. You use these identifiers in method code and in some instances as property settings.

Identifier	Description
self	Refers to the object itself.
container	Refers to the object's container.
topcontainer	Refers to the form or report in which the object appears.

Using The Object Containment Methods

You have two options for calling the containment-related methods in your code: assigning an object reference to a variable, or chaining the method calls.

Assigning an Object Reference to a Variable

If you plan to refer to the same object repeatedly throughout your method code, you should assign the return value of the appropriate method to a variable of type `Object`.

For example, to change several different methods of the form in which an object appears, you might enter the following method code:

```
DIM vForm AS Object
vForm = self.GetTopContainer()
vForm.Label = "Working..."
vForm.ColorFill = 1
vForm.PositionX = 10
vForm.PositionY = 10
```

Chaining Method Calls

On the other hand, if you need to refer to the object only once, you can *chain* the calls to various containment-related methods. To chain method calls in this context, you use one method to get an object reference (for example, to a form), and then use the results of that method to get another object reference (to continue an example, to the form's recordset).

The following sample code illustrates this point by chaining some of these methods to move the pointer in a container's recordset to the first row:

```
self.GetContainer.GetRecordset.SetCurRow(1)
```

Or, if you want to add code to a pushbutton that calls the `CommitWork()` method of the form's session, you can enter the following code:

```
self.GetTopContainer.GetRecordset.GetSession.CommitWork()
```

As you can see, this technique gives you a quick shorthand for the layers of the object containment hierarchy, as well as the recordsets and sessions associated with containers.

Changing the Fonts on a Form

To illustrate how to use the object containment hierarchy, create a new class, `clsSetFont`, that lets you change the font used within a form. After you type in the name of a new font, the application cycles through all of the objects within the form and applies the new font to each one.

1. Create a new class named clsSetFont.
2. Add a text field to the class with the data type String and a DataSize of 32.
3. Add a static text object with the label New Font to the left of the text field.
4. Move and resize the class and its objects until it matches Figure 16.8.

Figure 16.8.
The clsSetFont class.

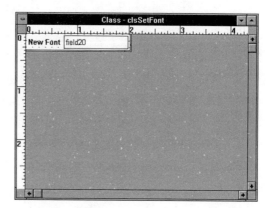

Because you can use the same procedure to change fonts in a form elsewhere in the application, you will create the procedure as a user-defined method.

5. Open the User Properties window and enter the following new method:

Section	Setting
Name	udmSetFont
Type	Subroutine
Arguments	ByVal vFontName As String, ByVal vContainer As Object

6. Add this new method to the text field appearing in the clsSetFont class.

Eventually, you will add code to call this method when the value in this text field changes. First, however, add the code to udmSetFont that changes the fonts used within a container.

7. Add the following method code to the udmSetFont method of the text field:

```
Sub udmSetFont (ByVal vFontName As String, ByVal vContainer As Object)
DIM vFlag AS Integer
DIM vControl AS Object
vFlag = 1
vControl = vContainer.FirstChild()
DO UNTIL x = 0
  IF ISNULL(vControl.NextControl()) THEN
    vFlag = 0
  ELSE
    vFlag = 1
```

```
' Get the type of control. If it's a text field, static
' text object, or something else that has a FontName property,
' change the font for that object
IF vControl.ControlType < 10 THEN
  vControl.FontName = vFontName
END IF
' Move to the next control in the container
vControl = vControl.NextControl()
  END IF
LOOP
```

8. Add the following method code to the PostChange() method of the text field in the clsSetFont class:

```
Sub PostChange()
Inherited.PostChange()
DIM vContainer AS Object
' Call the udmSetFont method on the class itself
vContainer =  self.GetContainer()
self.udmSetFont(self.Value, vContainer)

' Call the udmSetFont method on the form
vContainer = self.GetTopContainer()
self.udmSetFont(self.Value, vContainer)
```

9. Press Save.

10. Add an instance of the class to the form frmLogin.

11. Save and run the application.

   The Login form appears, including an instance of the new class, as shown in Figure 16.9.

Figure 16.9.

The Login form with an instance of clsSetFont.

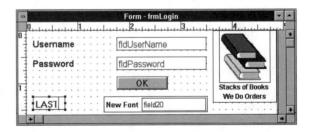

12. In the New Font field, enter Courier.

   The font used in all the static objects and text fields now changes to Courier.

13. Enter Arial for the new font.

14. Press Stop to end this exercise.

Because this class has been designed to be used on any report, you might experiment by adding it to other forms in the Bookstore application.

Creating a Customer Class

In both the Book Orders and Book Purchases forms, you needed to access records from the CUSTOMERS table. In both cases, you used an embedded form to display the customer information. Because you were adding essentially the same object—a container displaying customer records—you can replace the embedded form with a user-defined class bound to the same table.

When you develop applications, you often encounter cases in which information from the same table appears on several forms. By creating a class bound to this table, you simplify the task of adding this information to each form. If you decide to add further information about customers, such as their e-mail addresses, you only need to add a bound text field to the class to have this information available on every instance of the class. Similarly, if you want to remove customer information, such as that person's outstanding balance, you delete the appropriate text field from the master class definition.

If you want the information available without making it visible on the form, you add an instance of the class, and then set its `Visible` property to `FALSE`. As you saw in Day 15, invisible objects are often part of a scheme to enforce system security.

1. Create a new class, clsCustomerInfo.
2. Open the Table Editor window for CUSTOMERS.
3. Click and drag the following columns from CUSTOMERS onto the class: CUSTOMER_ID, LNAME, FNAME, and PHONE.

   The information from these columns represents the bare minimum of data you want to display about each customer.
4. Change the size, position, and appearance of the class and its objects until it looks like the one in Figure 16.10.

Figure 16.10.

The new customer information class.

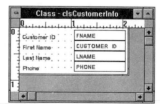

Because this class is designed to display information for a particular customer, represented by a CUSTOMER_ID value, you can design the class to be a detail of the form in which it appears. You can use the generic object identifier *container* to signify that the form in which an instance of this class appears is the master form in this relationship.

1. Set the following master-detail properties of the user-defined class:

Property	Setting
LinkMasterForm	CONTAINER
LinkColumn	CUSTOMER_ID
LinkDetailColumn	CUSTOMER_ID

2. Press Save to save the new class.

   Now that you have a generic class for displaying customer information, you can add the class to some forms.

3. Open the Book Orders form, frmBookOrders.

4. Delete the embedded form displaying customer information.

5. Add an instance of the new class, clsCustomerInfo, in the space previously occupied by the embedded form.

At this point, no further development work is necessary. The instance acts as a detail for the form, displaying the customer information matching whatever CUSTOMER_ID value you enter. To verify this, you can browse some of the orders already entered.

1. Save and run the form.

2. Use the scrollbar to move between records.

   As you move from one order to the next, the information about each customer appears in the instance of the clsCustomerInfo class.

3. Press Stop.

Next, you will add the new class to the Purchases form. Once again, no further work is needed to display information about each customer identified in the purchase.

1. Open the Book Purchases form, frmPurchases.

2. Remove the embedded form displaying customer information from frmPurchases.

3. Add an instance of clsCustomerInfo to the form.

4. Save and run the form.

5. Move among the purchases displayed in this form.

   As you scroll among purchases, the correct customer information appears in the class.

6. Press Stop to end this exercise.

Creating VCR Controls

Although scrollbars have been adequate controls for browsing records, they become less useful as the number of rows in a recordset increases. If you had over 1,000 orders entered through the

Book Orders form, you would not want to scroll through this many records to find a single purchase.

Instead of a scrollbar, you might use a VCR control to browse records. In this case, you would have four buttons:

- ☐ << takes you to the first record
- ☐ < takes you to the previous record
- ☐ > takes you to the next record
- ☐ >> takes you to the last record

The VCR type of control is common to many applications, including many database applications created with Microsoft Access or Microsoft Visual Basic. VCR controls do not provide every piece of functionality you need, but they are certainly better than scrollbars.

In this exercise, you will create two types of VCR controls. The first moves the pointer within the form to which an instance of the VCR control class has been added. The second is more generic and is capable of moving the pointer for any container's recordset.

1. Create a new class, clsVCR1.
2. Add four pushbuttons to the class, each with a SizeX and SizeY property of 0.25 inches.
3. Change the FontSize property of each pushbutton to 10, change the FontName property to Arial, and change FontBold to TRUE.
4. Add the following labels to the pushbuttons: <<, <, >, and >>.
5. Move the pushbuttons and resize the class so that it looks like the one in Figure 16.11.

Figure 16.11.
The finished appearance of clsVCR1.

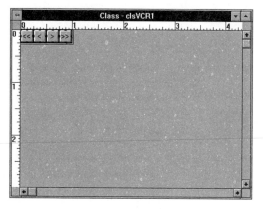

6. Add the following code to the `Click()` method of the leftmost pushbutton:

```
Sub Click()
' Move the pointer to the first record
self.GetTopContainer.GetRecordset.SetCurRow(1)
```

7. Add the following code to the `Click()` method of the next pushbutton to the right (displaying the label <):

```
Sub Click()
self.GetTopContainer.GoPrvLine()
```

In this case, you are calling a method of the form, `GoPrvLine()`, which moves the pointer in the form's recordset to the previous record.

8. Add the following code to the `Click()` method of the next pushbutton (displaying the label >):

```
Sub Click()
self.GetTopContainer.GoNxtLine()
```

9. Add the following method code to the `Click()` method of the last pushbutton:

```
Sub Click()
' Get the number of records in the recordset
DIM vNumRecs AS Long
vNumRecs = self.GetTopContainer.GetRecordset.GetRowCount()

' Move the pointer to the last row
self.GetTopContainer.GetRecordset.SetCurRow(vNumRecs)
```

10. Press Save.

11. Replace the scrollbar in the Employees form, frmEmployees, with an instance of the new class, clsVCR1.

12. Save and run the form.

13. Press the button labeled >> in the new VCR control.

    The pointer in the form's recordset moves to the last record.

14. Press the button labeled <.

    You now move the pointer to the previous record.

15. Press the << button.

    The pointer moves to the first record.

16. Press Stop.

17. Replace the scrollbar in other forms with the new VCR class.

18. Test the capability of the class to browse records in these other forms.

With a very small amount of work, you added a powerful alternative to the scrollbar.

Although the new control is very useful, it might not be generic enough. In some cases, you might want to use the VCR control to move among records displayed in any kind of container, including embedded forms and repeater displays. Therefore, in the next exercise, you will create a new VCR control class used to browse any container's recordset.

Creating a More Generic Browser

To create this more generic browser, follow these steps:

1. Create a new class, clsVCR2.
2. Copy the four pushbuttons you added to clsVCR1, and paste them into clsVCR2.
3. Resize the class so that its borders are flush against the four pushbuttons.

Again, you want a class large enough to contain these buttons, but no larger.

Before continuing work on the class itself, you need to add a new property to the class that identifies the container whose recordset you'll use the VCR control to browse.

1. Open the User Properties window and add the following entries:

Section	Setting
Name	udpContainer
Datatype	Object

2. Add this new property to the clsVCR2 class.

Be careful not to accidentally add the new property to one of the pushbuttons in the class.

Now that the class has this new property, you're ready to change the code appearing in the Click() methods of the four pushbuttons.

1. Replace the code for the << pushbutton's Click() method with the following code:

   ```
   Sub Click()
   DIM vContainer AS Object
   vContainer = self.GetContainer.udpContainer
   vContainer.GetRecordset.SetCurRow(1)
   ```

2. Replace the code in the < pushbutton's Click() method with the following code:

   ```
   Sub Click()
   self.GetContainer.udpContainer.GoPrvLine()
   ```

3. Next, replace the code in the Click() method of the > pushbutton with the following code:

   ```
   Sub Click()
   self.GetContainer.udpContainer.GoNxtLine()
   ```

4. Finally, change the code in the >> pushbutton's method to read as follows:

   ```
   Sub Click()
   DIM vContainer AS Object
   DIM vNumRecs AS Long
   vContainer = self.GetContainer.udpContainer
   vNumRecs = vContainer.GetRecordset.GetRowCount()
   vContainer.GetRecordset.SetCurRow(vNumRecs)
   ```

5. Press Save.

6. Open the form frmPubsBooks and add an instance of the new class just below the repeater display.

The form should now look like the one in Figure 16.12.

Figure 16.12.

The new VCR control class, clsVCR2, added to the form frmPubsBooks.

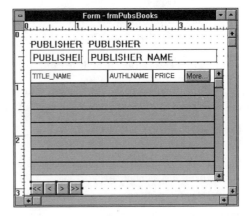

7. Open the Property sheet for the class instance and enter repBooks as the setting for the udpContainer property.

8. Save and run the form.

9. After the form appears, use the new VCR control to move the pointer among titles appearing in the repeater display.

10. Press Stop to end this exercise.

Adding an *ORDER BY* Capability to the Control

Next, you will add some more functionality to another incarnation of the VCR control. In this case, you add a pop-up list that lets you re-sort records in a container.

At this point, you want to keep the work you have done in clsVCR2, and simply add a list box to another version of this class. Therefore, instead of creating a brand new class, you will make the next set of VCR controls a subclass of clsVCR2. Therefore, if you make any changes to the code you added to the Click() method of each pushbutton, the subclass will inherit these changes.

1. In the application window, select the icon for clsVCR2.

2. Select the Edit | Create Subclass menu command.

Oracle Power Objects now creates a subclass of clsVCR2. Before continuing, you want to give this subclass a name that indicates its relationship to clsVCR2, as well as its special feature.

3. Give the subclass the name clsVCR2OrderBy.

4. Add two inches to the SizeX property of the subclass.

5. Move the > and >> pushbuttons to the right side of the subclass.

6. Add a new pop-up list to fill the space between the two pairs of pushbuttons.

7. Set the following properties of the pop-up list:

Property	Setting
Name	popOrderBy
Datatype	String
FontName	Arial
FontSize	10
FontBold	FALSE

Next, you need to add a user-defined method to the pop-up list. Whenever you make a selection from the pop-up list, the application calls this new method to re-sort the records in the container.

1. Open the User Properties window and add the following entries:

Section	Setting
Name	udmSortContainer
Type	Sub
Arguments	ByVal vContainer As Object, vOrderBy As String

2. Add the new method to the pop-up list.

Now that you have your method, you need a way to call it when the user selects something from the list.

3. In the PostChange() method of the pop-up list, enter the following code:

```
Sub PostChange()
Inherited.PostChange()

' Get a reference to the container
DIM vContainer AS Object
vContainer = self.GetContainer.udpContainer

' Call the method for resorting the container's recordset
self.udmSortContainer(vContainer, self.Value)
```

Next, you need to add code to the new method that sorts the container's recordset.

4. Add the following method code to the pop-up list's udmSortContainer() method:

```
Sub udmSortContainer(ByVal vContainer As Object, vOrderBy As String)
' Change the OrderBy property of the container
```

```
vContainer.OrderBy = vOrderBy

' Requery the container
vContainer.Query()
```

You now have finished developing the class itself. Although the point of this new subclass is to give the user the ability to re-sort records, you can't add this information to the master class definition. Instead, you will make the necessary adjustments to each instance of the class.

1. Add an instance of the class to the Book Orders form, frmBookOrders, just below the repeater display.

   The Book Orders form should now match Figure 16.13.

Figure 16.13.

The subclass clsVCROrderBy added to the Book Orders form.

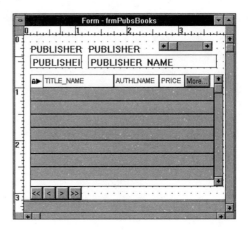

2. Open the Property sheet for the instance of clsVCROrderBy.

3. Set the udpContainer property to repTitles.

   The VCR control is now linked to the repeater display.

4. Open the Property sheet for the pop-up list in the class and enter the following code for its Translation property:

```
Translation
"Title" = TITLE_ID
"Number of copies" = QUANTITY
"Discount" = DISCOUNT
```

   In this syntax, the string values to the left of each equal sign define the display value for each item in the list, whereas the values on the right define the internal value.

5. Save and run the form.

6. Select an order with more than one line item.

7. In the VCR control's pop-up list, select each entry.

Figure 16.14.
Selecting the ORDER BY criterion through the class.

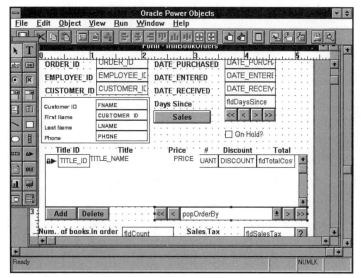

16

Each time you make a new selection, the application re-sorts the records in the repeater display according to the value in the TITLE_ID, QUANTITY, or DISCOUNT columns for each line item.

8. Press Stop to end this exercise.

Libraries

By now, you should be able to recite by heart the litany of reusability: "Whenever you design an object, property, or method, make it as reusable as possible." Keeping this litany in mind, you have designed classes generic enough to use on nearly all of the forms in the Bookstore application.

In fact, these classes are generic enough to use in *any* application. For example, the OK and Cancel pushbutton class, clsOKCancel, could easily appear in any type of application you design—from personal information managers to games, purchase order applications, and database administration tools.

Given that your classes have reached this pinnacle of reusability, they should no longer be defined within the Bookstore application. Instead, the definitions of the classes should live outside any one application, but should be usable in any application.

Oracle Power Objects lets you create a library as the repository for these types of highly reusable objects. A library is a file object, just like a session or an application. However, unlike applications, libraries can house only two types of objects—user-defined classes and bitmap

resources. Both classes and bitmaps can be designed for use in many different applications, so it makes sense that in many respects an Oracle Power Objects library serves the same purpose as a dynamic link library (DLL). As you learned on Day 11, DLLs store procedures that you can call from any application. Similarly, libraries in Oracle Power Objects store the definitions of objects that you can use in a variety of applications through dragging and dropping.

In future exercises, you will add the more generic classes to a new library, GENERAL.POL.

Summary

Today you learned about the following points:

☐ Classes are reusable application objects.

☐ When you want to add a copy of a class to a form or report, you are creating an instance of the class.

☐ Instances inherit changes to properties and methods in the master class definition.

☐ However, if you edit a property or method in an instance, that property or method no longer inherits the changes.

☐ You can add instances of classes to other classes, or you can create subclasses that inherit changes to the original class.

☐ Classes are bindable containers, so you can use them to display information from commonly used tables.

☐ Classes can also exist in a master-detail relationship with other containers.

☐ Some classes provide excellent replacements or enhancements to commonly used controls, such as recordset browsers or OK/Cancel buttons.

☐ The relationship between objects that contain other objects is called the object containment hierarchy. This hierarchy can be many levels deep.

☐ There are several standard methods in Oracle Power Objects for moving up and down the object containment hierarchy.

☐ The application itself is a type of container holding all the objects that comprise it.

What Comes Next?

Tomorrow, you will learn about a different type of reusability. Microsoft Windows has a technology called Object Linking and Embedding (OLE) that lets you use the same kinds of data across applications. Through OLE, you can paste an Excel spreadsheet into a Word document, or play a QuickTime for Windows movie in an Oracle Power Objects application.

OLE is one of the most versatile technologies in modern applications, so not surprisingly, it is highly popular among developers and users alike. You'll use some OLE data objects to jazz up the Bookstore application with graphics and sound, as well as add some new kinds of information to your book, customer, and order records.

Q&A

16

Q **Is there any theoretical limit to the number of classes I can add to a form?**

A Theoretically, there is no limit. However, if you add more than 10 or 15 classes, you might experience some drop in performance.

Q **Is there any limit to the length of the chain of propagation? Can I add one class inside another, inside another, *ad infinitum*?**

A Here is where you experience the greatest decrease in performance. If your object inheritance hierarchy is too deep, the application can slow down significantly as it tries to resolve references up and down the hierarchy. Therefore, although you should use classes liberally, you should be careful about creating too many subclasses and instances.

Q **Can I create too many classes?**

A As you saw in today's lesson, your application quickly fills up with classes after you learn to use them. That's fine. The more reusable your objects are, the more flexibility you enjoy as a developer. First-time developers are occasionally wary of adding too many new user-defined classes, but these are the building blocks of a good application. Also, remember that you can move some of the more generic classes into libraries for use in other applications.

Q **I'm having a hard time making a class more generic. What should I do?**

A You should always make your classes as reusable as possible, but you should not make your job as a developer harder by designing every one to be completely generic. If you find a particular class useful in one application but you can't easily generalize its design to work in other applications, that's fine. As long as the class simplified your work in one application, it has served its purpose.

Workshop

The Workshop consists of quiz questions to help you solidify your understanding of the material covered and exercises to give you experience in using what you've learned. Try and understand the quiz and exercise questions before you go on to tomorrow's lesson.

Quiz

1. What happens if you create a subclass, add it as an instance to another class, and then change a property in that instance?

2. Using what you know of classes, what is the most efficient way to create a set of controls for entering query conditions for a form?

Exercises

1. Replace the graphic appearing as the bookstore's logo with a new bitmap.

2. Create a class through which you can enter a query condition and then requery the container in which the instance appears.

Quiz Answers

1. The instance no longer inherits changes to the edited property made in either the original class or the subclass.

2. You can create the control as a class, used for selecting query conditions through list controls or entering them directly in a text field. You would then use the values from these controls to build a string that you pass to the `QueryWhere()` method or assign as the `DefaultCondition` property of the form.

17

Working with OLE Objects

You have already learned several ways to *extend* your application by adding new capabilities from outside the application itself. For example, you have learned how to call DLL procedures developed by other programmers to read and write .INI file entries, play sounds, and get the amount of available memory. Similarly, because user-defined classes can appear in any number of applications (if you design them correctly), you can use classes created by other developers in your application. Both kinds of extensibility (DLL procedures and classes) simplify your life as a developer by building on the work of others to add new features to your own application.

Today, you learn about the following topics:

- [ ] The fundamentals of OLE technology
- [ ] OLE and extensibility
- [ ] OLE data objects in your application
- [ ] OLE controls in Oracle Power Objects
- [ ] Storing OLE data in the database
- [ ] Using OLE for graphics
- [ ] Using OLE for charts
- [ ] Creating an employee performance report through OLE
- [ ] Adding sound through OLE
- [ ] Adding video through OLE
- [ ] OCX controls

What Users Want

From a user's standpoint, however, this kind of extensibility is totally invisible and mostly unappreciated. For users, an extensible application is one that incorporates features from other applications that they already know.

For example, nearly every Windows user has had some experience with Microsoft Word and Microsoft Excel. In fact, it's hard to find a Windows installation that does not include these two applications. What would make the user happy is to be able to use Microsoft Word (or some reasonable facsimile) inside another application to edit and format text. A user who already knows Word will be very happy not to have to learn some other text-editing tool, with its whole new array of commands and shortcuts, in order to handle some simple word processing chore.

Similarly, users might want to use Paintbrush to draw a simple graphic, or Excel to create a spreadsheet. In short, people do not like having to throw away their knowledge of other productivity applications such Word, Excel, PowerPoint, and others.

Although you might labor hard to add many of the capabilities of an application such as Excel, for the most part this work is wasted. Someone has already developed Excel, so why not use Excel itself? Thanks to OLE technology, you can.

What OLE Technology Can Do

An important technology underlying Microsoft Windows, *object linking and embedding (OLE)*, makes it possible to make Word, Excel, and similar applications part of your own application. Your application can store the word processing document, spreadsheet, or slide presentation, or provide a pointer to the file. You then view and edit this data through the application in which it was created (Word, Excel, PowerPoint, and so on). Figure 17.1 shows a Microsoft Word document appearing within an Oracle Power Objects application.

Figure 17.1.
A Microsoft Word document in an Oracle Power Objects application.

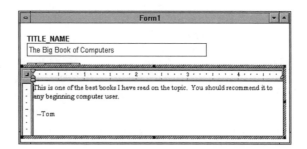

Not surprisingly, OLE technology is very popular. Application developers can take advantage of the powerful capabilities of complex applications such as Word and Excel to add features they would otherwise have to develop on their own. In turn, users can continue using their knowledge of these productivity applications.

In this lesson, you'll learn how to add OLE features to your application. Once again, you must learn some new concepts before adding a new feature to the Bookstore application.

OLE Technology: A Primer

As mentioned earlier, OLE stands for *object linking and embedding*. The name refers to two ways an application can provide access to data: by either *embedding* (that is, storing) it within the application itself, or providing a *link* to the file containing this data.

This might sound somewhat abstract at first. However, once you think about the relationship between your application and the productivity application used to view and edit the information, the concepts of linking and embedding should become clear.

Client and Server Applications

Unfortunately, the designers of OLE used the terms *client* and *server* to describe the two applications involved. However, in no way does this relationship resemble the client/server architecture of a database application. The server application is *not* a database, in the sense that the server in a client/server architecture is a relational database.

Instead, the *server* application is where OLE information is created and formatted. For Word documents, the server application is Word; for Excel spreadsheets, the server application is Excel.

The *client* application is a different application that stores or accesses the data created in the server application (or provides a link to it). When you add a Word document to an Oracle Power Objects application, your application becomes the client, and Word is the server. The only fair point of comparison between this use of the term *client* and its use in client/server computing is that the client application in OLE acts as a front end to the server application—a conduit through which you can access data defined according to the rules of the server application.

When you install an application that can act as an OLE server, it registers this fact with Microsoft Windows. Whenever you create a new OLE data object, the server application then appears in the list of data formats you can use. For example, after you install Microsoft Video for Windows, the entries QuickTime Picture and QuickTime Movie appear as formats for new OLE data objects. Figure 17.2 shows QuickTime movies registered as a type of OLE object in Microsoft Windows.

Figure 17.2.

QuickTime registered as an OLE data format.

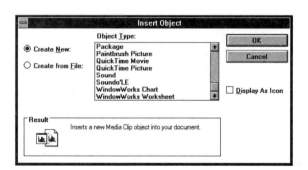

Practically speaking, it is possible to have never learned this terminology and still be able to use the OLE features of Oracle Power Objects. However, if you ever want to learn more about OLE, or use OLE features in other applications, you'll need to learn the standard language for describing OLE technology.

OLE Data Objects

What connects the client and server applications is an OLE data object. When you create a new graphic in Paintbrush, you are creating a piece of data in a special format. Because of this format, both the Windows environment and the many applications running under Windows can recognize this information for what it is—a graphic created in Paintbrush. Similarly, Word creates data objects formatted to be Word documents, and Excel creates data objects formatted to be Excel spreadsheets. You often store the data in a file—a .BMP file for Paintbrush; a .DOC file for Word; and an .XLS file for Excel.

However, as you will see, this is not the only place where this information can be stored. Therefore, it's important to remember the difference between the data itself and the file in which it might be stored. If you need to, chant this mantra to yourself: *The file is not the data; the file stores the data.*

Where else can you store this information? A database is one location, as you'll see in an exercise in today's lesson. In addition, the application itself can store the data by embedding it.

Embedded Objects

When you add an OLE data object to an application, you have the choice of linking or embedding it. If you embed it, the data object becomes part of the application object. For example, if you embed an OLE data object in a form, the OLE data is stored as part of the form's definition. When you save the form, the OLE data object is saved along with it.

Embedded objects can be edited at runtime, but you cannot save these changes when you close down the application. If you add an embedded Paintbrush graphic, the user might be able to edit the graphic. Once the application closes, however, the application would eliminate these changes.

Therefore, embedded objects are useful when you want to create an OLE object that the user can view, but should not edit. If you want to replace the imported bitmap you used as a logo with an OLE object, you should embed the object.

Linked Objects

In contrast, a *linked object* is actually stored in a file. When you add a linked OLE data object to your application, you are in fact storing a reference to where the application can find the file. (Therefore, you should not move this file into another directory, or accidentally delete it. For

example, if you create a Word document as a linked data object, the document would be stored in an operating system file somewhere on your hard disk or a network drive.

You use a linked object when you want to give the user of the application the ability to save changes to the data object. In a later exercise, you'll give the user the ability to add a personal icon to the Bookstore application. Because you need to be able to save the new bitmap, or save any later changes to it, you need to create it as a linked object. The .BMP file is then stored in a local or networked directory, available for further modifications.

Displaying the Data Object

After you add an OLE data object, whether it is embedded or linked, the application displays it in one of two ways:

- As an icon, using the matching icon for the server application
- As itself, including text for a word processor, a picture for a graphics editor, and so on

Figure 17.3 shows OLE data objects displayed normally and as an icon.

Figure 17.3.
Icons for OLE data objects.

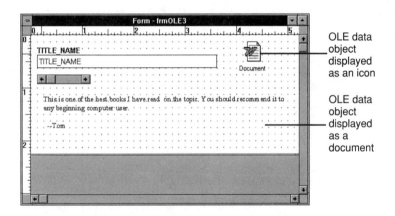

OLE data object displayed as an icon

OLE data object displayed as a document

Many data objects cannot be displayed as anything but an icon. A sound file cannot be displayed; it can only be played through its server application.

Launching the Server Application

Having the server application installed on the PC running your application is an important precondition of using an OLE data object. If you want to view a QuickTime video, for example, you need to have the QuickTime viewer installed on your system.

If you plan on adding OLE features to your application, you should make sure that everyone in your organization who might be using the application has the necessary server applications installed on their systems. Although you might make the courageous assumption that everyone has Word or Excel installed, you do not want to frustrate those users who for whatever reason (accidental deletion, a new PC, and so on) do not have these OLE server applications installed.

To launch the server application needed to view an OLE data object, you double-click the icon for the data object. In many cases, a simplified version of the server application's interface appears. For example, as shown in Figure 17.4, not all the components of the Microsoft Word interface appear when you double-click a Word document.

Figure 17.4.
The simplified OLE server interface for Word.

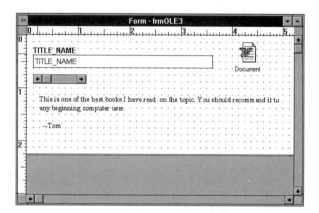

Not only can you view the OLE data object, but you can also edit it at this point. If the data object is linked, you can save your changes to the operating system file in which it is stored. In addition, if you are storing this object in a table, you can save your changes by committing them to the database.

A Quick Summary

Because there are a lot of potentially tricky concepts involved in OLE, I will stop to summarize them briefly before discussing how to use OLE in an Oracle Power Objects application.

- ☐ *OLE data objects* are pieces of data formatted for a particular application.
- ☐ The *server application* is where you define the new object. For example, a Word document uses Microsoft Word as its server application.
- ☐ The *client application* is where the OLE data object is used. Your Oracle Power Objects application will be the client for a Word document.
- ☐ OLE data objects are *embedded* when they are stored within the application itself.

☐ OLE data objects are *linked* when they are stored in an operating system file. In this case, the application contains a pointer to the location of the file.

☐ Before you can view and edit an OLE data object, you must have the server application installed on your system.

☐ To launch the server application from the client, you double-click the data object's icon.

With this knowledge under your belt, you're ready to see how to use OLE data objects in an Oracle Power Objects application.

OLE in Oracle Power Objects

You can use OLE data objects in Oracle Power Objects in a variety of ways. Before adding OLE capabilities to your application, however, you must have installed the special OLE DLLs that come with Oracle Power Objects. If you did not do a complete installation of Oracle Power Objects, including these DLLs, you need to run the Setup program again to add the necessary DLLs to your system.

OLE Controls

The primary vehicle for displaying OLE data objects is an *OLE control*, a special kind of standard control. The OLE control is itself one of the simpler standard controls, with only a few properties and methods. However, the variety of OLE data objects that you can store and display through this control is huge—limited only by the OLE server applications you have installed on your system.

OLE controls can display both linked and embedded objects. In addition, because the control is bindable, you can use it to store data objects in a table, and then query these objects for display in the application.

Binding OLE Controls

In a database application, the ability to store OLE data objects is crucial because it removes the two problems associated with saving OLE data in the client operating system. First, because the data is not stored in an operating system file, the user cannot unwittingly delete this file. Because the OLE data object is stored in the database, the user must explicitly delete this data and then commit the deletion before the data actually is deleted. Contrast this situation with how likely it is that a careless DEL command in DOS or a File Manager delete operation will eliminate a file containing a linked OLE data object.

Second, the OLE data stored in a database benefits from all the security features offered by the application and the server. For example, in an exercise in today's lesson, you'll write employee performance evaluations in Microsoft Word, but the Word documents themselves will be saved in the Blaze database BOOKS.BLZ. Getting the file out of Blaze takes more work than simply running Microsoft Word and looking for a likely DOC file on the hard drive. In the case of SQL Server and Oracle7, both of which require that you log in with a username and password before you access any data, the level of protection is that much higher.

Requirements for Bound OLE Controls

There are only two requirements for binding an OLE control to a column:

- ☐ The column must use the Long Raw data type.
- ☐ The OLE data object must be embedded, not linked.

OLE Resources

Like bitmaps, OLE data objects can be application resources. If you add an OLE data object as a resource, it appears in the Application window alongside imported bitmaps, classes, forms, and reports, as shown in Figure 17.5.

Figure 17.5.
An imported OLE
data object.

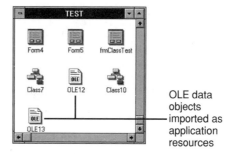

OLE data objects imported as application resources

Generally, you add an OLE object as an application resource only if you expect it to appear in many places in an application, but you do not want the user to edit it. (Once you import the OLE data object, it becomes compiled with the rest of the application.) For example, if you want to play an animation whenever the user opens one of several forms, you would import the OLE data object containing the animation into the application. You can then add the OLE resource to the forms in which you want the OLE data object to appear.

Launching the Server Application

As described earlier, you can launch an OLE data object's server application by double-clicking the icon for the data object. In fact, this icon is displayed in an OLE control, so you are actually

double-clicking the OLE control. Part of the `Double-click()` method's default processing is to open the appropriate server application if you are double-clicking an OLE control.

This situation gives you the ability to launch the server application from your own application through method code, or to make it impossible to launch the server application. As a developer, you can control whether the application launches the server application or not:

☐ To launch the server application, simply call the OLE control's `Double-click()` method.

☐ To prevent the server application from launching, add any code to the OLE control's `Double-click()` method that does not call the method's default processing. Note that setting the OLE control's `ReadOnly` property to `TRUE` or its `Enabled` property to `FALSE` does *not* prevent the user from launching the server application by double-clicking the OLE control.

The Flexibility of OLE Controls

When you create a new OLE control, Oracle Power Objects asks you about the type of OLE data you want to display in it (.WAV file, Paintbrush picture, Word document, and so on). However, the control can show any type of OLE object, not just the type you initially display in it.

This feature of OLE controls is especially important for bound controls. If you normally write your employee's performance evaluations in Word, you can switch to a different word processor, as long as it acts as an OLE server. The OLE control can store both documents, which can then be saved to the database.

In fact, you could store a QuickTime movie, a PowerPoint presentation, or a Paintbrush picture instead of a word processing document. The OLE control doesn't care, as long as the proper server application is installed.

Creating an OLE Graphic

Now that you know the basics of OLE controls in Oracle Power Objects, you are ready to create your first one. In this exercise, you'll add a personal icon to the Bookstore application.

First, however, you'll get some practice working with OLE data objects and controls. In this exercise, you'll add an embedded OLE data object to display a simple graphic on a form. Here are the steps to follow:

1. Launch the Microsoft Paintbrush application.

2. Select the Options | Image Attributes menu command.

3. Set the width and height of the new graphic to 1 inch.

4. Close Paintbrush.

   When you create the new OLE control, you need the size of the Paintbrush graphic already configured. Now that Paintbrush will use a default size of 1-inch by 1-inch the next time it creates a bitmap, you're ready to continue.

5. In Oracle Power Objects, open the splash screen form, frmSplash.

6. Select the OLE Control drawing tool from the Object palette.

7. Create a small OLE control somewhere on the form.

   The Insert Object dialog box now appears, as shown in Figure 17.6. This is a standard dialog box in Windows, used whenever you create new OLE data objects or copy them into an application. If you use the OLE features of other applications, such Microsoft Word, you'll see this same dialog box.

Figure 17.6.
The Insert Object dialog box.

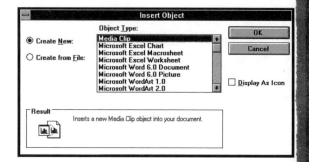

In the Insert Object dialog box, the type of OLE data object you want to create appears in the scrolling list. In addition, this dialog box asks whether you want to create a new data object or import the data from an operating system file. In this case, you want a brand new graphic; therefore, leave the Create New and Create from File radio button pair untouched.

8. From the scrolling list of object types, select Paintbrush picture.

9. Press OK. Windows now launches Paintbrush automatically.

10. In Paintbrush, draw a dollar sign ($) or some other icon for money. (You're not being graded on your artistic talents, so don't worry how your graphic looks.)

11. Select the File menu.

    As shown in Figure 17.7, the menu commands are different. Because Paintbrush has been opened as the interface for editing an OLE object, its menu options are slightly different.

12. Select File | Update. (This menu command updates the OLE data object stored in the OLE control.)

Figure 17.7.
The modified File menu for Paintbrush.

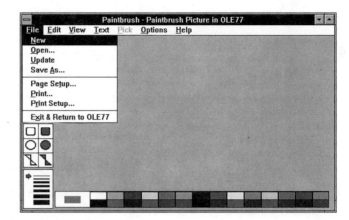

13. Close Paintbrush.

    The OLE control now displays the graphic you just drew. The data object is embedded, not linked, because you did not associate it with any operating system file that might contain a bitmap.

14. Open the Property sheet for the OLE control.

    As you can see, the OLE control has many of the familiar properties and methods associated with other objects. Most conspicuously missing, however, is a Value property.

15. Enter oleDollarBMP as the name of the OLE control.

    As you can tell, you'll be using the prefix ole in the naming convention for OLE controls. In addition, when appropriate, you'll add the filename extension for the type of data as a suffix. In this case, because the OLE data object is a Paintbrush picture, you are adding the BMP suffix to signify that this bitmap might be stored in a .BMP file.

16. Save and run the form. The new graphic now appears on the Book Purchases form.

17. Double-click the OLE control. Paintbrush now launches again.

18. Make some modification to the graphic and then select File | Update.

19. Close Paintbrush. Notice that the currency symbol icon you added is now changed.

20. Press Stop.

The form now returns to design mode. However, the changes you made to the graphic at runtime have disappeared. What happened?

As you should remember, embedded OLE data objects can be modified at runtime, but the application cannot save these changes. The OLE control gives you access to the data object, but it does not give you the means to save changes to it. However, you'll change that situation in the next exercise.

Caution: In the version 1.04 release of Oracle Power Objects, object linking does not work. If you plan to use this feature, you should download the patch that fixes this problem from the Oracle website, HTTP://WWW.ORACLE.COM.

Personalizing the Bookstore Application

As mentioned earlier, you'll be giving the user the ability to personalize the Bookstore application by adding an icon of the user's design. First, create the icon as a BMP file:

1. Open Paintbrush and select Options | Image Attributes.
2. Select 0.75 inches for both the width and height.
3. Save the file as C:\BOOKS\ME.BMP.
4. Delete the OLE control you added to the form frmSplash in the last exercise.
5. Add a new OLE control to this form. The Insert Object dialog box appears again (see Figure 17.8).

Figure 17.8.
The Insert Object dialog box, which appears when you create an OLE data object from a file.

6. Select the Create from File option. The scrolling list of data object types disappears; it is replaced by some new options.
7. Check the Link check box.
8. Press the Browse pushbutton. The common dialog box for selecting a directory and file appears.
9. Select the ME.BMP file you just created in the C:\BOOKS directory.
10. Press OK. The icon now appears in the form.

11. Make some room on the left side of the splash screen and position the OLE control there.

12. Save and run the form.

    As shown in Figure 17.9, the graphic appears in the splash screen when the application launches.

Figure 17.9.

The personalized graphic that appears in frmSplash.

OLE graphic
added to the form ————

Now, every time you run the application, the splash screen will appear with your personalized graphic.

13. Double-click the OLE control. Windows now launches Paintbrush, displaying ME.BMP.

14. Make some change to ME.BMP and save the file.

15. Close Paintbrush. The modified personal icon now appears in the form.

16. Press Stop, and then run the form again.

    Because you saved your changes to the graphic in the ME.BMP file, the modified graphic appears in the OLE control.

17. Press Stop to end this exercise.

Adding Sound to Your Application

In this exercise, you'll create your first OLE data object as an application resource. The goal is to play a sound whenever the user opens a form. To add this feature, you'll use the built-in sound features of Windows by playing a .WAV file.

Because .WAV files store sounds that are playable through Windows, they appear in the scrolling list of OLE data object types in the Insert Object dialog box. However, unlike many other OLE data object types, WAV sounds are not identified by the server application. Instead, .WAV files appear simply as *Sound* in this list.

Because you'll be adding the sound to several forms, you'll add the OLE control that stores the sound in a class instead of in the form itself. This makes it easier to change the sound later.

To add sound to the Bookstore application, follow these steps:

1. Launch the Windows application Sound Recorder and open the file C:\WINDOWS\TADA.WAV.

   The filename for Sound Recorder is SOUNDREC.EXE.

2. Select Edit | Copy; then close Sound Recorder.

3. Select the Application window for BOOKS.POA.

4. Select Edit | Paste Special.

   If there is an OLE data object in the Clipboard, this menu command is enabled. Once you select it, the Paste Special dialog box appears.

5. Without making any changes in this dialog box, press OK. A window containing an icon for the sound file now appears, as shown in Figure 17.10.

Figure 17.10.
TADA.WAV being added to the BOOKS.POA application.

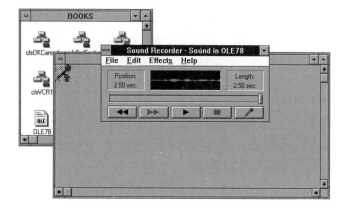

6. When Sound Recorder appears, select File | Update.

   Oracle Power Objects now asks whether you want to save this new OLE object as part of the application. Press OK to continue. The new OLE object now appears in the Application window as another resource (see Figure 17.11).

Figure 17.11.
The new OLE data object appearing as a resource in the Application window for BOOKS.POA.

7. Create a new class, clsStartupSound.

8. Drag into the class the icon for the new OLE resource.

   Oracle Power Objects now creates an OLE control containing the data object for TADA.WAV.

9. Resize the class until it is about 1-inch high by 1-inch wide.

10. Change its `Visible` property to `False`.

11. Drag into the class the OLE resource you just added to the application.

   An instance of this OLE data object now appears within the class. Oracle Power Objects automatically creates an OLE control to display this object.

12. Rename the OLE control `oleSound` and press Save.

Next, you'll add some instances of the class to forms in the application.

1. Open the form frmLogin.

2. Drag the class clsStartupSound from the Application window into this form to create an instance.

3. Add the following to the `OnLoad()` method for frmLogin:

   ```
   Sub OnLoad()
   clsStartupSound.oleSound.DoubleClick()
   ```

4. Open the Book Purchases form, frmPurchases, and add an instance of clsStartupSound to it.

5. Add the same line of code to the form's `OnLoad()` method.

6. Save and run the application.

   Now, when the application launches and opens the login form, the "tada" sound plays.

7. After logging in as `vbond/antwerp`, open the Book Purchases form. The sound plays again.

8. Press Stop to end this exercise.

Changing the Sound

You might decide that the "tada" sound will get annoying if it is played too often. Therefore, in this exercise you'll substitute a different sound for it. Follow these steps:

1. Repeat the steps in the earlier exercise to add CHORD.WAV to the application.

2. Drag the icon for the new OLE data object from the Application window into the OLE control in clsStartupSound.

Oracle Power Objects asks if you want to replace the contents of the OLE control with the new data object. That's the whole point of this exercise, so press OK to continue.

3. Save and run the application.

Now, when the login form appears, the application plays a different sound. The same sound will play when you open the Book Purchases form because the instance of clsStartupSound in that form inherits the change to the master class.

4. Press Stop.

Binding an OLE Control

Now that you have used an OLE control to add some trivial features to the Bookstore application, it's time to work on some more substantial applications of this technology. In this exercise, you'll write some employee performance evaluations using Microsoft Word as the server application. Once you have finished, you'll save these reports as part of an employee's record in the database.

Because Microsoft Word is one of the most popular word processors on the market, it makes sense to use it as the server application. However, if you do not have Word installed on your system, you can substitute some other OLE-enabled word processor for this exercise.

Because you might write several performance evaluations for an employee over the course of her career at the bookstore, you'll need to create a new table, EMPLOYEE_EVALS, to store this information. This table is designed to be a detail of the EMPLOYEES table, so it must have an EMPLOYEE_ID column in it to act as the foreign key. In addition, you'll add a date stamp for every evaluation. Follow these steps:

1. Open the session window for BOOKS.POS and double-click the Connector icon.

2. Add the following columns to the EMPLOYEES table:

Name	Data Type
EVAL_CREATED	Date
EVAL_LAST_REVISED	Date
EVAL_DOC	Long Raw

3. Save the modified table to the database.

4. Open the employees form, frmEmployees.

5. Drag the columns EMPLOYEE_ID, EVAL_CREATED, and EVAL_LAST_REVISED from the EMPLOYEE_EVALS table into the form.

6. Set the ReadOnly property of these fields to TRUE. (You'll set these dates automatically in the completed form.)

7. Add an OLE data control to the form.

8. For the OLE data object type, select Microsoft Word 6.0 document (or whatever OLE-enabled word processor you have installed).

9. Select the Display As Icon option and press OK.

The word processor now appears. Instead of entering the employee evaluation document now, you'll save a blank document in the control.

10. In Word, select File | Update to save the blank document in the control; then close Word. The new form should now look like the one shown in Figure 17.12.

Figure 17.12.
The Word document added to the form.

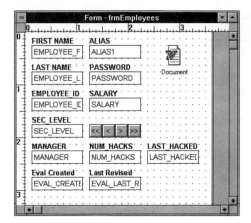

11. Select the new OLE control and open its Property sheet.

12. Name the control oleEvalForm and enter EVAL_DOC for its DataSource property.

The control is now bound to the EVAL_DOC column in the EMPLOYEE_EVALS table. Because this column uses the Long Raw data type, it can store the Microsoft Word document as an OLE data object.

13. Add the following method code to the InsertRow() method of the form:

```
Sub InsertRow()
' Allow the insertion of a new row into the recordset
Inherited.InsertRow()

' Enter today as the EVAL_CREATED date
EVAL_CREATED.Value = NOW()
```

14. Add the following method code to the form's ValidateRow() method:

```
Function ValidateRow(rownum As Long) As Long
' If the evaluation has been revised, record the date of the
' last revision in the EVAL_LAST_REVISED column
IF FORMAT(EVAL_CREATED.Value, "mm/dd/yy" <> FORMAT(NOW, "mm/dd/yy") THEN
  EVAL_LAST_REVISED = NOW
END IF
```

```
' Allow the change
ValidateRow = TRUE
Inherited.ValidateRow(rownum)
```

This code uses the Oracle Basic function FORMAT to trim the time from the date value before making the comparison. Otherwise, if you create the new evaluation at 10:00 a.m. and finish writing it at 11:00 a.m., the application will mistakenly conclude that the first draft was in fact a later revision!

15. Save and run the application.

16. Log in as jboss/daboss. (As store manager, you can open the Employees form.)

17. Select Setup | Employees to open frmEmployees.

18. In the form, double-click the OLE control for employee evaluations.

19. Type in a short hypothetical evaluation report and then select File | Update. Word now updates the OLE data object stored in the OLE control.

20. Close Microsoft Word. A new row now appears in the repeater display, including both the date you entered the evaluation as well as the Microsoft Word document.

21. Press the Commit pushbutton. The form now saves the evaluation in the EMPLOY-EES table.

22. Press Stop to end this exercise.

As you can see, with a trivial amount of work, you were able to add Microsoft Word to your application. In addition, you were able to save a new Word document in the database.

Creating a Template for Employee Evaluations

What if you want to use a standard format for employee evaluations? When you write evaluations in a standard format, you want to make sure that other managers also use this format. To standardize these documents, you can create a template, saved as an operating system file, that you apply to any new evaluation report.

To add this feature, you'll call some standard methods designed exclusively for manipulating OLE data objects and the files in which they are stored.

1. Launch Microsoft Word.

2. In the blank page, enter the standard sections that you want included in every employee evaluation. A sample template is shown in Figure 17.13.

3. Save the new document as C:\BOOKS\EVAL1.DOC.

4. Open frmEmployees and add a new OLE control to the lower-right section of the form. (The exact size and position of this object is unimportant because it will be invisible.)

Figure 17.13.

A sample employee evaluation template.

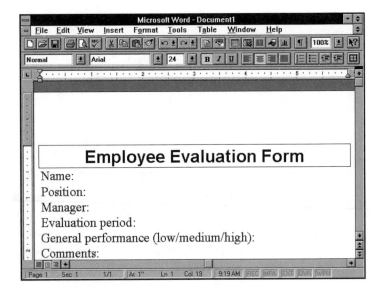

5. In the Insert Object dialog box, select the Create from File option, but do not check the Link check box.

6. After pressing Browse, select C:\BOOKS\EVAL1.DOC.

7. Press OK.

    You'll now add a new embedded OLE data object to the form, displayed in an OLE control. The OLE data object is a copy of the evaluation template you just created.

8. Name the OLE control oleTemplate and set its other properties to the following settings:

Property	Setting
Visible	False
ScrollWithRow	True

9. Add two new buttons, btnTemplate and btnSaveTemplate, to the lower-right side of the form.

10. For both buttons, set FontSize to 9, FontName to Arial, and FontBold to TRUE.

11. Set the Label property of btnTemplate to Template and the other pushbutton's to Save.

Before continuing, you need to create the file from which the application will read the template. Unfortunately, this file cannot be the original DOC file; instead, you need to create a new file that uses a special file format used by OLE controls in Oracle Power Objects.

With the pushbuttons added, the form should look like the one shown in Figure 17.14.

Figure 17.14.
*The modified form
frmEmpEvals.*

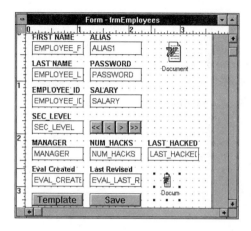

1. Add the following method code to the Click() method of btnSaveTemplate:

```
Sub Click()
' Open the file for access
DIM vFileNum AS Long
vFileNum = FREEFILE
OPEN "C:\BOOKS\TEMPLATE.TPL" FOR BINARY AS vFileNum

' Copy the template into the file
oleTemplate.WriteToFile(vFileNum)
CLOSE

' Disable the button
self.Enabled = FALSE
```

This code uses some Oracle Basic commands for changing the contents of an operating system file. In particular, the OPEN command opens the file for access or creates it if it cannot find the file in the specified directory.

2. Save and run the form.

3. Press the Save pushbutton.

Oracle Power Objects now creates the new file, TEMPLATE.TPL, containing the OLE data object contained in oleTemplate.

4. Press Stop.

5. Enter the following code in the Click() method of btnTemplate:

```
Sub Click()
' Open the file
DIM vFileNum AS Long
vFileNum = FREEFILE
OPEN "C:\BOOKS\TEMPLATE.TPL" FOR BINARY AS vFileNum

' Read the template from the file
oleTemplate.ReadFromFile(vFileNum)
CLOSE
```

```
' Enabled the Save pushbutton
btnSaveTemplate.Enabled = TRUE

' Open Microsoft Word
oleTemplate.DoubleClick()
```

6. Set the `Enabled` property of btnSaveTemplate to `FALSE`.

7. Open the Property sheet for the form.

8. Enter the following code in the form's `InsertRow()` method:

```
Sub InsertRow()
Inherited.InsertRow()

' Read the template from the file
DIM vFileNum AS Long
vFileNum = FREEFILE
OPEN "C:\BOOKS\TEMPLATE.TPL" FOR BINARY AS vFileNum

' Read the template from the file
oleEvalForm.ReadFromFile(vFileNum)
CLOSE
```

9. Save and run the application.

10. After logging in as the store manager, open the Employees form.

11. Press the Template pushbutton.

    Microsoft Word appears, displaying the current template for writing employee evaluations.

12. Make some change to the employee evaluation template.

13. Select File | Update, and then close Microsoft Word.

14. In the Employee Evaluations form, press Save.

    The application now saves the modified evaluation template to the TEMPLATE.TPL file.

15. Insert a new employee record.

16. Double-click the OLE control in the empty row to add a new evaluation for this employee. Microsoft Word now appears, displaying the modified template.

17. Enter some information about the employee and select File | Update.

18. After closing Word, press Commit. Another record for the employee is added to the EMP_EVALUATIONS table.

19. Press Stop to end this exercise.

OLE-Related Methods

The `WriteToFile()` and `ReadFromFile()` methods are two of several OLE-related standard methods in Oracle Power Objects. See Table 17.1 for the complete list.

Table 17.1. Standard methods related to OLE.

Method	Description
CanPasteFromClipboard()	Returns TRUE if an OLE data object is in the Clipboard; otherwise, returns FALSE.
OLEInsertObject()	Creates a new OLE data object by opening the Insert Object dialog box.
PasteFromClipboard()	Pastes an OLE object from the Clipboard into an OLE control.
ReadFromFile()	Reads the contents of a file into an OLE control. The file must have been created through the WriteToFile() method to have the proper format. This method takes a single argument: the file number of the file.
WriteToFile()	Writes the contents of an OLE object to a file. Again, this method's single argument is the file number of the file.

You call all of these methods from the OLE control itself. For example, in the previous exercise, you read the OLE data object stored in a file into of an OLE control with the following statement:

```
self.ReadFromFile(vFileNum)
```

In this case, vFileNum is a variable that holds the file number.

File I/O and Oracle Basic

You might be wondering why you needed to assign this file number. Why not use the filename instead?

Oracle Basic was designed to be 100 percent compliant with the standard Basic language promoted by Microsoft. The rationale was to make it easy for users of other development tools that use Basic as its coding language (such as Microsoft Visual Basic and Microsoft Access) to learn how to code in Oracle Power Objects. All of the commands, functions, and operators in Oracle Basic follow this standard.

Unfortunately, this means that you need to use the standard Basic commands for working with files. These commands have been part of Basic for decades, and they are undoubtedly the most confusing part of the language.

This section won't recap all of the file input and output (I/O) Basic commands. However, I'll take a moment to explain the ones used earlier in your method code.

Assigning a File Number

Before you can do anything with a file, you must reserve a number for it. In Oracle Basic, you can simply assign a number of your choosing, or you can use the FREEFILE function to return an available file number. FREEFILE returns 1 to start, but it increments the number returned by 1 each time it is called within the same method. If you call FREEFILE twice, it returns 2 the second time, 3 the third time, and so on.

Opening a File

Next, you need to open a file. When you use the OPEN command to open the file, you need to identify it by name, and you also need to specify the type of access you want to use. For example, your earlier code opened the file in BINARY access mode. Other modes include RANDOM, INPUT, OUTPUT, and APPEND. In addition, you can lock the file when you open it, preventing other applications from opening it.

For a full explanation of the options for OPEN, see the topic covering this Basic command in the online help.

Closing a File

Once you have finished reading data from a file or writing new data to it, you must close the file. Not surprisingly, you use the CLOSE command in this case, specifying the file by number you wish to close. (You could easily have several files open from within the same method, so you need to specifically identify any file you close.)

DO	DON'T

DO use OLE to add features to your application.

DO explain the OLE features of your application in your documentation. If users are not familiar with using OLE, they might be confused by seeing a hybrid interface: half your application, and half some other one.

DO use linked objects stored in files if you plan to display only a single version of the OLE control in the form.

DO use a Blaze database to store some multimedia OLE data objects to avoid too much traffic across the network. OLE data objects can be large, and querying a table with a large number of them stored in a Long Raw column can add a significant burden to the system.

DON'T rely too heavily on very complex OLE applications such as Word and Excel. Although you can use them judiciously in your application, adding OLE data objects for several such objects can slow down the application's performance significantly. If you want to perform some simple text editing, you don't need all the features of Word, so find an OLE server application that is less demanding on your users' systems.

DON'T add more than two OLE controls to a form. Not only will additional controls hurt performance, but having too many OLE server applications popping up from the same form can be confusing to the user.

Reading and Writing the Contents of a File

Earlier in this lesson, you used the methods ReadFromFile() and WriteToFile() to read and write the contents of a file containing an OLE data object. Although these methods were useful for working with OLE information, you could not use them to read other types of data stored in a file.

Instead, depending on the type of access mode you used to open a file, you want to use the GET, INPUT, or LINE INPUT command to read the contents of the file. Similarly, depending on the access mode, you want to use the PUT, WRITE, or PRINT command to write data to a file.

There are several other commands related to manipulating files. For a complete list, use the search keyword *file management* in the Oracle Power Objects online help.

Adding an OLE Spreadsheet to Your Application

By now, adding any type of OLE data to your application should be easy for you. To test this, you'll display the monthly store budget in an OLE spreadsheet. Follow these steps:

1. Create a new table, BUDGETS, with the following columns:

Column	Data Type	NOT NULL
BUDGET_ID	Number	No
DATE_CREATED	Date	Yes
DATE_LAST_REVISED	Date	No
BUDGET_XLS	Long Raw	No

2. Set the BUDGET_ID column as the primary key and then save the table.

3. Create a new form, frmBudgets.

4. Click and drag the BUDGET_ID, DATE_CREATED, and DATE_LAST_REVISED columns onto the form.

5. Add an instance of the class clsVCR2 to the form; set the form's `RowFetchMode` property to `Fetch all immediately`. (As you should remember, the clsVCR2 control class replaces the scrollbar for database browsing.)

6. Add a new OLE control to the form.

7. Set the OLE object type to Microsoft Excel Worksheet and then press OK. (You have now added an embedded Excel spreadsheet to the form.)

8. Name the OLE control `oleBudgetXLS` and set its `DataSource` property to `BUDGET_XLS`.

9. In BOOKS.POS, create a new index, SEQ_BUDGET_ID, with a starting number of 1 and an increment of 1.

   Now that you have the sequence, you'll use it to generate new BUDGET_ID values.

10. Open the Property sheet for the `BUDGET_ID` text field and set `CounterType` to `Sequence` and `CounterSeq` to `SEQ_BUDGET_ID`.

11. Add the following code to the form's `InsertRow()` method:

```
Sub InsertRow()
' Set the DATE_ENTERED to today's date
DATE_ENTERED.Value = NOW
```

12. Set the `ReadOnly` property of the `DATE_ENTERED` and `DATE_LAST_REVISED` fields to `TRUE`.

    Finally, you need to enter the code that updates `DATE_LAST_REVISED` whenever you edit a budget.

13. Enter the following code in the form's `ValidateRow()` method:

```
Function ValidateRow(rownum As Long) As Long
' If the evaluation has been revised, record the date of the
' last revision in the EVAL_LAST_REVISED column
IF FORMAT(DATE_CREATED.Value, "mm/dd/yy" <> FORMAT(NOW, "mm/dd/yy") THEN
   DATE_LAST_REVISED = NOW
END IF

' Allow the change
ValidateRow = TRUE
Inherited.ValidateRow(rownum)
```

14. Save and run the form.

15. Press Insert Row to create a new budget.

16. Select the OLE control and insert a new worksheet as an OLE object. (Remember, you select Edit | Insert Object to open the dialog box for inserting OLE data objects.)

17. When the spreadsheet appears, enter a sample budget.

18. In Excel, select File | Update and then File | Exit.

19. Press Commit to save the new budget to the database.

20. Press Stop to end this exercise.

At this point, you might also want to add a menu command to Setup for opening this form. If you do, you can protect this form from unauthorized access by using the techniques from Day 15. (Only the store manager and perhaps the assistant managers should view the store budget.)

OLE Charts Versus the Chart Control

At this point, you might be tempted to use the chart capabilities of Excel or a similar program to replace the Chart tool in Oracle Power Objects. However, keep in mind that you'll not be able to query information from the database through an Excel chart or some similar OLE tool. The chart control is designed to query data from a table or view; therefore, you should use this control if you plan to build a chart based on information in the database.

Other OLE Issues

Before finishing this lesson, there are a few other OLE-related issues to cover.

OLE and Multimedia

As you can probably guess, OLE provides the easiest means to add multimedia capabilities to your application. Many graphics, video, sound, and other applications can act as OLE servers. By using these multimedia applications, you can add a great deal of life and color (not to mention sound) to your own application.

As with any OLE data object, you must make sure that systems in which you install your application have the necessary OLE server applications to play these multimedia files. Windows already includes Sound Recorder (for playing .WAV files) and the Media Player (for playing sound in the .WAV and .MID format and video files in the AVI format). In addition, many PCs have Microsoft Video for Windows installed as part of the installation of another product.

OLE and the *Long Raw* Data Type

As you learned, columns to which OLE controls are bound must use the Long Raw data type. However, in Blaze databases (as well as other database formats), you can have only one Long Raw column per table. Therefore, although you might want several kinds of OLE data objects associated with a record (for example, a Word document for an employee evaluation and a bitmap of the employee's photograph), you'll need to break the OLE data into separate tables.

OLE and Performance

Although OLE provides enormous versatility, it also can degrade your application's performance. Graphics and video, in particular, can slow any application that uses them extensively, most significantly on older, slower PCs.

Therefore, use some discretion when you add OLE features to your application. In the case of bitmaps, for example, you might want to display this information in a picture control instead of an OLE control. This is another good reason for using the Oracle Power Objects chart control instead of OLE charts.

OLE and Custom Controls

A standard Windows 3.1 installation already includes the DLLs needed to use OLE in many applications. However, the newer OLE DLLs you installed with Oracle Power Objects are needed to run a special kind of custom control—an OCX file. Microsoft encourages these new kinds of custom controls as a replacement for the VBX files used in Visual Basic 3.0; they are a common feature of applications running under Windows 95. Therefore, Oracle has decided to keep up with this new standard by using OCXs as the basis for custom controls.

If you are not familiar with the concept of custom controls, imagine what it would be like to add a special control for displaying video clips, instead of relying on an OLE server application. The control would have properties and methods like standard Oracle Power Objects controls. For example, the Long Raw data comprising the video clip could be accessible through the control's Value property. In fact, the control could provide a miniature version of some larger applications, such as a word processor that might have enough features for simple text editing to replace Microsoft Word.

These types of custom controls are a common feature of development tools such as Visual Basic and Oracle Power Objects. Developers who create them as OCX, VBX, and DLL files distribute them as commercial software or, in some cases, as freeware. By purchasing one of these custom controls, you can add powerful features to your application. In Day 21, you'll add a simple OCX control to your application.

Summary

Today you learned about the following topics:

- [ ] OLE provides a further means to extend your application.
- [ ] In OLE terminology, an *OLE data object* is a piece of information formatted to be viewed and edited in a particular server application.

□ When you add OLE data objects to an Oracle Power Objects application, your application becomes the client of that server.

□ A wide variety of common applications can act as OLE servers, including many of the most popular productivity applications.

□ In an Oracle Power Objects application, OLE data objects are stored and displayed through OLE controls.

□ When the OLE data object is stored in the OLE control, it is embedded. If it is stored in an operating system accessed through the OLE control, it is linked.

□ Alternatively, the OLE data object can be stored in a Long Raw column in a table to which the OLE control is bound.

□ OLE technology is especially useful for adding multimedia capabilities to your application.

17

What Comes Next?

Tomorrow, you'll flesh out your knowledge of SQL. In particular, you'll get experience using the EXEC SQL command in Oracle Basic to execute SQL code for manipulating database objects. In addition, if you have an Oracle7 or SQL Server database, you'll have the chance to call some stored procedures through your Oracle Basic code.

Q&A

Q If I don't want to use OLE, what is the best way to add multimedia features to my application?

A Instead of adding multimedia OLE objects to your application, you have two options for relating sound, graphics, and video applications to your Oracle Power Objects application. First, you can use a multimedia OCX for playing multimedia files. Instead of calling a fully featured application, you can add a multimedia custom control that demands a lot less memory and other resources. In addition, the multimedia OCX is easy to distribute—simply make sure that you include the OCX or DLL file with your own application.

Second, you can use the Windows API procedure WinExec to launch a multimedia application. By declaring and calling WinExec, you can launch any Windows-based application. However, in most cases, you need only play a video or sound file or display a graphic, instead of giving the user the wide range of options available in a multimedia application like Adobe Photoshop or Creative WaveStudio.

Q **Can Oracle Power Objects documents act as OLE data objects?**

A Version 1.0 of Oracle Power Objects cannot create OLE server applications. However, Oracle plans to add this feature in a future release.

Workshop

The Workshop consists of quiz questions to help you solidify your understanding of the material covered. Try and understand the quiz answers before you go on to tomorrow's lesson.

Quiz

1. How does a Microsoft Word document differ from a DOC file created by Word?

2. How do you create a spreadsheet that you can edit both through Oracle Power Objects and the spreadsheet application itself?

Quiz Answers

1. The Word document is an OLE data object, whereas the DOC file is an operating system file in which it can be stored. However, the Word document can also be stored within another application as an embedded object, or in a database table. Therefore, it's important not to confuse the data object with the DOC file.

2. You should create the spreadsheet through the server application and then save it as an operating system file. Then, you should add the OLE data object as a linked object in your application. The OLE control displaying the spreadsheet provides a pointer to the operating system file, but the control does not store the actual spreadsheet object.

Writing SQL Code

Overview

Today, you learn about the following topics:

- [ ] The SQL language
- [ ] DDL, DML, and TPL commands
- [ ] Creating tables through SQL
- [ ] Inserting data into tables through SQL
- [ ] Updating records through SQL
- [ ] Deleting tables through SQL
- [ ] Using temp tables in your application
- [ ] Querying records into an array
- [ ] Do's and don'ts for arrays
- [ ] Transactions in SQL
- [ ] Calling a stored procedure

Because Oracle Power Objects applications use relational databases for their back end, they need to use the SQL language to work with database objects and their contents. To create a table, add a record to it, or delete the table, you must issue a SQL command to the database.

As described on Day 2, "Creating a Table," SQL is a very easy language to use because it is based on an English-like syntax. Additionally, SQL commands are fairly easy to understand—the purpose of CREATE TABLE, for example, is self-evident. As you will see later today, the arguments you pass to each of these commands are equally easy to understand.

However, writing SQL code can be a chore, particularly when you need to manage a large number of changes to tables. You also face the same challenge when you write SQL code that you face when you write any kind of code: How do you avoid program bugs? You want to be especially careful about any code that you write which affects the contents of the database.

Because Oracle Power Objects generates nearly all the necessary SQL code for your application, it removes a source of many potential headaches for you as a database application developer. Instead of you writing and debugging the SQL code for creating, changing, and deleting tables, for example, Oracle Power Objects writes all the necessary code for you and runs it behind the scenes. All you need to do is fill in the Table Editor window with the columns you want and save the new or modified table to the database.

Why Learn SQL?

However, if you do not learn some of the fundamentals of SQL, you put your application at risk, and you can miss some opportunities to improve the performance and features of your application.

SQL and Debugging

If some problem arises, you might need to write some SQL code to detect the source of the problem. When your view does not work as expected, you might need to write the SQL code that defines the view yourself, to see if the problem is in the database, Oracle Power Objects, or somewhere else.

Not knowing SQL is a bit like a truck driver not knowing how the truck's engine works. Most of the time, everything works fine. However, if the truck breaks down, being stranded without the necessary technical knowledge to fix the problem can be frustrating and costly. Similarly, as a database application developer, you need some greater knowledge of SQL.

SQL in Common Development Tasks

In addition, many development tasks are impossible unless you write SQL code. In order to implement the highly useful SQLLOOKUP command you must know how to write a SELECT statement in SQL. You cannot use the DefaultCondition property or the QueryWhere() method unless you know the proper syntax for a WHERE clause to be passed to a SELECT statement.

This is old news to you by now. What will be new today is how to use SQL code to define server-based procedures and to perform global operations on tables. Without knowing how to write SQL code, you cannot define a stored procedure to be executed on the server. You would also not be able to perform some global update on a table, such as giving everyone a raise. SQL is especially good at performing these global operations, so you should know how to take advantage of this feature of the language.

SQL and Oracle Basic

Like Basic, SQL is comprised of commands and operators. The Oracle Power Objects documentation also divides commands into regular commands (those that do not return any values) and functions (those that do return a value). However, for the sake of this lesson, we'll leave that intellectual distinction aside.

Many of these SQL commands and operators behave in much the same fashion as their counterparts in Basic. For example, the AVG function in SQL does what AVG in Oracle Basic does: You call this command to return the average of some values. In the case of the Oracle Basic AVG command, you are averaging the internal values of all instances of a control; in the case of the SQL AVG command, you are averaging the contents of a column.

There are occasional differences between the SQL command and its Oracle Basic counterpart, so you should always consult the SQL language reference in the online help before using a SQL command for the first time.

Many operators also behave differently. By now, you should know that the delimiter character you place at the beginning and end of a string is a double quotation mark (") in Basic, and a single quote (') in SQL. If you mistakenly use a double quote in SQL, you will get an error.

SQL and Database Objects

SQL has many commands that have no counterparts in Oracle Basic, all of which relate to database objects. Just as Oracle Basic has special object-oriented extensions for working with application objects, SQL has special commands for working with database objects. SQL also has a particular way of updating database objects, through *transactions*, designed to ensure the clarity, accuracy, and safety of changes to the database.

These database-related commands are the focus of today's lesson.

SQL in Oracle Power Objects

Before continuing, you should know that each relational database uses its own flavor of the SQL language. Although developers have been trying to reach a standard SQL language, there are still differences between implementations of SQL in different relational database engines.

For example, there are subtle but important differences between SQL in Oracle7 and Transact-SQL, the variation of SQL used in SQL Server. Additionally, the procedural language used in Oracle7, PL/SQL, differs from the procedural language in Transact-SQL.

For the most part, when you write SQL code in your application, you do not need to worry about these differences. For many common SQL commands, Oracle Power Objects lets you write a generic form of SQL. Your application then uses this "plain brown wrapper" version of SQL and makes slight modifications as needed to fit the database platform. In this sense, the application first interprets the SQL code you write before sending it to the database.

However, in many cases, you need to be aware of the special characteristics of SQL commands and operators in a particular database platform. Whenever you write a stored procedure, for example, you need to know the specifics of the procedural language (PL/SQL for Oracle7, or Transact-SQL in SQL Sever). Therefore, you should always have your database's SQL language manual handy. In the case of Blaze, the manual is the SQL language reference in the Oracle Power Objects online help.

Blaze and SQL

Blaze's version of SQL is the plain brown wrapper version used in Oracle Power Objects. You do not need to worry about how Blaze interprets the SQL code you write in sections of Oracle Basic method code, because the application does not interpret it at all. However, Blaze does not have a procedural language needed to write stored procedures and triggers. Otherwise, Blaze uses all of the SQL commands for working with database objects.

Database-Related SQL Commands

The database-related commands explained in the following sections are common to all versions of SQL, and are available when you write SQL code in an Oracle Power Objects application. These commands are divided into the following categories:

☐ Those that define database objects

☐ Those that change the contents of a database object

☐ Those that define a transaction

DDL Commands

SQL commands that define database objects are called *data definition language* (DDL) commands. These are described in Table 18.1.

Table 18.1. DDL commands.

Command	Purpose
CREATE	Creates a new object. For example, to create a new table, you would issue a CREATE TABLE command that gives the table a name and describes each of its columns.
ALTER	Changes some aspect of a database object. You would issue an ALTER TABLE command to add a UNIQUE constraint to a column or change the upper limit of numbers generated by a sequence.
DROP	Removes an object from the database. If you no longer need to maintain a particular index on a table, you would issue a DROP INDEX command.
GRANT	Grants users the privileges needed to view, insert, change, or update records.
REVOKE	Takes away privileges from a user.

DDL commands are fairly simple to use. For example, to create a table with two columns, you might write the following SQL code:

```
CREATE TABLE MYTABLE (COL_ONE NUMBER PRIMARY KEY,
➥COL_TWO VARCHAR2(256) NOT NULL)
```

As you can see, you specify the data type for each column, as well as any constraints you wish to apply. In this case, the column COL_ONE has the Number data type, and is the primary key for the table. The COL_TWO column uses the String data type, and it has the NOT NULL constraint applied to it.

Normally, you write the CREATE TABLE so that it looks like this:

```
CREATE TABLE MYTABLE &
  (COL_ONE       NUMBER       PRIMARY KEY,
   COL_TWO       VARCHAR(256) NOT NULL)
```

Obviously, this version is more readable.

Frequently, the most challenging DDL command is CREATE VIEW. Because multitable views must query, join, and sort records from separate tables, the SELECT statement behind a view can become extremely complex.

DML Commands

Data manipulation language (DML) commands let you read, write, and delete the contents of database objects. When you wrote SQL code for SQLLOOKUP, you were using the most common DML command, SELECT.

The list of DML commands is described in Table 18.2.

Table 18.2. DML commands.

Command	Purpose
SELECT	Retrieves records from a table or view. When you write a SELECT statement, you can add conditions through the WHERE clause and sort records using the ORDER BY and GROUP BY commands. In addition, you can nest one query within another, a procedure called a *subquery*.
DELETE	Deletes one or more rows from a table.
INSERT	Adds a new record to a table.
UPDATE	Changes values in a table. You can update a single record or many. Similarly, you can use this command to update values in multiple columns.

When you use DELETE and UPDATE, you can use a WHERE clause to apply a condition just as you do with SELECT. For example, to delete every discontinued item from the INV_ITEMS table, you might enter the following SQL code:

```
DELETE FROM INV_ITEMS WHERE DISCONTINUED = -1
```

Once you create the tables, views, sequences, indexes, and synonyms that comprise your database, the majority of SQL code that affects its contents will be DML commands.

TPL Commands

Relational databases use *transactions* to define the beginning and end of a particular task to perform, normally to make some change to the database. If you need to update the records of all employees, you would define this task as a transaction. Similarly, a small change to a single record, such as updating a customer's outstanding balance, can be a transaction.

When you begin editing a record, the application enables the Commit button. In essence, Oracle Power Objects is telling you that you are defining a transaction by editing the record. Whenever you insert, delete, or update a record, the Commit button also becomes enabled, because these are all transactions. Several SQL commands, explained in Table 18.3, control what happens to the transaction.

Table 18.3. TPL commands.

Command	Purpose
COMMIT	Commits a transaction. In Transact-SQL (the SQL used in SQL Server), the syntax is COMMIT TRANSACTION.
ROLLBACK	Rolls back a transaction. In Transact-SQL, the syntax is ROLLBACK TRANSACTION.
SAVE	Defines a savepoint, where the transaction saves all work done so far before continuing to the next set of changes to the database. In Transact-SQL, the syntax is SAVE TRANSACTION.

Creating a Table Through SQL

To let you practice with SQL, you will create a new table, PROMOTIONS, in which to store information about store promotions and sales. First, you need to define a new form for entering SQL code.

1. Create a new form, frmSQL, with the label Enter SQL Code.
2. Add a text field, fldSQL, to the form.

3. Stretch the field across the width of the form, and increase its height to about three inches.

4. Set the following properties of fldSQL:

Property	Setting
Datatype	String
DataSize	2048
FontName	Arial
FontSize	10
MultiLine	True
HasScrollBar	True

You now have a field in which you can enter many lines of SQL code, if necessary.

5. Add a pushbutton next to the text field labeled Execute SQL.

6. Add another text field to the bottom of the form.

7. Give this text field the following properties:

Property	Setting
Name	fldSQLError
ReadOnly	True
Datatype	Long Integer

This second text field will display a SQL error number if you make a mistake entering SQL code.

8. Add the following code to the Click() method of the pushbutton:

```
Sub Click()
' Get the SQL code entered in the field
DIM vStr AS String
vStr = fldSQL.Value

' Pass this code to the
EXEC SQL AT BOOKS :vStr

' Display the error code returned from this operation
' in the other field
fldSQLError.Value = SQLErrCode
```

9. Save and run the form.

You now have a simple form through which you can enter any SQL code you want the BOOKS database to execute (see Figure 18.1).

Next, you will enter the SQL code for creating a new table.

Figure 18.1.

The form frmSQL, used for entering SQL code.

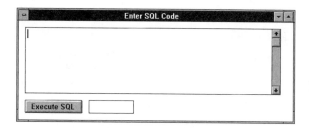

10. Type the following into the text field fldSQL:

```
CREATE TABLE PROMOTIONS
  (PROMOTION_ID              NUMBER         PRIMARY KEY,
   PROMOTION_DESC            VARCHAR2(128)  NOT NULL,
   LONG_DESC                 VARCHAR2(2056))
```

11. Press the Execute SQL pushbutton.

    The database has now added the PROMOTIONS table. The field fldSQLError displays the number 0, indicating that the CREATE TABLE operation was a success (see Figure 18.2).

Figure 18.2.

Executing a successful CREATE TABLE *command.*

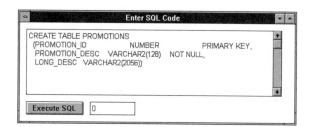

12. Press Stop.

    To verify that the table exists in BOOKS.BLZ, open a connection to the database.

13. Open the Session window for BOOKS.POS and double-click the Connector icon.

If you scroll down the list of database objects, you will find the PROMOTIONS table added to the database.

Adding Columns to the Table

The PROMOTIONS table was rather simple—in fact, too simple. For example, the table does not store information about the starting and ending dates of promotions, so you can't tell when sales begin and end. In the next exercise, you will use the DDL command ALTER to add two new columns to store this information.

1. Run the form frmSQL.

2. Enter the following text in the `fldSQL` field:

```
ALTER TABLE PROMOTIONS ADD (DATE_STARTED    DATE,
                            DATE_ENDED      DATE)
```

   These columns will store the beginning and ending dates of a promotion.

3. Press the Execute SQL button.

You have now added these columns to the PROMOTIONS table.

As you can see, creating the table using DDL commands was easy. So, too, will be creating the sequence for generating PROMOTION_ID values.

Creating a Sequence Through SQL

The CREATE SEQUENCE command creates a new sequence, a special kind of database object discussed on Day 12. The arguments you pass to this command define the beginning value, increment, and other features of the sequence. Instead of entering these features through the Create Sequence dialog box, you will define them through SQL code.

1. Delete the text in the field `fldSQL` and enter the following:

```
CREATE SEQUENCE SEQ_PROMOTION_ID
    START WITH 1
    INCREMENT BY 1
    NOMAXVALUE
    NOMINVALUE
```

   The line breaks and indentation are not necessary, but they do make your SQL code more readable. The NOMAXVALUE and NOMINVALUE arguments instruct the database to create a sequence without any maximum or minimum values.

2. Press the Execute SQL pushbutton.

Once again, the database returns an error code of zero, indicating that you did not make any mistakes in defining the new sequence.

Adding an Index

Finally, you will create an index for sorting promotions by their starting date.

1. Delete the text in the `fldSQL` field and enter the following:

```
CREATE INDEX IDX_DATE_STARTED
    ON PROMOTIONS (DATE_STARTED)
```

2. Press the Execute SQL pushbutton.

   The database now creates the index. Now you need to check your work so far.

3. Select the Session window for BOOKS.POS.

4. Select View | Refresh.

   Oracle Power Objects now updates the list of objects accessed through the Session window.

5. Scroll down the list of objects until you find SEQ_PROMOTION_ID and IDX_DATE_STARTED.

6. Close the Table Editor window for PROMOTIONS and re-open it.

The additional columns, DATE_STARTED and DATE_ENDED, are now part of the table.

Editing Records in a Table

The next step is to write some SQL code to add records to the PROMOTIONS table.

1. Run the form frmSQL and enter the following SQL statement:

```
INSERT INTO PROMOTIONS (PROMOTION_ID, PROMOTION_DESC,
   DATE_STARTED)
   VALUES (1, 'Mystery book sale', SYSDATE)
```

   In this code, the function SYSDATE returns the date and time, according to the operating system.

2. Press the Execute SQL pushbutton.

3. Replace the code in the field with the following:

```
INSERT INTO PROMOTIONS (PROMOTION_ID, PROMOTION_DESC,
   DATE_STARTED)
   VALUES (2, 'Computer book promotion', SYSDATE)
```

4. Press the Execute SQL pushbutton again.

5. Press Stop.

   You can now verify that these records have been added.

6. Run the PROMOTIONS table.

   The new records now appear in the Table Browser window (see Figure 18.3).

Figure 18.3.
Records added to the PROMOTIONS table through SQL code.

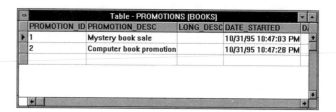

7. Press Stop to end this exercise.

Deleting Records from a Table

You can also use the DML command DELETE to remove records from a table. Because you want to be careful about what you delete, you will add a temporary record to the PUBLISHERS table before deleting it through SQL code.

1. Open and run the PUBLISHERS table.

2. Enter the following new record:

Column	Value
PUBLISHER_ID	99
PUBLISHER_NAME	Temporary Books

3. Press Commit to save the new record, and then press Stop.

4. Run the form frmSQL and enter the following code in the field fldSQL:

```
DELETE FROM PUBLISHERS WHERE PUBLISHER_NAME LIKE 'Temp%'
```

In this SQL code, you are using the SQL wildcard character % to search for all names that start with Temp.

5. Press the Execute SQL pushbutton.

6. Enter COMMIT in fldSQL and press Execute SQL again.

The record has now been deleted from the PUBLISHERS table. To confirm this, you can run the table and see that the record you just entered is no longer there.

Updating Records in a Table

The final test of your new SQL skills will be to give all the employees in the bookstore a 5 percent raise. In this case, you will be using the DML command UPDATE to change the values in the EMPLOYEES.SALARY column.

1. Enter the following SQL command in the fldSQL field:

```
UPDATE EMPLOYEES SET SALARY = SALARY * 1.05
```

2. Press the Execute SQL pushbutton.

All of the records in the EMPLOYEES table have now received this change. Once again, SQL is designed to make this type of global operation in the database fast and simple.

To further illustrate how to use UPDATE, you will take all orders from a particular customer off hold.

3. Enter the following SQL command:

```
UPDATE ORDERS SET ON_HOLD = 0 WHERE CUSTOMER_ID = 1
```

4. Press the Execute SQL pushbutton.

   As you might remember, this customer had her order placed on hold because of an outstanding balance owed to the store. If she had other orders on hold, this SQL command would have taken all of her orders off hold.

5. Press Stop to end this exercise.

The other DML command, SELECT, queries values from the database. Although you have some experience with SELECT statements already, using SELECT requires an additional step not required of INSERT, UPDATE, and DELETE. With SELECT, you must use a special kind of variable—a bind variable—to receive the values that are queried. Because multiple values might be returned from a query, you might need to define the variable as an array.

Writing a *SELECT* Statement

Because you have written the query strings for many SQLLOOKUP commands, the structure of a SELECT statement is old news to you. Because EXEC SQL is a multipurpose command for executing any type of SQL statement, you can use it to query data with a SELECT statement, instead of querying these values with SQLLOOKUP. However, the variable that receives this value must be defined as a bind variable.

Variables and *SELECT* Statements

Variables that receive values from a SELECT statement are called *bind variables*. You reference the bind variable within the SELECT statement itself, by using the INTO statement. For example, to query salary information into the variable vResult, you would enter the following SELECT statement:

```
SELECT SALARY INTO :vSalary FROM EMPLOYEES
```

Any Oracle Basic variable you use in any EXEC SQL statement must be preceded by a colon (:). This rule applies to bind variables, as well as strings you assign to part or all of the SELECT statement. If you were to enter a condition in a text field and then use that value in a SELECT statement, you would write something like the following method code:

```
' Declare the variables used to define the condition
' and capture values returned from the query
DIM vWhere AS String
DIM vResult AS Long

' Get the condition entered in the field
vWhere = fldCondition.Value

' Perform the query
EXEC SQL SELECT SAL INTO :vResult FROM EMP WHERE :vWhere
```

In this case, the SELECT statement uses two variables. The first, vResult, captures the value queried from the SAL column. The second, vWhere, defines the condition for the WHERE clause.

Capturing Values Returned from a Query

Whenever you capture values into a variable, you have two choices:

☐ By defining the variable as an array, you can capture all of the values queried from a column. In the case of the previous EXEC SQL statement, you could define vResult as an array, in which case it could capture all of the values queried from the SAL column.

☐ By not defining the variable as an array, you can capture only a single value. If you write the SELECT statement so that it will return only one value, then that value is assigned to the variable. However, if the SELECT statement returns multiple values, then the application assigns to the variable the last value queried from the column.

Obviously, in many cases, you will want to capture multiple values from the query, so you will define the bind variable as an array. However, arrays can be tricky to use, and they have some special requirements in Oracle Basic.

Before getting into the intricacies of arrays, however, you will first get a taste of how to use them. In the next exercise, you will use an array to display the results of a query in a text field.

Querying Values into an Array

For this exercise, you will need to create another text field in frmSQL for displaying the values returned from the query. The method code you will write is designed to capture values from a single column.

1. Open the form frmSQL and add a text field to the bottom of the form. Make the new field approximately the same size as fldSQL.

2. Give the text field the Name fldResult, the Datatype String, and the DataSize 2056.

   Next, you need to give the field the capability to display multiple lines of text.

3. Set the field's MultiLine and HasScrollBar properties to True.

4. Add a new pushbutton with the Label Query in the form.

5. Add the following method code to the Click() method of the second pushbutton:

```
Sub Click()
' Define the bind variables
STATIC vResult(1 TO 100) AS String

' Call EXEC SQL to perform the query
EXEC SQL AT BOOKS SELECT TITLE_NAME INTO :vResult FROM TITLES

' Display the results in the text field
```

```
DIM vTempStr AS String
vTempStr = ""
FOR x = 1 TO 100
  IF ISNULL(vResult(x)) THEN
      EXIT FOR
  ELSE
      vTempStr = vTempStr & vResult(x) & CHR(13) & CHR(10)
  END IF
NEXT X

fldResult.Value = vTempStr
```

6. Save and run the form.

7. Press the Query pushbutton.

   The application now performs the query and displays the result in the text field (see Figure 18.4).

Figure 18.4.

Displaying the result of a query in the field fldSQL.

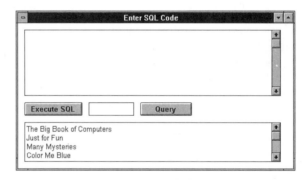

8. Stop the application.

9. Make the following change (in bold) in the code you just entered:

```
Sub Click()
' Define the bind variables
STATIC vResult(1 TO 100) AS String

' Call EXEC SQL to perform the query
EXEC SQL AT BOOKS SELECT TITLE_NAME INTO :vResult FROM TITLES
➥WHERE PRICE > 10

' Display the results in the text field
DIM vTempStr AS String
vTempStr = ""
FOR x = 1 TO 100
  IF ISNULL(vResult(x)) THEN
      EXIT FOR
  ELSE
      vTempStr = vTempStr & vResult(x) & CHR(13) & CHR(10)
  END IF
NEXT X

fldResult.Value = vTempStr
```

10. Run the form and press the Query pushbutton.

    A different set of results now appears in the text field.

11. After you stop the form, change the EXEC SQL statement to read as follows:

    ```
    SELECT ALIAS FROM EMPLOYEES WHERE SEC_LEVEL > 25
    ```

12. Run the form again and press Query.

    Results returned from a different table than TITLES now appear in the text field.

13. Press Stop to end this exercise.

An Important Critique of This Exercise

In this exercise, working with an array was a fairly simple task. However, you cheated slightly, because you declared the size of the array as a fixed amount. As part of the definition of an array, you need to tell the application the number of elements in that array. In this case, the number of elements should be the same as the number of values returned from the query.

Unfortunately, the application cannot know the number of elements necessary until it performs the query. If the SELECT statement returned more than 100 values, you would get an error. In this case, the values returned would exceed the upper bound you defined for the array (that is, the expected number of values), so the error message would read Array out of bounds.

In addition, your array only accepted values from a single column. However, many SELECT statements include multiple columns, a situation that your procedure could not accommodate.

How then do you write a better procedure? In part, the answer lies in the nature of arrays themselves.

Arrays in Oracle Basic

An *array* is a special type of variable that can hold multiple values. To better envision how an array works, think of a box separated into several identical compartments. The box can hold one object per compartment; if you have more objects than compartments, you have a problem. In addition, you would like to know the number of objects in advance so that your box is designed to have no empty compartments.

An array is much like this box. Each element of the array can hold a value. When you define the array, you need to tell the application the number of elements in the array, as well as their data type (which must be the same for all values). The array can use any type of data type, including more exotic ones like Longs and Objects.

Note: When you write the array, you always include the parentheses after its name. Without these parentheses, the application will not understand that a variable is an array; nor will it know how many elements will be part of the array.

When you declare the array, you have two options for defining the number of elements:

☐ Declare the number of elements when you declare the array. In this case, the number of elements will remain fixed throughout the procedure. For example, if you defined an array, vDays(), for holding the names of the days of the week, you would declare the array using the following syntax:

```
DIM vDays(7) AS String
```

When you define an array in this fashion, you place the number of elements between the parentheses as part of the declaration.

☐ Leave the number of elements blank when you declare the array. You use this technique when you cannot predict the number of elements, or you expect it to change. When you declare this type of array, you must use the GLOBAL or STATIC keywords instead of DIM. For example, to declare a dynamic array containing salaries queried from a table, you would enter the following:

```
STATIC vSalaries() AS Double
```

Later, you use the REDIM command to define the number of elements in the array. Until you REDIM the array in this fashion, you cannot assign values to the elements of the array, because the application does not know how many elements it should have.

This latter type of array is known as a *dynamic array*, to signify that you can define the array *dynamically* (that is, at runtime). In contrast, arrays that have their number of elements defined when you declare the array itself are called *static arrays*.

Identifying an Element in an Array

You can identify each element in an array by a number. This number is often called the *index*, and you can use it to both read values from that element and assign new values to it.

For example, to read the value in position one into a variable, you would enter something resembling the following method code:

```
vReceive = vGive(1)
```

Alternatively, if you wanted to assign a value to the element in position one, you might enter the following:

```
vGive(1) = vReceive
```

Setting the Upper and Lower Bounds of Elements

When you declare an array, by default the index values for each element start at zero. If there are 10 elements in the array, the index values for each element range from 0 to 9, not 1 to 10.

However, you can define the upper and lower bounds of the array differently, so that the beginning value is something other than zero. For example, the following array has 10 elements, with index values from 1 to 10:

```
DIM vArray(1 TO 10)
```

Similarly, the following array has index values from 50 to 99:

```
DIM vArray(50 TO 99)
```

In addition, either the upper or lower bound of the array can be a negative number:

```
DIM vArray(-10 to -1)
```

Although these examples use static arrays to illustrate this point, you can use the TO keyword when you REDIM a dynamic array to specify a range of index values for that array.

Multidimensional Arrays

Finally, arrays can have more than one dimension (that is, they can have a range of elements). Such arrays are called multidimensional; each set of elements comprises a different dimension of the array. For example, if you wanted to create an array of x and y coordinates for a graph, you might declare the array as follows:

```
DIM vCoord(1 TO 100, 1 TO 100) AS Long
```

In this case, the array has two dimensions, each indexed from 1 to 100.

Arrays and Recordsets

Arrays have a lot of potential uses, particularly when capturing values from a SELECT statement. (In fact, they provide the only means for capturing multiple values from a query, because SQLLOOKUP returns only the first value found.) However, having worked with an array as an imitation recordset in the last exercise, you might have asked yourself, "Why go through the bother of coding an array if you can use a recordset instead?"

This question is important, because Oracle Power Objects is designed to make working with recordsets easy. If you are collecting related pieces of information and placing them in one or more arrays, you should ask yourself why you didn't use a recordset instead. If you were storing the first and last names of customers in two arrays, then the extra code you need to write to synchronize values between the two arrays would seem to be reason enough to use a recordset instead. If you move to a particular index in one array, you then need to move to the same index in the other. As the number of arrays increases (one per column), the extra code for synchronizing all these values grows. In contrast, a single recordset method, SetCurRow(), moves the pointer to a particular record and synchronizes the values in all columns.

As powerful as recordsets are, arrays are often a useful or necessary replacement for them in the following circumstances:

☐ When writing the code for a recordset is more difficult than writing the code for an array. If you have a small and relatively simple range of values, you can save yourself some work by storing them in an array instead of a stand-alone recordset.

☐ When you SELECT values into a bind variable, you must use an array. Unfortunately, you cannot substitute a stand-alone recordset for an array as the bind variable in a SELECT statement.

Working with Arrays

18

To illustrate some of these points about arrays, you will write some code that creates an array of values queried from the EMPLOYEES table into two dynamic arrays.

1. Open the form frmSQL.

2. Add a button with the label Names to the form.

3. Enter the following method code in the Click() method of the pushbutton:

```
Sub Click()
STATIC vLname() AS String
STATIC vFname() AS String
DIM vNumRecs AS Long

' Get the number of employee records
vNumRecs = SQLLOOKUP(BOOKS, "SELECT COUNT(*) FROM EMPLOYEES")

' Set the dynamic arrays to the proper number of elements
REDIM vLname (1 TO vNumRecs)
REDIM vFname (1 TO vNumRecs)

' Read values from the EMPLOYEES table into the arrays
EXEC SQL AT BOOKS SELECT EMPLOYEE_LNAME, EMPLOYEE_FNAME &
    INTO :vLname, :vFname FROM EMPLOYEES

' Display the contents of the arrays in the field
FOR x = 1 TO vNumRecs
  fldResult.Value = fldResult.Value & vFname(x) & " "
  ➡& vLname(x) & CHR(13) & CHR(10)
NEXT x
```

4. Save and run the form.

5. Press the Names pushbutton.

    The names of all employees now appear in the text field.

6. Press Stop to end this exercise.

Working with Temp Tables

Frequently, you use DDL and DML commands to create database objects that have a very limited lifespan. These short-lived objects have a very specific and temporary purpose.

One frequent use of this technique is to increase performance while you generate reports. If you have to perform a large number of cross-table lookups, performance can suffer, particularly when you use SQLLOOKUP to find values in secondary tables. To circumvent this problem, developers often create temporary tables, populated with records from other tables, as the source of a report's records. Once you have finished generating the report, you then eliminate the table from the database. Tables created and destroyed in this fashion are called *temp tables* for obvious reasons.

When you create any kind of table, you can base it on the columns from another table or view. The new table not only copies the column descriptions from the other database object, but it also queries values from all of these columns. Therefore, the new table is a cut-and-paste job that includes the data queried through the table or view.

To create a table in this fashion, you use the following syntax:

```
CREATE TABLE table_name AS query_string
```

The query must identify by name all of the columns to be added to the new table. For example, to create a table that copies a few columns from the TITLES table, you would write the following DDL code:

```
CREATE TABLE SHORT_TITLES AS SELECT TITLE_NAME, AUTHLNAME, &
   AUTHFNAME, PRICE FROM TITLES
```

As you shall see, you can filter the queried records by adding a WHERE clause to this query. In addition, because you can use a view as the basis for a new table, you can easily create a new table that includes values queried from all the tables included in a multitable view.

Using a Temp Table for a Report

In this exercise, you will create a temp table for a simple listing of books, including their publishers and book types. Before writing the DDL code to create the temp table, you first must define a view that queries all the necessary information from the TITLES, PUBLISHERS, and BOOK_TYPES tables. Once you have defined this view, you can use the records queried through it as the basis for the temp table.

1. Open the Session window for BOOKS.POS and open a connection to the database.

2. Create a new view named VW_RPTBOOKS.

   The name indicates that the view will be used as the basis for the report rptBooks.

3. Add the TITLES, PUBLISHERS, and BOOK_TYPES tables to the view.

4. Join the columns TITLES.PUBLISHER_ID and PUBLISHERS.PUBLISHER_ID.

   As you should remember from Day 3, you join columns in separate tables by clicking a column from one table's window and dragging it onto the name of a column in a different table window.

5. Join the columns TITLES.TYPE_ID and BOOK_TYPES.TYPE_ID.

6. Add the following columns to the Column List area of the view:
   TITLES.TITLE_NAME, TITLES.AUTHLNAME,
   PUBLISHERS.PUBLISHER_NAME, TITLES.TYPE_ID, and
   BOOK_TYPES.TYPE_DESC.

   These are the columns that will be displayed when you query records through the view.

7. Save the view.

8. Create a new report, rptBooks, with the label Title Listing.

9. Click and drag all of the columns from VW_RPTBOOKS into the detail area of the report.

10. Adjust the appearance of the report until it meets your liking.

    Now, the report is bound to the VW_RPTBOOKS view. However, you want to bind this report to a temp table, so you will manually change the RecordSource property of the report to the name of the temp table.

11. Enter TP_RPTBOOKS as the RecordSource of the report.

    Next, you will make a special dialog box for opening this report. You also need to add a button for opening this dialog box from a form.

12. Open the form frmPubsBooks and a pushbutton at the bottom of the form.

13. Set the label of the pushbutton to Title Listing, and enter the following method code in its Click() method:

    ```
    Sub Click()
    frmReportDialog.OpenWindow()
    ```

14. Create a new form, frmReportDialog, with the label Title Listing.

15. Add three pushbuttons to the bottom of the form, labeled Generate, Display, and Close. Give the Display pushbutton the name btnDisplay.

16. Resize the form until it looks like Figure 18.5.

18

Figure 18.5.

The form frmReportDialog.

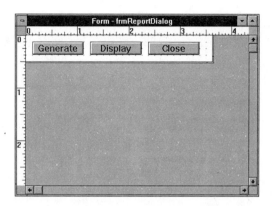

17. Set the Enabled property of the Display pushbutton to False.

18. Add the following code to the Click() method of the Generate pushbutton:

```
Sub Click()
' If the table already exists in the database, delete it
EXEC SQL AT BOOKS DROP TABLE TP_RPTBOOKS

' Create the temp table
EXEC SQL AT BOOKS CREATE TABLE TP_RPTBOOKS AS &
  SELECT TITLE_NAME, AUTHLNAME, PUBLISHER_NAME, TYPE_DESC &
  FROM VW_RPTBOOKS

' Enable the display pushbutton
btnDisplay.Enabled = TRUE
```

You first need to generate the temp table before you display it. If you were to open the report while the CREATE TABLE command was still executing in the database, the report could not find its table and would crash. To prevent this problem, this code ensures that you cannot open the report until the database is finished creating the temp table.

19. Add the following method code to the Display pushbutton's Click() method:

```
Sub Click()
' Open the report
rptBooks.OpenWindow()
```

Finally, you need to add some method code to delete the temp table when you close the rptRunReport dialog box.

20. Add the following code to the Click() method of the Done pushbutton:

```
Sub Click()
self.GetTopContainer.CloseWindow()
```

21. Add the following code to the CloseWindow() method of frmRunReport:

```
Sub CloseWindow()
' Drop the temp table
EXEC SQL AT BOOKS DROP TABLE TP_RPTBOOKS

' Close the form
Inherited.CloseWindow()
```

22. Save and run the application.

23. After logging in as vbond/antwerp (the username and password of an employee of the bookstore), open the form frmPubsBooks.

24. Press the Title Listing pushbutton.

    The dialog box you just created now opens.

25. In the dialog box, press the Run Report pushbutton.

    The application pauses momentarily while the database creates the temp table. After a second, the report opens, displaying all the records queried from the temp table (see Figure 18.6).

Figure 18.6.

Records queried for the Title Listing report from a temp table.

Title	Author	Type	Publisher
An English Garden	Throckmorton	Reference	Chatham House
The Big Book of Computers	Grant	Computer	Enigma Books
Development Made Easy	Fortran	Computer	Enigma Books
Many Mysteries	Lumley	Mystery	Maximum Books
Sleep No More	Black	Mystery	Maximum Books
Kiss Me Dead	Steele	Mystery	Chatham House
Just for Fun	Hartwell	Children's	Logos Press
Fun for Everyone	Hartwell	Children's	Logos Press
Color Me Blue	Leavitt	General fiction	Rollercoaster Boo
A Boy's Life in New Zealand	MacAvoy	General non-ficti	Enderby Press

Book Listing

26. Close the report, and then press Done to close the dialog box.

    Behind the scenes, the application tells the database to drop the temp table.

27. Press Stop to end this exercise.

Applying a Condition to the Report

Because the SELECT statement that queries values for the temp table can accept a WHERE clause, you can use this feature to apply a condition to the records queried for the report. In the next exercise, you will add the capability to display only particular types of books in the report.

1. Open the form frmReportDialog.

2. Add a check box, chkApplyFilter, to the form. Give this check box the label Select Book Type?.

3. Set the following properties of chkApplyFilter:

Property	Setting
DefaultValue	0
ValueOn	-1
ValueOff	0

4. Add the following code to the check box's PostChange() method:

```
Sub PostChange()
Inherited.PostChange()
IF NVL(self.Value, 0) <> 0 THEN
  popBookTypes.Enabled = TRUE
ELSE
  popBookTypes.Enabled = FALSE
END IF
```

This code will enable or disable a pop-up list displaying all the types of books.

5. Create a new pop-up list with the following properties:

Property	Setting
Name	popBookTypes
DefaultValue	1
Enabled	False
Label	(NONE)

6. Set the pop-up list's Translation property to the following:

```
= AT BOOKS BOOK_TYPES.TYPE_DESC = TYPE_ID
```

7. Change the code added to the Click() method of the Generate pushbutton to the following:

```
Sub Click()
' If the table already exists in the database, delete it
EXEC SQL AT BOOKS DROP TABLE TP_RPTBOOKS

' Create the temp table
IF chkApplyFilter.Value = 0 THEN
  EXEC SQL AT BOOKS CREATE TABLE TP_RPTBOOKS AS &
    SELECT TITLE_NAME, AUTHLNAME, PUBLISHER_NAME, TYPE_DESC &
    FROM VW_RPTBOOKS
ELSE
  DIM vTypeID AS Long
  vTypeID = popBookTypes.Value
  EXEC SQL AT BOOKS CREATE TABLE TP_RPTBOOKS AS &
    SELECT TITLE_NAME, AUTHLNAME, PUBLISHER_NAME, TYPE_DESC &
    FROM VW_RPTBOOKS WHERE TYPE_ID = :vTypeID
END IF

' Enable the display pushbutton
btnDisplay.Enabled = TRUE
```

8. Save and run the application.

9. Once again, open the form frmPubsBooks and press the Title Listing pushbutton.

10. Check the Select Book Type? check box.

    The pop-up list is now enabled.

11. In the pop-up list, select Computer.

12. Press the Generate pushbutton, and then press the Display pushbutton.

    The report appears again, as shown in Figure 18.7. This time, the temp table used as its record source has only computer books in it.

Figure 18.7.

Applying a filter to the report through the temp table.

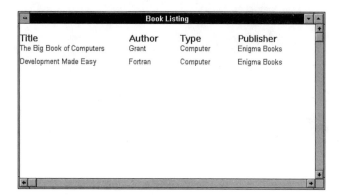

13. Close the report and the dialog box, and then press Stop.

As shown in this example, you must often use several DDL or DML commands together to accomplish a task. In this exercise, you first checked to see if a table existed, and dropped it if it did. After this preliminary step, you then created the temp table.

It makes little sense to see these two operations as separate, because they are part of the same task: creating a temp table. However, in your Oracle Basic code, these two operations (deleting the temp table if it exists, and then re-creating it) have no necessary connection to each other, except that they appear in the same method.

In contrast, you can write SQL code that makes these two operations part of the same task. In this case, you define the procedure as a transaction, including both dropping and re-creating the temp table.

DO	**DON'T**

DO use SQL commands through EXEC SQL to make rapid changes to the database.

DO use the CREATE VIEW command to design views that you cannot create through the View Editor window. As you shall see in Day 19, many views use aggregate functions like SUM, MIN, and MAX, as well as other SQL commands to define components of the view. The Table Editor window does not provide an easy way to write these views, so you must create them through your own SQL code.

DO use temp tables for other purposes, such as generating unique ID values without locking up a real table.

DON'T write SQL code that replaces what Oracle Power Objects already does to query and update records. This is especially true of DML commands. If you insert, delete, or update records through SQL code, you will not have the built-in transaction control that the application provides. In addition, you will not be able to enforce referential integrity unless you code it yourself, a completely unnecessary step.

DON'T forget to always start your code that creates a temp table with a command to drop the temp table if it already exists.

Database Transactions in SQL

When you perform any database operation, such as inserting a record or dropping a table, you are effectively defining a transaction. In SQL, you can define a whole set of operations as a single transaction, so that you can make sure that all or none of them are executed.

This feature is very important when you are dealing with information whose accuracy and safety you highly value. For example, if you move money between accounts, you effectively perform two operations:

1. Deduct the amount from one account
2. Add the same amount to the other account

If the computer crashes in step 1, however, you will have lost the money you were trying to move. Because you never reached step 2, the system never added the money you deducted from one account to the other account.

However, if you define the two steps as part of the same transaction, you can ensure that the system performs both operations, or neither. You write the transaction as a piece of SQL code with a distinct beginning and end. If you cannot perform all of the steps, then the transaction never happens.

This type of transaction logic is especially useful if you want to perform some checks before allowing any changes to the database. For example, in the case of moving money from one account to another, you might first see if there is enough money in the first account. If not, you would then roll back the transaction instead of committing it.

In addition to protecting your data in this fashion, transactions also help organize your thinking about database operations into logical steps. What are the tasks you need to perform when you move money between accounts, delete old purchases, or give everyone a raise? Because each group of tasks belongs together, you should define them as a transaction.

In SQL, transactions use particular commands to denote their beginning and end. After the BEGIN statement, the remaining SQL code defines whatever operations occur as part of the transaction. The END statement then identifies the end of the transaction. In the body of the transaction, SQL code can COMMIT or ROLLBACK changes made to the database.

Server-Based Procedures in SQL

When you perform checks within a transaction, you often need to code a procedure in the same fashion as an Oracle Basic procedure. You might need to use an IF...END IF block to perform a check, which might require using a FOR...NEXT loop to examine a series of values.

As described earlier, each relational database engine has its own procedural language. Many of the commands in these languages are similar to Basic, although they also might resemble Pascal or some other commonly used programming language.

The SQL code you write to perform the check can be part of a trigger or a stored procedure. Because both are defined and executed on the server, the only significant difference between them is the way in which they are triggered. Unless you call a stored procedure, it does not execute. In contrast, you can define a trigger that executes whenever a certain event (such as deleting a record in a particular table) occurs.

In Oracle7, the language added to SQL that makes it possible to write procedures is called PL/SQL. In SQL Server, the commands are part of the Transact-SQL language. Unfortunately, the current version of Blaze does not have procedural SQL commands, so you cannot do the next exercise unless you have access to a remote server such as Oracle7 or SQL Server.

The next exercise presupposes that you are familiar with the basics of writing PL/SQL code in Oracle7. If you are not familiar with this language, you should read your Oracle7 documentation before continuing.

Using PL/SQL in *EXEC SQL*

In this exercise, you will use some procedural language to insert 100 records into the CUSTOMERS table. You might insert records in this fashion if you needed to add a lot of test data to a table as quickly as possible.

If you have access to an Oracle7 server, this will give you your first experience with migrating (that is, copying) your database objects to another database platform. In many cases, you will be using Blaze to develop the application, but then deploying the final version on a remote server such as Oracle7. (This way, you can develop and test database objects without tampering with the real corporate database until you are ready to deploy the application.) Therefore, this exercise will also give you a sense of what deploying an Oracle Power Objects application on a remote server is like.

If you are using SQL Server, you can substitute many of the PL/SQL commands with their Transact-SQL equivalents. In addition, you can enter a SQL Server connect string for the new session you must create for this exercise.

1. Create a new session, BOOKS2.POS.

2. In the Create Session dialog box, select Oracle7 as the database engine, and enter the connect string of an available schema for the `DesignConnect` property.

   Again, if you want to use SQL Server, you would enter a different database engine and connect string.

3. Press OK to open the dialog box for creating the session file object, and then enter `C:\BOOKS\BOOKS2.POS` as its filename and directory.

   After you press OK, you create the new session (see Figure 18.8).

Figure 18.8.

Creating a new session, BOOKS2, for remote server access.

4. Double-click the Connector icon for the session to open a connection.

5. Open the Session window for BOOKS.POS and double-click its Connector icon.

6. Select all of the database objects in the BOOKS session.

7. Click and drag these objects into the Oracle7 session.

   Oracle Power Objects now copies all the database objects from BOOKS.BLZ, including the records in each table, to the Oracle7 database. Clearly, deploying all the objects for a simple application like this is a no-brainer; once again, all Oracle Power Objects asks you to do is click and drag.

8. Create a new form, frmTestSP.

9. Add a pushbutton to the form with the label Add Data.

   When you press this pushbutton, it will add new data in the CUSTOMERS table.

10. Enter the following method code in the pushbutton's Click() method:

```
Sub Click()
' Insert the records
EXEC SQL AT BOOKS2                                      &
  BEGIN                                                 &
  FOR x = 101 to 200                                    &
    INSERT INTO CUSTOMERS (CUSTOMER_ID,                 &
       LNAME, FNAME) VALUES (x, 'Holmes', 'Sherlock')   &
  END LOOP;                                             &
  COMMIT;                                               &
  END;

' Requery the repeater display showing these records
repCustomers.Query()
```

Note: In PL/SQL, the semicolon (;) denotes the end of a command. For example, after you have inserted values into the PUBLISHERS table, you end that command with a semicolon. The database then understands where one command ends and the next begins.

Next, you need to add a repeater display to display customer records. You have already referenced this repeater display in the code you just wrote.

11. Add a new repeater display, repCustomers, to the form.

12. Click and drag the CUSTOMER_ID, FNAME, and LNAME columns into the repeater display.

    Finally, you'll add a button to delete these records when you're finished.

13. Add a new pushbutton labeled Delete Data to the form.

14. Enter the following code in this button's Click() method:

```
Sub Click()
' Delete the records
EXEC SQL AT BOOKS2                                      &
  BEGIN                                                 &
  DELETE FROM CUSTOMERS WHERE CUSTOMER_ID > 100;        &
```

18

```
        COMMIT;                                          &
        END;

      ' Requery the repeater display
      repCustomers.Query()
```

15. Save and run the form.

16. Press the Add Data pushbutton.

    The repeater display now fills with additional customer records.

17. Press the Delete Data pushbutton.

    The new records now disappear.

18. Press Stop to end this exercise.

A Last Word on SQL and Databases

This lesson gave you the briefest of introductions to SQL and how to write SQL code for particular relational database engines. Many hefty tomes have been written on this subject, so I suggest that you consult some of these if you want to become a "power" SQL programmer.

Without this level of expertise, however, you have already met the goal of this chapter: You now better understand some of the important issues about using SQL to work with database objects. Even if you never become an advanced SQL programmer, you now have firmer grounding for testing and fine-tuning your database applications.

Summary

Today, you learned about the following topics:

☐ SQL includes commands for creating and manipulating database objects.

☐ In addition, SQL contains many recognizable commands and operators, similar to those used in Oracle Basic.

☐ You can enter SQL code within your method code by using either the SQLLOOKUP or EXEC SQL commands.

☐ Bind variables receive values queried through a SELECT statement.

☐ Often, you use an array to receive the values returned from the query.

☐ Arrays are composed of elements and dimensions.

☐ Arrays can have a fixed number of elements (a static array), or you can resize the dimensions of the array at runtime (a dynamic array).

☐ You can use SQL DDL commands to create temp tables.

☐ You can define procedures on the server through SQL code. Both stored procedures and triggers then execute on the server, not the client (unlike Oracle Basic method code).

☐ SQL can define blocks of related commands as transactions. Either all of these commands execute and are committed, or none are.

What Comes Next?

Tomorrow you will learn some final touches to the Bookstore application. Although the lessons so far have focused on adding functionality to this application, they have not done much to enhance the usability of the application. In other words, although the Bookstore application does a lot of different tasks, it is not designed to make learning how to use these features easy for the first-time user. In the next two days, you will spend much of your time improving the usability of your application.

Q&A

Q **Are there any dangers to using SQL code to delete, update, and insert records?**

A Because SQL is designed to work on groups of records, you can mistakenly delete or update more records than you intended. To avoid these problems, look carefully at the WHERE clauses you apply to UPDATE and DELETE statements, particularly when you are generating WHERE clauses "on the fly" (that is, specifying new conditions while the application is running).

Q **Is there any reason to create database objects through SQL code, instead of using the graphical editors in Oracle Power Objects?**

A Except in the case of complex views that the View Editor window cannot create, you should always create your database objects through these graphical editor windows. An additional exception is when you need to specify constraints that are not covered by these windows (for example, FOREIGN KEY), but are available in a particular database engine.

Q **I'm running SQL code successfully, but the changes don't appear in the database. What am I doing wrong?**

A When you insert, delete, or update records through SQL code, you need to issue a COMMIT command to instruct the database to save these changes.

Workshop

The Workshop consists of quiz questions to help you solidify your understanding of the material covered today and exercises to give you experience in using what you've learned. Try and understand the quiz and exercises before you go on to tomorrow's lesson.

Quiz

1. What type of database operations is SQL best suited to perform?
2. What is a stored procedure? A trigger?
3. What is the difference between a DDL and a DML command?
4. From the standpoint of SQL, what is a transaction?
5. If you get an `Array out of bounds` error, what happened?

Exercises

1. Write an `EXEC SQL` statement that deletes all purchases over two weeks old. Remember that when you issue a `DELETE` command, you can specify conditions using a `WHERE` clause.
2. Create a temp table for generating new unique ID numbers for the EMPLOYEES, PUBLISHERS, and TITLES tables. (Hint: You might need to use the `MAX` function in SQL to determine the largest value currently in the primary key column for each of these tables.)

Quiz Answers

1. SQL is well-suited to perform global operations on records, such as updating the salary of all employees. In addition, SQL is designed to make joining information from different tables and views through a query easy.
2. Both are procedures defined through SQL code that are defined and executed on the server. You must call a stored procedure, whereas triggers execute in response to some system event.
3. DDL commands create, alter, and delete database objects, whereas DML commands change their contents.
4. A transaction is a set of related commands that start with a `BEGIN` command and end with an `END` command. The transaction can include one operation or several; the only requirement is that you clearly identify the beginning and end of the transaction.
5. The application discovered that it was trying to add more values to an array than the number of elements in the array.

Usability Enhancements

Overview

Today, you learn about the following topics:

- ☐ Setting the tab order in a form
- ☐ Adding help text to your application
- ☐ Adding online help to your application
- ☐ Creating a wizard for a form
- ☐ Adding error handlers to your code

Frequently, the usability of an application is something of an afterthought. While developers race to meet deadlines, their primary focus is making sure that all the promised features are included in an application, and that these features work as expected. In these all-too-frequent occurrences, the ease with which someone can use the application becomes secondary.

Applications are designed to be used by people, however, not simply to be finished by a deadline. As demonstrated repeatedly in Macintosh and Windows applications, users want to be able to perform tasks quickly and easily. However, if the developers have not put enough emphasis on usability, users might have a hard time figuring out how to perform a task, or they might have to go through too many steps to complete it.

Consider the popularity of toolbars in GUI applications: To print a document, you need only press the pushbutton with the picture of a printer on it. Users immediately understand this convention in Windows and Macintosh applications: To print, press the button with the icon of a printer.

For similar reasons, context-sensitive help is a standard feature of GUI applications, because it gives users fast answers to questions while they are using the application. If you are stuck at a particular point in an application, you can press the F1 key to see the online help file associated with that application. The help file then opens to the topic appropriate to what you are doing. For example, if you are adding code to the `Validate()` method and are unsure about the specifics of this method, you can press F1 to see the topic describing `Validate()` in the Oracle Power Objects online help file.

During the last several years, software developers have invented other ways to make it easier for people to use their applications. An increasing number of applications use "wizards" to walk you through all the steps needed to complete a task. The wizard in Microsoft Publisher, a relatively simple desktop publishing tool, can automatically generate a greeting card or a flyer for you, using the text and graphics you select for it.

So far, your work in the Bookstore application has not emphasized usability. In this lesson, you will work on flattening the learning curve for new users of this application.

We will focus our attention on the Book Purchases form. Because the bulk of the bookstore's revenue comes from in-store purchases, you need to make sure that employees can quickly and accurately enter information in this form.

Changing the Tab Order in a Form

The first change might seem nit-picky, but from a user's standpoint, it can be very important. When you are entering information as quickly as possible, it is faster to use the Tab key to move between controls, instead of using the mouse. If you are entering a purchase as quickly as possible, so that customers do not have to be kept waiting while you are typing information about the sale, you cannot afford the time to click every control with the mouse. In any form you create, you should take time to set the tab order, to make moving quickly from one control to the next easier.

The *tab order* in a form is the sequence of controls through which the focus moves when you tab. If the CUSTOMER_ID field in the Book Purchases form has the focus, and you press the Tab key, the focus does not move to a random field. Instead, the application uses the TabOrder property of controls within the form to determine which object then receives the focus.

Most controls and several kinds of containers have the TabOrder property. When you tab, the application looks at the setting for the TabOrder property of the control you are leaving and then finds the control with the next highest value for TabOrder. The focus then moves to this second control. If you tab again, the application performs the same comparison among the TabOrder properties of various objects within the form. Once you have reached the control with the highest value for TabOrder, the focus moves to the object with the lowest TabOrder value if you tab again. Figure 19.1 shows the tab order of a form.

Figure 19.1.

The tab order in a simple form.

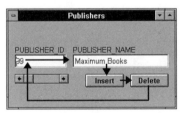

Tab order

In the case of controls, it is easy to understand why they are part of the tab order. The reason for including certain containers—embedded forms, repeater displays, and instances of user-defined classes—is less obvious. Because these containers within a form can contain other objects, however, you need to determine how the focus moves in and out of each container as the user tabs. Figure 19.2 shows how the tab order can move in and out of one such container, an embedded form. It makes sense to include a container in the tab order, to direct the focus to the controls within the container.

Figure 19.2.

Tabbing in and out of an embedded form.

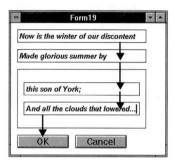

Unfortunately, there is no easy shortcut to setting the tab order. Instead, you must set the TabOrder property of each control manually through the Property sheet.

In addition, the TabEnabled property determines whether a control or container is part of the tab order. If you set the TabEnabled property to FALSE, the application ignores that object in the tab order, even if it has a value assigned to its TabOrder property.

Setting the Tab Order

In this exercise, you will set the tab order within the Book Purchases form.

1. Open the form frmPurchases.

2. Open the Property sheet for the PURCHASE_ID field.

3. Set this control's TabEnabled property to False, and its TabOrder property to 99.

   Because a sequence generates the PURCHASE_ID value, you do not ever want this control to be part of the tab order. You set its TabOrder property to 99 so that this value will not conflict with any TabOrder values you assign to other controls. Every TabOrder value must be unique to make sense of the sequence for tabbing.

4. Open the Property sheet for CUSTOMER_ID and set its TabOrder property to 1.

   This text field is now the first control in the tab order.

5. Set the TabOrder property of other objects in the form to the following settings:

Name	Object Type	TabOrder
DATE_PURCHASED	Text field	2
ORDER_ID	Text field	3
repTitles	Repeater display	4
TITLE_ID	Text field	5
NUM_COPIES	Text field	6
DISCOUNT	Text field	7
button1	Pushbutton (in the class instance)	8
button2	Pushbutton (also in the class instance)	9

You have left the EMPLOYEE_ID text field out of the tab order, because the application automatically sets this value to the ID of whomever is currently logged into the application. Similarly, you will leave the various text fields that use derived values out of the tab order, because the application also sets the values of these controls automatically.

6. Set the TabEnabled property of all other controls in the form to FALSE.

   Before finishing, you need to move the focus to the CUSTOMER_ID text field whenever you begin entering a new purchase. This code will save the user the added step of clicking in the CUSTOMER_ID field for every new purchase record.

7. Add the following bold lines to the method code appearing in the InsertRow() method of the form:

```
Sub InsertRow()
Inherited.InsertRow()

' Get today's date
DATE_PURCHASED.Value = Application.udmGetNow()

' Assign the employee's ID number to the record
EMPLOYEE_ID.Value = Application.udpEmployeeID

' Move the focus to the CUSTOMER_ID field
CUSTOMER_ID.SetFocus()
```

8. Save and run the form.

9. Press the Insert Row button to enter a new purchase.

   The focus automatically moves to the CUSTOMER_ID text field.

10. After entering a customer ID number, press the Tab key.

    The focus moves to the next control in the tab order, ORDER_ID.

11. Continue filling out the order, tabbing as you go.

    Eventually, the focus will move into the repeater display.

12. Press Commit to save the new purchase, and Stop to end this exercise.

As you can see, a relatively simple change to the form made it much easier to enter all the information for a new purchase.

Help Text in an Oracle Power Objects Application

Although the tab order determines where the focus moves, it does not tell you what to do when you get there. To give you hints about the purpose of a control, many applications add *summary help* (also called *status-line hints*, *micro-help*, and a variety of other names), which is displayed on the application's status line.

To see how help text works, move the mouse around the Oracle Power Objects desktop. As you move over buttons in the toolbar, the text appearing on the status line tells you what will happen when you press each button. If you move the cursor over the Property sheet, the help text briefly describes each property or method. As you move the cursor over the buttons in the Object palette, the text describes the type of object you create with each type of drawing tool. Figure 19.3 shows summary help appearing in Oracle Power Objects.

Figure 19.3.

Summary help in Oracle Power Objects.

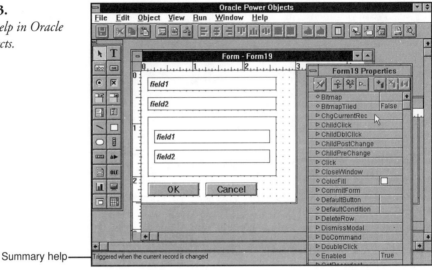

Summary help

Summary help gives you an instant indication of the purpose of a particular object in an application. If you don't understand one of the icons on a toolbar button, the summary text explains what that button does. This feature saves you the few seconds needed to find the right topic in the online help, or the minute or two required to find the relevant information in the printed documentation.

You can add summary text to any Oracle Power Objects application. At runtime, as the focus moves over each object within a form, summary text explaining the purpose of that object appears in the status line. To display these tips, you add the text of the summary help to the HelpText property of a control.

Adding Summary Help to the Book Purchases Form

Once again, you will use the Book Purchases form to learn how to add some usability features to an Oracle Power Objects application.

Unfortunately, applications do not include a status line by default. You need to add a status line to the Bookstore application, using some of the same techniques for adding a custom menu bar or toolbar.

> **Note:** Summary text does not work in the production release of Oracle Power Objects. However, a recent patch has fixed this problem. You can download the patch from the Oracle Web site, http://www.oracle.com.

1. Open the Property sheet for the application.

2. Add the following line to the (Declarations) section:

   ```
   GLOBAL gStatBar AS Object
   ```

3. Add the following code to the InitializeWindow() method of the form frmPurchases:

   ```
   Sub InitializeWindow()
   ' Create a new status line
   gStatBar = NEW StatusLine

   ' Use the default status line
   gStatBar.SysDefaultMenuBar()

   ' Associate the new status line with the form
   self.SetStatusLine(gStatBar)
   ```

4. Open the Property sheet for the PURCHASE_ID field.

5. For the HelpText property, enter Displays a unique purchase ID.

6. Set the HelpText property of other controls in the form to the following settings:

Object	Setting for Help Text
CUSTOMER_ID	Enter the customer ID number
DATE_PURCHASED	The date of the purchase
ORDER_ID	Enter the ID of the order, if any, being purchased
EMPLOYEE_ID	Your employee ID number
TITLE_ID	Enter the ID number of a book
TITLE_NAME	The book's title
PRICE	The book's price
NUM_COPIES	Enter the number of copies purchased
DISCOUNT	Enter the discount applied, if any
fldAdjPrice	The adjusted price of the books

19

continues

Object	*Setting for Help Text*
`fldSubTotal`	`The subtotal for all books`
`fldTaxAmount`	`The amount of sales tax`
`fldTotal`	`The total cost of the purchase`

7. Save and run the form.

8. Move the cursor across the different objects in the form.

    As you move the mouse, the help text for the object currently underneath the cursor appears on the status line.

9. Press Stop to end this exercise.

Although this summary help can be useful, it often cannot impart all the information someone needs. For example, when you pass the cursor over the `Validate()` method in the Property sheet, the Oracle Power Objects summary help cannot give you information about the argument passed to this method, its return value, or the related `ValidateMsg` property. To access this information quickly, you need to consult the online help file.

Adding Online Help to Your Application

Online help files are used almost universally in Macintosh and Windows applications. They have become such an accepted and expected part of productivity applications that you immediately notice when one does not have online help. Although some online help files provide only scant reference information, others give you detailed step-by-step instructions and comprehensive descriptions of important concepts and features of an application.

Online help files created for Microsoft Windows often use the same format. You can design such a help file to be context sensitive by making a few adjustments to the online help and the application itself.

Authoring Online Help

Standard Windows online help is first authored as a document formatted in a particular way so that it can be converted into a help file (.HLP). Saved in rich text format (.RTF), the online help document includes a variety of codes for determining all of the features of each help topic, such as hypertext links and search keywords. After you finish writing the formatted help text, you use one of several standard help compilers (HCP.EXE, HC31.EXE, and so on) to convert the .RTF file into a Windows help file.

Opening Online Help Files

To make the help context sensitive, you call a Windows API procedure, WinHelp, to open the online help file. WinHelp takes as an argument the unique ID number identifying a topic. When Windows opens the online help file, the appropriate topic appears immediately.

A detailed explanation of how to create an online help file is beyond the scope of this lesson, because the process involves a wide array of special codes and formatting needed by the help compiler. In many respects, creating an online help file is like developing an application: You need to apply the exact syntax and formatting conventions before the compiler can create the finished .HLP file.

For the sake of the next exercise, you will use the Oracle Power Objects online help file to learn how to implement context-sensitive help. In your own application, you would work with the documentation writers (or whoever else wrote the online help) to generate the list of context IDs, and then pass these IDs to WinHelp whenever you open an online help file.

Adding Help to the Bookstore Application

The easiest way to add online help to the Bookstore application is to create a small pushbutton and place it next to each control that might need further explanation. When you press the pushbutton, the application opens the online help file at the appropriate topic.

Because this pushbutton will appear throughout the application, you will create it as a user-defined class. This class will have a user-defined property, udmHelpID, that stores the ID number of the help topic to display after you press the pushbutton.

WinHelp is a DLL function, so you need to add its API declaration to the application.

1. Open the (Declarations) section of the application's Property sheet and add the following:

   ```
   (Declarations)
   DECLARE Function WinHelp LIB "USER.EXE" ( ByVal hwnd AS  &
     Long, ByVal help AS String, ByVal command AS Integer, &
     ByVal add AS Long ) AS Long
   CONST cHelpFile = "PWROBJX.HLP"
   ```

   If you had an online help file for your application, you would substitute its filename (and perhaps its path) for the value assigned to the constant cHelpFile.

2. Create a new user-defined class, clsHelpBtn.

3. In the new class, add a small pushbutton with the label ?.

4. Move the pushbutton to the upper-left corner of the class, and resize the boundaries of the class until it has the same height and width as the pushbutton (see Figure 19.4).

19

Figure 19.4.

The new class clsHelpBtn.

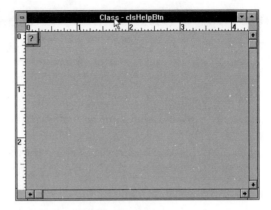

5. Add the following entries to the User Properties window:

Component	Setting
Name	udmHelpID
Type	Property
Datatype	Long

6. Add the new property to the pushbutton in the class.

7. Add the following method code to the `Click()` method of the pushbutton:

```
Sub Click()
' Get the help ID
DIM vHelpID AS Long
vHelpID = self.udmHelpID

' Call the WinHelp procedure, passing the help ID
x = WinHelp( 0, cHelpFile, 1, vHelpID )
```

8. Save the class.

9. Add an instance of the class to the form frmPurchases.

10. Position the instance so that it appears to the right of the PURCHASE_ID field.

    The left edge of the instance should be touching the right edge of the field.

11. Set the udmHelpID property of the instance to 1.

12. Save and run the form.

13. After the form appears in runtime mode, press the Help button.

    The application calls the WinHelp procedure to open the online help file PWROBJX.HLP (see Figure 19.5).

14. Press Stop to end this exercise.

Figure 19.5.

The Oracle Power Objects online help file, opened from the Book Purchases form to a particular topic.

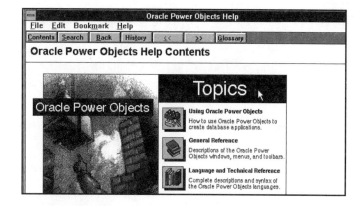

DO	DON'T

DO add summary text to all the objects in your application.

DO be descriptive in the summary text about what users should do when a control is selected.

DO add online help to your application.

DON'T try to cram too much information into summary help. You should always depend on the online help and documentation to provide an explanation.

DON'T write summary help that fills up more than two-thirds of the section of the status line where it appears. If your application will be translated into other languages (especially German and Finnish), you need to leave extra space for the translated text.

DON'T make online help the last part of development. It takes time to write and test online help, particularly if you want to make it context-sensitive.

In a finished application, the opened online help topic would explain something about the PUBLISHER_ID field—why it's there, when and how the application generates new values, and so on. However, what the user might really want is a step-by-step guide for filling out a purchase.

This information would be useful in other forms as well, because new users might not know all the steps needed to complete a record. If a column represented on the form has the NOT NULL or UNIQUE constraint applied to it, there should be some warning to this effect in the instructions. Although applying these constraints in the application is useful, the user has no idea they exist until the application fails to commit the record to the database.

Adding a Wizard to Your Application

In other words, what you need is a wizard. In this exercise, you will add a wizard to the Bookstore application for every major form, describing how to view and edit records through the form. The easiest way to store this information is in the database, so you'll use a bound form to display the instructions.

1. Open the Session window for BOOKS.POS and double-click its Connector icon.

2. Create a new table, WIZARDS, with the following columns:

Name	Data Type	Size	NOT NULL	UNIQUE
FORM_NAME	Varchar32	64	Yes	Yes
WIZARD_TEXT	Varchar32	900		

3. Save the new table to the database.

4. Create a new form, frmWizard, with the label Need Help?.

5. Click and drag the two columns from the WIZARDS table onto the form.

6. Resize the WIZARD_TEXT field until it covers nearly all the form.

   You need to keep a small amount of space at the bottom to add an OK pushbutton.

7. Set the HasScrollBar and MultiLine properties of the field to TRUE.

   Because the text for the wizard might be lengthy, you want to be able to scroll through a large number of steps documented in the wizard.

8. Run the form and enter the following record:

   For FORM_NAME:

   frmPurchases

   For WIZARD_TEXT:

   ```
   1. Enter a CUSTOMER_ID number. If the customer does not
   exist in the database, select Setup ¦ Customers to enter
   this information. You cannot leave this section blank.
   2. If the customer is buying books that he or she ordered,
   enter the ID number of the order.
   3. Enter the ID number of the first book.
   4. Enter the number of copies to be purchased.
   5. Enter the discount, if any, applied to this title.
   6. Continue entering new books.
   7. When finished, press OK to save the new purchase, or
   Cancel to delete it.
   ```

9. Press Commit, and then press Insert Row.

10. Enter frmBookOrders for the FORM_NAME and some instructions for using this form in the WIZARD_TEXT field.

    You're not required to enter a lengthy set of instructions at this point, but you must enter something.

11. Repeat this process for other forms in the application.

12. Press Stop.

    Because you have entered all the instructions you want, you will now remove the FORM_NAME field from the user's view.

13. Set the Visible property of the FORM_NAME text field to FALSE.

14. Set the ReadOnly property of the WIZARD_TEXT field to TRUE.

15. Delete the static text objects from the form.

16. Add a pushbutton labeled OK to the bottom of the form, and enter code in its Click() method to close the form when you press the button.

17. Set the WindowStyle property of the form to Fixed Size Dialog.

    Next, you will create a class for opening the wizard form from any other form in the application. When opened, the wizard will display the correct instructions.

18. Create a new class, clsWizard.

19. Add a pushbutton to the class with the label Instructions.

    Instead of this label, you might display a bitmap on the pushbutton. The bitmap should evoke the idea of step-by-step instructions, such as a series of footsteps.

20. Reposition the pushbutton and resize the class so that it looks like Figure 19.6.

Figure 19.6.

The clsWizard class, used to open the Wizard form.

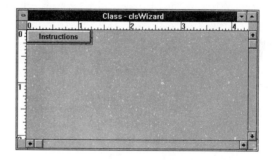

21. Add the following method code to the Click() method of the pushbutton:

```
Sub Click()
' Open the window
frmWizard.OpenWindow()

' Apply the condition
DIM vQueryStr AS String
vQueryStr = "FORM_NAME = '" & self.GetTopContainer.Name & "'"
frmWizard.QueryWhere(vQueryStr)
```

This code filters out all instructions queried from the WIZARDS table except for the one matching the form.

22. Save the class, and then add an instance of it to the Book Purchases form.

23. Save and run the application.

24. Open the Book Purchases form and the press the Instructions pushbutton.

    The form frmWizard now appears, displaying instructions for entering a new purchase.

25. Press Stop to end this exercise.

This wizard is fairly simple, providing some quick guidelines for filling out the form. However, you could easily create a wizard that actually sets values as you go. Although such a wizard might be overkill in a simple form like Book Purchases, it might be very handy in a larger, more complex form.

Error Handlers in Oracle Basic

Very often, users need the greatest amount of hand-holding when something goes wrong in the application. In these cases, you don't want to keep the nature of the problem a mystery; if you do not make some extra effort in your application, users might be left without a clue as to why things don't work as expected. If they press the Commit button and the application shuts down, they need to understand what happened and why.

On Day 13, "Enforcing Business Rules," you already provided some of this feedback. Whenever the Validate() method returned FALSE, you displayed the text entered for the ValidateMsg property. Similarly, the message defined for ValidateRowMsg appeared whenever ValidateRow() returned FALSE. If you broke some business rule by leaving a field blank, or by entering a negative discount, then the application immediately informed you of your mistake.

Validating the data in controls or records does not solve the entire universe of errors, however. For example:

☐ When the application tries to insert more values into an array than there are elements in the array, the application displays the Array out of bounds error message. Although this should be meaningful to a developer who knows something about arrays, the user is unlikely to understand the message. What's more, as the developer responsible for fixing the problem, you need to know which array is out of bounds and why.

☐ When the database returns a SQL error code because it cannot update a table, the user will not know that this happened. If your EXEC SQL statement that includes the UPDATE command cannot find the table, the application does not automatically display an error message. Users that encounter this situation won't realize that updates to the database are not happening as expected.

In the first example, the problem might simply puzzle the user. If the application were in the middle of an important operation, however, such as entering a large number of new orders into the database, the application error would be more than a little annoying. Equally dangerous is the second situation, when no one is aware the information is not being added or updated. In this case, the problem worsens every day until information in the database becomes wholly unreliable.

To summarize, there are three cases in which you need to provide extra information about problems:

☐ When the application fails mysteriously. You need to replace default error messages that are understandable only by a developer with something the user can comprehend. You might also want to add some information to help you debug the problem.

☐ When the application fails unexpectedly. Don't let the user think she was doing everything right if her actions caused the application to fail. You need to explain why the problem occurred.

☐ When the application fails silently. If the application does not display any error message when some operation fails, you need to warn users that a problem is occurring.

In addition, you need to write error handlers to prevent the application from shutting down. When an Oracle Basic error occurs, the application normally stops running. If you write an error handler routine to detect and respond to the error, however, you can avoid this situation.

The process of detecting (or *trapping*) problems and responding to them is called *error handling*. As with other usability related features, this aspect of development often does not receive the attention it deserves. Once you have made the application work to your satisfaction, you might not be excited about taking extra time to add error handler routines to manage the expected and unexpected situations in which the application might fail. If people in the organization depend on the application to do their jobs, however, you don't want to leave them high and dry whenever a problem surfaces. You always need to devote some development time for error handling.

In the next few exercises, you will get experience writing error handlers for both Oracle Basic and SQL errors. In Basic, there is a standard way to handle both types of errors.

Error Handlers in Oracle Basic

The Oracle Basic ON ERROR command lets you respond to a problem with an Oracle Basic routine. Instead of letting the application use drastic measures to handle an error, such as shutting down the application or preventing the operation from continuing, you can use ON ERROR to let an error handler, a special kind of procedure, take care of the situation. ON ERROR handles only problems with Oracle Basic commands and operators; it does not trap SQL errors.

Often, the ON ERROR command is followed by a GOTO statement that moves the point of program execution to the error handler. In other words, the GOTO command lets you jump to a particular line of code within the same method.

When it comes to good coding practices, using a GOTO statement in an ON ERROR command represents an exception to the important rule: Avoid GOTO statements. GOTO statements can make it difficult to track program execution from one section of code to another. Code written like this is called *spaghetti code*, and can be extremely hard to unravel. Therefore, you should use GOTO *only* in ON ERROR commands and nowhere else if you can avoid it.

Writing Your First Error Handler

To give you some familiarity with error handlers, you will start with a relatively simple one. Suppose that you wanted to display a scrolling list of customer names in a form. To implement this, you plan to read values queried from the CUSTOMERS table into an array, and use that array to determine the contents of the scrolling list (in this case, a text field). You will deliberately write the code, however, so that there will be too many customer names for the array to handle.

1. Open the form frmCustomers.

2. Add a new text field, fldNames, to the bottom of the form.

   You might need to lengthen the form to add enough space for this field.

3. Expand the text field until it is about 1.5 inches high.

4. Set the HasScrollBar and MultiLine properties of this text field to TRUE, and its ScrollWithRow property to FALSE.

   The ScrollWithRow property determines whether the contents of a control are linked with the currently selected record. By setting this property to FALSE, you are telling the application to keep the contents of this field the same regardless of where you move in the form's recordset.

5. Set the Datatype property of the text field to String, and its DataSize property to 1024.

   Next, you need to display names queried from the CUSTOMERS table.

6. Set the form's RowFetchMode to Fetch All Immediately.

   This step ensures that the application queries all the records for the form's recordset before you run the method. Without changing this property, the form's recordset might have only a few records queried from the CUSTOMERS table, instead of all of them.

7. Create a new user-defined method, udmNameList, as a subroutine with no arguments.

8. Add the new method to the text field.

9. Add the following method code to the field's `OnLoad()` method:

```
Sub OnLoad()
Inherited.OnLoad()
self.udmNameList()
```

10. Add the following method code to `udmNameList()`:

```
Sub udmNameList()
STATIC vNames(1 TO 3) AS String  ' The array to contain customer names
DIM vNumRecs AS Long        ' The number of customer records
DIM vRecSet AS Object       ' The form's recordset

'Get the number of customer records from the form's recordset
vRecSet = self.GetTopContainer.GetRecordset()
vNumRecs = vRecSet.GetRowCount()

' Iterate through all the records to get the customer's last name,
' and then add them to the array
FOR x = 1 TO vNumRecs
  vRecSet.SetCurRow(x)
  ON ERROR GOTO Handler
  vNames(x) = vRecSet.GetColVal("LNAME")
NEXT x

' Display the values in the text field
DIM vTemp AS String
vTemp = ""
FOR x = 1 to vNumRecs
 vTemp = vTemp & vNames(x) & CHR(13) & CHR(10)
NEXT x

' Return the pointer to the first record
vRecSet.SetCurRow(1)

' Display the names in the list
self.Value = vTemp
EXIT SUB

Handler:
  MSGBOX "Too many customer names to display at the bottom of this form"
```

In the FOR...NEXT loop, the code switches execution to the error handler if the number of customer records exceeds the number of elements in the array (three). After displaying the error message, execution moves down to the bottom of the method code. Because there's nothing past this point, the method stops execution.

The error handler is preceded by the EXIT SUB statement to keep it separate from the rest of the code. After you finish running all the code except the error handler, the application reaches the EXIT SUB command, which stops running any code in this subroutine. (If you added this code to a method with a return value, you would use the EXIT FUNCTION command instead.)

11. Save and run the form.

While the form is opening, the application displays the error message defined in the error handler (see Figure 19.7).

19

Figure 19.7.
The Customers form,
displaying the error message
defined in the error handler.

12. Press Stop to end this exercise.

Polishing this Error Handler

This error handler keeps the application running, even if you exceed the bounds of an array. Unfortunately, it does not let you display the names queried from the form's recordset until you reach the point of exceeding the array's upper bound. When the FOR...NEXT loop fails, it fails completely—you cannot display a partial list of names in the list.

You'll make it possible to view the partial query by modifying the code you just wrote. Most significantly, you need to make it possible for the code to continue executing after the problem occurs. The Oracle Basic RESUME NEXT command tells the application to continue running the method code after the error has been detected.

Note: There are other options for RESUME, as described in its topic in the Oracle Power Objects online help.

If the code continues executing, however, it will run into the same problem several times. Because the error handler displays an error message every time an error occurs, this message will appear several times. To help display the message only once, you will add a variable, vDispMsg, to indicate whether the error message has already been displayed. The code will read vDispMsg before displaying the error message.

1. Add the following bold code to the udmNameList() method:

```
Sub udmNameList()
STATIC vNames(1 TO 3) AS String  ' The array to contain customer names
DIM vNumRecs AS Long             ' The number of customer records
DIM vRecSet AS Object            ' The form's recordset
DIM vDispMsg AS Integer          ' The new flag

vDispMsg = FALSE

'Get the number of customer records from the form's recordset
vRecSet = self.GetTopContainer.GetRecordset()
vNumRecs = vRecSet.GetRowCount()

' Iterate through all the records to get the customer's last name,
' and then add them to the array
FOR x = 1 TO vNumRecs
```

```
      vRecSet.SetCurRow(x)
      ON ERROR GOTO Handler
      vNames(x) = vRecSet.GetColVal("LNAME")
   NEXT x

   ' Display the values in the text field
   DIM vTemp AS String
   vTemp = ""
   FOR x = 1 to vNumRecs
    ON ERROR GOTO Handler
    vTemp = vTemp & vNames(x) & CHR(13) & CHR(10)
   NEXT x

   ' Display the names in the list
   self.Value = vTemp
   EXIT SUB

   Handler:
     IF vDispMsg = FALSE THEN
       MSGBOX "Too many customer names, some not displayed in the scrolling
       ➥list"
       vDispMsg = TRUE
     END IF
     RESUME NEXT
```

2. Save and run the form.

   The error message appears again. This time, the text field at the bottom of the form displays some of the customer names queried from the CUSTOMERS table (see Figure 19.8).

Figure 19.8.

A truncated list of customer names appearing after the error handler has executed.

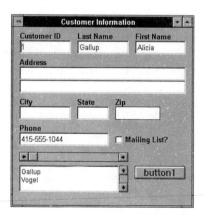

3. Press Stop to end this exercise.

A Different Way to Handle Errors

The error handler you wrote in the last exercise worked fine, but it only applied to a single method. Other method code you write might also have arrays that run out of bounds, mistaken attempts to divide a value by zero, or other common errors that can arise in method code.

In other words, you once again need to design some reusable piece of code instead of duplicating the same work in several different places. Instead of writing an individual error handler for every attempt to divide by zero, you can write a single procedure to handle every time that this happens. You still need to add a short error handler to the method containing the code that encounters the divide by zero error; however, what the application does in response to this error is defined somewhere else.

To make error handling more generic, you will create a new user-defined method, udmBasicErrors, that determines how the application handles several common basic errors. This method will have the following characteristics:

- ☐ An error code passed to the user-defined method as an argument. These error codes will be defined as constants, each corresponding to a different type of Oracle Basic error.

- ☐ The name of the object where the error occurred, passed as an argument. In other words, if code in the Click() method of a pushbutton fails, you will pass the name of the pushbutton to the method as an argument. If you need to use this information to help debug your code, you can display the object name as part of the error message.

- ☐ Within the error handler method, a SELECT CASE statement that uses the error code to detect which kind of error has occurred, and respond accordingly.

- ☐ A return value indicating whether the application needs to take some additional action. To provide this information, our error handler method will return TRUE or FALSE.

This method lets you define and maintain your error handling routines in a single place. If you decide that having a SQLLOOKUP command fail is a relatively benign error, you might instruct the method to return TRUE every time the application encounters a SQLLOOKUP error. If you later decide that this error can cause more damage to your application than you originally realized, then you need only set the return value of udmBasicErrors to FALSE, halting execution of the method in which the SQLLOOKUP problem occurred. Obviously, defining how you respond to SQLLOOKUP failures in a single location is far easier than updating your error handlers in every method that calls SQLLOOKUP.

In the next exercise, you create this new method and add it to the application. Although an actual error handler of this type would include dozens of entries in the SELECT CASE statement, you will keep the range of Basic errors it handles to a much smaller number.

Before beginning this exercise, you should look at the online help topic summarizing all of the Oracle Basic errors to get some sense of the range of situations you might wish to cover with error handlers. Once you start defining error handlers in your own applications, you can create an expanded version of this method to cover more of these Oracle Basic errors.

1. Open the application's Property sheet.

2. In the (Declarations) section, enter

```
(Declarations)
CONST cOBErrors = 9000
CONST cArrayOOB = cOBErrors + 1
CONST cDivByZero = cOBErrors + 2
CONST cSQLLOOKUP = cOBErrors + 3
```

These constant declarations resemble what you did to define the command codes for menu commands and toolbar buttons. You are setting a range of values identifying Oracle Basic errors, starting at 9001 and incremented by 1 for each new Basic error you wish to handle.

3. In the User Properties window, create a new method with the following characteristics:

Characteristic	*Setting*
Name	udmBasicErrors
Type	Function
Datatype	Boolean
Arguments	ByVal vErrCode As Long, vObjName As String

4. Add the new method to the application.

5. Open the Code Editor window for udmBasicErrors() and enter

```
udmBasicErrors(ByVal vErrCode As Long, vObjName As String) As Boolean
DIM vErrorMsg AS String

SELECT CASE vErrCode
  CASE cArrayOOB
    ' Build the error message, including the object name
    vErrorMsg = "Error in " & vObjName & ":" & CHR(13) & CHR (10)
    vErrorMsg = vErrorMsg & "You have exceeded the number
    ➥of elements in an array"
    ' Display the message
    MSGBOX vErrorMsg
    ' Allow execution to continue
    udmBasicErrors = TRUE
  CASE cDivByZero
    MSGBOX "You cannot divide by zero"
    udmBasicErrors = FALSE
  CASE cSQLLOOKUP
    ' Build the error message, including the object name
    vErrorMsg = "Error in " & vObjName & ":" & CHR(13) & CHR (10)
    vErrorMsg = vErrorMsg & "Problems looking up a value from a table
    ➥or view"
```

```
      vErrorMsg = vErrorMsg & CHR(13) & CHR(10) & "SQLLOOKUP Error"
      ' Display the message
      MSGBOX vErrorMsg
      ' Stop execution of the method
      udmBasicErrors = FALSE
END SELECT
```

For two Basic errors, the application builds a lengthy error message providing a lot of information about the nature of the error and where it occurred. The method returns TRUE or FALSE, depending on the kind of error encountered.

Now that you have your generic error handler method, you can put it to work. To avoid complicating this exercise, you will create a new form to test the error handler's capability to deal with these three types of errors.

6. Create a new form, frmTestErrors.

7. Add a new text field, fldTitleID, to the form.

8. Add another text field, fldPrice, with the following property settings:

Property	Setting
Datatype	Double
Format Mask	Currency

This text field will display book prices queried from the TITLES table.

9. Add a pushbutton next to fldTitleID with the label Go!.

10. Add the following method code to the Click() method of this pushbutton:

```
Sub Click()
ON ERROR GOTO Handler
fldPrice.Value = SQLLOOKUP(BOOKS, "SELECT PRICE WHERE
➥TITLE_ID = " & STR(fldTitleID.Value))

EXIT SUB

Handler:
DIM vName AS String
DIM vResult AS Integer
vName = self.Name
vResult = Application.udmBasicErrors(cSQLLOOKUP, vName)
IF vResult THEN
  RESUME NEXT
END IF
```

As you might notice, this code has accidentally omitted the name of the table from which the SQLLOOKUP command should query PRICE values. When the application discovers this defect in the SELECT statement, program execution moves to the error handler, which then calls the new error handling method. If udmBasicErrors does not return TRUE, execution stops in the Click() method.

11. Save and run the form.

12. Enter 1 in the field `fldTitleID` and press the Go! pushbutton.

The application now displays the error message you defined in the error handler, including the name of the text field where the problem occurred (see Figure 19.9).

Figure 19.9.

Displaying an error message from `udmBasicErrors`.

13. After closing this dialog box, press Stop.

Next, you will fix this problem and create the means to handle the divide-by-zero problem.

14. Add the name of the table to the `SQLLOOKUP` statement you entered in the `Click()` method of the pushbutton.

The `SQLLOOKUP` statement should now look like this:

```
fldPrice.Value = SQLLOOKUP(BOOKS, "SELECT PRICE FROM TITLES WHERE
➥TITLE_ID = " & STR(fldTitleID.Value))
```

15. Add two new text fields, `fldDivideBy` and `fldResult`, to the form.

16. In the `PostChange()` method of the `fldDivideBy` field, enter

```
Sub PostChange()
Inherited.PostChange()
ON ERROR GOTO HANDLER
fldResult.Value = fldPrice.Value / self.Value

EXIT SUB

Handler:
DIM vName AS String
DIM vResult AS Integer
vName = self.Name
vResult = Application.udmBasicErrors(cDivByZero, vName)
```

In this case, you have omitted the check to see if the code should continue executing after the error. In the case of a divide-by-zero error, the application will continue trying to divide the price by zero if you use the `RESUME` command to continue program execution. Needless to say, you want to avoid infinite loops like this.

Before you run the form, you will add an additional test for array overflow errors.

17. Add a pushbutton with the label `Array` to the form.

18. Enter the following code in the pushbutton's `Click()` method:

```
Sub Click()
STATIC vArray(1 to 5) AS Long
```

```
FOR x = 0 to 5
  vArray(x) = x
  ON ERROR GOTO Handler
NEXT x
MSGBOX "All done!"

EXIT SUB

Handler:
DIM vName AS String
DIM vResult AS Integer
vName = self.Name
vResult = Application.udmBasicErrors(cArrayOOB, vName)
IF vResult THEN
  RESUME NEXT
END IF
```

The code accidentally tries to insert an extra value into the array. Although the array has five elements, incremented from 1 to 5, the code tries to insert values from 0 to 5 (that is, six values) into the array.

19. Save and run the form.

20. Enter 1 in the fldTitleID field.

    Because you fixed the SQLLOOKUP statement, it queries the price of a book and displays it in the fldPrice field.

21. In the fldDivideBy field, enter 0.

    Your error handling routines take care of this divide-by-zero error, in part by displaying the error message shown in Figure 19.10.

Figure 19.10.

The error message for the divide-by-zero error.

22. Enter 2 in the fldDivideBy text field.

    No error has occurred, so the message does not reappear.

23. Press the Array pushbutton.

    Because you have exceeded the upper bound of the array, the error message you defined as part of your error handler appears, as shown in Figure 19.11.

Figure 19.11.

The error message for the array out of bounds error.

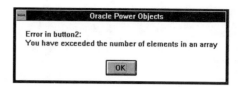

24. After closing this dialog box, press Stop.

    The `All done!` message appeared after the error message because in `udmBasicErrors`, you returned `TRUE` in the case of array-out-of-bound errors. To make sure that your error handling method is working properly, change it to return `FALSE`. If you look at the code in the `Click()` method of the button, you will see that the `All done!` message will not appear in this case, because program execution will not return to the `FOR...NEXT` loop. If you're confused at this point, take a moment to read this code carefully to understand how it works.

25. Open the Property sheet for the application and enter the following bold change in the `udmBasicErrors()` method:

```
udmBasicErrors(ByVal vErrCode As Long, vObjName As String) As Boolean
DIM vErrorMsg AS String

SELECT CASE vErrCode
  CASE cArrayOOB
    ' Build the error message, including the object name
    vErrorMsg = "Error in " & vObjName & ":" & CHR(13) & CHR (10)
    vErrorMsg = vErrorMsg & "You have exceeded the
    ➥number of elements in an array"
    ' Display the message
    MSGBOX vErrorMsg
    ' Allow execution to continue
    udmBasicErrors = FALSE
  .
  .
  .
```

    This code fragment does not include the remaining lines appearing in this method.

26. Save and run the form.

27. Press the Array pushbutton.

    As expected, the error dialog box message appears, but the other message does not.

28. Press Stop to end this exercise.

You now have the means to trap and respond to a wide array of Oracle Basic errors. You could easily add this method and the code behind it to another application, to give you some general routines for error handling that you add to all your development projects.

19

DO	**DON'T**

DO write error handler routines for a wide range of errors.

DO migrate your error handling routines to a generic error handler such as `udmBasicErrors`.

DON'T try to trap and respond to every conceivable Oracle Basic error. Instead, you should plan for the most likely errors to occur in your application.

DON'T make your error handler routines too generic. You often want to have some flexibility in how you respond to different types of errors. Although you never want to resume execution after a divide-by-zero error, you might be able to live with the consequences of a failed `SQLLOOKUP`. In other cases, an error in `SQLLOOKUP` might be catastrophic enough that you want to stop executing method code at that point.

In the next exercise, you add similar capabilities for trapping SQL errors in your application.

Trapping a SQL Error

Every computer language needs some error trapping commands. SQL has several designed to handle errors in SQL code, as well as problems with database objects.

When you execute DDL, DML, or TPL commands in a database, the database engine can return a code indicating whether the operation was successful. If the command failed, the code returned is the ID number for a particular type of error, explaining the reasons for the failure.

In Oracle Power Objects, you have two types of error IDs that you can trap:

☐ Codes indicating the general class of SQL error. The `SQLERRCLASS` function returns a number between 0 and 13 that describes what happened when it tried to execute some piece of SQL code. These IDs apply to all database engines. `SQLERRCLASS` returns the code for the last SQL operation executed.

☐ Codes returned from a particular database engine. Each relational database has its own range of SQL error codes. The `SQLERRCODE` function returns this database-specific ID, instead of the generic number returned by `SQLERRCLASS`. `SQLERRCODE` often gives you more specific information about a database operation than `SQLERRCLASS`. You need the documentation for that specific database engine, however, to interpret the error code. As with `SQLERRCLASS`, `SQLERRCODE` returns the code for the last SQL operation executed.

You can also use the `SQLERRTEXT` function to display the text associated with a particular database error. This error message is returned by the database, so `SQLERRTEXT` gives you platform-specific information about errors.

In the next exercise, you create a new form for executing SQL commands. This form includes fields displaying SQL error codes and text, as returned by the SQLERRCLASS, SQLERRCODE, and SQLERRTEXT functions.

1. Create a new form, frmSQL2, with the label Run SQL Commands.

2. Add a text field to the top half of the form with the following properties:

Property	Setting
Name	fldSQL
Datatype	String
DataSize	2056
HasScrollBar	True
MultiLine	True

3. Add another text field below fldSQL2, called fldErrText, with the same properties (except for its name).

   Leave space between the two fields to add other controls.

4. Add a pushbutton with the label Go to the space between the two fields.

5. Add two more text fields, fldErrClass and fldErrCode, to the same area.

6. Use static text objects to label fldErrClass as Error Class, and fldErrCode as Database Error Code.

7. Set the ReadOnly property of fldErrClass, fldErrCode, and fldErrText to True.

   Add the following method code to the Click() method of the pushbutton:

```
Sub Click()
DIM vCommand AS String
vCommand = fldSQL.Value

' Run the SQL command
EXEC SQL AT BOOKS :vCommand
fldErrClass.Value = SQLERRCLASS
fldErrCode.Value = SQLERRCODE

' Display the error text, if any
IF fldErrCode.Value <> 0 THEN
   fldErrText.Value = SQLERRTEXT
ELSE
   fldErrText.Value = "Operation successful"
END IF
```

8. Save and run the form.

9. Enter the following text in the field fldSQL:

```
CREATE TABLE FOO
    (FOO_ID      NUMBER,
     FOO_DESC    VARCHAR2(64))
```

10. Press Go.

    The form now tells you that the CREATE TABLE operation was successful.

11. Replace the text in `fldSQL` with the following:

    ```
    INSERT INTO BOO (FOO_ID)
       VALUES (1)
    ```

    The misprint in this SQL code is deliberate, because you want to see what happens when the database encounters a problem.

12. Press Go.

    The form now displays error codes and an error message returned from the database (see Figure 19.12).

Figure 19.12.

Error codes and text returned from the database.

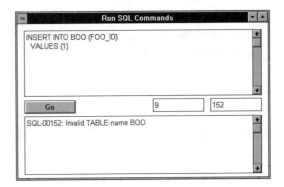

13. Replace the text with the following:

    ```
    INSERT INTO FOO (BOO_ID)
       VALUES (1)
    ```

    Again, you have made a deliberate mistake to test your SQL error trapping capabilities.

14. Press Go.

    The form displays a different set of error codes and messages, as shown in Figure 19.13.

Figure 19.13.

New error codes and text.

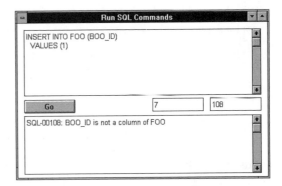

15. Correct the mistaken column name and press Go.

16. Replace the text with the command COMMIT and press Go.

    You have now committed your first change to the new table. You'll make another deliberate error in the next step.

17. Enter the following SQL code, and then press Go:

    ```
    DROP FROM FOO WHERE FOO_ID = '1'
    ```

    You use the DELETE command to remove rows, and the DROP command to delete database objects. Because you used the wrong command, you see another error.

18. Enter the command DROP TABLE FOO and press Go.

    You don't want to leave this table in your database, so delete it before finishing.

19. Press Stop to end this exercise.

DO	DON'T

DO warn users about database errors.

DO shut down the application if these errors threaten "mission-critical" information.

DO leave users some way to continue to use other parts of the application if there is a database error.

DO substitute your own error messages for those returned from SQLERRTEXT, if you need a more "user-friendly" message.

DON'T end program execution for every database error.

DON'T leave out critical information about the state of the database that developers and MIS personnel need to address the problem if you write your own error messages.

DON'T make it too easy for users to continue, especially if someone else in the organization needs to know about problems with the database.

19

An Alternative Way to Display SQL Error Messages

If you do not have fields especially designed for displaying error codes and messages, how do you tell the user when a database error has occurred? The easiest way is to use the SQL command WHENEVER, which can display an error message whenever the database encounters a problem. You use the WHENEVER command as part of an EXEC SQL statement, so that you can communicate directly with the database to discover the last error encountered there.

For more information on the WHENEVER command, consult the Oracle Power Objects user's guide or online help.

Error Handling and Usability

You now have the means to handle a wide range of problems that can occur in your application, on both the front and back ends.

- [ ] Using `Validate()`, `ValidateRow()`, and similar methods, you can detect when users have broken business rules and tell them what they did wrong.

- [ ] Using the `ON ERROR` command, you can trap and respond to Oracle Basic errors.

- [ ] Using the `SQLERRCLASS`, `SQLERRTEXT`, `SQLERRCODE`, and `WHENEVER` commands, you can inform the user about SQL errors.

These features of your application help users understand what to do when a problem occurs. Instead of wasting time trying to puzzle out the nature of the problem, they can quickly move toward resolving it. Therefore, error handling is an important kind of usability feature: Rather than confusing your users and wasting their time, you give them immediate and useful feedback about a problem. No matter whether they can solve these problems themselves, or they need the help of a developer or MIS specialist, they are not left in the dark about what to do next. This approach eliminates a great deal of frustration for users when problems inevitably arise.

Summary

Today, you learned about the following points:

- [ ] Usability is an important consideration in any application.

- [ ] Usability often depends on the ability to give instructions through summary help, online help, and wizards.

- [ ] To add summary help, set the `HelpText` property of objects within a form.

- [ ] To add context-sensitive online help, first write and compile the online help file. You can then use the `WinHelp` API procedure to open the online help file to a particular topic.

- [ ] A wizard is a set of instructions that walk the user through all the steps needed to fill out a form. A wizard can be relatively simple, just displaying the instructions. It can be more sophisticated, entering values in controls as you go.

- [ ] You can further enhance your application's usability by setting the tab order in all its forms.

- [ ] Error handling enhances usability by giving users information about problems that arise and what to do next.

- [ ] You can use the `ON ERROR` command to trap Oracle Basic errors.

- [ ] You can use several SQL error-trapping commands to respond to database errors.

What Comes Next?

Tomorrow, you will add one of the most important usability enhancements in your application: performance. Another source of frustration for users is waiting too long for the application to perform simple tasks such as querying records, enforcing business rules, and running reports.

In any application, you can improve performance by making adjustments to both the front and back ends. Some of these adjustments will look familiar, because they use techniques learned in earlier lessons. Some of the newer techniques will take advantage of the client/server architecture of an Oracle Power Objects application to speed access to information. In this program architecture, sometimes the server can perform some tasks faster than the client; at other times, the client is more efficient.

Therefore, you can attack system performance from several different angles at once. Your ultimate goal is to reach a point where the application responds so fast that users no longer think about performance as an issue.

Q&A

Q Are there ever reasons not to display error messages?

A In some cases, you might not want to display a SQL error message, which can include the exact names of database objects. If you are concerned about system security, you might want to keep users from seeing the exact names of database objects.

Q Is there any way to detect an error before Oracle Power Objects displays its built-in error messages?

A Not in the current version of Oracle Power Objects.

Q When you are adding usability features, are there any special considerations for internationalization?

A When you are adding error handlers, you might want to read the actual text of error messages from a separate file, instead of hard coding the messages in your Oracle Power Objects application. When you need to translate these messages into a different language, you can edit them in this file, instead of revising them in the application itself (requiring you to recompile the application every time you add, change, or translate error messages).

Q Can I make it possible for my application to display an online help file when the user presses the F1 key?

A Not in the current version of Oracle Power Objects, although you will be able to capture key presses in the next version.

Usability Enhancements

Workshop

The Workshop consists of quiz questions to help you solidify your understanding of the material covered and exercises to give you experience in using what you've learned. Try and understand the quiz and exercises before you go on to tomorrow's lesson.

Quiz

1. What is the difference between SQLERRCLASS and SQLERRCODE?
2. What kind of value do you need to pass to the WinHelp procedure to open a particular online help topic?
3. What is summary help?
4. If you want to remove a control from the tab order, what do you do?
5. Can you use ON ERROR to respond to a SQL error?

Exercises

1. Set a meaningful tab order in other forms in the application.
2. Add help text to these forms.
3. Add some additional error handler routines to udmBasicErrors to manage a broader range of Oracle Basic errors.

Quiz Answers

1. SQLERRCLASS returns a generic error code applicable to all database platforms, whereas SQLERRCODE returns the error ID generated by the database itself, specific to that database engine.
2. A numeric ID identifying a particular online help topic.
3. The hints that appear on the status line of your application.
4. Set its TabEnabled property to FALSE.
5. Yes and no. In some cases, you can detect whether the EXEC SQL and SQLOOKUP commands have experienced problems. However, the error is a Basic error, not a SQL error from the database.

624

Improving System Performance

Today, you learn about the following topics:

- ☐ Accelerated development
- ☐ Creating mini-applications
- ☐ Performance in a client/server environment
- ☐ Where performance suffers most
- ☐ Incremental fetching
- ☐ Maintaining local recordsets
- ☐ Creating client-enforced privileges
- ☐ Collapsing data into a single column
- ☐ Global changes to tables
- ☐ Migrating procedures to the server
- ☐ Improving reporting speed
- ☐ Classes and performance
- ☐ Graphics and performance
- ☐ OLE data objects and performance
- ☐ Streamlining your Oracle Basic code

This lesson is unlike others in this book, in that more time is spent on lecture than lab exercises. This variation is necessary because many performance enhancements require a lot of work throughout your application. You will hear about these enhancements first, therefore, and then try to implement many of them in your own application.

If every performance tip had an exercise, this would be a very long chapter! Nevertheless, this lesson does include several exercises that demonstrate how to improve the performance of an Oracle Power Objects application.

Overview

Performance is an important consideration in any application. In database applications, there are many additional performance challenges posed by the relationship between the front and back ends of such applications. What is the fastest way to query records? How can I get my reports to run faster? If I have a lot of transactions to send to the server, is there any way to free my client to perform other tasks while the server is finishing?

Although client/server applications have these additional challenges, they also provide some important opportunities. For example, you can frequently reassign the responsibility for a particular task from the client to the server, or vice-versa, depending on which end of the application would handle the task with the greatest speed and efficiency.

When you need to look up the title of a book, where should the application store book titles, and how should it get this information? The most obvious option is to use SQLLOOKUP to query the title from the TITLES table in the database. However, SQLLOOKUP slows down the application for every lookup it has to make. The loss of speed in running forms and reports can increase exponentially with the number of lookups you add.

The basic problem with SQLLOOKUP is that it must perform a new query every time it looks up a value from a table. If you could find some way to maintain all of the relevant information from that table on the client, you would reduce drastically the number of queries the application would make of the server. Instead of many little queries, the application could issue a single query and then maintain the resulting values somewhere on the client. Rather than making the database responsible for answering every lookup, you shift that responsibility to the application itself for maintaining the list of book titles. Consequently, the server has less work to do, and the amount of network traffic decreases as well.

Where Performance Suffers Most

This example illustrates both the challenges and opportunities for fine-tuning system performance in an Oracle Power Objects application. Because your application will be communicating with a database (or perhaps several databases) every minute, you need to think about how to avoid the following situations:

- Burdening the server with too many requests for data.
- Adding too much traffic to the network. Your application can get information across the network only as fast as the network itself is able to provide it.
- Occupying either the client or the server with lengthy processing tasks, such as performing large numbers of calculations or checks.
- Returning too much information from the server. Not only does this add to the load of the server and the network, but it also requires extra memory for the client to maintain information it might not use.
- Tying up either the client or the server when it could be performing other tasks.

As you shall see, these are only a few of the potential performance problems your application can face. In this chapter, you will use a variety of different measures to improve the speed and efficiency of the Bookstore application.

Speeding Development

Before you improve the application's performance, there are some steps you can take to cut down the time it takes to launch and run Oracle Power Objects.

The Main Window

When you first install Oracle Power Objects, all of the sample applications included with the product appear in the Main window. As you add your own sessions, libraries, and applications to this window, you not only face the clutter of too many icons (many of which represent sample applications you're not using), but you are also slowing down Oracle Power Objects.

Whenever Oracle Power Objects launches, it loads a reference to each object in the Main window. The amount of information it loads is substantial, so each object appearing in this window adds noticeably to the time it takes to launch and run Oracle Power Objects.

Before you do anything else, therefore, you should delete the icons for the sample applications from the Main window. By selecting an icon for an object in Main and pressing the Cut button, you remove the reference to the object, but you do not delete its file from the operating system. If you need something from that library, session, or application, you can always select the File | Open command (or press the Open button) to add it to the Main window again. If you want to use the class clsTab from the sample applications, you can add the library in which it is stored to the Main window temporarily.

You should apply the same rule no matter what objects appear in the Main window. If you are not currently using an application, library, or session in the Main window, you should remove its icon. Although it might seem useful to have all of these objects handy, the cost in system performance offsets any gain in convenience.

The Application

As you have noticed already, the more objects you add to the application, the longer it takes to launch. At startup, the application needs to load references to forms, reports, classes, OLE data resources, bitmap resources, and other features of the application. In addition, it needs to generate any recordsets, menu bars, toolbars, and status lines you create for the application, and it might open connections to the database through sessions used by the application.

In other words, while you're still developing the application, you might need to find a faster way to test and run some of its forms and reports. Although the Run Form button lets you run a single form or report at a time, you often need to run several at the same time. If a form shares a recordset, opens a dialog box or another form, opens a report, or makes reference to any other form in the application, you need to run the application to test the form.

If you run the application now, however, you must wait a few extra seconds while it creates a custom menu bar, calls some methods, and performs other tasks. In addition, you need to go through the splash screen and the login dialog box to open the form or report you want.

One way around this problem is to move groups of forms into a separate dummy application for testing. This secondary application has fewer objects in it, and it might not create custom

toolbars and menus, stand-alone recordsets, and other objects at startup. Therefore, the tests you run on objects in this dummy application go faster than if you tested them in the real application. You always want to test all objects in the real application before you finish, however, to make sure everything works as expected.

Mini-Applications

Not only can you create mini-applications for testing, but you might also enhance the performance of a large application by breaking it down into two or three smaller ones. Each mini-application serves a very limited purpose and runs faster than a larger application combining all the separate executables. If you need to launch another application, you can call the WinExec API procedure.

Calling *WinExec* to Launch an Application

On Day 11, "Graphics and Other Matters," you used the Windows API procedure WinExec to launch applications. In the next exercise, you will use WinExec again to launch a mini-application used to enter employee information.

1. Create a new application, EMP.POA, and save it to the C:\BOOKS directory.

2. In this new application, add a single form, frmEmployees2.

3. Click and drag the EMPLOYEES table into the form.

4. Set the RowFetchMode of the form to Fetch all immediately, and then add an instance of one of the VCR control classes to the form.

5. In the BOOKS.POS application, open the Property sheet for the application and enter the following bold change to its DoCommand() method:

```
Function DoCommand(cmdCode as Long) As Long
.
.
.
CASE cEmployees
' frmEmployees.OpenWindow()
WinExec("C:\BOOKS\EMP.EXE", 9)
```

Once again, we are showing only a portion of the code in this method. In this fragment, you have commented out the code you might have added to open the form frmEmployees when the user selects the Setup | Employees menu command.

At this point, you would usually run the application to test the new feature you added. However, you would need to compile the EMP.POA application to perform the test, and you will not be learning how to compile this until the next lesson. Therefore, take out this feature temporarily, although you can test it after you finish Day 21's lesson.

6. In the DoCommand() code just described, comment the line that calls WinExec, and uncomment the line that opens frmEmployees.

Tip: If you are having trouble running some method code, the problem might not lie with the line of code you think is the cause. Execution can stop at the line before the one with the problem, or the difficulty might be with a variable, property, method, or object reference in the code. Therefore, deleting this line might be a hasty measure you will regret later when you discover the real problem (such as entering the wrong name for an object, or trying to store a value in a variable that doesn't fit that variable's data type). If you comment the code instead of deleting or replacing it, you can simply uncomment it to activate it again.

7. Press Save.

Some Database-Related Performance Tips

As mentioned earlier, there are several ways in which you can improve your application's capability to communicate with the database.

Improving Query Performance

The most noticeable enhancement you can make is to improve the speed with which the application queries records. As the number of records returned from a query increases, so does the time needed to finish returning records from the database.

The *RowFetchMode* Property

The first step you can take is to make sure that your forms have the correct setting for the RowFetchMode property. This property of all bindable containers determines how many records from a table or view the application initially queries for the container's recordset. In other words, you do not need to query all the records to begin with; instead, you can query only a few at a time. If you scroll through the container's recordset, the application then fetches each new batch of records as needed, until ultimately all of the records from the table or view are queried. However, there are cases in which you need to query all of the records immediately, as described next.

The RowFetchMode property has the settings outlined in Table 20.1.

Table 20.1. `RowFetchMode` settings.

Setting	Description
Fetch as needed	Fetches only a few records at a time. For most containers, the application fetches 10 records at a time. For repeater displays that show more than 10 records in their scrolling list, the application queries enough records to fill the repeater display.
Fetch count first	Queries the total number of records to be queried when the application fetches the first group of records. The reason for having this information is that a scrollbar used as a recordset browser can set the proper number of records as its upper range (as stored in the control's `ScrollMax` property).
Fetch all immediately	Fetches all of the records from the recordset.

The first two settings keep the number of records in the application's memory as low as possible, while reducing to a minimum the amount of information across the network. As the user scrolls through a form's recordset, the application can then fetch a few more records, adding only a small packet of information to the traffic across the network.

As useful as these settings for `RowFetchMode` can be, there are situations in which the application must query all of the records:

☐ If you perform any kind of global calculation involving values in the recordset, the application must query all the records. For example, if you use the `SUM` function to add all the values displayed in a bound text field, then the application must query all of the records to do the addition.

☐ If you perform any kind of global operation on the recordset, then the application queries all remaining records.

☐ If you need to know the actual number of rows to be queried from the recordset, you need to set the `RowFetchMode` to `Fetch all immediately`. The VCR control class you created on Day 16, "User-Defined Classes," had one pushbutton that moved the pointer to the last record in a container's recordset. The code that moved the pointer assumed that it had an accurate count of the number of records in the recordset, and then used the `SetCurRow()` method to move to the last record (identified by row number). However, if the container has its `RowFetchMode` set to anything but `Fetch all immediately`, the `GetRowCount()` method returns the number of the last row fetched, which is not necessarily the last row in the table or view.

You should take time to go through the application and set the `RowFetchMode` property of any form not using one of the VCR controls to `Fetch as needed`. Remember, however, that if you use this setting in a form containing an instance of one of the VCR control classes, the control cannot work properly.

Using Stand-Alone Recordsets

One way to reduce the number of times the application requests the same information from the database is to create a stand-alone recordset containing the data. For example, you often need the name of a customer to display in a text field. Instead of using SQLLOOKUP or a master-detail form, both of which require frequent queries of the same information from the CUSTOMERS table, you can instead read the information from the stand-alone recordset. When the application launches, it creates the stand-alone recordset and queries values from a table or view to populate it.

To illustrate how to use a stand-alone recordset in this fashion, you will create one containing descriptions of different types of books. When the application needs to find the description of a title's topic, it looks up this information in the bound stand-alone recordset, instead of in the BOOK_TYPES table.

1. Create a new form, frmStandalone.

2. In the BOOKS.POS session, open the Table Editor window for TITLES.

3. Click and drag the following columns from this table onto the form: TITLE_ID, TITLE_NAME, and TYPE_ID.

4. Add another text field to the form with the following properties:

Property	Setting
Name	fldType
Datatype	String
DataSize	32

5. Add a scrollbar to the form for browsing.

6. Open the Property sheet for the application and add the following line to the (Declarations) section:

   ```
   (Declarations)
   GLOBAL gTypeRecs AS Object
   ```

7. At the end of the code appearing in the OnLoad() method, add

   ```
   Sub OnLoad()
   .
   .
   .
   ' Create the stand-alone recordset containing book types

   gTypeRecs = NEW DBRecordset(BOOKS, TRUE)
   gTypeRecs.SetQuery("select TYPE_ID, TYPE_DESC from BOOK_TYPES", FALSE)
   gTypeRecs.ReQuery()
   gTypeRecs.FetchAllRows()
   ```

This method code includes the following sections:

- [ ] The NEW DBRecordset statement, declaring gTypeRecs as a new stand-alone recordset that will query records from the table.
- [ ] A call to the recordset's SetQuery() method, which defines the query used to populate the recordset. The columns identified in the SELECT statement become the columns in the recordset.
- [ ] A call to the ReQuery() method, which instructs the application to perform the query for the stand-alone recordset.

8. Open the Property sheet for the TYPE_ID field and enter the following code in its PostChange() method:

```
Sub PostChange()
Inherited.PostChange()
IF NOT ISNULL(self.Value) THEN
  DIM vNumRecs AS Long
  DIM vTypeID AS Long
  vNumRecs = gTypeRecs.GetRowCount()
  ' If there is a matching TYPE_ID value in the standalone
  ' recordset, display its corresponding TYPE_DESC value in
  ' the field fldType
  FOR x = 1 to vNumRecs
  gTypeRecs.SetCurRow(x)
    IF gTypeRecs.GetColVal("TYPE_ID") = self.Value THEN
      fldType.Value = gTypeRecs.GetColVal("TYPE_DESC")
      EXIT FOR
    END IF
  NEXT x
END IF
```

9. Save and run the form.

10. Scroll among the records displayed in the form.

   As you move to each record, the application looks up the correct description of each book in the stand-alone recordset and displays it in the fldType field.

11. Press Stop to end this exercise.

This technique improves performance only in cases in which the number of records is relatively small—no more than 50 to 100. If the recordset is any larger, the application needs more time to loop through all the records looking for a value than if you were to query it directly from the database. Therefore, it works best in situations like this example, where you expect only a small number of records to appear.

Shared Recordsets

Another way to keep a single recordset in memory for reference is to create a hidden form bound to a frequently used table like BOOK_TYPES, CUSTOMERS, or EMPLOYEES. The application loads and hides this form at startup, and then uses it to look up values in that form's recordset.

The trick to making this work is to share this hidden form's recordset with other containers in the application. This technique reduces the number of instances of the same recordset that you need to maintain in the application at any time. Rather than one instance per container, you keep a single copy of the recordset, bound to the hidden form, in memory at all times.

To illustrate this principle, you will create a hidden form that queries records from the CUSTOMERS table, as well as two visible forms for displaying customer information. These visible forms will share a recordset with the hidden form.

You will add these forms to a new mini-application, CUST.POA, to avoid cluttering the BOOKS.POA application any further. In addition, you need to avoid adding more code to the OnLoad() method to open these forms, or more menu commands to open forms you do not intend to keep in your application.

1. Create a new application, C:\BOOKS\CUST.POA.

2. Add a new form to this application, frmCustHidden.

3. Click and drag the icon for the CUSTOMERS table from the BOOKS.POS session onto the form.

4. Create a new form, frmCustVisible1.

5. Drag the icon for CUSTOMERS onto this form.

6. Create another form, frmCustVisible2, and drag CUSTOMERS onto this form as well.

7. Add scrollbars to both forms.

8. Add the following lines of method code to the application's OnLoad() method:

```
Sub OnLoad()
frmCustHidden.HideWindow()
frmCustVisible1.OpenWindow()
frmCustVisible2.OpenWindow()
```

9. Save and run the application.

   Both frmCustVisible1 and frmCustVisible2 appear. As you scroll through the records in one form, the same records appear in the other form. Because the forms share the same recordset, the pointer for all of them moves to the same record as you scroll in either form.

10. Press Stop to end this exercise.

The one serious limitation of this approach is that you cannot apply it to containers displaying detail records in a master-detail relationship. For example, if you were to keep the records from TITLES in a hidden form, you could not share its recordset with a form using TITLES as the source of detail records. One such form is frmPubsBooks, in which PUBLISHERS records displayed on the form comprise the master, and TITLES records in the repeater display comprise the detail.

Although you might be tempted to write method code that maintains the master-detail relationship between these recordsets, bypassing the `LinkMasterForm`, `LinkMasterColumn`, and `LinkDetailColumn` properties, you should be skeptical about this solution for the following reasons:

☐ Creating a master-detail relationship through the `LinkMasterForm`, `LinkMasterColumn`, and `LinkDetailColumn` is a "bullet-proof" (that is, tested and reliable) measure. Unlike your own method code, you do not have to worry about extensively testing these properties to feel confident that the application is properly maintaining the relationship between master and detail records.

☐ The amount of code you would need to write is considerable, especially if you are going to maintain referential integrity among master and detail records.

☐ The code that would synchronize the master and detail records would be far slower than using these built-in features of Oracle Power Objects, particularly when there are large master or detail recordsets.

However, if you design several forms for displaying the same information, you should consider sharing a recordset among them. Before finishing your application, you should examine your forms for opportunities to share recordsets among them.

Storing Data in a Blaze Database

One way to query records quickly into the client and then store them in a format easily read by the application is to maintain local copies of these records in a Blaze database. For example, when you start the application or load a particular form, the application can query records from frequently used tables like CUSTOMERS, TITLES, and BOOK_TYPES, and then save this information to copies of these tables in a Blaze database located on the client system.

The method code needed to perform this operation is relatively simple. You can use several shortcuts, such as the `CopyColFrom()` method, which copies all the data from a column in one recordset to a column in a different recordset. Once the information has been copied from the table on the remote server, you do not need to continue querying the server for this information. To reduce network traffic and the number of queries the remote server needs to handle, you instead look for the same information in the Blaze database.

This technique works best when you expect the records from a table to remain unchanged while the application is running. For example, while you are entering orders into the system, you do not expect anyone to be adding new categories of books to the BOOK_TYPES table. It is relatively safe, therefore, to copy the records from BOOK_TYPES in an Oracle7 session into the same table in a Blaze session. When you need to find a book category through SQLOOKUP or some other means, you can use the BOOK_TYPES records in the Blaze database to provide this information. You would never use this technique on a table that changed regularly, however, such as the PURCHASES and ORDERS tables.

If you do not expect the contents of the table to change very often, you might not need to query the server every time the application launches. Instead, you can add a procedure to your application that checks every day or so to see if the contents have changed, and then update the contents of the Blaze database if necessary.

Views and Master-Detail Relationships

If you need to show a master-detail relationship in a form, one option is to use a view as the underlying record source. If you use a multitable view instead of several separate tables, the database queries and joins records in the database before handing them off to the application. Frequently, the database can perform the join faster than the application, especially when you are running against a powerful remote server like Oracle7 or SQL Server.

This technique works best in one-to-one relationships, in which there is one matching record in the detail recordset for a master record. In other words, in cases when you need to perform a lookup into a foreign table to find a value (such as the description of a book's topic, read from the BOOK_TYPES table), you can often use a view to get this information.

You can apply this technique only in forms used to display records, but not to edit them. Because you cannot insert, delete, or update records through a multitable view, you should not use a view as the record source for a form in which users need to enter data. For browser forms, however, views are an excellent record source.

Caching Records to Disk

Bindable containers have a property, `RecSrcMaxMem`, that determines the amount of information the application maintains in the container's recordset before caching this information to disk. To save memory, you can set the value for `RecSrcsMaxMem` so that the application regularly copies the contents of large recordsets to a temporary operating system file. You will never see this file, nor will the user. When the application is finished working with a recordset, it deletes the temporary file.

The value you enter for `RecSrcMaxMem` is the number of kilobytes of information the recordset can contain before the application starts caching it to disk. The default setting for `RecSrcMaxMem` is 0, so the application will not use disk caching unless you tell it to. Standard settings for `RecSrcMaxMem` depend on the type of computer you plan to use. For low-end computers with less memory, 64 to 128KB are common settings; for high-end computers, the amount of memory set as the upper limit before caching can be measured in megabytes.

Global Updates to the Database

Because the SQL language is written to simplify any general change to the database, you should leap at the chance to use this capability. For example, if you need to delete all orders that are on hold, you can use the SQL command DELETE to quickly move through the table and perform the necessary deletions. The EXEC SQL statement that performs this operation might look like this:

```
EXEC SQL AT BOOKS DELETE FROM ORDERS WHERE ON_HOLD = -1
```

This is a simple piece of code to write, and fast for the database to execute. In contrast, here is the code that you would write to iterate through all the records in a form's recordset and delete the orders on hold:

```
' Get a reference to the recordset object
DIM vRecSet AS Object
vRecSet = self.GetTopContainer.GetRecordset()

' Delete all records on hold from the recordset
FOR x = 1 TO vRecSet.GetRowCount()
  vRecSet.SetCurRow(x)
  IF vRecSet.GetColVal("ON_HOLD") = -1 THEN
    vRecSet.DeleteRow()
  END IF
NEXT x
```

To showcase SQL's capability to make global changes to a table, you will add to your application the capability to delete all orders on hold, or take them all off hold.

1. Open the form for reviewing orders on hold, frmOrderReview.

2. Give the repeater display in this form the name frmOrders.

   When you created this form on Day 15, "Adding Security to Your Application," you had not named this repeater display. Because you need to refer to it in some later method code, give it a descriptive name now.

3. Add a pushbutton with the Label property Delete All.

4. Add the following code to the pushbutton's Click() method:

```
Sub Click()
' Ask whether you really want to do this
DIM vResult AS Integer
vResult = MSGBOX ("Do you want to delete all these orders?",
➥36, "Deleting orders on hold")

' If so, delete the records and requery the repeater display
IF vResult = 6 THEN
  EXEC SQL AT BOOKS DELETE FROM ORDERS WHERE ON_HOLD = -1
  repOrders.Query()
END IF

' Display the number of records deleted
DIM vNumRecs AS Long
DIM vMsg AS String
vNumRecs = SQLROWCOUNT
vMsg = STR(vNumRecs) & " orders deleted..."
MSGBOX (vMsg, 64, "Orders deleted")
```

20

5. Add another pushbutton, labeled `Release All`, next to the Delete All pushbutton.

   When you press this pushbutton, the application takes all the orders displayed in the repeater display off hold.

6. Add the following code to the second pushbutton's `Click()` method:

```
Sub Click()
' Ask whether you really want to do this
DIM vResult AS Integer
vResult = MSGBOX ("Do you want to release all these orders?",
➥36, "Releasing orders on hold")

' If so, release the records and requery the repeater display
IF vResult = 6 THEN
  EXEC SQL AT BOOKS UPDATE ORDERS SET ON_HOLD = 0 WHERE ON_HOLD = -1
  repOrders.Query()
END IF

' Display the number of records updated
DIM vNumRecs AS Long
DIM vMsg AS String
vNumRecs = SQLROWCOUNT
vMsg = STR(vNumRecs) & " orders released..."
MSGBOX (vMsg, 64, "Orders released")
```

7. Save the form.

That's all you need to do. If you want to test the form, enter some new orders for a customer with a large outstanding balance, run the form, and press the Update All pushbutton to take the orders off hold.

Migrating Procedures to the Server

If you are performing any kind of general change to a table, such as deleting old purchases or redefining everyone's security rating, you should create a stored procedure or trigger to handle this task. When you are running your application against Oracle7 or SQL Server, you can take advantage of the greater processing power of the server, as well as the powerful capabilities of the SQL language itself.

Instead of defining the SQL code through an `EXEC SQL` statement, you should use SQL to call a stored procedure within the database. In the case of complicated procedures that contain many lines of SQL code, you can save some space within your application by moving this code to the server. The `EXEC SQL` statement would then contain a single line calling the procedure, instead of many lines defining the SQL operations you want to perform.

As an additional benefit, other applications can call the stored procedure. Rather than adding the same procedure to several applications, you can define the procedure on the server as a stored procedure or trigger that is usable by all applications.

Keep in mind, however, that not every database-related operation is best handled on the server. For example, many business rules are better enforced through the Validate() and ValidateRow() methods. You can refer to Day 13, "Enforcing Business Rules," for some of the basic guidelines for deciding whether to migrate procedures to the server.

Compacting Data into a Single Column

Very often, records contain several columns worth of relatively simple information. For example, the ORDERS.ON_HOLD column stores only a TRUE or FALSE value. The same record might include several other TRUE/FALSE or YES/NO values: Has the order been received? Did all of the books arrive? Has the customer purchased this order?

If each of these values is stored in a different column, every one of these columns adds to the amount of querying done by the database, the amount of traffic across the network, and the amount of memory the application must reserve for these columns in a form's recordset.

In other words, these separate pieces of information add to the workload of every part of an application. If your application queries, sorts, and updates large recordsets, the additional work can slow down your application and the database.

Fortunately, there is a relatively easy solution to this performance problem. Because YES/NO and TRUE/FALSE values are all simple, you can compact them into a single column's worth of information. When the application needs one of these bits of data, such as the flag for whether the customer has paid for the order, it could look at just that piece of the data in the column.

Developers use different strategies for compacting data in this fashion. In the case of yes/no and true/false information, you could combine them into a single string of values. For example, the string YNYYNYN could store seven different pieces of yes/no information. If the fifth value represented whether the customer had purchased the order, you could write some simple code for finding the fifth character in this string.

Another way of compacting information is to add numeric values in a way that ensures that every sum of values will be unique. You have already seen this strategy in action in the MSGBOX command. As you remember, MSGBOX takes as an argument a numeric value indicating the number and type of buttons appearing in the dialog box, as well as the icon displayed. When you want to create a message box with Yes and No buttons that displays the stop sign icon, you simply add the numeric ID for Yes/No buttons to the numeric ID for the stop sign icon. The range of IDs for this argument is shown in Table 20.2.

20

Table 20.2. Numeric IDs for MSGBOX Components.

ID	Description
0	OK button
1	OK and Cancel buttons
2	Abort, Retry, and Ignore buttons
3	Yes, No, and Cancel buttons
4	Yes and No buttons
5	Retry and Cancel buttons
16	Stop sign icon
32	Question mark icon
48	Exclamation point icon
64	Information icon button

To display Yes/No buttons and a stop sign, therefore, you add 4 + 16 = 20, and pass this sum as an argument to MSGBOX. If you look carefully at all these values, you can see that any sum of the ID for an array of buttons plus the ID for an icon will be unique. The developer who designed MSGBOX ensured that the application would need only a single argument to handle two different kinds of information, reducing the amount of system resources and memory required to create a message box.

Although this approach is the most efficient way to compact information, it does not work well in situations in which you have several pieces of information compacted into the same numeric value. Ensuring that the sum of all of these values will be unique becomes more difficult as you add each new piece of information to be represented by this sum. If you're not careful, you might face a situation in which two different sets of values, representing two very different situations, have the same sum.

In the case of interpreting whether an order is on hold, has been received, and has been purchased, you do not want to confuse these values. Although your computer might interpret a value to mean that an order has been received and purchased, and is not on hold, you might by accident design the numeric values so that the sum really means that the order is on hold, not received, and not purchased.

If this sounds confusing, then you actually already understand the basic point. The more pieces of information you try to compact into this numeric ID, the harder it is to keep them all straight.

Creating a Database Privileges System

In the next exercise, you will use the first strategy for compacting data by taking several YES/NO values and combining them into a single string. Every employee record will have a new column,

PRIVILEGES, containing this string, which determines whether that person can insert, delete, or update a record. The string will always have three characters, one for each database operation.

The PRIVILEGES column will use the CHAR data type, which always stores a fixed number of characters. (In contrast, VARCHAR2 stores a variable number of characters, up to the limit you define for the column.) Because there are three characters in the string defining database privileges, you will define the column as CHAR(3).

1. Open the EMPLOYEES table and add the following column:

Characteristic	Setting
Name	PRIVILEGES
Datatype	CHAR
Size	3

2. Save and run the table.

3. Enter the following values for PRIVILEGES for the bookstore's employees:

EMPLOYEE_ID	PRIVILEGES
1	YYY
2	YYN
3	NNN
4	NNN
5	NNN
6	YYY

4. Press Commit, and then Stop.

Once again, to keep the example simple, you will create a new form instead of using one of the existing forms in BOOKS.POS.

1. Create a new form, frmPrivileges.

2. Add an embedded form, embPrivs.

3. Click and drag the EMPLOYEE_ID and PRIVILEGES columns into the embedded form.

4. Add three new text fields—fldInsert, fldUpdate, and fldDelete—to the embedded form.

5. Set the Datatype property of these three fields to String, and their DataSize property to 1.

6. Label these three fields Insert, Update, and Delete.

7. Add a scrollbar to the embedded form.

8. Add the following method code to the PostChange() method of the PRIVILEGES field:

```
Sub PostChange()
Inherited.PostChange()
```

20

```
' Parse the PRIVILEGES string so that the user's rights to
' insert, update, and delete records are displayed in the
' three text fields
IF NOT ISNULL(self.Value) THEN
  fldInsert.Value = LEFT(self.Value, 1)
  fldUpdate.Value = MID(self.Value, 1, 1)
  fldDelete.Value = RIGHT(self.Value, 1)
END IF
```

This code uses the Oracle Basic string functions LEFT, MID, and RIGHT to read different parts of the string. For the syntax of these functions, see the Oracle Power Objects online help.

9. Click and drag the LNAME and FNAME columns from the CUSTOMERS table onto the form.

Be sure to drag them onto the form, not into the embedded form.

The form should now look like Figure 20.1.

Figure 20.1.

The form frmPrivileges.

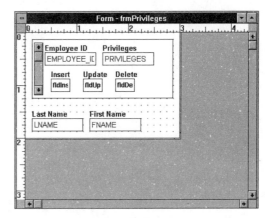

10. Add the following code to the form's DeleteRow() method:

```
Sub DeleteRow()
IF embPrivs.fldDelete.Value = "N" THEN
  MSGBOX ("You do not have rights to delete records",
  ➥16, "Insufficient privileges")
ELSE
  Inherited.DeleteRow()
END IF
```

11. Add the following method code to the form's InsertRow() method:

```
Sub InsertRow()
IF embPrivs.fldInsert.Value = "N" THEN
  MSGBOX ("You do not have rights to insert records",
  ➥16, "Insufficient privileges")
ELSE
```

```
    Inherited.InsertRow()
END IF
```

12. Add the following code to the form's `ValidateRow()` method:

```
Function ValidateRow(rownum as Long) As Long
IF embPrivs.fldUpdate.Value = "N" THEN
  MSGBOX ("You do not have rights to update records",
  ➡16, "Insufficient privileges")
ELSE
  ValidateRow = TRUE
  Inherited.ValidateRow(rownum)
END IF
```

13. Save and run the form.

14. In the embedded form, scroll until you find the employee record with an employee ID of 3.

    This person does not have privileges to make any changes to records in this form.

15. Click the field displaying a customer's last name.

    You need to perform this step to make sure that you are changing a row in the form's recordset, not in the embedded form's.

16. Press the Insert Row button.

    The application prevents you from inserting a new record, because the selected employee does not have the rights to do so (see Figure 20.2).

Figure 20.2.

Preventing the user from inserting a record.

17. After closing the message box, press the Delete Row button.

    Once again, the application tells you that you lack the rights to perform this database operation.

18. Enter a different name for the customer and press Commit.

    Because you do not have rights to update records, you see a third error message.

19. Press Stop to end this exercise.

Adding This Feature to an Application

Databases already grant privileges to different users and schemas for inserting, deleting, and updating records. So why duplicate this feature in the application?

In some cases, it might be easier to update the employee's record than to redefine the schema. If several users share the same schema, you might want the flexibility to grant or revoke privileges on a user-by-user basis without having to define a new schema for each of them, or granting or revoking privileges for all of them simultaneously. Additionally, enforcing privileges through the application gives immediate feedback, without having to send the request for a change to a table to the database and wait for a reply. By removing work from the network and the database, this approach also helps streamline the performance of the system.

In your own application, you might read the PRIVILEGES string into a user-defined property akin to udpSecLevel, the property you added to the application on Day 15. When the user logs into the application, your method code can assign the value read from PRIVILEGES for that user into this new property. In any bound form, the application could quickly read the privileges stored in this property to determine if it should let the user insert, update, or delete a record.

Speeding Reports

Because you cannot apply to reports many of the techniques described earlier to increase the performance of forms, reports represent a special challenge. Reports usually need to query most or all of the records from a table or a view, often joining the contents of several tables. On the surface, it seems as though there are no easy ways around the inherent performance problems of reports: Because they query so much information, how can you generate reports quickly?

Views and Reports

The most obvious way to enhance performance is to use a view as the RecordSource of your form. Views query and join records from multiple tables at the server, which often can perform these joins faster than the client.

Looking up information through a view is certainly faster than using SQLLOOKUP. Take, for example, a report from the TITLES table. If you want to display the name of a book's publisher, you have two options:

- [ ] Create a view that includes the column PUBLISHERS.PUBLISHER_NAME.
- [ ] Add a field to the form that uses the SQLLOOKUP command to find the PUBLISHER_NAME value in the PUBLISHERS table that matches a PUBLISHER_ID value for a book.

Both techniques work, but as described earlier, the SQLLOOKUP solution can be very slow. Every time the application queries a new title record, it must stop and perform the lookup through SQLLOOKUP to find the name of the book's publisher. In contrast, if you use a view instead, the database queries and joins the information from TITLES and PUBLISHERS, including the publisher's name, and then passes this information along to the application.

For this reason, views are nearly always the preferred record source for a report, except in the rare case of a single-table report. If you have properly normalized your database, however, you will be hard pressed to create a report that does not need to perform lookups to find descriptive values (such as a publisher's name, a book's category, and so on) in a foreign table.

SQL Functions and Reports

When you create the view for a report, you can often take advantage of aggregate SQL commands like AVG, MIN, MAX, and SUM. By using these aggregate commands in the definition of a view, you can make it easier to display the result of an aggregate value calculation in your report.

If you want to show the total price of all books in inventory, how should you do this? One technique is to add a text field outside the Detail portion of the report that would use a derived value calculation to determine the total value of all books. The DataSource property of such a control might look like this:

```
=SUM(Detail.PRICE)
```

A faster way to get the same information, however, is to create a column in the report's underlying view that adds the value of all books while the database is querying records. When the application populates the report with data, the total value has already been calculated.

To get some experience writing views that use aggregate values in this fashion, you will create a new report, rptTitles2, and a new view, VW_TITLES_VALUES.

1. Run the form frmSQL2.

    You need to use this form to enter the SQL text that defines the view. Unfortunately, the View Editor window does not let you enter calculations as part of the view definition.

2. Enter the following text to create a new view:

    ```
    CREATE VIEW VW_TITLES_PRICES AS
      SELECT BOOK_TYPES.TYPE_ID, TYPE_DESC,
        SUM(PRICE) "SUM_PRICE"
      FROM TITLES, BOOK_TYPES
      WHERE BOOK_TYPES.TYPE_ID = TITLES.TYPE_ID
      GROUP BY BOOK_TYPES.TYPE_ID, TYPE_DESC
    ```

    This view will add together the price for each type of book. For example, when it queries children's books, it will display the total price of all children's books in the TITLES table.

3. Press the Go pushbutton, and then press Stop.

4. Create a new report, rprBookPrices.

5. Select the Session window for BOOKS.POS, and then select the View | Refresh menu command.

    The new view appears in the session.

20

6. Drag the icon for the view into the Detail section of the new report.

7. Make whatever cosmetic adjustments you want to improve the appearance of the report.

8. Save and run the report.

   Now, the report displays the total value of books in inventory at the top of the report (see Figure 20.3).

Figure 20.3.

Displaying a sum at the top of a report.

TYPE_ID	TYPE_DESC	SUM_PRICE
1	Reference	$9
2	Computer	$58
3	Mystery	$17
4	Science fiction	$5
10	Children's	$14
11	General fiction	$4
12	General non-fiction	$12

9. Press Stop to end this exercise.

Summary: Databases, Recordsets, and Performance

Because the ability to manage records is the core feature of database applications, the designers of Oracle Power Objects have provided several ways for you to improve your application's performance when you are querying, joining, and modifying records, as well as when you are maintaining these records in memory. The measures described in this section represent some of the most common techniques. As you work with Oracle Power Objects further, you will discover additional ways to improve the performance of your database applications.

The remaining performance tips in this lesson focus less on the database-related features of Oracle Power Objects, and more on other facets of your application.

Improving the Performance of Application Objects

This section discusses some techniques for addressing performance problems caused by two types of application objects: OLE controls and their associated server applications—and any application object displaying graphics.

Replacing OLE Controls with OCX Controls

Although OLE can enhance your application significantly, it can seriously degrade performance if you rely on it too much. The process of loading an OLE data object and launching its server application can take a great deal of time, as well as require a great deal of memory. This is especially true in the case of graphical OLE data objects, or especially large and complex server applications such as Microsoft Word.

If you are making choices between functionality and performance, you face a real dilemma when you try to decide what to do with OLE features in your application. Although you might want to speed up your application by removing some memory-intensive OLE data objects, you nonetheless want to give the user the capabilities of the server application behind these data objects. Although it might cost your application a great deal in performance to include Microsoft Word documents, you might want to give your application word processing capabilities.

Fortunately, there is a way out of this dilemma. Oracle Power Objects applications can use a special type of custom control to provide the features of many OLE server applications. A custom control cannot be run on its own, but it can provide new functionality (graphics, word processing, sound, animation, and so on) to any application to which it is added. In some respects, a custom control is much like a DLL, because it is a modular piece of code that you can use in several applications. (In fact, many OCX files use the .DLL extension for this reason.)

Unlike DLLs, however, OCXs provide more than procedures. When you incorporate an OCX into your application, you add a new control to the Object palette in Oracle Power Objects. You can then add the new custom control to your application in the same fashion as you would a pushbutton, radio button, or embedded form—by clicking and dragging across a form, report, or class. An OCX has Property sheets like any other type of control. An OCX also has many of the standard properties and methods of other controls, as well as unique properties and methods. OCX-specific properties and methods have the small letters ocx next to their names in the Property sheet.

OCX controls are based on OLE technology, so you might often see them referred to as OLE controls. In fact, when you add a new OCX control to your application, you use the menu command File | Import OLE Control in Oracle Power Objects.

You can think of an OCX as a mini-application added to your own, or as just another type of control. OCXs exist for a variety of purposes, that can be both modest (such as a simple graphics viewer) and ambitious (a full-featured word processor within a single OCX).

Getting OCXs

Like many other features of contemporary software technology, OCXs are designed to be used in a variety of software development tools. The OCX you learn to use in Oracle Power Objects can be part of an application you create with Visual Basic 4.0 or another tool that has OCX support.

Because there is a wide market for OCXs (and their predecessors, VBXs), it's easy to find freeware, shareware, and commercial OCXs. You can download many of them from commercial networks such as CompuServe and America OnLine, as well as from various World-Wide Web sites.

In the next exercise, you will use a freeware OCX. If you want a copy of it, you can locate it at the URL http://www.soe.bcit.ca/ocx/. This is a very simple OCX, designed to display text at various rotations. You'll add this OCX as a label to some forms.

1. Add a copy of the OCX to your Oracle Power Objects directory.

    When you download a copy of this OCX from a web site, you might need to use the PKUNZIP.EXE utility to decompress it.

2. Open the form frmBookOrders.

3. Select File | Load OLE Control.

    The standard Windows dialog box for selecting a file appears. In this case, you are looking for an .OCX or .DLL file.

4. Select SPINLBL.OCX and press OK.

    A new button appears on the Object palette for the OCX.

5. Press this button to select the drawing tool for this OCX, and then click and drag in the area to the immediate left of the repeater display.

    The new OCX control appears on the form.

6. Open the Property sheet for this OCX.

    As you can see, it has many of the same standard properties and methods of other controls.

7. Enter the following settings for its properties:

Property	Setting
Caption	Line Items
TextOrientation	1
BackgroundColor	(Light gray)

8. Press Save.

9. Select and copy the OCX control.

10. Open the form frmPurchases and paste a copy of it next to the repeater display in this form.

    At this point, you can also test whether the standard properties and methods of this OCX behave as they do on standard Oracle Power Objects controls.

11. Open the Code Editor window for the OCX control's Click() method and enter

```
Sub Click()
MSGBOX "Click indeed!"
```

12. Save and run the form.

13. Click the OCX label.

    The message box appears, as expected.

14. After closing the message box, press Stop.

Graphics and Performance

Undoubtedly, the greatest performance-killers in your application are graphics. If you make graphical data part of a recordset with many rows, you should expect the system to respond sluggishly. Graphics can potentially slow down any kind of application, but database applications are particularly vulnerable because they need to query large chunks of information to display pictures stored in the database. As pictures are added to a form's recordset, browsing between records slows down. When you display pictures in a report, the time it takes to generate the report increases markedly.

Therefore, follow these rules when you add graphics to your application:

☐ Show graphics at the minimum resolution needed for readability. If the graphic looks good in 16 colors, use 16 colors. If the graphic needs 256 colors, use that many. Only use higher resolutions when absolutely necessary, such as when you are displaying photo-realistic graphics. Remember, too, that many printers might not support the resolution of many graphics.

☐ In forms displaying graphics queried from a table, always set the `RowFetchMode` property to `Fetch as needed`. Because graphics place such a large demand on the system, you need to use incremental fetching.

☐ As soon as you are finished displaying a graphic, eliminate it. For example, if you want to show an animated or complex graphic in the application's splash screen, make sure that you close the form when you are finished showing it. Otherwise, the application will keep the graphic in memory along with the form.

☐ Always ask yourself, "Do I really need this graphic?" Although there's always the temptation to add as many graphics as possible to your application, you need to justify the loss in performance that every graphic causes.

☐ Keep your graphics small, or limit their number. Frequently, you can achieve the effect you want with only a few graphics or with smaller-sized graphics. If you look at the Oracle Power Objects interface, you see a large number of small icons everywhere in the desktop, from the Object palette to the toolbar. Each of these small graphics conveys enough information about the purpose of a pushbutton, or the state of a property in the Property sheet, that a larger graphic isn't needed.

☐ Use graphics sparingly in reports. Generally, one type of graphic per report, such as an employee's picture, is enough. Adding more graphics, such as a large number of icons

20

identifying different sections of the report, might add too much visual information in the report, at a potentially high cost in performance.

Oracle Basic Performance Tips

There are several ways to streamline your Oracle Basic code to improve the performance of your application.

Eliminate Dead Code

When you finish your application, you often find that you have code left over in several methods that the application never uses. No matter why the code is there, you should eliminate it if you do not plan to execute it. The unused code is compiled with the application, adding to the amount of hard disk space needed to store the executable and the amount of memory needed to run it.

Clear Out Arrays

When you have finished using an array, use the ERASE command to eliminate the data stored in its elements. After you clear out the array in this fashion, the application will no longer reserve memory for these values. (You can repopulate the array later, if needed.)

Delete Unused In-Memory Objects

You create many objects through method code, including custom menus, toolbars, and status lines, as well as stand-alone recordsets. Once you create one of these objects through the NEW command, the application keeps them in memory as long as the application is running.

You might find, however, that the application reaches a point at runtime when it no longer needs a particular in-memory object. In this case, you should use the DELETE command to eliminate the object, freeing the memory previously reserved for it.

In addition, if only a single form or report ever uses a particular in-memory object, you might want to create the object only when the user opens that form or report. For example, if you use a status line to display a text message indicating whether an order is on hold, you might create and display the status line through the form's OnLoad() method, instead of adding it to the application's.

Don't Use Too Many Variables

As a beginning Basic programmer, you might be using more variables than you need. Although this might seem harmless at first, consider that the application needs to reserve a small amount of memory space for every variable you declare. As your method code becomes longer and more sophisticated, the amount of memory needed to execute the code and manage all the variables referenced in it increases markedly.

To illustrate this point, the following is a piece of method code that uses too many variables:

```
DIM vRecSet AS Object
DIM vRecNum AS Long
DIM vString AS String
vRecSet = self.GetRecordset()
vRecNum = vRecSet.GetRowCount()
FOR x = 1 TO vRecNum
  vRecSet.SetCurRow(x)
  vString = vRecSet.GetColVal("CUST_NAME")
  MSGBOX vString
NEXT x
MSGBOX vString
```

Here is a slightly better way of writing the same code:

```
DIM vRecNum AS Long
vRecNum = self.GetRecordset.GetRowCount()
FOR x = 1 to vRecNum
    self.GetRecordset.SetCurRow(x)
    MSGBOX vRecSet.GetColVal("CUST_NAME")
NEXT x
```

The code has exactly the same result, but it uses one variable instead of three.

> **Note:** After examples of high-performance code, you might notice that some of the sample code in this book is not written this way. The sample code is meant to clarify for the beginning Oracle Basic programmer how the code works, rather than optimizing it for performance. This less-optimized code serves its purpose in these exercises, but your own code should be far more streamlined.

20

Avoid Redundant Procedures

One of the principles you've learned in this book is *design everything to be reusable*. This maxim applies to the procedures you write: Rather than duplicating your work in several places, define and maintain a procedure in one place.

Applying this rule simplifies development, and it also improves performance. If you are writing many, roughly similar procedures, you are adding unnecessary code to your application. When you combine these procedures into a single method, the application needs to keep in memory only a single set of code.

Use the Right Scope for a Variable

An important rule of programming in any language is, don't give a variable a larger scope than it needs. If you define a variable as local to a method, the application needs to maintain that variable only as long as the method is running. By contrast, variables declared as GLOBAL or STATIC stay in memory for as long as the program is running. (STATIC variables, however, are stored in memory only after the first time the application calls the method in which they are defined.)

Use Variables Instead of Properties

If your application repeatedly evaluates the same property, you might consider assigning its value to a global variable. Although this approach breaks the object-oriented model of development somewhat by moving information about an object from a property to a variable, you might need, in rare cases, to use this technique to enhance performance. The application can read the value in a variable slightly faster than it can evaluate the same value assigned to a property. If the application is reading the property thousands of times, then you might want the small improvement in performance that moving the value to a variable would give you.

Avoid the *Variant* Data Type

As discussed earlier, the Variant data type can handle any kind of data. However, Variant variables require more memory than other variables. If you do not need the flexibility that the Variant data type provides, you should substitute a different data type.

Classes and Performance

Although classes can be one of the most important development tools at your disposal, you need to be careful about some performance pitfalls involving classes and their instances. One of the greatest losses in application speed can occur when the object inheritance hierarchy has too many levels, either by subclassing or by adding instances of one class inside of another. Additionally, if you add too many instances of other classes within a single class, performance can suffer.

For example, one way to make a daily schedule class is to make a different class for each day of the week, and then add instances of all seven classes to another class. Next, you would add instances of the schedule class to forms in your application. If you wanted to create some modified versions of this scheduler, you could create a subclass of it that would include the seven instances as well.

On slower machines, the subclass might cause the forms in which it appears to load and display more slowly. If you think about how classes work, you can see why this is the case. When the

application loads an instance of the scheduler subclass, it must evaluate the properties and methods of the subclass and its instance. In addition, it must figure out the relationship between the scheduler subclass and its master class. At the next level of the hierarchy, the application then looks at the master scheduler class and the seven other classes appearing within it.

When you create user-defined classes, therefore, you should be aware that as the complexity of the object inheritance hierarchy increases, the performance of the application decreases slightly.

Summary

This lesson has covered too many points to summarize them all. However, major hints for enhancing performance include the following:

- [ ] Take advantage of performance-enhancing properties such as `RowFetchMode` and `RecSrcMaxMem`.

- [ ] Use views, shared recordsets, and other techniques to accelerate the application's capability to query records and maintain them on the client.

- [ ] During development, you can break up your application into mini-applications to increase performance during testing. You can apply the same technique to the finished applications themselves, by breaking up a large application into smaller ones.

- [ ] In cases where SQL can best handle a database operation, move the procedure to code in an `EXEC SQL` statement, a stored procedure, or a trigger.

- [ ] Streamline your Oracle Basic method code.

- [ ] Be judicious when adding graphics to your application, because graphics often slow performance.

- [ ] To add OLE functionality to your application without suffering a loss in performance, you can often replace OLE data objects and their associated server applications with OCX controls.

- [ ] Avoid creating an overly complex object inheritance hierarchy.

What Comes Next?

Tomorrow, you will take the final steps needed to finish the Bookstore application. Before compiling the application, you will make sure that you have preserved your work, including your classes, generic procedures, database objects, and test data. You can use this information when you need to make changes to the Bookstore application, or when you add similar features to other applications you write.

Q&A

Q How high should I rate performance as a priority when I develop my application? When in the development cycle should I begin working on performance?

A Performance should be a high priority, because the user will notice any performance shortcomings every time the application launches.

Although you can wait until just before you finish your application to apply some performance-enhancing techniques, other measures require that you start working on performance from the very beginning. For example, if you decide to use views as a report's record sources, you need to design these views before you create the report. If you plan to move some procedures to the server, you should do so immediately, instead of creating some temporary version of them in your method code as a quick solution. Because you need time to test the stored procedure, you should not waste any of this time using an Oracle Basic procedure you do not intend to keep.

Q Are there any reasons to avoid moving procedures to a stored procedure or trigger?

A Because triggers execute in response to system events, such as deleting a record from the TITLES table, you might not want to create any application-specific triggers if you expect other applications to be interacting with the same table.

Workshop

The Workshop consists of quiz questions to help you solidify your understanding of the material covered and exercises to give you experience in using what you've learned. Try and understand the quiz and exercises answers before you go on to tomorrow's lesson.

Quiz

1. If you need to perform a large number of lookups in a report, what is the best way to ensure that the application can generate the report quickly?

2. In what way did the method udmBasicErrors enhance performance?

3. If you write a user-defined method for changing a particular customer's credit limit, should the method code change this value through an EXEC SQL statement? (Assume for this question that the employee increasing the customer's credit limit might need to undo this change, if the store manager does not approve of the credit increase.)

Exercises

1. Apply the techniques described in this lesson to streamline the method code in the Bookstore application.

2. Add the following feature to the Bookstore application: At startup, the application creates a bound stand-alone recordset that reads the columns EMPLOYEE_ID, ALIAS, and PASSWORD from the EMPLOYEES table. When the user logs in, the application looks for the correct username and password combination in the recordset.

Quiz Answers

1. You should use a view as the report's record source, including all the columns of information needed for these lookups. This technique is faster than adding fields to the report that use the SQLLOOKUP command to look up values.

2. By defining what the application does in response to Oracle Basic errors in a single place, this all-inclusive method reduces the amount of error-handling code in the application.

3. You should not perform the change through EXEC SQL for two reasons. First, you want to use EXEC SQL when you have a change to make to many or all of the records in a table, because these global changes are what SQL code does best. Second, if you want to give the user the ability to undo this change, you do not want to bypass the application's Commit and Rollback buttons, which give the employee the chance to reconsider the change to a customer's credit limit.

Finishing Your Application

Overview

Today, you learn about the following topics:

- ☐ Creating a tabbed form
- ☐ Writing SQL scripts
- ☐ Creating a generic session
- ☐ Preparing for later development projects
- ☐ Moving objects to libraries
- ☐ Warehousing your user-defined methods
- ☐ Compiling the final application
- ☐ Files included with the compiled application

In the last two days you learned some final steps you need to take before declaring your application finished. Without giving some thought to usability, your application might work but your users might not like or understand what it does. If you don't spend time improving performance, users might not be patient enough to wait and see all the things the application can do.

In addition, before you compile the final application, you need to make some backups of your application and the database. Obviously, you do not want to accidentally lose all your work at any point—but especially when you are about to finish. Although you should create regular backups of your application, library, and session files throughout development, there are other steps you need to take to preserve your work. Some of these steps simply preserve your work from hard disk errors and other whims of the gods, while others make the more reusable pieces of your application available for future development projects.

For example, you should save the descriptions of all your database objects (or at least the most important ones) in a SQL script. As shown in a later exercise, "Backing Up Your Database," you can run the script to re-create all of the database objects and even insert your test data into the tables. If some misfortune befalls the Blaze database you were using to prototype the database objects, you always have an additional backup—the SQL scripts. As an additional benefit, the SQL scripts are simple text files, so they require less space to store than a backup Blaze database.

In addition to backing up your files and your database objects, you also need to complete the following tasks:

- ☐ Store the generic procedures you added to the application in some easily accessed location.
- ☐ Create a generic session so that you can open a connection to any available database. This generic session makes it easy for you to add your database objects anywhere you want, simply by entering a username and password as well as the location of the server.

☐ Move your generic classes into a library. By maintaining these classes in a library, instances of the classes added to several applications immediately receive whatever changes you make to the master class definition.

☐ Make sure that you or another developer can return to your application and make changes as needed. Because every application needs some debugging after it is deployed, you need to make it as easy as possible for you or someone else to fix any unexpected problems. Even if the application needs no debugging, you might need to make adjustments to it to meet the changing needs of the organization.

After taking these steps, you need to decide how to compile the application. Oracle Power Objects offers two options:

☐ A fully independent .EXE file

☐ A smaller compiled application that you launch with the Oracle Power Objects Runtime Application, PWRRUN.EXE

As the final step, you need to consider the best way to distribute your application, and you need to make sure that all the necessary files are included with it.

In this chapter, you will take all of the steps needed to finish the Bookstore application and make it ready for deployment. First, however, you will add one final feature to the Bookstore application—a tabbed form.

Creating a Tabbed Form in Oracle Power Objects

A tabbed form is a popular kind of form or dialog box appearing in an increasing number of applications. If you look at products such as Microsoft Word 6.0, Excel 5.0, and the Control Panel dialog boxes in Windows 95, you will see that many mimic the appearance of a set of tabbed folders. To select a particular virtual folder, you click its tab and the contents of that folder appear. Figure 21.1 shows a typical tabbed form.

Tabbed forms are easy to understand, and they can compact a large number of controls into a small space. Only the controls for the selected tab appear; all others remain invisible until their tabs are selected.

Microsoft is promoting this interface convention for its own applications and the Windows 95 operating system, and an increasing number of other applications for both Windows and the Macintosh are also using it. Although future versions of Oracle Power Objects will also have tab controls that you can add to your applications, the current version does not.

Figure 21.1.

A tabbed dialog box from Microsoft Word.

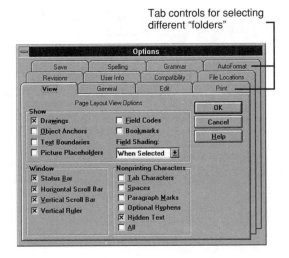

Tab controls for selecting different "folders"

Fortunately, tab controls are easy to develop on your own. In fact, the sample applications included with Oracle Power Objects have their own tab control, clsTab, created as a user-defined class. This class has the appearance and behavior expected of a tab control:

- [ ] Each tab has a 3-D look and feel.

- [ ] When you select a tab, the black line beneath it disappears, to make it look as though you have selected a particular folder.

- [ ] Clicking the tab makes the contents of one folder appear, while others remain invisible.

- [ ] When you resize the folder, the tabs shrink or stretch to reflect this change.

To demonstrate how a tab control works, however, you will create a much simpler version of a tab control.

A New Tabbed Form

Your version of a tabbed form will display publishers and books in a master-detail relationship. When you select the Publishers tab, the folder containing publisher records appears; when you select the Books tab, the folder displays the corresponding titles from that publisher.

The form will contain the following objects:

- [ ] One rectangle comprising a folder. This folder never actually changes, although the behavior of the tabs and other objects in this form give the illusion that a different folder has appeared when you select a tab.

- [ ] Two rectangles comprising the folder tabs.

☐ A line for each tab that disappears when the tab is selected and reappears when a different tab is selected.

☐ Two embedded forms within the folder rectangle. These containers will display records from the PUBLISHERS and TITLES tables. When you select a tab, one embedded form will become visible, and the other invisible.

With this in mind, you're ready to get started.

1. In the Bookstore application, create a new form—frmTabPubs.

2. Set the `ColorFill` property of the form to light gray.

   Tabbed forms use a 3-D look and feel, so you should apply this GUI convention throughout frmTabsPubs.

3. Add a new rectangle, rctFolder, to the form.

4. Add two smaller rectangles, rctPubs and rctBooks, just above rctFolder.

5. Outside these rectangles, create two lines, linPubs and linBooks.

6. Set the `ColorBrdr` property of these two lines and the `ColorFill` property of the rectangles to light gray.

   It is hard to see these lines on the form. If you ever lose track of them, you can tab through the objects in the form until you select one of them.

7. Position all the objects in the form in the following way:

   ☐ The tab rectangles should be flush against the top of the folder rectangle, with their bottom edges slightly lower than the top edge of the folder (about 1 pixel difference).

   ☐ The lines should be positioned on top of the lower edge of the folder rectangles. Because these lines are the same color as the light gray background, the lower edge of the tab disappears.

   In positioning and sizing these objects, you can exert fine control by holding down the Ctrl key as you click and drag.

   The form should now look like the one in Figure 21.2.

8. Add a static text object with the label `Publishers` to the left tab, and one with the label `Books` to the other tab.

   Make sure that you select each rectangle before you add the label to it. For the tabbed form to work, the labels must be inside the rectangles and not on top of them. Additionally, the label must fill the entire tab.

9. Add a new embedded form in the rctFolder rectangle.

21

Figure 21.2.

The preliminary appearance of the tabbed form.

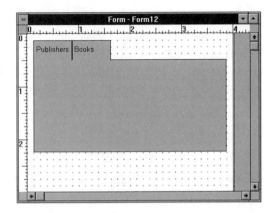

10. Give this embedded form the following properties:

Property	Setting
Name	embPubs
ColorFill	(light gray)
HasBorder	FALSE

11. In the Session window for BOOKS.POS, open the Table Editor window for PUB-LISHERS.

12. Click and drag the columns PUBLISHER_ID and PUBLISHER_NAME into the embedded form.

13. Give the newly created text fields a DrawStyle of 3D control.

14. Add a scrollbar to the embedded form.

15. Select the rectangle rctFolder and add a second embedded form to it.

16. Give this new embedded form the same properties as emPubs, but name it embBooks.

17. Add a repeater display, repBooks, to this new embedded form.

18. Open the Table Editor window for TITLES and drag the columns TITLE_NAME, AUTHLNAME, and PRICE into the repeater display.

    Now that the embedded forms are bound to the PUBLISHERS and TITLES tables, it's time to make the TITLES records a detail of the PUBLISHERS records. As you scroll between publishers in the tabbed form, you can select the Books tab to see all the titles published by that company.

19. Open the repeater display's Property sheet and enter the following settings for its master-detail properties:

Property	Setting
LinkMasterForm	embPubs
LinkDetailColumn	PUBLISHER_ID
LinkMasterColumn	PUBLISHER_ID

20. Open the Property sheet for the rectangle rctPubs and enter the following code in its `ChildClick()` method:

```
Sub ChildClick(child as Object)
linPubs.Visible = TRUE
linBooks.Visible = FALSE
rctFolder.embPubs.Visible = TRUE
rctFolder.embBooks.Visible = FALSE
```

This method executes whenever the user clicks on an object within the container. Because the static text object displaying the label Publishers fills the rectangle, you trigger `ChildClick()` whenever you click on the label to select the tab.

As you can see, the code makes the line and embedded form associated with Publishers visible when you select the tab. When the line appears, it covers the lower edge of the tab rectangle, making it look like the folder containing publisher information has appeared.

21. Enter the following method code in the `ChildClick()` method of the rectangle rctBooks:

```
Sub ChildClick(child as Object)
linPubs.Visible = FALSE
linBooks.Visible = TRUE
rctFolder.embPubs.Visible = FALSE
rctFolder.embBooks.Visible = TRUE
```

The last step is to indicate which folder should appear to be selected when the form opens.

22. In the `OnLoad()` method of the form, enter the following:

```
Sub OnLoad()
Inherited.OnLoad()
linPubs.Visible = TRUE
linBooks.Visible = FALSE
rctFolder.embPubs.Visible = TRUE
rctFolder.embBooks.Visible = FALSE
```

23. Save and run the form.

The tabbed form (shown in Figure 21.3) makes it look as though the folder containing publisher information is now selected.

24. Click on the Books tab.

The application makes it appear that the Titles folder is now moved to the front to display the books manufactured by the publisher selected in the other folder.

25. Select the Publishers tab, and then scroll to a different publisher record.

21

Figure 21.3.
*The final tabbed form
at runtime.*

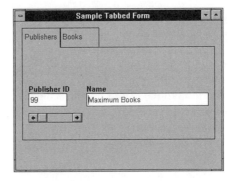

26. Select the Books tab to see the books from that publisher.

27. Press Stop to end this exercise.

Although you managed to implement a simplified version of a tabbed form, this is not the most elegant solution imaginable. Without a tab control, however, you have little choice within the range of existing Oracle Power Objects features. Fortunately, because Oracle Power Objects is extensible, you add an OCX control to add this capability.

An OCX Tab Control

Given the recent popularity of both tabbed forms and OCX controls, it's not surprising to find more than one tab control OCX on the market. Surprisingly, almost no development tools have added tab controls to the collection of standard controls they provide, so OCX developers have leaped at this opportunity. The http://www.soe.bcit.ca/ocx/ OCX web site mentioned on Day 20 provides a link to a site containing a tabbed form OCX.

Backing Up Your Application

With these final features added to the Bookstore application, your actual development is finished. Before you compile, however, you want to take time to back up all of your work.

Because you might want to reuse some of the user-defined classes and methods you added to the Bookstore application, you should take some additional steps to store them in a central repository where you can find and maintain them easily. In addition, you should take some steps to store the descriptions of database objects in a platform-independent way, so that you can quickly re-create them on any type of database.

The easiest step in backing up your work is to copy all of the file objects comprising the front end of your application into a backup directory. The files you need to copy include the following:

☐ The application file (.POA) itself

☐ All libraries (.POL) containing objects used in the application

☐ All sessions (.POS) used in the application

You should already be regularly copying these and your Blaze database file into a backup directory so that you can recover your work in case of a hard-disk error or some other problem. If you have not, you have been living dangerously for too long. Before continuing, create a backup directory, C:\BOOKS\BACK, and copy all of the .POS, .POL, and .POA files created during these lessons.

Backing Up Your Database

Because database objects are half your application, you need some easy way to back them up. The format in which these objects are stored should make it easy for you to re-create them on any database platform (Blaze, Oracle7, or SQL Server).

The easiest way to create a backup copy of your database objects is to create a new Blaze database for storing copies of these objects. By clicking and dragging the database objects from one Blaze session to another, you can copy these objects with a minimum of effort.

1. Create a new Blaze database, BOOKS_BK.BLZ.

   The name indicates that this file contains the backup copy of all your database objects for the Bookstore application. By adding the suffix _BK to its filename, you ensure that you cannot accidentally replace BOOKS.BLZ if you move the backup database into the same directory as the original.

2. Create a new Blaze session, BOOKS_BK.POS, for this database.

3. Double-click the Connector icon for both the BOOKS and BOOKS_BK sessions.

4. Select all of the database objects in BOOKS.POS.

5. Hold down the Ctrl key, drag these objects into the BOOKS_BK session, and release the mouse button.

   Oracle Power Objects starts copying these objects and (in the case of tables) their records into the BOOKS_BK.BLZ database. You might need to wait a minute or two for this process to finish.

6. Close the Session window for BOOKS_BK.POS.

Because you might use the real database further, you need to close the backup so that you do not accidentally start working with the backup copy instead of the original.

Writing SQL Scripts

Dragging and dropping is easy, but it is not always the best way to reproduce tables, nor should it be the only way. For example, your Blaze tables cannot use a multisegmented primary key (one that uses more than one column), but you can add this feature to tables in SQL Server and Oracle7. If you click and drag a table with a single-column key from Blaze into an Oracle7 session, you must then change the table description in Oracle7 to add the multisegmented key.

There are also cases when you want to preserve the query behind a view. If you cannot create the view through the View Editor window, you want to keep the text of the CREATE VIEW command handy in case you need to modify the view somehow. If you click and drag the view between sessions, you can copy the view, but you cannot easily access the SQL query that defines its contents.

In the last lesson, you created a view through SQL code that used the aggregate command SUM to add the values of all the books found in the TITLES table. To add an additional column to the view, you would need to drop it from the database, and then re-create it through essentially the same CREATE VIEW command, with one small modification. However, editing the CREATE VIEW command and running it again presumes that you have the SQL code handy.

For these and other reasons, experienced database application developers write their database object descriptions in plain text files, and then use some utility (such as SAF.EXE for SQL Server) to read the contents of the script and execute the DDL and DML commands in them. In Oracle Power Objects, you can create a database administration form to do exactly this, running the script against the database through a series of EXEC SQL commands.

In the Bookstore application, the logical place to add this feature is the form frmSQL2, which already can run DDL, DML, and TPL commands for you.

Special Considerations for Running SQL Scripts

Before you add this feature to frmSQL2, you should know a few facts about SQL scripts.

- [ ] The standard way of identifying the end of a SQL command is a semicolon. Unfortunately, Blaze does not recognize the semicolon, so you need to design some way of executing DDL and DML commands without depending on the semicolon to instruct the database to execute one command and start reading the next.

- [ ] The SQL script must be a plain text file. You cannot save it as a Microsoft Word, Microsoft Write, or other formatted word processing document. Therefore, you should use Notepad to write the SQL script, or be sure to save the script in your word processor as plain text.

- [ ] The beginning of every SQL script should drop all the objects it will then re-create. If any of the objects created through the SQL script already exist in the database, the SQL script will not be able to reproduce them.

- [ ] The definition of a view must include the query that defines all the tables and columns included in the view. If you have created a view through the View Editor

window, you can find its query in the SQL_TEXT column of the ALL_VIEWS view in the SYS schema. You can copy this text into your SQL script that creates the view.

Running a Simple SQL Script

The first step in this exercise is to create a new Blaze database and its associated session for testing SQL scripts. You do not want to use the BOOKS.BLZ database, because any mistakes you make might destroy records or database objects used in the Bookstore application.

1. Select the File | New Blaze Database menu command to create a new Blaze database.

2. Name the file TEST_SQL.BLZ, and save it in the C:\BOOKS directory.

3. Create a new Blaze session, TEST_SQL.POS, with the connect string
   `C:\BOOKS\TEST_SQL.BLZ`.

   Next, you create your first SQL script.

4. Open Notepad and enter the following text:

```
DROP TABLE FOO;
DROP TABLE BOO;
DROP VIEW VW_BOOFOO;

CREATE TABLE FOO
    (FOO_ID      NUMBER          PRIMARY KEY,
     FOO_DESC    VARCHAR2(64)    NOT NULL);
CREATE TABLE BOO
    (BOO_ID      NUMBER          PRIMARY KEY,
     BOO_DESC    VARCHAR(64)     NOT NULL,
     FOO_ID      NUMBER);

CREATE VIEW "VW_BOOFOO" AS (SELECT "BOO"."BOO_DESC", "FOO"."FOO_DESC"
FROM "BOO", "FOO" WHERE "BOO"."FOO_ID" = "FOO"."FOO_ID");

INSERT INTO FOO (FOO_ID, FOO_DESC) VALUES (1, 'One');
INSERT INTO FOO (FOO_ID, FOO_DESC) VALUES (2, 'Two');
INSERT INTO FOO (FOO_ID, FOO_DESC) VALUES (3, 'Three');

COMMIT;

INSERT INTO BOO (BOO_ID, BOO_DESC, FOO_ID) VALUES (1, 'Uno', 1);
INSERT INTO BOO (BOO_ID, BOO_DESC, FOO_ID) VALUES (2, 'Dos', 2);
INSERT INTO BOO (BOO_ID, BOO_DESC, FOO_ID) VALUES (3, 'Tres', 3);

COMMIT;
```

This script creates two tables, BOO and FOO, as well as a view based on both of them. It also inserts some test data into the two tables.

5. Save this text file as TEST.SQL in the C:\BOOKS directory.

   Now you can add the capability to run this SQL script to the form frmSQL2.

6. Add a new pushbutton labeled Run Script to the bottom of the form.

21

7. Next to the pushbutton, add a text field with the following properties:

Property	Setting
Name	fldFile
Datatype	String
DataSize	256

8. Give the Go pushbutton the name btnGo.

9. Add a static text object with the label SQL Script next to the text field.

   You'll call the Click() method of this pushbutton in some method code, so you need to give it a descriptive name.

   The form should now look like the one in Figure 21.4.

Figure 21.4.

The modified form frmSQL2, with the new section for running a SQL script.

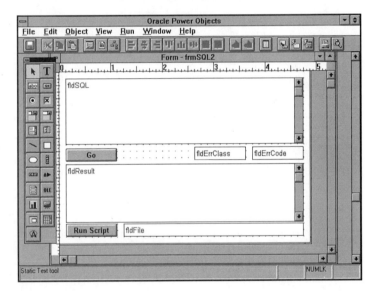

10. Add the following code to the Click() method of the Run Script pushbutton:

```
Sub Click()
DIM vLine AS String
DIM vFileName AS String
DIM vCommand AS String

' Get the filename and directory entered by the user
vFileName = fldFile.Value

' Read through the file and execute each command
ON ERROR GOTO Handler
OPEN vFileName FOR INPUT AS #1
  DO UNTIL EOF(1)
```

```
      LINE INPUT #1, vLine
   IF RIGHT(vLine, 1) = ";" THEN
     vLine = LEFT(vLine, (LEN(vLine) -1))
     vCommand = vCommand & vLine
     fldSQL.Value = vCommand
     btnGo.Click()
     vCommand = ""

   ELSE
     vCommand = vCommand & vLine
   END IF

LOOP

IF vCommand <> "" THEN
  fldSQL.Value = vCommand
  btnGo.Click()
END IF

EXIT SUB

Handler:
  MSGBOX ("File not found or not available", 48, "Error opening file")
```

Ideally, the error handler routine should call udmBasicErrors, in which you would add the code needed to handle situations in which the application could not open an operating system file. However, for the sake of simplicity, that step is left out of this exercise.

Once again, the Basic commands for file input and output reappear. In this case, you are using the OPEN command to access the SQL script, from which you are reading each line of text. Therefore, you are opening this file in INPUT mode, and you are using the LINE INPUT command to read each line of text. When the code reaches the end of this file (EOF), the application knows to stop trying to read any further lines.

As you can see, the code keeps building a command string until it finds a semicolon. At that point, it assigns this string to the fldSQL field and calls the Click() method of btnGo to start executing the command. The code then starts building the next command string until it finds another semicolon, and so on through the SQL script.

1. Add the code in bold in the Click() method of btnGo:

```
Sub Click()
DIM vCommand AS String
vCommand = fldSQL.Value

' Run the SQL command
EXEC SQL AT TEST_SQL :vCommand
fldErrClass.Value = SQLERRCLASS
fldErrCode.Value = SQLERRCODE

' Display the error text, if any
IF fldErrCode.Value <> 0 THEN
  fldErrText.Value = SQLERRTEXT
ELSE
```

```
    fldErrText.Value = "Operation successful"
END IF
```

You needed to change the name of the session so that you would run the script against the TEST_SQL.POS session, instead of BOOKS.POS.

2. Save and run the form.

3. In the field `fldFile`, enter `C:\BOOKS\TEST.SQL.`

4. Press the Run Script pushbutton.

    The application pauses temporarily while it runs the SQL script.

5. Press Stop to stop running the form.

6. Double-click the Connector icon for the session TEST.SQL.

    After you open the connection, you can see the new database objects appearing in the session, as shown in Figure 21.5.

Figure 21.5.
The two new tables and the view created through the TEST.SQL script.

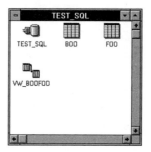

7. Open the View editor window for VW_BOOFOO and run the view.

    This simple multitable view queries related records from BOO and FOO, joined by FOO_ID. Figure 21.6 shows how this view queries records from these two tables.

Figure 21.6.
Running the view you created.

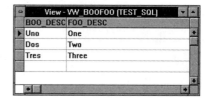

8. Press Stop to end this exercise.

Writing Your Own SQL Scripts

As you can see, writing a SQL script is a relatively easy task, but it is one that can save you a great deal of headaches if your database is deleted, corrupted, or otherwise unavailable. Through frmSQL2, you can run any SQL script for dropping and re-creating database objects.

Before you write your own scripts, you should review the SQL language reference in the Oracle Power Objects online help, as well as the chapter covering the SQL language in the *User's Guide*. SQL is a powerful language, but like all languages, it demands precision in your use of its commands and operators.

You should regularly update your SQL scripts to reflect changes you make to the set of database objects used by your application. Before you declare the application finished, you should also make one final update to the SQL script so that you are certain to have the script needed to populate the database for the final application.

Creating a Generic Session

The only adjustment you need to make to frmSQL2 is to add the capability to open a connection to any database. This additional feature will make it possible to add the database objects described in your SQL script to any database, simply by entering the location of the database, a username (or schema name), and password.

Oracle Power Objects sessions already have this feature. You can open a generic database connection dialog box by entering a question mark (?) for the DesignRunConnect and RunConnect properties of the session. Whenever the application tries to open a connection through the session, this dialog box appears.

1. Select the Session window for TEST_SQL.POS.

2. If there is an open connection to the database, double-click the Connector icon to disconnect.

3. In the Property sheet for the session, enter ? as its DesignRunConnect and RunConnect properties.

4. Save the modified session.

5. Select and run the form frmSQL2.

6. In the fldFile field, enter C:\BOOKS\TEST_SQL.SQL.

   The Database Logon dialog box now appears, as shown in Figure 21.7.

7. For the database type, select Blaze.

8. Leave the Username and Password fields blank.

9. For the address of the database, enter C:\BOOKS\TEST_SQL.BLZ.

10. Press OK.

    The application now opens the connection to the database and runs the SQL script.

11. Press Stop to end this exercise.

Any form, report, or Oracle Basic code that uses the TEST_SQL session will open the Database Logon dialog box whenever the application needs to open a connection to a database. You can use TEST_SQL for development, or you can even incorporate it into your application if you want to give your users the ability to log into any database they can access. However, unless the database objects used by the application are part of a database, your users will be unpleasantly surprised when the application cannot query records from the database. Therefore, although this dialog box can add some flexibility to your application, it might cause some frustration for users, particularly for those new to using the system who might need help entering the correct address of a database usable by the application.

Figure 21.7.

The Database Logon dialog box, which lets you open a connection to any available database.

The biggest advantage of displaying this logon is to build in flexibility for your application to accommodate changes to the network. Over time, you should expect your MIS department to be making changes to the network. If a database moves to a new server, your users need to access the database without waiting for you to recompile the application with the new connect string. Therefore, many sessions use ? for their connect strings to make it easier to adapt to changes in the corporate network.

Backing Up Your Classes

If you have taken care to design your user-defined classes to be as generic as possible, you might want to use them in other applications. Instead of storing them in BOOKS.POA, you should keep these classes in a library. When you want to add an instance of one of these classes to an application, you can click and drag the class from the library into a form or report.

In the following exercise, you create a library for storing generic classes:

1. Press the New Library button, or select the File | New Library command.

   The common dialog box for creating new file objects appears. In this case, you want to give the file the extension .POL to indicate that it is a library.

2. Give the library the name GENERAL.POL, and save it in the C:\BOOKS directory.

3. Open the Application window for BOOKS.POA.

4. Select all of the user-defined classes you added to the library.

5. Hold down the Ctrl key, and drag the classes into the new library.

   Copies of the classes now appear in the library.

6. With the Library window for GENERAL.POL selected, press Save.

You now have a repository for the classes you might use in other applications.

A Word of Warning

As copies, the user-defined classes you added to GENERAL.POL have no relationship with instances of the original classes in BOOKS.POA. In fact, if you try to delete the classes from BOOKS.POA, Oracle Power Objects displays an error message telling you that it cannot remove them because instances of them appear in the application.

If you want to delete the classes from BOOKS.POA, you first need to delete their instances. When the classes are gone from BOOKS.POA, you then add new instances to the forms or reports in which they appeared. Unfortunately, any changes you make to the original instances will be lost, so you will have to re-enter these changes (if you can remember them!).

> **Note:** For this reason, if you create a generic class, you should move it immediately into a library before you add an instance of it anywhere.

Backing Up User-Defined Methods

When you have taken great pains to design user-defined methods to be general enough to handle a wide range of cases, a copy of these methods should be stored outside of the application. Instead of wading through a host of forms and classes in which they are defined, you need to create one location for storing all your generic methods. When you work on future development projects, you can quickly find an instance of the methods, including the method code you wrote for them.

A library seems like the logical place to store methods. Unfortunately, the method code for a user-defined method cannot exist on its own. You need to add the code to an instance of the method in some object.

Although you cannot store a method in a library on its own, you can add the method to a class contained in the library. Your version of GENERAL.POL can contain a single class that includes every generic user-defined method you have designed, including the method code you wrote for each method. When you add an instance of the method to a new application, you can copy its code from the instance in the warehouse class.

As your collection of generic user-defined methods grows (a sign that you're doing a good job as a developer), you might need to organize them into several different classes, each designed to

21

hold a different category of user-defined methods. For example, you might design one class, clsErrHandler, to contain all your error handler methods and another class, clsSecurity, to store your security-related methods.

In the following exercise, you create a single class, clsMethods, to contain all of the user-defined methods in your application.

1. In the library GENERAL.POL, create a new class, clsMethods.
2. Open the User Properties window and select the method udmGetNow().
3. Drag the method onto the new user-defined class.
4. Open the Property sheet for the application BOOKS.POA.
5. Open the Code Editor window for udmGetNow() and select all of the code in this method.
6. Press the key combination Ctrl+C to copy this code (see Figure 21.8).

Figure 21.8.

Copying the code for
udmGetNow().

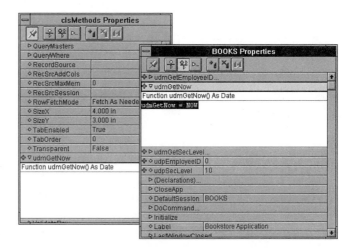

7. Open the Code Editor window for the same method in the class clsMethods.
8. Press Ctrl+V to paste the code.
9. Add an instance of the udmGetEmployeeID() method to the class.
10. Copy the code for this method from the application's Property sheet and paste it into the new instance appearing in clsMethods.
11. Repeat this process for all of the other user-defined methods you added to the Bookstore application.
12. With the class selected, press Save.

You now have your warehouse class for storing generic user-defined methods.

An Alternative Way to Warehouse Methods

This approach has one important shortcoming: There is no automatic way to update the code in the library as you change it in the application. If you find you need to modify the code somehow, you must stop and manually cut and paste the code from the application into the library. If you are working late or you get distracted, you might forget this step, in which case the warehoused version of the method in the library will not include the most recent version of the code.

The solution to this problem is simple, however. If you think about it, there is no reason to keep two copies of the same method code if you add one instance of the method to a class. If you add an instance of the class to an object, you can call the method from that instance to execute the code. If you added an instance of clsMethods to a form, you can call `clsMethods.udmGetNow()` to get the current date and time.

This technique makes it possible to maintain the code behind a user-defined method in a single location. Instead of copying and pasting updated code between different copies of the same class, you simply enter your changes in the method as it appears in the class. All instances of the class then inherit the new behavior of the method. You can still customize the method to handle a special case in your application by entering a modified version of the code in an instance of the class.

Categorizing Warehouse Classes

However, if you use this approach, you do not want to create a single class, like clsMethods, containing all your user-defined methods. If you have only one class containing all your generic methods, you will be adding the code for every user-defined method in this class when you create an instance of it, even if you plan to use only a few of these methods in the application. If you are writing a simple application in which security is not a concern, you don't need all of the methods you created to enforce system security. Instead, you should be able to add a smaller class that contains only the methods you need, instead of one monolithic class.

Adding the Class to an Application

When you created `udmGetNow()`, you added the method to the application, so that you could call it from anywhere, regardless of which forms are currently open. However, an instance of this "method warehouse" class needs to go somewhere in your application. Therefore, you need to create a form that stays in memory.

In the Bookstore application, the best place to put an instance of clsMethods is the splash screen. As you should remember from Day 9, "Menus and Toolbars," you kept a hidden copy of the splash screen in memory at all times so that the custom menu you created would remain even if you closed all other visible forms. In another application, you might need to create a different form, which is loaded and hidden (using the `HideWindow()` method) when the application

21

launches, containing an instance of the class. To use the method, you call it from the instance within the hidden form.

Adding clsMethods to an Application

In the following exercise, you add a new form to the mini-application, EMP.POA, you created in the last lesson. This form will contain an instance of clsMethods, which then makes all of the user-defined methods accessible to the application. In a different form, you take advantage of this feature by calling udmGetNow() to help display today's date on a different form.

1. Open the Application window for EMP.POA.

2. Create a new form, frmMethods, and add an instance of clsMethods to it.

3. Change the method code in the application's OnLoad() method to read as follows:

```
Sub OnLoad()
Inherited.OnLoad()
frmMethods.HideWindow()
frmVisible1.OpenWindow()
```

This code loads both forms but hides frmMethods.

4. Add a new text field, fldToday, to the form frmVisible1.

5. Set the new field's Datatype property to Date.

6. Open the form's Property sheet and enter the following code in its OnLoad() method:

```
Sub OnLoad()
Inherited.OnLoad()

' Get today's date by calling the udmGetNow() method in the
' instance of the warehouse class
fldToday.Value = frmMethods.clsMethods.udmGetNow()
```

7. Save and run the application.

The form frmVisible1 appears, including the new text field displaying today's date.

8. Press Stop to end this exercise.

Compiling the Final Application

With everything in your application backed up, you can take the final step—compiling your application. At this point, you have two options for compiling.

☐ Compile as a runtime file. When you choose this option, Oracle Power Objects compiles everything that comprises the application, including all library objects and sessions used in the application. The compiled file cannot run on its own, however; you need to launch your own application from the Oracle Power Objects runtime application, PWRRUN.EXE. Applications compiled in this fashion have the filename extension .PO on Windows.

☐ Compile as a stand-alone executable. In this case, you are compiling an .EXE file that can run independently, without launching PWRRUN.EXE. However, because the compiled .EXE file includes all the additional code needed to run the application, the .EXE file is significantly larger than the .PO file.

You compile the application as a .PO file if you expect to be running more than one Oracle Power Objects application on the same system. If you create purchase order and order entry applications, you can launch both of them from PWRRUN.EXE. To save disk space, you should compile both as .PO files instead of much larger .EXE files.

However, if there will be only one Oracle Power Objects application running on the system, you should compile it as an .EXE file. Users are less likely to delete files that they know they need to run an application, and an .EXE file is unambiguously important. A .PO file, on the other hand, looks less significant to the user, who might not understand that this is the actual application.

In the following two exercises, you compile the Bookstore application as both a .PO file and an .EXE file.

Compiling a .PO File

To compile BOOKS.POA as a .PO file, follow these steps:

1. Select the Application window for BOOKS.POA.

2. Press the Compile pushbutton.

   If there are any errors in the application, such as references to objects that do not exist, Oracle Power Objects detects them before compiling the application. You might need to fix some problems before continuing. Because you have a backup copy of BOOKS.POA, the simplest way to handle a problem is to delete the object where it occurred.

   Oracle Power Objects now displays a dialog box, shown in Figure 21.9, asking whether you want to compile the application as a stand-alone executable or a separate application file (a .PO file).

Figure 21.9.

The dialog box for selecting compile options.

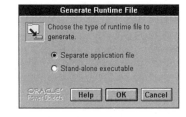

3. Select the Separate application file option and press OK.

   Oracle Power Objects now displays a dialog box for entering the filename and directory of the compiled application. By default, it uses the name of the .POA file, which in this case is BOOKS.

4. Press OK.

   At long last, the Bookstore application is compiled and ready to run.

5. From the Program Manager group for Oracle Power Objects, double-click the icon for Oracle Power Objects Runtime.

   As shown in Figure 21.10, the runtime application now launches and asks for the name of a .PO file to run.

Figure 21.10.
Launching the Oracle Power Objects Runtime application.

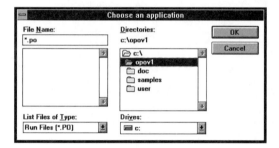

6. Select C:\BOOKS\BOOKS.PO and press OK.

   The compiled Bookstore application is now running.

7. Select File | Exit to close the application.

Compiling an .EXE File

Next, you compile the Bookstore application as a stand-alone executable.

1. With the Application window for BOOKS.POA selected, press the Compile pushbutton.

2. In the dialog box that appears, select Stand-alone executable and press OK.

3. For the filename and directory, enter C:\BOOKS\BOOKS.EXE and press OK.

   After a few moments, Oracle Power Objects finishes compiling the application. You can add the Bookstore application as a Program Manager icon and run it.

4. In the Program Manager, select the Oracle Power Objects program group.

5. While still in Program Manager, select File | New.

6. In the dialog box that appears, select Program Item and press OK.

7. In the Description field, enter The Bookstore Application.

8. In the Command Line field, enter `c:\BOOKS\BOOKS.EXE` and press OK.

An icon for the Bookstore application now appears in the Program Manager.

Unfortunately, you cannot create a custom icon for the application, so the Program Manager uses the building blocks icon for Oracle Power Objects.

9. Double-click the icon for this application.

BOOKS.EXE now launches.

10. Choose File | Exit to close the application.

All done! The application is compiled and runs as both a .PO and an .EXE file. The last step is distributing the application to your users. However you handle this process, you need to make sure that everyone using the application has all the files they need and that the database is populated with the necessary database objects.

Distributing Your Application

Now that you have compiled your application, you need to distribute it to your users. The easiest distribution strategy is to place it in a network directory where users can simply copy all the files into their systems. If you distribute the application on floppies, you might need to use a compression program such as PKZIP.EXE to fit the application file on a single disk, especially if you compiled the application as a stand-alone executable.

If you hard coded the directory in which a file exists, you must be sure that your users place all the necessary files in an identical directory on their systems. For example, the Blaze session BOOKS.POS looks for the Blaze database file BOOKS.BLZ in the directory C:\BOOKS\BOOKS.BLZ. If that directory does not exist, the application won't be able to find the database. Obviously, you can avoid this problem by not hard coding the directory in which a Blaze database or other file is located.

Required Files

When you distribute the application, you need to make sure that all the required files are included with it. Shown here is a checklist of all the files you might need to install with your application:

☐ If you compile the application as a .PO file, you must include the files PWRRUN.EXE, SYSDLG.X, and PWROBJX.MSB.

☐ If the application accesses an Oracle7 database, you must include the ORACLE71.POD driver.

☐ If the application accesses SQL Server, you must include the DBLIB.POD driver.

☐ If your application includes a Blaze database, you need to add this file to your installation.

21

☐ If the application uses an OCX control, you must distribute the .OCX or .DLL file.

☐ If the application calls a dynamic link library procedure (.DLL), you must include the DLL. However, if you call a Windows API procedure, you do not need to include any DLLs because these procedures are accessible in any system running Windows.

☐ If the application includes OLE data objects, you must make sure that the OLE server applications are installed on your user's PC.

☐ If you used any special fonts in your application, you need to install these fonts on your user's system.

☐ If your application uses an .INI file to save application configurations, you need to add a copy of this file to the WINDOWS directory.

☐ If your application uses other operating system files, such as a file containing a linked OLE data object, you need to include these files in your installation.

Database Objects

How you create the necessary database objects depends on whether you are running your application against Blaze or a remote server.

☐ If you are using Blaze as the back end of the application, you can simply copy the Blaze database file containing all the database objects to the application's directory. No further work is required, but you might want to add to your application a procedure that automatically copies the Blaze database to a backup directory. Although remote servers have backup features, Blaze databases do not. Therefore, you need to make sure that the application regularly backs up the Blaze database because you cannot count on the user to perform this step.

☐ If you are using Oracle7 or SQL Server as the back end, you can use Oracle Power Objects to add the tables, views, sequences, indexes, and synonyms to the database. By dragging these objects from a Blaze session into an Oracle7 or SQL Server session, you create these database objects in the remote server. In addition, Oracle Power Objects copies all the records from the Blaze database into the new tables on the remote server. Your test data therefore becomes part of the database, so you might need to delete some of these records in the final tables.

☐ Alternatively, you can run a SQL script against the remote server, using the database administrator utility included with Oracle7 or SQL Server, or an Oracle Power Objects form like frmSQL2.

After migrating the objects to a new database, you should test the application running to make sure that everything works as expected.

Remember that the compiled application uses the connect string specified in a session's RunConnect property. (If you did not enter a connect string here, the application uses whatever you entered for DesignConnect or DesignRunConnect.)

Summary

Today you learned about the following points:

☐ You should always back up your work before finishing the application.

☐ Part of saving your work is making it available for future development projects. You can create a library that contains your generic user-defined classes, as well as classes designed to be the central repository for your generic user-defined methods.

☐ In addition, you need to back up your database objects in a separate Blaze database file.

☐ You should also write some SQL scripts for creating these objects through a database utility or a form designed for this purpose. The SQL scripts give you a lightweight file with all the database object descriptions, as well as the means to generate the objects on any database platform.

☐ You can compile an application as a .PO file or as a stand-alone .EXE file.

☐ When you distribute your application, you must make sure that all the required files are included with it.

☐ In addition, you must add the database objects to whatever database you plan to use, either by running the SQL script or dragging the icons from one Session window into another.

What Comes Next?

Your own applications come next! You now have both the tool and the skills, so there is no reason to delay. Clear the Main window, add your own application, and dive right in!

Q&A

Q How can I create a setup disk for the Windows version of my application?

A Unfortunately, using SETUP.EXE can be a fairly involved process because you need to script the files to be installed and the directories in which to place them. For a full explanation of SETUP.EXE and its options, consult the appropriate Microsoft manual, or consult a third-party book on the topic.

Q Should I use tabbed forms as my standard form layout?

A Although tabbed forms are increasingly common GUI components, you do not need to use them in every form. However, you should look at some of your related forms to see if it makes sense to collapse them into a single tabbed form. For example, forms with pop-up dialog boxes can be made into a tabbed form, as can separate system configuration dialog boxes.

21

Workshop

The Workshop consists of quiz questions to help solidify your understanding of the material covered and exercises to give you experience in using what you've learned. Try and understand the quiz and exercise answers before you go on to tomorrow's lesson.

Quiz

1. If you plan to deploy several mini-applications instead of one larger one, how should you compile them?

2. If you are backing up your prototype Blaze database, should you copy the file, or should you write a SQL script describing all the database objects?

3. Suppose you write a generic procedure for writing entries to an .INI file. Where should you add the method code that defines the procedure?

4. When you add OLE features to your application, how does this complicate the task of distributing the application?

Exercises

1. Currently, when you run a SQL script through frmSQL2, the field fldResults displays the results of only the last SQL command executed in the script. Modify the code in the btnOK pushbutton's Click() method so that you can display the results of every SQL command executed.

2. Add 3-D lighting effects (a highlight on the top and left edges, a shadow on the bottom and right edges) to the tabbed folder in frmTabPubs.

3. Write the SQL script needed to reproduce every database object you have added to BOOKS.BLZ.

4. Compile the mini-application EMP.EXE, and then launch it from the Bookstore application.

Quiz Answers

1. You should compile these mini-applications as .PO files and launch them from PWRRUN.EXE. Because you will have several Oracle Power Objects applications running on the same system, you don't need to compile them as separate .EXE files.

2. A trick question! The answer is that you should always do both. Copying the Blaze database is an obvious step. However, for the reasons outlined earlier in this lesson, you should also write the SQL script.

3. If this method is generic enough to be used across applications, you should add it to a class in a library. After you add an instance of the class to an application, you can call the method from that instance.

4. When you distribute the application, you need to make sure that users have the OLE server application required to view and edit all the OLE data objects in the application.

21

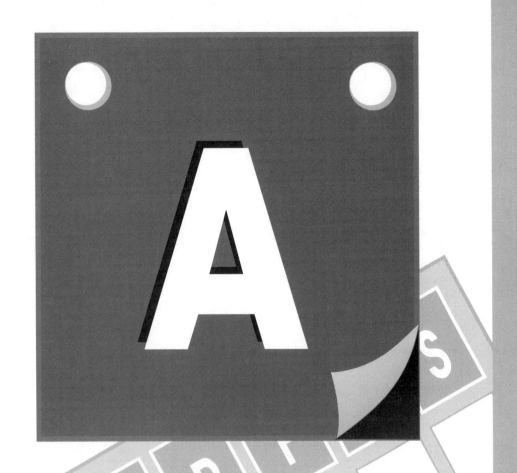

User-Defined Property and Method Worksheet

The following worksheets are designed to help you document your own user-defined methods and properties. Even if you develop your applications on your own, you might need to keep this information on file for later reference. You don't want to be perplexed by your own work long after you've finished it and you need to fix or update some portion of the application. In addition, someone else might inherit responsibility for maintaining your application, so you should help them learn how your methods and properties are supposed to work.

It's especially important to document user-defined methods. Although you can view the API for the method (its name, return value, and arguments) in the User Properties window, the code that defines what the method does is located somewhere in your application. If you do not make a note to yourself where to find it, you might waste a great deal of time searching through objects to find where it resides.

Worksheet for User-Defined Methods

Method Name

Designed by   **Last revised**

Purpose

Return Value

Arguments

Name	Datatype	ByVal?

Where applied

_____
_____
_____
_____
_____
_____
_____

General Notes

_____
_____
_____
_____

Development Notes

Date	Note

A

Worksheet for User-Defined Properties

Property Name

Designed By

Purpose

Datatype

Where Applied

_____

_____

_____

_____

_____

_____

General Notes

_____

_____

_____

_____

_____

_____

Development Notes

Date   *Note* _____

_____

_____

_____

_____

From Visual Basic
to Oracle Power
Objects

Visual Basic users will find a lot of familiar terrain in Oracle Power Objects, but they'll also encounter some unfamiliar features. This appendix is designed to help Visual Basic developers get their bearings when using Oracle Power Objects for the first time.

Getting Started

There are several steps you can take to prepare for developing your first Oracle Power Objects application. As a Visual Basic user, you will find many points of similarity between the two products. However, in many key areas, you will need to reconsider how you think about the development process, or how you put together the different pieces of a database application.

Object-Oriented Development

The object-oriented approach to developing Oracle Power Objects will be familiar to you as a Visual Basic developer. Methods, however, are handled somewhat differently.

As with Visual Basic, both properties and methods are inherent parts of an object's definition. The Property sheet in Oracle Power Objects should look very familiar: a scrolling list of alphabetically sorted properties of the object. However, all the methods of the object also appear in the Property sheet.

As described on Day 1 in this book, "Your First Form," both properties and methods define what characteristics an object has and what actions it can take. For example, a form has a width and height (properties), and it can open or close (methods). Because these are all features of a form, they should be part of the form's Property sheet, to reinforce the object-oriented model.

Methods Instead of Events

More importantly, placing the method on the Property sheet lets you redefine what the method does when it is called. Instead of coding around an event, you code around a method. To illustrate how this works, here is how the two products handle the same situation: Before opening a form, the application checks to see if the user has the rights to view that form.

In Visual Basic, you add code to an event procedure that calls the form's `Open()` method. You add code around this call to see if the user has the necessary rights.

In Oracle Power Objects, you add code to the form's `OpenWindow()` method to see if the user can open the form. If the user has sufficient rights, the code lets the default behavior of `OpenWindow()` occur (that is, displaying the window).

Although this might seem like a distinction without a difference, it is important to understand what this feature of Oracle Power Objects means to you as a developer. When you want to perform a check before opening a form, the check is an intrinsic part of the act of opening the form. By adding the code to the OpenWindow() method, you perform the check regardless of where you call the form's OpenWindow() method. Whether you open the form by pressing a pushbutton or by selecting a menu command, the check occurs.

This approach makes perfect sense, from both a practical and an object-oriented perspective. You want to make it easy to perform the check, so you add it to the method that opens the form. Both the check on the user's privileges and the act of opening the window are part of the definition of the form itself. Therefore, instead of placing this information in something separate from the form, you make it part of the form itself.

The only adjustment you need to make as a developer is to rethink how you capture events. Many methods execute in response to an event. For example, the PostDelete() method always occurs after a record is deleted. More importantly, however, the default processing of a method determines what system event occurs when you call the method (opening a form, deleting a record, and so on). In the case of the OpenWindow() method, you can add code completely around the event:

☐ Before opening the window, you perform a check.

☐ You then call the default processing to open the form (a system event).

☐ You can add additional code that performs other tasks after this event, related to the act of opening the form.

As you work more with Oracle Power Objects, you will learn to appreciate how this particular interpretation of the object-oriented model (closer to the ideal than Visual Basic) simplifies your life as a developer.

The Building Blocks of an Application

As with Visual Basic, this object-oriented approach to development trains you to think of an application as a collection of objects. Rather than focusing on the code needed to create objects, tools like Oracle Power Objects predefine these building blocks for you. When you build a form, a report, or a class, you need only ask yourself the following question: What do I want this object to do? Everything you do from that point on, from adding new controls to a form to writing method code to binding, should flow from that question.

This maxim is equally true when you design objects for the back end of the application, in the database.

The Data Model

Undoubtedly, the most important first step in designing your new application is to create a preliminary data model (that is, a plan for all the tables, views, synonyms, sequences, and indexes in the database). This data model does not have to be complete, but you should have some sense of the tables you wish to create and the columns they include. You should go through the exercise of normalizing your database as far as possible, breaking down the information into separate tables.

At this point, your chief concern is the set of tables to be included in the database. As you consider issues of security, you might also plan some views to limit access to information in these tables, or move some of these tables to different schemas.

Even the tiniest amount of forethought about the data model can save you endless headaches later in development. If you have some picture of the database-to-be, you can begin designing the front end of the application. Once you create some of the core tables in the database, such as the TITLES table in BOOKS.BLZ, you can begin creating forms and reports that are bound to these tables. If the information in these core tables appears frequently throughout the application, you can develop a strategy for displaying this information in different forms. For example, by building a class for displaying customer information (queried from the CUSTOMERS table), you can drastically reduce the amount of work needed to include this information throughout the application.

More significantly, by developing at least the key parts of the data model first, you save yourself the trouble of rebinding controls to columns. For example, if you create a form bound to the CUSTOMERS table, you will undoubtedly use the drag-and-drop features of Oracle Power Objects to bind the text fields and other controls to columns in the table. However, if you later redefine the CUSTOMERS table, you must then rebind some or all of these controls.

In many cases, the type of information displayed in a control might have changed to the point where you want to substitute a different type of control. If you were saving TRUE and FALSE values in a column, you would bind the column to a check box. However, if you change the column to store Yes, No, and Maybe information, the check box would be less useful than a pop-up list or radio button group.

As this example illustrates, even small changes to a table can force you to redesign important parts of your application. Therefore, if your application uses more than a few tables, you should start development by sitting down with the original word processor—a piece of paper and a pencil—or its modern equivalent and writing the descriptions of some of the core tables and views. This exercise will save you the messy task of redefining database objects and then rebinding them to forms and reports. When you are prototyping your application on Blaze, this rule is especially important, because you cannot modify or drop columns after you have created them.

As a Visual Basic developer, you might have been accustomed to building the front end of the application first. In fact, many developers use VB as a prototyping tool, mocking up the appearance and general behavior of the application before using a higher-end tool such as PowerBuilder or Visual C++ to develop the final application. In Oracle Power Objects, to save yourself extra work, you should be designing the back end from the beginning of development.

Reusable Application Components

When you are working on the front end of the application, you need to perform the same mental exercise before you dig too deeply into actual development. The biggest work-saving feature of the application is your ability to create user-defined classes as reusable objects. As demonstrated on Day 16, "User-Defined Classes," you make it easy to develop and maintain commonly used application objects by creating them as classes. The master class definition provides a central point for any work you do on identical objects used throughout the application. The best example of this principle from this book is the VCR database control developed on Day 16.

Similarly, you need to think about the best way to design reusable properties and methods. User-defined properties are somewhat easier to design in this respect, because they normally define some relatively simple characteristic of an object: What is the security rating needed to open a form? Which form's records can you use this VCR control to browse? How many times have you inserted a new record in a form's recordset since you opened the form?

User-defined methods require a bit more thinking to make them generic. Although there is a temptation to write a method as quickly as possible for a specific task, you actually save yourself time by trying to design the method to be more generic. You might discover yourself needing to add a similar method for a different object, so why not save yourself some trouble by designing a generic method in the first place? For example, you might need to check the user's security rating several times throughout the application, or look up some other important piece of information about that person.

Incremental Development

Like Visual Basic, Oracle Power Objects is designed to let you develop an application incrementally. You build your application a form, a report, or a class at a time, testing as you go. Because you can use drag-and-drop techniques to bind objects to tables and views, it's equally easy to build database objects incrementally. Although you might need some idea of your data model before you build the application, your picture of the database does not need to be 100 percent complete to continue.

Projects with Multiple Developers

Like Visual Basic, Oracle Power Objects is primarily designed for single-developer projects. However, if several developers are working on the same application, here are some hints on how to proceed:

☐ Once again, start by developing the data model and as many user-defined classes as possible. If you have a relatively stable database, then everyone can start building forms and reports bound to objects in it. If everyone is using the same set of user-defined classes, it's easy to maintain a consistent look and feel throughout the application. In addition, every instance of the class will have the same behavior, so that pressing an OK button in Frank's purchase order form has the same effect as pressing the same button in Shannon's vendor information form.

☐ You need to be especially scrupulous about documenting user-defined properties and methods, so that the other developers in the team understand how they work.

☐ You might want to create a warehouse class for storing user-defined methods and their codes, as described on Day 21, "Finishing Your Application." If someone needs to debug your code, they can find a copy of the method in this class. However, that developer needs to tell you about the changes to the method, so that you can update it in your own copy of the application.

☐ To work on different portions of the application, you can create separate application files (.POA) for each person. Each person works on a different set of forms, reports, and other objects, and saves them in this temporary application. When your work is finished, you can copy all the objects from these separate applications into the final application.

☐ If security is a concern, you need to discuss your strategy for enforcing system security as early as possible. For example, if you create a user-defined property like udpSecLevel to store the security rating needed to open and view a form, you need to make sure that everyone on the development team adds this property to their forms and uses the proper scale of security ratings.

Reports

Unlike Visual Basic, the report writer is an intrinsic part of Oracle Power Objects. The good news is that you use the same techniques to bind a report to a record source that you use to bind a form to a table or view. By dragging the icon for a table or view onto the report, you automatically create text fields to display information queried from the database. By setting the DefaultCondition and OrderBy properties of the report, you can filter and sort these records as needed. Therefore, the learning curve for the report writer function is much less steep.

The bad news is that the report writer does not have some of the features of Crystal Reports, the report writer included with Visual Basic. For example, the Suppress if option does not exist in the Oracle Power Objects report writer. However, both report writers have the same core features:

☐ The capability to sort records according to report groups, defined by columns in the record source.

- [ ] Support for multitable reports. In both cases, you can use a multitable view as the basis for the report. In addition, you can create a master-detail relationship between an embedded form within the report and the report itself.

- [ ] The capability to display calculated values. In the case of Oracle Power Objects, you define the calculation as a derived value, by entering the expression in the control's `DataSource` property. The expression can use values in other controls, or it can look up values in a table with the `SQLLOOKUP` command. For more information on derived value calculations, see Day 8, "Derived Values."

- [ ] The division of the report into different functional areas (Report Header, Detail, and so on).

- [ ] The capability to display graphs, charts, and graphics in your report. You can add a chart control to an Oracle Power Objects report to display a chart or graph. To show a graphic, you can use the picture control.

To get the most out of your reports, you need to master report groups. As in Crystal Reports, report groups sort records according to values in a particular column. For example, to show employees by department, you would create a report based on the EMP table that uses the DEPTNO column in its report group for sorting. If you want to sort by multiple columns, you nest one report group inside another. To sort by department number and manager, you would add two report groups, one that sorts by `DEPTNO`, and the other by `MANAGER`.

In addition, you need to use report groups to create a master-detail report. The embedded form that displays detail records must use a group header or footer as its master. Without knowing how to create a report group, you will not be able to design master-detail reports.

Writing Code

As described earlier in this chapter, you code around methods instead of events in Oracle Power Objects. Unlike Visual Basic, there is no separation between event procedures and methods in Oracle Power Objects; instead, you write code within the method that determines what happens when the method is called. Applications are still event-driven, in that many methods are triggered by system events, or trigger events when called.

The following sections discuss some other important points about coding in Oracle Power Objects.

Calling Methods

You use the same object-oriented syntax to trigger a method on an object: `object.method_name([arguments])`.

Redefining Methods

The code you add to a method can completely replace that method's default processing with your own behavior. More commonly, your code calls the default processing only after other code has executed, or some check has been performed. To call the default processing, you use the `Inherited.`*`method_name()`* statement.

To use the earlier example, the following is some code that opens a form only if the user has the correct privileges:

```
Sub OpenWindow()
IF Application.udmSecLevel > 25 THEN
  Inherited.OpenWindow()
ELSE
  MSGBOX "You do not have privileges to open this form"
END IF
```

Creating New Procedures

Writing your own procedures (called *user-defined methods* in Oracle Power Objects) is a different experience than in Visual Basic. Instead of adding the method to a module (which does not exist in Oracle Power Objects), you add it as a new method of an object. After you define the API for the procedure (its name, return value, and arguments), you add it to the object, and then enter the code that defines its behavior. To call the method from another object, you use the same *`object.method`*(`[`*`arguments`*`]`) syntax used for calling standard methods.

In many cases, you want to enter the code defining the procedure in only one instance of that procedure. If you enter code in separate instances, you have to revise the code in all these places whenever you make modifications. Fortunately, you can call the user-defined method added to an object from anywhere within the application, because properties and methods are global to the application.

Programming Language (Oracle Basic)

The version of Basic used in Oracle Power Objects is fundamentally the same as the programming language in Visual Basic. To be compliant with the Visual Basic for Applications (VBA) standard definition of Basic commands, functions, and operators, language components such as FOR...NEXT, FORMAT, NOW, and ON ERROR behave exactly as they do in Visual Basic. Therefore, you do not need to re-learn the fundamental constructs of the programming language in Oracle Power Objects. Whether you are evaluating properties through a SELECT CASE statement or creating a dynamic array, the syntax and techniques are the same in both products.

The two versions of Basic differ in their *extensions*, the additions to the language specific to each product. Although there are points of similarity (see Table B.1), the properties and methods in

Oracle Power Objects often vary in many critical ways from their Visual Basic counterparts. Because Oracle Power Objects emphasizes database connections more than Visual Basic, the Basic extensions in Oracle Power Objects have more commands and functions for working with recordsets and databases.

Adding SQL Code

If you are working with any relational database, it is impossible to be completely ignorant of SQL. However, to use Oracle Power Objects effectively, you need to learn more SQL than you would use in Visual Basic. Some commonly used properties and methods, such as DefaultCondition and QueryWhere(), require some knowledge of basic SQL syntax, such as how to write the contents of a WHERE clause. As you become more familiar with the product, you will be using the SQLLOOKUP and EXEC SQL commands more frequently, both of which require a greater command of SQL than you would need to write a WHERE clause.

Although becoming an expert in SQL is not a requirement for Oracle Power Objects development, more knowledge can't hurt. In situations in which you might profit by defining a view yourself through SQL code, or improving performance by executing database commands through EXEC SQL, you do not want to be hindered by ignorance of SQL. Although you do not need to become an advanced SQL programmer, you should push yourself to learn at least the basics of SQL programming. Once you can write a three-table view and a fairly complex stored procedure, you have learned enough SQL to take full advantage of Oracle Power Objects.

Automated SQL Operations

Although you might need to use an increasing amount of SQL as you dig deeper into Oracle Power Objects, you might find yourself ultimately writing less SQL code than you would have as a Visual Basic database developer. Many recordset-related operations that you would code yourself in Visual Basic are completely automated in Oracle Power Objects. Most obviously, establishing a master-detail relationship and then maintaining referential integrity between master and detail recordsets requires a great deal of coding in Visual Basic. In Oracle Power Objects, you set three properties to establish a master-detail relationship, and two more to define the type of referential integrity you wish to enforce.

Similar Properties and Methods

Tables B.1 and B.2 summarize some properties, methods, and event procedures in Visual Basic that have equivalents in Oracle Power Objects. Sometimes, the Oracle Power Objects version of a property, method, or event is an exact duplicate; in others, it is a rough approximation. Before you write code using these properties and methods, you should read their descriptions in the Oracle Power Objects online help so that you don't make courageous but mistaken assumptions about how they work.

697

From Visual Basic to Oracle Power Objects

Table B.1. Visual Basic properties and their Oracle Power Objects equivalents.

Visual Basic	Oracle Power Objects
BackColor	ColorFill
BackStyle	Transparent
BorderColor	ColorBrdr
Caption	Label
Checked	ValueOn
Connect	DesignConnect, DesignRunConnect, RunConnect
DataChanged	Validate(), PostChange()
Database	RecordSource, RecSrcSession
DataField	DataSource
Default	DefaultButton
EditMode	GetRowStat()
Enabled	Enabled
FillColor	ColorFill
FontBold	FontBold
FontItalic	FontItalic
FontName	FontName
FontSize	FontSize
FontUnderline	FontUnderline
hWnd	GetWindowHandle()
ItemData	Translation
List	Translation
ListIndex	Value
MaxLength	DataSize
MinButton	WindowStyle
MousePointer	SetCursor()
MultiLine	MultiLine
Name	Name
NoMatch	SQLROWCOUNT, SQLERRCODE, SQLERCLASS
PasteOK	CanPasteFromClipboard()
Picture	Value

698

Visual Basic	Oracle Power Objects
ReadOnly	ReadOnly
RecordCount	GetRowCount()
Recordset	GetRecordset()
RecordSource	RecordSource
Scrollbars	HasScrollBar
Selected	GetFocus()
Sort	OrderBy
TabIndex	TabOrder
TabStop	TabEnabled
Text	Value
Type	Datatype
UnLoad	CloseWindow()
Value	Value
Visible	Visible

Table B.2. Visual Basic events and methods and their Oracle Power Objects equivalents.

Visual Basic	Oracle Power Objects
Change()	PostChange()
Click()	Click()
Close	Disconnect()
CommitTrans	CommitForm(), CommitWork()
CreateDynaSet	NEW DBRecordset, NEW Recordset
CreateQueryDef	EXEC SQL CREATE VIEW
DblClick()	DoubleClick()
Delete	DeleteRow()
DeleteQueryDef	EXEC SQL DROP VIEW
DragDrop()	MouseDown(), MouseMove(), MouseUp()
Execute	EXEC SQL
ExecuteSQL	EXEC SQL
FreeLocks	LockRow()

continues

Table B.2. continued

Visual Basic	Oracle Power Objects
GotFocus()	FocusEntering()
Hide()	HideWindow()
Load	OnLoad(), Initialize(), InitializeWindow()
LostFocus()	FocusLeaving()
MouseDown()	MouseDown()
MouseMove()	MouseMove()
MouseUp()	MouseUp()
MoveFirst	SetCurRow(1)
MoveLast	SetCurRow()
MoveNext	GoNxtLine()
MovePrev	GoPrvLine()
OpenDatabase	GetSession(), Connect()
PrintForm	OpenPrint(), OpenPreview()
Reposition()	ChgCurrentRec()
Rollback	RollbackForm(), RollbackWork()
Seek	QueryWhere()
SetFocus	SetFocus()
Show	OpenWindow()
UnLoad()	CloseWindow()
Update	CommitForm(), CommitWork()
UpdateRecord	CommitForm(), CommitWork()
Validate()	Validate(), ValidateRow()

Databases and Development

Oracle Power Objects was designed to hit the ball out of the park when it came to database access. The tool is designed to simplify many of the most painful aspects of writing database applications, such as maintaining referential integrity between two recordsets. For Visual Basic developers, here is where you'll find the best news of all about using Oracle Power Objects.

Viewing and Editing Database Objects

Probably the first enhancement you will notice as a database application developer is that you can view and edit all of the database objects through a series of windows from within the same tool you use to design the front end. If you want to see the structure of the EMP table, you double-click its icon in the Database Session window to open a spreadsheet containing all the columns in EMP. To add, modify, or delete a column, you select a row in this spreadsheet and enter your modifications.

Oracle Power Objects has other windows for designing views, sequences, indexes, and synonyms. When created, all of these objects appear in the same Database Session window. You can use another window, the Table Browser, to enter data into a table, to give you the ability to populate your tables with test data very quickly.

Binding Forms to Tables and Views

In Visual Basic, you use the data control as the primary tool for connecting a form to a record source (a table or view). The data control is central to database connectivity, identifying the database (the DatabaseName property), connect string (Connect), and table or view (RecordSource). Once you have set these properties and bound the form to a record source, you can bind a control to a column by setting its DataSource property to the name of the column.

In Oracle Power Objects, there is no equivalent to the data control. In many respects, the Oracle Power Objects methodology makes more sense: Rather than using a data control as a middleman for binding a form to a table or view, you set properties of the form itself to establish the connection. These properties include the following:

Property	Description
RecordSource	The name of the table or view to act as the form's record source.
RecSrcSession	The session through which the form accesses its table or view.

Sessions and Connectivity

The session is a separate object, invisible at runtime, whose sole job it is to establish and control the connection to the database. Keep in mind that when you establish the connection, you log into the database as a particular user, or using a particular schema.

The session, not the form, has a property containing the connect string. In fact, it has three such properties, to cover three different situations in which you might be establishing a connection:

- ☐ At runtime, for the application (the RunConnect property)
- ☐ At design time, for running a single form or the entire application (the DesignRunConnect property)

☐ At design time, for viewing and editing database objects through Oracle Power Objects (the `DesignConnect` property)

The session also has two methods, `Connect()` and `Disconnect()`, for opening and closing a connection.

The Logic of This Architecture

This relationship between forms and sessions creates a sensible division of labor between application objects.

☐ The form queries and displays records and lets the user edit these records. The records displayed in the form are maintained in a recordset, a local copy of records queried from a table or view.

☐ The session manages interactions between the form and the database. The session queries records to populate a recordset, and flushes changes to tables to the database.

From a development standpoint, this model gives you greater flexibility in determining where the application gets data. You can use any number of sessions, each connected to a different schema and perhaps a different database, in your application. In addition, the same form can have data from several sessions displayed in it.

Recordsets and Dynasets

One major advantage of database programming in Oracle Power Objects over Visual Basic is that you do not have to write any code to create a dynaset (called a *recordset* in Oracle Power Objects). By setting the `RecordSource` property, you tell the application to query records from a particular table or view. The application then queries the records, applying whatever conditions you might define (through the `QueryWhere()` method or the `DefaultCondition` property), and then creates a local copy of these records in memory. You can edit the contents of this recordset/dynaset through the controls connected to columns in the recordset, or you can make programmatic changes directly through code.

If you want to create a recordset not associated with any form, you can write code to create a stand-alone recordset. The code involved is relatively simple, and you can make these recordsets read-only recordsets to define them as snapshots.

Transaction Logic and Recordsets

The application automatically handles a large number of other database-related operations. For example, instead of coding each transaction so that the application knows that the user has inserted, deleted, or updated a record, an Oracle Power Objects application has this transaction logic already built into it. As soon as you start making changes to a recordset, Oracle Power

Objects is aware that you are entering a change. The Commit and Rollback buttons on the application's toolbar become enabled, letting you save your changes to the database or roll them back. In fact, if you try to begin editing another record or close down the application, a message appears telling you that you must commit or roll back the transaction before moving on.

If you want to define your own transaction, you can use the EXEC SQL command to run native SQL code. You can use the BEGIN and END commands (BEGIN TRANSACTION and END TRANSACTION in SQL Server) to define the beginning and end of the transaction. In addition, you can use the SAVE (or SAVE TRANSACTION) command to define savepoints within the body of the transaction. However, these situations are the exception that define the rule: Most of the time, your forms will be using the automated transaction processing built into Oracle Power Objects.

SQL Code in Power Objects

If you want to write native SQL code for defining transactions, calling stored procedures, creating database objects, or performing some other database operation, you can use the EXEC SQL command to run this code against the database. Therefore, if you want to use some of the SQL code you wrote for a Visual Basic application, you can still run this code in Oracle Power Objects through the EXEC SQL command.

The only shortcoming of EXEC SQL is that you cannot run your SQL code asynchronously. If you start a long process on the server, your application won't be free until it finishes. Therefore, you might consider breaking up very large database operations into several smaller ones, if possible.

Master-Detail Relationships

One of the most difficult recordset operations to code yourself is establishing a master-detail (or one-to-many) relationship between two recordsets. Not only must you synchronize records through their primary and foreign keys, but you must maintain referential integrity between the two recordsets.

Although you might be proud of the code you wrote for establishing and maintaining master-detail relationships in a Visual Basic application, you can throw it away in Oracle Power Objects. By setting a few properties, you can establish the master-detail relationship and maintain referential integrity. Using the same technique on several containers, you can display several levels of a master-detail relationship. Oracle Power Objects makes developing a drill-down form extremely easy, because no scripting is involved.

ODBC Access

Most Visual Basic programmers are accustomed to accessing databases through Open Database Connectivity (ODBC). However, the current version of Oracle Power Objects does not have an ODBC driver, but future versions of the product will include ODBC support.

Database Prototyping and Local Data Access

OraclePowerObjectscomeswith
Blaze, a fully ANSI SQL-compliant relational database engine. Like the Microsoft Jet Database Engine provided with Visual Basic, you can use Blaze to prototype database objects for later deployment on a remote server, or to store data locally on a client system. If you are designing a single-user application, or you want to store part of the information used by the application (such as system configuration options) locally in a relational database format, you can use Blaze for both of these purposes.

Like Jet, Blaze has its limitations:

- [ ] It does not support multisegmented keys, the FOREIGN KEY constraint, and some other constraints used in remote servers.
- [ ] Blaze does not have a procedural language, so you cannot write stored procedures and triggers for a Blaze database.
- [ ] Blaze databases are single-user only.

Where Blaze proves its worth, however, is when you need to deploy database objects from Blaze to a remote server. Once you have finished prototyping your database objects in Blaze, you drag them from the Session window for Blaze to an Oracle7 or SQL Server session. Oracle Power Objects copies all the database objects on the remote server, and adds your test data to all the tables. Although you might want to write SQL scripts for defining these objects, you can use simple drag-and-drop techniques to create copies of your prototyped database objects.

Controls

Oracle Power Objects has many of the same controls as Visual Basic, with some minor differences in naming:

Visual Basic	Oracle Power Objects
Check box	Check box
Combo box	Combo box
Command button	Pushbutton
Frame	Radio button frame
Horizontal/vertical scroll bar	Horizontal/vertical scrollbar
Image	Picture control
Label	Static text object

Visual Basic	Oracle Power Objects
Line	Line
List box	List box
OLE control	OLE control
Option button	Radio button
Shape	Rectangle, oval
Text box	Text field

Visual Basic controls included in the Professional Edition that do not have equivalents in Oracle Power Objects include data controls, directory list boxes, drive list boxes, file list boxes, grids, picture boxes, and timers.

Dynamically Created Controls

Oracle Power Objects does not let you create new controls at runtime through code. The workaround for this is simple: Add several similar controls to the form, but make each one invisible if it is not needed. As soon as it becomes invisible, the control becomes unavailable to the user.

Indexes for Controls

In addition, you cannot create indexed controls as in Visual Basic.

The *Value* Property

Controls that store values (for example, text fields and check boxes) all have a `Value` property. In contrast, some Visual Basic controls, most notably text boxes, have a `Text` property instead of a `Value` property.

Printing Object Descriptions

Unlike Visual Basic, you cannot print an object's description, including its property settings and Basic code, to the printer or an ASCII text file.

Menus, Toolbars, and Status Bars

Oracle Power Objects has no graphical menu designer. However, a default menu always appears when the application is running, as does a default toolbar. If you want to replace the default menu with one of your own, you define the toolbar entirely through code, following these steps:

☐ Create a new menu bar object. This remains invisible until you add menus to it and associate it with a form.

☐ Create menus and add menu commands to them. Each menu command needs a command code (a unique ID).

☐ Add the menus to the menu bar.

☐ Associate the menu bar with a form. The menu then appears whenever that form is selected.

Two methods of the application determine the appearance and behavior of the toolbar. TestCommand() enables or disables a menu command, and can display a check mark next to it. DoCommand() determines what happens when the user selects a menu command. Both methods take the menu command's unique ID as an argument.

You create custom toolbars and status bars (called *status lines* in Oracle Power Objects) using the same sequence of steps. In place of menu commands, you add buttons to a toolbar, or panels to a status bar.

Files

When you compile a Visual Basic application, the .EXE file has a smaller imprint on your hard disk than an Oracle Power Objects executable. Oracle Power Objects applications do not have a DLL like VBRUN300.DLL in which all the procedures needed to run an application are defined, nor do they have a modular program architecture using VBXs to add in controls and features as needed. When you compile an Oracle Power Objects application, you get everything. It should be no surprise, therefore, that the average Oracle Power Objects executable is larger than its Visual Basic equivalent.

However, Oracle Power Objects has an option for creating a much smaller executable file. If you plan to have several Oracle Power Objects applications running on the same system, you can save hard disk space by compiling them as .PO files instead of stand-alone executables (.EXE files). The Oracle Power Objects Run-Time application, PWRRUN.EXE, includes everything you need to launch and run an application—in other words, everything you would add during the compile to create a stand-alone executable file, but don't need if you create a .PO file.

During development, Oracle Power Objects applications create fewer operating system files than Visual Basic applications. Several types of objects, some of which are stored in separate files in Visual Basic, are combined in the same application file in Oracle Power Objects, including

☐ Forms

☐ Reports

☐ Imported bitmaps

- [ ] OLE data objects
- [ ] User-defined classes

In addition, an Oracle Power Objects application has an additional file object containing the description of a session. This much smaller file (with a .POS extension) includes the information needed to connect to a database, as well as some code you might add to control what happens when the application opens or closes this connection.

A third type of file, a library (.POL), contains some reusable application objects, including bitmaps and classes. However, an object in this file is compiled only if you add an instance of it to the application. In this sense, classes stored in a library are as modular as VBXs or OCXs, in that they become part of the application only if you use them. Unlike VBXs and OCXs, classes are compiled into the application, so you do not have to worry about distributing an extra file for each of them.

The lesson on Day 21, "Finishing Your Application," describes how .POA, .POS, and .POL files are compiled. To summarize:

- [ ] When you compile the .POA file, you can create a stand-alone executable (.EXE file) or a smaller runtime file (.PO file). If you compile the smaller version, you launch it from the PWRRUN.EXE application.
- [ ] Any sessions (.POS files) referenced in the application are compiled with it.
- [ ] In addition, any bitmaps or classes used from a library (.POL) are also added.

For a checklist of files you need to distribute with your application, see Day 21.

Extensibility

Oracle Power Objects provides extensibility in three ways familiar to Visual Basic Developers:

- [ ] DLL procedure calls—You can call procedures defined in dynamic link libraries (DLLs), including the Windows API procedures.
- [ ] Custom controls—You can use OCX custom controls in an Oracle Power Objects application. However, you cannot use VBX controls. (Oracle decided to follow Microsoft's lead in this matter by embracing OCXs as the new standard for custom controls.)
- [ ] OLE data objects—You can include OLE data objects in your application. These data objects can be displayed and accessed through an OLE control. Because this control is bindable, you can use it to store OLE objects in a database. Oracle Power Objects applications cannot act as OLE servers.

Graphics

You have four options for displaying graphics in an Oracle Power Objects application:

☐ Imported bitmaps—You can import a bitmap and display it as the background of a form, embedded form, user-defined class, or pushbutton. The palette for imported bitmaps is limited to 256 colors, and you must use the .BMP format.

☐ Picture controls—The picture control can display bitmaps (256-color .BMP format again) in this control. Because it is a bindable control, you can save these graphics in a column that uses the Long data type.

☐ OCX controls—Many OCX controls are graphics editors for .BMP, .PCX, .JPG, and .GIF files. By adding these custom OCX controls to your application, you provide a wider range of graphics capabilities. However, OCX controls are not bindable, so you will not be able to store the graphic in a database.

☐ OLE controls—You can display a graphical OLE data object, such as a Paintbrush picture, through an OLE control. The resolution, color palette, and editing capabilities added to your application are determined by the OLE server application. OLE controls are bindable, so you can save the OLE data objects stored in them in a column using the Long Raw data type.

If you want to manipulate the appearance of a graphic, you can use the GetWindowHandle() method to return the Windows handle for an object displaying the graphic. You can pass the handle as an argument to the Windows API procedure bitBlt to edit the graphic, including writing your own animation routines.

GUI Standards for Oracle Power Objects Applications

This appendix gives you some suggestions for improving the appearance of your application.

3-D Look and Feel

You can use the 3-D look and feel common to many contemporary Windows, Windows 95, and Macintosh applications. To create this appearance, you should do the following:

- ☐ Set the DrawStyle property of controls to 3-D control whenever possible.
- ☐ Set the ColorFill property of forms, embedded forms, and user-defined classes to light gray.
- ☐ Use 3-D lines, rectangles, and frames to separate sections of a form.

You should not apply the 3-D look and feel within a repeater display.

Controls

The following GUI design guidelines apply to controls.

Alignment

You should left-align controls that are vertically stacked. You might also right-align as many of them as possible, to eliminate the "ragged right" appearance of stacked controls.

Grouping

You can group controls that have a logical relationship (for example, all related to customers or all related to shipping) in the following ways:

- ☐ Place them in the same rectangle or radio button frame. To avoid confusion in the object containment hierarchy, the controls should not be contained within the frame.
- ☐ If the values queried for these controls come from a different table or view than the main form, you would place them in an embedded form, repeater display, or user-defined class.
- ☐ Use lines as separators. To create a 3-D line (a groove), first create a line that has a ColorBrdr property which is set to light gray. Then place a white line of the same length immediately beneath it. Instead of copying and pasting these lines, you might create them as a simple user-defined class.

Read-Only and Disabled Controls

You should make controls read-only if the user can never edit their contents. If the user can access the control at some times but not at others, you should disable the control. The grayed appearance of the disabled control suggests that there are times when you can edit its contents.

Stacking Controls

When you stack controls vertically, you can often save space by leaving no vertical separation between them. In the case of stacked text fields, you should also limit the number of different values for SizeX to no more than two or three different settings, to avoid a wildly ragged right edge.

OLE Controls

When you add an OLE control to a form, you should label it clearly. The appearance of an OLE control can be confusing, whether it displays the data object or an icon for the server application.

In most cases, displaying the icon is preferable to showing the object. The space you allot for displaying a Word document will never be enough to show it completely or clearly. Therefore, you can save yourself some valuable real estate on the form and make it look better in the process by displaying an icon for an OLE data object.

Labels

Static text objects and the intrinsic labels of other controls (check boxes, pop-up lists, and so on) should follow these conventions:

- ☐ Text should be initial capped (for example, Purchase Order Number).
- ☐ The label may or may not include a colon (:) at the end of the text. If you choose to display a colon, always display it.
- ☐ The static text object's FontBold property should be set to TRUE.

Controls in Repeater Displays

The following controls are not recommended for placement in standard repeater displays: list boxes, scrollbars, radio buttons, and radio button frames.

To fit the text of some controls within the repeater display, you might want to switch to a FontSize of 9, or possibly even 8.

List Controls

There is an effective maximum to the number if items you can easily view in the list portion of a combo box, list box, or combo list.

- ☐ For combo boxes and list boxes, the maximum is between 10 and 15.
- ☐ For list boxes, the maximum is between 20 and 40.

If you need to display more items, you should use a pop-up dialog box or some other mechanism for displaying and selecting the list of values. If you reduce the control's font, you can squeeze more items into the list, but you sacrifice readability.

Pushbuttons

When you add pushbuttons to the bottom of a form, you should make sure that they always appear in the same location. Your application looks unpolished if the OK button roams across the bottom of forms, appearing at a different location in each one. Commonly, pushbutton groups are centered at the bottom of a form, but left-aligning or right-aligning them at the bottom of the form are common conventions as well.

Whenever you have more than one pushbutton displayed in the same area of a form, you need to keep the same amount of space between them. Needless to say, the pushbuttons should also be the same width and height if they are part of the same group.

Fonts

You should choose fonts for readability. Sans serif fonts such as Arial and Helvetica are usually the most readable on a form, especially when a large number of controls appear within it. If you are developing cross-platform applications, you should choose a scaleable font that appears in both Mac and Windows (Arial is highly recommended for this reason).

Using several fonts can be dramatic, but you should not overuse this technique, particularly on simple forms. Using a different font for a particular section of a form attracts the eye to it, and identifies it as something deserving special attention. You dilute this effect by using too many different fonts.

Colors

The same principle applies to colors. You can color-code labels to identify different types of controls or sections of the form. For example, if you want to identify the controls your user cannot leave blank while editing a record, you can make the label red. Once again, a little bit goes a long way: if you add too many colors, your form simply becomes colorful, not dramatic.

You should be careful about the colors you use for text. Yellow can be striking against a light gray background, but nearly invisible against a white one.

Forms

The following GUI design guidelines apply to forms.

Breaking Up Large Forms

A form should be designed to fit within a 640 × 480 display, because many laptops and older desktop machines still use this resolution. If you cannot fit all the fields in the form at this size, you have several options for handling this situation:

- ☐ Create dialog boxes for displaying additional information. These dialog boxes can share their recordset with the main form.
- ☐ If the additional information is a detail of the main form (for example, line items for an invoice), you can display it in a repeater display on the main form, or in a separate dialog box.
- ☐ Create a tabbed form.

Avoid adding a scrollbar to a form to handle this problem. If the user doesn't notice the scrollbar, he might miss the fact that there are more fields below the visible area of the form.

Browser or Value List Forms

When a form has a large (over 50) recordset, the scrollbar should be replaced with a browser form (also known as a *value list form*). This form pops up when the user presses a button adjacent to a primary key field, such as DEPTNO, or some other field for which the user can select from a wide range of possible values. The browser form displays a scrolling list of the primary key values for the form in a scrolling list (a repeater display or list box), a descriptive explanation of a numeric primary key value (for example, DNAME), or a combination of the two. By clicking one of these records, or a current row control within this repeater display, the user selects the record to be displayed on the form.

A standard feature of browser forms should be a text field at the bottom in which the user can enter a condition.

Tabbed Forms

To create a tabbed form, each "folder" should be an embedded form. The sample applications include a tab control class, and later versions of Oracle Power Objects will provide a standard tab control. Alternatively, you can use one of many OCX tab controls, or some version of the faux tab controls from Day 21, "Finishing Your Application."

Menus

Menus for Windows applications should include the following headings: File, Edit, View, Database, Window, and Help. Any additional menus must be placed between the Database and Window menus.

Menus for Macintosh applications should include the following headings: Apple, File, and Edit. Any further menus should be added after these items.

There are two schools of thought about the order in which you add menus:

☐ Order by the frequency of use, with the more frequently used menus appearing to the left.

☐ Order by the steps needed to set up information, with the menus that open setup forms and system configuration dialog boxes appearing to the left.

Either convention is fine, as long as you apply it consistently.

Repeater Displays

The following GUI guidelines apply to repeater displays.

Labeling Controls Within the Repeater Display

Because you usually find yourself trying to squeeze several controls into a single row in a repeater display, you don't want to add the labels for these controls within the repeater display itself. Instead, you can add the label for a control just above the repeater display, aligned with the control.

Multiple Rows of Controls

You can create multiline repeater displays, in which rows of controls are stacked within the repeater display panel, to display a large number of controls within the panel. However, the number of rows should not exceed three, and cleaving to a two-row limit is highly recommended.

Status Lines

The standard status line should display the date and time, help text, and the status of the keyboard (NUM LOCK, INSERT, CAPS LOCK) in separate panels.

Index

Data Model

SAMS
PUBLISHING

Sams
Learning
Center

data types

tables

Add to Your Sams Library Today with the Best Books for Programming, Operating Systems, and New Technologies

The easiest way to order is to pick up the phone and call

1-800-428-5331

between 9:00 a.m. and 5:00 p.m. EST.
For faster service please have your credit card available.

ISBN	Quantity	Description of Item	Unit Cost	Total Cost
0-672-30681-6		Oracle DBA Survival Guide (Book/CD-ROM)	$49.99	
0-672-30757-X		Developing Personal Oracle7 Applications (Book/CD-ROM)	$45.00	
0-672-30873-8		Essential Oracle7	$25.00	
0-672-30609-3		Teach Yourself ODBC Programming in 21 Days	$29.99	
0-672-30832-0		Teach Yourself Database Programming with Visual Basic 4 in 21 Days (Book/CD-ROM)	$39.99	
0-672-30789-8		Developing Client/Server Applications with Visual Basic (Book/CD-ROM)	$49.99	
0-672-30833-9		PowerBuilder 4 Unleashed (Book/CD-ROM)	$49.99	
0-672-30837-1		Visual Basic 4 Unleashed (Book/CD-ROM)	$45.00	
0-672-30851-7		Teach Yourself Database Programming with Delphi (Book/CD-ROM)	$39.99	
0-672-30771-5		Essential Visual Basic 4	$25.00	
0-672-30511-9		Developing SQLWindows Applications (Book/CD-ROM)	$45.00	
0-672-30613-1		Database Developer's Guide with Visual C++ (Book/CD-ROM)	$49.99	
❏ 3 ½" Disk		Shipping and Handling: See information below.		
❏ 5 ¼" Disk		TOTAL		

Shipping and Handling: $4.00 for the first book, and $1.75 for each additional book. Floppy disk: add $1.75 for shipping and handling. If you need to have it NOW, we can ship product to you in 24 hours for an additional charge of approximately $18.00, and you will receive your item overnight or in two days. Overseas shipping and handling adds $2.00 per book and $8.00 for up to three disks. Prices subject to change. Call for availability and pricing information on latest editions.

201 W. 103rd Street, Indianapolis, Indiana 46290

1-800-428-5331 — Orders   1-800-835-3202 — FAX   1-800-858-7674 — Customer Service

PLUG YOURSELF INTO...

MACMILLAN INFORMATION SUPERLIBRARY™

que · SAMS PUBLISHING · Hayden Books · que COLLEGE · NRP · alpha books · Brady · ADOBE PRESS

THE MACMILLAN INFORMATION SUPERLIBRARY™

Free information and vast computer resources from the world's leading computer book publisher—online!

FIND THE BOOKS THAT ARE RIGHT FOR YOU!

A complete online catalog, plus sample chapters and tables of contents give you an in-depth look at *all* of our books, including hard-to-find titles. It's the best way to find the books you need!

- **STAY INFORMED** with the latest computer industry news through our online newsletter, press releases, and customized Information SuperLibrary Reports.

- **GET FAST ANSWERS** to your questions about MCP books and software.

- **VISIT** our online bookstore for the latest information and editions!

- **COMMUNICATE** with our expert authors through e-mail and conferences.

- **DOWNLOAD SOFTWARE** from the immense MCP library:
  - Source code and files from MCP books
  - The best shareware, freeware, and demos

- **DISCOVER HOT SPOTS** on other parts of the Internet.

- **WIN BOOKS** in ongoing contests and giveaways!

TO PLUG INTO MCP: ➤

GOPHER: gopher.mcp.com

FTP: ftp.mcp.com

WORLD WIDE WEB: http://www.mcp.com

Home Page · What's New · Bookstore · Reference Desk · Software Library · Macmillan Overview · Talk to Us